THE ELEMENTS
OF
ARTIFICIAL
INTELLIGENCE

An Introduction Using LISP

PRINCIPLES OF COMPUTER SCIENCE SERIES
ISSN 0888-2096

Series Editors
Alfred V. Aho, *Bell Telephone Laboratories, Murray Hill, New Jersey*
Jeffrey D. Ullman, *Stanford University, Stanford, California*

*These previously-published books are in the *Principles of Computer Science Series* but they are not numbered within the volume itself. All future volumes in the *Principles of Computer Science Series* will be numbered.

OTHER BOOKS OF INTEREST

THE ELEMENTS
OF
ARTIFICIAL
INTELLIGENCE
An Introduction Using LISP

Steven L. Tanimoto

Department of Computer Science, FR-35
University of Washington
Seattle, Washington 98195

Computer Science Press

Computer Science Press, Inc.
1803 Research Boulevard
Rockville, Maryland 20850

1 2 3 4 5 6   92 91 90 89 88 87

Library of Congress Cataloging-in-Publication Data

Tanimoto, S. (Steven)
   The elements of artificial intelligence.

   Includes bibliographies and indexes.
   1.   Artificial intelligence—Data processing.
2. LISP (Computer program language)   I. Title.
Q336.T36 1987   006.3   86-31044
ISBN 0-88175-113-8
ISSN 0888-2096

To my parents
Taffee and Mary-Mae Tanimoto

PREFACE

Today there is a growing recognition of computer science as a *laboratory* science. In addition to the mathematical theory that supports techniques in subareas such as artificial intelligence, the student needs to work with actual programs and problems to get a feel for the technology. This book grew out of the perception that hands-on experimentation coordinated with textbook explanations of principles and of actual programs can provide an ideal learning combination for students of artificial intelligence.

The purpose of this book is to provide an up-to-date and didactically coherent introduction to the principles and programming methods of artificial intelligence. It is appropriate for an undergraduate or first-year graduate course. While it is possible for the student to get acquainted with artificial intelligence in a single quarter or semester, a sequence of two to three quarters or semesters is preferable. The author covers most of the material in two academic quarters at the University of Washington. During the first quarter, Chapters 1 through 6 or 7 are tackled, laying a foundation of symbol manipulation, knowledge representation and inference. The second quarter takes on the more advanced topics: learning, natural language understanding, vision and the integration of AI technology into expert systems.

If programming is to be given a heavy emphasis, the material can be spread over more than two quarters; more of the problems may be assigned, and the instructor may wish to spend some time discussing various aspects of the assignments. In the final term of a two- or three-course sequence, a term project by each student, which can grow out of one of the programs provided in the text, can be very successful.

Unlike other AI texts, *The Elements of Artificial Intelligence* integrates the presentation of principles with actual runnable LISP illustrations. I have attempted to implement a large enough fraction of these ideas in fully-presented LISP programs to allow the student to gain enough intuition through experiment to support his/her understanding of all the principles covered.

While the LISP examples encourage an experimental study of the subject, theory is not avoided. The student needs to gain an appreciation for the interplay between theory and practice. Logical reasoning plays a key role in much of AI today, and other formalisms such as various probabilistic reasoning methods are also important. Various mathematical ideas come up in practically all areas of AI, and a study of AI can serve as an invitation to the student to investigate some of these formalisms further.

The prerequisites for a course based on this book are: (a) an intuitive understanding of how a computer works; this is normally the result of programming experience, (b) an exposure to mathematical logic, at least at the level of the propositional calculus, and preferably some experience with the predicate calculus, (c) high-school algebra, and (d) some familiarity with data structures such as strings, trees, arrays and graphs. Some of the techniques and examples in this book may require an understanding of essential aspects of other subjects: an understanding of what it means to take a derivative of a function (something normally taught in freshman calculus) is needed to appreciate the LEIBNIZ program in Chapter 3; some exposure to mathematical logic would facilitate an understanding of Chapter 6; an exposure to elementary concepts of probability is recommended for students embarking on Chapter 7; and Chapter 10 makes occasional use of several kinds of mathematics, including the integral calculus and computational geometry. However, most of the examples do not require more than common knowledge (e.g., the rules of chess) to understand.

The Elements of Artificial Intelligence is designed to be a self-contained text. However, if a separate, deeper treatment of LISP is desired, there are several books on LISP that could be used in a supplementary fashion. One of these is *LISP* by Winston and Horn; another is by D. Touretsky, and a book particularly suited to students using the Franz Lisp implementation was written by R. Wilensky.

The use of programs to illustrate elements of artificial intelligence seems essential if students are to get a practical view of the field. Courses in AI today can more and more easily have access to sufficient computational facilities, and in the opinion of the author, it is inadvisable to neglect the experience of interaction with computers in introducing AI.

At the same time, a course on artificial intelligence should be an enjoyable one. A primary source of students' pleasure is the chance to write, play with, and modify programs that seem to be clever, and to understand what makes them work or not work. To this end, many of the exercises in the book consist of experimentation with or modification of the programs presented in the text, or explaining aspects of their behavior.

Various implementations of LISP may be used to run the examples, including several excellent microcomputer LISP's. One implementation has been developed by the author specifically to support the examples used in this text; it is the intention of the author and publisher to make this software available at a cost much less than what commercial systems typically cost.

The chapters are intended to be treated in the order given. However, the instructor may choose to omit or supplement material to his or her own taste, as artificial intelligence is a subject of broad scope.

Chapter 1 provides a general introduction addressing the popular question of what intelligence is and the question of how AI is related to other fields. Chapter 2 is a brief but self-contained introduction to interactive programming with the LISP language. This chapter can be skipped by students already familiar with the language. Programming tools and methodology are further developed in Chapter 3. There, a pattern-matching function, MATCH, is described that facilitates several subsequent programs. The chapter illustrates the application of LISP to simple AI problems: carrying on a dialog, and manipulating mathematical formulas according to rules of the differential calculus. The emphasis is on programming techniques.

In Chapter 4 (Knowledge Representation), we begin to explore possibilities for structuring simple factual knowledge to support subsequent inference, using concrete LISP data structures. The example program LINNEUS, described at length, builds upon the MATCH function of the previous chapter to illustrate both the representation of knowledge in an ISA hierarchy, and elementary inference based on that knowledge. The program includes a simple conversational interface. Several issues are raised here which are discussed further in subsequent chapters: search, theorem proving and natural language understanding.

The notion of search, introduced briefly in the previous chapter, is elaborated in Chapter 5 with concepts of state space, evaluation functions, etc. The importance of pruning to fight the combinatorial explosion is explained. Alternative algorithms for searching are presented and compared. Planning is presented as direct application for search algorithms. The chapter closes with a discussion of minimax search and its application in programs to play games such as checkers and chess.

The subject of Chapter 6 is reasoning with the propositional and predicate logics. This is taken to include the more general issue of mathematical logic as a means for representation and inference in AI. To show how search applies to deduction, automatic techniques are presented based on both the propositional calculus and the predicate calculus. The "Logic-Theory Machine" is presented to show a more "human" way to find proofs: to search using subgoals. Presenting unification, we elaborate on the notion of pattern matching (from Chapter 3) and introduce the PROLOG language. A "mock-PROLOG" interpreter written in LISP is presented, and several of the chapter's exercises require the student to use it or modify it. The subject of non-monotonic reasoning wraps up the chapter.

Chapter 7, in contrast to 6, deals with knowledge in which probabilities or certainty values play a crucial role. Bayes' rule is presented, as are some of the epistemological considerations for applying it. We illustrate probabilistic inference networks in the style of PROSPECTOR, and give some guidelines for constructing them. A complete example program is presented which computes probabilities for various hypotheses about the quality of a restaurant, given the values of some observable variables. Finally, the Dempster-Shafer calculus is described.

In Chapter 8 (Learning) we change our perspective. In preceding chapters the concern was with using general knowledge to prove specific theorems, diagnose particular symptoms and solve particular puzzles and problems. Not treated was the question of where the general knowledge comes from. Here the problem of going from specific facts to general knowledge is treated. Starting with empirical data, one can derive hypotheses, rules of inference and classification rules using automatic means. A logical approach to single-concept learning is described, and this leads into a presentation the version-space method. Automatic theory formation is described, and a program PYTHAGORUS is presented which explores a space of concepts about geometry using a heuristic search algorithm.

Chapter 9 addresses the subject of natural-language understanding. Beginning with design criteria for language understanding systems, the notions of syntax, semantics and pragmatics are discussed. Augmented transition networks and semantic grammars are presented as two powerful techniques for building useful systems. An interactive program "Stone World" that allows the user to communicate with a simulated character to achieve action through a subset of natural English demonstrates the power of these methods as well as their limitations.

Machine vision is the subject of Chapter 10. The chapter covers the underlying image representation problems as well as high-level vision techniques. The complexities of interpreting scenes in the midst of ambiguities and incomplete information require that vision call upon many other areas of artificial intelligence to help solve its problems. Computer-vision research has pursued two related but fundamentally different approaches. One of these is the development of algorithmic or architectural models to explain how human vision works; this approach has been labelled "computational vision" by some of its proponents. The other approach is the inventing of techniques for performing useful tasks; this approach includes image processing and robotic vision. While this chapter presents ideas from both approaches, the emphasis is distinctly on the machine, rather than the human, side of vision. This is consistent with the theme of the book that artificial intelligence is in large part a design and programming activity. Two LISP programs are included in Chapter 10, one for connected-components analysis of binary images, and another for polygonal approximation of two-dimensional shapes.

While Chapters 2 through 10 present "elements" of artificial intelligence, Chapter 11 (Expert Systems) discusses the problem of combining the elements into useful compounds. This chapter touches upon such issues as tools and shells for building expert systems, special hardware, and limitations of expert systems.

A closing chapter suggests directions in which artificial intelligence may move in the future, and it mentions some of the technical and social challenges that artificial intelligence raises or may help solve.

S. L. T.

Seattle, Washington

Acknowledgements

I received kind assistance in various aspects of preparing this text from a number of people, especially my students, some of whom had to suffer through very rough early drafts. I am grateful to them for their patience. Particularly helpful were Agnes Andreassian, Wayne Backman, John Ballard, Ron Blanford, Philip Harrison, Tom Holman, Shu-Yuen Hwang, Brian Koblenz, Kuo-Lung Ku, Debora Lilly, Clifford Neuman, Douglas Pan, Joseph Pfeiffer, Harry Plate, Scott Rose, Robert Shields, and Ricky Yeung.

Some of my friends and professional colleagues who made helpful suggestions or provided encouragement are Jean-Loup Baer, Gerald Barber, Alan Borning, Y. T. Chien, Norbert Cot, Per-Erik Danielsson, Gösta Granlund, Alistair Holden, Ramesh Jain, Simon Kasif, Robert Matthews, Ryszard Michalski, Michael Morgan, Charles Osborne, John Palmer, Theo Pavlidis, Ira Pohl, Richard Rice, Alan Shaw, Robert Simmons, Jean-Claude Simon, George Stockman, Imants Svalbe, Leonard Uhr, and Walter Wolnik. I must apologize in advance for failing to incorporate all of the good suggestions I have received. My hope is that the book will survive to a second edition, at which point the additional improvements can be made.

I am indebted to Jeffrey Ullman for numerous constructive comments, and to Art and Barbara Friedman, and Elizabeth Mergner of Computer Science Press for their encouragement during the final stages. For help with the cover design, I would like to thank Jessie Phillips Pearson. Pierre MacKay's TEX-pertise and patient instruction on the use of an aging Alphatype phototypesetter were invaluable. Finally I would like to thank my wife Gunnel and daughter Elise for their patience and love that made it possible for me to undertake and complete this project.

Contents

Chapter 1

INTRODUCTION

1.1 An Intellectual and Technical Challenge

The practice of designing systems that possess and acquire knowledge and reason with that knowledge is perhaps the ultimate intellectual challenge. What could be a more intense intellectual experience than creating an intellect? Human intelligence is applied in every aspect of our culture. In building an intelligent machine, one might become involved in any aspect of human culture.

Like statistics, artificial intelligence brings a collection of techniques that can be applied in other fields such as history, biology, or engineering. Like philosophy and mathematics, it is concerned with reasoning, but unlike either statistics or philosophy, artificial intelligence gets deeply involved with the theories and meanings in the subjects to which it is applied. The application of artificial intelligence to history might easily require that a theory of the rise and fall of nations be reworked and formalized and that new representations be designed for describing historical events such as battles. Whereas statistics may help to justify or refute a hypothesis, artificial intelligence may produce the hypothesis or show an inconsistency with it. Its wide applicability and the great depth with which it can embrace a subject make artificial intelligence unique and powerful, and for this reason artificial intelligence may be the most interdisciplinary field of study taught in universities.

1.1.1 They Said It Couldn't Be Done

It is not possible for a machine to think.
Computers can only deal with zeros and ones.
Only natural things like people and animals can have intelligence.

The prospect of intelligence in machines has produced widespread skepticism. There are two main reasons for this. First, until recently, there have been

1

relatively few examples of machine expertise that were in the public eye. Furthermore, AI is sufficiently complicated that it is difficult for the uninitiated to understand. Without seeing any artificial thing behave intelligently, and without understanding how AI techniques work, it is hard to believe that it could be possible.

A second reason for the skepticism has to do with people's perception of themselves. Most people hold their own intelligence close to their hearts. People often feel that intelligence is what gives them their significance and their identity in our complicated world. The possibility that a machine might possess intelligence can be frightening. "If intelligence is something mechanical, then am I nothing better than a machine?" Machines are supposed to be subservient to humans. What is to be the status of human beings if we can no longer claim to be the smartest of earthly beings? Many people would rather belief that machine intelligence is impossible than try to answer some of these questions.

1.1.2   Artificial Intelligence In Action

Let's consider some systems that have been developed in research centers which incorporate artificial intelligence.

MOLGEN is a program that assists a molecular geneticist in planning scientific experiments. It was developed by M. Stefik at Stanford University in 1979. A typical experiment for which MOLGEN successfully devised a plan was one for the production of insulin by bacteria. Since no natural bacteria can do this, it was necessary to provide a way to splice an insulin-production gene into the genetic material of a bacterium. MOLGEN used a problem-solving technique called "planning" guided by "means-ends analysis" to generate a small sequence of general steps, and then it expanded these general steps into detailed ones, introducing constraints and propagating them as it progressed. A large knowledge base about molecular genetics is built into MOLGEN, and this was consulted frequently by the program as the plan was refined. MOLGEN was actually able to devise four different plans for the insulin-production experiment.

ACRONYM was developed by R. Brooks and T. Binford at the Stanford Artificial Intelligence Laboratory around 1981. Provided with an image (such as an aerial photograph of an airport) and geometric models for each of a set of objects (such as Boeing 747 and Lockheed L-1011 planes), ACRONYM is capable of locating objects (in the image) for which it has models. In order to accomplish this, it uses each model to predict invariant features of the corresponding object that will occur in an image, it computes a description of the image in terms of line segments and other graphical primitives, and finally, it determines an interpretation of the image by putting portions of the image description into portions of the models. Two subsystems are employed: a geometric reasoning system and an algebraic reasoning system. ACRONYM has been successful in interpreting airport images; it distinguished airplanes from surrounding structures such as gate ramps and pavement markings, and it correctly identified a plane as an

L-1011 rather than a Boeing 747.

AM is an experimental program which performs a kind of automatic theory formation in mathematics. Given a starting knowledge base containing concepts about elementary set theory and arithmetic, AM produced new concepts and conjectures by using a heuristic-search algorithm to explore a concept space. AM is guided by a mechanism that directs it to perform the task on its list of things to do that has the highest "interestingness" value. In this way it attempts to explore the most interesting examples and concepts, and to find the most interesting conjectures it can. The program managed to synthesize the concept of prime numbers and to make conjectures about them. AM was developed as part of the doctoral research of D. Lenat, also of Stanford, in 1976.

These three systems exemplify relatively recent progress in three areas of AI: plan-generation systems, computer vision, and machine learning. Much progress has also been made in other areas of AI including logical inference and consistency systems, probabilistic reasoning, speech understanding, and text understanding. Let us mention just a few of the many other accomplishments of AI.

In the late 50's and early 60's, much of the research that went by the name of artificial intelligence was concerned with getting machines to play games. An early success was the checkers-playing program of Samuel[1]. It could beat most humans at the game, and it could improve its technique through automatic learning. Today computers play good games of chess, backgammon, and many other games.

AI programs have demonstrated that computers can reason effectively with uncertain information using Bayesian methods. The program MYCIN prescribes treatment for infectious diseases, after gathering information about symptoms in dialog with users. Another program, PROSPECTOR, analyzes geological information obtained from field observations, and makes predictions about minerals that might be found at a site. Both programs employ extensive knowledge bases built with the help of specialists ("experts"). Yet another program, called XCON, whose development was sponsored by Digital Equipment Corporation, automatically determines optimal configurations of VAX computers according to customer needs and the available options.

Translation of written documents from one language to another requires deep knowledge of both languages as well as about the subject matter under discussion. Machine-aided German/English translation is now performed in a practical way, combining the human's deep knowledge with the computer's speed and facility with dictionaries and syntax. Computers are also handling semantics; they translate questions phrased in English into database queries. This eliminates the need for users of a database to know a strange query language or to write programs.

---

[1]see *Computers and Thought* mentioned at the end of this chapter.

1.2   What Intelligence Is

1.2.1   Aspects of Human Intelligence

"She's intelligent." Different people will interpret this sentence in different ways. Some take this to mean, "she knows a lot." Others would say this means, "she thinks fast." People who have thought about thinking would probably find these interpretations somewhat lacking. Someone can be fast, yet stupid; and yet one can know a lot of facts, but be incapable of putting things together in a creative fashion. A somewhat more satisfactory interpretation would be, "her actions are appropriate to each situation." One, of course, might complain that this statement is overly general and does not concentrate on the concept of intelligence sufficiently.

Important aspects of human intelligence seem to be the following: the use of intuition, common sense, judgment, creativity, goal-directedness, plausible reasoning ("if A happens, then B might happen, and if so, then C might ..."), knowledge and beliefs. While human intelligence is powerful and deep, there certainly are limits to it; humans are intellectually fallible, they have limited knowledge bases (no man or woman can read every book or have every kind of experience), and information processing of a serial nature proceeds very slowly in the human brain when compared with today's computers. Thus, the meaning of "intelligence" is not the same as "the human brain's information-processing ability." However, intelligence is a quality that much of human information processing has and which one might hope to find in other creatures or in machines.

Two of the ways that people demonstrate their intelligence are by communicating effectively (through text, pictures, verbal expression, or other medium), and by learning; that is, acquiring new knowledge through experience, and then demonstrating that they have learned the knowledge by communicating.

1.2.2   Communication

Effective communication requires skills both in analysis of messages (reception) and in synthesis of messages (transmission). In order to communicate something effectively, one must be able to synthesize a message, whether that be a letter, a paper, poem, musical composition, painting, or other form of communication, in such a way as to express one's meaning to one's intended recipient or audience. Doing this well may require making judgments about the level of sophistication of a recipient, careful use of language, and proper speed of presentation.

On the other hand, understanding a message also requires intelligence. A listener must know the meanings of most of the words a speaker is using, and the listener must have some knowledge of the context for the message. It is usually necessary for the listener to use contextual knowledge to constrain the possible interpretations of a message. In addition, the receiving person may need to be able to formulate pointed questions to gather any bits of lacking information that are necessary to understand the message. In either synthesis or analysis of a message, skills are generally required in determining context and in altering the representation of information.

1.2.3 Learning

The ability to learn or adapt one's behavior to new situations is considered by many to be a vital component of intelligence. Those animals which can change in response to changes in their environment are considered generally to be more clever than those unable to change their behavior. The kind of learning that people do seems to be much more sophisticated than that which animals do; however, it is likely that many of the basic mechanisms of learning are common to both humans and lower animals.

What is involved in learning how to deal with a new kind of stimulus? One must first learn what the major concerns are in the new context. For example, a new soldier suddenly thrust into war must quickly perceive what his side's objectives are and use that information as a framework in which to insert knowledge he gains later. Another part of learning is finding out what the basic descriptive units are in a situation. For example, in learning language one must learn that phonemes (and at the next level words and then phrases and sentences) are structural units with which descriptions of experience can be formed. Learning these structural units is essential in all kinds of learning experience. In learning to see, one gradually becomes acquainted with such distinctive features as corners of man-made objects (such as buildings and furniture). Colors, textures, and shape features are gradually acquired as tools with which to describe (consciously or subconsciously) visual experience. The third part of learning is the acquisition of the rules for combining primitive descriptors. How do words go together? How can a description of an object be composed from shape, color, and texture features? Both syntactic models and semantic models must be acquired for each knowledge domain. Learning progresses as such models become more and more sophisticated in order to understand the domain more deeply.

Organizing knowledge is an important component of the learning process. Just how pieces of information are related to one another and arranged in a machine or person's memory is a very important issue. Facts must be accessible when needed. Skills must come into play readily when the appropriate situation arises. Knowledge must be structured in such a way that further learning can take place smoothly. Part of knowledge is a framework in which various facts and aspects of experience can be stored. The framework must make it possible for associations to be made between old and new when the old and new are related. The kinds of knowledge which must be stored in the framework must include both specific facts and general rules.

1.3   What Artificial Intelligence Is

1.3.1   A Field of Study

Artificial intelligence is a field of study that encompasses computational techniques for performing tasks that apparently require intelligence when performed by humans. Such problems include diagnosing problems in automobiles, computers and people, designing new computers, writing stories and symphonies, finding mathematical theorems, assembling and inspecting products in factories, and negotiating international treaties. It is a technology of information processing concerned with processes of reasoning, learning, and perception.

Fundamental issues of artificial intelligence involve knowledge representation, search, perception and inference. Knowledge can be available in many forms: collections of logical assertions, heuristic rules, procedures, statistical correlations, etc. Much of AI is concerned with the design and understanding of knowledge-representation schemes. How can knowledge be represented so that it (a) can be easily used in reasoning, (b) can be easily examined and updated, and (c) can be easily judged as relevant or irrelevant to particular problems?

Search is a key issue because it is usually easy to invent brute-force algorithms to solve problems, but they fail on all but "toy" problems. An understanding of search techniques can help us to avoid the "combinatorial explosion" that swamps the brute-force attempts.

Inference is the process of creating explicit representations of knowledge from implicit ones. It can be viewed as the creation of knowledge itself. Deductive inference proceeds from a set of assumptions called axioms to new statements that are logically implied by the axioms. Inductive inference typically starts with a set of facts, features or observations, and it produces generalizations, descriptions and laws which account for the given information and which may have the power to predict new facts, features or observations.

1.3.2   AI: Art or Science?

One difference between a science and an art is that a science consists, in good part, of a body of proved principles that have been abstracted from nature through processes of empirical inquiry and logical deduction. That physics is a science is not contested. On the other hand, an art is for the most part a collection of techniques, developed pragmatically to a sophisticated level, but not necessarily in a logical way. Most cooks would agree that cooking is an art rather than a science.

Artificial intelligence is both an art and a science. The activity of developing intelligent computer systems employs both proved mathematical principles, empirical results of studying previous systems, and heuristic, pragmatic programming techniques. Information stored in relational data structures can be manipulated by well-studied techniques of computer science such as tree-searching algorithms. At the same time, experimental or vaguely understood "rules of thumb" for problem solving are often crucial to the success of a system and must be carefully accommodated in intelligent systems.

The field of AI is fascinating because of this complementarity of art and science. There is a lot of room for creativity in AI, and yet there is a growing body of mature ideas that are beginning to give more rigorous support to the practice of AI.

1.3.3 A Purpose

The most important purpose of artificial intelligence is to increase man's understanding of reasoning, learning, and perceptual processes. This understanding is desirable for two reasons: it is needed in order to build useful new tools and it is needed in order to achieve a more mature view of human intelligence than currently exists. The development of new tools is important because they may have commercial value, they may improve the quality of our lives through better products or entertainment, or they may increase the efficiency of governments and companies. In the author's opinion, a deeper understanding of human intelligence and its limitations is extremely important, for it might lead to suggestions for partially resolving many of the political and religious disagreements in the world that currently pose a great threat to the human race.

1.4   Artificial Intelligence Comes of Age

1.4.1   Growth of the AI Research Community

While the intellectual challenge to designers of artificial intelligence has been with western civilization for centuries, it is only very recently that a glint of practical feasibility has shown on a wide variety of applications. During the early and mid-nineteen-sixties, overly ambitious projects in automatic English/Russian translation not only failed to produce the promised systems, but dampened respect and enthusiasm for AI as a field. Critics of AI, of whom some were very "anti-computer" as well, lambasted these early failures and claimed that AI is impossible, although their arguments, typically couched in the vague terminology of phenomenological philosophy, have always been fallacious.

Today, however, the field has recovered. Many numbers of scientists, engineers and programmers are studying AI techniques and building AI systems. National and international organizations dedicated to AI have been formed and are growing. In the U. S., the American Association for Artificial Intelligence now holds a conference each three out of four years, at which research results are reported, tutorials are offered, and an exhibition of equipment and books is held.

The pendulum may even have swung back too far. Amidst the current excitement about AI, some voices are making claims that cannot be substantiated.

It is the hope of the author that this book will help in some small way to keep
the field on an even keel by presenting the elements of artificial intelligence as
they are, describing their limitations as well as their assets.

1.4.2   The Industrialization of AI

Unlike the early sixties, today a much deeper understanding of the problems
and solutions in the major domains of AI provides a solid base for many AI
systems and ventures. The intricacies of natural language translation are not
yet completely understood. However, enough is known to permit useful systems
to be constructed; several commercial ventures have recently been launched in
computer-assisted language translation. Machine vision is now practical in areas
of robotics, biomedical microscopy, and materials analysis, even though a good
many basic questions of vision have yet to be answered. The market for expert
systems has begun to open up, and now we see only the first few houses of what
will become a large metropolis.

1.4.3   What An AI Practitioner Does

For the next decade, the majority of artificial intelligence engineers are likely to
be designing expert systems. Their jobs will often be to work with experts in
particular fields such as medicine, corporate finance, astrophysics and anthropology to develop suitable representations for the knowledge in each field. The
knowledge must be put into a form on which useful inferences can be made automatically. Such work is challenging and at the forefront of the information
revolution.

In addition to developing knowledge representations, suitable displays and
means of access must be designed for users. Natural language and CRT interfaces
must be designed, often with capabilities particular to each application.

After an expert system has been designed and debugged it may require maintenance. New knowledge must be added; heuristics found to be inferior need to
be replaced; new technology may need to be incorporated. There is usually room
for improvement in fields such as medical diagnosis, mathematical theorem proving, anthropology, etc. Post-installation changes to expert systems are likely to
keep AI practitioners in work for a long time to come.

Some AI people will be scientists continuing to study basic mechanisms of
machine learning and problem solving. The field is sufficiently rich that many
basic issues, such as optimal search, probabilistic reasoning and inductive inference, will provide open problems for many years.

1.5   Philosophical Challenges

The existence of artificial intelligence puts a new light on much of philosophy.
"Can a machine think?" People often feel threatened by the possibility that a

machine can think. It suggests that they, too, are machines or no better than machines. Without an understanding of how the machine works, the intelligence of the machine is a mystery to them, and the machine may seem to be an instrument by which the machine's creators might replace or overpower and control them.

People argue this question at higher levels of sophistication than in the past, but the debate continues. An excellent presentation of some of the views on this may be found in Pamela McCorduck's book *Machines Who Think*.

1.5.1   Turing's Test

One of the philosophical problems of AI is also a practical problem. How can one tell when artificial intelligence has been achieved? A manager who wants to evaluate an AI project may well need a way to answer this question. The traditional answer to this question is that artificial intelligence is manifested in a machine when the machine's performance cannot be distinguished from that of a human performing the same task. This answer is based on a suggestion by Dr. Alan Turing that comparison with a human be the criterion by which it is decided whether or not a machine can think. Turing's test is to put a human and a machine in one room, and another human, the "interrogator," in a separate room, perhaps as illustrated in Fig. 1.1. The interrogator may ask questions

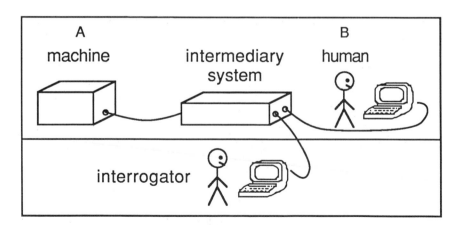

Figure 1.1: Turing's test. The interrogator (a human) must distinguish the other human from the machine.

to either the other human or the machine, referring to one as A and the other as B. However, the interrogator is not told which of A or B is the human or which is the machine. The interrogator cannot see or hear the others but passes messages through an intermediary, which could be an electronic mail system or could be another person. As they respond to questions, A and B each compete with one another to convince the interrogator that he/she or it is the human. If the machine can win, on the average, as often as the human, then it passes the "Turing test," and, by this particular criterion, can think. In practice, the outcome of such a test would probably depend heavily on the humans involved, as well as the machine.

As we grow more sophisticated, we realize that the question of whether a system is intelligent is a shallow one. We should be asking about the kinds, quality and quantity of knowledge in a system, the kinds of inference that it can make with this knowledge, how well-directed its search procedure is, and what means of automatic knowledge acquisition are provided. There are many dimensions of intelligence, and these interact with one another.

1.5.2   AI and Human Beliefs

Studies in several areas of AI—concept formation, abstraction hierarchies, belief representation, and truth maintenance systems—provide plausible explanations for some intellectual limitations of human beings. People develop prejudices by automatically forming generalizations even when it is statistically invalid to do so. People are willing to adopt fantastic beliefs and maintain them in light of serious inconsistencies, provided the beliefs supply plausible explanations for certain questions that are emotionally central. What are beliefs? Can they or should they be represented in systems as if they were knowledge? Is a man or a woman just the sum of his or her beliefs? Can a person or personality be represented in a machine? If so, does this permit a kind of morality or immorality to be manufactured? What kinds of laws should there be to regulate societies of intelligent machines?

The fact that AI brings up so many questions like these contributes to the excitement of an involvement with artificial intelligence. For years, most scientists have treated computers as fairly stupid tools. More and more people are realizing not only that computers are changing the way our society processes data, but that the ideas of computing are bringing some intellectual traditions into question, changing how we think about ourselves. AI is at the forefront of this computer revolution.

1.6   The Reference Literature

Beginning with the volume of collected papers, *Computers and Thought*, edited by E. Feigenbaum and J. Feldman in 1963, there has been a gradual growth of books that can be considered basic books in AI. *Computers and Thought* is not a text, but it introduced the subject of AI using two kinds of papers: (1) methodological articles such as A. Turing's "Computing Machinery and Intelligence," and M. Minsky's "Steps Toward Artificial Intelligence;" and (2) descriptions of computer programs. Some of the programs are (a) the "Logic Theory Machine" of A. Newell, J. Shaw, and H. Simon, and (b) a geometry theorem-proving program by H. Gelernter.

The first textbook was *Artificial Intelligence: The Heuristic Programming Approach*, by J. Slagle. This book surveys some of the programs for game-playing and problem-solving that had been completed by the early 1960's. The principle of minimax analysis of a game tree is presented there in a clear way.

A text by N. J. Nilsson entitled *Problem Solving Methods in Artificial Intelligence* appeared in 1971. It presented two key topics in a straightforward and pleasing way. The first topic is that of searching through a space of problem configurations called states. The second topic is the use of the predicate calculus in automatic reasoning. This text is mathematical in style when compared with most of the other AI texts.

The books by Slagle and Nilsson each treated relatively specific parts of AI as might be expected for the time. A book that covers cognitive models, perception and inductive methods such as clustering of patterns for subsequent recognition, in addition to theorem proving, was the book *Artificial Intelligence* by E. Hunt. This book covers a much greater variety of mathematical techniques than did its predecessors. Occasionally the treatment is dense, but the variety and depth of topics treated continue to make the book useful.

An introduction to AI suitable to readers who want a flavor for the issues and applications of AI without getting deeply involved in technique was written by P. Jackson in 1974. A book giving a similar variety of topics but including the basic techniques of AI was written by B. Raphael. It appeared in paperback form in 1976, and it was entitled *The Thinking Computer: Mind Inside Matter*.

A course for college undergraduates at MIT was developed by P. Winston, currently director of the AI laboratory there. This course concentrated on the systems and studies done at the MIT laboratory, nonetheless spanning a considerable range of topics. The course notes developed into the text *Artificial Intelligence* (bearing the same title as Hunt's book). This was the first AI text to include LISP programming techniques as part of the core material.

In 1981, Nilsson published a second AI text, entitled *Principles of Artificial Intelligence*. Like his earlier AI text, this one emphasizes search and the predicate calculus as the key components of AI systems. The treatment of both topics is expanded in the new book. In addition, the programming methodology called "production systems" is examined as a means of implementing the search and deduction methods espoused. Extensive bibliographical material on production systems, problem-solving, plan-generation and theorem proving is given.

A text, *Artificial Intelligence* by Elaine Rich, was published in 1983. It surveys AI in a style comparable to Raphael's *The Thinking Machine*. Although there is a relatively scanty treatment of vision, Rich's text has particular strength in knowledge representation. A graduate-level text *Introduction to Artificial Intelligence* by E. Charniak and D. McDermott emphasizes the computational modelling of human faculties.

The majority of writings on AI are research papers. Some good collections of these papers are the following:

1. *IJCAI Proceedings.* Every two years starting in 1969 there has been an "International Joint Conference on Artificial Intelligence." The proceedings of these contain many papers covering all the major topics in AI.

2. *AAAI Proceedings.* Starting in 1980, there has been a conference each year, (except years when the IJCAI is held in North America) sponsored by the American Association for Artificial Intelligence.

3. Technical Reports from major centers. During the 1970's most of the published research on AI came out of large centers that were sponsored by the Department of Defense. Some of these centers were the Stanford Artificial Intelligence Lab., the MIT AI Lab., and the Computer Science Department at Carnegie-Mellon University.

4. *Journal of Artificial Intelligence.* A limited number of papers of high academic quality are published in this journal by North-Holland Publishers.

5. *IEEE Transactions on Pattern Analysis and Machine Intelligence.* The majority of the papers published here have focussed on computer vision and pattern recognition, and this publication has more of an engineering orientation than the *Journal of Artificial Intelligence.*

6. *The AI Magazine.* This periodical contains semi-academic articles, book reviews, news items, and paid advertising. It is published by the AAAI.

7. *SIGART Newsletter.* News items and unrefereed articles can be found several times a year in this publication by the *Association for Computing Machinery* Special Interest Group on Artificial Intelligence.

The three AI programs mentioned earlier, MOLGEN, ACRONYM, and AM, are described in more detail in Volume 3 of the AI Handbook (edited by Cohen and Feigenbaum).

References

1. Barr, A., and Feigenbaum, E. A. (eds.) 1980, 1981. *The Handbook of Artificial Intelligence*, Volumes 1 and 2. Los Altos, CA: William Kaufman.

2. Charniak, E., and McDermott, D. 1985. *Introduction to Artificial Intelligence.* Reading, MA: Addison-Wesley.

3. Cohen, P. R. and Feigenbaum, E. A. (eds.) 1982. *The Handbook of Artificial Intelligence*, Volume 3. Los Altos, CA: William Kaufman.

4. Feigenbaum, E. A. and Feldman, J. (eds.) 1963. *Computers and Thought.* New York: McGraw-Hill.

5. Hunt, E. B. 1975. *Artificial Intelligence.* New York: Academic Press.

6. McCorduck, P. 1979. *Machines Who Think.* San Francisco: W. H. Freeman.

7. Rich, E. 1983. *Artificial Intelligence.* New York: McGraw-Hill.

8. Nilsson, N. J. 1971. *Problem Solving Methods in Artificial Intelligence.* New York: McGraw-Hill.

9. Nilsson, N. J. 1981. *Principles of Artificial Intelligence.* Palo Alto, CA: Tioga Press (1981); also Los Altos, CA: William Kaufman, 1983.

10. Raphael, B. 1976. *The Thinking Computer: Mind Inside Matter.* San Francisco: Freeman.

11. Slagle, J. 1967. *Artificial Intelligence: The Heuristic Programming Approach.* New York: McGraw-Hill.

12. Winston, P. H. 1977. *Artificial Intelligence.* Reading, MA: Addison-Wesley.

Chapter 2

PROGRAMMING IN LISP

2.1 Introduction

The programming language LISP was developed at the Massachusetts Institute of Technology in the late 1950's under the direction of J. McCarthy. It was designed specifically for list processing: that is, the manipulation of symbolic information (it does have a capability for numerical data handling as well, but it was designed primarily for non-numerical computation). The language was based in part on the "lambda calculus" of A. Church; the lambda calculus is a formal, applicative language with interesting theoretical properties. LISP is especially good for applications in artificial intelligence, and is the most widely used language for this purpose.

LISP gives the programmer great flexibility and power. Data structures are created dynamically without need for the programmer to explicitly allocate memory. Declarations for data are not necessary, and a LISP atom, acting as a variable, may represent one kind of object (e.g., an integer) at one time and a completely different kind of object (e.g., a binary tree) a little later. Using one basic data-structuring concept, the "S-expression," both programs and data are easily represented. Execution of programs written in LISP is normally accomplished by an interpreter program; thus a compiler is not necessary. Occasionally a compiler is used to optimize relatively fixed parts of a particular software collection.

A LISP program consists of several function definitions together with other statements which work together to perform the desired task. Usually, one writes the function definitions using a text editor or a structure editor. In MACLISP (and some of its derivatives) one edits function definitions in an external text editor. In UCILISP and most versions of INTERLISP there is a structure editor

15

built into the LISP system which may be used. In either case the programming
process usually proceeds through iterations of program modification and program
testing. The interactive nature of LISP makes it possible to enter definitions
directly into the LISP system, without the use of an editor. However, if there
is no editor within the LISP environment (of the implementation you are using)
as in MACLISP, it is usually too inconvenient to edit the functions within the
LISP system.

The program statements of LISP are essentially functional forms. However,
since these functional forms can and usually are nested to a large extent, one
normally does not refer to particular lines of LISP code as statements.

In this chapter the LISP language is presented, beginning with the underlying
representation for LISP programs and data: S-expressions. We then describe
how operations are expressed as functional forms. Gradually, we increase our
vocabulary of functional forms until we can conveniently understand and write
functions in LISP that are useful in artificial intelligence experiments.

2.2   S-Expressions

All data and program statements in LISP are represented in terms of S-
expressions. S-expressions often appear as lists of items enclosed in parentheses,
but they are actually more general. An *S-expression* is either an "atom" (see
below), a list of S-expressions, or a "dotted pair" (see below) of S-expressions.
(The definition for S-expression which will be stated more formally later is recursive.) Before defining each of these three types of S-expressions, let's consider
some examples of S-expressions.

A	a literal atom
SAMPLELITERALATOM	a literal atom
4	a numeric atom
(A B C D)	a list of S-expressions
(A (DOG CAT) 7)	a list of S-expressions
(A . B)	a dotted pair of S-expressions
(DOG . (CAT . MOUSE))	a dotted pair of S-expressions

The first three of these examples are atomic S-expressions while the last four are
composite.

"Atoms" are the basic building blocks of S-expressions. An *atom* is either a
"numeric atom" such as an integer (e.g., -25) or a floating point number (called
a FLONUM, e.g., 107.3), or a "literal atom," very much like an "identifier" of
other programming languages such as PASCAL. A literal atom is described as
a string of characters beginning with a letter, the characters generally being
restricted to letters, digits and a few other characters.

Let us now give a formal definition of "S-expression." The definition is recursive, and in its course are also defined the terms "dotted pair" and "list."

1. Any atom is an *S-expression.*

2. If X and Y are S-expressions then $(X . Y)$ is an *S-expression* and is also called a *dotted pair.*

3. If $S_1, S_2, \ldots, S_k$ are S-expressions, then $(S_1 S_2 \cdots S_k)$ is an *S-expression* and is also called a *list.*

4. Only an object formed by a finite number of applications of rules 1, 2 and 3 is an *S-expression.*

Thus atoms may be put together to form more complicated S-expressions using either the dotted-pair construction or the list construction. Although the list construction is far more common in actual usage of LISP, we begin here describing the dotted pair construction because understanding it gives a clear idea of how S-expressions are represented in a computer's memory, and it is then easy to understand how lists are represented, too. A LISP system can seem mysterious without some good notions of how its structures fit into the machine.

A dotted pair (as we have defined it) consists of an ordered pair of S-expressions, which by convention are written separated by a period and surrounded by parentheses. For example, two atoms A and B may be written in the following way to represent the dotted pair of A and B:

(A . B)

The resulting pair is an S-expression which may be further combined with other S-expressions to build larger ones.

2.2.1 Machine Representation of S-expressions

The main memory of a LISP system is logically divided up into "cells." A cell is typically two machine words of storage and represents a dotted pair. Denoting each cell by a rectangle with two halves containing arrows or atoms, the printed and the diagrammed representations for two dotted pairs are shown in Fig. 2.1. The letters A through D within the rectangles indicate the presence of pointers to literal atoms. The arrows represent pointers to subexpressions.

Before we expand on the nature of lists in LISP, we must mention a literal atom "NIL" which has special significance. The atom NIL is used in LISP for several purposes. The most important of these is as a marker at the end of a chain of pointers in memory. (In other words, NIL is used to terminate lists. Later in this chapter we shall see how NIL also serves to represent the boolean value "false" in many contexts.) The third diagram in Fig. 2.1 contains such a chain, and the diagonal slash is used to indicate NIL.

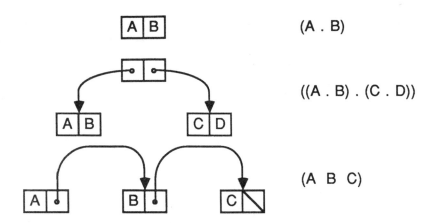

Figure 2.1: Printed and diagrammed representations of S-expressions in memory.

As defined above, a list is a sequence of S-expressions, separated by spaces, and surrounded by a pair of parentheses. When the number of S-expressions in the sequence is zero, the list is empty and may be written as:

()

The atom NIL is an alternative way to indicate the empty list. "NIL" and "( )" are equivalent.

2.2.2   Correspondence Between Lists and Dotted Pairs

Except for the empty list, NIL, a list is always equivalent to some dotted pair of a particular kind. The machine representation for a list and its corresponding dotted pair are identical. For example the list illustrated in the third diagram of Fig. 2.1 is equivalent to the dotted pair

(A . (B C))

Eliminating the sublists by converting into dot notation as far as possible yields the S-expression below, which is the dot-notation equivalent of the original list.

(A . (B . (C . NIL)))

Note that the last atom in the dotted-pair representation of a list is always the special atom NIL.

Using the fact that NIL is equivalent to ( ) and the fact that an expression of the form $(X$. NIL$)$ is equivalent to one of the form (X), it is not difficult to see that the following three S-expressions are equivalent:

```
(NIL . NIL)
(() . ())
(())
```

Here are some additional examples of dotted-pair expressions which have equivalent list forms:

in dot notation	in list notation
(A . NIL)	(A)
((X . NIL) . (Y . (Z . NIL)))	((X) Y Z)
((APPLE . BANANA) . NIL)	((APPLE . BANANA))

Any list can be re-expressed in dot notation (also called dotted-pair notation). However, only certain S-expressions in dot notation can be converted into list notation[1]. For example, the dotted pair (A . B) is not equivalent to any list. It doesn't even contain the atom NIL, which is a required terminator for any list. The third example above shows an S-expression which cannot be completely converted to list notation. The right-hand version is clearly a list, but one of its elements is a dotted pair that cannot be expressed as a list. Any S-expression which is not an atom is *composite*. In practice, lists probably account for 98% of all composite S-expressions that are actually used. Arbitrary dotted pairs, once common because they are more space-efficient, are used infrequently today, since list notation is a more convenient representation for the programmer to work with than is dot notation.

2.3   Functional forms

2.3.1   Some Forms and Their Evaluation

In order to get a computer system to perform operations, it is necessary to give it some instructions. In LISP, one does this by presenting the computer with special S-expressions called "functional forms." A functional form consists of a list whose first component is the name of a function and whose subsequent components are arguments to that function. An example is the following:

```
(ADD1 5)
```

Here "ADD1" is the name of a function and 5 is an S-expression that plays the role of an argument to the function. By typing in such an S-expression to the LISP system the programmer is requesting that LISP evaluate that function on those arguments. After typing it, LISP responds with "6."

---

[1] By examining the memory diagram for an S-expression in dot notation, we can determine whether or not it can be converted into list notation (such that the resulting expression contains no dots). The diagram may be viewed as an ordered binary tree. Each chain consisting only of arrows leaving right-hand sides of memory cells must terminate at a cell whose right-hand side contains NIL.

Most of the functions commonly provided in LISP systems are shown in Fig. 2.2. The various kinds of functions are described throughout this chapter. An alphabetical listing of LISP functions with brief descriptions is given in an appendix.

2.3.2 Nested forms

Arguments to functional forms can themselves be functional forms. For example, the following form produces the value 47:

```
(PLUS 2 (TIMES 5 9))
```

Thus, subexpressions such as (TIMES 5 9) in the form above are treated as functional forms themselves. When the LISP system computes the value of the whole expression, it first evaluates the subexpression (getting 45 in this example) and then this partial result is used as an argument to the outer function (here PLUS) and the final value is computed.

2.4 CONS, CAR and CDR

In our definition of "S-expression" we gave rules for composing dotted pairs and lists. There are functional forms that perform such construction and also for taking out the parts of a composite S-expression. The name for the operation of putting two S-expressions together to form a dotted pair is "CONS." CONS is a binary operation taking two S-expressions and returning a new S-expression. Here are two examples using CONS to build larger S-expressions:

```
(CONS 1 2)            produces the value (1 . 2)
(CONS 1 NIL)          produces the value (1)
```

When the CONS operation is performed, a cell of memory is allocated, and the contents of the left and right halves are set to the values of the two arguments. When the second argument to CONS is a list, the effect of the CONS is to create a new list in which the first argument to CONS is the element of the list, and the second argument is the remainder of the list. Thus, if x and y are S-expressions whose values are 1 and (4 5 6), respectively, then (CONS x y) produces the value (1 4 5 6).

Functions which extract the components of a dotted pair (and therefore also access parts of lists) are CAR and CDR. CAR takes a composite S-expression and returns as value the first component S-expression. Applying the CAR function to the dotted pair (A . B) produces A as value. The effect of CAR on a list is also to produce the first element of the list as value. Thus CAR applied to the list (X Y Z) produces X as value.

Input and Output:
(READ S)
(TYI)
(PRINT S)
(TERPRI)
(TYO N)

List Structure Manipulation:
(CONS S1 S2)
(CAR S)
(CDR S)
(CAAR S)
(CADR S)
(CDAR S)
(CDDR S)
(APPEND L1 L2 ... Lk)
(RPLACA S1 S2)
(RPLACD S1 S2)
(NCONC L1 L2)

Evaluation-related:
(EVAL S)
(APPLY F L)
(MAPCAR F L)
(LIST S1 S2 ... Sk)
(QUOTE S)
(FUNCTION S)
(SET S1 S2)
(SETQ A S)

Control Forms:
(COND (S1a S1b)
      (S2a S2b)
      ...
      (Ska Skb))
(PROG L S1 S2 ... Sk)
(GO A)
(RETURN S)

Predicates:
(NULL S)
(ATOM S)
(NUMBERP S)
(EQ A1 A2)
(EQUAL S1 S2)
(LESSP N1 N2)
(GREATERP N1 N2)
(ZEROP N)
(ONEP N)
(MEMBER S1 S2)

Logical Functions:
(AND S1 S2 ... Sk)
(OR S1 S2 ... Sk)
(NOT S)

Arithmetic:
(ADD1 N)
(SUB1 N)
(PLUS N1 N2 ... Nk)
(TIMES N1 N2 ... Nk)
(DIFFERENCE N1 N2)
(QUOTIENT N1 N2)
(REMAINDER N1 N2)
(MAX N1 N2 ... Nk)
(MIN N1 N2 ... Mk)

Function and Property Definition:
(DEFUN A L S)
(DEFEXPR A L S)
(LAMBDA L S)
(PUTPROP A S1 S2)
(GET A S)
(PLIST A)

Debugging:
(TRACE F1 F2 ... Fk)
(UNTRACE F1 F2 ... Fk)
(BREAK)

S — an S-expression
L — a list
N — a number
F — a function
A — a literal atom

Figure 2.2: Functions commonly provided in LISP systems. Note that the values of arguments have the types indicated.

Similarly, CDR produces the second component of the dotted pair as value.
CDR applied to (A . B) produces B. Applied to a list, CDR returns as value the
list, missing its first element. Thus the CDR of the list (X Y Z) is the list (Y Z).

In a sense, each of CAR and CDR is a partial inverse of CONS. Evaluating
the following functional forms illustrates this

```
(CAR (CONS 1 2))                    produces the value 1
(CDR (CONS 1 2))                    produces the value 2
```

However, as we shall see later when we discuss the special functional form
SETQ, neither CAR nor CDR nor both taken together necessarily undo the
effect of CONS.

Functional forms built up using CONS, CAR and CDR can be used to create
and access parts of arbitrarily complex S-expressions. By putting S-expressions
together with CONS, arbitrarily large S-expressions may be formed.

```
(CONS 5 (CONS (CONS 6 (CONS 1 2)) 8))
```

produces (5 . ((6 . (1 . 2)) . 8)).

Combinations of CAR and CDR are needed so often to access various components of S-expressions that additional functions are provided in most LISP
systems to abbreviate the more common combinations. The following twelve are
standard; some implementations provide more. Each combination is shown in
the left column and its corresponding abbreviation is in the right-hand column:

```
(CAR (CAR X))                      (CAAR X)
(CAR (CDR X))                      (CADR X)
(CDR (CAR X))                      (CDAR X)
(CDR (CDR X))                      (CDDR X)
(CAR (CAR (CAR X)))                (CAAAR X)
(CAR (CAR (CDR X)))                (CAADR X)
(CAR (CDR (CAR X)))                (CADAR X)
(CAR (CDR (CDR X)))                (CADDR X)
(CDR (CAR (CAR X)))                (CDAAR X)
(CDR (CAR (CDR X)))                (CDADR X)
(CDR (CDR (CAR X)))                (CDDAR X)
(CDR (CDR (CDR X)))                (CDDDR X)
```

The general rule for combining several CARs and CDRs together is that one
forms a string by concatenating the middle letters (A's or D's) of all the instances
in the same order that they appear in the expanded form, and then a C is prefixed
and an R suffixed to the string.

2.5 QUOTE and SETQ

There are exceptions to the general pattern of evaluating functional forms that has been described so far. For example, a special functional form is QUOTE. The QUOTE of something evaluates to itself. Another special form is SETQ, used for saving a value by associating it with an atom.

2.5.1 QUOTE

QUOTE is used to suppress the evaluation of an S-expression in a place in which it would otherwise be evaluated. Here are examples:

(PLUS 1 2)	produces 3
(QUOTE (PLUS 1 2))	produces (PLUS 1 2)
(QUOTE A)	produces A
(CAR (CONS 1 2))	produces 1
(CAR (QUOTE (CONS 1 2)))	produces CONS
'(PLUS 1 2)	produces (PLUS 1 2)

As the last example shows, there is an abbreviation for the QUOTE form. This is the single quote mark. Thus, 'X is equivalent to (QUOTE X). Note that the quote mark avoids having to use one pair of parentheses needed by the canonical version of the QUOTE form. It is often useful to precede an argument to a function by a quote mark so that the argument will evaluate to itself before the function is applied. Consider the next example.

(CONS (CAR '(A . B)) (CDR '(C . D)))

Here the top-level function in this functional form is CONS. There are two arguments to it. In this case the first is the smaller functional form (CAR '(A . B)) and the second is the functional form (CDR '(C . D)). Before the top-level function CONS can be applied to the arguments, those arguments must be evaluated. The first subexpression (CAR '(A . B)) produces A upon evaluation. The second subexpression, (CDR '(C . D)), produces D. The value of the top-level form is now equivalent to that of the form (CONS 'A 'D) which in turn is (A . D).

Note that the form

(CAR (X Y))

will usually cause an error (unless the programmer defines X to be a function), unlike the form

(CAR '(X Y))

which yields the value X.

2.5.2 SETQ

As we have already seen, (PLUS 5 7) is a sample functional form in LISP. When
LISP interprets this form, the function PLUS will be applied to the arguments
5 and 7. The value of this form, 12, will then be computed and returned. Such
a functional form may be typed directly into LISP and the system will evaluate
it and print its value.

If it is desired to have the system remember a value, a form such as the
following could be used.

```
(SETQ X (PLUS 5 7)).
```

This form first evaluates the PLUS expression and then assigns its value to the
atom X. After this form has been evaluated, the expression X may be evaluated
to recall the value 12. Note that there is no need to declare X to be a variable.
Its mere mention in the expression is sufficient to make LISP treat it as one.

Also, note that there is no need to quote the argument X here. The first
argument to SETQ is automatically quoted; in fact, SETQ is short for "SET
QUOTE."

The expression above has the same effect as the following one using SET,
which is not a special form:

```
(SET 'X (PLUS 5 7)).
```

2.6 Special Forms

Certain functional forms are called "special" forms. Special forms are either
those that take a variable number of arguments, rather than a number fixed by
the function definition, or those that do not have their arguments evaluated at
entry in the standard way. We have already seen two special forms, QUOTE and
SETQ. The single argument to QUOTE is not evaluated, and the first of the two
arguments to SETQ is not evaluated. An example of a form that is considered
special even though all its arguments are evaluated uses the arithmetic function
MAX. Any number (1 or more) of arguments may be supplied to MAX. For
example, (MAX 3 7 2 10 -3) produces the value 10. Actually, PLUS is also a
special form in most LISP implementations, so that, for example, (PLUS 1 3 6
10) is legal and produces the value 20.

Another special form is the AND function form. Evaluation of (AND
$E_1 E_2 \cdots E_k$) proceeds by successive evaluation of subexpressions E_1, E_2, until
one is found with value NIL, at which point the value NIL is returned as the
value of the whole form. If none of the subexpressions evaluates to NIL, then T
is returned as the value of the whole form. Like MAX, AND takes one or more
arguments. Unlike MAX, it is possible that some of the arguments to AND are
never evaluated.

LIST is a special form which takes any number of arguments and returns a list of their values.

(LIST 2 (PLUS 2 7) (CONS 'A 'B)) produces (2 9 (A . B))

Other special forms are COND and PROG, which control the evaluation of their enclosed subexpressions. These are described later.

2.7 Predicates

Predicates are functions that return values normally interpreted as Boolean truth values. For example, (LESSP 3 5) returns the value T, whereas (LESSP 3 3) returns value NIL. This predicate tests to see whether its first argument is less than its second argument. Another predicate (GREATERP 3 5) returns NIL in this instance. The special form AND described earlier may be considered to be a predicate. It is interesting to note that in most LISP implementations, any value not explicitly NIL is taken to mean "true" in any logical test. Consequently, a predicate may return any value except NIL to indicate a true condition. Thus (AND 'A 'B) may evaluate to T, to B or to any non-NIL value depending upon the implementation. Like AND, OR is a special form which produces a logical result. Other examples of predicates that are standard are ATOM and NULL. (ATOM X) evaluates to T if X is an atom, NIL otherwise. (NULL X) evaluates to T only if X is NIL, and NIL otherwise. Most LISP systems recognize NOT as a synonym for NULL. (NUMBERP X) yields T if X evaluates to a numeric atom.

The predicate EQUAL can be used to compare any S-expression with another. For example (EQUAL '(A B (C)) '(A B (C))) returns T. There is a more efficient function, EQ, that can be used if the arguments are literal atoms. For example, (EQ 'A 'A) produces T and (EQ 'A 'B) produces NIL. However, EQ may produce NIL even if given two arguments that are EQUAL, if the arguments are numeric or non-atomic[2].

2.8 COND

Several special forms are particularly useful in controlling the execution of LISP programs. One of these is COND. A COND form (or "conditional form") takes an arbitrary number of arguments called *clauses*, each of which is a list of two S-expressions. The general format of a COND form is as follows:

(COND $(C_1\ E_1)$ $(C_2\ E_2)$ $\cdots$ $(C_n\ E_n)$)

---

[2]In most LISP systems, EQ returns T if the two pointers that result from evaluating the two arguments are the same; thus two different pointers to similar structures would lead to EQ returning NIL.

The subexpressions C_i represent conditions, and the subexpressions E_i represent corresponding actions or results.

The value returned by the COND form depends upon the values of one or more of the C_i and precisely one of the E_i. Suppose that the first C_i whose value is not NIL is C_k. Then the value returned by COND is the value of E_k. If none of the C_i are true, the value returned by COND is undefined. In programming practice usually the last C_i is the constant T. Programming in this manner is analogous to the use of an ELSE clause with the IF construction in other programming languages.

For example,

```
(COND (NIL 1) (T 2) (T 3))
```

produces the value 2. As another example, the following sequence results in the value B.

```
(SETQ X 'A)
(SETQ Y NIL)
(COND (X 'B) (Y 'C))
```

Most modern LISP interpreters accept a more general format for COND. Instead of requiring that each E_i be a single S-expression, they permit one or more expressions to follow each C_i. A clause then has the form:

$(C\ E_a\ E_b\ \cdots\ E_k)$.

After a C_i is found to be the first condition that is not null, the corresponding sequence of expressions is evaluated in order, and the last one's value gives the value for the entire COND form. This feature is sometimes referred to as the "implicit PROG," and the reason for this will be clear later when the PROG form is discussed. We will occasionally rely on this feature in subsequent chapters because it helps make programs shorter and easier to read.

Many function definitions are based upon the COND form. In order to illustrate this, we turn now to the general problem of defining functions in LISP.

2.9   Defining Ordinary Functions

A LISP program consists primarily of a set of function definitions. The programmer writes these functions so that they work together to perform a given task. There are several ways in which functions can be defined, but the most common method is using DEFUN. (Later sections describe how special forms and LAMBDA expressions can be defined.)

2.9.1 DEFUN

To define a new function in LISP, the programmer gives the system a special form. The usual general format for a function definition is as follows:

(DEFUN *function-name argument-list function-body*)

When this form is evaluated, the LISP system will enter a function definition into the LISP system under the name represented by *function-name*. The list of arguments indicates what parameters used by the function are to be bound to values when the function is called. The body is a functional form which expresses the value that the function is to return in terms of its argument values when it is called. For example, we can define a function which computes the square of a number as follows:

(DEFUN SQUARE (X) (TIMES X X))

Once the definition has been evaluated, we can make use of it; for example, typing

(SQUARE 7)

would result in the value 49 being returned.

In most respects a LISP function is conceptually similar to a function or subroutine in a programming language such as PASCAL, FORTRAN, or PL/I. An interesting difference is that the arguments are not constrained by declarations to particular types; that is, each argument need only be some S-expression. When a function is called, the arguments in the calling form are paired ("bound") with the formal arguments in the definition. Then the body is evaluated. (If there is an incompatibility between an S-expression and an operation to be performed on it, such as in trying to add 5 to the literal atom A, a run-time error will be reported.)

2.9.2 Recursive Definitions of Functions

Functions to perform complex operations are generally defined in terms of simpler ones. However, it is often useful to define a function in terms of itself. More particularly, the function applied to a complex object can be defined as a combination of results of applying the same function to components of the complex object. Such function definitions are *recursive*.

Below is a function definition based upon COND. The function computes the length of a list (i.e., the number of top-level S-expressions).

```
(DEFUN LENGTH (LST)
   (COND ((NULL LST) 0)
         (T (ADD1 (LENGTH (CDR LST)))) ) )
```

This function may be applied to any list to return an integer. For example, the length of '(A B C D) is 4, and the length of '(THIS (IS (A (NESTED (LIST)))))) is 2. The function has one formal parameter, namely LST. The body consists of a conditional form (a "COND"), in this case having two clauses. Each clause has two parts, a condition and a result. The first clause has as its condition the expression (NULL LST) and the result 0. This specifies that when the functional form is evaluated, the argument, LST, is tested to see if it is null, and if so, the result 0 is returned. The second clause is there in case the first fails. Its condition is T, which is always true and thus forces its result to be returned if LST is not null. This second result expression, "(ADD1 (LENGTH (CDR LST)))", contains a recursive call to LENGTH, the function being defined. The argument for the recursive call is the original LST minus its first element. To evaluate the recursive call, the LISP system evaluates the argument, binds the argument value to LST after saving the old value of LST on a stack, and then starts a fresh pass through the body of the function, possibly making additional recursive calls, if the list whose length is to be determined is long enough. When the recursive call is finished, the value returned gets 1 added to it by the function ADD1, and this value is the result of the LENGTH computation. The sequence of recursive calls in such a situation is sometimes called a spiral of recursion. In this function, the spiral of recursion eventually starts to unwind when the list bound to the atom LST gets down to NIL.

A spiral of recursion for the LENGTH function applied to the list (A B C) is shown in Fig. 2.3.

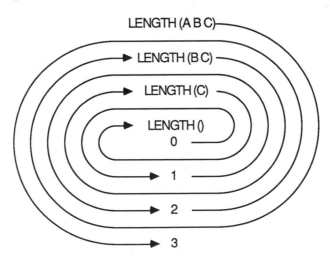

Figure 2.3: A spiral of recursion.

A similar but more interesting example of a recursive function is one that counts the number of sublists in a list. The list '(MEAT VEGETABLES

SWEETS) has no sublists, but the list

'((BEEF PORK) (POTATO CARROTS) ((APPLEPIE CHERRYPIE) CANDY))

contains four sublists (three of them at the top level, and one at the next level). A function to count the number of sublists in a list would be awkward to define without recursion. Here is a recursive definition of COUNTSUBLISTS.

```
(DEFUN COUNTSUBLISTS (LST)
  (COND ((NULL LST) 0)
        ((ATOM LST) 0)
        ((ATOM (CAR LST)) (COUNTSUBLISTS (CDR LST)))
        (T (PLUS 1
                 (COUNTSUBLISTS (CAR LST))
                 (COUNTSUBLISTS (CDR LST)) )) ) )
```

If we call COUNTSUBLISTS with the S-expression above with 4 sublists, first the test for null list fails, then the test for atomic argument fails, then the test for atomic CAR fails, since the CAR of that expression is (BEEF PORK). Finally the T clause of the COND has to succeed, with the result that three quantities are added together: the constant 1, the result of calling COUNTSUB- LISTS recursively on (BEEF PORK) which gives 0, and the result of call- ing COUNTSUBLISTS recursively on ((POTATO CARROTS) ((APPLEPIE CHERRYPIE) CANDY)) which returns 3.

Since the definition of COUNTSUBLISTS contains two recursive calls rather than one, not a spiral of recursion but a tree of recursive calls is followed. Each recursive call generates a separate branch of the tree. An example is shown in Fig. 2.4.

As a third example of recursive function definition, consider the function MATCHKTH below. This function takes three arguments: an "element," a list and an integer. It compares the element to the kth one in the list where k is specified by the integer. It returns the element if the match was successful and returns NIL otherwise.

```
(DEFUN MATCHKTH (ELT LST K)
  (COND ((NULL LST) NIL)
        ((LESSP K 1) NIL)
        ((AND (EQUAL K 1)
              (EQUAL (CAR LST) ELT) )
         ELT)
        (T (MATCHKTH ELT
                     (CDR LST)
                     (SUB1 K) ) ) ) )
```

We have defined MATCHKTH as a function of the arguments ELT, LST, and K. The body is a COND having four clauses. The first clause tests for LST

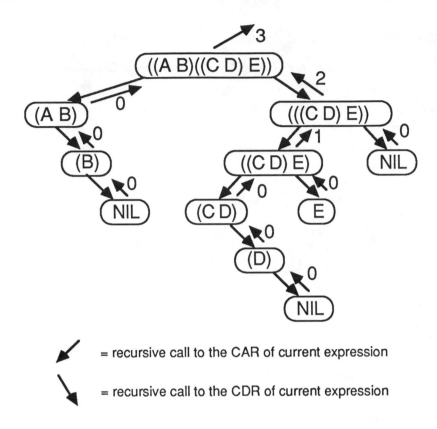

= recursive call to the CAR of current expression

= recursive call to the CDR of current expression

Figure 2.4: A tree of recursive calls for the evaluation of (COUNTSUBLISTS '((A B)((C D) E))).

being null and returns NIL if so. Otherwise, the next clause checks for K less than 1 and returns NIL if this is the case. If neither of those two hold, then the third clause tests first for K equal to 1. If this fails, control falls through to the fourth clause. However, if K equals 1 then an additional test is made to see if ELT is equal to the first item of LST. If this is true, the value of ELT is returned. If not, the fourth clause with condition T invokes a recursive call to MATCHKTH with a list one element shorter and with K reduced by one. The depth of the deepest recursive call will be the smaller of K and the length of LST.

Here are some examples of the behavior of MATCHKTH:

```
(MATCHKTH 'CROISSANT  '(BREAD  ROLL CROISSANT)  2)
```

produces NIL.

```
(MATCHKTH 'CROISSANT  '(BREAD  ROLL  CROISSANT)  3)
```

produces CROISSANT. The first result is NIL because CROISSANT does not appear as the second element of the list. If the last argument were changed to a 3, as shown in the second example, then the result would be CROISSANT.

2.9.3 Appending Lists Recursively

A useful function for concatenating two or more lists is provided by most LISP systems. To show how recursive definitions may help with list manipulation, a two-list version is defined below:

```
(DEFUN APPEND (L1 L2)
      (COND ((NULL L1) L2)
          (T (CONS (CAR L1)
                  (APPEND (CDR L1) L2) )) ) )
```

This definition says that in order to append list L2 onto the end of list L1, we first check to see if L1 is null. If it is, the answer is just L2. Otherwise, the answer is the result of appending L2 to the CDR of L1 and then CONS'ing the CAR of L1 back on.

It is possible to define APPEND as a special form so that it can take any number of arguments; to do this, one could use the function DEFEXPR, described later. In most LISP systems, APPEND is predefined and can take any number of arguments.

2.9.4 Commenting LISP Programs

Most LISP systems allow comments to be embedded in LISP functions. Comments have no effect on the functions; the LISP interpreter ignores them. However, they are helpful to the programmer in documenting and annotating the functions. The use of comments is encouraged. In this book, a semicolon is used to indicate that the remainder of a line of LISP code is a comment. For example, we could write

```
(SETQ X 5)   ; Set X equal to 5.
```

2.10 PROG

The LISP language was developed soon after FORTRAN. Some programmers, fluent in FORTRAN, found it difficult to design their programs as nested function calls. They thought in terms of a set of statements expressed and executed in a sequence, with possible branching using the GOTO statement. The PROG form allows FORTRAN-like control structure to be embedded in LISP programs. A sequence of functional forms may be grouped together to function like statements of a conventional programming language by the use of the PROG form. The general format of a PROG is:

(PROG L F_1 F_2 $\cdots$ F_n)

Here L is a list of local variables, and F_1 through F_n are individual functional forms (or they may be atomic "labels"), which may include nested forms within them. When the PROG is evaluated, local variables will be set up for all the elements in the list L. Note that L may be NIL. The values of these local variables will be initially undefined. (The values of any variables external to the PROG having the same names will be inaccessible within the PROG.) Then the forms F_1 through F_n will be evaluated in sequence unless special provisions have been made to alter that sequence.

In order to alter the flow of control within a PROG, one may use special control flow statements such as GO or RETURN. For example, (GO LOOP) when evaluated, results in control being transferred to the first functional form following the label LOOP. By nesting GO statements inside of COND arguments, it is possible to conditionally transfer control within a PROG.

The example PROG below contains two "PROG variables," X and Y, which are local to the PROG and have values that are accessible only within the PROG. The first expression in the PROG's sequence is (SETQ X 10), which causes X's value to be set to 10. The tag, "LOOP" is not evaluated but passed over, and it serves only to indicate a position in the sequence for use in the later expression "(GO LOOP)". The expression "(PRINT (TIMES Y Y))" first causes the square of Y to be computed and then causes that value to be printed (on the screen). The next expression first computes X−1. That value would be lost if it weren't then put somewhere; it is then made the new value of X, as prescribed by the SETQ form. Similarly, the value of Y is changed. The COND first has X checked to see if it is 0, and if so the RETURN causes the execution of the entire PROG to be terminated with the current value of Y passed back as the value of the PROG. If X is not zero, the second clause is activated. Here T evaluates to itself and forces (GO LOOP) to be evaluated. This simply causes a transfer of execution back to the expression (PRINT (TIMES Y Y)).

```
(PROG (X Y)
      (SETQ X 10)
      (SETQ Y 0)
 LOOP (PRINT (TIMES Y Y))
      (SETQ X (SUB1 X))
      (SETQ Y (ADD1 Y))
      (COND ((ZEROP X) (RETURN Y))
            (T (GO LOOP)) ) )
```

The result of evaluating this PROG is the following being printed out:

0
1
4

9
16
25
36
49
64
81

and then the value 10 is returned.

When the evaluator leaves the PROG (in this case via the RETURN), the values of the local variables are disposed of, and any previous values of atoms with the same names are accessible again (the local contexts are nested as execution enters functions and PROGs having local variables). Execution may exit a PROG not only by evaluating a RETURN expression, but also by "falling through." In this case, the value of the PROG is (for most implementations of LISP) the value of the last expression in it. For example, the following PROG returns the value 5:

```
(PROG (X)
      (SETQ X 10)
      (ADD1 4) )
```

However, the following PROG is preferable because it is less implementation dependent, and it makes the programmer's intentions more specific.

```
(PROG (X)
      (SETQ X 10)
      (RETURN (ADD1 4)) )
```

A PROG need not have any local variables:

```
(PROG NIL
      (PRINT 'NO)
      (PRINT 'LOCALS)
      (RETURN (SETQ X (ADD1 X))) )
```

The variable X here is from an outer context, either the global, or a local one in which this PROG is either embedded statically (via its physical placement within the S-expressions containing it) or embedded dynamically via function evaluation. The value of this PROG clearly depends upon the value of that X; it's the value of X plus 1.

2.11 EVAL and APPLY

2.11.1 EVAL

Before arguments are passed to most functions, they are evaluated. In fact, what happens is that a special function in LISP is applied to each argument

S-expression. That special function is called EVAL. EVAL computes the value
of an S-expression differently depending on whether the expression is a numeric
atom, a literal atom, or a functional form. If the S-expression consists of a
numeric atom, the value is the atom itself. If the expression is a literal atom, its
value is looked up using the current bindings. The S-expression may also be a
functional form. EVAL will first (recursively) evaluate all of the arguments in the
functional form, and then it will apply the function to the results of evaluating
the arguments. The final result will be returned as the value of the functional
form.

EVAL may also be used by the programmer directly to cause an extra evaluation to take place. For example, if the value of X is Y, and the value of Y is
Z, then the functional form (EVAL X) would evaluate to Z. (The S-expression
X by itself would evaluate to Y.) EVAL could be helpful in retrieving the value
of an atom whose name is not known until runtime.

EVAL can also be useful in letting LISP evaluate a functional form that
is constructed by the program at runtime rather than by the programmer at
programming time. For example, we could have:

```
(EVAL (LIST FN ARG1 ARG2))
```

2.11.2   APPLY

Part of EVAL's job is actually handled by the built-in function APPLY. The
function APPLY takes two arguments (and in some implementations a third),
and the form of a call is (APPLY *function arglist*). When this is evaluated, the
function which is the value of *function* is applied to the arguments that are the
elements of the list *arglist*. For example, the following form produces the value
5.

```
(APPLY 'DIFFERENCE '(12 7))
```

Some LISP systems allow APPLY to take a third argument which specifies a
list of bindings of variables to values, that are to be used during the application
of the function.

2.11.3   LAMBDA expressions

It is possible to specify a function in a LISP program without giving it a name or
calling it by name. This is sometimes convenient when a function is only needed
in one specific place, so that there is no economical advantage to defining it with
its own name. There is also an advantage of "locality"; it is easier to understand
programs whose functions are specified at the point of use than somewhere far
away.

A local function specification is accomplished by making a "LAMBDA expression." A LAMBDA expression is of the form,

(LAMBDA *argument-list body*)

For example, the function $x^2 + 2y$ is computed by

(LAMBDA (X Y) (PLUS (TIMES X X) (TIMES 2 Y)))

LAMBDA expressions are most commonly used as arguments to APPLY. For example, the following computes y^3:

(APPLY (FUNCTION (LAMBDA (X) (TIMES X X X))) (LIST Y))

Here the special form FUNCTION serves to quote the LAMBDA expression, preventing it from being evaluated.

2.11.4   Closures of functions

A feature of some implementations is the ability to specify a "closure" of a function in which all or a selected set of free variables of the function receive values from the environment in which the closure is performed, rather than the values they might get in the middle of evaluating the body of the function. Such a closure, if performed, is executed as an effect of FUNCTION. An example where closure makes a difference is the following:

(PROG ()
     (SETQ Y 5)
     (RETURN (APPLY (FUNCTION (LAMBDA (X) (PLUS X Y)))
                    (LIST (SETQ Y 7)))))

Without closure, the value of Y at the time the PLUS operation is performed is 7, as is the value of X. This is because the evaluation of (SETQ Y 7) takes place before the LAMBDA expression is actually applied to anything. The overall result is 14. However, with closure, when the FUNCTION expression is evaluated, the result is not merely that which would have been obtained by quoting the LAMBDA expression. It is a special LISP object referred to as a *funarg* (which is an abbreviation of "functional argument"). In creating the funarg, the free variable, Y, gets bound to its current value, 5, and that value is "closed into" the function. When the PLUS is performed, the value of X is 7 but that of Y is still 5 within the funarg, even though it has changed to 7 in the surrounding environment. The result of PLUS and of the overall expression is then 12 rather than 14.

Closure tends to be computationally expensive, and binding of all free variables at closure time is seldom necessary in practice. It is one solution to the so-called "funarg problem," where there may be a conflict between intended bindings of variables in a function definition, and the actual bindings those variables may get upon evaluation in an unforeseen environment.

An alternative solution is to allow FUNCTION to take an arbitrary number of arguments; the first is either the name of a function or a LAMBDA expression, and successive arguments are particular free variables in the function specification whose values are to be closed into the funarg. Any free variables not listed are treated as if there were no closure. This method is computationally more efficient yet allows the programmer to prevent binding conflicts.

2.12   Defining Special Forms

Functions (for user-defined functions) are of two types. Most frequently used are those of the "EXPR" variety. The other type is the "FEXPR" variety. Functions of the EXPR type are those having a fixed number of arguments. Functions of the FEXPR type have no restrictions on the numbers of arguments they can take. In addition, EXPR's always have their arguments evaluated as they are called. On the other hand, FEXPR's do not necessarily have their arguments evaluated; the evaluation is controlled in the definition of the FEXPR. In a FEXPR's definition, only a single formal parameter is given. When the FEXPR is called, all of the arguments in the call are bound as a list to the formal parameter.

The way to define a FEXPR is dependent upon one's LISP system. We use the convention that a special form DEFEXPR similar to DEFUN is used. A simple example of a FEXPR is the function MYSETQ below, which has behavior similar to that of the built-in function SETQ.

```
(DEFEXPR MYSETQ (L) (SET (CAR L) (EVAL (CADR L))))
```

A call such as (MYSETQ X 5) binds L to the list (X 5) and applies the function body, setting the value of X to be the result of evaluating 5 (which is 5). Note that if MYSETQ is called with fewer than two arguments, an error will result. If there are more than two arguments, the extra ones are ignored.

A more novel example of a FEXPR is a function we can call SETQ2 which, like SETQ, takes two arguments and assigns from right to left. However, where SETQ automatically quotes its first argument and evaluates the second, SETQ2 does the converse. It evaluates the first and quotes the second. Then, for example, we could have the following interactive sequence:

```
(SETQ X 'Y)                    ; produces value Y
(SETQ2 X (CAR Y))              ; produces value (CAR Y)
Y                              ; produces value (CAR Y) and
(EVAL Y)                       ; produces value CAR.
```

In order to define SETQ2, as with MYSETQ, we need control of argument evaluation. Therefore, we choose the FEXPR type of function rather than the normal EXPR. Our definition is as follows:

```
(DEFEXPR SETQ2 (L)   ; here L represents a list of the arguments.
  (COND ((NOT (EQUAL (LENGTH L) 2)) (PRINT '(ERROR IN SETQ2)))
        (T (SET (EVAL (CAR L))
              (CADR L) )) ) )
```

Since there is no way for the LISP interpreter to know how many arguments we intend SETQ2 to be called with, the first clause of the COND above checks to make sure the number is 2, causing an error message (which is specific to the problem) to print if not. Then, the arguments are accessed from the list L using CAR and CADR to pick off the first and second ones, respectively. The first one is evaluated as per our requirement. Since the second is not evaluated, we may think of it as automatically quoted. The assignment is acually performed by the general function SET.

Suppose we wish to define a special form taking any number of numeric arguments which computes the average of them. We may do this as follows:

```
(DEFEXPR MEAN (L)
  (QUOTIENT
    (APPLY (FUNCTION PLUS)
           (MAPCAR (FUNCTION EVAL) L) )
    (LENGTH L) ) )
```

The atom L gets bound to the entire list of unevaluated arguments when MEAN is called. In our case, we want those arguments evaluated. Therefore we use the subexpression (MAPCAR (FUNCTION EVAL) L) to give us this list of evaluated arguments (the function MAPCAR is described in the following section of this chapter). To get the sum of this list we apply the function PLUS to it. Note that the form (PLUS (MAPCAR (FUNCTION EVAL) L)) would produce an error since there would be only one argument to PLUS and this would be a list, not a number. Thus, we APPLY the function PLUS to the list of arguments. Finally, the length of L is unchanged by evaluating the elements of L, and we can therefore take LENGTH of L itself. The quotient of the sum and the length is the average.

2.13 MAPCAR

Sometimes one wants to apply a single function to each of the several elements in a list. Although one could use a PROG including a loop to iteratively process first one argument, then the next and so on, LISP provides a special form, "MAPCAR," to accomplish this in one fell swoop. For example, the form (ADD1 5) which returns value 6 can be expanded upon with MAPCAR to yield a form such as

```
(MAPCAR (FUNCTION ADD1) '(5 10 7 -2 101))
```

which returns as its value the list (6 11 8 -1 102). We see here that MAPCAR requires two arguments: the first is a function description, in this case the expression (FUNCTION ADD1). The second argument to MAPCAR is a list of inputs for the function.

It is often convenient to operate on lists using MAPCAR. The next example takes a list of words and changes some of them, so that if the input is an English sentence in the present tense, then the output will be in the past tense. This example shows how an embedded function definition can be included within a MAPCAR expression. The embedded definition uses the keyword "LAMBDA." The function could have been separately defined and named but was embedded instead (as a matter of style).

```
(DEFUN MAKEPAST (PRESENT)
        (MAPCAR (FUNCTION (LAMBDA (WORD)
                            (COND ((EQ WORD 'AM) 'WAS)
                                  ((EQ WORD 'ARE) 'WERE)
                                  ((EQ WORD 'IS) 'WAS)
                                  (T WORD) ) ))
                PRESENT) )
```

The function MAKEPAST takes a single argument, PRESENT, which is assumed to be a list of atoms. MAPCAR successively causes each word to be tested with the embedded function, and the word or a replacement for it is returned in the output list. Here is an example application of MAKEPAST to a data list:

```
(MAKEPAST '(MT ST HELENS IS AN ACTIVE VOLCANO))
```

which yields

```
(MT ST HELENS WAS AN ACTIVE VOLCANO)
```

2.14 READ and PRINT

A LISP function may obtain data in several ways: (a) the data may be passed as one or more arguments, (b) the data may be represented as global values of properties and accessed within the function by referencing the appropriate atoms, or (c) the function may accept data directly from the user or from a data channel connected through the operating system. In order to obtain data this third way, the function READ (or one of its variations) is used. READ takes no arguments. When it is called, evaluation is suspended until the user types in a syntactically valid S-expression at the console. When the input operation is complete, the value typed in is returned as the value of READ. For example, we might type

```
(CONS (READ) '(TWO THREE))
ONE
```

and get the result (ONE TWO THREE).

The results of a computation are commonly printed on the screen because LISP automatically prints the result of any top-level evaluation. However, any available S-expression can be printed at almost any point within a function using PRINT. PRINT takes one argument and prints the value of the argument on a new line on the screen or printer. For example, (PRINT '(A B (C))) produces output (A B (C)) and then returns a value. Consider also:

```
(MAPCAR (FUNCTION PRINT) '(A B (C . D)))
```

which produces the output:

```
A
B
(C . D)
```

and then the value of PRINT is returned. In some systems, PRINT always returns T. In others, it always returns NIL. In others, the value printed is what is returned.

An important variation of PRINT is PRIN1, which is like PRINT but does not go on to a new line.

Additional functions for reading and printing data are system dependent. However, two are described here which are very useful for interactive experiments.

TYI is a function of no arguments which waits for one character to be typed at the keyboard (or read from a data channel, in some systems) and returns a FIXNUM giving the ASCII code for the character typed. This function is useful for building keystroke-driven command interpreters.

TYO is a function which takes a single FIXNUM argument representing an ASCII character code. TYO causes that character to be "typed out" on the screen, printer, or data channel. It provides a simple way to get punctuation, special symbols, and control characters.

Some LISP systems provide functions for opening and manipulating logical windows on the display screen. One function used later in this book is LOCATE, invoked as (LOCATE I J). This positions the screen's cursor at row I, column J, where I and J must evaluate to FIXNUMs.

2.15 The Property List of an Atom

Each literal atom such as MTRAINIER is automatically given a property list by the LISP system as soon as the atom is first seen. The property list is a list of pairs of S-expressions which store information related to the atom. The built-in function PUTPROP is used to place such a pair on the list. For example, to associate with MTRAINIER a HEIGHT property of 14410, the following call could be used:

(PUTPROP 'MTRAINIER 14410 'HEIGHT)

The general format of this call is (PUTPROP *atom value property-type*)[3]. Subsequently, the information may be retrieved with the call:

(GET 'MTRAINIER 'HEIGHT)

which returns the value 14410. Any number of pairs may be associated with an atom. However, giving a new value for a previously stored property type will overwrite the previous value. Thus, evaluating the form

(PUTPROP 'MTRAINIER 4392 'HEIGHT)

which gives the height of Mt. Rainier in meters, effectively deletes the old value stored for the HEIGHT of MTRAINIER. Notice that the order in which the arguments are given is important. The result of evaluating

(GET 'HEIGHT 'MTRAINIER)

will be NIL, unless additional information is explicitly stored on the property list of the atom HEIGHT.

2.16   Replacing Pointers in LISP Memory

Normally, when a new list or dotted pair is created by LISP (as the result of a CONS or LIST form, for example) one or more new cells are allocated and pointers copied into their left and right halves, in such a way that no previous cells are altered. Thus if the value of X is the list (A B C) and the form (SETQ Y (CONS 'N (CDR X))) is evaluated, Y will receive the value (N B C) without any change being made to the value of X. On the other hand, there exist functions that have the effect of rewriting a pointer into a LISP cell, causing an alteration rather than allocation of new memory. The form (SETQ Y (RPLACA X 'N)) causes the CAR of X to be replaced by a pointer to the atom N, and the value of Y is this altered version of X. If X is now evaluated, the result is (N B C).

The function RPLACD is similar to RPLACA but causes the CDR rather than the CAR to be replaced. Note that circular lists can easily be created with RPLACA and RPLACD that may cause problems when they are given to PRINT. For example, (SETQ X '(A B C)) creates the list structure shown in Fig. 2.5. Evaluating the form (RPLACA X X) changes this to the structure shown in 2.6.

This structure prints as a long sequence of left parentheses, (((((((((((··· until the system stack overflows or the user turns off the computer. In a similar fashion, the sequence (SETQ X '(A B C)), (RPLACD X X) causes LISP to emit (A A A A A ..., without ever getting to a closing parenthesis.

---

[3]Note that some systems require that the property type be an atom.

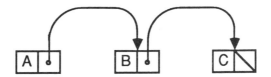

Figure 2.5: List structure created by (SETQ X '(A B C)).

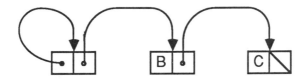

Figure 2.6: List structure resulting from (RPLACA X X).

The function (NCONC X Y) applied after (SETQ X '(A B C)) and (SETQ Y '(D E F)) makes a non-copying concatenation of X and Y. The last pointer in X (which points to NIL) is replaced by a pointer to the value of Y. The result is similar to that given by (APPEND X Y). However, as a side effect, X has been altered. The value of Y remains the same.

These functions are not recommended for general or casual use, since they easily create structures which are unprintable and make debugging difficult. However, they have some merits. It is possible to construct fairly compact representations in memory of arbitrary directed graphs, cycles permitted, using them. Also, since they do not cause new storage to be allocated, they may reduce the amount of time spent by LISP in garbage collection for some applications.

2.17   Debugging

Errors and oversights seem to be the rule in AI programming, largely because of the experimental nature of the field. Although the programming methodology ideas discussed elsewhere in this chapter will greatly assist in program development, the need still exists for occasional detailed observation of a program. Tools for examining the progress of a program are useful both in finding errors, in verifying correctness, and for human understanding.

LISP systems usually provide two kinds of debugging aids: TRACE capability for viewing function calls, and BREAK capability for examining the values of variables at selected breakpoints during the execution.

TRACE is a special form which takes any number of function names as (unevaluated) arguments. The general format for invoking it is (TRACE F_1 $F_2 \cdots F_n$). It causes those functions to be marked for automatic "tracing" whenever they are called. For example, (TRACE LENGTH) marks the LENGTH function, so that each time it is called, the name of the function and the particular values of the arguments in the call will be displayed. Also, when the function returns, the returned value is displayed. In some LISP systems, only EXPR's can be TRACEd. In others, any function can be traced.

The related form (UNTRACE F_1 $F_2 \cdots F_n$) turns off trace mode for each F_i. If no arguments are given, all traced functions are made untraced.

Suppose, for example, that we define FACT to compute the factorial of its argument. An appropriate definition is the following:

```
(DEFUN FACT (N)
  (COND ((ZEROP N) 1)
        (T (TIMES N (FACT (SUB1 N)) ))) )
```

If we cause FACT to be traced, and then invoke it:

```
(TRACE FACT)
(FACT 3)
```

we get a display such as the following one:

```
1 FACT:(3)
 2 FACT:(2)
  3 FACT:(1)
   4 FACT:(0)
   4 FACT=1
  3 FACT=1
 2 FACT=2
1 FACT=6
6
```

Such a display typically shows not only the function name, argument values and return value, but also the level of invocation of the function (here shown both with printed integers and with corresponding indentation). These extra features make it easy to see the correspondence between an entry to a function and the value which results.

Using TRACE, one can easily determine whether a particular function is ever reached, or ever reached with a particular set of arguments. TRACE is easy to use because no editing and subsequent un-editing of the functions to be traced are necessary, as they usually are with other debugging methods.

As convenient and useful as it is, TRACE does not provide a means of viewing the state of a computation at other than function entry and exit. It doesn't provide any way to see values of variables not directly connected with the function call, and it does not provide a way for the programmer to change variable values interactively during the computation. A function which permits these things to be done is BREAK. In a typical LISP system, when (BREAK X) is evaluated, the interpreter stops further evaluation and prints "BREAK:" followed by the result of evaluating X. It then enters a "Read-Eval-Print" loop similar to that at top-level. Local variable values can be examined or changed, and functions can be executed as if at top-level. To continue the evaluation of an expression after a BREAK, the programmer types a control character or a special atom such as RESUME.

If a BREAK function is not available in your LISP system, the following definition gives you one.

```
(DEFUN BREAK (S)                    ;program break utility function
   (PROG (BREAKVAL)                 ;local variable
         (PRIN1 'BREAK)             ;print out message
         (TYO 58)                   ;type a colon
         (TYO 32)                   ;type a space
         (PRINT S)                  ;print the argument
         (PRINT '(TYPE RESUME TO CONTINUE))
    LOOP (SETQ BREAKVAL (READ))     ;get an S-exp from the user
         (COND ((EQ BREAKVAL 'RESUME)
                (RETURN NIL)))      ;return if it's RESUME
         (PRINT (EVAL BREAKVAL))    ;otherwise evaluate and print it
         (GO LOOP) ) )              ;repeat
```

2.18　Programming Methodology

One tends to be concerned with slightly different issues when writing LISP programs than when writing payroll programs, or statistical packages. LISP programs are usually experimental, to test out new ideas, to model something one might not fully understand. Consequently, getting the program to work, gaining a better understanding of one's problem, and ease of development are usually more important to LISP programmers than speed.

2.18.1　Benefits of Programming in LISP

Some of LISP's strengths are the following:

Modularity: Since a LISP program consists of a set of function definitions, and it is very easy to have one function call another, it is also easy to fit a hierarchy of modules (functions) to the natural structure of a problem or problem-solving procedure.

Speed of development: LISP requires very few "declarations" of data or data types, as do languages such as PASCAL. There is time saved in not having to declare data and in not having to debug consistencies between data declarations and data usages. On the other hand, the LISP programmer is not prevented from writing procedures that test data for proper formats. The fact that LISP is usually interpreted means that the programmer can easily and frequently make

changes and try them without having to wait for a compiler to translate his
entire program each time. Debugging aids available in LISP allow location of
problems faster than do those for conventional languages. This is because the
debugging tools are integrated into the programming environment, have access
to all symbols and function definitions, and have the full power of LISP available
to them.

Functional Programming: It is relatively easy in LISP to write programs
whose correctness is relatively easy to prove mathematically. A style of programming in which no assignments or global properties are manipulated is called
"functional programming."

2.18.2   Stepwise Refinement

To have an orderly development of a program larger than a couple of pages, the
following suggestions are offered.

Use dummy functions in the beginning stages of coding, as "syntactic scaf-
folding" to verify correct data formats of functions that communicate with the
dummies. The dummies also serve to help verify proper execution order.

Alter only as many things at a time as you can mentally keep in mind at
once. Add roughly one new feature at a time, to make debugging simpler.

Thoroughly test each new feature under a variety of input configurations.

2.18.3   Ways to Keep Complexity Manageable

The potential confusion grows more than linearly with the size of a program.
This is just as true for LISP as for any other language. Here are some tips for
fighting the tendency.

Use simple functions (with good names) to construct and access data objects
of the types you need. For example, if dates are to be represented as lists of
the form (DAY MONTH YEAR), it clarifies programs to have defined special
accessing functions:

```
(DEFUN DAY (DATE) (CAR DATE))
(DEFUN MONTH (DATE) (CADR DATE))
(DEFUN YEAR (DATE) (CADDR DATE))
```

Keep function definitions from getting too big. For most functions, a screen-
ful is a good limit. The programmer's eye can then take in the entire function
definition at once. If needed, create helping functions. This also helps to keep
parenthesis balancing easy, and reduces the need for a large number of "indentation levels" for neatly formatting function definitions.

Use a formatting scheme in the source file that clarifies the structure of each
expression. A convention used in formatting the LISP expressions in this book
is that in a sequence of closing (right) parentheses, there is a space between

two right parentheses if the two left parentheses that they correspond to lie on separate lines. This makes it easier to see the right-to-left correspondences.

Comment the function definitions.

2.18.4 Pragmatics

Here are some general edicts of good programming practice:

Keep backups of your files and document them. Since they tend to be experimental, you may have more versions of your LISP programs around than one usually would have with programs in other languages. A backup should be made at the end of a day's work, after a bug has been completely eliminated, or after a certain amount of work. Usually, software backups suffice (e.g., extra disk files). But when in danger of magnetic media erasure, etc., an occasional paper printout is wise.

AI is almost by definition a field in which people try to automate intellectual tasks that are more and more difficult. When you bite off more than you can chew, spit it out and start over. That is, back off from your original ambitious plans when necessary.

2.19 Implementation of LISP

2.19.1 Representations of Literal Atoms, Numbers and CONS Cells

LISP interpreters generally consist of a memory management unit, a collection of core functions usually implemented in a low-level language for speed, and a library of functions that augment the core functions. Such functions may be written in LISP themselves. The core functions generally must include READ, EVAL, APPLY and PRINT or variants of them. Also CONS, CAR, CDR, SET, and DEFUN are core, as are NULL, ATOM, and various arithmetic functions and predicates. COND and PROG are core. The core functions form a basic group in terms of which the library functions can be implemented.

Memory is usually organized into cells, although some implementations provide a number of memory areas including non-cellular ones. The cells initially form a large pool of available storage. They are chained together into a long list called the freelist. Cells are taken off the freelist as needed to build atoms, build lists, etc. Literal atoms may require several cells to hold their definitions. Typically a cell consists of two or three machine words of memory. Small interpreters on microcomputers may use 4 bytes per cell, while larger lisp systems might use more than 8 bytes (64 bits) per cell. Each cell must be capable of being addressed by a pointer that fits in half a cell. This is because a "CONS cell" or cell representing a dotted pair, must store pointers to two other cells, one representing the CAR and one representing the CDR.

2.19.2   Garbage Collection

As evaluation in a LISP environment proceeds, cells are continually taken off
the freelist to make the list structure to represent results of function evaluations.
Many of these results are temporary and of no use after a brief moment. If there
were no way of reclaiming the space taken up by these old values, only LISP
programs making very light use of memory could run before the freelist would
be exhausted and all evaluation terminated. Thus, practically all LISP systems
have a "garbage collector" facility which causes the cells no longer in active use
to be identified and linked back into the freelist for reallocation.

The simplest kind of garbage collector uses a "mark and sweep" procedure.
Whenever the freelist becomes exhausted, evaluation is temporarily suspended.
Then the garbage collector begins its work by marking all literal atoms and the
cells accessible from them through their values and their property lists. Then all
temporary cells (in use by the evaluator) and their values are marked. All bindings of literal atoms must be marked (not just current local bindings). Marking
a CONS cell usually consists of the following: (1) checking to see if it is already
marked and passing it by if so, (2) setting a special bit in the cell (the mark bit)
to 1, (3) recursively marking the cell pointed to be the CAR pointer in the cell,
and (4) similarly marking the CDR cell. After the marking stage is complete, a
sweep is begun by starting at (say) the high end of cell memory space and examining the mark bit in each cell. Each cell not marked is assumed to be garbage,
and it is linked into the freelist. Each marked cell is assumed to be potentially
useful and is not changed (except that the mark bit is cleared in anticipation of
the next garbage collection).

A variation on the mark and sweep algorithm is to perform "compaction"
during the sweep phase. With this scheme the sweep is performed starting with
two pointers: one at the high end of cell memory and the other at the low
end. The pointer at the low end is advanced to locate a vacant (unmarked)
cell. Then the pointer at the top is moved down to find a marked cell. The
contents of the marked cell are moved to the vacant cell in low memory, and a
"forwarding address" is stored in place of the information that was just copied
down. The process continues until the pointers meet somewhere in the middle of
cell memory. Then all references to marked cells in the higher part of memory are
updated by replacing the referencing pointers by the forwarding addresses left
at each marked upper-part cell. Finally, all upper-part cells are joined to form
the new freelist. The main advantage of compacting is that it becomes easier
to allocate large-sized blocks of memory in LISP systems which can make use
of larger blocks. Another advantage may accrue in LISP systems having disk-
based virtual memory. By moving values of relatively permanent importance to
resident areas of memory (or by moving them close together), the frequency of
page faults may sometimes be reduced.

If the memory space is very large (as it often is on LISP machines using
disk-based virtual memory), a mark-and-sweep garbage collection might take

several minutes, causing an annoying interruption to the user. In response to this problem, designers of LISP machines have developed "incremental" garbage collection algorithms that perform a little bit of the work of recycling memory every time memory is allocated, rather than waiting to do it all at once. The result of this is slightly slower execution 95% of the time, but no long waits occurring as a result of a sudden need for a little memory to be allocated. The incremental algorithms are considerably more complicated than non-incremental ones.

Some LISP systems save some memory by storing lists in chunks bigger than CONS cells, when possible. For example, if a list of 7 elements is to be created, and a block of 5 contiguous half-cells (pointer containers) is available, a spare bit in each half-cell is used to indicate whether the next half-cell contains the pointer to the CDR (conventional) or it contains (a pointer to) the next element on the list. This technique is known as "CDR-coding" and can save almost 50% of memory when many long lists are represented with large blocks of memory.

2.20 Bibliographical Information

LISP was invented by McCarthy [McCarthy 1960], and it was based in part on the lambda calculus [Church 1941]. A clear introduction to the lambda calculus may be found in [Wegner 1968]. An early collection of application-oriented discussions of LISP is [Berkeley 1964]. Primers devoted to LISP are: [Weissman 1967], and [Friedman 1974] (both of these concentrate on basic aspects of the language which can be learned without experience on a computer). More advanced books on LISP (in order of increasing sophistication) are: [Siklossy 1976], [Winston and Horn 1981], [Charniak et al 1979] and [Allen 1978] (which deals in depth with the theory and implementation of LISP).

The methodology of structured programming in LISP was explained well in [Sandewall 1978]. Techniques of functional programming are presented in [Henderson 1980] (which also includes guidelines for implementing parts of LISP).

Since 1980 there has been a biennial conference sponsored by the Association for Computing Machinery on LISP and applicative programming. Research papers about new developments in LISP can be found in the proceedings of those conferences.

References

1. Allen, J. 1978. *Anatomy of LISP*. NY: McGraw-Hill.

2. Berkeley, E. C., and Bobrow, D. G. (eds.) 1964. *The Programming Language LISP: Its Operation and Applications*. Cambridge, MA: Information International, Inc.

3. Charniak, E., Riesbeck, C. and McDermott, D. 1979. *Artificial Intelligence Programming*. Hillsdale, NJ: Lawrence Erlbaum Associates.

4. Church, A. 1941. *The Calculi of Lambda-Conversion*. Princeton, NJ: Princeton University Press.

5. Friedman, D. 1974. *The Little LISPer*. Palo Alto, CA: Science Research Associates.

6. Henderson, P. 1980. *Functional Programming*. Englewood Cliffs, NJ: Prentice-Hall.

7. McCarthy, J. 1960. Recursive functions of symbolic expressions and their computation by machine, Part I. *Communications of the ACM*, Vol. 3, No. 4. pp185-195.

8. Sandewall, E. 1978. Programming in the interactive environment: The LISP experience. *ACM Computing Surveys*, Vol. 10, pp35-71.

9. Siklossy, L. 1976. *Let's Talk LISP*. Englewood Cliffs, NJ: Prentice-Hall.

10. Wegner, P. 1968. *Programming Languages, Information Structures and Machine Organization*. New York: McGraw-Hill.

11. Weissman, C. 1967. *LISP 1.5 Primer*. Belmont, CA: Dickenson Publishing Co.

12. Winston, P. H., and Horn, B. K. P. 1981. *LISP*. Reading, MA: Addison-Wesley.

Exercises

1. Which of the following are LISP atoms?

```
ATOM                17                  5
(0)                 ( )                 NIL
(A . B)             T                   4A
```

2. Convert the following S-expressions into list notation (insofar as it may be possible):

```
(A . (B . (C . NIL)))
(X . ((Y . Z) . NIL))
((A . B) . (C . D))
```

3. Convert the following S-expressions into dot notation:

```
(A)
((B))
(( )( ))
```

4. Describe the values of the following expressions:

```
(ADD1 (TIMES 4 5))
(CAR (QUOTE (A LIST)))
(CAR '(A LIST))
(CDR '(A LIST))
(CONS 'TO '(BE OR NOT TO BE))
(CONS (CDR '(CATS . DOGS))(CAR '(BEARS . LIONS)))
(COND (NIL 1)(T 2)(NIL 3)(T 4))
```

5. For the function COUNTSUBLISTS defined on page 29 determine how many recursive calls are made in order to evaluate the following expression:

```
(COUNTSUBLISTS '(A (B) (C (D))))
```

What is the argument to COUNTSUBLISTS in each case?

6. Write a recursive function EXIFY which takes any S-expression and converts it to a new one in which all atoms other than NIL have been replaced by X. Thus (EXIFY '(A (B . C) X Y NIL Z)) should produce (X (X . X) X X NIL X).

7. Write a recursive function REPLACE which takes three S-expressions (call them S1, S2 and S3). It replaces S2 by S3 wherever it occurs in S1. Use EQUAL to test for occurrences of S2 in S1. For example,

```
(REPLACE '((THIS 1) CONTAINS (2 OCCURRENCES (THIS 1)))
         '(THIS 1)
         '(THAT ONE))
```

should yield the value

```
((THAT ONE) CONTAINS (2 OCCURRENCES (THAT ONE))).
```

8. Using a recursive approach, write a function which prints the first fifteen cubes (1, 8, 27, 64, ..., 3375). Now write a non-recursive version, using PROG. Compare the lengths of the two definitions by counting the number of atom occurrences in each.

9. What is the result of evaluating the following?

```
(SETQ X '(EVAL '(SETQ X 'EVAL)))
```

What would be the value if the first quote mark were omitted?

10. Suppose an atom ILIST is bound to a list of integers such as (3 7 11 13) and a function is needed which returns the sum of all the elements of ILIST; that is, a function SUM is desired such that in our case (SUM ILIST) = 34. Use APPLY to define such a summation function.

11. Explain the difference between an EXPR and a FEXPR.

12. Define a LISP function (PALLINDROMEP LST) which returns T if and only if LST is a pallindrome; that is, if LST is the same after its top level elements have been put into reverse order.

13. Assume that (REVERSE L) takes a list L and reverses its top-level elements; for example (REVERSE '(A B (C D) E) produces the value (E (C D) B A). What is the value produced by the expression below?

```
(MAPCAR (FUNCTION REVERSE) '((A B) (C (D E)) (F G)))
```

14. Use MAPCAR to write a function that takes a list and creates a new list whose elements are lists obtained by repeating original elements. For example, if the old list was (X Y (Z W)) then the new list would be ((X X) (Y Y) ((Z W)(Z W))).

15. Define a function (EQUALELTS LST) which returns T if and only if all the top-level elements of LST are EQUAL to each other.

16. The list ((A B)(C D)(E F)) represents a "quasi-balanced" tree in the sense that:

    - all top-level sublists have the same length,
    - all top-level sublists have the same depth (depth is the maximum path length from the root to a leaf node), and
    - each sublist is also quasi-balanced.

    Write a function (QUASI_BALANCEDP LST) which returns T if and only if LST represents a quasi-balanced tree. You may use the function EQUALELTS of the previous problem.

17. A function may be recursive even though it does not contain a direct call to itself. Consider the tree structure of Fig. 2.7 and its representation as the list:

$$((3\ (2\ 5))(7\ (3\ 1)))$$

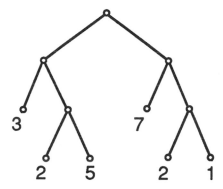

Figure 2.7: A tree for manipulation by indirectly recursive functions.

Suppose we want to compute a value at the root which is the *maximum* value for its two children, where each of those values is the *minimum* of its two children's, etc., alternating maximization and minimization at each level of the tree. Write definitions for two functions TREEMAX and TREEMIN that call each other to come up with the desired value. Your function should be able to handle binary trees of any depth. Note that the correct value for the example illustrated is 3. That is, (TREEMAX '((3 (2 5))(7 (2 1)))) should yield 3. Test your function on the example above and on the following two:

(((1 2)(3 4))((5 (6 7)) 8))
(1 (8 (2 (7 (3 (6 (4 5)))))))

This method of processing trees is developed further in Chapter 5 in connection with automatic game-playing programs.

18. Using the function MAKEPAST (described on page 38) as an example, write a function MAKEOPPOSITES which replaces some common words by their opposites.

19. Write and debug a LISP function "NEXT" which finds the next element in a sequence. The sequence is assumed to be a list of FIXNUMs. NEXT should perform correctly on arithmetic and geometric progressions, and it should give up gracefully on others. For example

- (NEXT '(2 4 6 8)) = 10
- (NEXT '(4 −12 36 −108)) = 324
- (NEXT '(3 1 4 1)) = UNKNOWN

Show the results your function gives on these examples and on five other diverse examples of your own fabrication.

20. Describe how property lists could be used in order to represent the information that daffodils are yellow and belong to a group of plants called bulbs. What is then necessary to retrieve this information?

21. Suppose that an arithmetic expression is any functional form using only PLUS and TIMES as functions, and using only constant numbers, variables (literal atoms), and (nested) arithmetic expressions as arguments. An example is the following:

    (PLUS X 3 5 (TIMES (TIMES X Y Z) 0))

    Write a function SIMPLIFY which takes an arithmetic expression and returns a new one in which the following improvements are made, if they are possible: (a) any subexpression consisting of the function TIMES followed by a list of arguments, one of which is 0, is replaced by 0; (b) any occurrence of 1 as an argument to TIMES is eliminated, and then, if possible, the occurrence of TIMES is eliminated, leaving only the other factor at that level; and (c) any occurrence of 0 as an argument to PLUS is eliminated, and if only one argument remains, the occurrence of PLUS is eliminated. If SIMPLIFY were run on the arithmetic expression above, it should give the expression:

    (PLUS X 3 5)

Chapter 3

Production Systems and Pattern Matching

3.1 Overview

In this chapter we further develop LISP programming methodology, and at the same time, we examine conceptual tools for designing AI systems. The previous chapter presented the main features and functions of LISP. However, in order to solve interesting problems, we need to be able to write LISP programs that are more complicated than those of Chapter 2. This chapter begins by describing "production systems," which provide a scheme for structuring AI programs. We then develop several LISP examples to illustrate the implementation of production systems. Next, pattern-matching techniques are presented and illustrated in LISP. In order to show how these ideas can be used in larger programs, we then apply both production systems and pattern matching in each of two simple AI systems: "SHRINK," a conversational simulator for a Rogerian psychiatrist, and "LEIBNIZ," a program which performs symbolic differentiation and simplification of mathematical formulas. The chapter closes with an introduction to unification, a pattern-matching technique for logical reasoning that is developed further in Chapter 6.

3.2 Production System Methodology

3.2.1 Modularity Revisited

As was mentioned in the previous chapter, LISP programs should be built up out of relatively small and understandable parts (modules). This necessity for simplicity and clarity becomes a challenging problem as the size of a program grows. One way to combat the problem is to adopt a simple structure for the

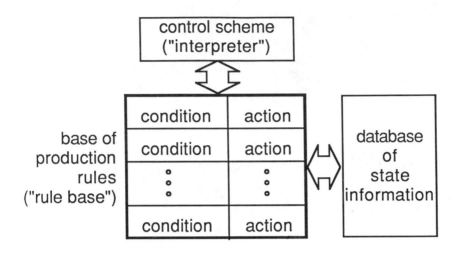

Figure 3.1: The structure of a production system.

entire program, called a "production system." A production system consists of a collection of condition-action pairs called production rules, together with a database of "state information" and a procedure for invoking the production rules. The overall structure of a production system is shown in Fig. 3.1.

Each production rule is much like a clause in a COND form. It contains a condition which must be satisfied before the action part is performed. In fact, we will often implement our production rules as actual COND clauses. The database of state information is just a collection of information tested and acted upon by the production rules. In LISP the database may consist of a list of variables (atoms), their values and their properties. The invoking procedure is often just a program loop which repeatedly tests the conditions of production rules and executes their actions when satisfied.

A simple example of a production system is now described. The job accomplished by the system is to take an integer x and produce its Roman numeral representation.

1. Production Rules:

   (a) If x is null then prompt the user and read x.

   (b) If x is not null and is bigger than 39 then print "too big" and make x null.

   (c) If x is not null and is between 10 and 39 then print "X" and reduce x by 10.

(d) If x is not null and is equal to 9 then print "IX" and reduce x to 0.

(e) If x is not null and is between 5 and 8 then print "V" and reduce x by 5.

(f) If x is not null and is equal to 4 then print "IV" and reduce x to 0.

(g) If x is not null and is between 1 and 3 then print "I" and reduce x by 1.

(h) If x is not null and is equal to 0 then print an end-of-line and make x null.

2. Database: The value of the sole variable x.

3. Control scheme: Test conditions in an arbitrary order until one is true; execute corresponding action; repeat indefinitely.

The control scheme here works by having an interpreter scan through a list of the production rules. The rules may be in the order given, or any other order. The condition part of each rule is tested in turn, until one of the conditions is found to be true. When one is true, we say that the production rule "fires" or "triggers." Then, the action for that rule is executed by the interpreting procedure. For example, if x has the value 7, then production rule e above would fire, causing the action

print "V" and reduce x by 5

to be performed. After the action is taken, the interpreting procedure starts testing production rule conditions once again. This process is repeated indefinitely (i.e., forever or until the interpreter is turned off).

An alternative to the indefinite repetition scheme could be to repeat until either no conditions are true any more or an action is taken which explicitly halts the interpreter. However, the particular set of production rules might not allow halting anyway.

The program ROMAN1 is a straightforward (though not the most efficient) implementation of this production system. Here is the LISP program ROMAN1:

```
; ROMAN1.LSP - unordered production system to
;convert to Roman numerals.

(DEFUN ROMAN1 ()
  (PROG(X)
    LOOP
    (COND
       ((NULL X) (PRINTM ENTER NUMBER) (SETQ X (READ)))
       ((AND (NOT (NULL X)) (GREATERP X 39))
        (PRINTM TOO BIG) (SETQ X NIL))
       ((AND (NOT (NULL X)) (LESSP X 40) (GREATERP X 9))
```

```
              (PRIN1 'X) (SETQ X (DIFFERENCE X 10)) )
           ((AND (NOT (NULL X)) (EQUAL X 9))
              (PRIN1 'IX) (SETQ X 0) )
           ((AND (NOT (NULL X)) (LESSP X 9) (GREATERP X 4))
              (PRIN1 'V) (SETQ X (DIFFERENCE X 5)) )
           ((AND (NOT (NULL X)) (EQUAL X 4))
              (PRIN1 'IV) (SETQ X 0) )
           ((AND (NOT (NULL X)) (LESSP X 4) (GREATERP X 0))
              (PRIN1 'I) (SETQ X (SUB1 X)) )
           ((ZEROP X) (SETQ X NIL) (TERPRI))
           )
        (GO LOOP) ) )
```

Thus ROMAN1 is defined as a function of no arguments (it gets its inputs through the action of one of the production rules – rule a). The body of RO-MAN1 consists of a PROG form, which allows the repetition of the control scheme to be easily implemented as a loop. There is a single local variable, X, for the PROG, and it is used to hold all the state information for this simple production system. The portion of the procedure for testing conditions and executing actions is implemented in ROMAN1 as a COND form. Each production rule is represented as one of the clauses of the COND form. (There are other ways to represent production rules in LISP; one alternative is used near the end of this chapter in the LEIBNIZ program). The production rules are examined in a fixed order here: the order in which they appear in the COND form. The repetition loop is completed by the form (GO LOOP).

3.2.2   Ordered Production Systems

The often-repeated test for X being not null is a symptom of LISP's need for arguments of the numeric type for its numeric predicates like LESSP and GREATERP. As we shall shortly see, the imposition of a planned ordering on the production rules can greatly reduce the redundancy of testing for such subconditions as whether or not a value is null, atomic, of a certain length, numeric, etc. The placing of the ordering on the production rules is no inconvenience in LISP, since the testing of conditions of production rules cannot be run in parallel without unusual hardware and nonstandard extentions to LISP.

ROMAN2 is a solution to the Roman numeral problem which uses a planned ordering in the production rules to streamline the condition-testing process. RO-MAN2 appears to be a better solution than ROMAN1. Now, in ROMAN2, only the first rule need test for X being null. If X is null, execution does not reach the production rules that follow, during this particular iteration of the PROG.

```
; ROMAN2.LSP - ordered production system to
;convert to Roman numerals.
```

```
(DEFUN ROMAN2 ()
  (PROG(X)
    LOOP
    (COND
        ((NULL X) (PRINTM ENTER NUMBER) (SETQ X (READ)))
        ((GREATERP X 39) (PRINTM TOO BIG) (SETQ X NIL))
        ((GREATERP X 9)(PRIN1 'X) (SETQ X (DIFFERENCE X 10)) )
        ((EQUAL X 9) (PRIN1 'IX) (SETQ X 0) )
        ((GREATERP X 4)(PRIN1 'V) (SETQ X (DIFFERENCE X 5)) )
        ((EQUAL X 4) (PRIN1 'IV) (SETQ X 0) )
        ((GREATERP X 0)(PRIN1 'I) (SETQ X (SUB1 X)) )
        ((ZEROP X) (SETQ X NIL) (TERPRI))
        )
    (GO LOOP) ) )
```

3.2.3   Limitations of Linear Production Systems

Any program can be reexpressed as some kind of production system, although perhaps in only a trival way.   For example, if we have a LISP function (BLACK_BOX X) that does something arbitrary, we can rewrite it in the production rule:

If true then compute (BLACK_BOX X).

This would seem to indicate that production systems per se do not buy us anything special. But, like "structured programming," the production system, when used appropriately, can be helpful in structuring large systems.

A problem with production systems, as we have presented them in examples ROMAN1 and ROMAN2, is that the selection of the rule to apply is done by making, in effect, a linear search through the list of productions each time one is needed. The amount of time spent testing each condition varies with the complexity of the condition and, in the case of a conjunction of subconditions, with the likelihood that the AND can be aborted early by a subcondition evaluating to NIL.

3.2.4   Discrimination Nets

It is well known that linear searching is usually slower than some sort of tree search. By making the subconditions select a path through a search tree that is balanced or nearly balanced, a lot of unnecessary computation can be avoided. To this end, builders of big production systems have employed "discrimination nets" of conditions to select production rules. The structure of such a net is like that of a decision tree, where the actions are all located at the leaf nodes.

We can reformulate our Roman-numeral conversion program as a discrimination net as shown in Fig. 3.2.

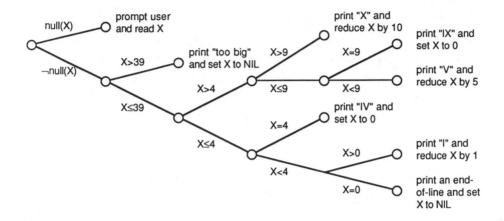

Figure 3.2: A discrimination net for the Roman Numerals problem.

This discrimination net reduces the maximum number of subcondition tests required from the eight of ROMAN2 to five in the process of determining the production rule which fires next. A program implementing this discrimination net is ROMAN3, and is shown in Fig. 3.3.

In using a discrimination net, we have reduced the redundancy of condition testing in our program. However, we have also lost some of the simplicity and modularity of the original production system. It is now a more complicated matter to add or delete a production rule from the program, because we have many nested COND's to keep balanced, and the placement of each clause bears heavily on the semantics of the program. By contrast, in our original system (ROMAN1) the adding or deletion of a rule could be done with relative ease.

Researchers have looked into ways to obtain both the modularity of pure production systems and the efficiency of discrimination networks. One solution is "compiled production systems" for which production rules are written in such a way that a compiling program can automatically transform them into an efficient program such as a discrimination net.

We shall be concerned less with efficiency than with making things work, and we will usually express production systems in the clearer "uncompiled" form.

3.3   Pattern Matching

3.3.1   Pattern Matching in Production Rules

As we shall see later in various examples, a good way to specify a condition in a production rule is by providing a pattern which the input should match if the

```
; ROMAN3.LSP -- discrimination net implementation

(DEFUN ROMAN3 ()
  (PROG(X)
    LOOP
    (COND
      ; 1st decision node:
      ((NULL X) (PRINTM ENTER NUMBER) (SETQ X (READ)))
      (T
       (COND
         ; 2nd decision node:
         ((GREATERP X 39) (PRINTM TOO BIG) (SETQ X NIL))
         (T (COND
              ; 3rd decision node:
              ((GREATERP X 4)
               (COND
                   ; level 4, first node:
                   ((GREATERP X 9)
                    (PRIN1 'X)(SETQ X (DIFFERENCE X 10)))
                   (T (COND
                         ; level 5, first node:
                         ((EQUAL X 9)
                          (PRIN1 'IX)
                          (SETQ X 0) )
                         (T
                          (PRIN1 'V)
                          (SETQ X (DIFFERENCE X 5)) ) )) ))

              (T (COND
                   ; level 4, second node:
                   ((EQUAL X 4) (PRIN1 'IV) (SETQ X 0))
                   (T (COND
                         ; level 5, second node:
                         ((GREATERP X 0)
                          (PRIN1 'I)
                          (SETQ X (SUB1 X)) )
                         (T (TERPRI) (SETQ X NIL))
                   )) )) )) )) )
    (GO LOOP)) )
```

Figure 3.3: ROMAN3: An implementation of a discrimination net.

condition is to be satisfied. Such a pattern may be a very particular one such
as NIL which only matches the input NIL or a general one such as ((* X) YES
(* Y)) which matches any (finite) list containing the atom YES as a top-level
element. We assume here that (* X) and (* Y) each match arbitrary sublists.
The act of matching is a comparison of a pattern S-expression with a subject
S-expression to find whether the subject has the form or elements required by
the pattern.

We will soon introduce a particular pattern-matching function MATCH which
has enough "power" to act as the basis for two interesting programs that we
describe later in this chapter. In order to test two S-expressions for similar
structure there are many possibilities. Some of these are demonstrated by the
functions MATCH1 through MATCH5.

3.3.2   The MATCH Function

The function (MATCH1 P S) defined below is too strict for our purposes and is
no better than EQUAL since it is EQUAL!

```
(DEFUN MATCH1 (P S) (EQUAL P S))
```

However, it should be clear that testing for equality is a form of matching, but
that we usually need more general capabilities for matching.

The next matcher, MATCH2, returns T if the list structures, disregarding
atom equality, of P and S are the same.

```
(DEFUN MATCH2 (P S)
  (COND
      ((ATOM P) (ATOM S))
      ((ATOM S) NIL)
      ((MATCH2 (CAR P) (CAR S))
       (MATCH2 (CDR P) (CDR S)) )
      (T NIL) ) )
```

Thus

```
(MATCH2 '(A (B) C) '(X (Y) NIL)     ; yields T,  but
(MATCH2 '(A (B) C) '(A B C))        ; yields NIL.
```

This is an interesting notion of matching but is still not very useful.

Rather than concern ourselves with isomorphism of list structures (which
MATCH2 essentially does) we shall assume that top-level structure is the important part, and that a greater degree of control is wanted in the matching of
pattern elements to subject elements at this level. We shall permit control of
matching at this level through the following mechanisms: equality, "variable"
constructs to match any element, match any sequence of elements, and match
any element satisfying a predicate. This assumption that top-level structure is

the only important one for matching is a powerful one, and it allows us to specify simple patterns that can match fairly complicated expressions, yet give the degree of control desired.

We first present a simple matcher which is capable of matching by equality and by a match-any-element construct in the pattern.

```
(DEFUN MATCH3 (P S)
  (COND
      ((NULL P) (NULL S))              ;null clause
      ((OR (ATOM P)(ATOM S)) NIL)      ;atom clause
      ((EQUAL (CAR P) (CAR S))         ;equal CAR clause
       (MATCH3 (CDR P) (CDR S)) )
                                       ;joker clause...
      ((EQ (CAR P) '?) (MATCH3 (CDR P) (CDR S)) )
      (T NIL) ) )                      ;extremal clause
```

The "joker" clause provides a "match-any-element" feature. When a question mark appears in the pattern, it matches whatever element occurs at the same position in the subject.

Thus MATCH3 says P matches S under the following conditions: (a) they are both null; (b) the CAR of P equals the CAR of S and their CDR's match (recursively); (c) the CAR of P is a question mark and the CDR's of P and S match recursively. Note: the atom clause rules out the possibility of any matching if P is not null and either P or S is an atom. This clause also "protects" successive clauses from the possibility of crash due to taking the CAR or CDR of an atom. Finally, the extremal clause declares that P and S do not match if none of the previous conditions holds. For example,

```
(MATCH3 '(A B ? D) '(A B C D))      ; yields T, but
(MATCH3 '(A B C D) '(A B ? D))      ; results in NIL.  Also,
(MATCH3 'A 'A)                      ; gives NIL but
(MATCH3 '((A)) '((A)))              ; yields T.
```

An improvement in MATCH3 would be the addition of a facility to remember the element(s) matched by the question marks in the pattern. We can provide such a capability. This would permit, for example, the form

```
(MATCH4 '((? X) B C (? Y)) '(A B C D))
```

to not only return T, but have the side effects of setting the value of X to be A and setting the value of Y to be D. In that way, if the match is used as a condition in a production rule, the action part of the rule can manipulate the values matching the variable elements in the pattern. To change MATCH3 into MATCH4, we replace only one clause of the COND: the joker clause. The replacement for the joker clause is:

```
((AND
    (EQUAL (LENGTH (CAR P)) 2)        ; subcondition a
    (EQ (CAAR P) '?)                  ; subcondition b
    (MATCH4 (CDR P) (CDR S)) )        ; subcondition c
  (SET (CADAR P) (CAR S))
  T)
```

Now, when the three subconditions are satisfied, the variable associated with
the question mark in the pattern can receive a value equal to the first element
of S. The three conditions are: (a) the first element of P must be a (sub)list of
length 2 – this prevents a possible error later in computing the CAAR of P; (b)
the first element of that sublist must be the question mark; and (c) the CDR of
P must match the CDR of S. The use of the AND form here is an example of
using "logic" forms to effect control structures. The outcome of the AND form
here controls whether the SET form is evaluated (since the whole expression
here is a clause of the big COND). At the same time, the AND plays the role of
several nested COND forms in the sense that only if subcondition *a* is not NIL
will there be an evaluation of subcondition *b*; and only if both subconditions *a*
and *b* are not NIL will there be an evaluation of subcondition *c*. MATCH4 looks
as follows:

```
(DEFUN MATCH4 (P S)
   (COND    ((NULL P) (NULL S))        ;null clause
       ((OR (ATOM P)(ATOM S)) NIL)     ;atom clause
       ((EQUAL (CAR P) (CAR S))        ;equal CAR clause
        (MATCH3 (CDR P) (CDR S)) )

                                       ;new joker clause...
       ((AND
           (EQUAL (LENGTH (CAR P) 2))  ;subcondition a
           (EQ (CAAR P) '?)            ;subcondition b
           (MATCH4 (CDR P) (CDR S)) )  ;subcondition c
        (SET (CADAR P) (CAR S))
        T)
       (T NIL) ) )                     ;extremal clause
```

We still want two more features for our MATCH function. The first of these
permits pattern elements similar to "(? X)" but gives us a finer degree of control over what it matches. The question-mark construct matches any element
appearing in the appropriate position in S. By specifying the name of a predicate
(the name must not be "?" or "*", which are reserved) in place of the question
mark, we may indicate a class of elements that can match. For example, we
would like

```
(MATCH5 '(A B (NUMBERP X) D) '(A B C D))
```

to yield NIL, but for

```
(MATCH5 '(A B (NUMBERP X) D) '(A B 17 D))
```

to give T, with the side effect of having the value of X set to be 17.

To obtain this feature, we add another clause to the COND of MATCH4, very much like the new clause in MATCH4. The difference is that instead of the second subcondition (labelled *b* above) (EQ (CAAR P) '?), we have the two subconditions:

```
(NULL (EQ (CAAR P) '?))              ; subcondition b1
(APPLY (CAR P) (LIST (CAR S)))       ; subcondition b2
```

making a total of four subconditions in the new AND form. The new clause is as follows, and it is *added* to the COND form of MATCH4, rather than replacing a clause.

```
((AND
    (EQUAL (LENGTH (CAR P) 2))        ; subcondition a
    (NULL (EQ (CAAR P) '?))           ; subcondition b1
    (APPLY (CAR P) (LIST (CAR S)))    ; subcondition b2
    (MATCH4 (CDR P) (CDR S)) )        ; subcondition c
 (SET (CADAR P) (CAR S))
 T)
```

Thus, a pattern element of the form (P X), where P is a predicate, matches an element S of the subject if P applied to S is T. When the entire match is successful, the value of S is assigned to X. Since MATCH5 is identical to MATCH4 except for the addition of this new clause, a complete listing for MATCH5 is not given. The function MATCH6, for which a complete listing is given below, includes the clause just discussed.

Our final feature is a new pattern construct to match any sequence of elements of S. We write this form (* X), and we call it a *wild sequence* construct. Unlike (? X) which matches one element of S and assigns it to X, the element (* X) may match zero or more elements of S and assigns a list of the matched elements to X. This feature makes the matching more powerful, although at the same time reducing the speed of matching. Once again, we are concerned now more with functionality than with efficiency.

The wild sequence construct is implemented by adding an additional clause to the COND of MATCH5. This clause is itself a COND with three clauses handling the various subcases. The new matching function is MATCH6, and is described in Fig. 3.4.

How the "*" construct works is as follows: subcase 1 allows the construct to match exactly one element of S, as if the construct were the "?" construct. Subcase 2 handles the situation in which the * construct should match zero elements of S, and so the overall match depends upon whether the (CDR P) matches S. Finally, subcase 3 takes care of the case when the * construct should match more than one element of S; it permits this by "eating up" one element of

```
; MATCH6.LSP -- a recursive pattern-matching function
; for use in production-systems programming.

(DEFUN MATCH6  (P S)
  (COND
      ((NULL P)(NULL S))      ;case with both P and S null
;from here on we can assume P is not null.
      ((ATOM (CAR P))         ;case when CAR P is an atom
       (AND S                 ;S must not be null.
         (EQUAL (CAR P) (CAR S))
         (MATCH6 (CDR P) (CDR S)) ) )
;from here on CAR of P is non atomic.
      ((AND                   ;case when P starts with ? form.
         S                    ;S must not be null.
        (EQ (CAAR P) '?) )
       (COND ((MATCH6 (CDR P)(CDR S))    ; rest much match, too.
            (SET (CADAR P) (CAR S))
            T)
            (T NIL) ) )
      ((EQ (CAAR P) '*)       ;case when P starts with * form.
       (COND
         ((AND S (MATCH6 (CDR P)(CDR S)))    ;subcase 1
          (SET (CADAR P) (LIST (CAR S))) T)
         ((MATCH6 (CDR P) S)                 ;subcase 2
          (SET (CADAR P) NIL) T)
         ((AND S (MATCH6 P (CDR S)))         ;subcase 3
          (SET (CADAR P) (CONS (CAR S)(EVAL (CADAR P)))) T)
         (T NIL) ) )

      ((AND     ;case when P starts with predicate form.
         S       ;S must not be null.
        (APPLY (CAAR P) (LIST (CAR S)))
        (MATCH6 (CDR P) (CDR S)) )
       (SET (CADAR P)(CAR S)) T)

      (T NIL) ) )
```

Figure 3.4: The definition for pattern-matching function MATCH6.

S (that is, calling recursively on its CDR), while not eating up the * construct itself, which is implemented by calling recursively with P rather than (CDR P).

MATCH6 is an implementation for a pattern matcher that is very much in the production-system style. The different cases for matching are handled independently. As a result, it is easy to add new pattern-matching features, while at the same time, there is some inefficiency, because the same subconditions may be tested repeatedly. It would not be difficult to rewrite MATCH6 as a discrimination net.

From this point on, we shall use the name MATCH to refer to the function defined in MATCH6 (one must imagine all occurrences of "MATCH6" as being replaced by "MATCH" in the definition).

The example use of MATCH below produces the value T:

```
(MATCH '((* X) WILD (? Y) (* Z))
       '(* SPECIFIES A WILD CARD SEQUENCE ELEMENT) )
```

Here (* X) matches and assigns to X everything up to WILD, and (? Y) matches and assigns to Y the atom CARD which follows WILD in the subject, and (* Z) matches and assigns to Z the rest of the subject.[1]

3.4 The "SHRINK"

We are now ready to describe a LISP program which simulates a Rogerian psychiatrist[2]. The simulation is crude, but illustrates well how the MATCH function can be put to good use. The program tries to make constructive comments in response to the patient's (the user's) input, to encourage him or her to reveal all inner conflicts and possible sources of frustration.

A session with the psychiatrist is started by typing

```
(SHRINK)
```

after the program has been loaded into LISP. Then the patient follows the doctor's instructions. The program enters an endless loop which repeatedly reads in a sentence and makes a response. It makes its response by trying to match patterns to the input. When a match is found, the corresponding scheme is used to construct a response. When no match is found, the DOCTOR "punts," and responds with a general remark such as "THATS VERY INTERESTING."

---

[1]It should be noted that MATCH treats the variables X, Y and Z as global variable. It is possible to write a matching function that passes the bindings of the matched fragments back in a list returned by the matching function to avoid the potential name conflicts that can arise with the use of globals.

[2]SHRINK is inspired by the ELIZA program of J. Weizenbaum.

3.4.1 Implementation of SHRINK

As in ROMAN2, SHRINK is implemented as an ordered production system in
which each production rule is represented by a clause in a COND form. A main
loop which includes the COND form is executed until a production rule fires that
causes a return (the "BYE" rule).

The main procedure here is SHRINK. MATCH is called by it and plays a
major role. PRINTL outputs a list without the usual enclosing parentheses.
WWORD returns a word like "WHEN," "WHERE," etc. GETNTH selects the
Nth element of a list. PUNTS is a list of pat phrases the psychiatrist uses to
keep the conversation going even though it hasn't found a more appropriate rule
to apply to the input. It always manages to at least blunder its way through
a conversation. YOUME translates any pronoun or BE-verb from first person
to second person or vice-versa. It is used by YOUMEMAP to roughly invert
a sentence so that the psychiatrist may incorporate parts of it in his response.
VERBP is a predicate which is T for any of a collection of commonly used verbs.
Here is the main function:

```
(DEFUN SHRINK ()     ; Simple Rogerian therapist simulation
  (PROG ()
      (SETQ WWORDCOUNT 0)           ; initialize counters
      (SETQ PUNTCOUNT 0)
      (PRINTM WELCOME TO MY SOFA) ; welcome message
      (PRINTM PLEASE ENCLOSE YOUR INPUT IN PARENTHESES)
 LOOP (SETQ S (YOUMEMAP (READ)))   ; get user input, invert person.
      (COND
 ; the production rules follow:
        ((MATCH '(BYE) S)
         (RETURN 'GOODBYE))
        ((MATCH '(YOU ARE (* X)) S)
         (PRINTL (APPEND '(PLEASE TELL ME)
           (LIST (WWORD))
           '(YOU ARE)
           X)))
        ((MATCH '(YOU HAVE (* X)) S)
         (PRINTL (APPEND '(HOW LONG HAVE YOU HAD) X)) )
        ((MATCH '(YOU FEEL (* X)) S)
         (PRINTM I SOMETIMES FEEL THE SAME WAY) )
        ((MATCH '(BECAUSE (* X)) S)
         (PRINTM IS THAT REALLY THE REASON) )
        ((MATCH NIL S) (PRINTM PLEASE SAY SOMETHING))
        ((MATCH '(YES (* X)) S)
         (PRINTL (APPEND '(HOW CAN YOU BE SO SURE) X)) )
        ((MATCH '(ME ARE (* X)) S)
         (PRINTL (APPEND '(OH YEAH I AM) X)) )
```

```
((MATCH '((VERBP V) (* X)) S)
 (PRINTL (APPEND '(OY YOI YOI HE WANTS THAT
   I SHOULD GO AND) (LIST V) X) ) )
((MATCH '((WPRED W)(* X)) S)
 (PRINTL (APPEND '(YOU TELL ME)(LIST W)) ) )
((MATCH '((DPRED W) ME (* X)) S)
 (PRINTL (APPEND '(PERHAPS I)(LIST W) X) ) )
((MATCH '(DO ME THINK (* X)) S)(PRINTM I THINK YOU
   SHOULD ANSWER THAT YOURSELF))
((MEMBER 'DREAM S)
 (PRINTM FOR DREAM ANALYSIS SEE FREUD))
((MEMBER 'LOVE S)
 (PRINTM ALL IS FAIR IN LOVE AND WAR))
((MEMBER 'NO S) (PRINTM DONT BE SO NEGATIVE))
((MEMBER 'MAYBE S) (PRINTM BE MORE DECISIVE))
((MEMBER 'YOU S) (PRINTL S))
; here's the rule that can't fail:
(T (SETQ PUNTCOUNT (ADD1 PUNTCOUNT))
   (COND ((EQUAL PUNTCOUNT 7)
     (SETQ PUNTCOUNT 0)))
   (PRINTL (GETNTH PUNTCOUNT PUNTS)) ) )
(GO LOOP) ))
```

The next function, PRINTL, prints a list without outer parentheses. It helps by making the output look more attractive than it would if PRINT were used in its place.

```
(DEFUN PRINTL (MESSAGE)
  (PROG ()
    (MAPCAR
      (FUNCTION (LAMBDA (TXT)
              (PROG () (PRIN1 TXT) (TYO 32)) ))
      MESSAGE)
    (TERPRI) ) )
```

WWORD is a function that returns WHEN, WHY or WHERE. It is used to make questions out of the user's input.

```
(DEFUN WWORD ()
  (PROG () (SETQ WWORDCOUNT (ADD1 WWORDCOUNT))
     (COND ((EQUAL WWORDCOUNT 3)(SETQ WWORDCOUNT 0)))
           (RETURN (GETNTH WWORDCOUNT
                     '(WHEN WHY WHERE) )) ) )
```

The predicate WPRED is true of the atoms WHY, WHERE, WHEN and WHAT, and it is used to help analyze an input sentence.

```
(DEFUN WPRED (W)
  (MEMBER W '(WHY WHERE WHEN WHAT)) )
```

The predicate DPRED is true of DO, CAN, SHOULD and WOULD. It is also used in input analysis.

```
(DEFUN DPRED (W)
  (MEMBER W '(DO CAN SHOULD WOULD)) )
```

The next function returns the Nth element of LST.

```
(DEFUN GETNTH (N LST)
  (COND ((NULL LST) NIL)
        ((ZEROP N)(CAR LST))
        (T (GETNTH (SUB1 N)(CDR LST))) ) )
```

The atom PUNTS is used to store the list of phrases that are used as responses of last resort.

```
(SETQ PUNTS
 '((PLEASE GO ON)
   (TELL ME MORE)
   (I SEE)
   (WHAT DOES THAT INDICATE)
   (BUT WHY BE CONCERNED ABOUT IT)
   (JUST TELL ME HOW YOU FEEL) ) )
```

The function YOUME translates some words from 1st to 2nd person or from 2nd to 1st person. For example, if the input is YOU, then the output is ME.

```
(DEFUN YOUME (W)
  (COND ((EQ W 'I) 'YOU)
        ((EQ W 'ME) 'YOU)
        ((EQ W 'YOU) 'ME)
        ((EQ W 'MY) 'YOUR)
        ((EQ W 'YOUR) 'MY)
        ((EQ W 'YOURS) 'MINE)
        ((EQ W 'MINE) 'YOURS)
        ((EQ W 'AM) 'ARE)
        (T W) ) )
```

In order to convert an entire sentence from the user's viewpoint to the SHRINK's viewpoint, the function YOUMEMAP applies the function YOUME to each word in the list that is input.

```
(DEFUN YOUMEMAP (LST) (MAPCAR (FUNCTION YOUME) LST))
```

VERBP is a predicate that is true of certain verbs.

```
(DEFUN VERBP (W)
  (MEMBER W '(GO HAVE BE TRY EAT TAKE HELP MAKE GET JUMP
              WRITE TYPE FILL PUT TURN COMPUTE
              THINK DRINK BLINK CRASH CRUNCH ADD) ) )
```

3.4.2 A Session with the SHRINK

The following is a sample dialog between a human user (the "patient") and the SHRINK. The patient's input is shown in lower case text while the SHRINK's responses are shown in capital letters.

```
(shrink)
WELCOME TO MY SOFA
PLEASE ENCLOSE YOUR INPUT IN PARENTHESES
(hello)
TELL ME MORE
(i have a small problem)
HOW LONG HAVE YOU HAD A SMALL PROBLEM
(ever since my girlfriend discovered my true love)
ALL IS FAIR IN LOVE AND WAR
(i see)
YOU SEE
(yes)
HOW CAN YOU BE SO SURE
(because i understand your comment)
IS THAT REALLY THE REASON
(perhaps not)
I SEE
(she wants me to give up computers)
SHE WANTS YOU TO GIVE UP COMPUTERS
(you got it)
WHAT DOES THAT INDICATE
(i cant see you anymore)
YOU CANT SEE ME ANYMORE
(no but)
DONT BE SO NEGATIVE
(but i will dream of you)
FOR DREAM ANALYSIS SEE FREUD
(bye)
GOODBYE
```

This session illustrates the flavor of a conversation with the SHRINK. One should not expect too much from a program as simple as the SHRINK; it doesn't have much of a knowledge base: eighteen production rules and a few odd bits of syntactic information, no grammar, and no dictionary.

On the other hand, this program illustrates at a simple level how a production system approach may be used to build a conversational program.

3.5   Mathematical Formula Manipulation

3.5.1   Motivation

While the SHRINK program shows how the production systems approach and pattern matching may be employed in building an AI program, the example does not illustrate how the database may be gradually transformed by a sequence of production-rule firings to work towards the solution of a problem. The SHRINK has a short attention span, using only one production rule on each new "problem" (i.e., the problem of generating a response to the user's input).

In this section, a program called "LEIBNIZ" is presented which shows how a production system may be set up so that each time a rule fires, a little progress is made towards the solution of a relatively complicated problem. The LEIBNIZ program also illustrates several other techniques, including:

1. the explicit representation of production rules as data rather than as clauses of a COND form;

2. the use of the function MATCH in examining the top *two* levels of list structure, rather than only the top level;

3. the use of production rules that can potentially be applied at any level of a data structure in the database; and

4. the use of the database to store the current goal that the system works toward, and the use of production rules to change that goal.

The LEIBNIZ program is capable of solving some of the following kinds of mathematical problems: (a) taking the derivative of a function such as a polynomial, and (b) simplifying an expression. For example, the function

$$f(x) = x^2 + 2x$$

has the derivative

$$\frac{d}{dx} f(x) = 2x + 2.$$

When $f(x)$ is suitably represented, LEIBNIZ can find a representation for its derivative. The representation for $f(x)$ above, that LEIBNIZ can work with, is:

(PLUS (EXP X 2) (TIMES 2 X)).

To express that we wish the derivative of $f(x)$, we write for LEIBNIZ:

(D (F X) X)

and in the case of our example, we would have

`(D (PLUS (EXP X 2) (TIMES 2 X)) X).`

Given this starting formula, LEIBNIZ would gradually transform it into the desired answer,

`(PLUS (TIMES 2 X) 2).`

LEIBNIZ also can simplify formulas. For example, it can reduce the formula

`(TIMES (EXP X 1) (PLUS 7 -6))`

to the much simpler formula,

`X.`

Differentiation of algebraic expressions is something commonly done by college freshmen in an introductory calculus course. Perhaps because it is rare to find much younger people doing it, differentiation has been thought to require intelligence. Differentiation and integration of formulas were items of study by AI researchers in the early 1960s. Today, techniques for mathematical formula manipulation are well understood and are not commonly discussed in the research literature. Nonetheless, the topic still provides suitable material for illustrating pattern matching and production systems in action.

3.5.2 Overall Structure of LEIBNIZ

LEIBNIZ is a collection of function definitions and SETQ forms which implement the three components of a production system: rule base of production rules, control scheme, and database of state information. Each of these three components is explicitly represented by some of the definitions and forms. In the next three subsections, these components and their implementations are described.

3.5.3 Production Rules for LEIBNIZ

The production rules for LEIBNIZ contain knowledge about how to take derivatives and simplify formulas. Therefore, most of these rules correspond to mathematical formulas; these are shown in Fig. 3.5.

Each production rule is represented as a 4-tuple of the form,

$$(current\_goal\ pattern\ transformation\ rule\_name)$$

where the current goal and pattern make up the "condition," the transformation specifies the action for the production rule, and the rule name is used in reporting progress. An example rule is the following:

Differentiation Rules

DIFF_PLUS_RULE $\quad\quad \frac{d}{dx}[u(x) + v(x)] = \frac{d}{dx}u(x) + \frac{d}{dx}v(x)$

DIFF_X_RULE $\quad\quad\quad\quad \frac{d}{dx}x = 1$

DIFF_CONST_RULE $\quad\quad\; \frac{d}{dx}c = 0$

DIFF_PRODUCT_RULE $\quad \frac{d}{dx}[u(x) \cdot v(x)] = v(x)\frac{d}{dx}u(x) + u(x)\frac{d}{dx}v(x)$

DIFF_POWER_RULE $\quad\quad \frac{d}{dx}[u(x)]^n = n[u(x)]^{n-1}\frac{d}{dx}u(x)$

Simplification Rules

EXP0_RULE $\quad\quad\quad\quad x^0 = 1$

EXP1_RULE $\quad\quad\quad\quad x^1 = x$

TIMES1_RULE $\quad\quad\quad x \cdot 1 = x$

ONE_TIMES_RULE $\quad\quad 1 \cdot x = x$

PLUS0_RULE $\quad\quad\quad\; x + 0 = x$

ZERO_PLUS_RULE $\quad\quad 0 + x = x$

TIMES0_RULE $\quad\quad\quad x \cdot 0 = 0$

ZERO_TIMES_RULE $\quad\quad 0 \cdot x = 0$

Figure 3.5: Mathematical rules used in LEIBNIZ. Not shown are three simplification rules that work by performing calculations rather than symbolic transformations. There is also a "goal-change" rule used for control.

> If the current goal is DIFFERENTIATE and there is a subformula of
> the form (D (PLUS E1 E2) V1) then replace the subformula by one of the
> form (PLUS (D E1 V1) (D E2 V1)); this is called DIFF_PLUS_RULE.

In this example, E1, E2, and V1 are arbitrary subexpressions; normally V1
represents the variable of differentiation, X. This rule says that in order to find
the derivative of a sum, take the sum of the derivatives of the constituents to
the sum. In other words,

$$\frac{d}{dx}[u(x) + v(x)] = \frac{d}{dx}u(x) + \frac{d}{dx}v(x).$$

As illustrated again in this rule, LEIBNIZ works with formulas expressed in
a LISP-like form. The following operations are supported as binary operations
(taking only two arguments): PLUS, TIMES, and EXP. Making LEIBNIZ work
with PLUS and TIMES allowing any number of operands is an exercise left to
the reader. The unary operation SUB1 is also supported, and it is useful in the
intermediate stages of differentiating polynomials.

We now give the LISP representations for all the production rules that LEIB-
NIZ uses. There are five rules for differentiation, one rule for changing the goal,
and eleven rules for simplification of formulas. The first representation is for the
rule just discussed. It uses a helping function PLUSFORM, which is a predicate
that is true whenever its argument has the form (PLUS E1 E2).

```
(SETQ DIFF_PLUS_RULE '(
   DIFFERENTIATE
   (D (PLUSFORM F1) (? V1))
   (LIST 'PLUS (LIST 'D E1 V1) (LIST 'D E2 V1))
   DIFF_PLUS_RULE
   ) )
```

Next, PLUSFORM, a helping function for DIFF_PLUS_RULE, is defined.
It is used to match certain second-level expressions:

```
(DEFUN PLUSFORM (F)
  (AND (NOT (ATOM F))
       (MATCH '(PLUS (? E1) (? E2)) F) ) )
```

The next rule says that the derivative of X with respect to X is 1. It will
work for X or any other variable.

```
(SETQ DIFF_X_RULE '(
   DIFFERENTIATE
   (D ((LAMBDA (V)(SETQ E1 V)) E1) ((LAMBDA (V) (EQ V E1)) E2))
   1
   DIFF_X_RULE ) )
```

The pattern for DIFF_X_RULE uses two local functions. The first causes the second subexpression (the function to be differentiated) to be immediately assigned as the value of E1. The second local function only succeeds if the subexpression there (telling which variable differentiation is with respect to) is the same as that saved in E1.

The rule DIFF_CONST_RULE says that if F is not a function of X, then its derivative with respect to X is 0.

```
(SETQ DIFF_CONST_RULE '(
   DIFFERENTIATE
   (D ((LAMBDA (F)(SETQ E1 F)) F)
      ((LAMBDA (V1) (NO_V1 E1 V1)) V1) )
   0
   DIFF_CONST_RULE ) )
```

The pattern for this rule also uses two local functions. The first saves the function to be differentiated (as in the previous rule). The second function is a predicate that is true only if the variable that differentiation is with respect to does not appear in the function to be differentiated.

The function NO_V1 is a helping function for DIFF_CONST_RULE; it returns T if V1 does not occur in F.

```
(DEFUN NO_V1 (F V1)
  (COND          ((NULL F) T)
       ((ATOM F) (NOT (EQ F V1)))
       ((NO_V1 (CAR F) V1) (NO_V1 (CDR F) V1))
       (T NIL) ) )
```

The next rule is for differentiating products:

```
(SETQ DIFF_PRODUCT_RULE '(
   DIFFERENTIATE
   (D
    ((LAMBDA (F)
             (AND (NOT (ATOM F))
                  (MATCH '(TIMES (? E1) (? E2)) F)) ) E3)
    (? V1) )
   (LIST 'PLUS
           (LIST 'TIMES E2 (LIST 'D E1 V1))
           (LIST 'TIMES E1 (LIST 'D E2 V1)) )
   DIFF_PRODUCT_RULE
   ) )
```

The rule for differentiating powers is DIFF_POWER_RULE; it says that the derivative of $[u(x)]^n$ with respect to x is equal to $n[u(x)]^{n-1}$ times the derivative of $u(x)$ with respect to x.

```
(SETQ DIFF_POWER_RULE '(
    DIFFERENTIATE
    (D
     ((LAMBDA (F)
              (AND (NOT (ATOM F))
                   (MATCH '(EXP (? E1) (NUMBERP E2)) F)) ) E3)
     (? V1) )
    (LIST 'TIMES E2
          (LIST 'TIMES (LIST 'EXP E1 (LIST 'SUB1 E2))
                (LIST 'D E1 V1) ) )
    DIFF_POWER_RULE
    ) )
```

The production rules for simplification are of two general kinds. Some actually perform arithmetic on constants. Others make use of properties of arithmetic to eliminate the need for operations in certain contexts. Here is a rule that actually performs arithmetic on constants; it's a simplification rule for subtracting 1:

```
(SETQ SUB1_RULE '(
    SIMPLIFY
    (SUB1 (NUMBERP E1))
    (SUB1 E1)
    SUB1_RULE
    ) )
```

A rule that makes use of a property of an operation is the following rule for simplifying an exponentiation by 0. It represents the fact that x^0 is 1.

```
(SETQ EXP0_RULE '(
    SIMPLIFY
    (EXP (? E1) 0)
    1
    EXP0_RULE
    ) )
```

It is also useful to use the fact that $x^1 = x$; here is the rule for exponentiation by 1:

```
(SETQ EXP1_RULE '(
    SIMPLIFY
    (EXP (? E1) 1)
    E1
    EXP1_RULE
    ) )
```

A rule that eliminates multiplications by 1 is the following:

```
(SETQ TIMES1_RULE '(
   SIMPLIFY
   (TIMES (? E1) 1)
   E1
   TIMES1_RULE
   ) )
```

Since the pattern-matching technique will match operands in the order specified, we need a variation of the rule for multiplication by 1 to handle the case
of (TIMES 1 X), rather than the case (TIMES X 1).

```
(SETQ ONE_TIMES_RULE '(
   SIMPLIFY
   (TIMES 1 (? E1))
   E1
   ONE_TIMES_RULE
   ) )
```

The rules for adding 0 are the next two:

```
(SETQ PLUS0_RULE '(
   SIMPLIFY
   (PLUS (? E1) 0)
   E1
   PLUS0_RULE
   ) )

; variation on rule for adding 0
(SETQ ZERO_PLUS_RULE '(
   SIMPLIFY
   (PLUS 0 (? E1))
   E1
   ZERO_PLUS_RULE
   ) )
```

Multiplication by 0 is another case where simplification can be made:

```
(SETQ TIMES0_RULE '(
   SIMPLIFY
   (TIMES (? E1) 0)
   0
   TIMES0_RULE
   ) )

; variation on rule for multiplication by 0
(SETQ ZERO_TIMES_RULE '(
```

```
SIMPLIFY
(TIMES 0 (? E1))
0
ZERO_TIMES_RULE
) )
```

More rules that do arithmetic on constants are the following ones. The next rule attempts to add constants when possible.

```
(SETQ CONSTANT_ADDITION_RULE '(
   SIMPLIFY
   (PLUS (NUMBERP E1) (NUMBERP E2))
   (PLUS E1 E2)
   CONSTANT_ADDITION_RULE
   ) )
```

Here is the rule to multiply constants when possible.

```
(SETQ CONSTANT_MULTIPLICATION_RULE '(
   SIMPLIFY
   (TIMES (NUMBERP E1) (NUMBERP E2))
   (TIMES E1 E2)
   CONSTANT_MULTIPLICATION_RULE
   ) )
```

The next rule is one which plays a role in directing the activities of the production system as a whole. It is placed after all the rules of differentiation, and when it fires, it causes the current goal to be changed to SIMPLIFY.

```
(SETQ GOAL_CHANGE_RULE '(
   DIFFERENTIATE
   ((* F))
   (PROG () (SETQ CURRENT_GOAL 'SIMPLIFY) (RETURN F))
   GOAL_CHANGE_RULE
   ) )
```

Now that all seventeen production rules are represented in LISP, they can be listed as the value of an atom RULES for easy manipulation by the control scheme. The following SETQ form makes a list of all the production rules. There is a certain amount of ordering that is intentional; the differentiation rules precede the simplification rules, and the goal-change rule separates them.

```
(SETQ RULES (LIST DIFF_PLUS_RULE DIFF_X_RULE DIFF_CONST_RULE
   DIFF_PRODUCT_RULE DIFF_POWER_RULE
   GOAL_CHANGE_RULE     ; this rule follows the DIFF rules
   SUB1_RULE EXPO_RULE EXP1_RULE
   TIMES1_RULE ONE_TIMES_RULE
```

```
TIMES0_RULE ZERO_TIMES_RULE
PLUS0_RULE ZERO_PLUS_RULE
CONSTANT_ADDITION_RULE CONSTANT_MULTIPLICATION_RULE
) )
```

This rule base can easily be enlarged, without a need to modify any of the rest of the production system.

3.5.4 Control Scheme for LEIBNIZ

In order to apply the production rules in an effective fashion to solve problems, a control scheme is needed. In the SHRINK program, all the rules were sequenced inside a COND form. By contrast, in LEIBNIZ, the rules are applied explicitly by a set of functions: CONTROL, TRY_RULES, TRY_RULE, TRY_RULE1, and TRY_RULE_ON_LIST. To make the production system start running, the function CONTROL is invoked with no arguments:

```
(CONTROL).
```

CONTROL causes TRY_RULES to try rules until one succeeds, then it starts again; when no rules fire, the current formula is returned.

```
(DEFUN CONTROL ()
  (PROG ()
  LOOP (COND ((NOT (TRY_RULES RULES))
             (RETURN CURRENT_FORMULA) ))
       (GO LOOP) ) )
```

TRY_RULES is a function that tries each rule on the list given to it until one succeeds, or the end of list is reached, or the current formula is no longer a list. If a rule fires, it returns the current formula; otherwise it returns NIL.

```
(DEFUN TRY_RULES (RULES_LEFT)
  (COND ((NULL RULES_LEFT) NIL)
        ((ATOM CURRENT_FORMULA) NIL)
        ((SETQ TEMP
              (TRY_RULE (CAR RULES_LEFT) CURRENT_FORMULA) )
         (SETQ CURRENT_FORMULA TEMP) )
        (T (TRY_RULES (CDR RULES_LEFT))) ) )
```

The next function, TRY_RULE, is one that tries to apply a single rule to an expression or one of its subexpressions. If the rule is successful, the transformed expression is returned; otherwise NIL is returned.

```
(DEFUN TRY_RULE (RULE EXPRESSION)
  (PROG (RULE_GOAL PATTERN ACTION)
        (SETQ RULE_GOAL (CAR RULE))
```

```
(SETQ PATTERN (CADR RULE))
(SETQ ACTION (CADDR RULE))
(COND ((NOT (EQ CURRENT_GOAL RULE_GOAL)) (RETURN NIL)))
(RETURN (TRY_RULE1 EXPRESSION)) ) )
```

The recursive slave of TRY_RULE, the function TRY_RULE1 does the real work of searching down through the current expression to see if the rule can be applied anywhere in it.

```
(DEFUN TRY_RULE1 (EXPRESSION)
  (COND ; make sure EXPRESSION is a list; return if not...
        ((ATOM EXPRESSION) NIL)
        ; attempt to apply rule to whole EXPRESSION...
        ((MATCH PATTERN EXPRESSION)
         (FIRE) )
        ; try rule on subexpressions...
        (T (TRY_RULE_ON_LIST EXPRESSION)) ) )
```

Helping in the recursive search of the expression is the following function that tries to apply the rule to each element on EXPRESSION_LIST. It returns NIL if the rule cannot be applied in any of the expressions or their subexpressions. Otherwise it returns the original list with one replacement: the first expression in which the rule can be applied is replaced by the result of applying the rule in it.

```
(DEFUN TRY_RULE_ON_LIST (EXPRESSION_LIST)
  (COND ((NULL EXPRESSION_LIST) NIL)
        ((SETQ TEMP (TRY_RULE1 (CAR EXPRESSION_LIST)))
         (CONS TEMP (CDR EXPRESSION_LIST)) )
        ((SETQ TEMP (TRY_RULE_ON_LIST (CDR EXPRESSION_LIST)))
         (CONS (CAR EXPRESSION_LIST) TEMP) )
        (T NIL) ) )
```

The next function is evaluated when a production rule fires. Its main purpose is to print a message on the console showing that a rule is firing and which rule it is.

```
(DEFUN FIRE ()
  (PROG ()
        (PRIN1 (CADDR (CDR RULE)))   ; print name of rule
        (TYO 32)                      ; print a space
        (PRINT 'FIRES)                ; print 'FIRES'
        (RETURN (EVAL ACTION))        ; do ACTION
        ) )
```

3.5.5   Database of State Information in LEIBNIZ

The database of state information consists of two items: the current formula and the current goal. The current formula reflects any transformations that have been made by the production rules, and it is the object being transformed into a solution to the original problem.

The current goal indicates whether the system is attempting to differentiate within the current formula or to simplify the current formula. This goal helps control the firing of production rules to implement a strategy for solving differentiation problems. The strategy is to do as much differentiation as possible first, and then simplify the result. The goal mechanism also serves to improve the efficiency of simplification by disabling the detailed condition testing for the differentiation rules.

Initializing the database is simply a matter of assigning values to two literal atoms CURRENT_GOAL and CURRENT_FORMULA. This can be accomplished by a set of SETQ forms such as the following three.

```
(SETQ CURRENT_GOAL 'DIFFERENTIATE)
(SETQ  F0 '(D (PLUS (EXP X 2) (TIMES 2 X)) X))
(SETQ CURRENT_FORMULA F0)
```

3.5.6   Performance of LEIBNIZ

A sample run of LEIBNIZ solving a differentiation problem is now shown. Let us assume that the database of state information has been initialized as explained above. This indicates that we want LEIBNIZ to compute the derivative of the function $x^2 + 2x$, and to simplify its result. After the user types (CONTROL), the following messages are displayed:

```
DIFF_PLUS_RULE FIRES
DIFF_PRODUCT_RULE FIRES
DIFF_X_RULE FIRES
DIFF_CONST_RULE FIRES
DIFF_POWER_RULE FIRES
DIFF_X_RULE FIRES
GOAL_CHANGE_RULE FIRES
SUB1_RULE FIRES
EXP1_RULE FIRES
TIMES1_RULE FIRES
TIMES1_RULE FIRES
TIMES0_RULE FIRES
ZERO_PLUS_RULE FIRES
```

and finally the simplified derivative of the original formula is returned as the value:

(PLUS (TIMES 2 X) 2).

From the record of rule firings we can see that only rules for differentiation fire before the change of goal. Thereafter, only rules for simplification fire. Interestingly enough, some of the rules fire more than once; DIFF_X_RULE fires twice, as does TIMES1_RULE. Other rules do not fire at all on this particular example.

Because the production rules of LEIBNIZ are in a fairly pure, uncompiled form (we have not used a discrimination net, for example), LEIBNIZ spends a lot of time testing and retesting production rule conditions that have little chance of being true. Thus it is not very efficient. However, the beauty of a production system is that one can easily introduce more production rules to expand the range of problems that the program can handle. The reader can add rules to LEIBNIZ without much trouble that will enable it to handle many formulas involving trigonometric functions, for example.

3.6   The Notion of Unification

In the function MATCH, a pattern is compared with a subject. At each step, the elements should be equal, or the pattern should have a "wild-card" element of the appropriate type. In the case of the "(* X) type of element, in a successful match, X would receive a value indicating what the element was put into correspondence with. The element (? X) can be considered as a variable, to which a value is given during the course of matching.

Let us now consider a different kind of matching problem: one in which no distinction is made between pattern and subject. Suppose we wish to match two expressions:

E1 = (A B (? X) D) and
E2 = (A (? Y) C D).

Then, with the right kind of matching function, we should find that they can indeed be matched, and that X corresponds to C and Y corresponds to B. On the other hand, if we had

E3 = (A (? Y) C (? Y))

there is a problem in matching E1 with E3. Even though at each position we have either an equality between elements or an element matched with a wild card, Y would have to have the value B at the same time as it has value D, an inconsistency! The pair E1 and E2 is said to be unifiable while the pair E1 and E3 is not unifiable. Suppose

E4 = ((? Z) B C D).

Then the set {E1, E2, E4} is unifiable since there exists a set of assignments of values to variables such that all the correspondences are consistent. We shall treat the subject of unification in Chapter 6 in detail when we see that this kind of pattern matching plays a crucial role in two areas: theorem proving using the "resolution" method, and general problem solving using the predicate calculus.

3.7   Bibliographical Information

Production systems are described in an article by Davis and King. The more general notion of pattern-directed control is treated in a book edited by Waterman and Hayes-Roth. Nilsson stresses production systems in his *Principles of Artificial Intelligence*. Discrimination nets are described in [Charniak et al 1979].

Pattern matching was recognized as important in the language SNOBOL. The function MATCH developed in this chapter is modelled after one presented by Winston, but avoids the use of functions that decompose atom names (EXPLODE, ATOMCAR, ATOMCDR).

Dialog was used as a means of demonstrating AI systems with Weizenbaum's ELIZA and later with Colby's PARRY. Today it is studied as a special topic in natural language understanding.

Early studies in formula manipulation for the calculus include [Slagle 1963]. A LISP-based system that has found widespread use for symbolic mathematics is MACSYMA [Mathlab 1975], [Moses 1976], [NASA 1977]. A more recent software system for symbolic mathematics is SMP, which is especially useful in scientific applications such as theoretical physics [Wolfram 1983, 1984]. The LEIBNIZ program presented in this chapter uses some of the differentiation and simplification rules used in a program in [Weissman 1967]; Weissman's program does not use the production-system approach, and was written for a dialect of LISP incorporating an "EVALQUOTE" feature, seldom found in today's implementations of LISP. Weissman's program, unlike LEIBNIZ, also supports the conversion of the mathematical formulas from infix notation to prefix notation and vice versa.

Unification is described further in Chapter 6, and references for it may also be found in that chapter.

References

1. Charniak, E., Riesbeck, C., and McDermott, D. 1979. *Artificial Intelligence Programming*. Hillsdale, NJ: Lawrence Erlbaum Associates.

2. Colby, K., Weber, S., and Hilf, F. 1971. Artificial paranoia. *Artificial Intelligence*, Vol. 2, pp1-25.

3. Davis, R., and King, J. J. 1977. An overview of production systems. In Elcock, E., and Michie, D. (eds.), *Machine Intelligence 8*. Chichester: Horwood.

4. Griswold, R. E., Poage, J. F. and Polonsky, I. P. 1971. *The SNOBOL4 Programming Language*, Second Edition. Englewood Cliffs, NJ: Prentice-Hall.

5. Mathlab Group. 1975. *MACSYMA Reference Manual*. Laboratory for Computer Science, Massachusetts Institute of Technology, November.

6. Moses, J. 1976. The current capabilities of the MACSYMA system. *Proceedings of the ACM National Conference*, October.

7. NASA. 1977. *Proceedings of the 1977 MACSYMA Users' Conference.* Washington DC: National Aeronautics and Space Administration report number NASA CP-2012, July.

8. Nilsson, N. J. 1980. *Principles of Artificial Intelligence.* Palo Alto, CA: Tioga Press.

9. Slagle, J. R. 1963. A heuristic program that solves symbolic integration problems in freshman calculus. In Feigenbaum, E. and Feldman, J. (eds.), *Computers and Thought.* New York: McGraw-Hill.

10. Weissman, C. 1967. *LISP 1.5 Primer.* Belmont, CA: Dickenson Publishing Co.

11. Weizenbaum, J. 1966. ELIZA—A computer program for the study of natural language communication between man and machine. *Communications of the ACM*, Vol. 9, pp36-45.

12. Winston, P. H. 1977. *Artificial Intelligence.* Reading, MA: Addison-Wesley.

13. Wolfram, S. 1983. *SMP Reference Manual.* Los Angeles: Inference Corp.

14. Wolfram, S. 1984. Computer software in science and mathematics. *Scientific American*, Vol. 251, No. 3, (Sept.) pp140-151.

Exercises

1. The production-system method of program organization is commonly used in AI systems.

    (a) List the components of a production system.

    (b) What is a production rule?

    (c) What is the principal advantage in using a production system?

2. Add new production rules (COND clauses) to ROMAN2 so that it handles numbers up to 399 instead of 39.

3. Modify ROMAN3 to handle numbers up to 3999. What is the maximum number of subcondition tests in the resulting discrimination net?

4. Production systems to determine representations for integers in the words of various foreign languages can range from straightforward to fairly complex. The case of German is not very difficult.

   (a) Write production rules to translate an integer in the range 0 to 99 into German words.

   (b) Implement your system in LISP.

5. French is slightly more complicated.

   (a) Make up a set of production rules for translating integers in the range 0 to 99 into the appropriate French-language words. For example 2 becomes DEUX and 75 becomes SOIXANTE QUINZE.

   (b) Implement your production system in LISP and demonstrate it on the numbers 0, 1, 9, 10, 16, 17, 19, 20, 21, 22, 30, 59, 60, 70, 76, 77, 80, 90, and 99. How many clauses are there in your principal COND form?

6. Using the TRACE option in LISP, determine the number of times the function MATCH is invoked (including all the recursive invocations) in evaluating the form

   (MATCH '((* X) B C (* Y)) '(A B C D E)).

7. The function MATCH assigns values to variables in successful matches involving joker, predicate, and wild sequence constructs. Is it possible for one (or more) of these variables ever to be assigned a value when the overall match is not successful? Explain.

8. As suggested on page 65, reimplement that MATCH function as a discrimination net.

9. Modify MATCH6 (creating MATCH7) in such a way that the application of predicates, rather than only to individual elements of S, can be to sequences of elements of S. For example, suppose that (INCREASING L) returns T if L is a list of increasing integers. Then we would like

   (MATCH7 '(101 (INCREASING X) (INCREASING Y))
           '(101 2 4 6 8 3 5 7))

   to return T and have the side effects of assigning the list (2 4 6 8) to X and the list (3 5 7) to Y.

10. After completing the previous problem, define a function DECREASING and a function SAME in the same spirit as INCREASING. These functions all will take a single argument, assumed to be a list, and return either T or NIL. For example,

```
(SAME '(3 3 3 3))        ; produces T
(SAME '(2 5))            ; produces NIL
(SAME '(4))              ; produces NIL
(SAME '( ))              ; produces NIL
(DECREASING '(5 4 1))    ; produces T
(DECREASING '(2))        ; produces NIL
(DECREASING '(10 10 9))  ; produces NIL
```

Then test your function MATCH7 with the following examples:

```
(SETQ P1 '((INCREASING X)(SAME Y)(INCREASING Z)))
(SETQ P2 '((DECREASING X)(DECREASING Y)))
(SETQ S1 '(1 2 3 3 3 2 1))
(SETQ S2 '(5 4 4 4 4 5))

(MATCH7 P1 S1)
(LIST X Y Z)
(MATCH7 P1 S2)
(LIST X Y Z)
(MATCH7 P2 S1)
(LIST X Y Z)
(MATCH7 P2 S2)
(LIST X Y Z)
```

11. Write a matching function MATCH8 whose behavior is similar to that of MATCH6 except that it passes the bindings (of matched fragments of the subject to variables in the pattern) back as a value, rather than by setting the global values of the variables.

12. Modify the SHRINK so that instead of always using a "punt" when no other productions match, it alternately uses a punt or a reference to previous items of the dialog. To do this you need the following: a way to remember some of the conversation (perhaps by using a SETQ to store some matched fragment in one of the production rules), a way to get alteration of the actions in the punt production rule (save a flag telling which action to next time, and complement the flag each time the punt production is reached), and a way to make reference to the stored fragment. The result of this enhancement might be the Shrink saying something like "EARLIER YOU MENTIONED YOU HATE HOMEWORK" or "LETS DISCUSS THE FACT THAT YOU ADORE VAN GOGH."

13. Design a new version of SHRINK which employs a discrimination net. Alter the production rules so that the net leads to a substantial increase in efficiency in finding the most suitable rule to fire.

14. Develop a dialog program in the style of SHRINK which portrays a personality of its own. Some suggestions: (1) a political candidate (or particular office-holder) who answers all questions in his/her own narrow way, (2) a paranoid, (3) a widget salesman.

15. To what extent does SHRINK use an *ordered* production system? Give an example of a user input that would generate different responses from SHRINK if the order of the production rules was changed.

16. To what extent does LEIBNIZ use an *ordered* production system? Reverse the order of the differentiation rules (leaving the other rules in the same order) and run LEIBNIZ on the same formula for which a run is described in the text. What differences do you find?

17. Run LEIBNIZ on the formula (D (PLUS (TIMES X 7) (TIMES 8 X)) X). What is the sequence in which the production rules fire?

18. Add new differentiation rules to LEIBNIZ so that it can handle mathematical expressions involving the function sin. An example of something that LEIBNIZ should be able to differentiate is

(PLUS X (SIN (TIMES 2 X))).

The chain rule for differentiating a composition of functions should be brought into play here.

19. As mentioned on page 73, LEIBNIZ allows only two operands with PLUS and TIMES in the formulas it manipulates. Develop the modifications that will permit LEIBNIZ to accept PLUS and TIMES with any number of arguments, as LISP does.

20. Develop a discrimination net that uses the same differentiation and simplification techniques that LEIBNIZ uses. Compare the running times for LEIBNIZ and your program on the example illustrated in the text.

21. One of LEIBNIZ's rules, DIFF_PLUS_RULE, uses a helping function, PLUSFORM, in the representation of the pattern part of the rule. On the other hand, DIFF_X_RULE uses local functions (with LAMBDA forms), avoiding the need for defining a named function. Rewrite the representation for DIFF_PLUS_RULE using local function definitions instead of PLUSFORM.

22. Devise a new control scheme which avoids testing the same productions on the same subexpressions over and over again. One way to do this is to keep track of subexpressions that have changed since each production rule was tried, and if the rule failed, only try the rule again if the subexpression has changed.

23. Some of the production rules for LEIBNIZ involve pattern matching at the top two levels of the current formula. Make up a pattern that actually performs matching at the top three levels of a formula.

24. A rational number may be represented by a dotted pair $(n \ . \ d)$ of integers (FIXNUMs) where n is the numerator and d is the denominator. Develop the following functions:

   (a) (REDUCE x) which simplifies the fraction, if possible,

   (b) (ADD x y) which computes the sum of rationals x and y, and

   (c) (MULTIPLY x y) which computes the product of rationals x and y.

25. Write down a set of rules that could be used to design a production system for symbolic integration of simple formulas.

26. Design and demonstrate a production system that uses rules of the previous problem to solve some freshman-calculus integration problems.

Chapter 4

KNOWLEDGE REPRESENTATION

4.1 Characteristics of Knowledge

One usually makes a distinction between "data" and "information." Data consists of raw figures, measurements, and files that do not necessarily answer the questions that its users may have. Information, on the other hand, is somewhat more refined. It is often the result of processing crude data, giving useful statistics for the data, or answering specific questions posed by users. In AI we usually distinguish a third kind of order in memory: "knowledge." We think of knowledge as a refined kind of information, often more general than that found in conventional databases. But it may be incomplete or fuzzy as well. We may think of knowledge as a collection of related facts, procedures, models and heuristics than can be used in problem solving or inference systems. Knowledge may be regarded as information in context, as information organized so that it can be readily applied to solving problems, perception and learning.

Knowledge varies widely in both its content and appearance. It may be specific, general, exact, fuzzy, procedural, declarative, etc. There are several commonly used methods to organize and represent knowledge. These are described in the following section.

4.2 Overview of Knowledge Representation Methods

Before describing a few methods in some detail, it is useful to consider briefly a number of the general approaches that have been used for representing knowledge. These include: production rules, inclusion hierarchies, mathematical logics, frames, scripts, semantic networks, constraints, and relational databases. Production rules, illustrated in Chapter 3, are a general method that is particularly appropriate when knowledge is action-oriented.

Inclusion hierarchies, described later in this chapter in some detail, handle a particular kind of knowledge very well: knowledge about objects that can be grouped into classifications, such that some categories are subcategories of others. Inclusion hierarchies may be used as an organizing scheme in connection with other methods, such as the predicate calculus.

Mathematical logics such as the predicate calculus provide a general and fundamental capability which supports general logical inference. However, these logics seldom provide organizational support for *grouping* facts so that the facts can be efficiently used. In this sense, mathematical logics are "low-level" representation schemes that do well with details but require additional support to be useful in building nontrivial systems.

Frames provide an organizational scheme for knowledge bases, but not much more than this; the detailed representations require other methods. Scripts have been used in some experimental systems for natural language understanding for representing scenarios with standard chronology such as what a person does when he/she goes to a restaurant: gets a table, waits for the menu, orders, eats, pays the bill, and leaves; scripts are like frames with additional support for describing chronology. Semantic networks, like frames, are a general organizational framework, but there is not necessarily any particular kind of low-level support in a semantic net system; any system in which the modules of knowledge may be described as nodes in a labelled graph may be called a semantic net, although it tends to be systems that attempt to mimic the neuronal interconnection structure of the biological brain that are most often labelled by their creators as "semantic networks."

A kind of knowledge that is often described as a representation method is "constraints." A *constraint* is a relationship among one, two or more objects that may be viewed as a predicate; the constraint is to be satisfied by the system in finding a solution to a problem. By emphasizing the use of constraints in representing a set of objects and their interrelations, a constraint-based approach to knowledge representation may be used.

Finally, relational databases can sometimes serve as a method for knowledge representation; as they are usually implemented, they are good at manipulating large quantities of regularly-structured information in certain, largely preconceived, ways. Relational databases have not been ideal for AI applications in the past because of their inefficiency in making large numbers of small inferences involving either very small relations or small parts of larger relations; there is currently research going on to make relational databases more suitable for AI applications.

This chapter presents the most important methods for knowledge representation. Inclusion hierarchies, the predicate calculus and frames are the methods treated here. After a brief discussion of production rules as a means of representing knowledge we focus on the problem of representing a single concrete, but very powerful, relation: the inclusion relation between classes of objects. Next, the use of propositional and predicate logics for representing knowledge is taken up. After examining semantic networks, we look at frames, schemata, and scripts. Then relational databases are considered. Finally, several issues related to knowledge representation are discussed and a comparative summary of the methods is given. Some of the other methods and several specialized techniques for such problem domains as computer vision and natural language understanding are presented in later chapters.

4.3 Knowledge in Production Rules

If we examine the SHRINK program to find the basis for its response-making ability, we would be hard-pressed to find anything but its production rules embedded into the big COND form. The knowledge of what to say when is almost all in these rules. Some of the SHRINK's knowledge, however, lies outside of the rules, although it is brought into play by the production rules. For example, the definition of the function VERBP is knowledge (albeit at a primitive level) about the English language and is represented separately from the production rules, but several rules contain patterns which use VERBP.

Similarly, the knowledge about differentiating formulas in LEIBNIZ lies almost entirely in its production rules. Some of LEIBNIZ's ability comes from the control scheme's method of trying to apply productions at many levels of the current formula, but if we wanted to increase the set of problems that LEIBNIZ could solve, we could simply add new rules.

In many of the expert systems described in the literature, such as MYCIN, AM and PROSPECTOR, much of the knowledge is represented within production rules. The left hand side of a production rule (the condition part) expresses the characteristics of a situation in which it is appropriate to perform the action (the right hand side) of the production rule. The testing of the condition as well as the execution of the action may involve the manipulation of other data structures (knowledge bases). Thus the production rules might not embody all of the knowledge in a system. Even when one plans to embed most of a system's knowledge in production rules, one should understand the use of other means of knowledge representation.

4.4 Concept Hierarchies

Much of man's knowledge about the world is organized hierarchically. All the "things" we know of we group into classes or sets. These classes are grouped into superclasses and the superclasses into even bigger ones. We associate with most of these classes names which we use to identify the classes. There is a class we call "dogs" and another we call "cats." These are grouped, with some other classes, into a superclass called "mammals." Plants, minerals, machines, emotions, information and ideas are treated similarly. Much of our knowledge consists of an understanding of the inclusion relationship on all these classes and cognizance of various properties shared by all members of particular classes. "All horses have four legs" states that the property "has four legs" is shared by each member of the class of horses.

4.4.1   Inclusion, Membership and "ISA"

The inclusion relation on a set of classes is very important in AI, and there are some interesting questions that arise when incorporating it into an AI system. Our first issue is deciding what statements of English express inclusion relationships. The sentence "A bear is a mammal" expresses that the class of bears is a subclass of the class of mammals. For this reason, the data structures used to represent inclusion relations are often called "ISA" hierarchies. The list (BEAR ISA MAMMAL) is one way of representing this inclusion relationship. One must beware of certain relationships which are similar in appearance to inclusion but are really quite different. "Teddy is a bear" does not really say that the class of Teddies is a subclass of the class of bears. Rather, it states that the particular object, Teddy, is a member of the class of bears. Using set notation we would write

BEARS $\subseteq$ MAMMALS

TEDDY $\in$ BEARS

The key clue that the first sentence gives us for distinguishing that case from the second is that "bear," preceded by the article "A," is indefinite and refers to any and presumably all elements of the class. The "A" before "bear" in the first sentence signals an inclusion relationship, whereas its absence before "Teddy" in the second sentence indicates that Teddy is a particular object rather than one representative of a class, and that "is a" means "is an element of the class" in this case. A list representing the membership relationship in this case could be (TEDDY ISIN BEAR).

The verb *to be* is used in various senses, also. "Happiness is a sunny day" illustrates the use of *to be* in expressing a metaphor. This expression would probably not be meant (by whoever uses it) to indicate that the set of happinesses is a subset of the set of sunny days. More probably, someone saying such a thing would intend that the listener understand him to mean that sunny days lead to happiness. "A hot fudge sundae is vanilla ice cream with chocolate sauce" uses *is* to mean *consists of*, making a kind of definition. These uses of *is* do not express inclusion, and so one must be careful when attempting to describe the meanings of English sentences that use *to be* (in its various forms) in terms of inclusion. This illustrates one of the many difficulties of dealing with natural language in a mechanized way.

Let us restrict ourselves to the inclusion relation for the time being. It has a very important property: transitivity. This indicates, for example, that if (BEAR

ISA MAMMAL) and (MAMMAL ISA ANIMAL) then (BEAR ISA ANIMAL). The fact that such a deduction can be made raises an important question: which assertions should be represented explicitly in a knowledge base and which should be deduced when needed; i.e., left implicit most of the time? The best answer is not always apparent. In order to illustrate the advantages and disadvantages of various alternatives we develop enough mathematical tools so that the properties and problems of various representations can be understood.

4.4.2 Partial Orders and Their Representation

Let S be a set. A set of ordered pairs of elements of S is a *binary relation* on S. A binary relation, $\leq$, on S is a *partial order* if and only if

1. for each $x, x \leq x$ (reflexive property),

2. for each x, for each y, if $x \leq y$ and $y \leq x$ then $x = y$ (antisymmetry), and

3. for each x, for each y, for each z, if $x \leq y$ and $y \leq z$ then $x \leq z$ (transitivity).

For example take $S = \{a, b, c, d\}$ and let $\leq$ be the relation

$$\{(a, b), (c, d), (b, d), (a, d), (a, a), (b, b), (c, c), (d, d)\}.$$

The graph[1] of this relation is shown in Fig. 4.1.

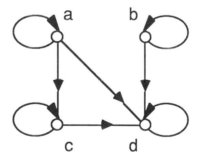

Figure 4.1: The ordinary graph of a relation.

It is customary to say that a *precedes* b and that c *precedes* d, etc. Since every node must have a self loop, these convey no information on the diagram and can be deleted. Next, if one positions the nodes of this graph so that whenever x precedes y, x is higher on the page than y, then one can dispense with the arrowheads and leave just the line segments, as shown in Fig. 4.2.

Noting that $a \leq d$ is implied by $a \leq b$ and $b \leq d$, the graph becomes less cluttered if the "redundant" segment is erased. The resulting picture is called

---

[1]The *graph* of a relation is a diagram in which each element of the set is shown by a *node*, and every pair of elements that is part of the relation is shown by an *arc* connecting the corresponding nodes. An arc connecting a node to itself is called a "self loop."

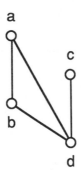

Figure 4.2: The graph with self loops and arc directions implicit.

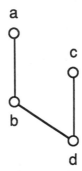

Figure 4.3: A Hasse diagram for a transitive relation.

a *Hasse diagram* for the partial order, and it is shown in Fig. 4.3. The ordered pairs of elements for which lines actually appear in a Hasse diagram constitute the covering relation $\lhd$ for the original relation $\leq$. The *covering* relation is also called the *transitive reduction*. The original relation $\leq$ may be derived from its covering relation $\lhd$ by taking the "transitive closure" of $\lhd$. The *transitive closure* of any relation is defined to be the smallest reflexive and transitive relation which includes the relation.

As an example of a partial order, let us consider the inclusion relation on some set. Let Ω be a universe of objects (i.e., some large set), and let S be the set of all subsets of Ω. If we consider any two elements x and y of S, then we have either $x \subseteq y$ or $y \subseteq x$, or $x \not\subseteq y$ and $y \not\subseteq x$. It is obvious that $\subseteq$ is a partial order. And thus when we have in LISP the expression (BEAR ISA ANIMAL), we have an explicit representation of one of the pairs in a partial order on some set of animal categories.

Suppose that a set of "facts" has been given, each of which is of the form "an X is a Y," and that inclusion is the relation expressed in each case. Two different approaches to the presentation of the set of facts are to store (1) the transitive reduction (covering relation) and (2) the transitive closure (all original and implied facts). The advantage of 1 is that less space is generally required in memory, since fewer graph arcs may be necessary. The advantage of 2 is that each fact is explicit and ready, so that less time may be required to respond to a question regarding the relationship of two entities. Presumably, the time necessary to deduce that $x \leq y$ (assuming that $x \leq y$ is true) depends largely upon the length of the path from x to y in the Hasse diagram. However, if the transitive closure is stored, one must consider that the additional arcs of the graph may necessitate additional time in verifying $x \leq y$ even though the path length from x to z is only one arc. That is to say, in a graph that is closed with respect to transitivity, each node is likely to have many neighbors (i.e., a high valence), and this high valence may cause some accesses to run more slowly.

For cases in which the transitive reduction and transitive closure are almost the same, it makes little difference which of the two representations is used; however, in practical situations the two graphs are almost always quite different. Depending upon how the search process is implemented, it may be possible to achieve a good compromise between the two approaches while holding both memory space and search time down. For example, by adding a few "short cut" arcs to the transitive reduction, expected path length can sometimes be reduced considerably without any considerable increase in the degree of the graph for the covering relation, and this can shorten the lengths of some searches; however, it may lengthen others. Optimal representation of ISA hierarchies under various assumptions is a subject for research.

4.5 An ISA Hierarchy in LISP

4.5.1 Preliminary Remarks

Knowledge of the inclusion relation among a set of categories is a very useful kind of information. Inclusion knowledge is instrumental in defining many nouns, and it can serve as the backbone of a representation system that incorporates other kinds of knowledge. Even without additional kinds of knowledge, however, inclusion knowledge can support a variety of types of queries. To illustrate some of the possibilities, a LISP program is presented that demonstrates first how the relation of inclusion can be conveniently represented, then how the information may be accessed and used for making limited inferences, and finally how these mechanisms may be integrated into a simple conversational program. Since the knowledge manipulated by the program is all related to categories of things, we refer to the program as "LINNEUS." This LISP program consists of the various functions that are explained subsequently.

4.5.2 The Use of Property Lists to Store Relations

The property lists of atoms offer a convenient facility for representing relations such as inclusion. To represent the set of elements $y_1, y_2, \ldots, y_k$, which are related to x by relation R, (that is, $x \, R \, y_i, i = 1, \ldots, k$), we use an S-expression of the form

4.5.2   The Use of Property Lists to Store Relations

The property lists of atoms offer a convenient facility for representing relations such as inclusion. To represent the set of elements $y_1, y_2, \ldots, y_k$, which are related to x by relation R, (that is, $x\ R\ y_i, i = 1, \ldots, k$), we use an S-expression of the form

(PUTPROP x (LIST y_1 y_2 $\cdots$ y_k) R).

For example, we might have,

(PUTPROP 'ANIMAL '(DOG CAT BEAR) 'INCLUDES).

The list of classes that ANIMAL includes may then be retrieved by

(GET 'ANIMAL 'INCLUDES).

The information, $x\ R\ y$, is accessible here by using x and R to formulate a GET expression, and then examining the list of atoms returned, which should contain y if $x\ R\ y$ is true. To make this information accessible more generally, it should be represented also in two other forms: on the property list of y and on that of R. This could be accomplished by the following:

(PUTPROP 'DOG '(ANIMAL) 'ISA)

which makes ANIMAL accessible from DOG via the ISA link, and

(PUTPROP 'INCLUDES
         '((ANIMAL CAT)(ANIMAL DOG)(ANIMAL BEAR))
         'PAIRS)

which makes all the pairs of the INCLUDES relation accessible from the atom INCLUDES.

In the demonstration program, we use the first two forms: the INCLUDES property and the ISA property, but not the PAIRS property. Another difference there is that we wish to add the knowledge gradually as it becomes available from the user. Thus we use special functions ADDSUBSET and ADDSUPERSET to put things on the property lists, since we do not want to clobber old information each time we add new information. These functions are defined in terms of a helping function ADDTOSET which is like CONS but avoids repeated elements in a list. The definitions of these functions follow:

```
(DEFUN ADDTOSET (ELT LST)
  (COND ((MEMBER ELT LST) LST) (T (CONS ELT LST)) ))

(DEFUN ADDSUPERSET (ANAME X)
  (PUTPROP ANAME (ADDTOSET X (GET ANAME 'ISA)) 'ISA))

(DEFUN ADDSUBSET (ANAME X)
  (PUTPROP ANAME (ADDTOSET X (GET ANAME 'INCLUDES)) 'INCLUDES) )
```

4.5.3 Searching a Base of Facts

Given a base of facts, "A turbot is a fish," "A fish is an animal," etc., represented in LISP as explained above, how can questions of the form "Is a turbot an animal?" be answered? Assuming that what is explicitly represented is a subrelation of the implied (transitive) one, and that this subrelation is not necessarily transitive, the program should begin a search (for example) for ANIMAL from TURBOT. It should look first on the list of things that a TURBOT is (as represented on its property list) and if ANIMAL is not found there, on the lists for each entry on TURBOT's list, recursively searching until either ANIMAL is found or all possibilities have been exhausted without finding it, or all alternatives to a given depth limit have been exhausted.

Such a search is performed by the function ISATEST described below:

```
(DEFUN ISATEST (X Y N)
  (COND ((EQ X Y) T)
        ((ZEROP N) NIL)
        ((MEMBER Y (GET X 'ISA)) T)
        (T (ANY (MAPCAR
                  (FUNCTION
                    (LAMBDA (XX) (ISATEST XX Y (SUB1 N))) )
                  (GET X 'ISA) ))) ) )
```

The function ISATEST takes three arguments, X, Y, and N where X and Y are atoms like CAT and ANIMAL, and N is a non-negative integer giving the maximum number of levels for the recursive search. The first clause, ((EQ X Y) T) tests to see if X is identical to Y and returns T if so. This corresponds to a search of depth 0. The next clause tests N for 0 and cuts off the search along the current branch if so. The third clause, ((MEMBER Y (GET X 'ISA)) T) performs a search of depth 1 from X looking for Y. If this fails, the last clause is tried. In the last clause, searches with maximum depth N−1 are initiated from each of the atoms appearing on X's "ISA" list. If any of these succeeds, ISATEST returns T.

For the ISA hierarchy shown in Fig. 4.4, the test (ISATEST 'LOBSTER 'ANIMAL 20) succeeds because there is a path from LOBSTER to ANIMAL going only upwards, and the length of the path is less than 20.

The supporting function ANY has the effect of applying the function OR to its argument list. It may be defined:

```
(DEFUN ANY (LST)
  (COND ((NULL LST) NIL)
        ((CAR LST) T)
        (T (ANY (CDR LST))) ) )
```

Note that ISATEST could be made more efficient by aborting the remaining

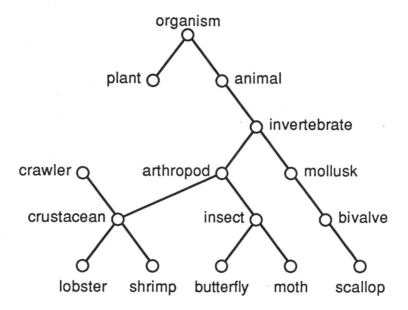

Figure 4.4: An ISA hierarchy for which the test (ISATEST 'LOBSTER 'ANI-MAL 20) succeeds.

subsearches as soon as Y is found in one of the subsearches (this is left as an exercise).

It may seem that the program might just as well have initiated a search from Y for X, traversing the inclusion arcs in the opposite direction. The length of the path from X to Y going forwards is the same as that from Y to X going backwards. However, the branching of the search may be drastically different in one case than the other. If X is a leaf node in a tree and Y is the root, it takes less searching in general to find Y from X than to find X from Y. This is because there are no choices when moving up a path of the tree. The strategy of searching forward from the present state or node (e.g., LOBSTER) toward the goal (e.g., ANIMAL) is called "forward chaining." The complementary strategy is to search from the goal back to the initial node or state, and this is called "backward chaining." Forward and backward chaining are described further in Chapter 5.

4.6   A Conversational Front End

The ability to store, retrieve, and perform simple inferences on relational data can support a variety of question-answering modes. LINNEUS demonstrates this by interpreting simple statements and questions and then invoking functions to search or manipulate the relational knowledge. The function INTER-

PRET (shown below) is the main component of the conversational front end (human-to-knowledge-base interface). INTERPRET consists of a large COND form embedding a number of clauses that are essentially production rules.

```
(DEFUN LINNEUS ()            ; This is the top-level procedure.
  (PROG ()
        (PRINT '(I AM LINNEUS))
        (PRINT '(PLEASE GIVE ME INFORMATION OR ASK QUESTIONS))
  LOOP  (SETQ TEXTIN (READ))  ; Get a sentence from the user.
        (INTERPRET TEXTIN)    ; Try to interpret it and act on it.
        (GO LOOP) ) )         ; Repeat until user aborts program.


(DEFUN INTERPRET (TEXT)      ; Here are the production rules...
  (COND
    ; rule for statements such as '(a bear is a mammal)' ...
    ((MATCH '((MATCHARTICLE ARTICLE1)(? X) IS
             (MATCHARTICLE ARTICLE2)(? Y))
           TEXT)
     (ADDSUPERSET X Y)     ; Create a link from X up to Y
     (ADDSUBSET Y X)       ; and a link from Y down to X.
     (PUTPROP X ARTICLE1 'ARTICLE) ; Save X's article
     (PUTPROP Y ARTICLE2 'ARTICLE) ; and Y's, too.
     (PRINT '(I UNDERSTAND)) )     ; Acknowledge user.

    ; rule for questions such as '(what is a bear)' ...
    ((MATCH '(WHAT IS (MATCHARTICLE ARTICLE1)(? X)) TEXT)
     (SETQ ISAFLAG NIL)       ; Default is 'no information
     (SETQ INCLUDEFLAG NIL) ; available'.
     (COND ((SETQ Y (GET X 'ISA))
            (SETQ ISAFLAG T) )       ; Y is a superset of X.
           ((SETQ Y (GET X 'INCLUDES))
            (SETQ INCLUDEFLAG T) ) ) ; ' subset '.
     ; Print out a reply based on one of the two relations...
     (PRINT (APPEND
             (LIST (GET X 'ARTICLE)); 'A' or 'AN',
             (LIST X)                ; whatever X is,
             (COND (ISAFLAG '(IS))   ; one of the two relations,
                   (INCLUDEFLAG
                    '(IS SOMETHING MORE GENERAL THAN) ) )
             (MAKECONJ Y) )) )       ; some things that X is or
                                     ; is more general than.

    ; rule for questions such as '(is a bear a mammal)' ...
    ((MATCH '(IS (MATCHARTICLE ARTICLE1) (? X)
```

```
              (MATCHARTICLE ARTICLE2) (? Y))
            TEXT)
    (COND ((ISATEST X Y 10)           ; Search for Y from X.
           (PRINT                     ; Reply affirmatively.
            (APPEND '(YES INDEED)
                    (LIST (GET X 'ARTICLE))
                    (LIST X)
                    '(IS)
                    (LIST (GET Y 'ARTICLE))
                    (LIST Y) )) )
          (T (PRINT '(SORRY NOT THAT I KNOW OF))) ) ) ; Negative.

    ; rule for questions such as '(why is a bear an animal)' ...
    ((MATCH '(WHY IS (MATCHARTICLE ARTICLE1) (? X)
             (MATCHARTICLE ARTICLE2) (? Y))
            TEXT)
     (COND ((ISATEST X Y 10) ; Is presupposition correct?
            (PRINT        ; Yes, prepare reply with explanation...
             (CONS 'BECAUSE
                   (EXPLAIN_LINKS X Y) )) ); Create explanation.
          (T (PRINT '(BUT IT ISN'T!)))  ) ) ; No, give reply
                ; indicating that the presupposition is false.

    ; rule that handles all other inputs:
    (T (PRINT '(I DO NOT UNDERSTAND))) ))
```

If the user types "(A BEAR IS AN ANIMAL)", the first production rule will fire. That is, the pattern:

```
((MATCHARTICLE ARTICLE1) (? X) IS
  (MATCHARTICLE ARTICLE2) (? Y))
```

will match the value of TEXT. The subpattern (MATCHARTICLE ARTICLE1) will match A because when the predicate MATCHARTICLE is applied to A the result is T. The subpattern (? X) will match BEAR and (? Y) will match ANIMAL. The action part of this production rule consists of five parts. (ADDSUPERSET X Y) causes ANIMAL to be entered onto the list of classes that are supersets of BEAR. (ADDSUBSET Y X) places the same relational information, but from the point of view of ANIMAL, on a list for ANIMAL. The next two subactions cause the articles (in this case A and AN) to be remembered in association with the nouns they precede (in this case BEAR and ANIMAL). The final subaction is to print (I UNDERSTAND), thus confirming the successful interpretation of the user's statement.

The second production rule handles user inputs such as (WHAT IS A BEAR). When the pattern is successfully matched to the input, X is bound to the atom (here BEAR) whose property list is to be examined. The action again consists of several subactions. First, two flags are reset. These flags control the form of the answer; the answer may report classes which are supersets of the value of X, or may report classes which are subsets. Thus the response to the question above might be (A BEAR IS AN ANIMAL). To the question (WHAT IS AN ANIMAL), the response might be (AN ANIMAL IS SOMETHING MORE GENERAL THAN A BEAR). If any supersets of X can be found, then ISAFLAG is set to T, and the immediate supersets are reported in the answer. If no supersets are found, the program looks for subsets.

The third production rule accepts queries of the form (IS A TURBOT AN ANIMAL). Its action is to search for Y (in this case ANIMAL) starting from X (here TURBOT) by invoking the function ISATEST, explained previously. If the search is successful, the relationship between X and Y is confirmed with the PRINT form. Otherwise the response is (SORRY NOT THAT I KNOW OF).

The fourth production rule provides explanations in response to questions such as "(WHY IS A TURBOT AN ANIMAL)" and makes use of the function EXPLAIN_LINKS. Before it does so, however, it uses ISATEST to make sure that a TURBOT really is an ANIMAL (or whatever the presupposition expressed in the question happens to be).

Let us now examine the definitions of the remaining functions for the LINNEUS program. The predicate MATCHARTICLE returns T if its argument matches one of the articles it knows about.

```
(DEFUN MATCHARTICLE (X)
  (MEMBER X '(A AN THE THAT THIS THOSE THESE)) )
```

In order to make a list of the form (DOG CAT AARDVARK) seem more like English, the function MAKECONJ transforms it into a list of the form (A DOG AND A CAT AND AN AARDVARK). The latter list is more obviously a conjunction than the original list.

```
(DEFUN MAKECONJ (LST)
  (COND ((NULL LST) NIL)
        ((NULL (CDR LST)) (CONS (GET (CAR LST) 'ARTICLE) LST))
        (T (CONS (GET (CAR LST) 'ARTICLE)
                 (CONS (CAR LST)
                       (CONS 'AND (MAKECONJ (CDR LST)))) )) ) )
```

The function EXPLAIN_LINKS works by checking for a couple of special cases and then, assuming neither holds, calling EXPLAIN_CHAIN. The first special case holds when the user has typed a question such as "(WHY IS A HORSE A HORSE)" in which case EXPLAIN_LINKS reports the reason: that they are identical. The second case holds when there is a single ISA link from X to Y, indicating that the fact in question was input by the user, rather than deduced by the program. LINNEUS would report "BECAUSE YOU TOLD ME SO" in such a case.

```
(DEFUN EXPLAIN_LINKS (X Y)
  (COND ((EQ X Y) '(THEY ARE IDENTICAL))        ; 1st special case
        ((MEMBER Y (GET X 'ISA))                ; 2nd special case
         '(YOU TOLD ME SO) )
        (T (EXPLAIN_CHAIN X (GET X 'ISA) Y)) ) ); General case
```

For the general case, the interesting part of the job is done by the recursive function EXPLAIN_CHAIN, with the help of TELL.

EXPLAIN_CHAIN takes three arguments: X, L, and Y. It gives a report about the first chain from X to Y that passes through a member of L. If there is a direct ISA link from X to Y (which is not the case in the top-level call, or else the second special case of EXPLAIN_LINKS would have held), then EX-PLAIN_CHAIN returns an explanation of that link, preceded by AND, thus providing the final part of an explanation onto which other parts can be AP-PENDed.

```
(DEFUN EXPLAIN_CHAIN (X L Y)
  (COND ((NULL L) NIL)            ; L should never be null.
        ((MEMBER Y L)             ; Is this the last link?
         (CONS 'AND (TELL X Y)) ) ; Yes, precede expl. by AND.
        ((ISATEST (CAR L) Y 10)   ; Does chain go through CAR L?
         (APPEND (TELL X (CAR L)) ; Yes, explain this link, etc.
                 (EXPLAIN_CHAIN (CAR L)
                                (GET (CAR L) 'ISA)
                                Y) ) )
        (T (EXPLAIN_CHAIN X (CDR L) Y)) ) ) ; else try next in L.
```

The function TELL takes care of the simple job of reporting about a single link. For example (TELL 'TURBOT 'FISH) would evaluate to (A TURBOT IS A FISH).

```
(DEFUN TELL (X Y)
  (LIST (GET X 'ARTICLE) X 'IS (GET Y 'ARTICLE) Y) )
```

The following illustrates a session with LINNEUS. The user's inputs are in lower case.

```
(linneus)
(I AM LINNEUS)
(PLEASE GIVE ME INFORMATION OR ASK QUESTIONS)
(a turbot is a fish)
(I UNDERSTAND)
(a fish is an animal)
(I UNDERSTAND)
(a fish is a swimmer)
(I UNDERSTAND)
```

```
(what is a turbot)
(A TURBOT IS A FISH)
(what is a swimmer)
(A SWIMMER IS SOMETHING MORE GENERAL THAN A FISH)
(is a turbot an animal)
(YES INDEED A TURBOT IS AN ANIMAL)
(why is a turbot a swimmer)
(BECAUSE A TURBOT IS A FISH AND A FISH IS A SWIMMER)
(why is a turbot a turbot)
(BECAUSE THEY ARE IDENTICAL)
(why is a turbot a fish)
(BECAUSE YOU TOLD ME SO)
```

There are a number of interesting extensions which can be made to LINNEUS. For example, "HAS" links can be incorporated; these are described in the next section. Other extensions are suggested in the exercises.

4.7   Inheritance

4.7.1   Inheritance from Supersets

With a representation of the inclusion relation on a set of classes based on the transitive reduction of the inclusion relation (or equally well by the "included by" relation), we can nicely handle additional relations with relatively little effort.

Let us consider the statements

```
(A PHEASANT IS A BIRD) and
(A BIRD HAS FEATHERS).
```

From these we normally conclude that

```
(A PHEASANT HAS FEATHERS).
```

That is, because the class PHEASANT is included by the class BIRD, certain properties of class BIRD are automatically "inherited" by class PHEASANT.

The general rule is: whenever we have x as a member of a set X which is a subset of a set Y, any property true of any member of Y must also be true of x. The fact that such a property of x can be determined by looking at Y means that the fact that x has this property need not be explicitly represented. As with the transitive reduction of a transitive relation, where it is only necessary to store a covering relation explicitly, we now may store some properties of classes only at "dominant" positions in the inclusion hierarchy.

4.7.2   HAS Links

Like the inclusion relation, the relation we call HAS is transitive. Here we use HAS to mean "has as parts." If a man has hands and a hand has fingers then we can infer that a man has fingers. We might express these relationships as follows

```
(MAN HAS HAND)
(HAND HAS FINGER)
```

therefore,

```
(MAN HAS FINGER).
```

By avoiding articles and plural forms here, we also avoid some problems of lexical analysis, which is more a subject in natural language understanding (see Chapter 9) than in the representation of knowledge.

The HAS relation is not only a transitive one by itself, and therefore capable of being efficiently represented by its transitive reduction, but it also may be viewed as a property that can be inherited with respect to the inclusion relation ISA. Let us write $X\ H\ Y$ to denote "X has Y"; i.e., members of class X have one or more members of class Y as parts. For example, HAND H FINGER means that a hand has one or more fingers. Then we note:

1. if $X \subseteq Y$ and ZHX then ZHY, and

2. if $X \subseteq Y$ and YHZ then XHZ.

Rule 1 may be called the rule of "generalizing HAS with respect to ISA," and Rule 2 may be called "inheritance of HAS with respect to ISA."

One can make inferences that involve sequences of these two rules and inferences by transitivity of ISA and HAS. For example, from the list of facts,

```
(A TURBOT IS A FISH)
(A FISH IS AN ANIMAL)
(ANIMAL HAS HEART)
(A HEART IS AN ORGAN)
(ORGAN HAS TISSUE)
(TISSUE HAS CELL)
```

we can infer

```
(TURBOT HAS CELL).
```

Thus ISA and HAS are two partial orders that interact through the rules of generalization and inheritance above.

4.7.3 Multiple Inheritance

When the ISA hierarchy (transitive reduction of the inclusion relation) forms a tree or a forest (collection of trees) such that each class X has at most one immediate superclass, then the test to see whether a class X has some property P is easy to do. Each Y along the path from X to the root of the tree containing X is examined to see if it has property P. If any does, then X also does, by inheritance. Inheritance by TURBOT and COD of the property of having scales, from FISH, is illustrated in Fig. 4.5.

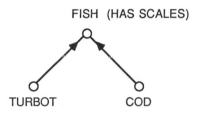

Figure 4.5: Inheritance of HAS relationships.

A more complicated search is required when each class may have more than one immediate superclass. This is to say, the covering relation branches upwards as well as downwards in the general case. The search for a property P must generally follow each upward branch until P is found or all possibilities are exhausted.

The possibility of multiple inheritance increases the potential for conflicting inherited values. Consider the example shown in Fig. 4.6. A decoy may be

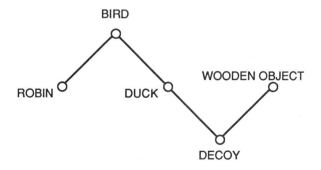

Figure 4.6: Multiple inheritance.

considered to be a kind of duck and in turn, a bird. It is also a kind of wooden object. As a duck, it has a bill, a head and a body. This is quite appropriate. As a bird, however, it ought to have a beating heart and be able to fly. But as a wooden object, it should not have a beating heart, nor should it be able to fly. The resolution of conflicts such as these may be difficult. In this particular case it is not; since a decoy is not truly a duck, the link between DECOY and DUCK should not be an inclusion link but a link such as RESEMBLES. A link of resemblance might only be allowed to pass inherited traits of certain types such as traits of appearance.

Generally speaking, properties are inherited from superclasses (i.e., along ISA arcs). However, they are not inherited along HAS arcs. Obviously the following "inference" is invalid:

```
(MAN HAS HAND)
(HAND SHORTER_THAN ONE_METER)
```

"therefore"

```
(MAN SHORTER_THAN ONE_METER).
```

Clearly one cannot treat HAS links in exactly the same manner as ISA links.

4.7.4   Default Inheritance

There are some domains of knowledge in which exceptions to general rules exist. For example, it is usually useful to assume that all birds can fly. Certain birds such as the ostrich and the kiwi, however, cannot fly (even though they really are birds, unlike wooden decoys). In such a case it is reasonable to use a representation scheme in which properties associated with atoms in a hierarchy are assumed to be true of all subclasses, unless specifically overridden by a denial or modification associated with the subclass. For example, see Fig. 4.7.

Under such a scheme, the fact that a woodpecker can fly is made explicit by following the (short) path from WOODPECKER to BIRD and finding there the property (CAN FLY). On the other hand, starting from OSTRICH, the property (CANNOT FLY) is found immediately, overriding the default which is further up the tree.

Although inclusion (ISA) hierarchies often provide a conceptual organization for a knowledge base, they give immediate support to inferences of only a rather limited sort. The inferences involve either the transitivity of the inclusion relation or the inheritance of properties downward along chains in the hierarchy. An inclusion hierarchy provides a good way to organize many of the objects and concepts in a knowledge base, but it does not provide a representation scheme for non-inclusion relationships, for logical or numerical constraints on objects or for descriptions of the objects.

One way to build an ISA hierarchy into a more powerful structure is to add many different kinds of links to the system. We have already seen ISA, IN-CLUDES, and HAS links. Some more that can be added include ELEMENT_OF

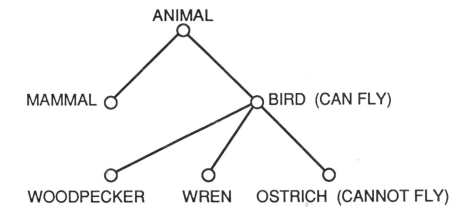

Figure 4.7: Default properties and exceptions.

and OWNS. A data structure consisting of nodes which represent concepts or objects, together with labelled arcs representing relationships such as these, is called a "semantic network" (or "semantic net" for short). Semantic nets are described later in this chapter.

In order to provide a general capability for representing many kinds of relations (rather than just inclusion and other binary relations), we turn to mathematical logic.

4.8 Propositional and Predicate Logic

4.8.1 Remarks

Mathematical logics are appropriate for representing knowledge in some situations. Two logics are commonly used. The propositional calculus is usually used in teaching rather than in actual systems; since it is essentially a greatly simplified version of the predicate calculus, an understanding of propositional calculus is a good first step toward understanding the predicate calculus.

On the other hand predicate calculus (or predicate logic) *is* often used as a means of knowledge representation in AI systems. Predicate logic is the basis for "logic programming" (as permitted by the programming language PROLOG, for example), and many specialists regard it as the single most important knowledge representation method. As we shall see, the predicate calculus is quite powerful but still has some serious shortcomings.

4.8.2   Propositional Calculus

Here we present a brief summary of the propositional calculus, its use in representing statements, and some simple ways in which the representations can be manipulated.

Let X represent the statement "it is raining today." Let Y represent the statement "the picnic is cancelled." Then the expression

$$X \wedge Y$$

represents the statement "it is raining today and the picnic is cancelled." The expression

$$X \vee Y$$

stands for: "it is raining today or the picnic is cancelled." The expression

$$X \Rightarrow Y$$

means "if it is raining today then the picnic is cancelled." The negation of X is written

$$\neg X$$

and means "it is not raining today," or equivalently, "it is not the case that it is raining today."

The symbols X and Y used here are called propositional symbols because each represents some proposition. The symbols

$$\wedge, \vee, \Rightarrow, \Leftrightarrow, \neg$$

are called *connectives* because they generally connect pairs of propositional symbols. An exception is $\neg$ which is a unary operator; although it is associated with only one propositional symbol, we still refer to it as a connective. The other connectives are binary operators.

The syntax of propositional calculus expressions can be formally described using Backus-Naur form (which may be regarded as a shorthand way of writing grammar production rules).

$$
\begin{array}{lll}
\langle\text{exp}\rangle & ::= \langle\text{prop symbol}\rangle \\
& ::= \langle\text{constant}\rangle \\
& ::= \neg\ \langle\text{exp}\rangle \\
& ::= (\langle\text{exp}\rangle\ \langle\text{binary op}\rangle\ \langle\text{exp}\rangle) \\
\langle\text{prop symbol}\rangle & ::= P|Q|R|X|Y|Z \\
\langle\text{constant}\rangle & ::= \mathbf{T}\ |\ \mathbf{F} \\
\langle\text{binary op}\rangle & ::= \wedge|\vee\ |\ \Rightarrow\ |\ \Leftrightarrow
\end{array}
$$

Parentheses may be omitted when the association of connectives with subexpressions is clear or is ambiguous but inconsequential.

Given an expression such as $((X \wedge Y) \Rightarrow Z)$, if we know the truth values for each of the propositions represented by X, Y, and Z, we can mechanically determine the truth value of the whole expression. Suppose that X and Y are each true, and Z is false. Then the overall expression's value becomes successively:

$$((\mathbf{T} \wedge \mathbf{T}) \Rightarrow \mathbf{F})$$
$$(\mathbf{T} \Rightarrow \mathbf{F})$$
$$\mathbf{F}.$$

The whole expression is false in this case. The rules for evaluating expressions are easily given in truth tables:

X	Y	$\neg X$	$X \wedge Y$	$X \vee Y$	$X \Rightarrow Y$
T	T	F	T	T	T
T	F	F	F	T	F
F	T	T	F	T	T
F	F	T	F	F	T

There are important things we can do with expressions of propositional calculus without needing to know whether the component propositions are true or false. That is, if we assume that some expressions are true, we can derive new ones which are guaranteed to be true if the assumptions are. To obtain new expressions which logically follow from the starting expressions we use one or more *rules of inference*. Some important rules of inference are stated below.

1. Modus Ponens:

$$\begin{array}{ll} \text{Assume:} & X \Rightarrow Y \\ \text{and} & X \\ \hline \text{Then:} & Y \end{array}$$

For example, suppose we know that if it snows today then school will be cancelled, and suppose we also know that it is snowing today. Then, by the rule of modus ponens, we can logically deduce that school will be cancelled today.

2. Disjunctive Syllogism

$$\begin{array}{ll} \text{Assume:} & X \\ \hline \text{Then:} & X \vee Y \end{array}$$

For example, suppose that you own a car. Then you can truthfully say that you either own a car or live in a 17th century castle (regardless of whether or not you live in any castle).

3. Resolution

$$\begin{array}{ll} \text{Assume:} & X \vee Y \\ \text{and} & \neg X \vee Z \\ \hline \text{Then:} & Y \vee Z \end{array}$$

For example, suppose that either John passes his final or John goes into seclusion. Suppose further that either John flunks his final or he misses Paula's pre-finals party. We can conclude that either John goes into seclusion or he misses Paula's pre-finals party.

Resolution is very important in automatic theorem proving and logical reasoning. In Chapter 6 we will see a more flexible kind of resolution in the predicate calculus.

Certain kinds of propositional calculus expressions deserve special names. An expression which is always true, no matter what assumptions one may make about the propositions represented, is a *tautology*. The expression $X \vee \neg X$ is a tautology. An expression which is always false (i.e., can never be true) is a *contradiction*. For example $X \wedge \neg X$ is a contradiction. An expression which is not a contradiction is said to be *satisfiable*.

The propositional calculus is very limited as a method of knowledge representation. Perhaps its primary use is in studying some aspects of the predicate calculus, which is much more powerful.

4.8.3   Predicate Calculus

One generally needs more expressive power in a knowledge representation language than is offered by the propositional calculus. There, one must build upon propositions, and one cannot "get inside" a proposition and describe the objects which make up the proposition. The predicate calculus, on the other hand, does allow one to work with objects as well as with propositions.

Because of its generality and the direct way in which it can support automatic inference, predicate calculus is probably the single most important method for knowledge representation.

Here we present the basics of the predicate calculus. This form of knowledge representation will be used in Chapter 6 in the discussions there of theorem proving and logic programming.

An expression in the predicate calculus is much like one of propositional calculus to which more detailed descriptions have been added. Where one might use the symbol P in the propositional calculus to represent the statement "the apple is red," in the predicate calculus, one separates the predicate (quality of being red) from the objects (or subjects, here the apple), and writes:

$$R(a)$$

or more explicitly,

$$\text{Red}(\text{Apple}).$$

Here, the symbol "Red" is a predicate and "Apple" is a constant that represents a particular object in a domain or universe of objects.

As another example, the propositional calculus doesn't provide a way to refer to specific objects within statements such as "the golden egg" in "The golden egg is heavy." On the other hand, the *predicate* calculus does provide for symbols to represent objects and then allows these to be used as components of statements. For example, the constant symbol a may refer to a particular golden egg and a predicate symbol P may assert that something is heavy. The statement $P(a)$ then could state that the golden egg is heavy. The *constant symbols* a, b, c, $\ldots$ are used in the predicate calculus to denote particular objects in some domain. The predicate symbols $P, Q, R, \ldots$ are used to denote qualities or attributes of objects or relationships among objects that are either true or false. For example $Q(x, y)$ might assert that x is less than y in some domain of numbers such as the reals. *Function symbols* $f, g, h, \ldots$ denote mappings from elements of the domain (or tuples of elements from the domain) to elements of the domain. For example, $P(a, f(b))$ asserts that predicate P is true on the argument pair "a" followed by the value of the function f applied to b. Logical connectives are the same as in the propositional calculus. *Variable symbols* x, y, z, x_1, x_2, etc. represent potentially any element of the domain and allow the formulation of general statements about many elements of the domain at a time. Two *quantifiers*, $\forall$ and $\exists$, may be used to build new formulas from old. For example $\exists x P(x)$ expresses that there exists at least one element of the domain that makes $P(x)$ true.

The rules for building up syntactically correct formulas are as follows:

1. Any constant or variable taken by itself is a term.

2. Any n-place function applied to n terms is a term.

3. Any n-place predicate applied to n terms is a well-formed formula.

4. Any logical combination of well-formed formulas is also a well-formed formula. (All the logical connectives of the propositional calculus may be used.)

5. Any well-formed formula F may be made into another well-formed formula by prefixing it with a quantifier and an individual variable; e.g., $\forall x(F)$. Parentheses should be used when necessary to make the scope of the quantifier clear.

The predicate calculus can be a convenient representation for facts and rules of inference, provided that a suitable set of functions and predicates is available with which to build formulas.

Predicates readily represent relations such as inclusion. For example,

Isa(Bear, Mammal).

The predicate calculus is an attractive representation mechanism for knowledge in AI systems because well-known techniques of logical inference can easily be applied to such a representation. One thing the predicate calculus does *not* provide is any particular set of given predicates with meanings, or functions or domain. These must be provided by the knowledge engineer in developing predicate calculus representations for knowledge.

The predicate calculus can be used to formalize the rules for inheritance that were discussed earlier in the chapter. Let us reconsider the specific syllogism: "A pheasant is a bird, and a bird has feathers implies that a pheasant has feathers." In general, when we have $X \subseteq Y$ and $\forall y \in Y$, $P(y)$, then we can infer $\forall x \in X$, $P(x)$. Since $\forall x \in X$, $P(x)$ is derivable from $X \subseteq Y$ and $\forall y \in Y$, $P(y)$, it need not be explicitly represented. (Logical inference techniques are discussed in Chapter 6.)

4.9   Frames of Context

Another problem with predicate calculus as a representation scheme is that it does not provide a means to group facts and rules together that are relevant in similar contexts. Such groupings may not be necessary in small knowledge bases. However, a lack of overall organization in large bases can have costly consequences. In order to provide organizational structure, various methods have been proposed including "partitioned semantic networks" (described later) and "frames."

By providing the knowledge in modules called "frames," the designer makes life easier for the algorithms that will access the knowledge. A frame is a collection of knowledge relevant to a particular object, situation, or concept. Generally there are many pieces of information in each frame, and there are many frames in a knowledge base. Some frames may be permanent in the system; others may be created and destroyed during the course of problem solving. The term "frame" appears to be borrowed from physics, where it usually refers to a coordinate frame or frame of reference in three-dimensional space. It suggests a concern with a subset of the universe, from a particular point of view.

A frame provides a representation for an object, situation, or class in terms of a set of attribute names and values for the attributes. A frame is analogous to a LISP atom with its property list, or to a "record" data type in PASCAL.

4.9.1   A "Kitchen" Frame

Let us suppose that we are designing a household robot. This robot should do useful things such as vacuum the living room, prepare meals, and offer drinks to the guests. If we ignore the mechanical aspects and consider only the problem of designing the knowledge base for this robot, we must find an overall organization for it. The robot should know about the living room and the things which are likely to be found there, such as the living room furniture. It should also know about the kitchen and all the key appliances there: stove, fridge, garbage disposal, dishwasher, and possibly fire alarm. Since our robot is to be designed not for one particular house but many, its knowledge base should not presuppose exact locations for these things. The exact coordinates for each item could be established at the time the robot is installed or delivered. A reasonable way of organizing such a knowledge base is according to the rooms of the house. We set up one module (frame) for each room. There can be a frame for the living room, a frame for the bathroom, a frame for the kitchen, etc. Our next step is to design each frame.

4.9.2 Slots and Fillers

A frame commonly consists of two parts: a name and a list of attribute-value pairs. The attributes are sometimes called "slot names" and the values called "fillers." Therefore a frame is a named collection of slots and the fillers associated with the slots. A frame can easily be represented in LISP using an atom for the frame name and part or all of its property list to hold the attribute-value pairs. For a kitchen we might have a frame as shown in Fig. 4.8.

slot name	*filler*
frame name:	KITCHEN-FRAME
FRIDGE_LOC	(3 5)
DISHWASH_LOC	(4 5)
STOVE_LOC	(5 4)
PANTRY_LOC	NIL

Figure 4.8: A frame representing a kitchen and its attributes.

It may be that a slot is to be filled with the name of another frame, or a list of other frames. If we add a slot named "ADJACENT_ROOMS" to the KITCHEN frame, it might get as value (DINING_ROOM BACK_HALL CEL-LAR_STAIRS). The interlinking of frames to one another creates a network that can be viewed as a semantic network. (However, the term "semantic network" is applied to a large variety of relational knowledge bases.)

4.9.3 Schemata

Often a frame is associated with a class of objects or a category of situations. For example, a frame for "vacations" may provide slots for all the usual important features of a vacation: where, when, principal activities, and cost. Frames

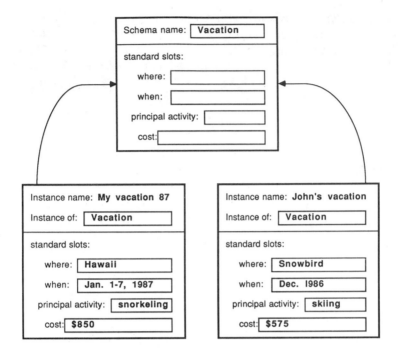

Figure 4.9: A schema and two instances of it.

for particular vacations are created by *instantiating* this general frame. Such a general frame is sometimes called a *schema*, and the frames produced by instantiating the schema are called *instances*. The process of instantiating the schema involves creating a new frame by allocating memory for it, linking it to the schema, such as by filling in a special "instance-of" slot, and filling in the remaining slots with particular information for the vacation in question. It is not necessary that all the slots be filled. The relationship between a schema and two instances of it is shown in Fig. 4.9.

Each schema in a collection of schemata gives the general characteristics which pertain to a concept, class of objects or class of situations. Therefore, a schema acts as a template or plan for the construction of frames for particular objects or situations.

4.9.4   Attachments to Slots

A slot may be provided with a default value and/or information related to the slot. Since such information is neither the value of the slot (which is "filled in") nor the name of the slot, the associated information is said to be *attached*. Attached information may be of kinds such as the following:

1. a constraint that must be satisfied by the filled-in value for the slot.

2. a procedure that may be used to determine the value for the slot if the value is needed (this is called an *if-needed* procedural attachment).

3. a procedure that is to be executed after a value is filled in for the slot (this is called an *if-added* procedural attachment).

By attaching procedures or constraints to slots, frames can be made to represent many more of the details of knowledge relevant to a problem, without losing their organizational effectiveness.

4.10 Semantic Networks

4.10.1 Motivation

Earlier in this chapter it was suggested that ISA hierarchies could be extended into more general "semantic networks" by adding additional kinds of links and nodes. In fact, such linked data structures have been used often to represent certain kinds of knowledge in AI systems. In this section, we present the rationale, methods, and an evaluation of semantic networks as an approach to knowledge representation.

Semantic networks were first developed in order to represent the meanings of English sentences in terms of objects and relationships among them. The neural interconnections of the brain are clearly arranged in some type of network (apparently one with a highly complex structure), and the rough similarity between the artificial semantic nets and the natural brain helped to encourage the development of semantic nets. The notion of accessing semantic information through a kind of "spreading activation" of the network, analogous to brain activity spreading via neurons, is still an appealing notion.

There are some more practical aspects to semantic nets, also. There is an efficiency to be gained by representing each object or concept once and using pointers for cross references, rather than naming an object explicitly every time it is involved in a relation (as must be done with the predicate calculus, for example). Thus it is possible to have very little redundancy in a semantic net. Not only can we get an efficiency in space, but search time may be faster as well; because the associations between nodes are represented as arcs in a graph, it is possible to use efficient graph-search methods to locate desired information. If the network structure is implemented with an adjacency list scheme, a search is likely to be much faster than if a long list of relationships has to be scanned every time an association is followed.

Semantic networks can provide a very general capability for knowledge representation. As we shall see, they can handle not only binary relations, but unary and higher-order relations as well, making them, in theory, as powerful as the predicates of the predicate calculus.

Unlike the predicate calculus, however, there is no standard semantic network, reasoning methods are not provided by the techniques themselves, and semantic net support for universally or existentially quantified statements is either not provided, nonstandard or messy. On the positive side, the semantic net approach is clearly valuable for providing a graphical way for the AI researcher or system designer to view knowledge, and it often suggests a practical way of implementing knowledge representations.

4.10.2   Representing Sentence Semantics

Since semantic nets were originally developed for representing the meanings of ordinary sentences, it is appropriate to consider an example in that vein.

Perhaps the simplest way to design semantic networks to represent sentences is first to restrict the allowable sentences to certain kinds that use only nouns, verbs and articles. Then one can set up a network node for each noun (including its article, if any) and a link for the verb. Such a net for the sentence "Bill killed the company" is shown in Fig. 4.10.

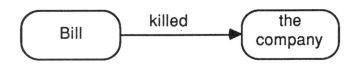

Figure 4.10: Simple semantic net for "Bill killed the company."

It is true that much can be done with such representations, as the LINNEUS program illustrates. Unfortunately, however, relatively few of the sentences we use are simple enough to be represented this way. Many verbs, for example, take both a direct object and an indirect object. Consider the sentence "Helen offered Bill a solution." Here the direct object is "a solution" and the indirect object is "Bill." In order to associate all three nouns and the verb, it is appropriate to create a node in a semantic net for the verb as well as each noun, and then to link the verb to each noun with an arc labelled with the relationship of the noun to the verb. In this case, the indirect object, Bill, plays the role of recipient of the offer (see Fig. 4.11).

If this fragment of a semantic net is to be a part of a large one representing the many aspects of a complicated story or situation, the nodes of the fragment are likely to duplicate existing nodes. If the repeated nodes are simply merged, there may be problems. For example, if the larger net also contains a similar representation of the sentence "David offered Bob a ride home," then merging the "offered" nodes would confuse the two offering events, possibly allowing the erroneous inference of "Helen offered Bob a ride home."

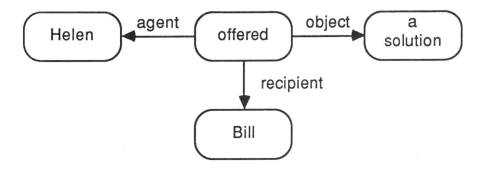

Figure 4.11: A semantic net for "Helen offered Bill a solution."

The situation is much improved if the specific offering events are represented as separate nodes, each of which is an instance of a general node representing the class of all offering events. Similarly, if there is another "solution" node in the network, it probably represents a different solution from the one Helen offered. Thus the noun phrase "a solution" should also be represented as an instance node linked to a node representing some class. It would be desirable for the sake of consistency for each particular nominal in the sentence to be represented as an instance. This leads to the net in Fig. 4.12.

Representing adjectives and prepositional phrases can be handled with additional nodes and links. For the example with an adjective: "The armagnac is excellent" a node for the attribute "excellent" is set up and a link labelled "quality" may be used (as in Fig. 4.13).

A prepositional phrase modifying a noun may be represented by a node for the nominal object of the preposition, pointed to by an arc from the noun that is modified, the arc being labelled with the relationship specified by the preposition. Thus for "the motor in the robot's wrist is dead" we have the net of Fig. 4.14.

It is not necessarily easy to build a useful semantic net representation for a sentence. Even when one is provided with a good set of class nodes and arc labels, it can be unclear which nodes and arc types to use, and how much of a sentence's meaning should be represented explicitly. Let us now consider a slightly more complicated sentence: "Laura traded her car for Paul's graphics board." A net for this is shown in Fig. 4.15.

The sentence suggests that Laura took the initiative in the trade. However, it is usual for a trade to be a cooperative activity, so that it would make sense to have an additional link from "Event#793" to "Paul" with the label "co-agent." But, since the sentence does not begin with "Laura traded *with* Paul," it appears to be safer not to infer that Paul was an active participant in the event.

This example contains another case that is difficult to decide. The sentence

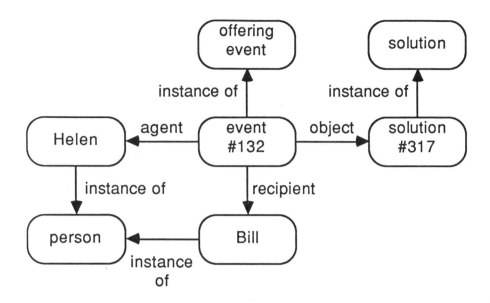

Figure 4.12: A net with class and instance nodes for "Helen offered Bill a solution."

makes clear that Laura was the owner of a car. Should an "owned" link be established from "Laura" to "car"? One problem with putting in such a link is the time-dependent nature of the truth of the fact it represents. After the trade was completed, Laura no longer owned the car. Anyway, the ownership information is implicit in the net because the node for the particular event is linked both to "Laura" and to "car" with appropriate labels on the arcs.

One thing that should be clear from this example is that there is a problem concerning time. In the representation of an event, one generally cannot represent the state of things before the event and the state of things after the event consistently without some kind of separation of representations. One way of maintaining consistency without physically separating the representations is to add temporal information to some or all of the links in a net. Then one could put a link between "Laura" and "car" with the label "owned before event#793" and a link between "Laura" and "graphics board" labelled "owned after event#793." This certainly complicates the representation of the links and is likely to slow down some inferences.

Should a semantic net represent the current states of the relevant objects or their histories or both? This depends on the kinds of inferences a system is supposed to make. If a system is to be able to answer questions such as, "What was the relationship between the defendant and the victim at the time of the crime?" then clearly temporal information must be incorporated. On the other hand, if a robot is expected only to be able to navigate through a room, and

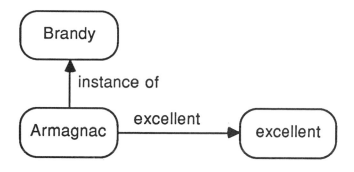

Figure 4.13: A net with an attributive node.

can see where all the obstacles are, it probably doesn't have to keep track of the history of its environment; it only needs to represent the current state of the environment it finds itself in.

4.10.3 Representing Non-Binary Relations

At first glance, semantic networks appear to be more effective in representing named binary relations (i.e., two-place predicates) than other kinds of relations. For example, Isa(dog, mammal) is represented as in Fig. 4.16. It should be made clear, however, that semantic networks are not limited in this respect; they can represent an n-ary relation with no loss of information. For example, consider the quaternary relationship expressed by the four-place predicate gives(John, Mary, book, today). A net representing this can be constructed with a node for the predicate symbol, a node for each argument, and an arc from the predicate node to each argument node labelled with the place number of the argument (as in Fig. 4.17). Of course, there may be more appropriate names for the arc labels than "place 1," etc. In this case, a better set of labels would be agent, recipient, object, when. The one disadvantage of using semantic nets to represent n-ary relations is that there is some overhead that results from the need to create these new arc labels.

4.10.4 Semantic Primitives and Combining Forms

The basic concepts necessary to represent everyday experiences are called "semantic primitives." Semantic primitives must be adequate for representing such things as events, stories and situations. Systems of such primitives have been proposed by Schank and by Wilks. Typically, each primitive is either an entity such as a man, a thing, or a part of another entity, an action such as to fly, to be, or to want, a case such as "on behalf of," "surrounding" or "toward," a qualifier such as "good," "much," or "unfortunate," or a type indicator such as "how,"

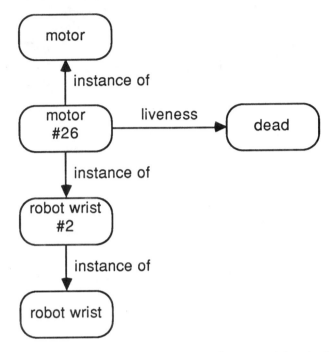

Figure 4.14: A net with a representation of a prepositional phrase.

which indicates that a related phrase modifies an action, or "kind" which indicates that a related phrase modifies an entity. A deeper treatment of semantic primitives is given in Chapter 9 as a basis for natural language understanding.

4.11 Constraints

A method for representing knowledge that is based on the predicates of predicate calculus, but that is augmented with procedural information, is "constraints." A constraint is a relationship between two or more items, which the system, in the course of solving a problem, must attempt to satisfy or keep satisfied.

4.11.1 Constraint Schemata

A constraint may be represented simply as a predicate of predicate calculus. However, it has proved useful to represent constraints as instances of "generalized constraints" or *constraint schemata*. A constraint schema may be represented by giving it a name, listing the formal parameters that represent the parts of each constraint modelled by the schema, and listing rules that allow any one of the parameters to be computed when the others are known.

An example of a constraint schema is the following one which could be used to represent Ohm's law in an electronics problem-solving system.

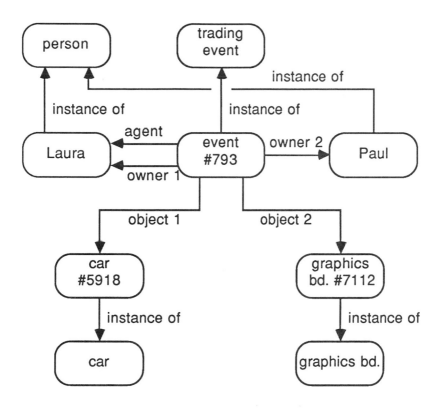

Figure 4.15: A net for "Laura traded her car for Paul's graphics board."

```
(CONSTRAINTS OHMS_LAW
    (PARTS (VOLTAGE CURRENT RESISTANCE))
    (RULES
            (TAKE VOLTAGE (TIMES CURRENT RESISTANCE))
            (TAKE CURRENT (QUOTIENT VOLTAGE RESISTANCE))
            (TAKE RESISTANCE (QUOTIENT VOLTAGE CURRENT))
    ) )
```

This constraint would make it easy for the current to be computed in a circuit if the voltage and resistance were known. Note that the constraint provides the knowledge in a form that can be used not just in updating a predetermined variable when the others change, but for whichever variable may have an unknown value at some time when the other variables have known values.

It is possible to make a constraint representing Ohm's law that is yet more useful by adding rules that allow updating with knowledge of only one variable, when that variable has the value zero and the variable is either CURRENT or RESISTANCE.

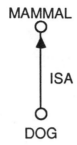

Figure 4.16: Semantic net for a named binary relationship.

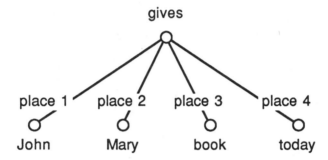

Figure 4.17: Semantic net for a four-place relationship.

```
(CONSTRAINTS OHMS_LAW
    (PARTS (VOLTAGE CURRENT RESISTANCE))
    (RULES
            (IF (EQUAL CURRENT 0) (TAKE VOLTAGE 0))
            (IF (EQUAL RESISTANCE 0) (TAKE VOLTAGE 0)
            (TAKE VOLTAGE (TIMES CURRENT RESISTANCE))
            (TAKE CURRENT (QUOTIENT VOLTAGE RESISTANCE))
            (TAKE RESISTANCE (QUOTIENT VOLTAGE CURRENT)))
    ) )
```

Both representations suffer from the problem that division by zero is not prevented. This could be fixed by modifying the last two rules, and is left as an exercise for the reader.

4.11.2   Using Constraints

In order to use a constraint schema such as this one in representing a complex situation, one or more instances of it may be used in conjunction with instances of other such schemata, and the instances may form a "constraint network." An example is shown in Fig. 4.18. This diagram represents an electronic-circuit problem in which one voltage and two resistance values are given, and the object

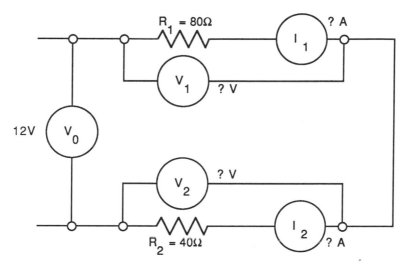

Figure 4.18: Constraint network for an electronic circuit.

is to determine the voltages and currents V_1, V_2, I_1 and I_2. The constraints for this problem, expressed as ordinary equations, are as follows:

$$
\begin{aligned}
V_0 &= 12 & R_1 &= 80 \\
R_2 &= 40 & V_0 &= I_0 R_0 \\
V_1 &= I_1 R_1 & V_2 &= I_2 R_2 \\
I_0 &= I_1 & I_1 &= I_2 \\
R_0 &= R_1 + R_2
\end{aligned}
$$

As instances of constraint schemata, the constraints are the following:

```
(INITIAL V0 12)
(INITIAL R1 80)
(INITIAL R2 40)
(OHMS_LAW V0 I0 R0)
(OHMS_LAW V1 I1 R1)
(OHMS_LAW V2 I2 R2)
(SERIES_CURRENT I0 I1)
(SERIES_CURRENT I1 I2)
(SERIES_RESISTANCE R0 R1 R2)
```

The designing of suitable representations for the schemata INITIAL, SE-RIES_CURRENT, and SERIES_RESISTANCE is left as a series of exercises for the reader.

4.11.3   Satisfying Constraints

Constraints are most frequently used as part of the representation of a problem. In the example of Fig. 4.18, the problem of finding the current through R1 may be solved by an iterative constraint-satisfaction procedure. Such a procedure repeatedly finds a variable for which the variables on which it depends have defined or updated values, and it computes a new value. If all constraints are satisfied, the procedure halts, and if the procedure ever detects that it is making no progress, it also stops. Sets of constraints may be inconsistent and thus have no solution. In some cases, a set of constraints may have a solution, but existing methods of constraint satisfaction are inadequate for finding it. Constraint-satisfaction procedures can be quite involved, and they continue to be a subject of active research.

Constraints have been most successful in representing numerical relationships. However, they have also been used successfully in combinatorial relationships involving finite sets of objects or labels. In such a situation, they may be used to filter out particular combinations of labels or partial states to arrive at a solution. Visual scene analysis and natural language understanding are two areas where combinatorial constraints have been useful.

4.12   Relational Databases

4.12.1   Remarks

It would do justice neither to AI nor to the field of database systems to omit relational databases from a serious survey of knowledge representation methods. Database techniques, while they have not been widely used in AI experiments, are fairly mature, well understood and are now being brought into AI systems. The relational database approach is particularly good at handling large, regularly structured collections of information. As with other representation methods, relational databases are set up to store some relationships explicitly and to permit implicit relationships to be recovered through computation. Capability for certain useful transformations is generally provided by relational database systems; selection, projection, and joining, for example, are common. These can be used both for access to and, to a limited degree, for inference on the database. However, these operations may be used in connection with more powerful inference methods (such as resolution in the predicate calculus) to attain a combination of intelligence and efficiency in a knowledge-based system.

4.12.2 n-ary Relations

Database management systems frequently are based on the "relational approach." A relation in the database sense is more general than the binary relations that we discussed in Section 4.4 on concept hierarchies. Rather than a set of ordered pairs, when talking about relational databases, the term "relation" refers to a set of ordered n-tuples, where n may vary from one relation to the next. For example, a 3-ary relation is the following:

$$\{(a, a, b), (a, c, d), (d, c, d), (d, c, e)\}.$$

It is customary to display such relations in tabular form:

a	a	b
a	c	d
d	c	d
d	c	e

In an n-ary relation there are n "fields." Each field has a name and a "domain." The *domain* is the set of values from which elements in the field may be drawn. The first field is sometimes called the primary key of the relation. Not only do the fields have names, but the entire relation usually has a name also. For example, consider the relation "Angiosperms" shown in Fig. 4.19.

ANGIOSPERMS			
Plant name	*General Form*	*Seed body*	*Products*
Wheat	Grass	Grain	Bread
Corn	Grass	Kernel	Meal
Potato	Tuber	Eye	Fries
Oak	Tree	Acorn	Floors
Oak	Tree	Acorn	Desks

Figure 4.19: A relation in a relational database.

The relational method is convenient insofar as certain standard operations on relations tend to be supported by database management systems. The operations are useful not only for querying and updating the database, but also for extracting subrelations, and merging relations to form composites.

It is interesting to note that binary and ternary relations can be easily represented in LISP using the property lists of atoms. Relations of higher order can also be represented in LISP as lists of tuples which are themselves lists.

4.12.3 Selection

With the relation in Fig. 4.19 we ought to be able to find the answer to a question such as: "What is the name of each angiosperm which is a grass?" The procedure is simply to scan top-to-bottom looking at the "general form" attribute of each tuple, and whenever the value "grass" is found, output the value of the "Plant name" field in the same row. A somewhat more general formulation of this kind of process is the following: the *selection* from an n-ary relation R according to a predicate $P(x_1, \ldots, x_n)$, is a new relation R' which is a subset of R, each of whose tuples satisfies P. The effect of a selection, therefore, is to extract some (and possibly none or possibly all) of the rows of R. Of course, the predicate P can be designed to ignore most of its arguments, and if it is understood which argument a unary predicate is to be applied to, it is not necessary to specify an n-ary one.

4.12.4   Projection

In a relation having n fields, it may be the case that only k of them are relevant to a particular application. A new relation, generally smaller than the original, can be obtained by making of copy of the original, but deleting the fields that are not wanted. At the same time, any duplications in the set of k-tuples thus formed are removed. For example, projecting the relation ANGIOSPERMS above, with respect to the first two fields, yields the new relation R2 shown in Fig. 4.20.

R2	
Plant name	*General Form*
Wheat	Grass
Corn	Grass
Potato	Tuber
Oak	Tree

Figure 4.20: The projection of "Angiosperms" onto "Plant name" and "General form."

The effect of projection is to extract one or more columns of the table representing the relation, and then to remove any redundant rows. Projection is analogous to selection, except in this possibility of having to remove redundant rows.

4.12.5   Joins

Two relations can be combined by the *join* operation if they share one or more common domains—that is, one can find a column in one relation whose elements are drawn from the same set as those in some column of the other relation. In such a case, the join is obtained by finding all "compatible pairs" of tuples and merging such pairs into longer tuples. A tuple from one relation is *compatible* with a tuple of the other relation if for each shared domain the first tuple's value matches the second tuple's value. In the tuples of the join, each shared field is represented once, so that length of a tuple of the join is strictly less than the sum of the lengths of the tuples used to produce it. Note that any tuple in one of the two initial relations does not participate in the join if its values in the common fields do not match those of some tuple in the other relation. Consider

R3	
General Form	*Size*
Grass	Small
Tree	Large
Bush	Medium

Figure 4.21: A two place relation containing a field "size."

the relation R3 shown in Fig. 4.21. The join of R2 with R3 is the relation R4, shown in Fig. 4.22. If one starts only with R2 and R3, then the join of R2 and

R4		
Plant Name	*General Form*	*Size*
Wheat	Grass	Small
Corn	Grass	Small
Oak	Tree	Large

Figure 4.22: The join of R2 and R3.

R3 is required before selection can be applied for answering the query: "What are the names of the small plants." This is because selection must be applied to a relation that contains both the "plant name" field and the "size" field, in order to obtain the answer to the question.

The relational approach to knowledge representation does not seem as appropriate for complicated semantic knowledge of the sort that could support dialogs in natural language, as other schemes such as those organized by frames or by class hierarchies. Although the relational approach is general enough to represent anything, the operations typically available (projection, join and some others for updating relations), are not very helpful for solving problems and making inferences.

On the other hand, relational databases do well at handling bulky bodies of information that have regular, homogeneous structure, and they can well be useful as components of intelligent information systems.

4.13   Problems of Knowledge Representation

Some of the problems for knowledge representation have already been mentioned: handling defaults and exceptions, explicit vs. implicit representations (e.g., transitive closures vs. transitive reductions). Here, some additional problems are discussed. These problems are related to the quality, completeness, and acquisition of knowledge.

4.13.1   The Closed-World Assumption

It is difficult to believe that a doctor knows everything there is to know about treating a common cold. There are lots of aspects of viruses that scientists, let alone doctors, do not understand that might be relevant to treating colds. Similarly, in playing a game of chess, a player may see very well where all the pieces are and be able to foresee various possible unfoldings of the game, but he/she probably does not know his/her opponent well enough to predict the reply to each move. The opponent may be thinking about his/her love life and suddenly make some unexpected move.

Except in very artificial situations, a person or machine doesn't have all the knowledge it needs to guarantee a perfect performance. As a result, the system or the designer of the system needs to recognize the limits of the system's knowledge and avoid costly errors that might result from assuming it knew all there was to know.

The LINNEUS program stays within its limits when it responds negatively to a question such as, "Is a house an animal?" Its reply is, "SORRY NOT THAT I KNOW OF." This points up a limitation of LINNEUS in not providing a way to represent negative information; e.g., "a house is not an animal." The program does, however, avoid concluding falsely that, for example, "a house is not a building" only because it hadn't been told that a house is a building.

There are times, however, when it is reasonable to assume that the system knows everything there is to know about a problem. For example, if the classical problem of missionaries and cannibals[2] crossing a river is posed, it would be "cheating" to propose a solution using a bridge, since no bridge is specifically mentioned in the problem. Thus, it can be appropriate to make use of the *closed-world assumption* that anything which cannot be derived from the given facts is either irrelevant or false.

When the closed-world assumption can be made, that is very nice, because it implicitly represents a whole lot of things that might otherwise have to be explicitly stated (e.g., "You may not use a bridge," "You may not drug the cannibals," etc.).

There is another way, though, that the closed-world assumption can lead to trouble. Its use could imply that, "if you can't find a solution to a problem then

---

[2]The missionaries and cannibals problem is stated as follows: There are three missionaries and three cannibals on one bank of a river that they must cross. There is a rowboat there that can carry up to two people, including the one who rows. If there ever are more cannibals than missionaries on one side of the river, then the missionaries on that side (if any) will be eaten. Otherwise, all will cooperate in peaceful transport. What is the plan by which the entire party of six can cross the river uneaten?

there is no solution." This may often be true, but might be false even more often. For example, if a system is inefficient at finding solutions and doesn't try long enough to find one, it could mistakenly infer that no solution exists. Even if the system is a good one, it might not be able to verify a true statement, as Gödel showed in his famous work on the incompleteness of arithmetic.

In designing a system for representing knowledge, one should decide whether a closed-world assumption can be used. If not, then it may be necessary to provide ways to represent negative information (e.g., "A house is not an animal"). Alternatively, compromises are possible where the absence of an explicit or derivable fact *suggests* that the negation may be true but does not assure it. Information obtained from suggestions would always be qualified when reported to the user, but could be used freely by the system for the purpose of directing search where it would be helpful if true but have little effect if false.

4.13.2 Knowledge Acquisition

The question of how knowledge should be represented is related to the questions of where the knowledge comes from and how it is acquired. Here are three reasons why these questions are related:

1. because the representation chosen may affect the acquisition process (this is discussed further in Chapter 8),

2. because the acquisition process can suggest useful representations (tools exist that build up knowledge structures from dialogs with human experts), and

3. because it is possible that some of the knowledge that a system is to use should stay in the form in which it is available (e.g., text files representing books and reports).

Methods for building knowledge structures automatically or interactively are discussed in Chapter 8.

4.14 Summary of Knowledge Representation Schemes

Eight of the methods discussed in this chapter are compared in Fig. 4.23.

A serious system for knowledge-based reasoning must combine two or more of the basic approaches. For example, a frame system may be organized as an ISA hierarchy whose nodes are schemata with instance frames linked to them. The slots of the frames may be considered to represent predicates, and the filled-in values and frame names may be viewed as arguments (terms) to the predicates, so that logical inference may use the knowledge in the frames. At the same time,

Method	Relations Handled	Inference Mechanisms	Strong Organization?	Principal Shortcomings
Propositional logic	Boolean truth functions	Modus ponens, etc.	No	Models only boolean truth relationships but not the statements themselves
Concept hierarchy	"ISA"	Graph search and transitive closure	Yes	Limited to one relation
Predicate logic	Any predicate	Resolution & others	No	Lacks facilities for organizing knowledge; awkward for control information
Frames	Binary or ternary	Not provided	Yes	Only a methodology; not an actual rep. system
Semantic nets	binary or ternary	Not provided	No (except with partitioning)	No standard
Constraints	Any predicates	Propagation; satisfaction	No	No standard
Production rules	If-then	Rule activation	No	Awkward for non-procedural knowledge
Relational database	n-ary	Selection, projection, join	Somewhat	Awkward for control information

Figure 4.23: A summary and rough evaluation of eight methods for representing knowledge.

a base of production rules may encode the procedural knowledge and heuristics that use the knowledge base to manipulate the state information to solve particular problems. Thus, in this example, four of the basic knowledge representations are used: frames, ISA hierarchies, predicate logic, and production rules.

4.15   Bibliographical Information

A very readable introductory article on knowledge representation is [McCalla and Cercone 1983]. That article is also an introduction to a special issue of *IEEE Computer* devoted to knowledge representation. The issue contains fifteen additional articles that collectively present a good survey of knowledge representation.

Elementary properties of binary relations (reflexiveness, symmetry, antisymmetry, and transitivity, for example) are treated by many texts on discrete mathematics, such as [Tremblay and Manohar 1975]. An algorithm for computing the transitive closure of a relation was developed by Warshall and is given in [Aho, Hopcroft and Ullman 1974]. For an intriguing treatment of the semantics of "ISA" see [Brachman 1983].

A collection of research papers that address the issue of representation of knowledge is [Bobrow and Collins 1975]. One of those papers is particularly good as an introduction to the problems of representing the kinds of knowledge that can support dialogs in natural language [Woods 1975].

The use of the predicate calculus as a knowledge representation method is described in [Nilsson 1981]. The frames approach to knowledge organization was presented in [Minsky 1975]. A formalism called KRL, which stands for "knowledge representation language" was developed [Bobrow and Winograd 1977] for expressing knowledge in a frame-like way.

Constraints were used extensively as a means of knowledge representation in [Borning 1979]. A good overview of the use of constraints is [Deutsch 1981].

Relational databases, developed in large part by [Codd 1970], are introduced in [Date 1976] and [Ullman 1982]. A thorough theoretical treatment is provided by [Maier 1983]. Many of the issues common to database systems and knowledge representation are treated in papers that were presented at a Workshop sponsored by three ACM special interest groups [Brodie and Zilles 1981].

References

1. Aho, A., Hopcroft, J. E. and Ullman, J. D. 1974. *The Design and Analysis of Computer Algorithms*. Reading, MA: Addison-Wesley.

2. Bobrow, D. G., and Collins, A. 1975. *Representation and Understanding: Studies in Cognitive Science*. New York: McGraw-Hill.

3. Bobrow, D. G., and Winograd, T. 1977. An overview of KRL: A knowledge representation language. *Cognitive Science*, Vol. 1, No. 1., pp3-46.

4. Date, C. J. 1976. *An Introduction to Database Systems*. Reading, MA: Addison-Wesley.

5. Borning, A. 1979. ThingLab: A constraint-based simulation laboratory. Ph.D. Dissertation, Stanford Univ. Dept. of Computer Science.

6. Brachman, R. J. 1983. What IS-A is and isn't: An analysis of taxonomic links in semantic networks. *IEEE Computer*, Vol. 16, No. 10, October, pp30-36.

7. Brodie, M. L., and Zilles, S. N. 1981. *Proceedings of the Workshop on Data Abstraction, Databases and Conceptual Modelling*, Pingree Park,

Colorado, June 23-26, 1980. published jointly as *ACM SIGART Newsletter*, No. 74 (January 1981), *SIGMOD Record*, Vol. 11, No. 2 (February 1981), and *SIGPLAN Notices*, Vol. 16, No. 1 (January 1981).

8. Codd, E. F. 1970. A relational model for large shared data banks. *Communications of the ACM*, Vol. 13, No. 6, pp377-387 (June).

9. Deutsch, P. 1981. Constraints: A uniform model for data and control. In [Brodie and Zilles 1981], pp118-120.

10. Maier, D. 1983. *The Theory of Relational Database Systems*. Rockville, MD: Computer Science Press.

11. McCalla, G., and Cercone, N. 1983. Approaches to knowledge representation. *IEEE Computer*, Vol. 16, No. 10, October, pp12-18.

12. Minsky, M. 1975. A framework for representing knowledge. In Winston, P. H. (ed.), *The Psychology of Computer Vision*. New York: McGraw-Hill, pp211-277.

13. Nilsson, N. J. 1981. *Principles of Artificial Intelligence*. Palo Alto, CA: Tioga Press; (also Los Altos, CA: William Kaufman, 1983).

14. Quillian, M. R. 1968. Semantic memory. In Minsky, M. (ed.), *Semantic Information Processing*. Cambridge, MA: MIT Press, pp27-70.

15. Raphael, B. 1976. *The Thinking Computer: Mind Inside Matter*. San Francisco: W. H. Freeman.

16. Tremblay, J.-P., and Manohar, R. P. 1975. *Discrete Mathematical Structures with Applications to Computer Science*. New York: McGraw-Hill.

17. Ullman, J. D. 1982. *Principles of Database Systems*, Second Edition. Rockville, MD: Computer Science Press.

18. Woods, W. A. 1975. What's in a link: Foundations for semantic networks. In [Bobrow and Collins 1975], pp35-82.

Exercises

1. Imagine a computer network of the future in a large hospital, that includes patient-monitoring devices, medical records databanks, and physicians' workstations. Explain some possible uses of data, information and knowledge in this environment.

2. Describe how knowledge may be represented in each of the three parts of a production system.

3. For each of the following, determine which of the two relations "subset-of" or "element-of" is being represented, and reformulate the statement to make this clearer. The first one is done for you. If you find genuine ambiguity in a statement, justify each of the possible interpretations.

   (a) Fido is a dog.   Fido $\in$ dogs

   (b) A parrot is a bird.

   (c) Polly is a parrot.

   (d) David Jones is a Jones.

   (e) "George Washington" is a great name.

   (f) Artificial intelligence is a state of mind.

4. For each of the following relations, state whether or not it is reflexive, whether or not it is symmetric, whether or not it is transitive, whether or not it is antisymmetric, and whether or not it is a partial order. For each example, let the set S on which the relation is defined be the set of elements mentioned in that example.

   (a) $\{(a, a)\}$

   (b) $\{(a, b), (a, c), (b, c)\}$

   (c) $\{(a, a), (a, b), (b, b), (b, c), (a, c), (c, c)\}$

   (d) $\{(a, b), (b, c)\}$

   (e) $\{\}$

5. Let R be the relation $\{(a, b), (a, c), (b, c)\}$. Draw the graph of this relation. Draw the Hasse diagram for this relation.

6. Give an example of a transitive relation on a set of people. Is the "ancestor-of" relation transitive? How about "parent-of," "cousin-of," "sister-of," and "sibling-of?" Assume that these are "blood-relative" relations rather than the more general ones that include adoptions, etc.

7. Write a LISP program that takes a binary relation, and computes its transitive reduction.

8. Write a LISP function which determines whether the input relation is reflexive or not.

9. Improve the efficiency of the ISATEST function in the LINNEUS program by having it terminate the search as soon as the goal is reached.

10. Let us assume that "HOUSE HAS ROOF" means that a house has a roof as a part. Suppose we want to extend LINNEUS to know about and reason with HAS links as well as ISA links.

(a) Let Isa(x, y) mean "an x is a y," and let Has(x, y) mean "an x has a y as a part." New HAS links may be inferred from combinations of existing ISA and HAS links. For example,

$$\text{Has}(x, y) \wedge \text{Isa}(y, z) \Rightarrow \text{Has}(x, z).$$

Complete the predicate calculus formulation of the rules for inferring HAS relationships described on page 104.

(b) Just as (ISATEST X Y N) succeeds if there is a path from X to Y of length N or less, following only ISA links, one can imagine a function (HASTEST X Y N) that tests for an implied HAS relationship between X and Y. Exactly what kind of path between X and Y implies that the test should succeed?

(c) Extend the LINNEUS program to properly handle HAS links. Allowable inputs should include expressions such as:

(DOG HAS SNOUT)

which expresses the fact that a dog has a snout, and

(DOG HAS LEG)

which says a dog has a (at least one) leg, and

(HAS DOG PAW)

which asks "Does a dog have a paw?" or equivalently, "Do dogs have paws?"

11. Extend the LINNEUS program to automatically maintain its inclusion hierarchy in transitive reduction (Hasse diagram) form. In connection with this, the conversational front end should handle the following new kinds of responses:

```
(I ALREADY KNOW THAT BY INFERENCE)
(I HAVE BEEN TOLD THAT BEFORE)
(YOUR EARLIER STATEMENT THAT A MOUSE IS AN ANIMAL IS NOW
     REDUNDANT)
```

You may name your new program whatever you like. Suppose it is called "SMARTY." If you tell SMARTY that "(A DOG IS A MAMMAL)" and then later tell it exactly the same thing, it should respond "(I HAVE BEEN TOLD THAT BEFORE)". If you tell it something that it can already deduce, it should respond "(I ALREADY KNOW THAT BY INFERENCE)" and if you tell it something new (not already implied) that makes a previously input fact redundant, SMARTY should reply with a statement such as (YOUR EARLIER STATEMENT THAT A MOUSE IS AN ANIMAL IS NOW REDUNDANT). Furthermore, the redundant link should then be removed, so that the internal data structure is kept non-redundant. Test your program on the following sequence of facts plus another sequence of your own creation.

```
(A LION IS A CARNIVORE)
(A LION IS A CARNIVORE)
(A CARNIVORE IS AN ANIMAL)
(A LION IS AN ANIMAL)
(A LION IS A THING)
(A DOG IS A THING)
(A MAMMAL IS A THING)
(A DOG IS AN ANIMAL)
(AN ANIMAL IS A THING)
(A DOG IS A MAMMAL)
```

12. By including more kinds of links in an ISA hierarchy, we can obtain a more general kind of semantic network.

    (a) Extend the program LINNEUS to properly handle the ELE-MENT_OF relation expressed by user inputs such as "(JANET IS A WOMAN)" and "(LARRY IS A LOBSTER)". Your program should correctly handle questions such as:

        i. (WHO IS JANET),
        ii. (WHAT IS LARRY),
        iii. (IS LARRY AN ANIMAL), and especially
        iv. (IS A LARRY AN ANIMAL), and
        v. (WHAT IS A JANET)

        These last two types should be answered with a message that indicates that they contain a false presupposition.

    (b) Further extend the program to handle the ownership relation as in (LARRY OWNS A CLAM) or (JANET OWNS A PORSCHE). Allow the user to type appropriate statements and questions and get answers that are reasonable. Note that if Janet owns a Porsche and a Porsche is a car, then Janet owns a car.

13. Draw a semantic network representing the sentence, "Artificial Thought, Inc. bought a controlling interest in Natural Ideas, Inc. for the sum of $23 million." Include nodes for each object or event and the class to which it belongs.

14. Suppose that we wish to represent some notion of the ISA hierarchy of Fig. 4.4 using propositional calculus. It is very difficult to represent the hierarchy in a way that would let us do reasoning based on inheritance of properties, for example. However, consider the following statements:

P1: "Larry is a lobster." (i.e., Larry is a member of the class lobster)
P2: "Larry is a crustacean."
P3: "Larry is an arthropod."
etc.

Class inclusion may be represented (in this very specific case of Larry) by the expressions:

P1 ⇒ P2
P2 ⇒ P3
etc.

This knowledge can be used to infer "Larry is an arthropod" from the statement that "Larry is a lobster."

(a) If we add the statement, P4: "Louise is a lobster," what can be inferred about Louise?

(b) Give additional propositions to support inferences about Louise.

(c) Give a set of *predicate* calculus expressions for the knowledge that allows some inferences about both Larry and Louise.

15. The predicate calculus supports certain kinds of quantification quite nicely, but not all kinds.

(a) For each of the statements below, give a predicate calculus formula that represents its meaning.

   i. There exists a white elephant.
   ii. There uniquely exists a white elephant.
   iii. There are at least two white elephants.
   iv. There exist exactly two white elephants.

(b) Describe a scheme that, for any given n, can be used to create a formula to represent the statement, "There exist exactly n white elephants."

(c) What does your answer to part (b) suggest about the predicate calculus in representing numerically quantified statements?

16. By using the symbol P to represent the statement "It is raining today," so much of the detail of the sentence has been lost in abstraction that nothing is left that represents the objects or actions that make up the statement. In the predicate calculus, on the other hand, we might represent the statement with "Weather(Today, Raining)" which provides representational components for important parts of the statement. However,

if the symbol P were replaced by the identifier "Raining" and the predicate "Weather(Today, Raining)" were redescribed as $P(a, b)$, then the predicate calculus representation would seem less informative than the propositional one. Explain the cause of this apparent paradox and which representational scheme provides a more informative representation.

17. Describe how the knowledge necessary to drive a car might be organized in a collection of frames.

18. Write representations for the following constraint schemata mentioned on page 123:

    (a) INITIAL

    (b) SERIES_CURRENT

    (c) SERIES_RESISTANCE

19. Design, implement, and test a LISP program that accepts a list of constraint schemata and a list of constraints and then determines the values of uninitialized variables by applying the constraints in a systematic fashion. Demonstrate your procedure on the circuit problem described in Fig. 4.18.

20. Consider the following problem. Let $\{(x_1, y_1), (x_2, y_2), (x_3, y_3)\}$ be the set of vertices of a triangle whose perimeter is P and whose area is A. Suppose $x_1 = 0, y_1 = 0, x_2 = 6, y_2 = 0$, and $A = 30$.

    (a) Develop constraint schemata and instances to represent the problem.

    (b) Which variables are forced to particular values? Which are not forced? What, if anything, can be said about the ranges of possible values for the variables which are not forced?

21. Relational databases are frequently incorporated into intelligent systems.

    (a) Project the relation ANGIOSPERMS (on page 125) to obtain a new relation employing only the attributes "General Form" and "Seed Body."

    (b) Compute the join of the relation you just found in part (a) with the relation R3 on page 127.

    (c) What is the sequence of selections, projections, joins and counting operations necessary to process the query: "How many products are made from small plants?" using the relations ANGIOSPERMS and R3?

22. Relational database operations can be coded in LISP to demonstrate question-answering capabilities.

(a) Design a LISP scheme for representing n-ary relations.

(b) Write one or a collection of LISP functions to compute the projection of a relation (onto any given list of attributes).

(c) Write a LISP function to compute the join of two relations.

(d) Add whatever functions and other representations may be necessary to automatically handle queries such as that of the previous problem, part (c). Assume these queries are presented in the form (A1 A2 V2) which means "How many different values of A1 can be found in tuples whose A2 value is V2?"

23. Suppose a system uses a small knowledge base consisting of the following statements in the predicate calculus, and suppose it is capable of making logical deductions, but does not know anything special about any of the predicates such as "Color" or "Equal" that might appear in its knowledge base.

- Color(Apple1, Red)

- Color(Apple2, Green)

- Fruit(Apple1)

- Fruit(Apple2)

- $\forall x\{[\text{Fruit}(x) \land \text{Color}(x,\text{Red})] \Rightarrow \text{Ripe}(x)\}$

Assume the system makes the closed-world assumption. For each of the predicate calculus statements (a) through (h) tell whether the system would assign to it a value of *true*, *false*, or *unknown*:

(a)	Color(Apple3, Red)	(e)	¬Color(Apple1, Red)
(b)	Fruit(Apple2)	(f)	Color(Apple1, Blue)
(c)	Ripe(Apple1)	(g)	NotEqual(Red, Blue)
(d)	Ripe(Apple2)	(h)	Equal(Red, Blue)

(i) To what extent does the system make a consistent interpretation of the statements (a) through (h)?

(j) Is there any inconsistency?

Chapter 5

Search

5.1 The Notion of Searching in a Space of States

Methods for searching are to be found at the core of many AI systems. Before knowledge representation became the key issue of AI in the 1970's, search techniques were at the center of attention in research and in courses on AI. They are still of central importance in AI not only because most systems are built around them, but because it is largely through an understanding of search algorithms that we are able to predict what kinds of AI problems are solvable in practice.

The idea of searching for something implies moving around examining things and making decisions about whether the sought object has yet been found. A cave explorer searching for treasure moves around from one underground place to another, looking to see where he is going and to see if there are any valuables around him. He is constrained by the geometry (or topology) of the cave; he must follow passageways provided by nature. A chess player searching for the best move in the middle of a game mentally makes moves and countermoves, finding the merits of resulting board positions and, in the process, finding the degree to which he can control the game to reach some of these positions. An engineer who designs integrated-circuit layouts considers sequences of design choices that lead to acceptable arrangements of components and electrical connections; he searches through spaces of possible designs to find those that have the required properties.

Many computer programs must also search along constrained paths through intricate networks of knowledge, states or conditions to find important information or to reach a goal position. In general such a network can be described as a graph: a set of nodes together with a set of arcs that connect pairs of nodes. The nodes represent "states" of a space of possible configurations. The transitions or moves that go from one state to another are represented by arcs of the graph.

The choice of a search method is often a critical choice in the design of an AI program. A poor choice can ensure that the program will always flounder in the "combinatorial quagmire" before it can find a solution to any nontrivial problem. Exhaustive techniques can be appropriate for small problems, but the human user will become exhausted waiting for a machine that uses a "British Museum" search method on only a moderately-complicated problem. A good search method typically uses some particular information about the problem or some general knowledge to focus the search for a solution on areas of the state space that have a reasonable chance of containing the solution.

In AI systems, the networks to be searched may be represented either explicitly or implicitly. For example, the inclusion hierarchy used by the LINNEUS program in Chapter 4 is an explicit network, where each arc is stored using relational information on the property list of an atom. However, many AI programs must search networks whose arcs are not explicitly stored and which must be generated from rules, one at a time. A computer program that plays chess explores a game tree in which each node corresponds to a board position and each arc corresponds to a legal move. The complete tree of all possible games is so huge that it cannot be explicitly represented. Rather, parts of it must be generated when needed according to the rules for moving pieces. The goal, of course, is to choose best moves by evaluating the consequences of each possible move from the current position. This search is for more than just a good node in the tree; it is, in a sense, for the best "subtree" from the current position. In this chapter we work with examples of both implicitly and explicitly represented search spaces.

There are several key notions connected with search. The most important of them, just mentioned above, is the concept of a *state space*: the set of all the possible states for a problem together with the relations involving states implied by the moves or operators. The graph, whose nodes represent states and whose arcs represent the relations, provides a good abstract representation for a state space. Another key notion is that of a *move generator*: a way to obtain the successors of a given state or node. The third key notion is the *search method*, or kind of algorithm that is used to control the exploration of the state space. A fourth idea is that of *search heuristics*; these are guiding principles, often of a pragmatic nature, that tend to make the search easier. A common way of controlling a search is to employ an "evaluation function" which computes an estimate of the merits of a particular successor to the current state or node.

Puzzles are easy to understand and describe, and they provide a good starting point for studying search methods. We shall begin our discussion of search with an analysis of a simple class of puzzles called "painted square" puzzles. Although this class of puzzles is elementary, it is a good vehicle for examining some subtle issues in the description of operators. The class is general, in that particular versions of the puzzle may have zero, one, or many solutions. This feature makes the puzzles somewhat more realistic as problems than the "15" puzzle or "Towers of Hanoi" puzzle that are sometimes used for teaching elementary search techniques.

We will describe a procedure for solving painted square puzzles which works by searching a space of configurations (which may be regarded as potential solutions).

5.2 The Painted Squares Puzzles

5.2.1 A Kind of Geometrical Puzzle

Given a set of N square blocks with painted sides, it is desired to place the squares adjacent to one another to form one large rectangle (of given dimensions), such that adjacent sides of the squares always match. A sample game for $N = 4$ and dimensions 2 by 2 is shown in Fig. 5.1.

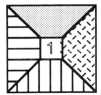  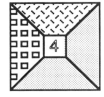

Figure 5.1: Pieces for one of the "Painted Squares" puzzles.

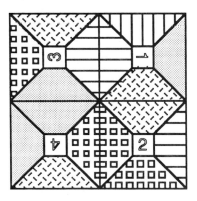

Figure 5.2: A solution to the sample puzzle.

We should note that such puzzles may or may not have solutions, depending upon how the squares have been painted. For example, if all four sides of piece 1 were striped, all four sides of 2 boxed, all four of 3 gray and all four of 4 hashed, no two squares could be placed together, let alone all four of them.

5.2.2   Solution Procedure

A solution, when one exists, can be found by the following procedure: enumerate the vacant positions in the rectangle with the numbers 1 to N, using a left-to-right, top-to-bottom order. Starting with vacant position 1, select the first painted square and place it in its first orientation (each square can be rotated into four different orientations). At each successive step, after having filled the ith vacancy with the jth square in the kth orientation, attempt to fill the $i + 1^{st}$ vacancy with the lowest numbered unused square in the first orientation. If this new placement does not match sides with previously placed squares, the following alterations are tried: successive orientations of the same square, successive unused squares, and retraction of the most recently placed square (backtracking). This procedure eventually either finds a solution if one exists, or exhausts all the possibilities without finding a solution. Backtracking can often be very inefficient. In the case of the painted squares puzzles it is generally much more efficient than an obvious alternative, which is to generate all possible arrangements of the squares in the rectangular space, testing each one to see whether it is a solution to the puzzle!

5.2.3   States and Operators

We may think of each partial (or complete) arrangement of squares in vacancies as a "state." A *state* is one of the possible configurations of the puzzle. It is a snapshot of one situation. A state is a configuration that could be reached using a sequence of legal moves or decisions, starting from an initial configuration. The sequence of steps that leads to a state is not part of the state. There may be more than one way to get to the same state.

Once again, the *state space* for a puzzle consists of the set of all the states for a puzzle, together with the relation implied by the legal moves for the puzzle. Each legal move from a state leads to a single new state. The pair (current state, new state) form one element in the move relation. For the painted squares puzzle of Fig. 5.1, a portion of the state space is shown in Fig. 5.3.

The *representation* of a state is an embodiment of the essential information about a state; the representation distinguishes the state from all others. A good representation also does more: it facilitates the application of operators to compute successive states; it is understandable by the scientist or programmer; it is efficient, etc. In the painted squares puzzle, we may represent a state by a list of pairs, each pair indicating a piece and an orientation. For example, piece 1 in the second orientation (i.e., rotated 90 degrees counterclockwise) is represented by the pair (P1 2), and the state consisting of this one piece being placed in the first enumerated vacancy of the rectangle, in this orientation is

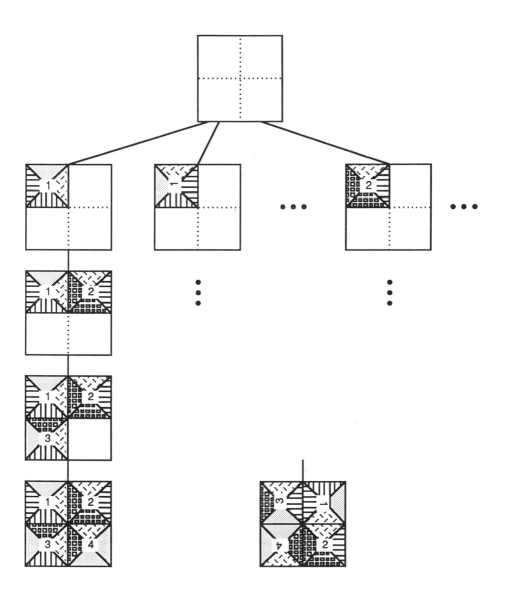

Figure 5.3: A portion of the state space for the sample puzzle.

indicated by ((P1 2)). The list () represents the starting state for the puzzle (no pieces placed). The solution shown above is represented by

((P2 1)(P4 3)(P1 4)(P3 2)).

The reason we list the pairs in reverse order will be apparent later, when we code our algorithm.

A state can be changed by placing a new square into the next vacancy, or by removing the most recently placed square. More generally, we say that states are changed by applying operators. Operators are transformations that map one state to another.

An example operator is "place piece 3 in the second place with the third orientation." This operator is a rather specific one, and is only applicable if the current state satisfies some stringent conditions: the first place must be full; the second place must be empty; piece 3 must not have been used already to fill place 1 and when rotated to the third orientation, the side of piece 3 that would touch the piece in place 1 must match there.

A more general operator is "place the first unused piece in the next vacant position in the first orientation that makes all the adjacent pieces match." There are still conditions for the applicability of this operator, but they are not so restricting. There must be an unused piece (if not, the puzzle has been solved!); there must be at least one orientation of the piece such that its placement in the next vacant position does make all adjacent sides match.

There is obviously quite a variety of operators one could imagine that could be used to describe moves in our puzzle. To put some order on them, we will consider general schemes for making state changes that may "generate" operators when called upon. The backtracking procedure sketched out earlier does essentially that. It produces new operators in an orderly sequence in order to search for a goal state.

5.2.4   Representation of the Puzzle and Its States in LISP

Let us work out a LISP program to implement the backtracking search procedure for the painted squares puzzles. We need a representation for the pieces, and a procedure to generate operators (these operators may only produce legal states—those in which adjacent sides of placed squares match).

Each piece can be represented as an atom with a property PATTERN which describes how its sides are painted. Let ST, BX, GR, and HA indicate striped, boxed, gray and hashed, respectively. Then we establish our piece representations (for the example shown) by the following LISP expressions:

```
(PUTPROP 'P1 '(ST HA GR ST) 'PATTERN)
(PUTPROP 'P2 '(BX ST HA BX) 'PATTERN)
(PUTPROP 'P3 '(ST HA BX GR) 'PATTERN)
(PUTPROP 'P4 '(GR GR HA BX) 'PATTERN)
```

Our convention is that the sides are ordered starting from the south, moving then east, north, and finally west. The list of pieces available starts out with all of them:

```
(SETQ PIECES_AVAIL '(P1 P2 P3 P4))
```

The dimensions of the rectangle to be filled are 2 and 2:

```
(SETQ BOX_WIDTH 2)
(SETQ BOX_LENGTH 2)
```

To orient a piece we rotate its pattern by one rotation less than the orientation number:

```
(DEFUN ORIENT (PIECE ORIENTATION)
    (ROTATE_LIST (GET PIECE 'PATTERN) (SUB1 ORIENTATION)) )
```

The helping function ROTATE_LIST moves elements from the end to the beginning with the help of functions LAST and ALL_BUT_LAST.

```
(DEFUN ROTATE_LIST (L N)
  (COND ((ZEROP N) L)
        (T (ROTATE_LIST
               (CONS (LAST L)
                     (ALL_BUT_LAST L) )
               (SUB1 N) )) ) )

(DEFUN LAST (L)
  (COND ((NULL (CDR L))(CAR L))
        (T (LAST (CDR L))) ) )

(DEFUN ALL_BUT_LAST (L)
  (COND ((NULL (CDR L)) NIL)
        (T (CONS (CAR L)(ALL_BUT_LAST (CDR L)))) ) )
```

To find out whether a new piece will match adjacent sides in the current configuration we use a function SIDESOK. If the current state is null, no pieces have been placed, and the new piece is OK. Otherwise, there are three cases that must be contended with. If the new piece is in the leftmost column, it only has a neighbor to the north that it must match. If the new piece is in the first row it only has a neighbor to the west that it must match. In any other case it must match both a neighbor to the north and a neighbor to the west.

```
(DEFUN SIDESOK (NEW_PIECE ORIENTATION CUR_STATE)
  (COND ((NULL CUR_STATE) T)      ;no pieces previously placed
        (T (PROG (TRIAL LEN)      ;some  "        "          "
```

```
(SETQ TRIAL (ORIENT NEW_PIECE ORIENTATION))
(SETQ LEN (LENGTH CUR_STATE))
(COND
     ;case of leftmost column:
     ((ZEROP (REMAINDER LEN BOX_WIDTH))
      (RETURN (MATCHNORTH TRIAL CUR_STATE)) )
     ;case of top row
     ((LESSP LEN BOX_WIDTH)
      (RETURN (MATCHWEST TRIAL CUR_STATE)) )
     ;general case:
     (T (RETURN
         (AND (MATCHNORTH TRIAL CUR_STATE)
              (MATCHWEST TRIAL CUR_STATE) ) ))
) )) ) )
```

This uses the helping functions MATCHNORTH and MATCHWEST. The job of MATCHNORTH is to find the square which is just to the north of the trial square and to see if its south side matches the north side of the rotated new piece. In the example, BOX_WIDTH is 2 and the neighbor to the north is in the second element of the current-state list.

```
(DEFUN MATCHNORTH (TRIAL STATE)
  (EQ (CADDR TRIAL)      ;north side of rotated new piece
      (CAR (APPLY 'ORIENT
                (GETNTH BOX_WIDTH STATE) ))
                    ;south side of square to the north.
) )
```

Similarly we define MATCHWEST so it returns T when the trial placement agrees with the neighboring piece to the west.

```
(DEFUN MATCHWEST (TRIAL STATE)
  (EQ (CADDDR TRIAL)     ;west side of rotated new piece
      (CADR (APPLY 'ORIENT
                (CAR STATE) ))
                    ;east side of square to the west
) )
```

The reason for representing states in backwards order is now apparent. With the most recent placement first, the act of checking to see whether a trial will match requires accessing recent additions to the state list. In LISP it is easier to get them near the front of a list than near the end of a list.

5.2.5   A Backtracking Search Procedure in LISP

So far we have defined a representation for states of our problem, and we have described functions that test trial placements for consistency in matching of sides of pieces. We now need a procedure to drive the overall search, generating the possible placements and backtracking when impasses are reached. Let us call our general searching procedure SOLVE_SQUARES. At the top level it would be invoked with

```
(SOLVE_SQUARES NIL PIECES_AVAIL)
```

We assume this invocation is done from a function TEST which also initializes a solution counter. It calls a helping function TRYPIECE which implicitly generates classes of operators to try placing pieces in the next vacant position. The helping function SHOW numbers and prints out solutions.

```
(DEFUN SOLVE_SQUARES (CUR_STATE UNUSED_PIECES)
   (COND ((NULL UNUSED_PIECES) (SHOW CUR_STATE)) ;sol'n found
         (T (MAPCAR 'TRYPIECE UNUSED_PIECES)
            NIL) ) )

(DEFUN SHOW (SOLN)
   (PROG () (SETQ COUNT (ADD1 COUNT))
           (PRIN1 'SOLUTION)
           (TYO 32)
           (PRIN1 COUNT)
           (TYO 58)
           (PRINT SOLN) ) )

(DEFUN TEST ()
   (PROG (COUNT)
          (SETQ COUNT 0)
          (SOLVE_SQUARES NIL PIECES_AVAIL) ) )
```

The function TRYPIECE fans out the search for a solution using a given piece in the next vacant place, in four directions, one for each possible orientation of that piece.

```
(DEFUN TRYPIECE (PIECE)
   (MAPCAR 'TRYORIENTATION '(1 2 3 4)) )
```

Control is then passed to TRYORIENTATION. Here a call is made to SIDESOK to check a specific trial placement for side-matching consistency. If consistent, the search is made to continue with a new current state that includes the new piece placed in the given orientation.

```
(DEFUN TRYORIENTATION (ORIENTATION)
   (COND ((SIDESOK PIECE ORIENTATION CUR_STATE)
          (SOLVE_SQUARES
                (CONS (LIST PIECE ORIENTATION) CUR_STATE)
                (DELETE PIECE UNUSED_PIECES) ) )
         (T NIL) ) )
```

If the trial placement is inconsistent with the currently-placed squares, the second clause of the COND returns NIL, effectively pruning the search along the current branch (by not pursuing it any further) and backtracking up the search tree (by returning from the call to TRYORIENTATION).

The helping function CADDDR may have to be defined for some LISP systems:

```
(DEFUN CADDDR (X) (CADDR (CDR X)))
```

The search is started by the user's typing:

```
(TEST)
```

5.2.6   Remarks on Efficiency

Evidently, SOLVE_SQUARES keeps searching for more solutions even after it finds one. The number of solutions is always even, since a rectangle can be rotated 180 degrees and still fit on itself; in the case of a square rectangle (as in our 2 by 2 example) the number of solutions is a multiple of 4. In fact, there are 24 different solutions to our example.

It is interesting to note that the number of calls made to TRYORIENTATION before the first solution is found generally depends not only upon the data (the pieces and the manner in which they are painted) but also on the order in which they are listed.

A note about the efficiency of our program is in order. The functions MATCHNORTH and MATCHWEST have a disadvantage: they apply ORIENT to pieces already placed, needlessly repeating work that was already performed. This redundant work can be avoided by making the state representation a little more ugly but explicit. Rather than describe each oriented piece as an atom-integer pair, one may describe it as an atom-list pair, where the list is the result of applying ORIENT to the atom-integer pair. Then minor changes must be made to MATCHNORTH, MATCHWEST, TRYORIENTATION, and SIDESOK. This optimization is left as an exercise for the reader.

5.3   Elementary Search Techniques

5.3.1   A Search Problem

In order to illustrate several different search techniques, we shall use a map of cities of France, transformed into a graph. This graph serves as an *explicit* representation of a state space. The search techniques we describe will be general, and can also work in a state space that is implicit. In that case, the states would be generated gradually by applying operators rather than pre-existing. (When search techniques are used for theorem proving, in Chapter 6, the search space is implicitly represented.)

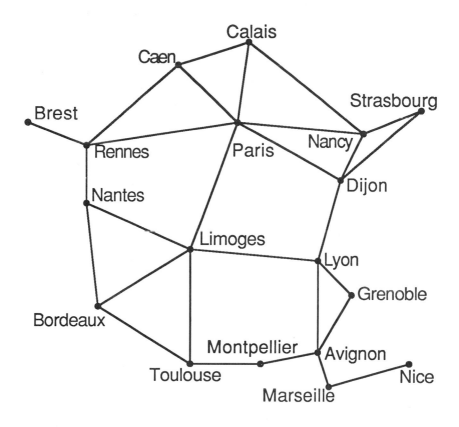

Figure 5.4: The state space for comparing algorithms.

Here, the use of an explicit state space helps us to understand the behavior of the search algorithms by making it obvious (to us humans) what kinds of paths to a solution exist. This is particularly helpful when alternative algorithms are compared, as is the case in this chapter. In our space, the roles of states are played by cities (the nodes of the graph, and the nodes, in turn, are later represented as LISP literal atoms), and the moves are transitions along arcs of the graph. Although we put an explicit representation of the graph into the machine, our search procedures only have access to a portion of the representation at any particular time. The algorithms search from a starting point in the graph outward to find a goal node. The algorithms may or may not actually explore the entire graph; for example, if the goal is found after only a few transitions, the majority of the nodes may remain unexplored.

Figure 5.4 illustrates the search space.

We may represent the adjacency data in the map by listing for each city the other cities directly connected to it, and putting this on the property list:

```
(PUTPROP 'BREST '(RENNES) 'ADJCNT)
(PUTPROP 'RENNES '(CAEN PARIS BREST NANTES) 'ADJCNT)
(PUTPROP 'CAEN '(CALAIS PARIS RENNES) 'ADJCNT)
(PUTPROP 'CALAIS '(NANCY PARIS CAEN) 'ADJCNT)
(PUTPROP 'NANCY '(STRASBOURG DIJON PARIS CALAIS) 'ADJCNT)
(PUTPROP 'STRASBOURG '(DIJON NANCY) 'ADJCNT)
(PUTPROP 'DIJON '(STRASBOURG LYON PARIS NANCY) 'ADJCNT)
(PUTPROP 'LYON '(GRENOBLE AVIGNON LIMOGES DIJON) 'ADJCNT)
(PUTPROP 'GRENOBLE '(AVIGNON LYON) 'ADJCNT)
(PUTPROP 'AVIGNON '(GRENOBLE MARSEILLE MONTPELLIER LYON) 'ADJCNT)
(PUTPROP 'MARSEILLE '(NICE AVIGNON) 'ADJCNT)
(PUTPROP 'NICE '(MARSEILLE) 'ADJCNT)
(PUTPROP 'MONTPELLIER '(AVIGNON TOULOUSE) 'ADJCNT)
(PUTPROP 'TOULOUSE '(MONTPELLIER BORDEAUX LIMOGES) 'ADJCNT)
(PUTPROP 'BORDEAUX '(LIMOGES TOULOUSE NANTES) 'ADJCNT)
(PUTPROP 'LIMOGES '(LYON TOULOUSE BORDEAUX NANTES PARIS) 'ADJCNT)
(PUTPROP 'NANTES '(LIMOGES BORDEAUX RENNES) 'ADJCNT)
(PUTPROP 'PARIS '(CALAIS NANCY DIJON LIMOGES RENNES CAEN) 'ADJCNT)
```

Let us suppose that we wish to find, with the help of a program, a route from Rennes to Avignon. There are several approaches we might take.

5.3.2 Hypothesize and Test

If one has very little knowledge about the space one must search, one may be inclined to explore it at random. Beginning from Rennes one could roll dice to choose which road to begin with. It is possible that a random decision sequence might lead one to the goal state (Avignon). Without an informed way of generating hypotheses (trial routes), however, one can expect to waste a lot of time with this approach. The first obvious improvement we can make is to systematize the search so that the various possible alternatives are tried in an orderly fashion.

5.3.3 Depth-First Search

We can proceed by listing the cities directly accessible from Rennes and then going to the first of these (taking us to Caen), and then adding to the list the new places one could go to directly from there, and moving to the first of those, etc., until we have either found Avignon or reached a dead end. If a dead end is reached, we can back up to the last city visited from which we had a choice of new cities and try the next alternative. Such a search technique is analogous to the backtracking search used in our solver for the painted squares puzzles. There are some subtle differences, however; for example, the new procedure avoids repeatedly examining nodes via an explicit test, whereas SOLVE_SQUARES avoided repetitions implicitly (if the pieces were all different). We can describe this *depth-first* search algorithm as follows:

1. Put the start node on a list OPEN and associate a null pointer with the node.

2. If OPEN is empty, output "FAILURE" and stop.

3. Select the first node on OPEN and call it N. Delete it from OPEN and put it on a list CLOSED. If N is a goal node, output the list obtained by following the chain of pointers beginning with the pointer associated with N.

4. Generate the list L of successors of N and delete from L those nodes already appearing on list CLOSED.

5. Delete any members of OPEN which occur on L. Concatenate L onto the front of OPEN and to each node in L associate a pointer to N.

6. Go to step 2.

This may be described in LISP as follows:

```
(DEFUN DEPTH_FIRST_SEARCH (START_NODE GOAL_NODE)
  (PROG   (OPEN CLOSED N L)
          (SETQ OPEN (LIST START_NODE))            ;step1
          (PUTPROP START_NODE NIL 'POINTER)
   LOOP   (COND ((NULL OPEN)(RETURN 'FAILURE)))    ;step2
          (SETQ N (CAR OPEN))                      ;step3
          (SETQ OPEN (CDR OPEN))
          (SETQ CLOSED (CONS N CLOSED))
          (COND ((EQ N GOAL_NODE)(RETURN (EXTRACT_PATH N))))
          (SETQ L (SUCCESSORS N))                  ;step4
          (SETQ L (SET_DIFF L CLOSED))
          (SETQ OPEN (APPEND L (SET_DIFF OPEN L)));step5
          (MAPCAR '(LAMBDA (X) (PUTPROP X N 'POINTER)) L)
          (GO LOOP)                                ;step6
          ) )
```

The helping function EXTRACT_PATH follows the pointers to produce a list of nodes on the path found:

```
(DEFUN EXTRACT_PATH (N)
  (COND ((NULL N) NIL)
        (T (APPEND (EXTRACT_PATH (GET N 'POINTER))
                   (LIST N) )) ) )
```

The function SUCCESSORS gets the cities adjacent to N:

```
(DEFUN SUCCESSORS (N) (GET N 'ADJCNT))
```

The other nonstandard function used is SET_DIFF, which returns the first list, but omits members which are also members of the second list.

```
(DEFUN SET_DIFF (L1 L2)
  (COND ((NULL L1) NIL)
        ((MEMBER (CAR L1) L2) (SET_DIFF (CDR L1) L2) )
        (T (CONS (CAR L1) (SET_DIFF (CDR L1) L2))) ) )
```

One problem with this method of finding a path is that it doesn't necessarily find the shortest one. Let us make the simple assumption (for the moment) that the length of a route is equal to the number of arcs in the graph along the route. The depth-first search method may just as well find a longest path between two points as find a shortest path. In fact, evaluating

```
(DEPTH_FIRST_SEARCH 'RENNES 'AVIGNON)
```

gives us the rather roundabout route

```
(RENNES CAEN CALAIS NANCY STRASBOURG DIJON LYON
        GRENOBLE AVIGNON)
```

which is five arcs longer than necessary.

We can alter our searching procedure to find shortest paths; we shall turn the function into a "breadth-first" search procedure.

5.3.4   Breadth-First Search

A more conservative style of searching a graph is to search along all paths of length 1 from the start node, then along all paths of length 2, length 3, etc., until either the goal is found or the longest possible acyclic paths have been tried. In actuality, when we search along paths of length k, we need not re-examine the first $k - 1$ nodes of each such path; we need only take one step further in each possible direction, from the nodes newly reached in iteration number $k - 1$. This method is called *breadth-first* search.

A minor modification in our function DEPTH_FIRST_SEARCH makes it become BREADTH_FIRST_SEARCH. In steps 4 and 5, we change the way the list L is merged with the list OPEN. Rather than concatenate L at the front, we put it at the back. That is, we replace

```
(SETQ L (SET_DIFF L CLOSED))
(SETQ OPEN (APPEND L (SET_DIFF OPEN L)))      ;step5
```

with

```
(SETQ L (SET_DIFF (SET_DIFF L OPEN) CLOSED))
(SETQ OPEN (APPEND OPEN L))                    ;step5
```

thus putting the newly reached nodes on the end of OPEN, for processing after all the nodes at the current depth are finished.

Now, the possible routes from the start node are explored in order of increasing length, so that as soon as the goal node is found, we know we have constructed a minimum-length path to it. The result of evaluating

```
(BREADTH_FIRST_SEARCH 'RENNES 'AVIGNON)
```

is the much more reasonable route,

```
(RENNES PARIS DIJON LYON AVIGNON).
```

Of course it is possible that DEPTH_FIRST_SEARCH might stumble upon the shortest path by some coincidence, and it might do so in many fewer iterations than BREADTH_FIRST_SEARCH requires. On the other hand, if the path is short, DEPTH_FIRST_SEARCH might not find the goal right away, whereas BREADTH_FIRST_SEARCH would find it very quickly.

5.4 Heuristic Search Methods

5.4.1 Evaluation Functions

Both the depth-first and breadth-first methods are "blind" in the sense that they use exhaustive approaches that can't "see" where they are going until they get there. That is, they don't have any sense of where the goal node lies until they find it. Consequently, they often spend a lot of time searching in totally fruitless directions. If some general guiding information is available, the searching can be biased to move in the general direction of the goal from the very beginning. For example, when a friend hides a present for you in the house and then gives you clues of "warmer" and "colder" as you move closer or farther away from the cache, you will have a much easier time locating the present than without such feedback.

A function f that maps each node to a real number, and which serves to estimate either the relative benefit or the relative cost of continuing the search from that node, is an *evaluation function*. In the remainder of this section, we consider only evaluation functions which are cost functions. Typically $f(N)$ is designed to estimate the distance remaining between N and the goal node. Alternatively $f(N)$ might estimate the length of a path from the start node to the goal node which passes through N. The evaluation function is used to decide the order in which nodes are to be considered during the search. A search method which tends to first expand nodes estimated to be closer to the goal is likely to reach the goal with fewer steps.

For the problem of finding a route from Rennes to Avignon, we now introduce an evaluation function to provide some rough guidance to the search. Suppose that the longitude of each city is available. We make $f(N) = \text{LongitudeDiff}(N,$ Avignon) which we define to be the absolute value of the difference between the longitude of N and the longitude of Avignon. We can now arrange to have the nodes on OPEN kept ordered by increasing f value, so that the most promising node to process next always appears at the front. The procedure for exploiting the new information, called "best-first" or "ordered" search, is described in the next section. Before proceeding there, we give the additional LISP representations that will be required.

First we store the longitude data required in computing f:

```
; Store the longitude (in tenths of a degree) of each city:
(MAPCAR '(LAMBDA (X) (PUTPROP (CAR X)(CADR X) 'LG))
        '((AVIGNON 48)(BORDEAUX -6)(BREST -45)(CAEN -4)
          (CALAIS 18)(DIJON 51)(GRENOBLE 57)(LIMOGES 12)
          (LYON 48)(MARSEILLE 53)(MONTPELLIER 36)
          (NANTES -16)(NANCY 62)(NICE 73)(PARIS 23)
          (RENNES -17)(STRASBOURG 77)(TOULOUSE 14) ) )
```

Now we define three functions used in computing f:

```
(DEFUN LONGITUDE_DIFF (N1 N2)
       (ABS (DIFFERENCE (GET N1 'LG) (GET N2 'LG))) )

(DEFUN ABS (X)
       (COND ((GREATERP X 0) X)(T (DIFFERENCE 0 X))))

(DEFUN F (N) (LONGITUDE_DIFF N GOAL_NODE))
```

We know that GOAL_NODE will be bound to AVIGNON when the search for AVIGNON from RENNES is begun.

5.4.2   Best-First (Ordered) Search

Let us first describe the general procedure for best-first search, and then we shall discuss its application to increasing the efficiency of finding a route from Rennes to Avignon.

With the aid of an evaluation function f on the nodes of a graph it is desired to find a goal node starting from a start node S.

We begin by placing node S on a list called OPEN. Then we successively process the node(s) on OPEN by examining them to see if they are goal nodes, and if not, transfering them to another list CLOSED while placing their successors on OPEN, all the while avoiding redundant processing, updating $f(N)$ for each node N processed, and treating nodes on OPEN in an order that gives priority to the node having lowest $f(N)$. More precisely:

1. Place the starting node S on OPEN, compute $f(S)$ and associate this value with S. Associate a null pointer with S.

2. If OPEN is empty, return "FAILED" and stop or exit.

3. Choose a node N from OPEN such that $f(N) \leq f(M)$ for each M on OPEN, and such that N is a goal node if any goal node achieves that minimum f value.

4. Put N on CLOSED and remove N from OPEN.

5. If N is a goal node, return the path from S to N obtained by tracing backwards the pointers from N to S. Then stop or exit.

6. For each successor J of N that is not already on OPEN or on CLOSED:

    (a) compute $f(J)$ and associate it with J.

    (b) put J on OPEN,

    (c) associate a pointer with J pointing back to N.

7. For each successor J that is already on OPEN, recompute $f(J)$ and compare it to its previous f value. If the new value is smaller, associate this new value with J and reposition J on OPEN.

8. Go to Step 2.

This general procedure may be used to search arbitrary graphs or trees such as those that describe the possible sequences of moves in puzzles. The search is said to be ordered (or "best-first") because at each iteration of Step 3, it chooses the best or one of the best alternative directions for searching, according to the evaluation function f. The efficiency of the search depends upon the quality of this function. This function should yield relatively low values along the shortest path to a goal node, if it is to make the search efficient.

Let us now apply the best-first searching method to finding AVIGNON from RENNES, using LONGITUDE_DIFF as the basis for evaluating nodes on OPEN. Here is the main procedure:

```
(DEFUN BEST_FIRST_SEARCH (START_NODE GOAL_NODE)
  (PROG   (OPEN CLOSED N L)
          (SETQ OPEN (LIST START_NODE))     ;step1
          (PUTPROP START_NODE (F START_NODE) 'FVALUE)
          (PUTPROP START_NODE NIL 'POINTER)
   LOOP   (COND ((NULL OPEN)(RETURN 'FAILURE)));step2
          (SETQ N (SELECT_BEST OPEN))        ;step3
          (SETQ OPEN (DELETE N OPEN))        ;step4
          (SETQ CLOSED (CONS N CLOSED))
          (COND ((EQ N GOAL_NODE)            ;step5
```

```
                (RETURN (EXTRACT_PATH N))))
        (SETQ L (SUCCESSORS N))            ;step6
        (MAPCAR 'OPEN_NODE
                (SET_DIFF (SET_DIFF L OPEN) CLOSED))
        (GO LOOP)                          ;step7
        ) )
```

The main procedure employs two special functions. These functions are SE-
LECT_BEST and OPEN_NODE which in turn use helping functions BETTER
and INSERT:

```
; Function to choose node in step 3...
(DEFUN SELECT_BEST (LST)
  (COND ((EQ (CAR LST) GOAL_NODE)(CAR LST))
        (T (BETTER (CAR LST)(CDR LST))) ) )

; Helping function for SELECT_BEST checks to see if there is a
;   goal node on LST with FVALUE as low as that of ELT.
(DEFUN BETTER (ELT LST)
  (COND ((NULL LST) ELT)
        ((LESSP (GET ELT 'FVALUE)(GET (CAR LST) 'FVALUE)) ELT)
        ((EQ (CAR LST) GOAL_NODE)(CAR LST))
        (T (BETTER ELT (CDR LST))) ) )

; For use in step 6:
(DEFUN OPEN_NODE (M)
  (PROG (VAL)
        (SETQ OPEN_COUNT (ADD1 OPEN_COUNT))
        (PUTPROP M (SETQ VAL (F M)) 'FVALUE)
        (SETQ OPEN (INSERT M OPEN))
        (PUTPROP M N 'POINTER) ) )

; Put NODE onto LST, which is ordered by 'FVALUE property.
;        This value is precomputed for NODE in VAL.
(DEFUN INSERT (NODE LST)
  (COND ((NULL LST)(LIST NODE))
        ((LESSP VAL (GET (CAR LST) 'FVALUE))
         (CONS NODE LST))
        (T (CONS (CAR LST)(INSERT NODE (CDR LST)))) ) )
```

In order to test BEST_FIRST_SEARCH we define a function TEST:

```
(DEFUN TEST ()
  (PROG (OPEN_COUNT)
        (SETQ OPEN_COUNT 1)
        (TRACE OPEN_NODE)
```

```
(PRINT (BEST_FIRST_SEARCH 'RENNES 'AVIGNON))
(PRINT (LIST OPEN_COUNT 'NODES 'OPENED)) ) )
```

The number of nodes opened during this test is 13. Thus, the incorporation of the evaluation function led to an improvement over the number, 16, of nodes opened by BREADTH_FIRST_SEARCH (a blind method).

5.4.3 Searching Graphs with Real Distances

In the previous section, we made the assumption that the length of a route from one city to another is equal to the number of arcs in the path. The actual road distances were not considered. These distances would, of course, provide a much better basis for the problem of finding a shortest driving route, than can the number of graph arcs on the path. Assuming that we have a measure of the kilometers along each arc of the graph, the total distance for a route is the sum of the distances of the arcs that constitute it.

Adding distance information to our graph of French cities, we have the labelled graph of Fig. 5.5.

We may represent this labelled graph by the following:

```
(PUTPROP 'BREST '((RENNES . 244)) 'ADJDST)
(PUTPROP 'RENNES '((CAEN . 176)(PARIS . 348)
       (BREST . 244)(NANTES . 107)) 'ADJDST)
(PUTPROP 'CAEN '((CALAIS . 120)(PARIS . 241)
       (RENNES . 176)) 'ADJDST)
(PUTPROP 'CALAIS '((NANCY . 534)(PARIS . 297)
       (CAEN . 120)) 'ADJDST)
(PUTPROP 'NANCY '((STRASBOURG . 145)(DIJON . 201)(PARIS . 372)
       (CALAIS . 534)) 'ADJDST)
(PUTPROP 'STRASBOURG '((DIJON . 335)(NANCY . 145)) 'ADJDST)
(PUTPROP 'DIJON '((STRASBOURG . 335)(LYON . 192)(PARIS . 313)
       (NANCY . 201)) 'ADJDST)
(PUTPROP 'LYON '((GRENOBLE . 104)(AVIGNON . 216)(LIMOGES . 389)
       (DIJON . 192)) 'ADJDST)
(PUTPROP 'GRENOBLE '((AVIGNON . 227)(LYON . 104)) 'ADJDST)
(PUTPROP 'AVIGNON '((GRENOBLE . 227)(MARSEILLE . 99)
       (MONTPELLIER . 91)(LYON . 216)) 'ADJDST)
(PUTPROP 'MARSEILLE '((NICE . 188)(AVIGNON . 99)) 'ADJDST)
(PUTPROP 'NICE '((MARSEILLE . 188)) 'ADJDST)
(PUTPROP 'MONTPELLIER '((AVIGNON . 91)(TOULOUSE . 240)) 'ADJDST)
(PUTPROP 'TOULOUSE '((MONTPELLIER . 240)(BORDEAUX . 253)
       (LIMOGES . 313)) 'ADJDST)
(PUTPROP 'BORDEAUX '((LIMOGES . 220)(TOULOUSE . 253)
       (NANTES . 329)) 'ADJDST)
(PUTPROP 'LIMOGES '((LYON . 389)(TOULOUSE . 313)(BORDEAUX . 220)
```

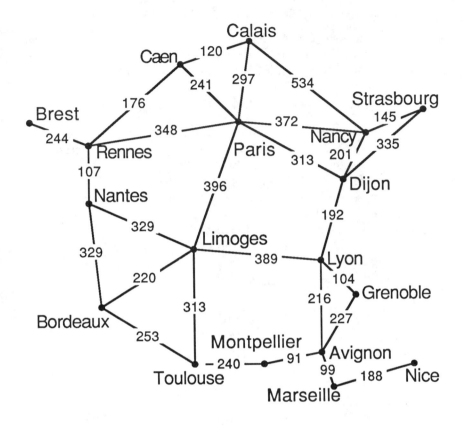

Figure 5.5: State space graph with distance ("cost") information.

```
              (NANTES . 329)(PARIS . 396)) 'ADJDST)
(PUTPROP 'NANTES '((LIMOGES . 329)(BORDEAUX . 329)
              (RENNES . 107)) 'ADJDST)
(PUTPROP 'PARIS '((CALAIS . 297)(NANCY . 372)(DIJON . 313)
              (LIMOGES . 396)(RENNES . 348)(CAEN . 241)) 'ADJDST)
```

In order to apply the breadth-first search method here, it should be modified so that it opens new nodes in order of their minimum distance from the start node. Thus, each time a successor node M of a node N is generated, we should (a) see whether M is on CLOSED and if so, not consider it further, and if not, (b) compute its distance from the start node along the path just followed as Temp = NodeDistance(N) + ArcDistance(M, N), and (c) examine OPEN for an occurrence of M and if present, compare the value of NodeDistance(M) with Temp, and if Temp is smaller, delete the old occurrence of M on OPEN, and finally (d) set NodeDistance(M) = Temp, and insert M into its position in OPEN according to increasing values of NodeDistance.

Note that although this method, which we shall call UNIFORM_COST is actually blind (there is no evaluation function biasing it to move more quickly toward the goal), it does bear some similarity with BEST_FIRST_SEARCH. In fact, the only substantial difference is in the meaning and computation of the node-distance function. In the best-first method, it gave an estimate of a node's proximity to the goal; here it reflects a node's distance from the start node. Besides the difference in where the distance is to or from, there is also a distinct difference, in that best-first search uses estimated distances or heuristic ordering values, whereas uniform-cost search uses (in theory) exact distances.

Let us now illustrate the effect on the solution to the French route problem brought about by the use of actual road distances and the uniform-cost algorithm.

```
; The main searching procedure:

(DEFUN UNIFORM_COST (START_NODE GOAL_NODE)
  (PROG   (OPEN CLOSED N L)
          (SETQ OPEN (LIST START_NODE))    ;step1
          (PUTPROP START_NODE 0 'FVALUE)
          (PUTPROP START_NODE NIL 'POINTER)
   LOOP   (COND ((NULL OPEN)(RETURN 'FAILURE)))    ;step2
          (SETQ N (SELECT_BEST OPEN))        ;step3
          (SETQ OPEN (DELETE N OPEN))        ;step4
          (SETQ CLOSED (CONS N CLOSED))
          (COND ((EQ N GOAL_NODE)            ;step5
               (RETURN (EXTRACT_PATH N))))
          (SETQ L (SUCCESSORS N))            ;step6
          (MAPCAR 'OPEN_NODE
               (SET_DIFF (SET_DIFF L OPEN) CLOSED))
          (GO LOOP)                          ;step7
          ) )
```

The supporting functions which are new or have definitions that supersede those used previously are the following:

```
(DEFUN SUCCESSORS (N) (MAPCAR 'CAR (GET N 'ADJDST)))

(DEFUN ARC_DIST (N1 N2) (CDR_SELECT N2 (GET N1 'ADJDST)))

(DEFUN CDR_SELECT (KEY LST)
  (COND ((NULL LST)            ; if KEY not found
         9999)                 ; return a very large value
        ((EQ KEY (CAAR LST)) (CDAR LST))
        (T (CDR_SELECT KEY (CDR LST))) ) )
```

```
(DEFUN F (NODE) (PLUS (GET N 'FVALUE) (ARC_DIST N NODE)))

(DEFUN TEST ()
 (PROG  (OPEN_COUNT)
        (SETQ OPEN_COUNT 1)
        (TRACE OPEN_NODE)
        (PRINT 'UNIFORM_COST_SEARCH:)
        (PRINT (UNIFORM_COST_SEARCH 'RENNES 'AVIGNON))
        (PRINT (LIST OPEN_COUNT 'NODES 'OPENED)) ) )
```

The result of applying the uniform-cost method here is the path

(RENNES NANTES LIMOGES LYON AVIGNON)

with 16 nodes being opened. As one might expect, the optimal route is different when real distances are used (as just done here) rather than the number of arcs along a path in our particular graph.

5.4.4   The A* Algorithm

If the exact distances from the start node can be determined when nodes are reached, then the uniform-cost procedure can be applied, as we have just seen. When additionally, some heuristic information is available relating the nodes visited to the goal node, a procedure known as the A* (pronounced "Eh star") algorithm is usually better.

The A* algorithm opens nodes in an order that gives highest priority to nodes likely to be on the shortest path from the start node to the goal. To do this it adds g, the cost of the best path found so far between the start node and the current node, to the estimated distance h from the current node to some goal node. Provided that the estimate h never exceeds the true distance between the current node and the goal node, the A* algorithm will always find a shortest path between the start node and the goal node (this is known as the *admissibility* of the A* algorithm).

In a sense, the A* technique is really a family of algorithms all having a common structure. A specific instance of an A* algorithm is obtained by specifying a particular estimation function h.

If the estimate h is always zero, A* is certainly admissible. In fact, A* then is no different from the uniform-cost method. In this case the search algorithm is called *uninformed*. The most informed algorithm possible would have h being the exact distance from the current node to the goal. An algorithm A_1 is said to be *more informed* than an algorithm A_2 if the heuristic information of A_1 permits it to compute an estimate h_1 that is everywhere larger than h_2, that computed by A_2.

The assumption that h never exceeds the true distance between the current node and the goal allows admissibility to be assured. An additional constraint

ALGORITHM A*
begin
   input the start node S and the set GOALS of goal nodes;
   OPEN $\leftarrow \{S\}$; CLOSED $\leftarrow \phi$;
   $G[S] \leftarrow 0$; PRED$[S] \leftarrow$ NULL; *found* $\leftarrow$ **false**;
   while OPEN is not empty and *found* is **false do**
     begin
       L $\leftarrow$ the set of nodes on OPEN for which F is the least;
       if L is a singleton **then** let X be its sole element
         else if there are any goal nodes in L
           then let X be one of them
           else let X be any element of L;
       remove X from OPEN and put X into CLOSED;
       if X is a goal node **then** *found* $\leftarrow$ **true**
         else begin
           generate the set SUCCESSORS of successors of X;
             for each Y **in** SUCCESSORS **do**
               if Y is not already on OPEN or on CLOSED **then**
                 begin
                   $G[Y] \leftarrow G[X] + distance(X, Y)$;
                   $F[Y] \leftarrow G[Y] + h(Y)$; PRED$[Y] \leftarrow X$;
                   insert Y on OPEN;
                 end
               else /* Y is on OPEN or on CLOSED */
                 begin
                   $Z \leftarrow$ PRED$[Y]$;
                   $temp \leftarrow F[Y] - G[Z] - distance(Z, Y) +$
                      $+ G[X] + distance(X, Y)$;
                   if $temp < F[Y]$ **then**
                     begin
                       $G[Y] \leftarrow G[Y] - F[Y] + temp$;
                       $F[Y] \leftarrow temp$; PRED$[Y] \leftarrow X$;
                       if Y is on CLOSED **then**
                         insert Y on OPEN and remove Y from CLOSED;
                   end;
               end;
         end;
     end;
   if *found* is **false then** output "Failure"
   else trace the pointers in the PRED fields from X back to S, "CONSing"
     each node onto the growing list of nodes to get the path from S to X;
end.

Figure 5.6: The A* algorithm. It uses real distances and an estimation function h to efficiently search a state space.

called the *consistency assumption* will allow us to assert a kind of optimality
for A*. The consistency assumption is satisfied provided that for any two nodes
n_1 and n_2, the difference in values of h for those nodes never exceeds the true
distance between n_1 and n_2. The A* method is optimal in the sense that if A_1
is more informed than A_2, and the consistency assumption is satisfied, then A_1
never opens any node not opened by A_2.

The general form of the A* algorithm is given in Fig. 5.6. Here uppercase
non-italic identifiers represent either fields of nodes or variables whose values are
sets of nodes (e.g., OPEN, L); italic uppercase letters represent variables whose
values are nodes (e.g., X); and italic lowercase identifiers represent real-valued
or boolean-valued variables (e.g., *temp, found*) or functions of nodes or pairs
of nodes (e.g., h, *distance*). In this formulation, each node X has three data
fields associated with it: G[X], the distance from the start node to X along the
shortest path found so far; F[X], the sum of G[X] and $h(X)$; and PRED[X],
the predecessor of X along the shortest known path to X. It is assumed that
distance(X, Y) gives the length (or cost) of the arc from X to Y.

We now provide a LISP implementation of the A* algorithm.

```
; ASTAR.LSP -- The A* Search Algorithm in LISP.
; Finds a minimum-cost path using an evaluation function
; to make the search efficient.
```

The road distances between cities in kilometers are as for uniform-cost search.
The longitudes (in tenths of a degree) of each city are as for best-first search.

```
; Let G represent the actual distance from the start node.
; Let H represent the estimated remaining distance to the goal.
; We make F(N) = G(N) + H(N), and use it as an eval. function.
; H is defined to be LongitudeDiff * 10.


; The main searching procedure:

(DEFUN A_STAR_SEARCH (START_NODE GOAL_NODE)
  (PROG (OPEN CLOSED N L)
        (SETQ OPEN (LIST START_NODE))            ;step1
        (PUTPROP START_NODE 0 'GVALUE)
        (PUTPROP START_NODE (F START_NODE) 'FVALUE)
        (PUTPROP START_NODE NIL 'POINTER)
   LOOP (COND ((NULL OPEN)(RETURN 'FAILURE)))    ;step2
        (SETQ N (SELECT_BEST OPEN))              ;step3
        (SETQ OPEN (DELETE N OPEN))              ;step4
        (SETQ CLOSED (CONS N CLOSED))
        (COND ((EQ N GOAL_NODE)                  ;step5
               (RETURN (EXTRACT_PATH N))))
        (SETQ L (SUCCESSORS N))                  ;step6
```

```
                (MAPCAR 'OPEN_NODE
                        (SET_DIFF (SET_DIFF L CLOSED) OPEN) )
                (MAPCAR 'UPDATE_OPEN
                        (INTERSECT L OPEN) )              ;step7
                (MAPCAR 'UPDATE_CLOSED   ;This can sometimes be eliminated.
                        (INTERSECT L CLOSED) )
                (GO LOOP)                                 ;step8
                ) )
```

The supporting functions are largely those used previously, with a few modifications:

```
; For use in step 6:
(DEFUN OPEN_NODE (X)
 (PROG  (VAL)
        (SETQ OPEN_COUNT (ADD1 OPEN_COUNT))
        (PUTPROP X (G X) 'GVALUE)
        (PUTPROP X (SETQ VAL (F X)) 'FVALUE)
        (SETQ OPEN (INSERT X OPEN))
        (PUTPROP X N 'POINTER) ) )
```

```
; For use in step 7.  Node X, presumably already on OPEN, gets
; its GVALUE recomputed and if the new value is less than
; than the old, the new value is stored and the node is
; repositioned on OPEN.
(DEFUN UPDATE_OPEN (X)
  (PROG (VAL)
        (SETQ VAL (G X))
        (COND ((LESSP VAL (GET X 'GVALUE))
               (PUTPROP X VAL 'GVALUE)
               (PUTPROP X (F X) 'FVALUE)
               (PUTPROP X N 'POINTER)
               (SETQ OPEN (INSERT X (DELETE X OPEN)))
        )) ) )
```

The following function is only necessary if the consistency assumption is *not* satisfied.

```
(DEFUN UPDATE_CLOSED (X)
  (PROG (VAL)
        (SETQ VAL (G X))
        (COND ((LESSP VAL (GET X 'GVALUE))
               (PUTPROP X VAL 'GVALUE)
               (PUTPROP X (F X) 'FVALUE)
               (PUTPROP X N 'POINTER)
```

```
                (SETQ OPEN (INSERT X OPEN))
                (SETQ CLOSED (DELETE X CLOSED))
          )) ) )
```

Here are the functions F, G, and H, and a function TEST which uses
A_STAR_SEARCH to find a path from Rennes to Avignon:

```
(DEFUN F (N) (PLUS (GET N 'GVALUE) (H N)))

(DEFUN G (M) (PLUS (GET N 'GVALUE) (ARC_DIST N M)))

(DEFUN H (N) (TIMES 10 (LONGITUDE_DIFF N GOAL_NODE) ))

(DEFUN TEST ()
  (PROG (OPEN_COUNT)
        (SETQ OPEN_COUNT 1)
        (TRACE OPEN_NODE)
        (PRINT (A_STAR_SEARCH 'RENNES 'AVIGNON))
        (PRINT (LIST (GET 'AVIGNON 'GVALUE) 'KILOMETERS))
        (PRINT (LIST OPEN_COUNT 'NODES 'OPENED)) ) )

(TEST)
```

By using ten times the absolute value of the longitude difference to estimate
the distance from the current node to the goal, we obtain a more informed
algorithm than the uniform-cost method. For the test above, we achieve the
same (shortest) route, but we only open 15 nodes, instead of 16. In a more
complicated graph or state space, the savings could well be more dramatic.

5.5   Planning

5.5.1   Problem Solving Before Action

The term *planning* is used for problem-solving activity whose purpose is to produce a tentative procedure or guide for accomplishing some task. The tentative
procedure is called a *plan*. The activity of planning usually involves searching a
space of configurations to find a path that corresponds to the desired sequence
of operations.

We note that ordinary people usually make a clear distinction between
"planning" an action and "performing" an action; planning is regarded as an
information-processing activity whereas performing is considered something mechanical. In a computer, the distinction is often unclear, since computers perform
only information-processing actions (unless they are controlling peripheral devices such as robot arms). Consequently, when we describe some problem-solving

activity as "planning" we imply that there is some separate activity (which may well be information processing, or even problem solving) which is to be guided by the results of the planning.

Planning is sometimes carried out with detailed representations of the problem domain. In other instances, planning may work only with approximations or even grossly simplified models of the problem domain.

5.5.2 A Robotics Example

Some problems in robotics may be solved by finding a sequence of operations that leads from an initial state to a goal state. An example of such a problem is illustrated in Fig. 5.7. In this situation, there are three blocks, A, B, and C, on

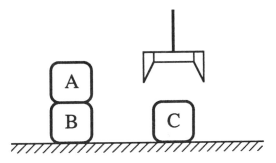

Figure 5.7: Robot hand and blocks on a table.

a table top with A stacked on top of B, and there is a robot capable of grasping one block (from the block's top only) and moving right or left and up or down and ungrasping. The problem is to find a way for the robot to stack block C on top of block B. A solution to this problem may be regarded as a plan since it could be used to guide the robot through the mechanical actions to achieve the physical goal of having C stacked on B. The process of finding such a plan is an example of planning.

Although there are many methods that could be used to solve this problem, the most straightforward one is to search in the space of configurations of blocks and the gripper for a path that leads from the initial configuration to a goal configuration. The arcs in the state-space graph correspond to operations that the robot can perform.

Let us consider a set of such operations:

G (Grasp)	Close the gripper fingers.
O (Open)	Open the gripper fingers.
U (Up)	Move up one vertical unit (= height of a block).
D (Down)	Move down one vertical unit.
R (Right)	Move right one horizontal step (= width of a block plus ϵ).
L (Left)	Move left one horizontal step.

If we choose a random sequence of operations and apply them, there is a high likelihood that there will be a collision of the robot with the table, with a block, or a block with the table or another block. For purposes of this example, we assume that any collision will cause damage and therefore any plan to stack C on B must avoid collisions.

A breadth-first search method could be used to find the plan

$$ULLDGURDDOURDGUULLDO.$$

However, since this plan is one of 6^{20} sequences of length 20, the computational cost of such a search is high.

This planning problem could be made more tractable by making the operators conditional. This provides a way to restrict the state space to configurations that do not involve collisions. Then the operator *Down* would have a *precondition* that defines the configurations at which it can be applied:

Precondition for *Down*:

If   the gripper is open then
       a.   the space directly beneath the gripper is open, and
       b.   the space directly beneath that one is either open or contains a block (so that the fingers do not collide with the table);

Else   if the gripper is carrying a block then
         the space directly beneath the block being carried is open;

       else   the space directly below the space which is directly under the gripper is open (i.e., the fingers will collide neither with the table nor with a block).

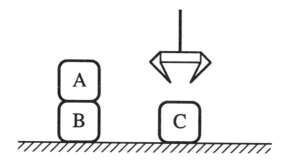

Figure 5.8: A configuration of the blocks and gripper that violates the precondition for *Down*.

Notice that the precondition for *Down* is not satisfied in the configuration of Fig. 5.8. Here the fingers, since closed, would collide with C.

5.5.3 Hierarchical Planning

As we have seen earlier in the chapter, blind search can be improved upon by incorporating heuristic evaluation functions. Another method to reduce the computational demands of search is to use a hierarchical approach. In order to develop a plan for a task such as a robot's establishing block C on top of block B, it is often possible to identify subtasks for which plans can be developed more easily, or for which plans or plan generators have been developed in advance. The plans for the subtasks are then combined, with any adjustments necessary to make them mutually compatible, to obtain a plan for the full task. Possible subtasks for the robotics problem are these:

- Clear the top of block B (or more generally, clear the top of any specified block).

- Move C onto B (or more generally, move any specified block onto any other specified block).

These two subtasks can themselves be divided into tasks of the following types:

- Move empty gripper to block x.

- Grasp the object under the gripper (making sure the gripper is open prior to attempting to grasp).

- Put down the block currently being held, without dropping, in order to free the gripper to grasp something else.

A procedure which generates a plan for a subtask is sometimes called a "macro-operator." For example, one macro-operator is a routine CLEARTOP(x), which creates a plan to remove any blocks that happen to be on top of block x; this macro-operator handles the first subtask listed above.

Although in our example so far we have considered a plan to be a sequence of elementary operations (arcs in the original state space), we may also consider a sequence of macro-operators to be a plan. Thus, another plan for putting C on B is the following:

```
CLEARTOP(B)
PUTON(C,B)
```

As with elementary operators, a macro-operator generally has one or more preconditions which must be true of a state in order to make the macro-operator applicable. Because a macro-operator can be complicated, it is also useful to associate "postconditions" with it. A *postcondition* is a property of the state that results from the operator or macro-operator which is guaranteed to hold. In addition, it is sometimes useful to associate "invariants" with macro-operators; an *invariant* is a feature of a state which is not affected by the macro-operator. Since, in practice, most state variables are unchanged by any one operator, only the possible exceptions to the invariances normally need be listed. For the macro-operator PUTON(x, y) we can easily imagine two preconditions: that x be clear (no blocks on top of it) and that y be clear. It would be reasonable to assume that all aspects of the state other than those involving x, y and the gripper remain unchanged by an application of PUTON(x, y).

In the two-step plan above for putting C on B, a postcondition of CLEARTOP(B) could assure us that B is clear after CLEARTOP has been applied. However, there is no corresponding postcondition assuring that C is clear, as required for PUTON(C, B). This indicates that the plan may fail when invoked in some situations. The plan may be regarded as correct if we decide that it will never be used in situations where C is not clear. However, if these situations are not ruled out, then the plan contains a *bug*. In this case, the bug can easily be fixed by adding the macro-operator CLEARTOP(C) before the call to PUTON(C, B). To a certain extent, bugs can be prevented by guaranteeing that as many as possible of the preconditions of operators in a plan are satisfied in advance. It is also possible to detect many bugs through testing, and then corrective changes to the plan can be administered.

If the designer of a problem-solving system can include a good set of macro-operators and a mechanism to apply them, this is a good way to fight the combinatorial explosion. Better yet is a system which combines macro-operators with good heuristics that suggest the situations and orders in which the macro-operators should be applied.

Planning is not fundamentally different from other kinds of problem solving; the techniques useful in planning are the same techniques useful in most other kinds of problem solving, e.g., heuristic search.

5.6   Two-Person, Zero-Sum Games

In games like checkers, chess, Go, and Tic-Tac-Toe, two players are involved at a time. If player A wins, then B loses, etc. Such a game is called a two-person, zero-sum game. The fact that a gain by one player is equivalent to a loss by the other leads to a sum of zero overall advantage.

The state-space graphs for two-person, zero-sum games are generally regarded differently from other state-space graphs. From any particular position in the game (that is, a state), at issue are the possible moves one or one's opponent can make, and what the consequences of each move may be.

In Tic-Tac-Toe, one must try to get three X's in a line, or three O's in a line, while preventing one's opponent from attaining such a line. One may settle for a draw, alternatively. The states from which no further move can be made may be called *final states*. The final states fall into three categories: win for X, win for O, or draw. When a win is impossible or unlikely, the objective may be to attain a draw. By assigning values to the possible states, the problem of playing the game becomes one of trying to maximize or minimize the value of the final state. Let us now examine a procedure for this.

5.6.1 Minimaxing

If a player has found a path from the current state to a goal state (or a state with high value), that is not an adequate basis on which to choose a move. Generally speaking, the opponent does not cooperate; it is necessary to take the opponent's probable reactions into account in choosing a move.

The set of states reachable from a given state (using only legal moves of a game) may be arranged into a *game tree*. If a particular state is reachable along two or more alternative paths, we may replicate the state enough times to allow a tree rather than a general graph to represent the current set of game potentialities ("If he goes there, then I could go here," etc.). Let us call the two players "Max" and "Min." We can generally assign a value to each possible state of a game in such a way that Max desires to maximize that value and Min wants to minimize it. Such an assignment of values is a kind of evaluation function. In games whose states are defined by the placements of pieces on boards (like checkers and chess), such an assignment is often called a "board evaluation function."

For the game of Tic-Tac-Toe, a board evaluation function is the following: $100A + 10B + C - (100D + 10E + F)$ where A is the number of lines of three X's, B is the number of unblocked lines with a pair of X's and C is the number of unblocked lines with a single X. Similarly E, F, and G give numbers of lines of O's in various configurations.

A game tree for Tic-Tac-Toe is shown in Fig. 5.9. Each level of nodes in the tree is called a *ply*. Ply 0 contains only a single node, corresponding to the current board position. Ply 1 contains the children of the root of the tree. Typically, a game-playing program will generate all the board positions for nodes down to a particular ply such as 4. It will then evaluate the leaves (tip nodes) of that 4-level tree with the board evaluation function, obtaining what are called *static* values. Then a process of backing values up the tree is begun. If the root corresponds to a position where it is Max's move, then all even-numbered ply contain "Max nodes" and all odd-numbered ply contain "Min nodes." To back up the value to a Max node, the maximum child value is written into the node. For a Min node, the minimum child value is taken. Backing-up proceeds from the leaf nodes up, until the root gets a value. Max's best move (given, say, a 4-ply analysis) is the move which leads to the largest value at a leaf node, given that Max always will maximize over backed-up values and that Min will always minimize. The value thus associated with each non-leaf node of the tree is the node's "backed-up value." While the backed-up value for a node is being computed, and after the backed-up value for the node's first descendant has been computed, the node has a "provisional backed-up value," which is the current minimum (or maximum, depending on whose move it is at the node). The positions shown in Fig. 5.9 are numbered according to the order in which they would be generated. The six

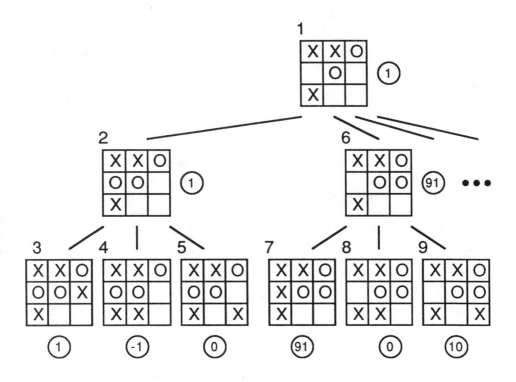

Figure 5.9: Game tree for Tic-Tac-Toe.

leaf nodes are labelled with their static values. Nodes 2 and 6 are labelled with their backed-up values. Since the root corresponds to a position where O, the minimizing player, is to move, choosing between positions 2 and 6, it is clear that O prefers 2 with value 1 over position 6 with a value of 91.

5.6.2   AND/OR Graphs

Game trees with Min and Max nodes have a counterpart in problem-solving; they are called AND/OR trees, and more generally, AND/OR graphs. An AND/OR tree expresses the decomposition of a problem into subproblems, and it allows alternative solutions to problems and subproblems. The original problem corresponds to the root of the AND/OR tree. At an AND node, all the child nodes must be solved in order to have a solution for the AND node. At an OR node, at least one of the children must be solved, but not necessarily any more than one. An AND/OR tree is illustrated in Fig. 5.10. The overall goal for this example is to prepare a main course for a dinner. Disjunctive subgoals of the main goal are "make hamburgers" and "make roast turkey." Conjunctive subgoals of "make hamburgers" are "prepare patties" and "toast buns." In an AND/OR tree (or

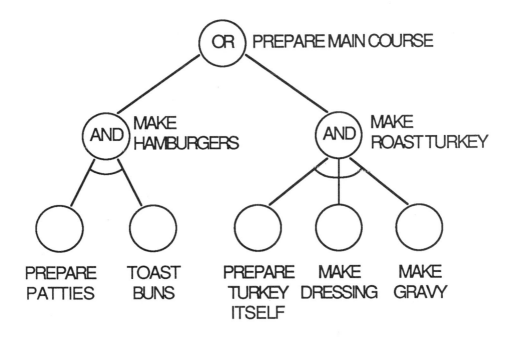

Figure 5.10: An AND/OR tree.

for that matter, an AND/OR graph), a node is *solved* if

- it is an OR node and at least one of its children is solved, or

- it is an AND node, and all of its children are solved, or

- it is a leaf node, and problem-dependent criteria associated with the node are satisfied.

In the above example, the problem-dependent criteria are "patties prepared," "buns toasted," etc.

A *solution graph* for an AND/OR graph (or tree) is a subgraph of the original consisting of a set of solved nodes and the arcs connecting them that make the root node solved. The root of the original graph is a necessary part of a solution graph. For the example of Fig. 5.10, there are two solution graphs; one of these consists of the nodes, PREPARE MAIN COURSE, MAKE HAMBURGERS, PREPARE PATTIES, and TOAST BUNS, together with the arcs that connect these nodes. The *solution* to the problem (or to any subproblem) may be defined recursively: if the (sub)problem corresponds to a leaf node N, then its solution is given by the satisfaction of the appropriate problem-dependent criteria; otherwise, the (sub)problem corresponds to an interior node N, and its solution consists of the subproblems which correspond to the children of N contained in the solution graph, together with their solutions. In this example, the solution may be considered to be a set of plans one of which is simply MAKE HAMBURGERS, and another of which is PREPARE PATTIES *and* TOAST BUNS.

An AND/OR graph may sometimes be used to represent the state space for a game. For example, in a game of Tic-Tac-Toe, we may consider the objective to be solving a problem; that problem is to win the game. For the "X" player, the problem is clearly solved if the current position contains three X's in a row and does not contain three O's in a row. Any position is solved if X has a win at it or can force a win from it, and otherwise, it is not solved. If it is X's move, X can force a win if *any* of the successor positions to the current one is solved. If it is O's move, then X can force a win only if *all* of the successors of the current position are solved. In order to use an AND/OR graph as a basis for playing the game, it must be computationally feasible to generate the entire graph for the current position. Consequently, AND/OR graphs are usually of use only for relatively simple games, for which the number of moves in a game can never get larger than, say, 15 or 20. On the other hand, the minimaxing approach can handle more complex games, because it allows the use of heuristic evaluation functions that avoid the necessity of constructing the entire game tree.

5.6.3   Alpha-Beta Search

In order to play well, a program should examine alternative lines of play to ply as deep as possible. Unfortunately, the number of possible board positions in a game tree tends to grow exponentially with the number of ply. It is usually possible to prune off subtrees as irrelevant by looking at their roots in comparison with alternative moves at that level. For example, in chess, one may be examining a line of play in which it suddenly is discovered that the opponent could capture the queen, while nothing would be gained, and actually a better move is available. Then there is no point to examining alternatives in which the opponent kindly does not take the queen. By assumption, each player is trying to win: one by maximizing and one by minimizing the evaluation function value. When such an irrelevant subtree is discovered, it is generally called a "cutoff." A well-known method for detecting cutoffs automatically is the "alpha-beta" method.

Let us consider an example in a game of checkers. We assume that the game has progressed to the position shown in Fig. 5.11, with black to move. The three-ply game tree for this position is shown in Fig. 5.12. The moves are examined in an order that considers pieces at lower-numbered squares first, and for alternative moves with the same pieces, considers moves to lowest-numbered squares first. Black has four possible moves from the position shown, and so there are four branches out from the root of the tree. The first move to be considered is to

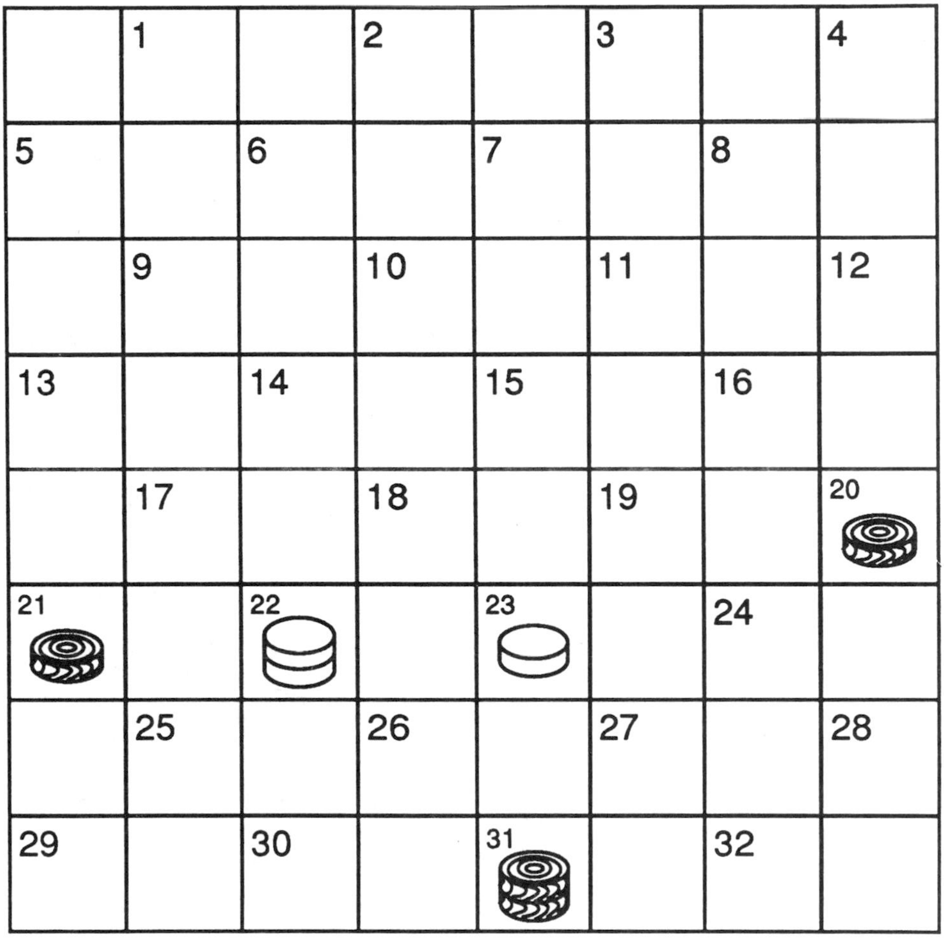

Figure 5.11: Checkers position with Black to Move.

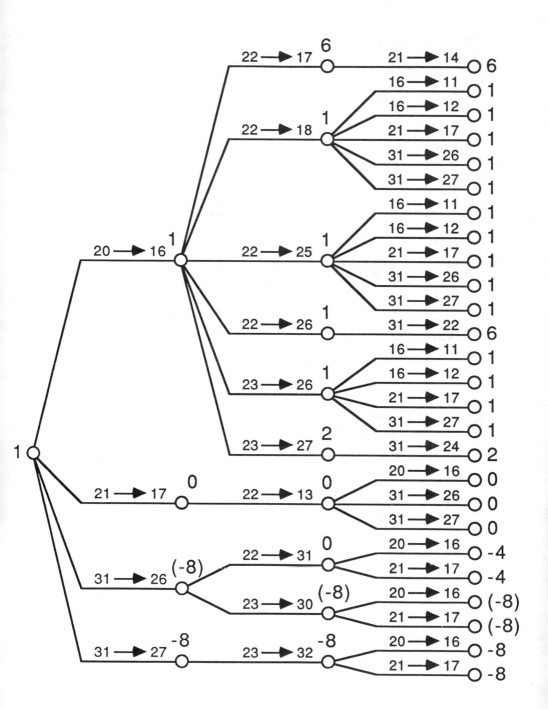

Figure 5.12: A three-ply game tree for the checkers position.

move the man at square 20 to square 16. To this, Red has six possible replies, the first of which is $22 \rightarrow 17$. In this case, Black must then jump with $21 \rightarrow 14$. This position is in ply 3 and should be evaluated statically. We use the following evaluation function:

$$5x_1 + x_2$$

Here x_1 represents Black's king advantage (the number of black kings minus the number of red kings), while x_2 represents Black's single-man advantage.

The static value of the first ply-3 position is therefore 6. This value is backed up to the previous node, and it also becomes the provisional backed-up value for the predecessor of that node (the first descendant of the root). The second Red reply to Black's $20 \rightarrow 16$ is now considered; $22 \rightarrow 18$ leads to five alternatives for Black, each of which results in some position with static value 1. The maximum of these is, of course, also 1, and this value is the backed-up value of the position resulting from Red's second alternative. This value, 1, is less than the provisional backed-up value (6) of the predecessor node, and since Red is minimizing, replaces 1 as the provisional value. Red's four other alternatives lead to backed-up values of 1, 6, 1, and 2, and since none of these is less than the current provisional backed-up value of 1, the final backed-up value for the first descendant of the root is 1.

Black's second alternative ($21 \rightarrow 17$) leads to a position with backed-up value 0. Since Black is maximizing, this move is clearly inferior to the first.

Black's third alternative, $31 \rightarrow 26$, brings out an interesting phenomenon. Red's first alternative for a reply gives Black two choices, each leading to a static value of -4. Thus Red can force Black into a situation much less favorable than if Black were to choose the first or second move in the first place. In other words, after computing the backed-up value of the position after Red's first (and in this case, only) alternative ($22 \rightarrow 31$), this value becomes the provisional value of the preceding position; but here a comparison is made: if this provisional value is less than any of the backed-up values already determined for this ply, the move is certainly inferior, and further evaluation of positions in this subtree can be bypassed. We say here that an *alpha cutoff* occurs at this node. Were the other positions of this subtree to be evaluated, the result would be that the backed-up value of the position after $31 \rightarrow 26$ is -8, which is even worse than the provisional value of -4. But, even if the other positions had high values, the effort to evaluate these positions would be wasted, since Red would always choose the alternative least favorable to Black.

Black's fourth alternative (the last) is $31 \rightarrow 27$. This leads to ply-3 positions of value -8, making this move inferior. Black's best move is clearly the first, according to the 3-ply analysis we have performed.

We saw how an alpha cutoff was used in analyzing Black's third alternative, to avoid evaluating some of the positions in the full 3-ply tree. Such cutoffs can be systematically determined with the *alpha-beta pruning* procedure. Alpha cutoffs are used at minimizing levels, while beta cutoffs are used at maximizing levels. Let A be a maximizing-level node for which k alternatives have been tried, the maximum backed-up value of these being alpha. Let B be the minimizing-level node which is the result of the next alternative from A. As soon as any immediate descendant of B receives a backed-up value that is less than alpha, further consideration of the subtree at B is unnecessary (an alpha cutoff occurs).

Similarly, let C be a minimizing-level node for which k alternatives have been tried, the minimum backed-up value of these being beta. Let D be the maximizing-level node which is the result of the next alternative from C. As soon as any immediate descendant of D receives a backed-up value which is more than beta, the remaining positions in the subtree at D can be ignored (a beta cutoff occurs).

If the search tree is explored in an order that improves the likelihood of cutoffs, the alpha-beta pruning procedure can typically eliminate more than half of the nodes that would have to be evaluated in checkers and chess situations. One way to increase the chances of getting useful cutoffs is to apply the evaluation function to each of the ply-1 positions and to order the exploration of the corresponding subtrees in a best-first fashion.

5.7   Bibliographical Information

Depth-first, backtracking search was used extensively in early problem-solving systems such as GPS ("General Problem Solver") [Newell et al. 1959]. Heuristic search techniques were studied by Pohl [Pohl 1969] and Sandewall [Sandewall 1969]. AND/OR trees and graphs were studied by Slagle and Dixon [Slagle 1963], [Slagle and Dixon 1969]. A thorough presentation of problem representation and state-space search, including proofs for the admissibility and the optimality of the A* algorithm, may be found in [Nilsson 1971]. Section 5.4.3 on pruned, best-first search is based upon material from [Nilsson 1971] and from [Barr and Feigenbaum 1981]. A good source of heuristics for mathematical problem solving is [Polya 1957].

Research in automatic planning for robots has derived benefit from, and had a positive impact upon general problem-solving technology [Newell and Simon 1963], [Fikes and Nilsson 1971]. Hierarchical planning was explored with the ABSTRIPS system [Sacerdoti 1974] and in NOAH [Sacerdoti 1977]. Together with hierarchical planning, the use of constraints in developing plans for genetic engineering experiments was demonstrated in the MOLGEN system [Stefik 1981a, b].

A successful checkers-playing program was developed in the late 1950's [Samuel 1959], and chess has received substantial attention since then [Newborn 1975], [Berliner 1978]. Efforts have also been made to computerize the playing of backgammon [Berliner 1980] and Go [Reitman and Wilcox 1979]. Go is considerably different from chess and checkers in that the game trees for it are so wide (there are typically hundreds of alternatives from each position) that normal minimax search is impractical for it. It has been suggested that principles of perceptual organization be incorporated into Go-playing programs [Zobrist 1970]. The use of plans in playing chess is described in [Wilkins 1980]. The efficiency of alpha-beta search is examined in [Knuth and Moore 1975].

References

1. Barr, A. and Feigenbaum, E. A. (eds.), 1981. *The Handbook of Artificial Intelligence.* Los Altos, CA: William Kaufman.

2. Berliner, H. J. 1978. A chronology of computer chess and its literature. *Artificial Intelligence*, Vol. 10, No. 2, April, pp201-214.

3. Berliner, H. J. 1980. Computer backgammon, *Scientific American*, June.

4. Fikes, R. E., and Nilsson, N. J. 1971. STRIPS: A new approach to the application of theorem proving to problem solving. *Artificial Intelligence*, Vol. 2, pp189-208.

5. Knuth, D. E., and Moore, R. W. 1975. An analysis of alpha-beta pruning. *Artificial Intelligence*, Vol. 6, No. 4, pp293-327.

6. Newborn, M. 1975. *Computer Chess.* New York: Academic Press.

7. Newell, A., Shaw, J., and Simon, H. 1969. Report on a general problem-solving program. *Proceedings of the International Conference on Information Processing*, UNESCO House, Paris, pp256-264.

8. Newell, A., and Simon, H. A. 1963. GPS, a program that simulates human thought. In Feigenbaum, E. A., and Feldman, J. (eds.), *Computers and Thought.* New York: McGraw-Hill, pp279-293.

9. Nilsson, N. J. 1971. *Problem Solving Methods in Artificial Intelligence.* New York: McGraw-Hill.

10. Pohl, I. 1969. Bidirectional and heuristic search in path problems. Ph.D. Dissertation, Dept. of Computer Science, Stanford University.

11. Polya, G. 1957. *How to Solve It*, Second Edition. Garden City, NY: Doubleday.

12. Reitman, W. and Wilcox, B. 1979. The structure and performance of the Interim.2 Go program. *Proceedings of the Sixth International Joint Conference on Artificial Intelligence*, Tokyo, pp711-719.

13. Sacerdoti, E. D. 1974. Planning in a hierarchy of abstraction spaces. *Artificial Intelligence*, Vol. 5, No. 2, pp115-135.

14. Sacerdoti, E. D. 1977. *A Structure for Plans and Behavior.* New York: North-Holland.

15. Sandewall, E. 1969. Concepts and methods for heuristic search. *Proceedings of the First International Joint Conference on Artificial Intelligence,* Washington, D.C.

16. Slagle, J. 1963. A heuristic program that solves symbolic integration problems in freshman calculus, *Journal of the ACM,* Vol. 10, No. 4, pp507-520.

17. Slagle, J., and Dixon, J. 1969. Experiments with some programs that search game trees. *Journal of the ACM,* Vol. 16, No. 2, pp189-207.

18. Stefik, M. 1981a. Planning with constraints (MOLGEN: Part 1). *Artificial Intelligence,* Vol. 16, pp111-139.

19. Stefik, M. 1981b. Planning meta-planning (MOLGEN: Part 2). *Artificial Intelligence,* Vol. 16, pp141-169.

20. Wilkins, D. E. 1980. Using patterns and plans in chess. *Artificial Intelligence,* Vol. 14, pp165-203.

21. Zobrist, A. L. 1970. Feature extraction and representation for pattern recognition and the game of Go. Ph.D. Dissertation, Dept. of Computer Science, University of Wisconsin, Madison.

Exercises

1. Define the following terms:

   (a) "state space"
   (b) "goal state"
   (c) "move generator"
   (d) "heuristic"
   (e) "backtrack search"

2. Brute-force approaches to searching can even get swamped by "toy" problems.

   (a) How many distinct states are there in the state space for the version of the painted squares puzzle shown in Fig. 5.1?
   (b) What are the maximum and minimum numbers of states that there might be in a 4-square case of the puzzle?

(c) Suppose that each square in Fig. 5.1 can be flipped over, and that each side is painted with the same pattern on both faces of the square. What is the number of distinct arrangements of the four pieces in the 2×2 space?

(d) Let us define a "quadramino" as any arrangement of four of the squares of a square tiling of the plane, such that the four form a single connected group. Two such arrangements that are alike except for a translational displacement will be considered as equivalent. If the four pieces of Fig. 5.1 may be placed in any quadramino arrangement and the pieces may be flipped, what is the total number of distinct arrangements of the four squares?

3. What is the maximum distance (where distance is measured as the number of arcs in the shortest path between two nodes) between the initial state and a goal state, in a 4-square version of the painted squares puzzle (assuming that there *is* a goal state for the version!).

4. The way in which the squares are painted in a version of the painted squares puzzle apparently affects not only the number of solutions that exist, but the efficiency with which the backtracking algorithm finds a solution. Give an example of a version of the puzzle in which many solutions exist, but for which a lot of backtracking is required.

5. The solution to the painted squares puzzle in the text suffers from an inefficiency: pieces already placed are repeatedly rotated by the ORIENT function. Implement a version of the solution which avoids this redundancy. Determine experimentally how many calls to ROTATE_LIST are used by the old and new versions.

6. Suppose that the rules for the painted squares puzzles are changed, so that (a) a starting configuration consists of all the squares placed to fill the rectangular space, but not necessarily having their sides matching, and (b) two kinds of moves are allowed: (i) the rotation of a piece clockwise 90 degrees and (ii) interchanging a piece with an adjacent piece. What is the maximum number of states that there could be in the state space for an instance of this puzzle having a 4 by 4 rectangle (16 squares)? What is the minimum number of states that there might be?

7. In Chapter 4, it was shown how knowledge about objects could be organized in an inclusion hierarchy. Suppose that it is desired to build a more knowledge-based solver for the painted squares puzzles. The (hypothetical) approach is to first classify the squares according to types, where the types are based on the ways the squares are painted. Then, when a vacancy is to be filled that requires a particular kind of piece, the program examines various kinds of pieces that it has examples of, testing to see if

the kind of piece found "ISA" piece of the type required. Describe how types of painted squares could be defined so that an interesting inclusion hierarchy could be set up (without doing any programming).

8. A "straight-line dominoes" puzzle consists of a set of dominoes, and the object of the puzzle is to lay all the dominoes in a straight line so that the adjacent ends match. Discuss the difficulty of this kind of puzzle. How would a program to solve such puzzles be constructed?

9. The Four-peg version of the Towers of Hanoi puzzle is stated as follows: Four pegs, called A, B, C, and D, can each hold n rings at a time. There are n rings, $R_1, R_2, \ldots, R_n$, such that R_i is smaller than R_j whenever $i < j$. A legal placement of the rings on the pegs requires that (1) whenever any two rings appear on the same peg, the smaller one is above the larger one, and (2) all n rings must be on pegs. The starting placement consists of all rings placed on peg A. The goal placement consists of all rings placed on peg D. Describe a representation for the states of the space to be searched. Describe a procedure that generates the successors of a state.

10. Using the data and function definitions in the text, compare the solutions found by the method DEPTH_FIRST_SEARCH with those found by BREADTH_FIRST_SEARCH for the problems of finding paths from PARIS to STRASBOURG, STRASBOURG to PARIS, BORDEAUX to LYON, and LYON to BORDEAUX.

   (a) What are the paths found?

   (b) What conclusions can you make?

   (c) Which procedure is more sensitive to the order in which the cities neighboring each city appear on the property list?

   (d) Describe alternative data for which the two procedures would perform equally efficiently.

11. Modify the function DEPTH_FIRST_SEARCH, and thus create a new function QUASI_DEPTH_FIRST_SEARCH, by having the list L concatenated onto the beginning of OPEN after culling members which are also present on either OPEN or CLOSED. The result of evaluating

        (QUASI_DEPTH_FIRST_SEARCH 'RENNES 'AVIGNON)

should be

        (RENNES CAEN CALAIS NANCY DIJON LYON AVIGNON).

Find the result of evaluating:

(QUASI_DEPTH_FIRST_SEARCH 'AVIGNON 'RENNES).

If the adjacency information were reordered, would it be possible for QUASI_DEPTH_FIRST_SEARCH to ever find the longest path from Rennes to Avignon? (Such a longest path has 13 arcs.) Describe the kinds of paths that can be found with this variation.

12. Figure 5.13 shows the board and initial configuration for the puzzle "Cycle-Flip." The object is to transform the initial configuration into the goal configuration through a sequence of legal moves. The lettered nodes are called *islands* and the lines connecting them are called *gaps*. An oval on a gap indicates a *bridge*. For example, in the initial configuration there is a gap A-B, but A-C is not a gap. The gap B-C is bridged, but A-B is not. A

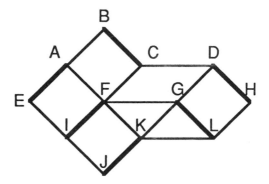

Figure 5.13: Initial configuration for "Cycle-Flip."

cycle is a sequence of gaps that are alternately bridged and unbridged that progress from island to island, forming a circuit of even length with no subcircuits. For example, (A-E, E-I, I-F, F-A) is a cycle, but (A-B, B-C, C-F, F-A) is not. Note that the former can be expressed more concisely as AEIF. We consider AEIF to be equivalent to EIFA, etc. A *flip* along a cycle is the act of making all the bridged gaps on the cycle unbridged and vice-versa. A legal move in Cycle-Flip is a flip along a cycle of length 4 or 6. The goal configuration is illustrated in Fig. 5.14.

(a) Describe a state-space representation for the game.

(b) Draw a piece of the state-space graph for the game which contains a solution path.

(c) Explain how this solution could be found automatically.

(d) Decide whether the solution is unique and explain why or why not.

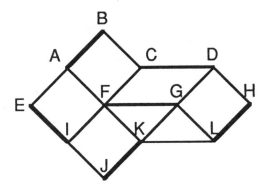

Figure 5.14: Goal configuration for "Cycle-Flip."

13. The plan for placing block C atop B on page 165 requires that 20 operations be performed by the robot. Suppose that the robot need not lift a block off a surface to move it left or right, but may slide it along. Give a shorter sequence of operations that accomplishes the task. Finally, suppose that no damage is done either by sliding or dropping blocks. What is the shortest plan that can be used now?

14. Develop a LISP program that uses breadth-first search to solve the robot planning problem in the text, employing preconditions on the operators. Explain and demonstrate how the choice of preconditions affects the time required to find a plan.

    (a) Use only preconditions that prevent collisions and prevent attempts to close the gripper when it is already closed or to open it when already open.

    (b) Add preconditions that allow the robot only three legal horizontal positions.

    (c) Add a precondition that allows the robot only three legal vertical positions.

    (d) Add preconditions that prevent opening or closing the gripper if there is no block between the fingers.

15. The (n, k) version of "Last One Loses" starts with a stack of pennies, n high. Two players, "Plus" and "Minus," alternate moves with Minus making the first move. In each move, a player may remove up to k pennies from the stack, but he must remove at least 1. The player stuck with the last move is the loser. Let the game configuration be represented

as $W(N)\sigma$, where N denotes the current number of pennies left, and σ is either "+" or "−" and indicates whose move it is. Note that $W(0)+$ and $W(0)−$ can never be reached, since $W(1)+$ and $W(1)−$ are terminal configurations.

(a) Draw the AND/OR graph for the case $(n, k) = (9, 3)$.

(b) Superimpose the solution graph for the same case (by hatching selected arcs of the AND/OR graph) that proves Plus can always force a win.

(c) For which (n, k) pairs is Last One Loses a determined game? Who wins in each case? By what strategy?

16. The game tree in Fig. 5.15 illustrates the possible moves, to a depth of 4, that can be made from the current position (at the root) in a hypothetical game between a computer and a human. The evaluation function is such that the computer seeks to maximize the score while the human seeks to minimize it. The computer has 5 seconds to make its move and 4 of these have been allocated to evaluating board positions. The order in which board positions are evaluated is determined as follows: The root is "searched." A node which is at ply 0, 1, 2, or 3 is *searched* by

- generating its children,
- statically evaluating the children,
- ordering its children by static value, in either ascending or descending order, so as to maximize the probability of alpha or beta cutoffs during the searches of successive children,
- searching the children if they are not in ply four, and
- backing up the minimum or maximum value from the children, where the value from each child is the backed-up value (if the child is not in ply four) or the static value (if the child is in ply four).

The computer requires 1/7 seconds to statically evaluate a node. Other times are negligible (move generation, backing up values, etc.). The computer chooses the move (out of those whose backed-up values are complete) having the highest backed-up value.

(a) Give the order in which nodes will be statically evaluated (indicate the ith node by putting the integer i in the circle for that node). Hint: the first 8 nodes have been done for you. Be sure to skip the nodes that alpha-beta pruning would determine as irrelevant. Indicate where cutoffs occur.

(b) Determine the backed-up values for the relevant nodes. (Fill in the squares.) Node Q has been done for you.

(c) Keeping in mind that it takes 1/7 seconds per static evaluation, what will be the computer's move?

(d) Now assume that it takes 1/8 seconds per static evaluation. What will be the computer's move?

17. Write a LISP program that plays "Tic-Tac-Toe" according to the scheme described on page 169 in the notes.

- You should be able to easily set the maximum depth of the program's search to any given ply.

- Include a function PRINTBOARD which shows a given board position in a neat format.

- Illustrate your program's behavior for 8 games as follows: 2 games at each of the four following maximum search depths: 1, 2, 4, and 6. In each pair, the human should play differently. In each game, show the board position after each of the actual moves chosen by your program. You may have the program play either O's or X's, but indicate which side the program is playing.

- After each board position printed, print out the number of times the evaluation function was computed to determine the move just made.

- At the end of each game, print out the number of times the evaluation function was applied to board positions during that game.

- Describe the tradeoff you observe between computation time (as measured by the number of computations of the evaluation function) and the skill of the program.

18. (term project) Write a program to play "Baroque Chess." This game is played with conventional chess pieces and set up as usual, except that the King's side rook for each player is turned upside-down. However, the names of pieces are changed, as are the rules of the game. The Baroque Chess names of the pieces are given below following their common names.

Pawn	= "Squeezer"
Knight	= "Leaper"
Bishop	= "Imitator"
(right-side-up) Rook	= "Freezer"
(upside-down) Rook	= "Coordinator"
Queen	= "Step-back"
King	= "King"

Most of the pieces may move like the Queens of ordinary chess. Exceptions are the Squeezers, Leapers (when capturing) and the Kings. However, many pieces have special requirements for making captures. The particular characteristics of each kind of piece are now given.

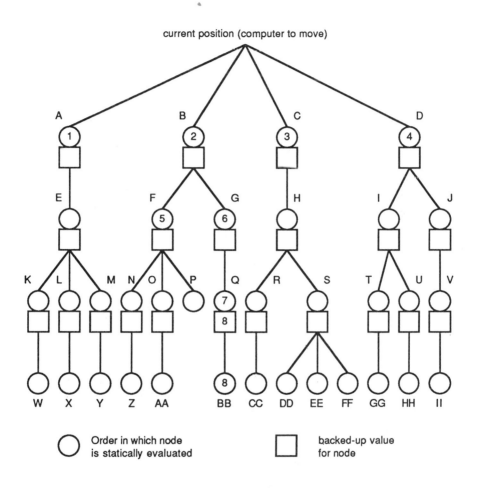

current position (computer to move)

Static values for nodes: A 4, B 15, C 13, D 10, E 20, F 9, G 8, H 10, I 10, J 8, K 5, L 20, M 3, N 7, 0 6, P 0, Q 9, R 12, S 10, T 15, U 10, V 9, W 7, X 22, Y 2, Z 7, AA 5, BB 8, CC 15, DD 12, EE 13, FF 13, GG 20, HH 22, II 18.

Figure 5.15: A hypothetical game tree.

- Squeezer—moves like a rook of ordinary chess, vertically or horizontally any number of squares. In order to capture an opponent's piece, the Squeezer must be moved so as to "sandwich" the piece between the Squeezer and another Squeezer. Two Squeezers sandwich an opposing piece by being on either side of it, either horizontally or vertically.

- Freezer—moves like a Queen. It does not capture other pieces. However, when it is adjacent (in any of the 8 neighboring squares) to an opponent's piece, the opponent may not move that piece.

- Coordinator—moves like a Queen. The Coordinator's row and the same player's King's column determine the location of a square on the board. If the coordinator is moved so as to make this square one where an opponent's piece stands, the piece is captured.

- Leaper—moves like a Queen, except that when capturing, it must complete its move by jumping over the piece it captures to the next square in the same line; that square must be vacant to permit the capture.

- Step-back—moves (and looks) like a Queen. However, in order to capture a piece, it must begin its move in a position adjacent to the piece (i.e., in any of the 8 neighboring squares), and then it must move exactly one square in the direction away from the piece.

- King—moves (and looks) like a normal chess King, and it captures like a normal chess King; (however, there is no "castling" move in Baroque Chess). The game is finished when a King is captured (there is no checkmating or need to say "check" in Baroque Chess).

- Imitator—normally moves like a Queen. However, in order to capture a piece, an Imitator must do as the captured piece would do to capture. In addition, if an Imitator is adjacent to the opponent's Freezer, the Imitator freezes the Freezer, and then neither piece may be moved until one of the two is captured.

Making the game even more interesting is a rule which makes all the captures implied by a move effective. For example, a Squeezer may move to simultaneously sandwich two opposing pieces and capture both of them. Another example would be a situation where an Imitator, in one move, steps back from a Step-back (capturing it) and in its new position sandwiches a Squeezer and captures it.

Chapter 6

Logical Reasoning

6.1 Motivation

In Chapter 4 we saw how deductions of the following form could be made by a computer program: Given that a dog is a mammal and a mammal is an animal, it may be concluded that a dog is an animal. This deduction was performed by simply applying the transitivity rule known to hold for the ISA relation. While useful, this kind of deduction is relatively restricted, and a more general capability is usually needed. By using mathematical logic, we will gain a good measure of generality.

There are several pioneers of artificial intelligence who believe that mathematical logic provides the best knowledge representation language. Some groups, such as the leaders of Japan's "Fifth Generation Project" are betting that programming in languages that resemble or are based on the predicate calculus will be the way of the future. Whether or not they are right, logic and algorithms for working with logic are important. There can be no doubt, however, that the methods of logic are powerful and that they are worth careful study by anyone interested in automatic problem solving.

We begin our exploration of the use of mathematical logic in computer deduction by illustrating several simple approaches that use the propositional calculus. Then we turn to the more powerful predicate calculus and examine some heuristics and strategies for trying to prove proposed conclusions.

6.2 Proofs in the Propositional Calculus

6.2.1 Perfect Induction

The propositional calculus provides a relatively simple framework within which basic concepts of automatic theorem proving can be illustrated. Below is an example of some statements that express information from which we wish to answer a question.

> If *thunk* is an English verb, then *thunk* is an English word. If *thunk* is an English word, then *thunk* is in *Noah's Lexicon*. *Thunk* is not in *Noah's Lexicon*.
>   Is *thunk* an English verb?

In order to express these statements (and a statement derived from the question) in the propositional calculus, we must agree on a set of atomic propositions. One suitable set of atomic propositions is the following:

- P: *Thunk* is an English verb.

- Q: *Thunk* is an English word.

- R: *Thunk* is in *Noah's Lexicon*.

The original statements we call *premises*. The premises expressed in propositional calculus are now as follows:

$$P \to Q, Q \to R, \neg R$$

The question would be answered if we could prove the proposition P from the premises, or alternatively if we could prove $\neg P$. Since this is a small problem, we can easily employ an exhaustive examination of all possible assignments of truth values to the propositions P, Q and R to check for the validity of either possible conclusion. All the possible combinations are listed in the *truth table* shown in Fig. 6.1.

Variables			Premises			Trial Conclusions	
P	Q	R	$P \to Q$	$Q \to R$	$\neg R$	P	$\neg P$
T	T	T	T	T	F	T	F
T	T	F	T	F	T	T	F
T	F	T	F	T	F	T	F
T	F	F	F	T	T	T	F
F	T	T	T	T	F	F	T
F	T	F	T	F	T	F	T
F	F	T	T	T	F	F	T
F	F	F	T	T	T	F	T

Figure 6.1: Truth table used in answering the question of whether or not *thunk* is an English verb.

We first check the validity of P as a conclusion by examining every row in which all three premises are true. The conclusions must also be true in these rows. In this example there is only one row where all premises are true (the bottom row). We see here that the potential conclusion P is false here (and therefore not the correct answer) whereas $\neg P$ is true and corresponds to the correct answer: *Thunk* is not an English verb.

The truth-table method just illustrated is called *perfect induction*. Constructing truth tables can easily be a big job even for a computer if there are more than just a few propositional symbols. With n symbols, a truth table requires 2^n rows. Consequently, other methods have been developed for proving conclusions from premises. One of these is Wang's algorithm. While in the worst case, Wang's algorithm may still require $O(2^n)$ time to prove a theorem, it usually is much faster.

6.2.2 Wang's Algorithm

To begin proving a theorem with Wang's algorithm, all premises are written on the left-hand side of an arrow that we may call the "sequent arrow" ($\Rightarrow_s$). The desired conclusion is written to the right of the sequent arrow. Thus we have:

$$P \rightarrow Q, Q \rightarrow R, \neg R \Rightarrow_s \neg P.$$

This string of symbols is called a "sequent." This particular sequent contains four "top-level" formulas; there are three on the left and one on the right. (It contains more than four formulas if we count embedded ones such as the formula P in $P \rightarrow Q$.)

Successively, we apply transformations to the sequent that break it down into simpler ones. The general form of a sequent is:

$$F_1, \ldots, F_m \Rightarrow_s F_{m+1}, \ldots, F_{m+n},$$

where each F_i is a formula. Intuitively, this sequent may be thought of as representing the larger formula,

$$F_1 \wedge \cdots \wedge F_m \rightarrow F_{m+1} \vee \cdots \vee F_{m+n}.$$

Here are the transformation (R1 through R5) and termination (R6 and R7) rules:

- R1: If one of the top-level formulas of a sequent has the form $\neg X$, we may drop the negation and move X to the other side of the sequent arrow. Here X is any formula, e.g., $(P \vee \neg Q)$. If the negation is to the left of the sequent arrow, we call the transformation "NOT on the left;" otherwise it is "NOT on the right."

- R2: If a top-level formula on the left of the arrow has the form $X \wedge Y$, or on the right of the arrow has the form $X \vee Y$, the connective may be replaced by a comma. The two forms of this rule are called "AND on the left" and "OR on the right," respectively.

- R3: If a top-level formula on the left has the form $X \lor Y$, we may replace the sequent with two new sequents, one having X substituted for the occurrence of $X \lor Y$, and the other having Y substituted. This is called "splitting on the left" or "OR on the left."

- R4: If the form $X \land Y$ occurs on the right, we may also split the sequent as in Rule R3. This is "splitting on the right" or "AND on the right."

- R5: A formula (at any level) of the form $(X \to Y)$ may be replaced by $(\neg X \lor Y)$, thus eliminating the implication connective.

- R6: A sequent is considered proved if some top-level formula X occurs on both the left and right sides of the sequent arrow. Such a sequent is called an *axiom*. No further transformations are needed on this sequent, although there may remain other sequents to be proved. (The original sequent is not proved until all the sequents obtained from it have been proved.)

- R7: A sequent is proved invalid if all formulas in it are individual proposition symbols (i.e., no connectives), and no symbol occurs on both sides of the sequent arrow. If such a sequent is found, the algorithm terminates; the original "conclusion" does not follow logically from the premises.

We may now proceed with the proof for our example about whether *thunk* is an English verb. We label the sequents generated starting with S_1 for the initial one. The proof is shown in Fig. 6.2.

Wang's algorithm always converges on a solution to the given problem. Every application of a transformation makes some progress either by eliminating a connective and thus shortening a sequent (even though this may create a new sequent as in the case of R3), or by eliminating the connective "$\to$". The order in which rules are applied has some bearing on the length of a proof or refutation, but not on the outcome itself.

6.2.3   Wang's Algorithm in LISP: "PROVER"

The program PROVER, which is listed below, provides an implementation of Wang's algorithm. Like the programs SHRINK and LEIBNIZ of Chapter 3, it uses the function MATCH extensively.

The first function, "PROVER," has the same name as the program as a whole, and it is the top-level function. To run the program the user types (PROVER) and responds to the prompts it gives. PROVER consists of a PROG form that implements an indefinite loop. In each cycle, a logical expression is accepted from the user; then it is checked for being well-formed, and it is converted so that the logical connective IMPLIES is eliminated, and then it is passed to VALID1 as the right-hand side of a sequent whose left-hand size is NIL. If the result is that

Label	Sequent	Comments
S1:	$P \to Q, Q \to R, \neg R \Rightarrow_s \neg P$	Initial sequent.
S2:	$\neg P \vee Q, \neg Q \vee R, \neg R \Rightarrow_s \neg P$	Two applications of R5.
S3:	$\neg P \vee Q, \neg Q \vee R \Rightarrow_s \neg P, R$	R1.
S4:	$\neg P, \neg Q \vee R \Rightarrow_s \neg P, R$	S4 and S5 are obtained from S3 with R3. Note that S4 is an axiom since P appears on both sides of the sequent arrow at the top level.
S5:	$Q, \neg Q \vee R \Rightarrow_s \neg P, R$	The other sequent generated by the application of R3.
S6:	$Q, \neg Q \Rightarrow_s \neg P, R$	S6 and S7 are obtained from S5 using R3.
S7:	$Q, R \Rightarrow_s \neg P, R$	This is an axiom.
S8:	$Q \Rightarrow_s \neg P, R, Q$	Obtained from S6 using R1. S8 is an axiom. The original sequent is now proved, since it has successfully been transformed into a set of three axioms with no unproved sequents left over.

Figure 6.2: A proof using Wang's algorithm.

the expression is a tautology, then the PROVER prints "VALID" and otherwise it prints "(NOT VALID)".

```
; PROVER.LSP -- Verifies propositions using Wang's algorithm
(DEFUN PROVER ()
  (PROG (S)
  LOOP (PRINT '(PLEASE ENTER PROPOSITION OR H OR R))
       (TERPRI)
       (SETQ S (READ))
       (COND ((EQ S 'H)                     ; H is the HELP command...
              (PRINT '(HERES AN EXAMPLE))
              (PRINT '((A AND (NOT B)) IMPLIES A)) )
             ((EQ S 'R) (RETURN NIL))   ; R is the RETURN command.
             (T (COND ((VALID1 NIL (LIST (FORMAT S)))
                       (PRINT 'VALID)
                       (TERPRI))
                      (T (PRINT '(NOT VALID)))) )) )
       (GO LOOP) ) )
```

Although the function PROVER is the top-level function, the recursive function
VALID1 does most of the work. It is implemented in a production-rule style
where each production rule is one of Wang's rewriting rules, except the first
production rule, which tests to see if a sequent is an axiom (i.e., that there is a
nontrivial intersection of the left-hand and right-hand sides of the sequent).

```
(DEFUN VALID1 (L R)       ;check validity with Wang's rules.
                          ; L is the left side of the sequent.
                          ; R is the right side of the sequent.
  (PROG (X Y Z)
    (RETURN
      (COND
        ((INTERSECT L R) T)      ;test for axiom
            ;NOT on the left...
        ((MATCH '((* X) (NWFF Y) (* Z)) L)
              (VALID1 (APPEND X Z)
                      (APPEND R (CDR Y)) ) )
            ;NOT on the right...
        ((MATCH '((* X) (NWFF Y) (* Z)) R)
              (VALID1 (APPEND L (CDR Y))
                      (APPEND X Z) ) )
            ;OR on the right...
        ((MATCH '((* X) (ORWFF Y) (* Z)) R)
              (VALID1 L
                (APPEND X (LIST (CAR Y)) (CDDR Y) Z) ) )
            ;AND on the left...
        ((MATCH '((* X) (ANDWFF Y) (* Z)) L)
              (VALID1 (APPEND X (LIST (CAR Y)) (CDDR Y) Z)
                      R) )
            ;OR on the left...
        ((MATCH '((* X) (ORWFF Y) (* Z)) L)
              (AND (VALID1 (APPEND X (LIST (CAR Y)) Z) R)
                   (VALID1 (APPEND X (CDDR Y) Z) R) ) )
            ;AND on the right...
        ((MATCH '((* X) (ANDWFF Y) (* Z)) R)
              (AND (VALID1 L (APPEND X (LIST (CAR Y)) Z))
                   (VALID1 L (APPEND X (CDDR Y) Z)) ) ) ) ) ) )


(DEFUN INTERSECT (A B)   ;return T if lists A and B have at
                         ;least one top-level element in common.
  (COND ((NULL A) NIL)
        ((NULL B) NIL)
        ((MEMBER (CAR A) B) T)
        (T (INTERSECT (CDR A) B)) ) )
```

The following functions manipulate a formula or part of a formula. WFF checks
that it is syntactically correct, i.e., a well-formed formula. FORMAT calls WFF
to verify the syntax and then transforms the formula into one that does not use
the implication operator IMPLIES. ORWFF, ANDWFF, and NWFF determine
whether or not a formula is a disjunction, conjunction or negation, respectively.
OP returns T if its argument is a valid binary operator.

WFF is a predicate that is true if its argument is a well-formed formula of the
propositional calculus. That is, the argument is either a variable (the first clause
tests this, although it doesn't make sure that the atom is not numeric or NIL), or
it is a compound well-formed formula that involves the unary operator NOT, or
it is compound with a binary operator, with a form (*WFF1 OP1 WFF2*) where
WFF1 and *WFF2* are well-formed formulas and *OP1* is one of the allowed binary
operators AND, OR, or IMPLIES.

```
(DEFUN WFF (X)      ;return T if X is a well-formed formula
   (COND ((ATOM X) T)
         ((MATCH '(NOT (WFF DUM)) X) T)
         ((MATCH '((WFF DUM) (OP DUM) (WFF DUM)) X) T)
         (T NIL) ) )

(DEFUN ORWFF (X) (COND ((ATOM X) NIL) (T (EQ (CADR X) 'OR))))

(DEFUN ANDWFF (X) (COND ((ATOM X) NIL) (T (EQ (CADR X) 'AND))))

(DEFUN NWFF (X) (COND ((ATOM X) NIL) (T (EQ (CAR X) 'NOT))))

(DEFUN OP (X)       ; test if X is a binary operation.
   (MEMBER X '(AND OR IMPLIES)) )

(DEFUN FORMAT (X)    ;check syntax and eliminate IMPLIES.
   (COND ((ATOM X) X)
         ((NULL (WFF X))
          (PRINT '(SYNTAX ERROR))
          (RETURN NIL))
         ((NWFF X) (LIST 'NOT (FORMAT (CADR X))))
         ((EQUAL (CADR X) 'IMPLIES)
          (LIST (LIST 'NOT (FORMAT (CAR X)))
                'OR
                (FORMAT (CADDR X)) ) )
         (T (LIST (FORMAT (CAR X))
                  (CADR X)
                  (FORMAT (CADDR X)) )) ) ) )
```

Here is another example problem. This example is used to illustrate the
PROVER. Let us assume the following: Either Jan buys a loaf of bread to-

day or she eats yogurt for breakfast. Jan doesn't eat yogurt and eggs at the same meal. We wish to prove that if Jan eats eggs for breakfast today, then she buys a loaf of bread. Our first task is to re-express our assumptions and desired conclusion in the form of primitive statements and logical relations among them. In order to keep our descriptions reasonably short, we use capital letters to abbreviate the primitive statements. Here are the primitive statements.

A. Jan buys a loaf of bread today.
B. Jan eats yogurt for breakfast today.
C. Jan eats eggs for breakfast today.

Here are the premises:

```
(A OR B)
(NOT (B AND C))
```

and the desired conclusion is

```
(C IMPLIES A)
```

The problem of showing that Jan buys bread today can be given to the prover in the following form:

```
(((A OR B) AND (NOT (B AND C))) IMPLIES (C IMPLIES A)).
```

When the program is invoked by typing (PROVER), the input S-expression is read and assigned as the value of the atom S. In the PROVER function, the input expression is compared with the atoms H and R to check for a help request or a command to return to top-level LISP. In the case of our example, VALID1 is called with two arguments: NIL and the result of applying FORMAT to S. FORMAT eliminates occurrences of the IMPLIES connective. The result of this is

```
((NOT ((A OR B) AND (NOT (B AND C)))) OR ((NOT C) OR A))
```

VALID1 is called with L equal to NIL and R equal to the above expression. The production which matches is the rule for OR on the right. This results in a call at level 2 to VALID1 with R as before but the OR dropped (and a set of parentheses dropped also). The next production which is applied is that for NOT on the right, leading to a level-3 call with

```
L = (((A OR B) AND (NOT (B AND C))))
R = (((NOT C) OR A))
```

"OR on the right" is applied again, making (NOT C) and A separate formulas in the list R. Then "NOT on the right" is again applied, resulting in a level-6 call to VALID1 with

```
L = ((A OR B) (NOT (B AND C)) C)
R = (A)
```

Next, "NOT on the left" is applied, making R = (A (B AND C)). A level-7 call with L = ((A OR B) C) and R = (A (B AND C)) brings about an application of "OR on the left" which yields two recursive calls at level 8 to VALID1. The first of these occurs with L = (A C) and R = (A (B AND C)). The sequent represented by this pair of L and R is an axiom, since A occurs as a top-level element of each, and this is noticed by the first production, and it therefore causes a return with T. The second recursive call at level 8 proceeds with L = (B C) and R = (A (B AND C)). The rule for "AND on the right" fires, and there are then two recursive calls at level 9. The first of these, with L = (B C) and R = (A B) returns T, since the intersection of L and R is (B) and therefore nonempty. The second of these finds that lists (B C) and (A C) share an element in common, and also returns T. From here on, the recursion unwinds, and the value T works its way up to the top-level call of VALID1. Then, the expression (PRINT 'VALID), in the function PROVER, is activated, and the atom VALID is printed, followed by a blank line. PROVER then loops back and prompts for another formula from the user.

While somewhat more efficient than the method of perfect induction, Wang's algorithm does not employ the kind of problem-solving strategy that humans seem to use. A system based upon a more strategic approach is described next.

6.2.4 The "Logic Theory Machine"

One of the earliest investigations in artificial intelligence was a study of automatic deduction using problem-solving heuristics [Newell et al 1957]. The objective of this study was to develop a program that could prove simple theorems from *Principia Mathematica* by Russell and Whitehead, using a human-like approach. The program achieved the objective and illustrates a different approach to theorem proving. The program was an improvement over the "British Museum algorithm." That brute-force algorithm attempted to prove a theorem by the following procedure:

- Start with the axioms and consider these to be one-step proofs of themselves.

- At the nth step, generate all theorems derivable in n steps by applying the "methods" to the theorems at the $n - 1^{th}$ step, exhaustively.

- At each step, eliminate duplicates and check to see whether or not the desired formula has been proved.

The methods consist of *substitution*, *replacement*, or *detachment* and are described below.

Needless to say, the British Museum algorithm leads to a combinatorial explosion: although there are only 5 one-step proofs (which correspond to the five axioms listed below), there are 42 four-step proofs, 115 six-step proofs, and 246 eight-step proofs, etc.

The Logic Theory Machine (as the program by Newell *et al* was called), used a more sensible approach. It attempted to do such things as to break the problem to be solved into subproblems and solve each one in turn. It used the following methods:

Substitution: From any known theorem one can get a new one by replacing all occurrences of a particular variable by some arbitrary formula.

Detachment: If B is to be proved and $A \to B$ is a theorem or axiom, then it suffices to prove A.

Chaining: If $A \to C$ is to be proved and $A \to B$ is a theorem or axiom, then it suffices to prove $B \to C$. This is called *forward chaining*. Alternatively, if $A \to C$ is to be proved and $B \to C$ is a theorem or axiom, then proving $A \to B$ is enough. Naturally, this is called *backward chaining*.

The axioms from *Principia Mathematica* used by the Logic Theory Machine are the following (for the propositional calculus):

Axiom	Name
$P \vee P \to P$	"Taut"
$Q \to P \vee Q$	"Add"
$P \vee Q \to Q \vee P$	"Perm"
$P \vee (Q \vee R) \to Q \vee (P \vee R)$	"Assoc"
$(Q \to R) \to ((P \vee Q) \to (P \vee R))$	"Sum"

The following example illustrates how a proof is done with the system of *Principia Mathematica*.

To Prove: $(P \to \neg P) \to \neg P$

formula	how derived
$\neg P \vee \neg P \to \neg P$	Subst. $(\neg P/P)$ in Taut.
$(P \to \neg P) \to \neg P$	Def. of "$\to$", Q.E.D.

As an exercise, the reader is encouraged to try to prove the following theorem.

$$P \to \neg(\neg P)$$

The Logic Theory Machine began by putting the formula to be proved on a list called the *subproblem list*. It went into its general loop, where it would examine a problem on the subproblem list, and try to work with it using substitution, detachment and chaining. The length of the subproblem list would grow and occasionally shrink (when subproblems were actually solved), and a list of theorems would grow. The program was successful in proving a large number of the theorems listed in *Principia Mathematica* in a reasonable amount of time. This study was important in demonstrating that strategy could be effectively employed in proof finding.

Before we examine logical reasoning methods for the predicate calculus, it is helpful to see the "resolution" method in the propositional calculus, where its mechanics are relatively simple.

6.2.5 The Resolution Principle in the Propositional Calculus

Another method for proving theorems of the propositional calculus makes use of the "resolution principle." This method, unlike Wang's algorithm, extends nicely to handle problems in the predicate calculus as well as the propositional calculus. It is very important for that reason. A very simple form of the resolution principle is

$$P \vee Q, \neg P \vee R \to Q \vee R.$$

More generally, resolution allows us to take two "parent clauses" that share a complementary pair of "literals" and obtain a new "resolvent clause." In the propositional calculus, a *literal* is a proposition symbol (a variable such as P) with or without a negation sign in front of it (e.g., P, $\neg Q$, and $\neg R$ are literals). A *clause* is a formula which is a sum of literals, e.g., $P \vee \neg Q \vee \neg R$. A complementary pair of literals is a pair such that one literal is the negation of the other, e.g., P and $\neg P$. A general expression of the resolution principle for propositional logic is

$$L_1 \vee L_2 \vee \ldots \vee L_k, M_1 \vee M_2 \vee \ldots \vee M_m \to L_2 \vee \ldots \vee L_k \vee M_2 \vee \ldots \vee M_m$$

where $M_1 = \neg L_1$ (i.e., the first literal of one clause complements the first of the other clause).

If $k = 1$ or $m = 1$, this rule still makes sense. If both $k = 1$ and $m = 1$, the resolvent is called the *null clause* and denotes a contradiction. (If this seems mysterious, it may help to note that $\mathbf{F}$ is the identity element for disjunction; $L_1 \vee L_2 \vee L_3 = L_1 \vee L_2 \vee L_3 \vee \mathbf{F}$, and that if we remove all the L_i we are left with $\mathbf{F}$.) The null clause is denoted by the box symbol, "$\square$".

We now illustrate theorem proving by resolution with the example previously introduced.

Premises: $P \to Q, Q \to R, \neg R$
Clause form: $\neg P \vee Q, \neg Q \vee R, \neg R$
Desired Conclusion: $\neg P$

Traditionally, proof by resolution uses the *reductio ad absurdum* method, whereby the conclusion is negated and added to the list of premises with the aim of deriving a contradiction. Therefore we have an additional clause (in some cases several additional clauses) P for this example. We number our clauses C1 through C4.

Label	Clause	Where From
C1:	$\neg P \vee Q$	premise
C2:	$\neg Q \vee R$	premise
C3:	$\neg R$	premise
C4:	P	negation of conclusion
C5:	Q	resolve C1 with C4
C6:	R	resolve C2 with C5
C7:	$\square$	resolve C3 with C6

Since C7 is the null clause, we have derived a contradiction from the clauses C1 through C4 and proved that the desired conclusion $\neg P$ follows from the original premises.

6.3   Predicate Calculus Resolution

6.3.1   Preliminary Remarks

As discussed in Chapter 4, one cannot describe the inner structure of propositions using the propositional calculus. One can only manipulate whole statements and not the objects and predicates which constitute them. On the other hand, the *predicate* calculus does allow explicit expression of objects and predicates. It also provides for manipulations of objects using functions, and for making general statements using the universal quantifier, and also for existence statements using the existential quantifier.

6.3.2   An Example

Now we consider an example problem to illustrate how the resolution principle is applied in a predicate-calculus setting. This example deals with properties of numbers, including primality and oddness.

Let us suppose that the following premises are given: Any prime other than 2 is odd. The square of an odd number is odd. The number 7 is a prime. The number 7 is different from 2.

From these premises it is to be proved that the square of 7 is odd.

We can represent the premises and the conclusion in the predicate calculus; we begin by choosing predicates and functions with which to build up formulas. A reasonable set is the following group of three predicates and one function:

- $P(x)$: x is prime.

- $O(x)$: x is odd.

- $E(x, y)$: $x = y$

- $s(x) = x^2$

Now we may express the premises in the predicate calculus as follows:

- $\forall x((P(x) \land \neg E(x, 2)) \to O(x))$

- $\forall x(O(x) \to O(s(x)))$

- $P(7)$

- $\neg E(7, 2)$

The negation of the conclusion is represented by the formula: $\neg O(s(7))$.

Before we can apply the resolution principle, the premises and the negation of the conclusion must be in clause form (the process of obtaining clause form in the predicate calculus is explained in the next section). The clauses that we get are these:

- C1: $\neg P(x) \lor E(x, 2) \lor O(x)$

- C2: $\neg O(x) \lor O(s(x))$

- C3: $P(7)$

- C4: $\neg E(7, 2)$

- C5: $\neg O(s(7))$

We may now attempt to derive new clauses using the resolution principle. In order to obtain matching literals, it is usually necessary to make substitutions of terms for some of the variables in each clause. This substitution process is explained in detail in Subsection 6.3.4. The proof that the square of 7 is odd is shown here:

new clause	how derived
C6: $E(7, 2) \lor O(7)$	C1, C3 ($x = 7$)
C7: $O(7)$	C6, C4
C8: $O(s(7))$	C7, C2 ($x = 7$)
C9: $\square$	C8, C5

Now let us consider the steps required for predicate-calculus resolution in more detail, beginning with the job of obtaining clause form.

6.3.3   Putting a Formula into Clause Form

There are a number of details that must be attended to in order to put an arbitrary formula of the predicate calculus into clause form. We shall explain the sequence of steps required, considering them one at a time, on an example expression.

As in the propositional calculus, a clause consists of zero or more literals, connected by "$\vee$". Transforming a formula into clause form requires elimination of quantifiers (according to strict rules) as well as getting it into conjunctive normal form. The elimination of quantifiers must usually be performed first, since so doing often introduces negation signs that apply to the entire scopes of eliminated quantifiers.

Let us consider the formula

$$(\forall x)\{P(x) \rightarrow (\exists y)\{Q(x,y)\}\} \wedge (\forall x)\{\neg P(x) \rightarrow \neg(\exists y)\{Q(x,y)\}\}.$$

One interpretation of the predicates in this formula is: $P(x)$ iff x is composite (i.e., x is divisible by some number other than 1 or itself); $Q(x,y)$ iff x is not equal to y, and y divides x with no remainder.

Our first order of business in converting this to clause form is to eliminate the implication connectives ("$\rightarrow$"), using the rule $(P \rightarrow Q)$ iff $(\neg P \vee Q)$. This gives us

$$(\forall x)\{\neg P(x) \vee (\exists y)\{Q(x,y)\}\} \wedge (\forall x)\{\neg\neg P(x) \vee \neg(\exists y)\{Q(x,y)\}\}.$$

Next we reduce the scope of each negation sign. Two rules that help here are DeMorgan's laws:

$$\neg(P \wedge Q)\text{iff}\neg P \vee \neg Q$$

$$\neg(P \vee Q)\text{iff}\neg P \wedge \neg Q$$

However, these are not applicable in the example here. Two rules regarding negations that precede quantifiers are the following:

$$\neg(\forall x)P(x)\text{iff}(\exists x)\neg P(x)$$

$$\neg(\exists x)P(x)\text{iff}(\forall x)\neg P(x)$$

Of course we reduce $\neg\neg P$ to P whenever we get the chance. Now we transform the negated existential quantification to get the new formula:

$$(\forall x)\{\neg P(x) \vee (\exists y)\{Q(x,y)\}\} \wedge (\forall x)\{P(x) \vee (\forall y)\{\neg Q(x,y)\}\}$$

Next we standardize the variables of the formula, giving each quantifier a variable with a different name. This renaming cannot change the meaning of the formula since each variable acts as a "dummy" for its corresponding quantifier anyway. Our formula is now:

$$(\forall x)\{\neg P(x) \vee (\exists y)\{Q(x,y)\}\} \wedge (\forall z)\{P(z) \vee (\forall w)\{\neg Q(z,w)\}\}$$

Next we eliminate the existential quantifiers using a technique known as Skolemization[1]. This works as follows. Suppose we have $(\forall x)(\exists y)\{P(x,y)\}$. This states that for each value of x we can find a y such that P of x and y. That is to say that one can imagine a function $f(x)$ which returns a value y that makes $P(x,y)$ true. If we allow ourselves the liberty of writing $(\forall x)\{P(x,f(x))\}$, then we obtain an expression logically equivalent to the former; however, the new formula uses a function symbol rather than a quantifier. Of course, if the existential quantifier had not been in the scope of the universal quantifier, there would be no functional dependency, and a constant symbol such as a could be used to replace the existentially quantified variable. That is, $(\exists x)\{P(x)\}$ is Skolemized to $P(a)$. Applying Skolemization, our example formula becomes:

$$(\forall x)\{\neg P(x) \lor Q(x,f(x))\} \land (\forall z)\{P(z) \lor (\forall w)\{\neg Q(z,w)\}\}$$

The functions introduced by Skolemization are called Skolem functions, and the constants are called Skolem constants. If several functions or several constants are introduced into a formula by Skolemization, they must each be given distinct symbols (e.g., f_1, f_2, etc., and a, b, c, etc.).

We now adopt the convention that all variables in the formula are universally quantified, so that the universal quantifiers themselves can be removed. The result for our example is:

$$\{\neg P(x) \lor Q(x,f(x))\} \land \{P(z) \lor \neg Q(z,w)\}.$$

Normally, at this stage, we would have to put the formula into conjunctive normal form. Coincidentally, our example is already in this form. In general, however, some changes to the formula are necessary. The distributive laws are generally helpful at this stage, and can be expressed in their propositional-calculus form as follows:

$$
\begin{aligned}
P \lor (Q \land R) &= (P \lor Q) \land (P \lor R) \\
P \land (Q \lor R) &= (P \land Q) \lor (P \land R)
\end{aligned}
$$

The final step is breaking up the formula into separate clauses. To do this we simply remove the conjunctions and list each conjunct as a separate clause. For our example, this results in the two clauses:

$$\neg P(x) \lor Q(x,f(x))$$

$$P(z) \lor \neg Q(z,w)$$

---

[1] named after the mathematician Thoralf A. Skolem.

6.3.4   Unification

In applying the resolution principle to clauses of the predicate calculus, detection
of complementary pairs of literals is more complicated than in the propositional
calculus, because the predicates take arguments, and the arguments in one literal are required to be compatible ("unifiable") with those in the corresponding
literal. For example, the pair of clauses

$$P(f(a), x) \vee Q(x)$$

$$\neg P(g(a), x) \vee R(x)$$

cannot be resolved because the first argument of P in the first clause is incompatible with that of P in the second clause; $f(a)$ and $g(a)$ don't match and can't
be made to match using any substitution of terms for variables. On the other
hand, the pair of clauses

$$P(f(a), x) \vee Q(x)$$

$$\neg P(y, g(b)) \vee R(g(b))$$

can be resolved. First, an operation called "unification" is performed: a new
version of the first clause is obtained by substituting $g(b)$ for x; also, a new
version of the second is obtained by substituting $f(a)$ for y. The two resulting
clauses, now unified, have a complementary pair of literals and resolve to yield
$Q(g(b)) \vee R(g(b))$.

6.3.5   A Unification Algorithm

In order to test a pair of clauses for resolvability, we apply the operation known as
unification, described in the preceding paragraphs. This testing process works
by matching one literal to another and performing substitutions of terms for
variables along the way. If at any point the process fails, the pair of literals
is not unifiable. On the other hand, it is often the case that there exists a
multitude of different substitutions that can unify a pair of literals. Some of these
substitutions can have further substitutions performed on them to yield some of
the others, and some substitutions are more useful than others for purposes of
deriving the null clause in a proof by resolution.

Let us assume that we have a whole set of literals to be unified (not just two):
$\{L_i\}$ where $i = 1, \ldots, k$. We seek a substitution

$$\Phi = \{(t_1, v_1), (t_2, v_2), \ldots, (t_n, v_n)\}$$

such that $L_1\Phi = L_2\Phi = \cdots = L_k\Phi$. In this notation $L_i\Phi$ is used to indicate
the result of making all the replacements of terms t_j for variables v_j specified
in Φ in all the variables' occurrences in L_i. As an example, we may take $L =
P(x, y, f(y), b)$ and $\Phi = \{(a, x), (f(z), y)\}$. Then $L\Phi = P(a, f(z), f(f(z)), b)$. In

addition, if S is a set, then $S\Phi$ denotes the set of literals formed by applying Φ to each member of S.

Let Φ be a substitution. Then Φ is a *most general unifier* of $S = \{L_1, L_2, \ldots, L_k\}$ provided that for any other unifier Φ' of S, there is some Φ'' such that $S\Phi' = S\Phi\Phi''$. That is, the effect of any unifier Φ' can be achieved by applying the most general unifier, Φ, followed by some additional substitution. A most general unifier leaves as many variables in the resulting literals as possible, but without introducing any unnecessary function symbols.

In order to find a most general unifier we proceed as follows. Let $\Phi \leftarrow \{\}$. We regard each L_i as a string of symbols and move left-to-right examining the corresponding symbols until a "disagreement" is found. The terms in this position form a *disagreement set*. If none of the terms in the disagreement set consists of a variable by itself, we give up because the set of literals cannot be unified by any substitution. Otherwise, we "convert the variables into terms" by adding pairs to the substitution of the form (t_p, v_p) where v_p is one of the variables and t_p is one of the terms. In order to add a pair (t_p, v_p) to a substitution $\Phi = \{(t_1, v_1), (t_2, v_2), \ldots, (t_k, v_k)\}$ it must be the case that v_p is not equal to any of $v_k, i = 1, \ldots, k$; we first apply the substitution $\{(t_p, v_p)\}$ to each of the $t_i, i = 1, \ldots, k$, and then we insert it into the resulting set. We continue to add such substitutions and simultaneously perform them on the literals until either the disagreement set is no longer a disagreement set, or no variables remain (in this case, we also give up). Once the disagreement has been taken care of, symbol examination is resumed (including the examination of symbols recently inserted by substitution). When and if the matching reaches the right end of all the literals, a unifier has been found (Φ). This unifier also happens to be a most general unifier. It can readily be seen that Φ actually is a unifier for the set of literals. In addition, we note that the algorithm for finding the unifier can be made to require time only proportional to the combined lengths of the literals in the input set.

Here is an example in which a unifier is found for a pair of literals. The two literals are:

$$L_1 = A(x, f(y))$$
$$L_2 = A(a, f(g(z)))$$

As the scan proceeds from left to right, the set Φ of substitutions gets larger each time a disagreement set is found and put into agreement.

$$\Phi \leftarrow \{\}$$
$$\Phi \leftarrow \{(a, x)\}$$
$$\Phi \leftarrow \{(a, x), (g(z), y)\}$$

This last substitution is a most general unifier for $\{L_1, L_2\}$. Another unifier for this set is

$$\Phi' = \{(a, x), (g(b), y), (b, z)\}.$$

However, this is not a most general unifier. It is possible to get Φ' from Φ by
making the additional replacement of b for z, but one cannot get Φ from Φ'
because variables may not be substituted for terms (the constant b is a term).

As previously mentioned, any given pair of clauses may yield zero, one, two
or many more resolvents. These can be found by finding complementary pairs
of literals and determining any existing most general unifiers for them and then
applying resolution.

6.3.6   A Unifier in LISP

Let us now examine a LISP program that implements one variation of the algorithm given above. The variation works with only a pair of literals rather than
an arbitrarily large set.

The program we give is reasonably efficient, although it could be made more
so (at a cost of reduced readability). It may attempt to perform substitutions
that have already been made; the removal of this redundancy is left as an exercise
for the reader.

The top-level function, UNIFY, initializes (to the empty list) a variable U
which is used to store the unifier (if any) as it is constructed. This function also
tests the predicate symbols for equality, and if successful, calls UNIFY1 to unify
the lists of arguments. Note that UNIFY and UNIFY1 may return either a list
of substitutions, which is possibly null, or the atom NOT_UNIFIABLE. If NIL
is returned, it means that the (sub)expressions are unified with no substitutions.

The program uses a straightforward representation for literals. The following
two statements set up test data corresponding to the literals $P(x, f(a))$ and
$P(b, y)$:

```
(SETQ L1 '(P X (F A)))
(SETQ L2 '(P B Y))
```

The program assumes that any negation signs have already been stripped off the
literals, and it therefore does not check for complementarity.

Further description of the functions is given in the comments.

```
; UNIFY.LSP
; A program that demonstrates unification of
; literals in the predicate calculus.

; The top-level procedure is UNIFY.
; It finds a most general unifier for 2 literals.
(DEFUN UNIFY (L1 L2)
  (PROG (U)
        (SETQ U NIL)  ; unifier is initially null.
        (RETURN
          (COND         ; make sure predicate symbols match:
```

```
              ((NULL (EQ (CAR L1) (CAR L2))) 'NOT_UNIFIABLE)
                 ; if all arguments can be unified,
                 ; return the list of substitutions:
              ((NULL (EQ (UNIFY1 (CDR L1) (CDR L2))
                        'NOT_UNIFIABLE))
               U)
              (T 'NOT_UNIFIABLE) ) ) ) )
```

```
; Recursive function UNIFY1 unifies lists of terms.
(DEFUN UNIFY1 (EXP1 EXP2)
  (COND ; if atomic and equal, no substitution necessary:
        ((EQ EXP1 EXP2) NIL)
        ; check for list length mismatch (a syntax error):
        ((OR (NULL EXP1) (NULL EXP2)) 'NOT_UNIFIABLE)
        ; if EXP1 is a variable, try to add a substitution:
        ((VARIABLEP EXP1) (ADD_PAIR EXP2 EXP1))
        ; handle the case when EXP2 is a variable similarly:
        ((VARIABLEP EXP2) (ADD_PAIR EXP1 EXP2))
        ; now, if either expression is atomic, it is a
        ; constant and there's no match since they're not EQ:
        ((OR (ATOM EXP1) (ATOM EXP2)) 'NOT_UNIFIABLE)
        ; the expressions must be non-atomic; do recursively.
        ; apply current substitutions before unifying the CARs.
        ((NULL (EQ (UNIFY1 (DO_SUBST (CAR EXP1) U)
                           (DO_SUBST (CAR EXP2) U) )
                   'NOT_UNIFIABLE))
         (UNIFY1 (CDR EXP1) (CDR EXP2)) )
        ; if the CARs are not unifiable, return NOT_UNIFIABLE:
        (T 'NOT_UNIFIABLE) ) )
```

```
; The function ADD_PAIR attempts to add a (term-variable)
; pair to the the substitution list.  If the variable occurs
; in the term, then it returns NOT_UNIFIABLE.  Otherwise it
; substitutes the term for any occurrences of the variable
; in terms already in U, and puts the new pair on the front
; of the list.
(DEFUN ADD_PAIR (TERM VAR)
  (COND ((OCCURS_IN VAR TERM) 'NOT_UNIFIABLE)
        (T (SETQ U (CONS (LIST TERM VAR)
                         (SUBST U TERM VAR) ))) ) )
```

```
; Do all substitutions in L on EXP in reverse order:
(DEFUN DO_SUBST (EXP L)
  (COND ((NULL L) EXP)
```

```
        (T (SUBST (DO_SUBST EXP (CDR L))
                  (CAAR L)
                  (CADAR L) )) ) )

; Substitute X for each occurrence of Y in L:
(DEFUN SUBST (L X Y)
  (COND ((EQ L Y) X)
        ((ATOM L) L)
        (T (CONS (SUBST (CAR L) X Y)
                 (SUBST (CDR L) X Y) )) ) )

; Test EXP to see if it is a variable:
(DEFUN VARIABLEP (EXP)
  (MEMBER EXP '(X Y Z W)) )

; Test to see if ELT occurs in EXP at any level.
; ELT is assumed to be atomic:
(DEFUN OCCURS_IN (ELT EXP)
  (COND ((EQ ELT EXP) T)
        ((ATOM EXP) NIL)
        (T (OR (OCCURS_IN ELT (CAR EXP))
               (OCCURS_IN ELT (CDR EXP)) )) ) )
```

The following statements provide some tests for the program:

```
(TRACE UNIFY UNIFY1 DO_SUBST)
(UNIFY L1 L2)

(SETQ L3 '(P (F X) (G A X)))
(SETQ L4 '(P (F (H B)) (G X Y)))
(UNIFY L3 L4)

(SETQ L5 '(P X))
(SETQ L6 '(P (F X)))
(UNIFY L5 L6)

(SETQ L7 '(P X (F Y) X))
(SETQ L8 '(P Z (F Z) A))
(SETQ U (UNIFY L7 L8))
(DO_SUBST L7 U)
(DO_SUBST L8 U)
```

The example with L5 and L6, above, demonstrates that the program correctly performs the "occurs check" and reports that L5 and L6 are not unifiable. The last example demonstrates that substitutions are performed correctly. If the substitution list were reversed, the results of making the substitutions in U on L7 and L8 would no longer match.

6.3.7 Factors and Resolvents

It sometimes happens that two or more literals within the same clause may be unified. For example, the clause $C = P(x) \vee Q(x) \vee Q(f(a))$ contains two literals which can be unified with the substitution $\Phi = \{(f(a), x)\}$. The result of applying this unifying substitution to the clause and removing the redundancy in the literals is called a *factor* of the original clause. In this example, the factor is $C\Phi$ or $P(f(a)) \vee Q(f(a))$.

Suppose that we have two parent clauses C_1 and C_2, with no variables in common, such that L_1 is a literal of C_1 and L_2 is a literal of C_2, and such that L_1 and $\neg L_2$ have a most general unifier Φ. Then the following clause is a *binary resolvent* of C_1 and C_2:

$$(C_1\Phi - L_1\Phi) \vee (C_2\Phi - L_2\Phi)$$

where $C - L$ denotes the clause obtained from C by removing literal L.

We define a *resolvent* of parent clauses C_1 and C_2 to be a binary resolvent either of C_1 and C_2, of C_1 and a factor of C_2, of C_2 and a factor of C_1, or of a factor of C_1 and a factor of C_2. For example, if $C_1 = P(x, f(a)) \vee Q(x) \vee Q(f(y))$ and $C_2 = \neg Q(f(b)) \vee R(z)$, then $C_3 = P(f(y), f(a)) \vee Q(f(y))$ is a factor of C_1 and $C_4 = P(f(b), f(a)) \vee R(z)$ is a binary resolvent of C_3 and C_2. Thus C_4 is a resolvent of C_1 and C_2.

The definition of *resolvent* just given is known as the "resolution principle," or simply "resolution." It is an inference rule that can yield new clauses from an initial set of clauses. Resolution is sufficiently powerful that no other rule is needed in order to assure that all logically implied clauses can be obtained. This may be stated another way: the resolution principle is logically complete; if a set of clauses is inconsistent (logically implies a contradiction) then the resolution principle is sufficient to demonstrate the inconsistency. As we shall see later, a restricted form of resolution is the basis of the PROLOG language.

We may now define the term "deduction." Let S be a set of clauses. A *deduction* of a clause C from S is a finite sequence $C_1, C_2, \ldots, C_k$, where each C_i is either a member of S or a resolvent of two clauses preceding it in the sequence, and $C_k = C$.

In the next section we prove that the resolution principle is logically complete. In order to do so, we first prove a result known as Herbrand's theorem.

6.4 The Logical Completeness of Resolution

In this section, we justify the claim behind the power of the resolution principle: that the resolution principle is logically complete. The fact that resolution is complete, in turn, makes it possible to build automated reasoning systems that require only one inference rule (resolution), yet provide as much power as any other predicate-calculus inference system.

6.4.1   Semantic Trees

In order to provide something of a foundation on which to base our discussion of the resolution method, we will begin with the notion of a "semantic tree." Then we will introduce some tools for establishing logical validity of a formula, and finally show how resolution provides a reliable method for finding logical inconsistency when such inconsistency is present.

Before we discuss semantic trees for predicate-calculus formulas, we present the propositional-calculus version. Consider the propositional calculus expression $P \vee Q$. A *semantic tree* for this consists of a balanced binary tree, each level of which is associated with some variable, here either P or Q. This is illustrated in Fig. 6.3. Each path from the root to the bottom of the tree corresponds to an assignment of truth values to proposition symbols (such an assignment is called an "interpretation" for the symbols). At the leaves of the tree, the truth values for the given expression appear.

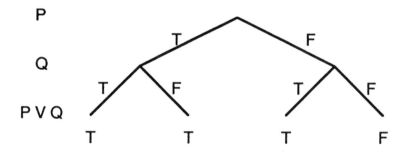

Figure 6.3: A semantic tree for $P \vee Q$.

There is a similarity between semantic trees and truth tables. They generally carry the same information. However, as we shall see, there is an advantage in using the idea of semantic trees when we explain how resolution works.

6.4.2   The Herbrand Universe and Herbrand Base

Let us now turn to the predicate calculus. In order to construct semantic trees for expressions of the predicate calculus, we must be able to assign truth values to the component parts. When variables are involved, one cannot easily do this, as the truth of a predicate usually depends upon the particular values of its arguments, and variables are simply not particular enough.

Suppose our predicate calculus expression is $P(x) \vee Q(y)$. If it is understood that x and y refer to positive integers, a semantic tree for this expression would require two levels for every positive integer (an infinite tree). The beginning of this tree might look like Fig. 6.4.

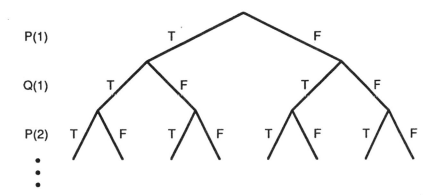

Figure 6.4: Top of semantic tree for $P(x) \vee Q(y)$.

In this example, the positive integers are playing the role of the *universe* of objects. If the universe were something finite, the job of constructing a complete semantic tree might be possible. On the other hand, it still might be made difficult by the fact that one must consider the results of applying functions to objects as though they were new objects.

Logical consistency of a set of formulas should not depend in any way upon the particular universe of objects one may wish to consider. As a result of this observation, we are free to choose a universe to suit our purpose. Such a universe should be as simple as possible, except that it should contain enough objects in it to ensure that we can establish logical inconsistency by looking at a semantic tree based on that universe.

We say that a formula is a *sentence* iff all its variables are quantified. Then, the "Herbrand universe" for a particular sentence Ψ is precisely the suitable universe we need. It is defined as follows: Let G be the set of constants appearing in Ψ. If G is empty, then let G be $\{a\}$. Here "a" is an arbitrary symbol. Let F_1 be the set of unary functions appearing in Ψ, and in general let F_i be the set of i-ary functions in Ψ. The *Herbrand universe* is defined to be the closure of G with respect to all the functions in all the F_i's.

If there is at least one function of arity 1 or more (that is, taking k arguments for some $k \geq 1$), then the Herbrand universe is necessarily infinite. For example, the Herbrand universe for the sentence $(\forall x)(\forall y)P(f(x), y)$ is

$$\{a, f(a), f(f(a)), \ldots\}.$$

If there are no functions, although there may be constants, then the Herbrand universe is finite.

The Herbrand *base* for a sentence Ψ is the set of all variable-free atomic formulas that one can construct by substituting elements of the Herbrand universe for variables in the propositions of Ψ. For the sentence $(\forall x)(\forall y)P(f(x), y)$ we have the following Herbrand base:

$$\{P(f(a), a), P(f(f(a)), a), P(f(a), f(a)), P(f(f(a)), f(a)), \ldots\}.$$

As a second example, consider the formula, $(\exists y)(\forall x)(P(x) \rightarrow Q(x, y))$ The Herbrand universe now is finite: $\{a\}$, and the Herbrand base is also finite:

$$\{P(a), Q(a, a)\}.$$

6.4.3   Herbrand's Theorem

An *interpretation* is defined to be a mapping which assigns either the value **T** or the value **F** to each element of the Herbrand base. If n is the number of elements in the Herbrand base, then there are 2^n possible interpretations. When the Herbrand base is infinite, the number of possible interpretations is vastly more infinite (uncountably infinite). In this case, there is no possibility of enumerating each interpretation and attempting to verify the validity of a sentence by perfect induction.

A *model* for a sentence or set of sentences is an interpretation which makes the sentence (or all the sentences in the set) true. For a sentence to be logically valid, every interpretation for the sentence must be a model. If no models exist for a sentence, then it is a contradiction, and it is unsatisfiable.

Resolution makes use of an essential result known as *Herbrand's theorem*. This theorem is stated as follows:

Herbrand's Theorem: Let Ψ be a formula in conjunctive normal form. Then Ψ is a unsatisfiable if and only if there exists an inconsistent finite set of variable-free instances of clauses of Ψ.

Proof: We first prove the forward implication. Suppose that Ψ is unsatisfiable. Let T be a semantic tree for Ψ based upon the Herbrand universe for Ψ. Then each path from the root in T must eventually reach a node at which one of the members of Ψ is falsified; otherwise, there would exist an interpretation of Ψ and Ψ would be satisfiable. Let Ψ' be the set of variable-free instances of members of Ψ that are falsified at these nodes. The number of these instances is finite, since none of them is infinitely far down the tree. The members of Ψ' form an inconsistent set since each interpretation of Ψ' falsifies at least one of them.

To prove the reverse implication, let us suppose that Ψ' is a finite, inconsistent set of variable-free instances of members of Ψ. Then every interpretation of Ψ'

falsifies a member of Ψ'. Any interpretation that falsifies a member C of Ψ' also falsifies the member of Ψ of which C is an instance. But every interpretation of Ψ is an interpretation of Ψ', and hence every interpretation of Ψ fails to satisfy Ψ' and also fails to satisfy Ψ. Thus Ψ is unsatisfiable. *Q. E. D.*

In order to illustrate the meaning of Herbrand's theorem, we present an example of a formula, its expression in conjunctive normal form, and a finite collection of variable-free instances of its clauses that are mutually inconsistent. The formula is: $(\forall x)[(P(x) \vee Q(f(x))) \wedge (\neg P(x) \wedge \neg Q(x))]$. In conjunctive normal form, its clauses are the members of the set S:

$$S = \{P(x) \vee Q(f(x)), \neg P(x), \neg Q(x)\}.$$

The following set of variable-free instances of these clauses is inconsistent:

$$\{P(a) \vee Q(f(a)), \neg P(a), \neg Q(f(a))\}.$$

Notice that the substitutions made to produce such an inconsistent set do not necessarily have to be the same. In the first two clauses, x was replaced by a, whereas in the third, $f(a)$ was used.

6.4.4   The Completeness of Resolution

Before we state and prove the completeness theorem for resolution, it is helpful to consider an example that shows the relationship between the resolution principle and Herbrand's theorem. In the example, the progress of the deduction procedure may be observed by visualizing particular subtrees of semantic trees called "failure trees."

Let us continue with the preceding set of clauses to build a semantic tree. This particular semantic tree is infinite since the Herbrand base is infinite (there is a function symbol f present in the original sentence).

To show that the original formula is unsatisfiable we must show that no interpretation of the Herbrand base is a model for S. This is equivalent to showing that each path from the root in the semantic tree runs into a node where some ground instance of some member of S is falsified by the partial interpretation defined by the path to that node. If S is unsatisfiable then each path from the root must eventually reach such a node; otherwise, an infinite path could be found that would correspond to an interpretation that satisfied S, and thus S would be satisfiable. The first node found along each path causing at least one clause of S to be false is called a *failure node*. Failure nodes are illustrated with circles around them in Fig. 6.5. The subtree (of the semantic tree) whose leaves are all failure nodes is called a *failure tree* for S. Assuming that S is unsatisfiable, there is a failure tree for each semantic tree for S; however, we need only find one failure tree to establish that S is unsatisfiable.

At least one of the interior nodes of a failure tree has leaves for its two children; that is, it is a parent of two failure nodes. Such a node is called

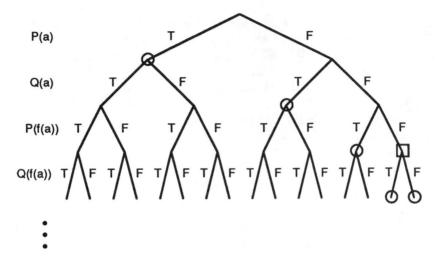

Figure 6.5: Top of a semantic tree for $\{P(x) \vee Q(f(x)), \neg P(x), \neg Q(x)\}$, showing failure nodes and inference nodes.

an *inference node*. The preceding diagram shows inference nodes with squares around them. The children n_1 and n_2 of an inference node represent points at which two partial interpretations, each consistent with S up to the inference node, both suddenly make ground instances of one or more members of S false. Let C_1 be the clause (or one of them, if several exist) made false at n_1, and let C_2 be the (or a) clause made false at n_2. For example, the inference node in the figure has two children, the left of which falsifies $\neg Q(f(a))$, which is a ground instance of $\neg Q(x)$, and the right of which falsifies $P(a) \vee Q(f(a))$, which is a ground instance of $P(x) \vee Q(f(x))$. Clauses C_1 and C_2 must always contain literals that can be unified to form a complementary pair. That is, there must be a literal in C_1 that can be unified with a literal in C_2, such that one literal is a negated proposition while the other is unnegated. Note that before attempting unification we should rename the variables in one of the clauses, if necessary, so that all the variables in that clause are distinct from those in the other clause; this process is called *standardizing the variables apart*. (Here $\neg Q(x)$ becomes complementary to $Q(f(x))$ after the x's have been standardized apart and the literals are unified.)

If resolution were performed on C_1 and C_2 to eliminate the complementary literals, a new clause C' would be obtained. Note that the partial interpretation defined by the path from the root to the inference node fails to satisfy C'. In our example $C' = P(f(x))$. The failure to satisfy C' occurs because at failure node n_1, all the literals of C_1 are falsified, and at n_2 all the literals of C_2 are falsified. At the inference node, all the literals except the complementary pair (and possibly some other literals that can be unified with the complementary ones) have been falsified, but C' is nothing but a disjunction of substitution instances of these falsified literals!

The inference node in the failure tree for S is therefore a failure node in a failure tree for $S \cup \{C'\}$. This new failure tree is slightly smaller than the one for S; it has one less failure node and one less interior node. Since there must be at least one inference node in the new tree (unless the tree is a trivial one—having only a single failure node—the root), we can repeat the process. Eventually we must end with a set of clauses that includes the null clause; the failure tree for such a set is the trivial tree, whose root is a failure node and which contains no other nodes. At that point it becomes obvious that we do indeed have a failure tree.

Resolution works by building up the set of clauses until the set has a trivial failure tree. Of course, if the original set of clauses is satisfiable, no failure tree can ever be found for it; successive resolution steps will lead nowhere.

Let us now state and prove the completeness theorem for the resolution principle.

Resolution Completeness Theorem: A set S of clauses is unsatisfiable if and only if there exists a deduction of the null clause from S.

Proof: Let us prove the reverse implication first. Suppose that there exists a deduction $C_1, C_2, \ldots, C_k$ of the null clause from S. If S were satisfiable then there would exist some interpretation that not only satisfies S but all resolvents derived from clauses in S. Since the null clause is one of these resolvents, and no interpretation can satisfy the null clause, there can be no interpretation that satisfies S.

To show that unsatisfiability implies the existence of a deduction of the null clause, let us assume that S is unsatisfiable. From the proof of Herbrand's theorem, there must be a failure tree T for S. If T has only one node, then S contains the null clause, since it is the only clause that can be falsified without assigning truth values to any atomic formulas. For the case when T has more than one node, there must be at least one inference node. As discussed above, there is a resolvent C' of the two clauses falsified at the two failure nodes below this inference node, such that C' is falsified at the inference node. The tree T' obtained by deleting these two failure nodes from T is a failure tree for $S \cup \{C'\}$, and has two fewer nodes than T does. By induction on the size of the failure tree, it can be seen that any failure tree can be reduced to the one-node failure tree by a sequence of such resolution steps. The sequence consisting of the members of S followed by the sequence of resolvents produced by this process constitutes a deduction of the null clause. *Q. E. D.*

6.5   Resolution Strategies

In any realistic theorem-proving situation, we find that a large number of possible resolvents can be obtained even from a relatively small number of original clauses. However, the vast majority of such resolvents are useless in deriving a contradiction. Some of the clauses may be tautologies. For example, the two clauses $P(x) \vee Q(x)$ and $\neg P(x) \vee \neg Q(x)$ yield the two resolvents $P(x) \vee \neg P(x)$ and $Q(x) \vee \neg Q(x)$; these are generally worthless in a deduction using resolution, and they should be eliminated.

Many of the clauses may be redundant; there may be exact duplicates of clauses, duplicates under reordering of literals, and there may be redundancy in the form of clauses being "subsumed" by other clauses. A clause C_1 is *subsumed* by a clause C_2 if there is a substitution Φ such that the literals of $C_2\Phi$ are a subset of those in C_1. For example, $P(a) \vee Q(y)$ is subsumed by $P(x)$ since the substitution of a for x makes the latter one of the literals of the former. It makes sense to delete any clause that is subsumed by another, since it cannot play any useful role in deducing the null clause that cannot be played by the shorter clause more efficiently.

Even if all tautologies and redundant clauses are removed, including those subsumed by others, there are still combinatorially imposing choices to be made in the selection of resolvents. The problem is in determining which ones to use. A number of strategies have been devised to guide the search for the null clause in an ocean of possible resolvents. Three of these are known as "set of support," "linear format," and "unit preference."

6.5.1   Set of Support

It is usually fair to assume that the negation of the original conclusion will play a key role in making a contradiction, if one exists. Therefore it seems reasonable to give priority to examining resolvents derived from the clauses that express the negation of the conclusion. The *set of support* consists of all those clauses which either are part of the negation of the conclusion, or are resolvents with a parent in the set of support (a recursive definition).

6.5.2   Linear Format

In order to avoid the aimless behavior that seems to result without some imposed direction, one can insist that each resolution step build on the results of the last, rather than do something completely unrelated to the last. A simple way to force this is to only consider, at any given moment, making resolvents that use the most recent resolvent as one of their parents. It has been proved (see [Anderson and Bledsoe 1970]) that there always exists a proof of this form for any provable theorem in the predicate calculus. Of course, this does not guarantee that following any particular chain of resolvents generated in this way will lead in the right direction! It is still very difficult to know how to build the chain to find a proof.

6.5.3 Unit Preference

The goal in resolution theorem proving is to derive $\square$, the null clause. This clause is one containing zero literals. It seems natural, therefore, that one should strive to derive new clauses containing fewer and fewer literals, until one with zero literals suddenly pops out. If we take two random clauses (random except for the assumption that they *can* be resolved), one might contain 4 literals and the other, 7. How many literals will be in one of their resolvents? Usually there will be 9 in such a case. That is, out of n literals of one parent and m of the other, $n + m - 2$ literals will make up the resolvent in the majority of cases. Clearly, for most values of n and m, this new resolvent will be longer than either of its parents. A case in which the number of literals in a resolvent can actually be lower than the number in one of its parents is when one parent consists of a single literal[2]. A clause consisting of just one literal is a *unit clause*. The *unit preference* strategy consists of always preferring to resolve with unit clauses when doing so will lead to something new.

6.6 Solving Problems With Resolution

We have seen how resolution in the predicate calculus is used to prove that a given conclusion follows logically from a set of premises. The same kind of deductive procedure can also be used to find solutions to many problems that can be expressed in logic. Here is an example of such a problem.

> Sally is studying with Morton. Morton is in the student union information office. If any person is studying with another person who is at a particular place, the first person is also at that place. If someone is at a particular place, then he or she can be reached on the telephone at the number for that place.
> What is the number where Sally can be reached?

Let us express the information about the situation in the predicate calculus. We use the following three predicates and one function:

- $SW(x, y)$: x is studying with y.

- $A(x, y)$: x is at place y.

---

[2]It is sometimes possible to reduce the number of literals by more than one in a single resolution step. For example, the first two literals of C_1 below are complementary to C_2 under the substitution $\{(a, y), (b, x)\}$, and both are absent in the resolvent:

$$\begin{aligned} C_1 &= P(a, x) \vee P(y, b) \vee Q(x) \\ C_2 &= \neg P(a, b) \\ C' &= Q(b) \end{aligned}$$

However, this situation is relatively uncommon.

- $R(x, y)$: x can be reached (by telephone) at number y.

- $ph(x)$: the telephone number for place x.

The logic formulations are as follows:

- SW(Sally, Morton)

- A(Morton, UnionBldg)

- $\forall x \forall y (SW(x, y) \wedge A(y, z) \rightarrow A(x, z))$

- $\forall x \forall y (A(x, y) \rightarrow R(x, ph(y)))$

In order to determine the sequence of substitutions that will provide an answer to the problem, we represent the question as a statement that the solution exists. Then we negate it and use resolution to derive the null clause. The negation of the existence statement is:

- $\neg \exists x R(\text{Sally}, x)$

In clause form, we have:

P_1: SW(Sally, Morton)

P_2: A(Morton, UnionBldg)

P_3: $\neg SW(x, y) \vee \neg A(y, z) \vee A(x, z)$

P_4: $\neg A(u, v) \vee R(u, ph(v))$

P_5: $\neg R(\text{Sally}, w)$

The resolution steps that produce the null clause are as follows:

Label	Clause	Where From
C_1:	$\neg A(\text{Sally}, v)$	P_4, P_5 {(Sally, u), (ph(v), w)}
C_2:	$\neg SW(\text{Sally}, y) \vee \neg A(y, v)$	P_3, C_1 {(Sally, x), (v, z)}
C_3:	$\neg SW(\text{Sally}, \text{Morton})$	P_2, C_2 {(Morton, y), (UnionBldg, v)}
C_4:	[]	P_1, C_3

Now that the null clause has been derived, we know a sequence of resolution steps that can be reapplied to a slightly different set of clauses to give us a solution. The sole modification we make to the original set of clauses is to change the negation of the existence statement into a tautology by OR'ing it with the unnegated statement. Thus Premise 5 is now:

$$\neg R(\text{Sally}, w) \vee R(\text{Sally}, w)$$

Now we apply the same sequence of resolution steps as before. Each resolvent derived from Premise 5 (all of them, in our case) will contain one more literal than before. All of the extra literals are substitution instances of R(Sally, w). The final resolvent, instead of being the null clause, will contain a single resolvent, R(Sally, ph(UnionBldg)). This literal says that "Sally can be reached by phone at the phone number for the student union building information center," and thus represents the solution to the problem.

6.7 Logic Programming and PROLOG

6.7.1 Introduction

A theorem-proving program takes as input a set of axioms and some formula to be proved. The output generally consists of information about whether a proof was found, and if so, what unifications were used to derive it. If we consider the input axioms to be a kind of program, and the theorem prover a kind of interpreter, then we can "program in logic." By suitably adding some extra language features to help the interpreter prove the theorem and to print out various things along the way, we may attain a programming language that is theoretically as general as any other. Such a language is PROLOG.

6.7.2 Horn Clauses

Logic programming is commonly done using predicate calculus expressions called "Horn clauses" (named after Alfred Horn, who first studied them). Horn clauses are clauses that satisfy a particular restriction: at most one of the literals in the clause is unnegated. Thus, the following are Horn clauses (assuming that $P, Q, P_1, P_2, \ldots, P_k$ represent propositions each consisting of a predicate and the required number of terms):

$$\neg P \vee Q$$
$$\neg P_1 \vee \neg P_2 \vee \ldots \vee \neg P_k \vee Q$$
$$\neg P_1 \vee \neg P_2 \vee \ldots \vee \neg P_k$$
$$P$$

These can be rewritten:

$$P \rightarrow Q$$
$$P_1 \wedge P_2 \wedge \ldots \wedge P_k \rightarrow Q$$
$$P_1 \wedge P_2 \wedge \ldots \wedge P_k \rightarrow F$$
$$P$$

The third of these expressions employs F to indicate falseness or the null clause. These are often written in a "goal-oriented" format in which the implied literal (the goal) is on the left:

$$Q \leftarrow P$$
$$Q \leftarrow P_1, P_2, \ldots, P_k$$
$$\leftarrow P_1, P_2, \ldots, P_k$$
$$P \leftarrow$$

The third and fourth examples above show cases in which the goal arrow has nothing to its left (in the former case) and nothing to its right (in the latter case). The null clause is a Horn clause, and can be written:

$$\leftarrow$$

Horn clauses in the goal-oriented format are used to program in PROLOG.

6.7.3   A Simple Logic Program

An example of problem solving using resolution on Horn clauses is offered below. The premises, stated in English, are: (1) X is a grandson of Y if for some Z, X is a son of Z and Y is a parent of Z; (2) Walter is a son of Martha; and (3) Jonathan is a parent of Martha. The question we wish to answer is: who is the grandson of Jonathan? We will now use the symbol ":-" of the PROLOG language (Edinburgh dialect) instead of the left arrow, "$\leftarrow$".

```
grandson(X,Y) :- son(X,Z), parent(Y,Z).
son(walter, martha).
parent(jonathan, martha).
```

```
?- grandson(W, jonathan).
```

The system attempts to satisfy the goal(s) preceded by "?-". The way it proceeds is similar to a sequence of resolution steps. In the course, it eventually performs a unification that substitutes walter for W, thus solving the problem.

Starting with the question *?- grandson(W, jonathan)*, the system attempts to justify each right-hand-side literal (and there is only one in this question). It does this by finding a matching left-hand-side literal in another clause. In this example, it finds the first clause, performing the unification of $\{W/X, jonathan/Y\}$. Now the system must justify the literals: *son(W, Z), parent(jonathan, Z)*. The first of these is attempted using the second clause and the substitution $\{walter/W, martha/Z\}$. The second literal of the first clause, to which the same substitution must be applied, is now: *parent(jonathan, martha)*. Fortunately, this literal matches the third clause exactly, and the justification of Clause 1 and in turn, the goal, is complete.

A program in PROLOG consists of a list of clauses. The program is executed as the PROLOG intepreter applies a form of resolution known as *Lush resolution*[3], using a depth-first search strategy implemented with backtracking.

---

[3]*Lush* is an acronym for "*Linear resolution with unrestricted selection function for Horn clauses.*"

This is only one of many possible algorithms to search for proofs. Although linear-format resolution (discussed on page 214) is complete, Lush resolution is not complete. The built-in logical reasoning engine in PROLOG is weak in this sense. However, the PROLOG language provides a good base on which to implement more powerful reasoning systems.

In order to be practically useful, PROLOG contains some theoretically impure language constructs. Special directives to the interpreter may occur within clauses or on separate lines. One of these features is the "cut," described later. Others directives handle input and output.

Typically, PROLOG is implemented so that upper and lower-case ASCII characters are used, with the convention that words starting with capital letters denote variables, and words starting with lower-case letters denote constants and "functors." *Functor* is the PROLOG name for a predicate symbol. (This usage is consistent with the Edinburgh PROLOG dialect [Pereira et al 1978].) In general, each clause has a *head* and a *body*. The head is the part to the left of the ":-" and the body is the right-hand part. The head or the body may be null. The programmer has reasonable leeway in formatting the clauses; the head and subgoals of a clause may be on the same or on separate lines, and several short clauses can be placed together on one line.

6.7.4 Another PROLOG Example

A more interesting example program is the one below, which combines facts, rules, and information about a current situation to choose an appropriate wine to go with a meal. The first eight statements of the program declare facts, e.g., "Beaujolais is a red wine." The next two statements give general rules which encode the "knowledge" that a red wine goes well with a main course of meat, whereas a white wine goes well with a main course of fish. The symbols *Wine* and *Entree* are variables. The declaration "maincourse(salmon)" provides the information particular to the one situation for which the advice is sought. The last line of the program is the query. A value of *Wine* is sought that will satisfy the conditions for being a good wine for the meal.

```
redwine(beaujolais).
redwine(burgundy).
redwine(merlot).

whitewine(chardonnay).
whitewine(riesling).

meat(steak).
meat(lamb).

fish(salmon).
```

```
goodwine(Wine) :- maincourse(Entree),meat(Entree),redwine(Wine).
goodwine(Wine) :- maincourse(Entree),fish(Entree),whitewine(Wine).

maincourse(salmon).

?-goodwine(X).
```

6.7.5   A Mock PROLOG Interpreter in LISP

In order to elucidate the process of answering a query using goal-driven resolution with Horn clauses, we present a LISP program which carries out the main function of a PROLOG interpreter. This program shows that the heart of a PROLOG interpreter is relatively simple; yet it indicates that there are some technical challenges in making such an interpreter efficient.

This interpreter is capable of executing the two example logic programs (after some syntactic changes) given above. The intepreter works by attempting to satisfy the literals on the list of current subgoals, in left-to-right order. If it succeeds in unifying the head of a rule with the first subgoal on its list, the literals in the tail of the rule are put on the front of the list of subgoals and the interpreter attempts to satisfy the new list recursively. Whenever the list is reduced to NIL, the current bindings of variables are printed out as a solution, since all the original subgoals have been satisfied.

This program makes use of the following functions defined in UNIFY.LSP and whose definitions are not repeated here: UNIFY1, DO_SUBST, SUBST and OCCURS_IN. The function UNIFY2 used here is a modification of the function UNIFY in UNIFY.LSP, and the version of ADD_PAIR given here omits the "occurs check" of the version in UNIFY.LSP. Although this version of ADD_PAIR does not use OCCURS_IN, the function PRINT_PAIR does use it.

```
; PROLOG.LSP - a mock PROLOG interpreter.
; This program demonstrates goal-driven logical inference
; using Horn clauses.
```

The top-level function is QUERY. When this function is called, the input goal clause is bound to the atom GOAL, and QUERY invokes SOLVE with initial binding list NIL and recursion level 0:

```
(DEFUN QUERY (GOAL)
  (SOLVE GOAL NIL 0) )
```

SOLVE uses all the rules in the database to attempt to solve the current subgoals. L is list of current subgoals. B is a list of all the current bindings. LEVEL is an integer indicating recursion depth.

```
(DEFUN SOLVE (L B LEVEL)
  (PROG (NEWB)
       (COND ((NULL L)(PRINT_B B))
             (T (SOLVE1 DB)) ) ) )
```

Solve simply calls SOLVE1 with the entire database (DB) as the list of rules to be tried. R is a list of remaining clauses from the database to be tried in order to satisfy the current subgoals. SOLVE1 first checks to see if there are any rules left to be tried. If not, it returns NIL. Otherwise it attempts to apply the next rule (the first element of R). If the head of this rule can be unified with the current subgoal (after all the current bindings have been applied), then a recursive call to SOLVE is made with a new list of subgoals in which the one just matched has been replaced by all those in the tail of the rule. (If there is no tail, then the new list of subgoals is shorter than before.) This call to SOLVE includes the new bindings (NEWB), and the recursion level is one more than before. Whether or not the unification in SOLVE1 is successful, a recursive call is made to SOLVE1 with (CDR R) so that all the rules (or facts) get tried, and all solutions are found.

```
(DEFUN SOLVE1 (R)
  (COND
    ((NULL R) NIL)   ; no rules left, return.
                     ; else try next rule:
    (T (COND ((NEQ (SETQ NEWB
                        (UNIFY2 (CAAR R) ; trial head
                                (CAR L)  ; current subgoal
                                B) )     ; current bindings
                  'NOT_UNIFIABLE)
             (SOLVE (APPEND (COPY (CDAR R) (ADD1 LEVEL))
                           (CDR L) )
                    NEWB
                    (ADD1 LEVEL) ) ))
       (SOLVE1 (CDR R)) ) ) ) )
```

The functions PRINT_B and PRINT_PAIR are used to report solutions:

```
; Print out the bindings in B:
(DEFUN PRINT_B (B)
  (PROG NIL (MAPCAR (FUNCTION PRINT_PAIR) B) (TERPRI)) )
```

```
; Helping function for PRINT_B prints out a term-variable pair
; in the form "X=MARY; ", provided the variable occurs in the
; original query GOAL.
(DEFUN PRINT_PAIR (P)
  (COND ((OCCURS_IN (CADR P) GOAL)
         (PROG NIL (PRIN1 (CADR P)) (TYO 61)
```

```
                        (PRIN1 (CAR P)) (TYO 59) (TYO 32) ) )
        (T NIL) ) )
```

The function NEQ gives a convenient way to say (NULL (EQ X Y)). It returns T if X is not EQ to Y.

```
(DEFUN NEQ (X Y) (NULL (EQ X Y)))
```

UNIFY2 is a version of UNIFY that postpones the substitutions required by SOLVE1 (done by COPY and DO_SUBST) until after the the test for matching predicate symbols, often avoiding some time-consuming, yet fruitless work. When UNIFY2 returns a unifier, it is appended with the previous bindings. UNIFY2 calls UNIFY1, defined in the program UNIFY.LSP.

```
(DEFUN UNIFY2 (L1 L2 B)
   (COND ; make sure predicate symbols match:
        ((NULL (EQ (CAR L1) (CAR L2))) 'NOT_UNIFIABLE)
        (T (PROG (U)
                 (SETQ U NIL)   ; unifier is initially null.
                 (RETURN
                   (COND
                     ((NEQ (UNIFY1 (COPY (CDR L1) (ADD1 LEVEL))
                                   (DO_SUBST (CDR L2) B) )
                           'NOT_UNIFIABLE)
                      (COMPOSE U B))
                     (T 'NOT_UNIFIABLE) ) ) )) ) )
```

During unification, a new (*term, variable*) pair must frequently be "added" to the existing substitution. The test to see whether the variable occurs in the term is time-consuming and seldom of use in correct programs. The version of ADD_PAIR here differs from the one in UNIFY.LSP by omitting this test.

```
(DEFUN ADD_PAIR (TERM VAR)
   (SETQ U (CONS (LIST TERM VAR)
                 (SUBST U TERM VAR) )) )
```

The function COMPOSE combines two substitutions S1 and S2, adding pairs from S1 to S2 in a manner similar to that of ADD_PAIR.

```
(DEFUN COMPOSE (S1 S2)
   (COND ((NULL S1) S2)
         (T (CONS (CAR S1)
                  (SUBST (COMPOSE (CDR S1) S2)
                  (CAAR S1)
                  (CADAR S1) ) )) ) )
```

The function COPY replaces all the variables in its argument L (which is normally bound to part of a rule) by new variables for the current level, thus assuring that the same rule may be used in different ways at different levels of recursion. COPY is supported by COPY1, GETVAR, GETNTH, and the PUTPROP statements that set up the lists of variables.

```
(DEFUN COPY (L LEVEL) (COPY1 L))

(DEFUN COPY1 (L)
  (COND ((NULL L) NIL)
        ((ATOM L)
         (COND ((VARIABLEP L)(GETVAR L LEVEL))
               (T L) ) )
        (T (CONS (COPY1 (CAR L)) (COPY1 (CDR L)))) ) )

; Get the version of variable V for the given LEVEL of recursion:
(DEFUN GETVAR (V LEVEL)
  (GETNTH LEVEL (GET V 'NEWVARS)) )

; Return the Nth element of list L:
(DEFUN GETNTH (N L)
  (COND ((NULL L)(PRINT '(N TOO LARGE FOR LIST)))
        ((EQUAL N 1)(CAR L))
        (T (GETNTH (SUB1 N) (CDR L))) ) )
```

In this implementation, the extra variables that may be needed are provided in advance. There is one group for each "original" variable (e.g., "X" has the group X1, X2, ..., X5). Each group is stored on the property list for its corresponding original variable. The variables given here support the two examples given further below.

```
(PUTPROP 'X '(X1 X2 X3 X4 X5) 'NEWVARS)
(PUTPROP 'Y '(Y1 Y2 Y3 Y4 Y5) 'NEWVARS)
(PUTPROP 'Z '(Z1 Z2 Z3 Z4 Z5) 'NEWVARS)
(PUTPROP 'W '(W1 W2 W3 W4 W5) 'NEWVARS)
(PUTPROP 'WINE '(WINE1 WINE2 WINE3 WINE4) 'NEWVARS)
(PUTPROP 'ENTREE '(ENTREE1 ENTREE2 ENTREE3 ENTREE4) 'NEWVARS)
```

Function VARIABLEP supports both UNIFY1 and COPY1. This version (unlike that given in UNIFY.LSP) supports the two examples given below.

```
(DEFUN VARIABLEP (X)
  (MEMBER X '(
  X X1 X2 X3 X4 X5
  Y Y1 Y2 Y3 Y4 Y5
  Z Z1 Z2 Z3 Z4 Z5
```

```
W W1 W2 W3 W4 W5
WINE WINE1 WINE2 WINE3 WINE4
ENTREE ENTREE1 ENTREE2 ENTREE3 ENTREE4
) ) )
```

Let us now give two examples. The database of clauses for Example 1 is set up
by:

```
(SETQ DB1 '(
 ((GRANDSON X Y) (SON X Z) (PARENT Y Z))
 ((SON WALTER MARTHA))
 ((PARENT JONATHAN MARTHA))
))
```

Here is the database of clauses for Example 2:

```
(SETQ DB2 '(
 ((REDWINE BEAUJOLAIS))
 ((REDWINE BURGUNDY))
 ((REDWINE MERLOT))

 ((WHITEWINE CHARDONNAY))
 ((WHITEWINE RIESLING))

 ((MEAT STEAK))
 ((MEAT LAMB))

 ((FISH SALMON))

 ((GOODWINE WINE)(MAINCOURSE ENTREE)(MEAT ENTREE)(REDWINE WINE))
 ((GOODWINE WINE)(MAINCOURSE ENTREE)(FISH ENTREE)(WHITEWINE WINE))

 ((MAINCOURSE SALMON))
))
```

When the following LISP expressions are evaluated, we get a demonstration of
sample inferences, and the sequences in which subgoals are attempted become
apparent.

```
(TRACE SOLVE UNIFY2)

(SETQ DB DB1)   ; use the database for Example 1.
; Who is the grandson of Jonathan?
(QUERY '((GRANDSON W JONATHAN)))

(SETQ DB DB2)   ; now use the database for Example 2.
```

```
; What is a good wine for dinner tonight?
(QUERY '((GOODWINE WINE)))
```

The answer to the first example is printed as:

```
W=WALTER;
```

Although there are other bindings in the environment at the time when the solution is found (Z1−MARTHA; Y1=JONATHAN), only the variable W occurs in the query, and thus only its binding is printed.

The two answers to the second example are printed as:

```
WINE=CHARDONNAY;
WINE=RIESLING;
```

Note that a query may involve several literals. For example, the question "what are the combinations of red wine and meat?" is handled by the query:

```
(QUERY '((REDWINE WINE) (MEAT ENTREE)))
```

and results in the six solutions:

```
ENTREE=STEAK; WINE=BEAUJOLAIS;
ENTREE=LAMB; WINE=BEAUJOLAIS;
ENTREE=STEAK; WINE=BURGUNDY;
ENTREE=LAMB; WINE=BURGUNDY;
ENTREE=STEAK; WINE=MERLOT;
ENTREE=LAMB; WINE=MERLOT;
```

6.7.6 PROLOG's List-Handling Facilities

Like LISP, PROLOG has essentially a single data type to represent both data and programs, and this data type is much like the S-expression of LISP. (The syntax of PROLOG programs hides this structure, however.) Although the Marseille dialect of PROLOG represents what in LISP would be $(X.Y)$ as $cons(X,Y)$, the Edinburgh dialect (which is more common) uses $[X|Y]$. The null list is denoted $[\,]$. The list containing A, B, and C is written $[A, B, C]$. Variables appearing in list expressions can be unified just as they can outside of lists. For example, the predicate $member(X, L)$ which is true if X is an element of L can be defined as

```
member(X, [X|Y]).
member(X, [Y|Z]) :- member(X, Z).
```

Here, the query

```
?-member(b, [a, b, c]).
```

fails to unify with the single literal of the first clause of the definition, since b and a are different constants. However, the head of the second rule unifies with the query with $\{b/X, a/Y, [b, c]/Z\}$. The subgoal, $member(b, [b, c])$, is solved recursively; this one does unify with the first rule and is satisfied. The query is found to be true.

A more interesting example is the definition of $append(L1, L2, L3)$ which is true if the bindings of $L1$ and $L2$, appended together, match the binding of $L3$.

```
append([], L, L).
append([X|L1], L2, [X|L3]) :- append(L1, L2, L3).
```

The first rule says that *append* is true if the first list is empty and the other two are the same. The second rule says that *append* is true if the heads of the first and third lists are the same and *append* happens to be true on the tail of the first list, the same second list, and the tail of the third list. The query,

```
?-append([a, b], [c], L).
```

results in $L = [a, b, c]$.

Unlike other programming languages, PROLOG makes it easy to compute functions "backwards." For example the query

```
?-append(L, [c], [a, b, c]).
```

results in $L = [a, b]$, and we can get all four pairs of lists that can be appended to give $[a, b, c]$ with the query

```
?-append(L1, L2, [a, b, c]).
```

The results are the following:

```
L1=[]; L2=[a, b, c];
L1=[a]; L2=[b, c];
L1=[a, b]; L2=[c];
L1=[a, b, c]; L2=[];
```

6.7.7   Cut and Other PROLOG Features

When PROLOG attempts to satisfy a goal P in a statement of form

```
P :- Q1, Q2, ..., Qn.
```

it attempts to satisfy subgoals $Q1$ through Qn with a common substitution, proceeding from left-to-right and backtracking (right-to-left) if necessary. If the special subgoal "!" occurs in the body of the clause, however, backtracking is restricted. For example, with the statement form

```
P :- Q1, !, Q2.
```

after $Q1$ is satisfied, the interpreter encounters the cut symbol, and, since this is the first time the cut is encountered for the interpretation of this clause, the cut subgoal is immediately satisfied with the current substitution, and then the interpreter attempts to satisfy $Q2$. If $Q2$ fails, the interpretation backs up. As it backs up past the cut, the attempt to satisfy the current goal is interrupted and treated as a failure.

Another special predicate is *fail*, which takes no arguments. Any attempt to satisfy *fail* fails and the interpreter tries to backtrack. A simple way to implement *fail* is to forbid its use on the left-hand side of any rule, so that a *fail* subgoal can never be satisfied.

Although it is easy with Horn clauses to state a positive fact (i.e., that some predicate is true on some arguments), one has a problem in stating a negative fact (i.e., that a predicate is false on some arguments). One way to obtain negation is to define it in terms of *cut* and *fail*:

```
not(X) :- X, !, fail.
not(X).
```

If X is true, then $not(X)$ fails because the subgoals X and *cut* are both satisfied, but *fail* causes backtracking into the cut, which causes the goal to fail. On the other hand, if X fails, then the second rule is tried and found to succeed, since it is a unit clause. Note that here, X plays the role of subgoal and argument to predicate *not* at the same time. By using this definition of *not*, one is making a kind of closed-world assumption called *negation as failure*.

PROLOG provides special predicates *assert* and *retract* that are used to add clauses to or delete them from the database. (Backtracking does not undo their effects, however.)

In order to do arithmetic, PROLOG provides an assignment operator *is* that takes two operands: a variable on the left and an arithmetic expression on the right (and thus it is an infix functor). The following definition of *factorial* uses it:

```
factorial(0, 1).
factorial(N, F) :- M is N-1, factorial(M, G), F is N * G.
```

Here $factorial(5, X)$ would be satisfied by binding N to 5, M to 4, G to 4 factorial (computed recursively), and F to the result of multiplying N by G, which is 120. Note that *is* fails if there is an unbound variable in its right-hand argument. Another limitation of *is* is that arithmetic with *is* does not permit backtracking, and the query

```
?-factorial(X, 120).
```

will fail to produce a solution.

6.7.8   LISP versus PROLOG

Both LISP and PROLOG are popular languages for artificial intelligence systems implementation. The unification and backtracking mechanisms built into PROLOG make development of problem-solving systems that use them easy. However, not all AI systems are based upon problem solving through predicate logic. For many systems, PROLOG does not seem as appropriate as LISP. Many consider LISP to be a more flexible language, albeit a somewhat lower-level one than PROLOG. In the late 1970's and early 1980's, LISP was more prevalent in the United States while Europe and Japan were more oriented towards PROLOG. However, the user communities have become more evenly distributed in recent years.

6.8   Non-Monotonic Reasoning

6.8.1   Motivation

The predicate calculus is an example of a "monotonic" logic. Suppose that S is the (possibly infinite) set of formulas provable from some set A of axioms. If A' is a larger set of axioms that includes A, then S', the set of formulas provable from A', is either a superset of S or is equivalent to S. That is, the set of theorems is monotonically nondecreasing as one adds to the set of axioms. None of the formulas in S have to be retracted as A is enlarged.

In everyday life, people seem to reason in ways that do not adhere to a monotonic structure. For example, consider the following:

> Helen was attending a party at her friend Jack's apartment. Jack ran out of wine and asked Helen to drive his car to the bottle shop to buy some Cabernet. He handed Helen the keys. She accepted the job and concluded that she would buy the wine. After she tried to start the car, however, it became apparent that the battery was dead. She revised her previous conclusion that she would buy the wine.

Here Helen has performed non-monotonic reasoning. As new information came in (that the car wouldn't start) she withdrew a previous conclusion (that she would buy the wine). Adding an "axiom" required the revocation of a "theorem."

There is good reason for people to employ such non-monotonic reasoning processes. We often need to jump to conclusions in order to make plans, to survive; and yet we cannot anticipate all of the possible things that could go wrong with our plans or predictions. We must make assumptions about things we don't specifically know.

Default attributes are a powerful kind of knowledge, since they permit useful conclusions to be made, even if those conclusions must sometimes be revoked. Here we examine means for AI systems to make defaults of a particular kind.

6.8.2 Circumscription

A formal method for non-monotonic reasoning using the predicate calculus has been proposed [McCarthy 1980] which has some elegant features. The method, called *circumscription*, is a mechanism for adding to a set of predicate-calculus formulas one or more new formulas which express a kind of default or closed-world assumption.

Let A be a formula containing an n-ary predicate symbol P. If Ψ represents a formula with n designated free variables, then we use $A[\Psi/P]$ to denote the result of substituting Ψ for each occurrence of P in A, such that the kth free variable in Ψ is replaced by the kth argument of P in the occurrence. If the occurrence of P has the form $P(x_1, \ldots, x_n)$, which can be abbreviated to $P(\bar{x})$, then the occurrence of Ψ that replaces it can be denoted $\Psi(\bar{x})$.

Then the circumscription of P in A is the following "schema" for generating formulas:

$$\{A[\Psi/P] \wedge \forall \bar{x}[\Psi(x) \to P(\bar{x})]\} \to \forall \bar{x}[P(\bar{x}) \to \Psi(\bar{x})].$$

This schema represents the assertion that the only objects $\bar{x}$ that satisfy P are those which *must* satisfy P, to avoid inconsistency, assuming A is true.

Let us illustrate how circumscription can be used to represent Helen's assumptions before she got into Jack's car. In order to drive a car there are a number of requirements, two of which are the following:

K: having the *keys* to the car, and

C: having physical access to the *car*.

That these conditions are prerequisites for driving a car is expressed by the formula

A: prerequisite(K) $\wedge$ prerequisite(C).

Helen assumed that if all the prerequisites were satisfied (that is, there were "no problems" with them), she could and would drive the car and buy the wine. This belief is expressed by the following:

α: $\forall x[\text{prerequisite}(x) \to \text{noproblem}(x)] \to \text{buy}(\text{Helen}, \text{wine})$.

When Helen arrived at the car, she had these prerequisites; thus we have:

$$\text{noproblem}(K) \wedge \text{noproblem}(C).$$

The circumscription of *prerequisite* in A is the schema:

$$\{[\Psi(K) \wedge \Psi(C)] \wedge \forall x[\Psi(x) \to \text{prerequisite}(x)]\} \to \forall x[\text{prerequisite}(x) \to \Psi(x)].$$

From this circumscription, it is a straightforward matter to "jump" to Helen's first conclusion. We begin by taking for Ψ the expression $(x = K) \vee (x = C)$.

The antecedent of the circumscription is clearly true, so we may conclude the right-hand side:

$$\forall x[\text{prerequisite}(x) \rightarrow ((x = K) \vee (x = C))]$$

which asserts that the keys and access to the car are the only prerequisites. This formula may be added to the set of theorems, and it can be used to deduce new theorems.

Now since K and C are the only prerequisites, and Helen has both of them, the antecedent of (α) is true, and the consequent, buy(Helen, wine), follows. Without the circumscription, there would be no basis for proving the antecedent of (α).

The non-monotonic retraction of Helen's initial conclusion was necessary after two additional facts became apparent:

prerequisite(B):   the battery must be functional, and
¬noproblem(B):   the battery is not functional.

A natural way to handle the retraction is to remove from the set of theorems the right-hand side of the circumscription of *prerequisite* in A as soon as the new fact involving *prerequisite* is encountered, also removing all formulas derived from the circumscription. Then the new fact may be conjoined with A to produce a formula

A': noproblem(K) $\wedge$ noproblem(C) $\wedge$ noproblem(B).

A new circumscription of *prerequisite* in A' may be constructed in the hope of deriving new useful conclusions, but it is no longer possible to prove the formula, buy(Helen, wine), since ¬noproblem(B) prevents the antecedent of (α) from being true.

A possible advantage of circumscription over some other methods for non-monotonic reasoning is that it is an augmentation of the first-order predicate calculus, which allows all the reasoning, except circumscription itself and the instantiation of the resulting schemata, to be handled by the methods already available (e.g., resolution). However, the practical application of circumscription appears awkward in comparison to the adoption of explicit defaults or the use of the negation-as-failure assumption in logic programming.

6.9   Bibliographical Information

A clear introduction to the propositional calculus with proofs of its consistency and completeness may be found in Part 2 of [Hunter 1971]. Wang's algorithm for proving theorems in the propositional calculus first appeared in [Wang 1960]. A thorough introduction to mathematical logic may be obtained using the text [Mendelson 1964]. An excellent text covering the basics of automatic theorem proving is [Chang and Lee 1973]. A newer text with an emphasis on applying theorem proving to mathematical problems is [Bundy 1983]. An introduction to logical reasoning by computer that is easy to read is [Wos et al 1984].

The mathematics underlying most modern approaches to automatic theorem proving in the predicate calculus was done in the early part of this century [Herbrand 1930]. The first program to prove theorems of the predicate calculus by applying Herbrand's theorem was that of [Gilmore 1960] which exhaustively generated sets of variable-free instances of a set of clauses, looking for an inconsistency. The more efficient resolution approach was first described by [Robinson 1965]. The "Logic Theory Machine" program [Newell et al 1957] used a subgoal approach to proving theorems in the propositional calculus taken from [Whitehead and Russell 1935]. The use of a "diagram" to control the search for a proof in geometry is illustrated in [Gelernter 1963]. A detailed account of a theorem-proving program widely considered to be successful is given in [Boyer and Moore 1979].

The notion of using a theorem prover as a program interpreter was incorporated in the PLANNER programming language [Hewitt 1971] embedded in LISP. Incorporating a predicate logic style into a programming language was first achieved in an accepted way in PROLOG [Warren et al 1977]. For a text on PROLOG, see [Clocksin and Mellish 1981], and for logic programming in general see [Kowalski 1977]. A concise introduction to PROLOG is the pair of articles [Colmerauer 1985] and [Cohen 1985], the latter also containing a bibliography of some 47 items related to the language. A collection of articles about logic programming and its uses is contained in [van Caneghem and Warren 1986].

Non-monotonic reasoning was the subject of a special issue of *Artificial Intelligence*, which contained the original article on circumscription [McCarthy 1980], as well as several other important papers, including [McDermott and Doyle 1980], [Reiter 1980] and [Winograd 1980]. A pragmatic approach to non-monotonic reasoning was developed by Doyle and called "truth maintenance systems" [Doyle 1979].

References

1. Boyer, R. S., and Moore, J. S. 1979. *A Computational Logic. ACM Monograph Series.* New York: Academic Press.

2. Bundy, A. 1983. *Artificial Mathematicians: The Computational Modelling of Mathematical Reasoning.* New York: Academic Press.

3. Chang, C.-L., and Lee, R. C.-T. 1973. *Symbolic Logic and Mechanical Theorem Proving.* New York: Academic Press.

4. Clocksin, W. F., and Mellish, C. S. 1981. *Programming in PROLOG.* New York: Springer-Verlag.

5. Cohen, J. 1985. Describing PROLOG by its interpretation and compilation. *Communications of the ACM*, Vol. 28, No. 12, December, pp1311-1324.

6. Colmerauer, A. 1985. PROLOG in ten figures. *Communications of the ACM*, Vol. 28, No. 12, December, pp1296-1310.

7. Doyle, J. 1979. A truth maintenance system. *Artificial Intelligence*, Vol. 12, No. 3, pp231-272.

8. Gelernter, H. 1963. Realization of a geometry theorem proving machine. In Feigenbaum, E. A., and Feldman, J. (eds.), *Computers and Thought*. New York: McGraw-Hill, pp134-152.

9. Gilmore, P. C. 1960. A proof method for quantificational theory. *IBM Journal of Research and Development*, Vol. 4, pp28-35.

10. Herbrand, J. 1930. Recherches sur la théorie de la démonstration, *Travaux de la Societé des Sciences et des Lettres de Varsovie, Classe III Sci. Math. Phys.*, no. 33. Also translated to: "Researches in the theory of demonstration," in van Heijenoort (ed.), *From Frege to Gödel: A Source Book in Mathematical Logic, 1879-1931*, pp525-581, Cambridge, MA: Harvard University Press.

11. Hewitt, C. 1971. Description and theoretical analysis (using schemas) of PLANNER: a language for proving theorems and manipulating models in a robot. Ph.D. dissertation, Massachusetts Institute of Technology.

12. Hunter, G. 1971. *Metalogic: An Introduction to the Metatheory of Standard First Order Logic*. Berkeley and Los Angeles: University of California Press.

13. Kowalski, R. A. 1977. *Predicate Logic as a Programming Language*. Amsterdam: North-Holland.

14. McCarthy, J. 1980. Circumscription—a form of non-monotonic reasoning. *Artificial Intelligence*, Vol. 13, pp27-39.

15. McDermott, D. V. 1980. Non-monotonic logic I. *Artificial Intelligence*, Vol. 13, No. 1 & 2, pp41-72.

16. Mendelson, E. 1964. *Introduction to Mathematical Logic*. New York: Van Nostrand Reinhold.

17. Newell, A., Shaw, J. C., and Simon, H. 1957. Empirical explorations with the Logic Theory Machine. *Proceedings of the Western Joint Conputer Conference*, pp218-230. Also, reprinted in Feigenbaum, E. A., and Feldman, J. (eds.), *Computers and Thought*. New York: McGraw-Hill, 1963.

18. Pereira, L. M., Pereira, F. C. N., and Warren, D. H. D. 1978. *User's Guide to DECsystem-10 PROLOG*. Dept. of Artificial Intelligence, University of Edinburgh.

19. Reiter, R. 1980. A logic for default reasoning. *Artificial Intelligence*, Vol. 13, No. 1 & 2, pp81-132.

20. Robinson, J. A. 1965. A machine oriented logic based on the resolution principle, *Journal of the ACM*, Vol. 12, pp23-41.

21. van Caneghem, M. and Warren, D. H. D. (eds.) 1986. *Logic Programming and its Applications*. Norwood, NJ: Ablex.

22. Wang, H. 1960. Towards mechanical mathematics. *IBM Journal of Research and Development*, Vol. 4, pp2-22.

23. Warren, D., Pereira, L. M., and Pereira, F. 1977. PROLOG—the language and its implementation compared with LISP. *Proceedings of the ACM SIGART-SIGPLAN Symposium on AI and Programming Languages*, Rochester, NY.

24. Whitehead, A. N., and Russell, B. 1935. *Principia Mathematica*, Second Edition, Vol. 1, Cambridge University Press.

25. Winograd, T. 1980. Extended inference modes in reasoning by computer systems. *Artificial Intelligence*, Vol. 13, No. 1 & 2, pp5-26.

26. Wos, L., Overbeek, R., Lusk, E., and Boyle, J. 1984. *Automated Reasoning: Introduction and Applications*. Englewood Cliffs, NJ: Prentice-Hall.

Exercises

1. Classify each of the following as either a contradiction, a tautology, or a satisfiable non-tautology. Justify each answer.

   (a) $P \to \neg P$

   (b) $(P \vee Q) \wedge (\neg P \vee \neg Q)$

   (c) $(P \to Q) \wedge (Q \to \neg P)$

   (d) $P \to (\neg P \to P)$

2. Use Wang's rules to prove $((P \to Q) \wedge (Q \to R)) \to (P \to R)$.

3. Find a proof for the following logical expression using Wang's rules. Compare your proof with the display you get when you set (TRACE VALID1) and then give the expression to PROVER to validate.

(((A IMPLIES B) AND (B IMPLIES C)) IMPLIES (A IMPLIES C)).

4. Explain why the PROG is used in the definition of the function VALID1.

5. Devise a valid logical expression of three variables A, B and C, which has only four occurrences of logical operators, which causes the maximum number of calls to VALID1 under these restrictions.

6. Enhance the FORMAT function so that it also can accept well-formed formulas of the form (A XOR B), meaning the exclusive-or of A and B, and translate them into equivalent formulas using only AND, OR, and NOT.

7. Is the implementation of the proposition verifier really a production system? Explain.

8. Using only the axioms of *Principia Mathematica*, prove that $P \rightarrow \neg(\neg P)$.

9. Prove the resolution principle of the propositional calculus (for three propositional symbols P, Q, and R) by perfect induction.

10. Consider the following statements:

    - "If the maid stole the jewelry, then the butler wasn't guilty."
    - "Either the maid stole the jewelry or she milked the cows."
    - "If the maid milked the cows, then the butler got his cream."
    - "Therefore, if the butler was guilty, then he got his cream."

    (a) Express these statements in the propositional calculus.

    (b) Express the negation of the conclusion in clause form.

    (c) Demonstrate that the conclusion is valid, using resolution in the propositional calculus.

11. Write a LISP program that takes a list of clauses of the propositional calculus and attempts to derive the null clause, using resolution.

12. Put the following predicate-calculus formulas into clause form:

    (a) $(\forall x)(\forall y)\{[P(x) \wedge Q(y)] \rightarrow \exists z R(x, y, z)\}$
    (b) $(\exists x)(\forall y)(\exists z)\{P(x) \rightarrow [Q(y) \rightarrow R(z)]\}$

13. For each of the following sets of literals, find a most general unifier or determine that the set is not unifiable.

    (a) $\{P(x, a), P(b, y)\}$
    (b) $\{Q(a), Q(f(x))\}$

(c) $\{P(x), P(f(y)), P(f(g(z)))\}$

(d) $\{P(x), Q(y)\}$

(e) $\{P(x, f(x), a), P(b, y, x)\}$

14. Prove the conclusion $(\forall x)L(x)$ from the premises $(\forall x)(S(x) \rightarrow L(x))$ and $\neg(\exists x)(\neg S(x))$, using predicate calculus resolution.

15. Consider propositions P1 through P4 below. Encode each proposition as a logical formula in the predicate calculus, choosing appropriate predicates. Then show that P4 is logically implied by P1, P2 and P3 using the resolution method.

   - P1: If something has hair and gives milk, then it is a mammal.
   - P2: Any coconut has hair.
   - P3: Any coconut gives milk.
   - P4: All coconuts are mammals.

16. (a) Determine the number of times UNIFY1 is called in the evaluation of the form:

```
(UNIFY '(P X Z Z A)
       '(P Y Y W W) )
```

   (b) Determine the number of times UNIFY1 is called in the evaluation of the form:

```
(UNIFY '(P X Y Z (F (F (F (G X Y Z)))))
       '(P (F A) (F A) (F A) W) )
```

   (c) Determine the computational complexity of the variation of the unification algorithm that is implemented in UNIFY and its supporting functions.

17. Write a function (FACTORS C) that uses UNIFY to find factors of a clause C, where C is given as a list of literals. FACTORS attempts to unify pairs of literals from C, and whenever successful, prints the corresponding factor; any factors of the factor are then computed recursively. Show your results for the clause $P(x) \vee P(f(y)) \vee P(f(a)) \vee Q(x) \vee \neg P(y)$.

18. Modify the UNIFY program to accept a list of two or more literals rather than only two literals.

19. Make the UNIFY program more efficient by avoiding the redundant attempts to perform substitutions that can take place before the recursive calls to UNIFY1. No term-variable substitution should be applied more than once to the same subexpression.

20. (a) Using the UNIFY program, write additional functions to produce a resolvent given two parent clauses. Test your program with the form

```
(RESOLVE '((P A X) (NOT (Q X Y)))
         '((Q (F Z) B) (P Z B)) )
```

(b) Improve your RESOLVE program to find a resolvent for each eligible complementary pair of literals from the parent clauses.

21. Explain the necessity of renaming variables with the COPY function in the program PROLOG.LSP. What would be the result for the following logic program if COPY were only an identity function?

```
; Database:
((GRANDPARENT X Y) (PARENT X Z) (PARENT Z Y))
((PARENT X Y) (FATHER X Y))
((FATHER SAM JOE))
((FATHER JOE DAVID))
; Query:
(QUERY '((GRANDPARENT SAM Y)))
```

22. Using each of the example logic programs presented for PROLOG.LSP, determine the number of successful unifications (performed by UNIFY2). Next, with tracing disabled, measure the time required by your computer to execute each of these two examples. For each, divide the time by the number of unifications to get a measure of the LIPS (Logical Inferences Per Second). Describe your results and discuss the factors that may or may not make this a fair measure of a system's execution speed.

23. The function UNIFY1 used in both UNIFY.LSP and PROLOG.LSP can run faster or slower depending upon whether the "occurs check" is made by the function ADD_PAIR.

(a) Measure the speed difference this makes in the execution of the good-wine example for PROLOG.LSP on page 224. Give your answer in LIPS (Logical Inferences Per Second).

(b) What is the danger in removing the occurrence check?

24. Add the following features to PROLOG.LSP:

(a) handling the special *cut* subgoal.

(b) handling of subgoals of the form (NOT X), where X is a subgoal.

(c) handling of arithmetic assignments of the form (IS X (PLUS Y 5)) as done by the PROLOG *is* operator. Demonstrate this feature using the factorial function on page 227 to compute 5!

25. Using the function PROLOG.LSP, implement the Horn-clause definitions of:

    (a) *member* given on page 225, and demonstrate it with the query

        ```
        (QUERY '((MEMBER JOHN
                         (CONS MARY (CONS X (CONS BOB NIL))) )))
        ```

        which should result in "X=JOHN;".

    (b) *append* given on page 226. By tracing the SOLVE function, determine the sequence of subgoals attempted for the query,

        ```
        (QUERY '((APPEND (CONS A (CONS B NIL))
                         (CONS C NIL)
                         X)))
        ```

        where A, B, C and NIL are constants and X is a variable.

26. (a) Develop a list of ten to fifteen Horn clauses that represents a set of constraints or preferences for restaurants or entertainment during a night on the town with a friend.

    (b) Demonstrate the solution to a problem using your rules (with PROLOG.LSP or a PROLOG interpreter).

27. (a) What is the circumscription of P in the formula below?

    $$P(a, b) \land P(a, c)$$

    (b) Demonstrate the steps required to use the circumscription to conclude that (a, b) and (a, c) are the only argument pairs that satisfy P.

28. Determine the circumscription of *buy* in (α) on page 229.

Chapter 7

Probabilistic Reasoning

7.1 Introduction

7.1.1 The Need to Represent Uncertain Information

In many practical problem-solving situations, the available knowledge is incomplete or inexact. Weather prediction and medical diagnosis are two kinds of such situations. In cases like these, the knowledge is inadequate to support the desired sorts of logical inferences. However, humans have ways of drawing inferences from incomplete, inexact or uncertain knowledge and information. Although our knowledge is not complete, we can and do make and use generalizations and approximations that help us summarize our experience and predict aspects of things we don't yet know. Generalizations are often subject to error, and yet we use them anyway.

The knowledge in a machine is always limited, too. Because intelligent machines should do the best they can when their knowledge is not complete and exact, we want them to use generalizations and approximations, too.

Probabilistic reasoning methods allow AI systems to use uncertain or probabilistic knowledge in ways that take the uncertainty into account. In addition, probabilistic methods can help us accumulate evidence for hypotheses in a fair way; they are appropriate tools in making "just" decisions. Decision theory, related to theory of probability, provides additional techniques that help to minimize risk in making decisions.

7.1.2 The Nature of Probabilistic Information

We often must deal with statements whose actual truth we don't know and don't have the resources to learn in a short period of time. Let us consider the statement "it will rain tomorrow in Walla Walla." Suppose that a resident of Walla Walla is planning a picnic and would indeed like to know whether or not it will rain. Suppose further that he has a feeling that it will rain, but is not sure. How might this feeling be related to the truth of the statement? How should (or does) this feeling affect his decision to have the picnic? What are the conscious or unconscious factors in his mind that give rise to his intuition? How can a computer program take such factors into account?

Asking such questions may seem to be stretching the importance of predicting the weather or of common intuition. However, we can ask the same questions about a doctor's intuition in diagnosing a patient, or a financial analyst's feelings about the stock market. In domains such as these, there may well exist formal criteria that complement intuition or which actually underlie the intuition. Furthermore, we may be able to design computational mechanisms which are consistent with both the formal criteria and the intuition.

The phenomenon of uncertainty can be studied mathematically drawing on the theory of probability and on theories of evidence.

7.2 Probability

7.2.1 The Notion of Certainty

To an arbitrary statement, anyone who knows what he believes can lend a judgment: "Sure," "Impossible," "Maybe," "I'll give you ten to one it's true," "Unlikely but possible," and perhaps even "I don't know and I don't care." If we require that the person choose a number in some range, say, 0 to 10, to indicate his degree of belief in the truth of the statement, we could interpret 0 as his certainty that the statement is false, 5 his belief that it may just as well be true as false, and 10 his certainty in its truth. The value he chooses represents his (subjective) belief in the statement. Since such a value is a belief rather than an actual representation of the truth of a statement, it is possible and permissible that someone assign a value of 10 to the statement "27 is a prime number."

On the other hand, regardless of what particular individuals may believe, certain statements are true, certain others are false, and others have basis for neither truth nor falseness to be ascribed to them. Regardless of one person's opinion, 27 is not a prime number. The statement, "The next time you flip a fair coin, it will come up tails," has no basis for being true or for being false. Consequently, to give a certainty value of 0 or 10 to this statement is to do an injustice to it. In cases such as this, truth or falseness seeming equally likely, 5 would be a fair certainty value[1]. There is thus a kind of ideal, "just" certainty value that some statements deserve.

Probabilities are numerical values between 0 and 1 (inclusive) that represent ideal certainties of statements, given various assumptions about the cir-

---

[1]There are other systems for assigning values to degrees of belief that are arguably more appropriate than probability or systems equivalent to probability. One of these, commonly known as "Dempster-Shafer theory," has received much attention recently, and it is described at the end of this chapter.

cumstances in which the statements are relevant. The concept of probability has been studied through the controlled circumstances of mathematically simple situations.

The mathematical theory of probability has evolved through the last three centuries. Notable landmarks are Pascal's study of binomial coefficients, which he did around the year 1650, and Laplace's formulation of probability as a ratio. Using numbers from Pascal's triangle, or by computing the binomial coefficient C_k^n directly with the formula $C_k^n = \frac{n!}{k!(n-k)!}$, one could easily determine that the number of ways to choose three books from a set of five is $(5 \times 4)/2 = 10$. Laplace's formula gives a way to compute a probability:

Probability = (number of desired outcomes) / (total number of outcomes)

For example, to determine the probability of drawing a card belonging to the diamonds suit out of a normal deck of playing cards, one divides the number of diamond cards (13) by the total number of cards (52), getting the value 1/4. Laplace's formula works under the assumption that each outcome is equally likely.

What is the probability of drawing, out of a hat containing a shuffled deck of playing cards, the ace of spades? In the absence of particular information about where in the hat the ace of spades lies (e.g., on top of all the other cards), it makes sense to treat each of the possible outcomes of the draw equally. That is, it is only fair that we ascribe to each of the 52 cards a probability of being drawn equal to 1/52. To do otherwise would be to act as if we had additional information when, in fact, we do not.

7.2.2   Axioms of Probability

In many situations the possible outcomes can be classified into categories called "events." For example, in drawing a card from a shuffled deck, there are 52 possible outcomes. Drawing a diamond is an event containing 13 outcomes. Drawing the ace of spades is an event containing one outcome.

It is possible to dispense with the notion of outcome entirely and deal only with events and their probabilities. For example, if John Doe has an upset stomach, some possible events are that John has a virus, John has food poisoning, John is seasick, etc. The probabilities for each event could be very unequal in a given context. In particular, if the context is a Caribbean cruise during hurricane weather, it is quite likely that John is seasick. Furthermore, these events are not mutually exclusive; John might suffer from several of the diseases simultaneously.

Probability values obey two laws: the additive law and the multiplicative law. Let A and B be events having probabilities $P(A)$ and $P(B)$, respectively.

1. Additive Law: $P(A \cup B) = P(A) + P(B) - P(A \cap B)$. If A and B do not have any outcomes in common, then $P(A \cup B) = P(A) + P(B)$.

2. Multiplicative Law: $P(A \cap B) = P(A) \times P(B|A) = P(B) \times P(A|B)$. Here $P(B|A)$ is $P(B$ given $A)$, which refers to the probability of event B under circumstances where event A is known to occur or be true. In the case where A and B are known to be statistically independent, the multiplicative law can be expressed more simply: $P(A \cap B) = P(A) \times P(B)$.

When we can describe a set of events for a situation, it is important that we see to it that probabilities are assigned to the events in such a way that these laws are satisfied. This helps to assure that any conclusions drawn from the probabilities are reasonable.

7.2.3   Bayes' Rule

It is very common to compute conclusions from premises. With mathematical logic, the rule of *modus ponens* allows us to take general knowledge of the form $P \to Q$ and a specific fact P and deduce Q. Often either the general rule or the specific information is uncertain, but we would still like to determine something about the consequence: the degree to which it can be believed. In this section, we treat degrees of belief as if they are probabilities values. Depending on the phenomena being described, the probability of a conclusion Q could be computed by any of an infinite number of different functions of the probability of P. A method that provides a sensible approach in many situations was developed by the British cleric and mathematician, Thomas Bayes.

Bayes' rule is well presented using a fictional medical-diagnosis problem. We wish to know the probability that John has malaria, given that he has a slightly unusual symptom: a high fever.

We assume that two kinds of information are available from which to compute this probability. First there is general knowledge: (a) the probability that a person (in this case John) has malaria, regardless of any symptoms, (b) the probability that a person has the symptom of fever, given that he has malaria, and (c) the probability that a person has the symptom of fever, given that he does not have malaria. Second, there is the information particular to John: that he has this symptom. Let us assign the symbol H to the hypothesis and the symbol E to the evidence:

- $H =$ "John has malaria," and

- $E =$ "John has a high fever."

Thus we begin with:

- general knowledge or "model" consisting of

  1. $P(H)$: probability that a person has malaria,

2. $P(E|H)$: probability that a person has a high fever, given that he has malaria, and

3. $P(E|\neg H)$: probability that a person has a high fever, given that he does not have malaria; and

- particular: the fact that John has the symptom of high fever.

We desire the value of $P(H|E)$ which represents the probability that John has malaria, given that he has a high fever.

This is obtained using Bayes' rule:

$$P(H|E) = \frac{P(E|H)P(H)}{P(E)}$$

where

$$P(E) = P(E|H)P(H) + P(E|\neg H)P(\neg H).$$

This is interpreted as saying: the probability that John has malaria given that he has a high fever is equal to the ratio of the probability that he has both the fever and malaria, to the probability that someone has a fever regardless of whether or not he has malaria. The probability of having a high fever is computed as the sum of the conditional probabilities of having the fever given malaria or given not malaria, weighted by the probability of malaria and not malaria, respectively.

To continue the example, let us suppose that the general knowledge is as follows:

$$P(H) = 0.0001 \qquad P(E|H) = 0.75 \qquad P(E|\neg H) = 0.14$$

Then we have

$$P(E) = (0.75)(0.0001) + (0.14)(0.9999)$$

which is approximately 0.14006 and

$$P(H|E) = (0.75)(0.0001)/0.14006 \approx 0.0005354.$$

Thus John's probability of malaria, given his fever, is about 0.0005. On the other hand, if he did not have the fever, his probability of having malaria would be

$$P(H|\neg E) = \frac{P(\neg E|H)P(H)}{P(\neg E)} = \frac{(1 - 0.75)(0.0001)}{(1 - 0.14006)} \approx 0.000029$$

or about 0.00003. We can say that knowledge of John's having a high fever increases his probability for malaria by a factor of 5 while knowledge of John's not having a high fever reduces the probability by a factor of 3.

We can generalize the example we have just presented by showing how evidence, prior and conditional probabilities, and Bayes' rule fit together as the first stage of a decision-making system. Figure 7.1 shows a diagram for a decision-making system. This system could be adapted (in theory) to any application

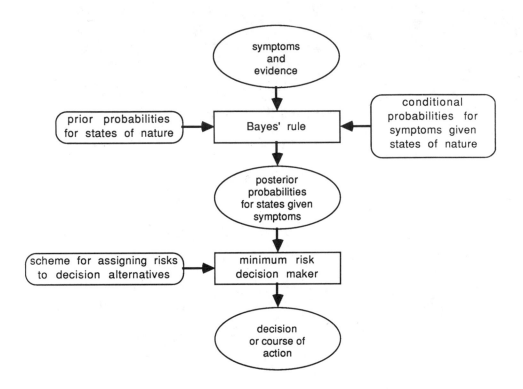

Figure 7.1: General form of an ideal decision-making system.

by changing only two boxes: the prior and conditional probabilities box and the risk-assignment-scheme box.

In Fig. 7.1 the components in rectangular or rounded-rectangular boxes are fixed parts of the system. In the ovals are the evidence, probabilities conditioned on the evidence, and decision based on the evidence.

If we always had accurate general knowledge for such inference problems, we could make simple and clean machines to compute probabilities for various things considering all the evidence. Unfortunately, we usually do not have accurate knowledge of the conditional probabilities of sets of symptoms (or evidence) given the state of health (the hidden truth), so that the ideal, all-Bayesian system of Fig. 7.1 cannot be successfully built. However, heuristic modeling tools can be used to represent known relationships between evidence and conclusion. The complex relationship between evidence and final conclusions can be expressed as a network of simpler relationships involving not only the evidence and final conclusions, but also intermediate assertions: partial conclusions and close consequences of the evidence. Such networks are called "probabilistic inference networks." Their design and construction are discussed in the following three sections of this chapter.

7.3 Probabilistic Inference Networks

7.3.1 Appropriate Domains

Making a decision means choosing among alternative courses of action with or without all the relevant information and often with uncertain information as well. The need for intelligent decision-making is omnipresent in intelligent beings. In people, the need arises at the simple level of choosing whether or not to step around a puddle on a rainy day, or at the complicated level of choosing a treatment plan for a medical patient. Animals need such abilities in order to find food and evade predators. A mathematician may need to choose among a set of possible directions in which to search for a proof.

We seek to model general decision-making in a computationally practical, yet mathematically meaningful way. Here "probabilistic inference network" structures are presented as formal structures for representing decision-making systems. They are good at handling information processing tasks with the following characterisitics:

1. pieces of information are available at various levels of certainty and completeness;

2. there is a need for optimal or nearly optimal decisions;

3. there may be a need to justify the arguments in favor of the leading alternative choices; and

4. general rules of inference (either based on scientific theory, or simply heuristic) are known or can be found for the problem.

Usually there must also be an economic need for the application of these techniques to a problem domain. Accurate models for complex phenomena take a significant effort to develop, even with the help of experts.

Some examples of actual or potential areas of practical application of inference networks are:

- medical diagnosis;

- fault diagnosis in machines and computer software (including automobiles, airplanes, computers, spacecraft, etc.)

- minerals prospecting;

- criminal investigations;

- military strategy formulation (including war-time decision-making);

- marketing strategy and investment; and

- decision-making in design processes (e.g., software design, suspension bridge design, VLSI circuit design).

7.3.2   Heuristical Components of Inference Networks

Because of the lack of knowledge of the exact conditional probability distribution for the various possible states of evidence (symptoms) given the various possible states of nature (e.g., having or not having malaria), successful inference networks cannot usually be developed directly from Bayes' rule. A reasonable alternative is to develop a hierarchy of "fuzzy" assertions or hypotheses and use substantiated hypotheses at level k to substantiate hypotheses at level $k+1$ (see Fig. 7.2). Bayes' rule can be used directly to substantiate (establish probability values for) level-1 hypotheses from the evidence if the evidence may be regarded as certain. Then "fuzzy inference rules" are used to obtain probabilities for other hypotheses, given the evidence. If there is uncertainty associated with the evidence, then fuzzy inference may be used at the first level as well.

7.3.3   Fuzzy Inference Rules

Fuzzy inference rules are functions for propagating probability values. The general form of such a function is:

$$f : [0,1]^n \to [0,1].$$

Thus a fuzzy inference rule takes some number n of probabilities as arguments and returns a single probability. The choice of f for a particular situation is a modelling decision that requires some understanding of the relationship among the phenomena described by the hypotheses.

Two sets of fuzzy inference rules analogous to operations in the propositional calculus have been found useful for building inference networks because they have behavior that follows intuition and they are easy to work with. These are shown in the bottom two rows of Fig. 7.3.

The system employing min and max is sometimes called a "possibilistic logic." Note that the value for $A \wedge B$ in the possibilistic system is *not* smaller than both the values for A and B. If $\min(a,b)$ is regarded as the probability of $A \wedge B$, then the propositions A and B should be regarded as *dependent*.

On the other hand, the second system, which assigns the value ab to the conjunction $A \wedge B$, gives a lower value to the conjunction than the values of either of the components. That is, $ab < a$ except when $a = 0$ or $b = 1$, and $ab < b$ except when $b = 0$ or $a = 1$. If ab is considered to be the probability of $A \wedge B$, then we must regard A and B as (statistically) independent.

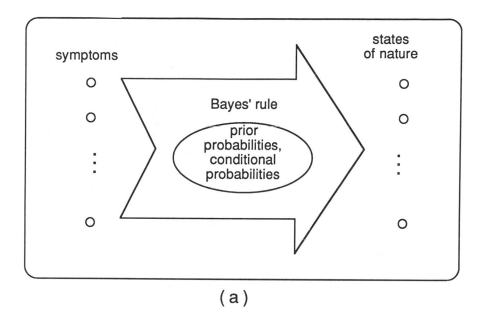

(a)

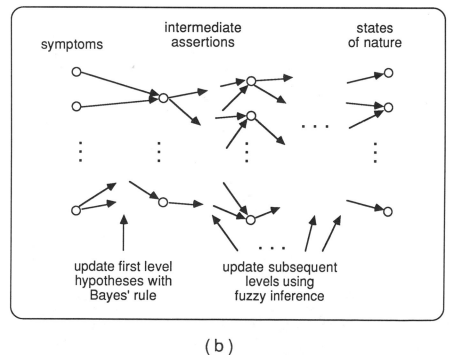

(b)

Figure 7.2: Pure Bayesian (a) and heuristic (b) inference systems.

A	B	$\neg A$	$A \wedge B$	$A \vee B$	$A \to B$	$A \oplus B$
F	F	T	F	F	T	F
F	T	T	F	T	T	T
T	F	F	F	T	F	T
T	T	F	T	T	T	F
a	b	$1-a$	$\min(a,b)$	$\max(a,b)$	$\max(1-a,b)$	$\mathrm{xor}(a,b)$
a	b	$1-a$	ab	$a+b-ab$	$1-a+ab$	$\mathrm{Xor}(a,b)$

Figure 7.3: Inference rules for propositional calculus and two fuzzy logics. The possibilistic logic rule for $A \oplus B$ is $\mathrm{xor}(a,b) = \max(\min(a, 1-b), \min(1-a, b))$. The probabilistic logic rule for $A \oplus B$ is $\mathrm{Xor}(a,b) = a+b-2ab+a^2b+ab^2-a^2b^2$.

In the examples involving fuzzy logic which follow, the possibilistic logic rules are employed.

Let us turn to the application domain of automobile repair for an example of an inference network with intermediate assertions. Let the possible symptoms be those described by the following four statements:

- S_1: There is a clanking sound in the engine.

- S_2: The car is low on pickup.

- S_3: The engine has trouble starting.

- S_4: Parts are difficult to obtain for this make of car.

The final state of nature whose probability we wish to infer is the truth of the statement

- C_1: The repair estimate is over \$250.

Because of the complexity in inferring C_1 directly from S_1, S_2, and S_3, five intermediate assertions are included which we believe relevant to the problem. The first three of these, which depend directly upon the evidence, are "first-level" hypotheses:

- H_1: A connecting rod is thrown in the engine.

- H_2: A wrist pin is loose.

- H_3: The car is out of tune.

The other two are a level removed from the first three, and they are thus at the second level:

- H_4: The engine needs replacement or rebuilding.

- H_5: The engine needs a tune-up.

Each first-level hypothesis is related to one or more of the symptoms. We may choose to express such a relationship so that Bayes' rule may be used to establish probabilities for the hypotheses that reflect a particular set of symptoms. In order to concisely express the prior and "class-conditional" probabilities for these relationships we may use a table such as that shown in Fig. 7.4. The rightmost column, labelled $P(S)$, gives values of the prior probability for each of the combinations of S_1, S_2 and S_3. We are using the symbol S as a variable that represents some combination of S_1, S_2, and S_3.

symptoms			$P(S|H_1)$	$P(S|H_2)$	$P(S|H_3)$	$P(S)$
S_1	S_2	S_3	$P(H_1) = 0.0001$	$P(H_2) = 0.0002$	$P(H_3) = 0.1$	
F	F	F	0.001	0.2	0.2	0.4405
F	F	T	0.003	0.1	0.2	0.25
F	T	F	0.006	0.1	0.2	0.109
F	T	T	0.15	0.1	0.396	0.20
T	F	F	0.04	0.125	0.001	0.0001
T	F	T	0.06	0.125	0.001	0.0001
T	T	F	0.11	0.125	0.001	0.0001
T	T	T	0.63	0.125	0.001	0.0002

Figure 7.4: Table of probabilities for the auto repair problem.

Using fuzzy logic rules we may model the dependence of H_4 and H_5 on H_1, H_2, and H_3 as follows:

$$H_4 = H_1 \vee H_2$$

and

$$H_5 = \neg(H_1 \vee H_2) \wedge H_3.$$

which, with the scheme of Fig. 7.3 (second-to-last row), means that

$$P(H_4|S) = \max[P(H_1|S), P(H_2|S)]$$

and

$$P(H_5|S) = \min\{1 - \max[P(H_1|S), P(H_2|S)], P(H_3|S)\}.$$

Finally, C_1 depends upon H_4, H_5, and S_4:

$$C_1 = H_4 \vee (H_5 \wedge S_4)$$

so that

$$P(C_1|S) = \max[P(H_4|S), \min(P(H_5|S), v)]$$

where:

$$v = \begin{cases} 1 & \text{if } S_4 \text{ is true;} \\ 0 & \text{otherwise.} \end{cases}$$

We may diagram our inference network as in Fig. 7.5. As an example for this inference network, let us consider the case when all of S_1, S_2, S_3 and S_4 are true. Then $P(S|H_1)$ is 0.604 and $P(S)$ is 0.0002. By Bayes' rule, $P(H_1|S) = 0.302$. Similarly, $P(H_2|S) = 0.125$, and $P(H_3|S) = 0.5$. Combining these using the fuzzy logic rules above leads to $P(H_4|S) = 0.302$, $P(H_5|S) = 0.5$, and $P(C_1|S) = 0.5$.

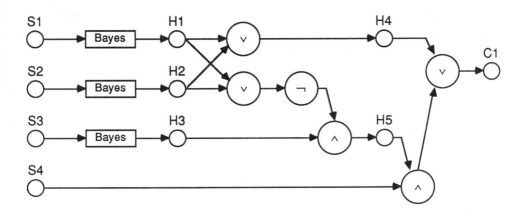

Figure 7.5: A probabilistic inference net for an automobile problem.

7.3.4   Steps in the Design of Inference Networks

The difficult problem of building an inference network appropriate to a given problem domain can be broken down into simpler steps. The basic steps are the following:

1. determination of the relevant inputs (i.e., set of possible evidence or symptoms),

2. determination of states of nature or decision alternatives,

3. determination of intermediate assertions that may be useful in the inference network,

4. formulation of inference links, and

5. tuning the probabilities and/or the fuzzy inference functions.

Let us address each of these steps in turn. The relevant inputs are usually properties of the object under study or of its environment. For automobile diagnosis, these are likely to be various aspects of the car itself: the condition of its various components, sounds, emissions, consumptions, and attributes of the make or type of car—availability of its parts, the propensity of parts from particular brands or year models to fail. In medical diagnosis, symptoms range from obvious fatigue, incapacity or infection to results of lab tests or descriptions of pain or medical history from the patient. One approach to the formation of the set of relevant inputs divides the process into two parts. First, a large set of possible inputs is determined by listing all known attributes of the object or situation under study. Second, this set is filtered to keep only those for which there is a hope of relevance to the problem. Relevance is established when a particular attribute's value has been correlated with the state of nature with a correlation coefficient beyond a threshold. Relevance may also be established through association with something else already known to be relevant. For example, if engine state is known to be relevant to the estimated cost of auto repair, then the sound of the engine may be declared relevant through correlation with the engine state. Relevance determination is nontrivial and would be an important part of any general system for inferring inference networks automatically or through interaction with an expert.

The states of nature, like the set of relevant inputs, are learned from experience or through training. For example, some of the conditions of an automobile engine may be found by taking some apart. Finding broken parts, one immediately is acquainted with one subset of states of nature for car engines: the set of states for which the engine contains broken parts. Additional experience with engines leads to further subdivisions of these sets of states. Eventually one has a suitably fine partition of the set of states of engines to support the reasoning in one's head or in an inference network.

The intermediate assertions may be established in a fashion like the establishment of the states of nature or the relevant inputs. Attributes (of the object or situation under investigation) which are not directly observable (but probabilistically related to the inputs and states of nature in some reasonably understood way) form the basis of intermediate assertions. Partial characterizations of the state of nature may be useful as intermediate assertions; for example, "the problem is in the engine."

Formation of inference links may be done on the basis of correlations among attributes. First a search is made for the simplest logical relationships, and then more and more complicated ones are sought. In order of increasing complexity we have

1. logical concurrence—e.g., an input highly correlated with a partial state of nature;

2. negative concurrence—strong negative correlation;

3. logical implication—whenever A occurs, B does too—this may be worth noting even when B is an input;

4. conjunction—C occurs whenever both A and B occur;

5. disjunction—C occurs whenever either A or B occur; and

6. exclusive disjunction—either A or B occurs but not both.

Whenever a sought logical relationship is found among a group of nodes (inputs, assertions or states), a link (possibly 3-way to involve A, B and C as above) can be added to the network with labels as to its type and/or appropriateness of fit. When the node(s) for the state of nature has been connected (possibly via intermediate nodes) to the inputs, the topological portion of an inference network has been constructed. Updating functions still need to be chosen to propagate the effects of inputs.

If Bayes' rule is to be used to make the first-level connections in the network, then there is no need for fuzzy inference rules at that level. But fuzzy logic and/or "subjective-Bayesian" updating functions (which are defined later) may be used at subsequent levels to represent the ways information is to propagate through those levels. Probability values associated with various parts of the network need to be tuned to give reasonable performance. Prior probabilities for states of nature and intermediate assertions must be specified if Bayesian or subjective-Bayesian updating is to be used. Class-conditional probabilities are also essential for Bayesian updating, and they must be well-chosen to give reasonable results. Statistical learning methods might be employed to obtain and to improve probability estimates. However, in most applications, there will not be enough trials (test cases) in which to get good values automatically, and this knowledge must be obtained from an expert or from compiled materials and directly incorporated to achieve a useful level of performance. For example, a new auto mechanic learning about Brand Q automobiles may learn from his own experience that 1971 was a bad year for transmissions; or he may learn this by word of mouth from a senior mechanic, and gain this bit of expertise in much less time. A computer system to diagnose car problems could be given *a priori* probability of 0.5 that any power train problem in '71 Brand Q cars is in the transmission, rather than have to process 20 power-train cases to find out.

We will assume that relationships and probabilities needed to construct an inference network are provided by an expert, either in collaboration with an AI programmer or with an interactive tool for building expert systems.

7.4 Updating in Inference Networks

In an inference network the general format of an inference rule is the following: "if E, then H," where E is the evidence and H is the hypothesis. In some cases, the evidence may be compound and instead of E we have $E_1, E_2, \ldots, E_n$. There

E_i is the ith piece of evidence bearing on the hypothesis. Each inference rule has a certain strength associated with it, which is the power of the evidence in that rule to confirm the hypothesis in that rule. Here we discuss means for updating probabilities associated with hypotheses on the basis of the certainty with which we know the evidence to be present. A family of such means often called "subjective-Bayesian" updating rules has proved to be useful in expert systems such as PROSPECTOR. We begin by formulating the "odds likelihood" version of Bayes' rule.

7.4.1 Odds and Bayes' Rule

As explained in Subsection 7.2.3, Bayes' rule is usually formulated as follows:

$$P(H|E) = \frac{P(E|H)P(H)}{P(E)}.$$

This expresses the probability of the hypothesis, given the evidence, as the product of the conditional probability for the evidence given the hypothesis, times the prior probability of the hypothesis all divided by the prior probability of the evidence. We may also express the probability for the negation of the hypothesis using Bayes' rule.

$$P(\neg H|E) = \frac{P(E|\neg H)P(\neg H)}{P(E)}$$

Now we obtain the *odds likelihood formulation* for Bayes' rule by dividing these two equations. Shortly, we will rewrite this odds-likelihood formulation by using the definition for the odds of an event. An event X having probability $P(X)$ has odds as follows:

$$O(X) = \frac{P(X)}{1 - P(X)}$$

This relationship can be inverted, allowing the probability to be computed from the odds:

$$P(X) = \frac{O(X)}{1 + O(X)}$$

Thus "50/50" odds (i.e., odds $= 50/50 = 1$) corresponds to a probability of one-half.

We may now express the odds-likelihood formulation for Bayes' rule very simply:

$$O(H|E) = \lambda O(H).$$

Here $O(H)$ is the *prior odds* on H and λ is defined to be the *likelihood ratio* $P(E|H)/P(E|\neg H)$. Thus, we update the odds on H in the light of evidence E by multiplying the prior odds on H by the likelihood ratio λ.

Presumably, in the construction of an inference network, an expert provides a value of λ for each rule. If λ is much greater than 1, the rule has a high strength indicating that the presence of the evidence E makes it much more probable that H is true. In such a case, we may speak of E as being "sufficient" for H. Thus, we may refer to λ as a *sufficiency* coefficient for the rule. Also, if λ is close to zero (significantly less than 1), then the presence of the evidence reduces the likelihood of H, and it would be reasonable to say that E is sufficient for $\neg H$.

Now, suppose E is false or known to be not present (rather than not known). Then we may write

$$O(H|\neg E) = \lambda' O(H)$$

where λ' is defined as

$$\frac{P(\neg E|H)}{P(\neg E|\neg H)} = \frac{1 - P(E|H)}{1 - P(E|\neg H)}$$

This provides a way to update the odds on H when the information about E is in the negative. Note that λ' cannot be derived from λ, and so it must also be provided by an expert. If $0 < \lambda' \ll 1$, (that is, λ' is between 0 and 1 but much closer to 0 than to 1), then we may say that E is "necessary" for H since the absence of the E (i.e., or the truth of $\neg E$) makes H very unlikely. We sometimes speak of λ' as the *necessity* coefficient for the rule.

Let us return to the example on page 242, where we computed the probability that John has malaria, given that he has a high fever. Since $P(H)$, the prior probability that John has malaria, is 0.0001, the odds, $O(H)$, is $0.0001/0.9999 \approx 0.0001$. We compute λ as $P(E|H)/P(E|\neg H) = 0.75/0.14 \approx 5.3571$ and λ' as $(1 - P(E|H))/(1 - P(E|\neg H)) = 0.25/0.86 \approx 0.2907$. If we know that John has a high fever, then we compute $O(H|E) = \lambda O(H) \approx 5.3571 \cdot 0.0001 \approx 0.000536$. If we know, to the contrary, that John does not have a high fever, we compute $O(H|\neg E) = \lambda' O(H) \approx 0.2907 \cdot 0.00001 \approx 0.000029$.

In a probabilistic inference network, an arc may be labelled with a pair of values for λ and λ' to indicate how the presence or absence of the evidence is to influence the odds on the hypothesis (see Fig. 7.6).

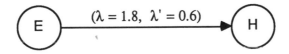

Figure 7.6: Arc in an inference network, labelled with the sufficiency and necessity coefficients.

Although λ and λ' are not functionally dependent on one another, they are not completely independent either. The following equation expresses λ' in terms of λ and the conditional probability of E given not H.

$$\lambda' = \frac{1 - \lambda P(E|\neg H)}{1 - P(E|\neg H)}$$

Now assuming that $P(E|\neg H)$ is neither 1 or 0, we find if λ is greater than 1, then λ' is less than 1 and vice versa. Note that it would not be entirely consistent to have λ greater than 1 and λ' equal to 1 or vice versa. Thus, if a rule states that the presence of some evidence enhances the odds for the hypothesis, then it should be the case that the absence of the evidence hurts the hypothesis at least to some extent. However, some systems such as MYCIN allow relationships in which positive evidence strengthens a hypothesis while negative knowledge of the same evidence has no effect on the hypothesis—in effect, allowing $\lambda > 1$ with $\lambda' = 1$.

The pair λ and λ' carries the same information as the pair $P(E|H)$ and $P(E|\neg H)$. To get the latter from the former we may use the two formulas:

$$P(E|H) = \lambda \frac{1 - \lambda'}{\lambda - \lambda'}$$

$$P(E|\neg H) = \frac{1 - \lambda'}{\lambda - \lambda'}$$

The formulas $O(H|E) = \lambda O(H)$ and $O(H|\neg E) = \lambda' O(H)$ give us a means to update the odds on hypothesis H given either knowledge that the evidence is present or knowledge that it is absent; if the evidence is present, we multiply the prior odds by λ, and if it is absent, we multiply it by λ'. However, most of the inference rules in an inference network must work with uncertain or incomplete evidence so that the rule must be capable of propagating probabilities in a more versatile fashion than we have just discussed.

7.4.2 Handling Uncertain Evidence

We may extend the foregoing discussion to handle the case of uncertain evidence by assuming that E above is in fact based on some observations E'. For example, if we say that we have 80 percent confidence in E, then we can re-express this as a statement that the probability of E given E' is 0.8. In order to develop some useful techniques for propagating probabilities, it helps to make the following simplifying assumption: Knowledge of E with certainty would allow us to forget about the observations E' for purposes of inferring the hypothesis H. Thus we are assuming that the only influence of E' on H comes through E. This allows us to have a fairly simple expression for the probability of H, given the observations E'.

It now appears reasonable to compute $P(H|E')$ as a linear convex combination of the two extreme values $P(H|E)$ and $P(H|\neg E)$. That is, for some value of t in the range $[0, 1]$, we have:

$$P(H|E') = tP(H|E) + (1 - t)P(H|\neg E)$$

Taking $P(E|E')$ as the value of t, we find that as $P(E|E')$ increases from 0 to 1, $P(H|E')$ goes from $P(H|\neg E)$ to $P(H|E)$. The two extreme values can, of

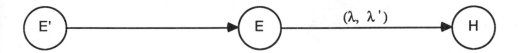

Figure 7.7: Inference with uncertain evidence.

course, be computed with Bayes' rule in a straightforward fashion. In order to determine the probability of H given the observations E' we interpolate the two extreme values using the conditional probability for E given E'. A diagram that illustrates this linear interpolation scheme is shown in Fig. 7.8.

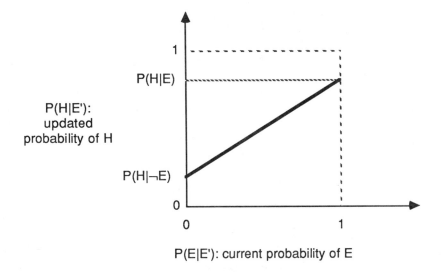

Figure 7.8: A linear interpolation function for computing $P(H|E')$ from $P(E|E')$.

Considering our example once again, let us assume that John's temperature is known to have been taken by an unreliable nurse, who, it is also known, takes correct readings 80 percent of the time. Here we have $P(E|E')$, the probability that John has a fever given that the nurse reports a fever, equal to 0.8. With the linear interpolation above, we compute $P(H|E')$, the probability that John has malaria given that the nurse reports a fever, as $P(H|E') \approx 0.8 \cdot 0.0005354 + 0.2 \cdot 0.000029 \approx 0.0004341$. This probability happens to be about 20 percent lower than that for the case in which the nurse is known to be reliable.

The choice of a linear function, rather than some curve, is an arbitrary one. It makes the updating computation simple. As we shall see, there is commonly

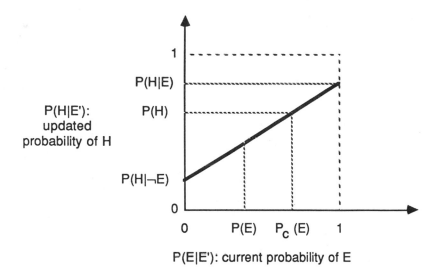

Figure 7.9: Inconsistency in prior probabilities for E and H.

a problem with this function, and some others may be better. In any case, it seems clear that such a function should be either monotonically nondecreasing or nonincreasing, depending upon whether E is supportive or detracting evidence for H, respectively.

An interesting dilemma arises from the fact that this equation places a constraint on the prior probabilities associated with H and E, and this dilemma is described in the next subsection.

7.4.3 The Bayesian Dilemma for Inference Networks

In order to apply Bayes' rule in a meaningful way in an inference network, it is necessary for the various prior probabilities in the network to be consistent with one another. In the absence of any observations E', if we use the prior probability for E to compute an updated probability for H, the "updating" should not give anything other than the prior probability for H. It would be easy indeed for an expert, subjectively assigning probabilities to various propositions in an inference network, to provide prior probabilities that do not meet this constraint. In such a case, the set of prior probabilities is called *inconsistent*.

For example, suppose that a physician assigns a prior probability of 0.3 to E, claiming that three out of ten of the patients he sees have fevers. If we use this value to obtain $P(H|\hat{E})$, the probability of H given the "expected" probability of E, then using the linear interpolation above, we obtain $P(H|\hat{E}) = 0.3 \cdot 0.0005354 + 0.7 \cdot 0.000029 \approx 0.000181$. This value should be equal to $P(H) = 0.0001$, but it is about 80 percent larger.

Although we could design tools that could make it easy for an expert to make up only consistent sets of prior probabilities, this may interfere with the already-difficult job of creating a good model of the expertise. Therefore researchers have explored the possibility of allowing the inconsistency and making the updating algorithms compensate for it. The inconsistency which can arise is illustrated in Fig. 7.9.

The prior probability for H should correspond to the prior probability for E along the line which interpolates the two extreme values. However, the two may not correspond, and $P_c(E)$, the prior probability of E which would be consistent with the prior probability for H, is somewhere to the right (as in the illustration) or left of the prior probabilty for E actually given by the expert. The resolution of this inconsistency is an important question because various forms of anomalous behavior need to be avoided. An example of undesirable behavior arises when the observations lead to a probability of E slightly greater than the prior one and yet less than the probability value that would be consistent with the prior probability of the hypothesis, and the result is that the probability for the hypothesis is actually lowered, even though the evidence is supposed to be supportive. Developers of early inference network systems (PROSPECTOR, MYCIN) have proposed some ways for getting around this inconsistency. They involve changing the function used to update the probabilities from the strictly linear one shown in Fig. 7.8 and Fig. 7.9 to some piecewise-linear one. Such a piecewise-linear function is designed to pass through the point whose coordinates are the prior on E and the prior on H as given by the expert. Two alternative functions are shown in Fig. 7.10 and Fig. 7.11. The function shown in Fig. 7.11 is designed so that the output remains stable for inputs anywhere within the "zone of inconsistency" between $P(E)$ and $P_c(E)$.

Two other piecewise-linear functions are of particular interest. Figure 7.12 illustrates an updating function which is flat for $P(E|E')$ below $P(E)$. If the evidence E is absent (i.e., the current probability of E is low, compared with the prior probability) then there is no effect on the probability of H; the prior probability of H remains constant. In this case the evidence E is somewhat sufficient for H but not at all necessary for H. This function is suitably called a "sufficiency-only" updating function.

On the other hand, the function of Fig. 7.13 causes a low value for $P(E|E')$ to negatively influence $P(H|E')$, but does not let a high value of $P(E|E')$ bring $P(H|E')$ above $P(H)$. Such a function is suitable when E is necessary for H but not sufficient for H. For this reason, the function can be called a "necessity-only" updating function.

7.4.4   Updating the Probabilities

The function in Fig. 7.10 provides a good practical method for updating the probability for a hypothesis in most situations. The steps for computing the

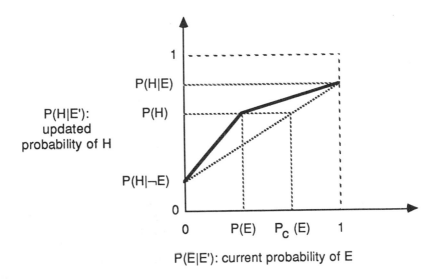

Figure 7.10: Piecewise-linear function for updating the probability of a hypothesis.

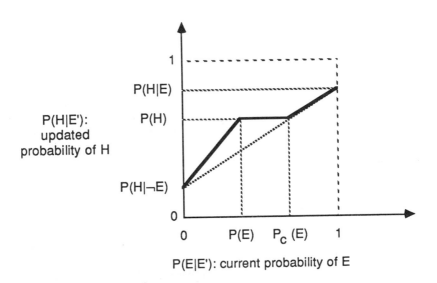

Figure 7.11: Alternative piecewise-linear function for probability updating.

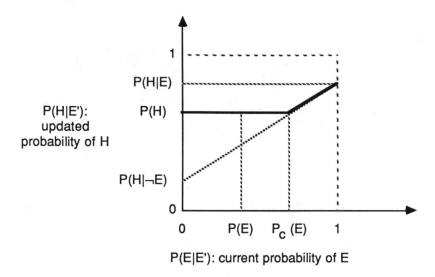

Figure 7.12: "Sufficiency-only" updating function.

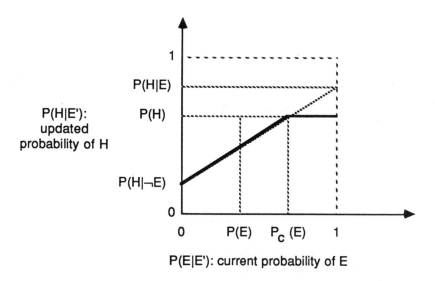

Figure 7.13: "Necessity-only" updating function.

posterior probability on H given the evidence E' whose influence is transmitted through E (see Fig. 7.7) are the following:

1. Compute $P(H|E)$. This depends only upon the prior at H and the λ values along the arc from E to H and can therefore be precomputed:

$$P(H|E) = \frac{O(H|E)}{1 + O(H|E)} = \frac{\lambda O(H)}{1 + \lambda O(H)}.$$

2. Compute $P(H|\neg E)$ with the formula:

$$P(H|\neg E) = \frac{O(H|\neg E)}{1 + O(H|\neg E)} = \frac{\lambda' O(H)}{1 + \lambda' O(H)}.$$

3. Compute $P(H|E')$ from $P(E|E')$ using the function shown in Fig. 7.10:

$$P(H|E') = \begin{cases} P(H|\neg E) + P(E|E')[P(H) - P(H|\neg E)]/P(E) \\ \qquad \text{if } P(E|E') \leq P(E); \\ P(H) + [P(E|E') - P(E)][P(H|E) - P(H)]/[1 - P(E)] \\ \qquad \text{otherwise.} \end{cases}$$

Note that most of the terms in Step 3 are independent of $P(E|E')$ and can therefore be computed in advance, saving time during the updating.

7.4.5 Combining Independent Evidence at a Node

Earlier we saw one way to have several pieces of evidence influence the probability of a single hypothesis. This was done by combining evidence using fuzzy logic rules. An alternative "multiple evidence" updating rule is now presented that is well-suited to the case when the items of evidence are to be considered independent for the purpose of computing their effects on the probability of the hypothesis. Such a situation is diagrammed in Fig. 7.14.

We update the odds on H by independently calculating "effective lambda values" along each arc: $\lambda_{e1}, \lambda_{e2}, \ldots, \lambda_{ek}$ and then multiplying them together to get an overall effective lambda:

$$\lambda_E = \lambda_{e1} \lambda_{e2} \cdots \lambda_{ek}$$

Then we can multiply $O(H)$ by λ_E to get the *a posteriori* odds on H.

The *effective lambda value* λ_e along an arc can be obtained from the posterior probability above as follows:

$$\lambda_e = \frac{O(H|E')}{O(H)}$$

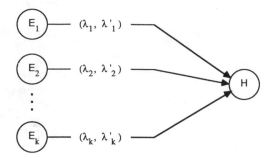

Figure 7.14: Combining independent evidence.

where $O(H|E') = P(H|E')/[1 - P(H|E')]$, and $P(H|E')$ is the probability of H given the evidence transmitted along the particular arc.

Even when $E_1, E_2, \ldots, E_k$ are not all mutually independent, this method may be useful. If E_i and E_j are highly correlated, then their λ and λ' values may be adjusted to moderate the effect of doubly supporting or doubly detracting influences.

7.5   An Inference Network in LISP

7.5.1   The Traveller's Restaurant Selection Problem

In order to illustrate some of these techniques for subjective-Bayesian inference, we consider a problem occasionally faced by travellers in unfamiliar towns.

> A traveller, without benefit of any guide book or particular restaurant advice, walks past several restaurants and takes a closer look at one of them. The traveller is hungry enough to eat but would like to think that he would get a good meal at this restaurant before committing himself to eating there. Several aspects of the restaurant are visible: its clientele, general atmosphere, menu, and some of the staff. The overall food quality is what is of most concern to the traveller; however, it is difficult to see the food or tell how it would taste. On the basis of what can be seen and heard, a prediction of the food quality must be made.

This problem is a rather fuzzy one, and there must accordingly be some arbitrariness in any solution for it. The solution presented here is clearly just one of many possible; it embodies one of many possible sets of heuristics for predicting food quality on the basis of pre-meal observations.

7.5.2   Heuristics for Restaurant Evaluation

Before actually making the committment to eat in the restaurant (i.e., asking for a table for dinner), there are several easily perceptible features of a restaurant, and then there are some which are perceptible with a little effort. Easily visible are these: the decor including the tastefulness of decor, and lighting; the atmosphere (smoky or not); the clientele (how many, how dressed and how behaved); and the menu with the prices. With a little effort, one can see these: the table settings including linen, plates, silverware, glasses, possible flowers, plants or candles, ashtrays and condiment vessels; the general cleanliness of all surfaces; the menu's details including the variety of dishes offered, the neatness and the artistry of the menu, and the existence of daily specialties; and the service: the number of waiters/waitresses in proportion to the number of clients; the dress and cleanliness of the staff, and the courtesy of the staff (as visible in gestures). Also perceptible is the noise level and the style of music, if any.

The chief variable to be predicted is the overall food quality of the restaurant. This comprises such features as taste, texture, appearance, portion sizes, correctness (consistency with traditions), nutrition and hygiene. Since it is certainly possible for a restaurant to have beautiful decor, cleanliness and good atmosphere, and yet have food which tastes terrible and is unhealthy, the inferences we make about the food from the observations can be probabilistic at best. Since it is difficult to know the statistical relationships among these variables with any degree of accuracy, the results cannot even represent true probabilities. All we can guarantee is this: our system will embody the judgment of an imaginary "expert."

Since each input variable (e.g., decor) can conceivably affect our estimate of the food quality, we shall design a network in which the various observations are inputs and the final node corresponds to overall food quality. In order to simplify the relationships between inputs and output to the point where we can rationally model them, we introduce a number of intermediate variables. The relationships between inputs and intermediates, between intermediates and other intermediates, and between intermediates and output(s) are easier to understand and describe than the relationship from inputs directly to output(s). In our case, the inputs are "primary evidential variables" (e.g., decor, etc.), and we introduce a set of four "lumped evidential variables" as intermediates: popularity, elegance, artistry and cleanliness. These are predicted directly from the primary evidential variables. The lumped evidential variables are then used, in our case, to predict seven "predicted component variables" which finally are used to predict the output, overall food quality.

Our nine primary evidential variables have the following significance:

1. DECOR is high when decor is tasteful.

2. TABLE_SETTING is highest when the tables are nicely set with respectable-looking dishes, silverware, glasses, table cloth, and flowers or

candles set out.

3. SURFACE_CLEANLINESS is high when tables, dishes, floors, etc., seem to be clean.

4. AIR is high when the air looks or smells clean and fresh.

5. SOUNDS is high when there is little noise, and any music playing is tasteful.

6. CLIENTELE is high when there are a good number of reasonably respectable people present in the restaurant and few or no rowdies or vagrants.

7. MENU is high when there is a reasonable variety of dishes available (not too many, as this would suggest the use of inferior ingredients or methods), the menu is clean, attractive, and tasteful.

8. PRICES is high when the listed prices seem reasonable for the dishes they represent.

9. SERVICE is high when the restaurant staff appears clean and attractive, courteous, and adequate for the number of people dining.

A diagram showing all the nodes and arcs of one probabilistic inference network for this problem is shown in Fig. 7.15. The prior probabilities on nodes are not shown, but are given in the section on implementation, as are the λ and λ' values for each arc.

7.5.3 Implementation

We now describe the LISP functions and other structures that constitute an implementation for the network we have just described.

```
; INFNET.LSP
; A LISP implementation of an INFerence NETwork that
;  uses subjective-Bayesian updating of certainty values.
; Given values of particular evidential variables,
;  the system determines the certainty value of several
;  intermediate variables and a summary variable.
; The problem solved is the prediction of food quality
;  in a restaurant:
;  The "Traveller's Restaurant Selection Problem"
```

The functions ODDS and PROB are used to convert between probability values (certainty values) and odds.

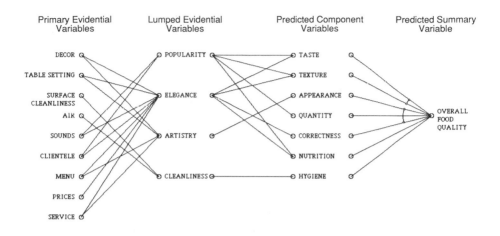

Figure 7.15: Probabilistic inference network for the Traveller's Restaurant Selection Problem.

```
; ODDS takes a probability value and returns an odds value:
(DEFUN ODDS (PROB)
  (QUOTIENT PROB (DIFFERENCE 1.0 PROB)) )

; PROB is the inverse of ODDS:
(DEFUN PROB (ODDS)
  (QUOTIENT ODDS (ADD1 ODDS)) )
```

The following function helps create the representation of the network by entering values onto the property list of the atom (node) being defined. The form of the argument list is this: L = (*atom prior-probability current-probability arc-expression*). The fourth argument to DEFINE_NODE is an "arc expression," which describes the incoming arcs and how their effects are to be combined.

```
; Each node of the inference network is represented by an
;  atom with its property list.  The next function helps
;  to set up these representations.
(DEFEXPR DEFINE_NODE (L)
  (PROG (ATOM_NAME)
        (SETQ ATOM_NAME (CAR L))
        (PUTPROP ATOM_NAME (CADR L) 'PRIOR_PROB)
        (PUTPROP ATOM_NAME (ODDS (CADR L)) 'PRIOR_ODDS)
        (SETQ L (CDDR L))
```

```
(PUTPROP ATOM_NAME (CAR L) 'CURRENT_PROB)
(PUTPROP ATOM_NAME (ODDS (CAR L)) 'CURRENT_ODDS)
(PUTPROP ATOM_NAME (CADR L) 'ARCS) ) )
```

The following functions allow abbreviation of the operations for accessing property lists and accessing components of arc descriptions.

```
(DEFUN CURRENT_PROB (N) (GET N 'CURRENT_PROB))
(DEFUN PRIOR_PROB (N) (GET N 'PRIOR_PROB))
(DEFUN CURRENT_ODDS (N) (GET N 'CURRENT_ODDS))
(DEFUN PRIOR_ODDS (N) (GET N 'PRIOR_ODDS))
(DEFUN SUFFICIENCY (ARC) (CADR ARC))
(DEFUN NECESSITY   (ARC) (CAR (CDDR ARC)))
```

Now the inference network is represented, beginning with the nodes for the primary evidential variables.

```
; Here we set up nodes for the Primary Evidential Variables:
(DEFINE_NODE DECOR 0.5 0.9 ())
(DEFINE_NODE TABLE_SETTING 0.5 0.8 ())
(DEFINE_NODE SURFACE_CLEANLINESS 0.8 0.8 ())
(DEFINE_NODE AIR 0.6 0.6 ())
(DEFINE_NODE SOUNDS 0.5 0.5 ())
(DEFINE_NODE CLIENTELE 0.5 0.9 ())
(DEFINE_NODE MENU 0.5 0.5 ())
(DEFINE_NODE PRICES 0.5 0.9 ())
(DEFINE_NODE SERVICE 0.3 0.9 ())
```

The first node, DECOR is defined with a prior probability of 0.5 and a current probability of 0.9. Since there are no incoming arcs for input nodes such as this, DECOR's arc expression is empty.

```
; Here are declarations for the Lumped Evidential Variables:
(DEFINE_NODE POPULARITY 0.5 0.6   (INDEP
                                  (ARC: SOUNDS 1.5 1.0)
                                  (ARC: CLIENTELE 1.0 0.24) ))
(DEFINE_NODE ELEGANCE 0.5 0.5     (INDEP
                                  (ARC: DECOR 3.0 0.5)
                                  (ARC: TABLE_SETTING 1.0 0.74)
                                  (ARC: SOUNDS 1.5 0.74)
                                  (ARC: CLIENTELE 1.0 0.5)
                                  (ARC: MENU 1.24 0.74)
                                  (ARC: PRICES 1.24 0.74)
                                  (ARC: SERVICE 1.0 0.5) ))
(DEFINE_NODE ARTISTRY 0.5 0.9     (INDEP
                                  (ARC: DECOR 1.0 0.5)
```

```
                              (ARC: TABLE_SETTING 1.0 0.5)
                              (ARC: MENU 1.5 0.74)
                              (ARC: SERVICE 1.0 0.5) ))
(DEFINE_NODE CLEANLINESS 0.7 0.7 (INDEP
                              (ARC: SURFACE_CLEANLINESS
                                    1.5 0.2)
                              (ARC: AIR 1.5 0.5) ))
```

Since the nodes corresponding to lumped evidential variables are not input nodes, they have arc expressions which are non-empty. In the case of the node POPU-LARITY, the arc expression contains two arcs, represented by the subexpressions (ARC: SOUNDS 1.5 1.0) and (ARC: CLIENTELE 1.0 0.24), respectively, and the atom INDEP indicates that the effects of these two arcs are to be combined with the method for independent influences. That is, SOUNDS and CLIEN-TELE are to be considered as independent pieces of evidence as far as their influence on POPULARITY is concerned. The first of these two arcs, (ARC: SOUNDS 1.5 1.0), is represented as a list of four elements: the atom "ARC:" identifies the arc expression as a *simple* one (not compound), representing an arc rather than a group of arcs and how they are to be combined; the atom SOUNDS is the name of node from which the arc emanates; the first number is the sufficiency factor associated with the arc—if the current probability of SOUNDS were 1.0, then the odds on POPULARITY would be multiplied by 1.5; the second number is the necessity factor.

```
; Here are node definitions for the Predicted Component Variables:
(DEFINE_NODE TASTE 0.6 0.6        (INDEP
                              (ARC: POPULARITY 1.5 0.7)
                              (ARC: ELEGANCE 1.5 0.8) ))
(DEFINE_NODE TEXTURE 0.6 0.6      (INDEP
                              (ARC: POPULARITY 1.5 0.7)
                              (ARC: ELEGANCE 1.0 0.5) ))
(DEFINE_NODE APPEARANCE 0.5 0.5   (INDEP
                              (ARC: ARTISTRY 3.0 0.4)))
(DEFINE_NODE QUANTITY 0.5 0.5     (INDEP
                              (ARC: POPULARITY 1.5 0.5)))
(DEFINE_NODE CORRECTNESS 0.5 0.5  (INDEP
                              (ARC: ELEGANCE 1.0 0.7)))
(DEFINE_NODE NUTRITION 0.6 0.6    (INDEP
                              (ARC: POPULARITY 1.1 0.7)
                              (ARC: ELEGANCE 1.8 0.8) ))
(DEFINE_NODE HYGIENE 0.8 0.8      (INDEP
                              (ARC: CLEANLINESS 1.0 0.1)))


; Here is the Predicted Summary Variable node:
```

```
(DEFINE_NODE OVERALL_FOOD_QUALITY 0.5 0.5
                            (INDEP
                            (AND
                             (ARC: TASTE 3.0 0.3)
                             (ARC: TEXTURE 1.0 0.5) )
                            (AND
                             (ARC: APPEARANCE 1.0 0.3)
                             (ARC: CORRECTNESS 1.3 0.8) )
                            (ARC: QUANTITY 1.2 0.8)
                            (ARC: NUTRITION 1.0 0.3)
                            (ARC: HYGIENE 1.5 0.2) ))
```

The function UPDATE_PROB below uses the formula on page 261 to compute an appropriate current probability of *H* using a piecewise-linear interpolation function.

```
; compute P(H | E') for a single arc.
(DEFUN UPDATE_PROB (H ARC)
  (COND
    ((GREATERP (CURRENT_PROB (CAR ARC))
               (PRIOR_PROB (CAR ARC)) )
     (REPORT_PROGRESS 'SUPPORTIVE)
     (PLUS (PRIOR_PROB H)
           (TIMES (QUOTIENT
                      (DIFFERENCE
                          (PROB (TIMES (SUFFICIENCY ARC)
                                       (PRIOR_ODDS H) ))
                          (PRIOR_PROB H) )
                      (DIFFERENCE 1.0 (PRIOR_PROB (CAR ARC))) )
                  (DIFFERENCE
                      (CURRENT_PROB (CAR ARC))
                      (PRIOR_PROB (CAR ARC)) ) ) ) )
    (T (REPORT_PROGRESS 'INHIBITIVE)
       (PLUS (PROB (TIMES (NECESSITY ARC) (PRIOR_ODDS H)))
             (TIMES (QUOTIENT
                        (DIFFERENCE
                            (PRIOR_PROB H)
                            (PROB (TIMES (NECESSITY ARC)
                                         (PRIOR_ODDS H) )) )
                        (PRIOR_PROB (CAR ARC)) )
                    (CURRENT_PROB (CAR ARC)) ) ) ) ) )
```

The following function helps to show the progress of computation through the inference network.

```
; if REPORTING is not NIL then describe progress of updating:
```

```
(DEFUN REPORT_PROGRESS (SUPP_INHIB)
  (COND ((NULL REPORTING) NIL)
        (T
         (PRINT (CONS SUPP_INHIB
                      (APPEND    '(PROBABILITY UPDATING FOR NODE:)
                                 (LIST H)
                                 '(ALONG ARC:)
                                 (LIST ARC)
                                 '(WITH PRIOR ODDS)
                                 (LIST (PRIOR_ODDS H)) ) ))
         (PRINT (APPEND '(PRIOR AND CURRENT PROBS OF E ARE:)
                        (LIST   (PRIOR_PROB (CAR ARC))
                                (CURRENT_PROB (CAR ARC))) ))
         ) ) )
```

In order to combine the effects of independent evidence, it is necessary to know the effective lambda values along each incoming arc, so that these can be multiplied to get an overall lambda value. The next function determines an effective lambda value.

```
; Determine the odds updating factor along the ARC specified,
; given the prior and current probabilities and odds for
; the predecessor node, the priors for the node H, and the
; SUFFICIENCY and NECESSITY values along the arc.
(DEFUN EFFECTIVE_ARC_LAMBDA (ARC)
  (QUOTIENT (ODDS (UPDATE_PROB H ARC))
            (PRIOR_ODDS H) ) )
```

The next function actually multiplies the effective lambda values together in order to combine their effects.

```
; Determine the updating factors for all arcs coming into H
; and multiply them to get an overall odds updating factor.
; This scheme assumes that the arcs are treated as if their
; influences were independent.
(DEFUN COMBINE_INDEP_LAMBDAS (ARC_EXP)
  (APPLY (FUNCTION TIMES)
         (MAPCAR (FUNCTION EVAL_ARC_EXP)
                 (CDR ARC_EXP) ) ) )
```

The function which follows evaluates a conjunctive arc expression, returning the smallest of the effective lambda values of the arc subexpressions.

```
(DEFUN COMBINE_CONJUNCTIVE_LAMBDAS (ARC_EXP)
  (APPLY (FUNCTION MIN)
         (MAPCAR (FUNCTION EVAL_ARC_EXP)
                 (CDR ARC_EXP) ) ) )
```

In a similar fashion, the next function evaluates a disjunctive arc expression. It returns the largest of the effective lambda values of the arc subexpressions.

```
(DEFUN COMBINE_DISJUNCTIVE_LAMBDAS (ARC_EXP)
  (APPLY (FUNCTION MAX)
         (MAPCAR (FUNCTION EVAL_ARC_EXP)
                 (CDR ARC_EXP) ) ) )
```

The function UPDATE_NODES updates the current odds and probabilities of all nodes on the list NODES (passed as an argument). The order of nodes on the list is important: they must be topologically sorted so that if there is an arc from A to B in the network, then either A precedes B in the list, or A does not appear in the list.

```
(DEFUN UPDATE_NODES (NODES)
  (COND ((NULL NODES) NIL)
        (T (UPDATE_NODE (CAR NODES))
           (UPDATE_NODES (CDR NODES)) ) ) )
```

```
; The function EVAL_ARC_EXP evaluates an arc expression, finding
;  an effective odds updating factor that takes effects of all
;  the arcs in the expression into account.
(DEFUN EVAL_ARC_EXP (ARC_EXP)
  (COND ((EQ (CAR ARC_EXP) 'ARC:)
         (EFFECTIVE_ARC_LAMBDA (CDR ARC_EXP)))
        ((EQ (CAR ARC_EXP) 'INDEP)
         (COMBINE_INDEP_LAMBDAS ARC_EXP) )
        ((EQ (CAR ARC_EXP) 'AND)
         (COMBINE_CONJUNCTIVE_LAMBDAS ARC_EXP) )
        ((EQ (CAR ARC_EXP) 'OR)
         (COMBINE_DISJUNCTIVE_LAMBDAS ARC_EXP) )
        (T (PRINT '(ILLEGAL ARC EXPRESSION:)) (PRINT ARC_EXP)) ) )
```

The following function causes one node's values to be updated.

```
(DEFUN UPDATE_NODE (H)
  (PROG NIL
        (PUTPROP H
                 (TIMES (PRIOR_ODDS H)
                        (EVAL_ARC_EXP (GET H 'ARCS)) )
                 'CURRENT_ODDS)
        (PUTPROP H (PROB (CURRENT_ODDS H)) 'CURRENT_PROB)
        (PRINT (APPEND '(UPDATED VALUE FOR NODE:)
               (LIST H)
               '(IS:)
               (LIST (CURRENT_PROB H)) )) ) )
```

In order to try out this inference network conveniently, the following TEST function is helpful:

```
; Make a pass through the non-input nodes,
;  updating their probabilities:
(DEFUN TEST ()
   (UPDATE_NODES '(POPULARITY ELEGANCE ARTISTRY CLEANLINESS
        TASTE TEXTURE APPEARANCE QUANTITY
        CORRECTNESS NUTRITION HYGIENE
        OVERALL_FOOD_QUALITY)) )
```

Finally, to help experiment with the program, a function is offered which makes it easy to interactively change the current probability (and, simultaneously, the current odds) of a node.

```
; To set the current probability and odds for a node,
;  use a form such as (SP DECOR 0.9) = (SP node prob)...
(DEFEXPR SP (L)
   (PROG NIL
        (PUTPROP (CAR L) (CADR L) 'CURRENT_PROB)
        (PUTPROP (CAR L) (ODDS (CADR L)) 'CURRENT_ODDS) ) )
```

In order to start a trial run, the following can be typed:

```
(SETQ REPORTING T)
(TEST)
```

7.6   The Dempster-Shafer Calculus

7.6.1   Motivation

The use of Bayes' rule for manipulating measures of belief is often regarded as inappropriate, because belief measures should not have to behave like probabilities. For example, suppose we let A represent the proposition "Acme computers are intelligent." The axioms of probability require that $P(A) + P(\neg A) = 1$. Suppose that some person, Sam, doesn't even know what a computer is. We can't really say that Sam believes the proposition if he has no idea what it even means. Neither is it fair to say that Sam believes that Acme computers are not intelligent. Denoting Sam's degree of belief by $B(A)$, it is reasonable to assign both $B(A)$ and $B(\neg A)$ a value of 0.

The Dempster-Shafer calculus is a system for manipulating degrees of belief which is more general than the Bayesian approach, and does not require the assumption that $B(A) + B(\neg A) = 1$. Because this system distinguishes the state of ignorance about a proposition from the relative weight afforded the proposition versus its negation, the Dempster-Shafer calculus is somewhat more complicated than the Bayesian approach. However, it allows a fairer, more precise kind of inference from uncertain evidence.

7.6.2 Definitions

As does the theory of probability, the Dempster-Shafer calculus deals with the possible values of an unknown variable, such as the two values *heads* and *tails* for the concealed face of a tossed coin. The set of possible values for a given variable is called the *universe* or the *frame of discernment*, and is usually (but not always) considered to be finite. For example, in the case of the rolling of an ordered pair of dice, the universe contains 36 elements.

Each subset of the universe corresponds to a proposition. Let A be a subset of a universe U. Then the proposition corresponding to A is "The unknown value is an element of A." To illustrate, if A is the set of rolls of the dice that total 7, then the proposition is that the roll is one of those six whose total of dots is 7. Since the correspondence between subsets and propositions is so tight, we will treat subsets as if they were propositions. Thus the set of all propositions is $\mathcal{P}(U)$, the power set of U. This includes the proposition U which may be considered certainly true, and the proposition $\emptyset$, which may be considered certainly false.

Let $m: \mathcal{P}(U) \to [0,1]$ be a function satisfying the two conditions:

$$m(\emptyset) = 0,$$

and

$$\sum_{A \subseteq U} m(A) = 1.$$

Here m maps each proposition to a value in the range zero to one; it maps the empty-set proposition to zero, and the sum of all the values of m is one. We call such a function m a *basic probability assignment*, and it may be considered as a representation of some uncertain evidence regarding the value of some variable X which takes values in U. Some evidence, represented by $F \subseteq U$, may be regarded as certain if $m(F) = 1$ and for all $A \subseteq U$ such that $A \neq F$, $m(A) = 0$; then the evidence claims that the value of X is in F with certainty. Only if F were a singleton would we know the value of X precisely. Note that $m(A)$ is *not* the value of the proposition "the value of X is in A," but is the probability mass ascribed to the particular subset A in $\mathcal{P}(U)$. Each subset F such that $m(F) > 0$ is called a *focal* element of $\mathcal{P}(U)$.

Another function, called a *belief* function, **Belief** : $\mathcal{P}(U) \to [0,1]$, is defined in terms of the basic probability assignment m.

$$\textbf{Belief}(A) = \sum_{B \subseteq A} m(B)$$

That is, the degree of belief associated with the subset A or U is the total of all the probability mass associated with A and its subsets. It is not hard to see that **Belief**(A) must be in the range $[0,1]$ since $\sum_{B \subseteq U} m(B) = 1$, by definition of m.

Having defined the belief function, we can also define the *doubt* and *plausibility* functions:

$$\textbf{Doubt}(A) \ = \ \textbf{Belief}(\neg A)$$
$$\textbf{Plausibility}(A) \ = \ 1 - \textbf{Doubt}(A)$$

The degree of doubt in A is thus defined as the degree of belief in the complement of A. The plausibility of A is 1 minus the degree of doubt in A. The plausibility function is sometimes called the *upper probability* function.

Belief and plausibility functions have the following relationships:

$$\textbf{Belief}(\emptyset) \ = \ 0 \qquad \textbf{Plausibility}(\emptyset) \ = \ 0$$
$$\textbf{Belief}(U) \ = \ 1 \qquad \textbf{Plausibility}(U) \ = \ 1$$

$$\textbf{Plausibility}(A) \ \geq \ \textbf{Belief}(A)$$
$$\textbf{Belief}(A) + \textbf{Belief}(\neg A) \ \leq \ 1$$
$$\textbf{Plausibility}(A) + \textbf{Plausibility}(\neg A) \ \geq \ 1$$

Also, if $A \subseteq B$ then the following two inequalities hold:

$$\textbf{Belief}(A) \ \leq \ \textbf{Belief}(B)$$
$$\textbf{Plausibility}(A) \ \leq \ \textbf{Plausibility}(B).$$

Here we can see that the Dempster-Shafer calculus allows the representation of ignorance since $\textbf{Belief}(A) = 0$ does not imply $\textbf{Doubt}(A) > 0$, even though $\textbf{Doubt}(A) = 1$ does imply $\textbf{Belief}(A) = 0$.

It is sometimes helpful to think of $\textbf{Belief}(A)$ as a measure of a mass of probability that is constrained to stay somewhere in A. The basic probability assignment m further specifies how the probability mass is distributed. If additional evidence is obtained, a new probability assignment comes into play, and a new value of $\textbf{Belief}(A)$ may be obtained. Dempster's rule of combination is used to obtain the new value.

7.6.3 Dempster's Rule of Combination

Suppose that we have two pieces of uncertain evidence relevant to the same universe U, and that they are represented by basic probability assignments m_1 and m_2, respectively. We wish to combine these pieces of evidence into a single new piece. The *orthogonal sum*, $m_1 \oplus m_2$, is given by

$$[m_1 \oplus m_2](A) = \frac{\sum\limits_{X \cap Y = A} m_1(X)m_2(Y)}{1 - \sum\limits_{X \cap Y = \emptyset} m_1(X)m_2(Y)}$$

whenever $A \neq \emptyset$. We define $[m_1 \oplus m_2](\emptyset)$ to be zero so that the orthogonal sum remains a basic probability assignment. The orthogonal sum is well defined provided that the "weight of conflict" is not equal to 1; that is, provided

$$\sum_{X \cap Y = \emptyset} m_1(X) m_2(Y) \neq 1$$

The denominator of the fraction above is sometimes called $1/K$ and is used as a normalization factor. If $1/K$ is zero, then the weight of conflict is equal to 1, m_1 and m_2 are said to be *flatly contradictory*, and $m_1 \oplus m_2$ is undefined. The formula for computing the orthogonal sum is also known as *Dempster's rule of combination*.

Let us consider a simple numerical example that illustrates Dempster's rule of combination. Suppose that the weather in New York at noon tomorrow is to be predicted on the basis of the weather there today. We assume that it is in exactly one of the three states: *snowing*, *raining*, or *dry*. This frame of discernment (universe) is represented by $U = \{S, R, D\}$. The power set of U therefore contains eight elements. Let us assume that two pieces of uncertain evidence have been gathered:

1. The temperature today is below freezing.

2. The barometric pressure is falling; i.e., a storm is likely.

These pieces of evidence are represented by the two basic probability assignments m_{freeze} and m_{storm} in the table of Fig. 7.16. By definition, neither m_{freeze} nor m_{storm} can place any probability mass in the proposition $\emptyset$. m_{freeze} distributes its mass among the remaining elements of $\mathcal{P}(U)$, with extra weight on $\{S\}$, $\{S, R\}$, and $\{S, R, D\}$. The function m_{storm} also distributes its weight over all the non-empty subsets of U, but it gives greatest weight to $\{S, R\}$ and some emphasis to $\{R\}$.

Let m_{both} represent the basic probability assignment that represents the combined evidence of m_{freeze} and m_{storm}. Assuming that m_{freeze} and m_{storm} represent items of evidence which are independent of one another, m_{both} is given by Dempster's rule of combination: $m_{\text{both}} = m_{\text{freeze}} \oplus m_{\text{storm}}$. The values obtained by computation show that m_{both} assigns more weight to each of the elements $\{S\}$, $\{R\}$, and $\{D\}$ than either of the starting basic probability assignments does. However, each of $\{S\}$ and $\{R\}$ has gained substantially more weight than $\{D\}$ has. The other elements of $\mathcal{P}(U)$ have net losses in weight.

The degree of belief in proposition $\{S, R\}$ based on the combined evidence $(0.282 + 0.282 + 0.180 = 0.744)$ is substantially higher than that based on m_{freeze}, 0.5 or based on m_{storm}, 0.6. The degree of belief in $\{S, R, D\}$ is, of course, unchanged and equal to 1.

7.6.4   Simple Evidence Functions

Because of the high computational cost of applying Dempster's rule of combination to arbitrary basic probability assignments, researchers have identified

	$\emptyset$	$\{S\}$	$\{R\}$	$\{D\}$	$\{S,R\}$	$\{S,D\}$	$\{R,D\}$	$\{S,R,D\}$
m_{freeze}	0.0	0.2	0.1	0.1	0.2	0.1	0.1	0.2
m_{storm}	0.0	0.1	0.2	0.1	0.3	0.1	0.1	0.1
m_{both}	0.0	0.282	0.282	0.128	0.180	0.051	0.051	0.026

Figure 7.16: Basic probability assignments for an example illustrating Dempster's rule of combination.

restricted classes of basic probability assignments that are useful but easy to work with.

Let m be a basic probability assignment mapping some $F \subseteq U$ to the value s, mapping U to $1 - s$, and mapping all other subsets to 0. Then we say that m corresponds to a *simple support function* with focus F.

Suppose that m_1 and m_2 each correspond to a simple support function (over the same universe U) with the same focus F. Then $m_3 = m_1 \oplus m_2$ also corresponds to a simple support function with focus F. If s_1 and s_2 are the values assigned to F by m_1 and m_2, respectively, then m_3 assigns F the value $s_1 + s_2 - s_1 s_2$, and it assigns U the value $(1 - s_1)(1 - s_2)$.

If $m_1, m_2, \ldots, m_k$ correspond to simple support functions (not necessarily with the same foci), then $m_1 \oplus m_2 \oplus \cdots \oplus m_k$ corresponds to a *separable support function*, provided $m_1 \oplus m_2 \oplus \cdots \oplus m_k$ exists. Here, each basic probability assignment must be over the same universe, even though the foci may be different.

Let us now consider the problem of accumulating some uncertain evidence for and against a particular member u of U. Assume that $m_1, m_2, \ldots, m_k$ correspond to simple support functions with common focus $\{u\}$ and that $m_{k+1}, m_{k+2}, \ldots, m_{k+l}$ correspond to simple support functions with common focus $U - \{u\}$. Thus $m_1, m_2, \ldots, m_k$ represent evidence in favor of u while $m_{k+1}, m_{k+2}, \ldots, m_{k+l}$ represent evidence against u. We say that $m = m_1 \oplus \cdots \oplus m_{k+l}$ corresponds to a *simple evidence function*. There are only three elements in $\mathcal{P}(U)$ to which m may assign non-zero values: $\{u\}, U - \{u\}$, and U. The value $p = m(\{u\})$ is called the measure of support for u. The value $c = m(U - \{u\})$ is called the measure of evidence against u, and the value $r = m(U)$ is the measure of the residue. To compute p, c, and r from $s_1, s_2, \ldots, s_{k+l}$, we first compute f, which is the value assigned to $\{u\}$ by $m_{\text{for}} = m_1 \oplus m_2 \oplus \cdots \oplus m_k$, and we compute a, which is the value assigned to $U - \{u\}$ by $m_{\text{against}} = m_{k+1} \oplus m_{k+2} \oplus \cdots \oplus m_{k+l}$. We compute a factor K, which takes into consideration the conflict in the evidence, using the formula

$$K = \frac{1}{1 - af}$$

Then we can easily obtain p, c, and r:

$$p = Kf(1 - a)$$
$$c = Ka(1 - f)$$
$$r = K(1 - f)(1 - a)$$

This value of K assures that $p + c + r = 1$.

Clearly, it is computationally straightforward to obtain p, c, and r for simple evidence functions. The assumption we had to make for the simplification is that each piece of evidence either bore directly upon a particular member u of the universe or it bore against it. The computations would be more complicated if the foci of the pieces of evidence were not so simple as a singleton set and its complement but were a number of overlapping subsets of U.

The Dempster-Shafer calculus provides a framework in which one can understand various more restricted computational systems for combining weights of evidence and hypotheses. It is very general, and if one does not impose some restrictions on the probability assignments one uses, the computational cost for combining weights of evidence by Dempster's rule of combination is a problem. Some restrictions have been mentioned that appear to be quite useful.

7.7   Bibliographical Information

A good reference on the theory of probability is [Feller 1968]. The material presented in this chapter is taken primarily from the work on PROSPECTOR as described in the papers by Duda and his coauthors. Another well-known system that uses probabilistic reasoning is MYCIN and it is described in [Shortliffe 1976]. The Bayesian approach developed for PROSPECTOR has its roots in Thomas Bayes' original work [Bayes 1763]. For an introduction to decision theory, see [Raiffa 1968].

The rigorous non-Bayesian system for manipulating degrees of belief, known as Dempster-Shafer theory, is described in [Shafer 1976] and is summarized in [Barnett 1981]. It grew out of [Dempster 1967, 1968]. A computationally tractable variation of Dempster's rule of combination is described in [Reynolds et al 1986]. A variation of the Dempster-Shafer system that incorporates a hierarchical approach is presented and illustrated in a medical-expert-systems context in [Gordon and Shortliffe 1985]. A brief, mathematically-unified treatment of approximate reasoning methods may be found in [Prade 1983]. The elements of fuzzy logic may be found in [Zadeh 1965] and [Kandel 1982]; the latter contains an extensive bibliography of "key references in fuzzy pattern recognition" with 3,064 entries.

References

1. Barnett, J. A. 1981. Computational methods for a mathematical theory

of evidence. *Proceedings of the Seventh International Joint Conference on Artificial Intelligence*, Vancouver, pp868-875.

2. Bayes, T. 1763. An essay toward solving a problem in the doctrine of chances. *Philosophical Transactions of the Royal Society*, Vol. 53, pp370-418, 1763. Reprinted in 1970 on pp131-153 of Pearson, E. S., and Kendall, M. G. (eds.), *Studies in the History of Statistics and Probability*, Hafner, Inc.

3. Dempster, A. P. 1967. Upper and lower probabilities induced by a multivalued mapping. *Annals of Mathematical Statistics*, Vol. 38, pp325-339.

4. Dempster, A. P. 1968. A generalization of Bayesian inference. *Journal of the Royal Statistical Society, Series B*, Vol. 30, pp205-247.

5. Duda, R. O., Gaschnig, J., and Hart, P. E. 1979. Model design in the PROSPECTOR consultant system for mineral exploration. In Michie, D. (ed.), *Expert Systems in the Microelectronics Age*. Edinburgh, Scotland: Edinburgh University Press, pp153-167.

6. Duda, R. O., Hart, P. E., and Nilsson, N. J. 1976. Subjective Bayesian methods for rule-based inference systems. *Proceedings of the AFIPS National Computer Conference*, Vol. 45, pp1075-1082.

7. Gordon, J., and Shortliffe, E. H. 1985. A method for managing evidential reasoning in a hierarchical hypothesis space. *Artificial Intelligence*, Vol. 26, pp323-357.

8. Feller, W. 1968. *An Introduction to Probability Theory and Its Applications*, Third Edition. New York: Wiley.

9. Kandel, A. 1982. *Fuzzy Techniques in Pattern Recognition*. New York: Wiley.

10. Prade, H. 1983. A synthetic view of approximate reasoning techniques. *Proceedings of the Eighth International Joint Conference on Artificial Intelligence*, Karlsruhe, pp130-136.

11. Raiffa, H. 1968. *Decision Analysis: Introductory Lectures on Choices Under Uncertainty*. Reading, MA: Addison-Wesley.

12. Reynolds, G., Strahman, D., Lehrer, N., and Kitchen, L. 1986. Plausible reasoning and the theory of evidence. Technical Report 86-11, Department of Computer and Information Science, University of Massachusetts at Amherst, Amherst, MA.

13. Shafer, G. 1976. *A Mathematical Theory of Evidence*. Princeton, NJ: Princeton University Press.

14. Shortliffe, E. H. 1976. *Computer-based Medical Consultations: MYCIN.* New York: Elsevier.

15. Zadeh, L. A. 1965. Fuzzy sets. *Information and Control,* Vol. 8, pp338-353.

Exercises

1. Compute the probability of drawing a card that is either an ace or a spade, from a normal shuffled deck of 52 playing cards.

2. Describe the difference between the probability of an event and someone's degree of belief in a statement.

3. Assume that the probability of a farmer having an apple tree is p_1, and assume that the probability of a farmer having a cherry tree, given that the farmer has an apple tree, is p_2. What is the probability that a farmer has both an apple tree and a cherry tree?

4. Suppose that $P \rightarrow Q$, and that the probability of P is 1. What is the probability of Q? Now suppose that the probability of P is 0.5. What might the probability of Q be? Justify your answer, but describe any anomalous aspect of this situation.

5. Consider the fuzzy logic rules of Fig. 7.3 on page 248 and the propositional calculus formula,

$$X \rightarrow (Y \vee Z).$$

Taking $P(X) = 0.5$, $P(Y) = 0.1$, and $P(Z) = 0.2$, compute the "probability" for the formula using

   (a) the rules in the second-to-last row of the chart, and

   (b) the rules in the bottom row of the chart.

6. Suppose that a three-valued logic is to be used for a type of "slightly-fuzzy" inferences. The three values that may be attributed to a statement are **T** (true), **M** (maybe), and **F** (false). Design a truth table for each of $\neg, \wedge,$ and $\vee$ which gives the truth values for logical combinations of statements in this system. Your system should be consistent with the propositional calculus and you should be able to justify your design.

7. Describe the characteristics of a problem domain for which probabilistic inference networks are appropriate.

8. Suppose the following:

(a) the prior probability that it will rain (tomorrow) in Seattle is 0.8;

(b) the probability that Canada geese are on Lake Washington given that it will rain tomorrow is 0.02; and

(c) the probability that Canada geese are on Lake Washington given that it will not rain tomorrow is 0.025.

Compute, using Bayes' rule, the *a posteriori* probability that it will rain tomorrow, given that there are Canada geese on Lake Washington.

9. (a) At a simulated horse race the odds are 10 to 1 in favor of Inference Engine. What is the probability with which Inference Engine is expected to win?

(b) At the same event, Bandwagon Joe, who always bets at double the odds on any horse rated better than fifty-fifty, places a bet. What is the probability corresponding to his bet on Inference Engine?

(c) If Inference Engine runs in all races Joe bets on, and he bets $20 on each race, what is the expected number of races Joe can bet on, assuming he starts with $200? (On each race, if Inference Engine wins, Joe receives $1, but if Inference Engine loses, Joe loses $20.)

10. Referring to Fig. 7.4, we note that certain useful probability values are not given explicitly.

(a) Give formulas that provides values of $P(S|\neg H_1)$, $P(S|\neg H_2)$ and $P(S|\neg H_3)$ from values that are given in the table.

(b) Compute $P(S|\neg H_1)$ for the case $S_1 = \mathbf{F}$, $S_2 = \mathbf{F}$, and $S_3 = \mathbf{F}$.

11. Using the inference network for the automobile repair problem, determine the values of $P(H_i|S), i = 1, \ldots, 5$ and $P(C_1|S)$ for the cases:

(a) $S_i = \mathbf{F}, i = 1, \ldots, 4$.

(b) $S_1 = \mathbf{F}, S_2 = \mathbf{T}, S_3 = \mathbf{T}, S_4 = \mathbf{T}$.

12. Let $O(H) = 3$, and let the sufficiency factor, λ, for H given E be 2. Compute $O(H|E)$ and $P(H|E)$.

13. Give a recursive definition for "arc expressions" and describe their representational capability, as they are used in the inference network for the Traveller's Restaurant Selection Problem.

14. Examine an execution of the test procedure on page 271 for the LISP inference network. Determine the node(s) of the net whose current value changes the most, as a result of the updating.

15. Design and implement a probabilistic inference network for one of the following kinds of problems:

(a) selecting a college elective course that is likely to be satisfying,

(b) choosing the menu for a dinner party,

(c) planning a vacation.

Include at least 8 nodes in 3 levels in your network. You may employ some of the functions given in the network for the traveller's restaurant selection problem. Give a diagram of your network. Show two runs that illustrate how changing the input values leads to a change in the output value(s).

16. Using the values of m_{freeze}, m_{storm}, and m_{both} in Fig. 7.16, compute the following:

   (a) **Belief**$(\{S, D\})$ based upon m_{freeze}.

   (b) **Belief**$(\{S, D\})$ based upon m_{storm}.

   (c) **Belief**$(\{S, D\})$ based upon m_{both}.

   (d) the *doubt* that there will be snow tomorrow, given both that it is freezing and that the barometric pressure is falling.

   (e) the *plausibility* that there will be snow tomorrow, given that it is freezing and the pressure is falling.

17. Suppose that you just purchased a birthday present for a business associate whom you do not know well but wish to please. You decided to buy a box of nice chocolates. In your mind, you set up a frame of discernment $\{L, D\}$, where L is the outcome that the associate likes the present and D that he/she dislikes it. Just after you arrive at the birthday party, you learn that the guest of honor likes gourmet food. Your hopes are raised that the birthday person will like your gift. However, you then overhear someone saying that the birthday person is allergic to chocolate. Your hopes fall.

   (a) Make up values for two basic probability assignments, $m_{gourmet}$ and $m_{allergic}$ that describe the separate effects each of these bits of evidence would bear on your belief in L or D.

   (b) Explain your choice of values in part *a*.

   (c) Apply Dempster's rule of combination to obtain the values of a function $m_{allergic+gourmet}$ that describes the combined effects of the evidence.

   (d) Explain your results for part *c*.

18. The presidential administration of Lower Slobovia is found to have committed an illegal act. The president either knew about the act and its illegality or he did not. Two independent witnesses have given testimony, and a legal AI expert has converted their testimony into basic probability assignments over the powerset of a binary frame of discernment:

	$\emptyset$	president knew	president didn't	either
Witness X	0.0	0.2	0.0	0.8
Witness Y	0.0	0.3	0.0	0.7

(a) (30 points) Compute the degree of belief for witness X that the president knew, the doubt that the president knew, and the plausibility that the president knew.

(b) (30 points) Compute the orthogonal sum of the assignments for witness X and witness Y.

Chapter 8

Learning

8.1 Introduction

8.1.1 Overview

Machine learning is the area of AI that focusses on processes of self-improvement. Information-processing systems that improve their performance or enlarge their knowledge bases are said to "learn." This ability is present in humans and many other living organisms, and it would clearly have value in computer systems. The primary objective of most research in machine learning has been to gain a better understanding of learning itself. Another objective of machine learning is to automate the acquisition of knowledge. Knowledge-based systems are expensive to construct because the process of extracting knowledge from experts and representing it in a form useful for inference is slow and requires the services of both the domain expert (e.g., a physician) and the AI specialist. By getting a machine to direct the knowledge transfer process and to construct its internal representations itself, one hopes to reduce the cost of new expert systems and provide efficient means for the systems to continually improve themselves.

Techniques for machine learning may be broadly classified as either numerical approaches or structural approaches (or a combination of the two). The numerical approaches include the kind of algorithm which automatically determines a threshold that distinguishes apples from bananas on the basis of their lengths, or which adjusts the coefficients of an evaluation function in a program that plays checkers.

Structural approaches are concerned with relationships, concepts, sets, trees and graphs, and they place relatively small importance on numerical values. One structural approach to learning is the use of heuristic search to explore a space of concepts in elementary number theory. Another structural approach is the use of combinatorial optimization techniques for the discovery of classification rules for classes of objects having various combinations of features (e.g., for classifying different hybrids of wheat), where it is the presences and absences of various attributes that matter.

There are many different levels of learning, the lowest of which is simply the acquisition of raw data, analogous to someone's going out and buying a library and then claiming to have a body of knowledge in his house. At a slightly higher level is the acquisition of information. Someone who memorizes facts may be said to be learning information. At yet a higher and more respectable level is acquisition of concepts, together with their interrelations to other concepts.

In this chapter, we begin by defining learning as an improvement in information-processing ability that results from information-processing activity. After a discussion of inductive and deductive transformations of information, we describe methods of machine learning based upon the notion of classification. This includes the automatic determination of classes or categories of objects, and also the automatic discovery of rules for classifying objects into classes. Next is a discussion of the principles of self-guided conceptualization systems. Such systems employ heuristic search to explore some of the concepts and relationships that can be automatically created in domains such as mathematics. Finally a LISP program, "PYTHAGORUS" is presented which explores a space of concepts having to do with geometric figures. Several of the problems of creating such a program are discussed.

8.1.2   What Learning Is

When a system learns, it improves its knowledge or its ability to perform one or more tasks[1]. The improvement comes about as a result of information-processing activity. The improvement may take many forms: enlargement of a knowledge base; reduction in size of a knowledge base through a refinement of existing knowledge; faster solution of problems through acquisition of heuristics or through a reordering of search alternatives; reduction in the space required to solve a problem through elimination of superfluous data; improvement of the quality of solutions found; or an increase in the set or class of problems that the system can solve. However, the improvement is most commonly some sort of increase in performance.

Learning may come about in many ways. These ways span a spectrum starting with those in which the system plays only a passive role and ending with those in which the system is self-sufficient for learning. The system may be operated upon; if a program is heavily modified by a programmer (possibly with source language editing and/or recompilation), its behaviour could change radically, but this kind of modification seems analogous to brainwashing or lobotomy. On the other hand, a system left to its own to learn by actively exploring an

---

[1]This is a "positive" definition of learning. According to Nilsson, "A learning machine, broadly defined, is any device whose actions are influenced by past experiences." Nilsson's may be considered a neutral definition, since the influence may be good, bad, or unimportant (see [Nilsson 1965]).

environment or a space of concepts may be likened to a child in a Montessori school without teachers. In the middle of the spectrum are systems that can accept guidance from teachers or that actively solicit knowledge.

Let us now put forth a slightly more formal definition of "learning." Let P be an information processing system. Let M be a function that measures the "merit" of P's computations or state. We say that P *learns* with respect to M over a period $[t_1, t_2]$, if the value of $M(P)$ at time t_2 is greater than the value $M(P)$ at time t_1, and the change is a result of P's processing information.

For example, let $M_{rules}(P)$ be the number of production rules in P's knowledge base. If the number of rules increases between noon Saturday and noon Sunday, and this increase is a result of P's information-processing activity, then P learns with respect to M_{rules} over this period.

Consider the following, somewhat different, example: Let P be a bottle of wine, and let M_{taste} be a measure of the quality of the wine. After the wine has been stored in a cellar for 5 years, the value of $M_{taste}(P)$ has increased. Has the bottle of wine learned? This example meets most of the given criteria for a learning situation. However, we would be stretching our imaginations to call the process by which the taste improved an "information processing" activity. It is certainly possible to view the chemical process inside the bottle as a kind of computation; however, we would soon be led to the useless conclusion that every chemical or physical process is an information-processing activity, and further that any physical process is a learning process if one chooses an appropriate merit function. Therefore we shall reject the improvement in the taste of the wine as an example of learning.

We often consider learning to be a monotonic progression from one intellectual or skill level to higher ones. However, it is common to speak of forgetting and unlearning, processes which appear to be the antithesis of progress. But it should be kept in mind that several merit functions may be applicable to a single system, and that as a system changes, some aspects may improve while others degrade. A human adult may acquire knowledge over a twenty-year period, and also experience a slowing of the rate at which he can recall or use that knowledge.

8.1.3   Inductive vs. Deductive Methods

Machine learning may involve two rather different kinds of information processing: "inductive" and "deductive." Inductive information processing is concerned with determining general patterns, organizational schemes, rules, and laws, from raw data, experience, or examples. Inductive computations perform abstraction, producing generalities from specifics. The creation of models and theories involves much inductive work.

On the other hand, the determination of specific facts using general rules is deductive information processing. Also, the determination of new general rules from old ones is usually termed "deductive." From the general rule that the circumference of a circle is pi times its diameter, we *deduce* that a circle of diameter 10 has circumference approximately equal to 31.4159. The proof of a theorem typically involves the use of rules of inference as well as previous theorems; the theorem is also *deduced.*

In any given computation, there may be many kinds of information processing: specific to general, general to specific, general to general, general to more general, etc. We note that "inductive" and "deductive" are broad terms and that it is often not possible to cleanly classify a computation as "inductive and not deductive" or the other way around.

When learning is concerned with enlarging a knowledge base, the question can be asked, "Is the new knowledge put in directly, is it induced from examples or experience, or is it deduced from existing knowledge?"

8.1.4   Knowledge Acquisition

The question of where a system's knowledge comes from is an appropriate one to begin with before examining any processes of knowledge acquisition. One of many possible classifications of knowledge sources is the following:

1. experts. This includes cases where the programmer is the expert.

2. books or textual files. Although books are usually written by experts, the process of obtaining knowledge from a book is significantly different from direct interaction with an expert.

3. direct experience. Although interacting with an expert and reading a book are forms of experience, by *direct experience* we mean interactions with the objects in the domain of learning (e.g., performing experiments with chemicals and test tubes), not interactions with teachers or pre-compiled representations of knowledge.

What are the processes for acquiring knowledge? Some general comments can be made before any detailed techniques are presented. The process depends on the source of knowledge and it depends on the representation to be used. For each representation scheme, we may consider the problems of forming a knowledge base that adheres to that scheme. Let us consider three cases:

1. production systems: In order to add knowledge to a production system, two discernible steps are:

   - to turn new knowledge into rules, and

   - to incorporate the new rules into the production system. If one is lucky, one can just add the new rules at the end of the existing list of rules. However, one may have to replace old rules with new, or revise the old and/or new rules if there is any interference among old and new rules. For example, if the system does non-monotonic reasoning, it may be necessary to retract old rules.

2. semantic nets: Adding knowledge to a semantic net typically requires creating new nodes and links to represent the new knowledge, and then tying the new structure into the existing network by either adding links, merging old and new nodes, or both.

3. frames: Expanding the knowledge of a frame-based system may be a simple matter of filling in some of the empty slots of existing frames. Alternatively, it may require creating new slots for existing frames or creating new frames. The creation of a new frame may just be the creation of a new instance of an old schema. However, it may require the creation of one or more new schemata.

An exciting topic currently receiving attention is the development of interactive tools for building knowledge bases. Some of these conduct interviews with experts while others provide visual views of the knowledge base being constructed.

Most knowledge acquisition systems are designed to assist in the transfer of knowledge rather than to create it; that is, they are not designed to induce facts and general rules from direct experience. If there are experts in the field of interest, it is usually easier to obtain the compiled experience of the experts than to try to duplicate the direct experience (of the experts, their teachers, or others) that gave rise to their expertise.

However, there are cases in which it is appropriate for a computer system to learn from direct experience. One family of techniques for learning directly from experience is described in the next section.

8.2 Learning Classification Rules

It is often useful to be able to classify objects according to their properties or the parts they contain. Consider the sentence, "Any animal with four legs and a tail, and which barks, is a dog." This can be represented in the predicate calculus as

$$\text{animal}(x) \wedge \text{quadruped}(x) \wedge \text{tailed}(x) \wedge \text{barks}(x) \rightarrow \text{dog}(x).$$

This formula is a classification rule having a conjunction of properties or tests on the left-hand side of an implication arrow and a classification on the right. A slightly more general form is exhibited by the following rule:

$$[\text{flies}(x) \wedge \neg\text{insect}(x) \wedge \neg\text{bat}(x) \wedge \text{animal}(x)] \vee \text{penguin}(x) \vee \text{ostrich}(x) \rightarrow \text{bird}(x).$$

This says that something which flies but is not an insect or bat, but is an animal, or something which is a penguin or an ostrich, is a bird. The left-hand side of this rule is a disjunction; in fact, it is in disjunctive normal form (DNF).

If enough suitable examples can be presented in a suitable way, classification rules such as those above can be determined algorithmically from the examples.

The derivation of such a rule is an inductive process, since it creates a generalization from a collection of specific cases; thus this sort of learning may be called "inductive learning."

8.2.1   General Rules from Fixed Examples

Let us explore machine learning of DNF classification rules with a simple example. The following describes a hypothetical situation that we will use to explore one variety of method for the automatic learning of classification rules.

> The night operator of an old-fashioned batch-style computer system, one of the early transistorized mainframes of the 1960's, is working late, as usual. Tonight, however, the machine exhibits some strange behavior. It prints a string of five characters, then computes for several minutes and does it again. After a few more such strings, a tape drive runs its tape off the end of the reel (this is an error condition), and the machine halts. Only one customer has left a job for that night, and five hours of CPU time were requested. The operator remounts the tape and reruns the job, but these problems persist, even though the strings are different each time. The operator thinks he sees a relationship between some of the strings and the tape's unwinding, and he would like to identify those strings that seem to warn that the tape unwinding is imminent so as to be able to stop the machine manually before the tape unwinds. After three halts, he divides the strings revealed into two sets: those from which the machine continued without problems (the "safe" strings) and those which immediately preceded the bad behavior (the "warning" strings).

Let us assume that these are the strings the operator sees:

$$\text{\textit{safe strings}}$$
$$s_1 = \text{DECCG}$$
$$s_2 = \text{AGDEC} \qquad \text{\textit{warning strings}}$$
$$s_3 = \text{GCFDC} \qquad w_1 = \text{CGCGF}$$
$$s_4 = \text{CDFDE} \qquad w_2 = \text{DGFCD}$$
$$s_5 = \text{CEGEC} \qquad w_3 = \text{ECGCD}$$

How can we mechanically find a rule that will correctly distinguish these warning strings from the safe ones, and also have a hope of performing correctly on new strings? One method is to begin with a logical description of the given examples that is so particular that it cannot possibly apply to other examples (whether they are positive or negative ones). To do this, let the predicate $M(x, n, c)$ be true if in string x, the nth character matches c. A thorough description of the first positive example of a warning string is

$$M(w_1, 1, \text{C}) \wedge M(w_1, 2, \text{G}) \wedge M(w_1, 3, \text{C}) \wedge M(w_1, 4, \text{G}) \wedge M(w_1, 5, \text{F}).$$

This statement is first generalized by "variablizing." The constant w_1 representing the particular example is replaced by x, and we build the formula into a classification rule, adding an implication connective and a right-hand side.

$$M(x, 1, \mathrm{C}) \wedge M(x, 2, \mathrm{G}) \wedge M(x, 3, \mathrm{C}) \wedge M(x, 4, \mathrm{G}) \wedge M(x, 5, \mathrm{F}) \rightarrow \mathrm{warning}(x).$$

In order to take all the positive examples into account, we create a disjunction in the left-hand side of the rule, in which each disjunct is a description of one of the examples.

$$[M(x, 1, \mathrm{C}) \wedge M(x, 2, \mathrm{G}) \wedge M(x, 3, \mathrm{C}) \wedge M(x, 4, \mathrm{G}) \wedge M(x, 5, \mathrm{F})]$$
$$\vee [M(x, 1, \mathrm{D}) \wedge M(x, 2, \mathrm{G}) \wedge M(x, 3, \mathrm{F}) \wedge M(x, 4, \mathrm{C}) \wedge M(x, 5, \mathrm{D})]$$
$$\vee [M(x, 1, \mathrm{E}) \wedge M(x, 2, \mathrm{C}) \wedge M(x, 3, \mathrm{G}) \wedge M(x, 4, \mathrm{C}) \wedge M(x, 5, \mathrm{D})]$$
$$\rightarrow \mathrm{warning}(x).$$

Next, this expression can be gradually simplified and generalized by testing each atomic proposition starting with $M(x, 1, \mathrm{C})$ and dropping it if it has no diagnostic value. That is, we remove the atom from the left-hand side, obtaining a new rule, provided that none of the safe strings would be classified as a warning string by the rule that remains. Thus, our classification rule must stay consistent with the constraint,

$$(\forall x)[\mathrm{safe}(x) \rightarrow \neg \mathrm{warning}(x)].$$

After as many atomic propositions have been dropped as possible, the resulting formula is a classification rule that has the possibility of handling (either correctly or incorrectly) more examples than just those used to obtain it. Like variablization, this process of *dropping conjuncts* is another method of generalization. In this example, the resulting classification rule is

$$M(x, 5, \mathrm{F}) \vee M(x, 5, \mathrm{D}) \rightarrow \mathrm{warning}(x).$$

The order in which conjuncts are considered can affect the resulting classification rule. For example, considering the atomic propositions from right to left (instead of left to right) would give us the classification rule

$$[M(x, 1, \mathrm{C}) \wedge M(x, 2, \mathrm{G})] \vee [M(x, 1, \mathrm{D}) \wedge M(x, 2, \mathrm{G})] \vee M(x, 1, \mathrm{E})$$
$$\rightarrow \mathrm{warning}(x).$$

Here the rules obtained by left-to-right and right-to-left scanning have considerably different lengths. Assuming that the most general rule is desired, there is a tendency to prefer a rule that has the fewest atomic formulas in it. In order to find the smallest rule, it may be necessary in some cases to try exhaustively to eliminate conjuncts in each of the possible orders ($n!$ where n is the number of atomic propositions in the formula). Thus, in the area of inductive learning as in many other areas of AI, we find the potential for a combinatorial explosion.

There are various ways to fight the combinatorial explosion in inductive learning. One of these is to apply domain knowledge by providing predicates which measure or test for features, in the hope that the space generated by the combinations of features will be smaller than the one generated by the combinations of components of the objects to be classified. For example, we might have the following contextual knowledge about the mysterious strings and the system producing them:

> The program running on the old-fashioned mainframe was written by a composer of music. It generates random motifs and tries to link them into melodies.

Some features of motifs are these:

1. tonic(x): true if all notes of x are in $\{C, E, G\}$,

2. symmetric(x): true if the motif is a palindrome, and

3. unfinal(x): true if the last note of x is in $\{D, F\}$.

If the set of features is discriminating enough, a new formulation may be made in terms of the features. A characterization is made for each positive example, and these are disjoined together to produce a classification rule:

$$\begin{aligned}
&[\neg\text{tonic}(x) \wedge \neg\text{symmetric}(x) \wedge \text{unfinal}(x)] \\
\vee&[\neg\text{tonic}(x) \wedge \neg\text{symmetric}(x) \wedge \text{unfinal}(x)] \\
\vee&[\neg\text{tonic}(x) \wedge \neg\text{symmetric}(x) \wedge \text{unfinal}(x)] \quad \rightarrow \quad \text{warning}(x).
\end{aligned}$$

Before simplification, this rule has only 9 atomic formulas, compared with the 15 of the formulation in terms of matching the components of the strings. In this particular case, the three disjuncts may be collapsed into a single one (since they are identical), before the generalization by elimination of conjuncts even begins. The resulting classification rule (after dropping conjuncts) is simply

$$\text{unfinal}(x) \rightarrow \text{warning}(x).$$

(The composer apparently had a fatal error in his program at a point where one motif is to be linked with another to produce a longer melody.) Interestingly, the first of the two classification rules found earlier, that is, $M(x, 5, F) \vee M(x, 5, D) \rightarrow$ warning(x), is equivalent to the feature-based rule that we just found.

The discovery of a classification rule, such as one of the simple ones we have obtained, may be viewed as an optimization; it is the finding of a minimal description of the given positive instances which excludes all of the given negative instances. Such a minimization problem can be attacked with search techniques. However, because the search for a minimal description can become bogged down in the quagmire of numerous possibilities, heuristics may be needed to reduce the size of the search space.

Although we have constructed our classification rules in this example in terms of the "warning strings," we could have used the same procedure on the "safe strings." This would have resulted in different rules. The rules based on the positive examples are not necessarily equivalent to those based on the negative examples (the verification of this statement is left as an exercise for the reader).

8.2.2 Incremental Learning

It is interesting to consider the behavior of the conjunct-dropping algorithm when it is applied repeatedly while the sets of positive and/or negative examples keep growing. Let us consider a situation in which one positive example of the concept of "arch" is given, and then negative examples are gradually introduced.

Our positive example of an arch, represented by the constant a_1, is shown in Fig. 8.1a. It is described by the predicate-calculus formula,

$$\text{On}(b_2(a_1), b_1(a_1)) \wedge \text{On}(b_2(a_1), b_3(a_1)) \wedge \neg\text{Adjacent}(b_1(a_1), b_3(a_1)).$$

Here the symbols b_1, b_2, and b_3 are function symbols; $b_1(a_1)$ refers to the first block of a_1, etc.

Our algorithm for constructing a rule replaces the constant a_1 by a variable, say x. It is assumed that x is universally quantified. Then it forms an initial rule by placing this formula on the left-hand side of an implication arrow and placing the predicate "arch(x)" on the right-hand side. With no negative examples, all atomic formulas on the left are eliminated, leaving the maximally general rule $\forall x \; \text{arch}(x)$.

Now let us introduce one negative example, c_1. Shown in Fig. 8.1b, it could be described by:

$$\text{On}(b_2(c_1), b_1(c_1)) \wedge \neg\text{On}(b_2(c_1), b_3(c_1)) \wedge \text{Adjacent}(b_1(c_1), b_3(c_1)).$$

Since the rule above classifies all objects as arches, it would certainly classify this negative example as an arch, and so it must be specialized; one or more of the conjuncts previously dropped must be put back into the rule. Alternatively, the algorithm may be re-run, starting again with the initial rule. With left-to-right consideration of the conjuncts, we get the new rule:

$$\neg\text{Adjacent}(b_1(x), b_3(x)) \rightarrow \text{arch}(x).$$

This rule is still quite general but does not make the mistake of classifying c_1 as an arch. If the conjuncts were considered in right-to-left order instead, we would obtain the rule,

$$\text{On}(b_2(x), b_3(x)) \rightarrow \text{arch}(x)$$

which is just as effective in handling the examples presented.

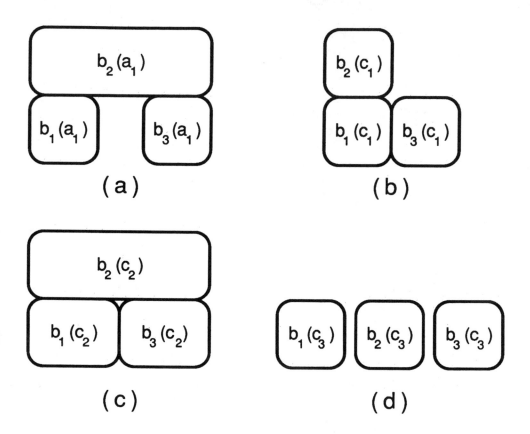

Figure 8.1: An example of an "arch" (a), and three negative examples (b–d).

After revising the rule to cope properly with two more negative examples, those shown in Fig. 8.1c and d, we obtain a rule which happens to be independent of the order in which the conjuncts are considered:

$$\text{On}(b_2(x), b_3(x)) \wedge \neg\text{Adjacent}(b_1(x), b_3(x)) \rightarrow \text{arch}(x).$$

Looking back upon this sequence of examples, one may note that the negative example c_3 could have been omitted without changing the final result. On the other hand, the negative examples c_1 and c_2 played an important role in getting the classification rule to converge to its final form. They have a notable property: they are negative examples which are almost positive examples. Such counterexamples are called *near misses*. It should be apparent that the learning of concepts is greatly facilitated when a suitable collection of near misses is presented early to the system.

8.2.3   Version Spaces

We have seen how a rule can be incrementally tightened to exclude new negative examples. Let us now consider a systematic method for keeping track of all rules consistent with a set of positive and a set of negative examples.

Let Arch^+ be a set of positive examples of arches and let Arch^- be a set of negative examples ("non-arches"). Then the *rule-version space* for Arch^+ and Arch^- is the set of all rules (that can be expressed in a particular system of features and logical operators) that classify all members of Arch^+ and Arch^- correctly. If we assume that each rule is a predicate, then this rule-version space (or simply "version space") is given by

$$V(\text{Arch}^+, \text{Arch}^-) = \{R \mid (\forall x \in \text{Arch}^+)R(x) \wedge (\forall x \in \text{Arch}^-)\neg R(x)\}$$

The process of learning a classification rule for arches may be considered as the problem of adjusting $V(\text{Arch}^+, \text{Arch}^-)$ as new positive and negative instances are encountered. If there are enough suitable examples and if the rule-description language is adequate, then the version space converges to a single rule. Naturally, if the examples were inconsistent (i.e., $\exists x, x \in \text{Arch}^+ \wedge x \in \text{Arch}^-$), then the version space would be empty.

The version space has a useful property that can reduce its computational requirements. A version space can be represented by explicitly listing only its extremal (most specific and most general) members. This is because the set of possible rules is partially ordered by the relation "$\leq$" defined by

$$R_1 \leq R_2 \iff \forall x[R_1(x) \rightarrow R_2(x)].$$

That is, rule R_1 is as general as or less general than rule R_2 whenever a positive classification by R_1 implies a positive classification of the same object by R_2. The set of possible rules and this ordering may be thought of as an inclusion hierarchy as discussed in Chapter 4.

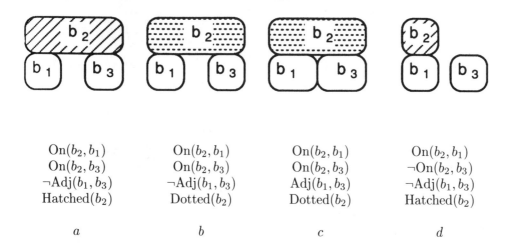

$$\begin{array}{cccc}
\text{On}(b_2, b_1) & \text{On}(b_2, b_1) & \text{On}(b_2, b_1) & \text{On}(b_2, b_1) \\
\text{On}(b_2, b_3) & \text{On}(b_2, b_3) & \text{On}(b_2, b_3) & \neg\text{On}(b_2, b_3) \\
\neg\text{Adj}(b_1, b_3) & \neg\text{Adj}(b_1, b_3) & \text{Adj}(b_1, b_3) & \neg\text{Adj}(b_1, b_3) \\
\text{Hatched}(b_2) & \text{Dotted}(b_2) & \text{Dotted}(b_2) & \text{Hatched}(b_2)
\end{array}$$

$$\begin{array}{cccc}
a & b & c & d
\end{array}$$

Figure 8.2: Two arches and two non-arches to illustrate version spaces.

A version space is thus a set of rules that is bounded above by the most general rules in the set and that is bounded below by the most specific rules in the set. The rules between the extremal ones need not be listed. Thus, if I^+ and I^- are the sets of positive and negative instances, we may represent version space $V(I^+, I^-)$ as $\mathcal{V}(R_s, R_g)$ where R_s is the set of most specific rules in the version space and R_g is the set of most general rules in it.

As appropriate new positive examples are assimilated, the lower bounds generally get moved up; with negative examples, the upper bounds come down. In order to have an effect, a new example must be *salient*; it should either be a near miss or an "unexpected hit."

Let us now consider another variation of the arch-learning problem. Suppose that we have two positive and two negative examples, as shown in Fig. 8.2.3. The notation is slightly simpler than that used above, since b_1, b_2 and b_3 are considered here as objects rather than functions; we ignore any potential problems of confusing the different occurrences of these symbols associated with the different examples of arches and non-arches.

Let us allow each rule to be either the constant symbol **T** or a conjunction of literals (i.e., excluding disjunctions), where each literal is one of those used in the partial descriptions given in the figure. Let us now assume that the examples are encountered in the order: a, c, b, d. It is instructive to express the version space before any examples and after each example is encountered.

$$V(\emptyset,\emptyset) \quad = \quad \text{all rules in the rule language.}$$

$$
\begin{aligned}
V(\{a\},\emptyset) \quad &= \quad \text{all rules except those that assign } \mathbf{F} \text{ to example } a.\\
&= \quad \mathcal{V}(\{\text{On}(b_2,b_1) \wedge \text{On}(b_2,b_3) \wedge \neg\text{Adj}(b_1,b_3) \wedge \text{Hatched}(b_2)\},\\
&\qquad \{\mathbf{T}\}).
\end{aligned}
$$

$$
\begin{aligned}
V(\{a\},\{c\}) \quad &= \quad \mathcal{V}(\{\text{On}(b_2,b_1) \wedge \text{On}(b_2,b_3) \wedge \neg\text{Adj}(b_1,b_3) \wedge \text{Hatched}(b_2)\},\\
&\qquad \{\neg\text{Adj}(b_1,b_3), \text{Hatched}(b_2)\}).
\end{aligned}
$$

$$
\begin{aligned}
V(\{a,b\},\{c\}) \quad &= \quad \mathcal{V}(\{\text{On}(b_2,b_1) \wedge \text{On}(b_2,b_3) \wedge \neg\text{Adj}(b_1,b_3)\},\\
&\qquad \{\neg\text{Adj}(b_1,b_3)\}).
\end{aligned}
$$

$$
\begin{aligned}
V(\{a,b\},\{c,d\}) \quad &= \quad \mathcal{V}(\{\text{On}(b_2,b_1) \wedge \text{On}(b_2,b_3) \wedge \neg\text{Adj}(b_1,b_3)\},\\
&\qquad \{\text{On}(b_2,b_3) \wedge \neg\text{Adj}(b_1,b_3)\}).
\end{aligned}
$$

Note that all the rules in one of these version spaces can be obtained by dropping conjuncts from the specific rule (there can only be one with this rule language), such that all the conjuncts of one of the general rules remain.

The last version space here, $V(\{a,b\},\{c,d\})$, contains only two rules, the general one being only slightly more general than the specific one. By including an additional example in either Arch$^+$ or Arch$^-$ it is possible to make this learning sequence converge (this is suggested in the exercises at the end of this chapter).

The version-space method has an advantage over the simpler incremental method of finding rules: backtracking is unnecessary. However, the version-space approach has some difficulty handling rules that allow disjunction (details may be found in the references).

Our discussion in this section has focussed on learning a classification rule for distinguishing the members of a set of objects from nonmembers. This kind of learning is sometimes called "single-concept" learning. A related, but more complex, kind of learning requires that the system take a larger role in the knowledge-formation process. This requires *creating* concepts as well as learning about their properties, their relationships and rules for distinguishing them. This "concept-exploration" kind of learning is described in the next section.

8.3   Self-Directed Conceptualization Systems

8.3.1   Piaget's Circular Reaction Paradigm

Out of the painstaking observations of children by Jean Piaget, one can discern
a pattern of learning that recurs throughout the process of intellectual development. This pattern has been referred to as the "circular reaction paradigm."[2]
We are interested in it as a guide for writing programs to perform structural
learning.

As an example of the circular reaction paradigm, imagine a child of approximately six months lying in a crib on its back, with a bell hanging overhead and
a string hanging down from the bell ending about twenty centimeters above the
head. The child knows how to flail its arms about quite actively, and it does so
repeatedly. Suddenly, as the child accidentally grabs and pulls the string, the
bell rings distinctly. In surprise, the child freezes. Soon, however, the child is
flailing away trying to make it happen again. Eventually it does happen again
and again. Gradually the child refines the flailing to the point where ringing the
bell is a reasonably controlled action. The child may rest at this point; the set
of available mechanisms now includes the ability to ring the bell. The next time
the child plays, it begins to explore again, and bell-ringing is one of the facilities for exploration. The cycle is complete. It began with available mechanisms
(e.g., flailing arms), which were exercised until something detectably unusual
happened (the bell sounded). After a pause, an attempt was made to repeat the
event. Successive iterations converged on a refined, relatively coordinated new
ability (ringing the bell). This ability became part of the repertoire of actions
to be used in further explorations.

The phases of the learning cycle are as follows:

1. exercising of actions in repertoire;

2. evaluation of results of those actions with particular attention devoted to
   detecting the unusual;

3. determination of the relationship between the actions exercised and the
   unusual condition, possibly through repeated attempts to produce the
   unusual; and

4. cataloging of the new ability (or concept) as a member of the repertoire.

An oversimplified model of intellectual development is a long sequence of
these cycles, one beginning exactly where the last ends. This model might be
good for designing science laboratory sequences for school curricula. However,
a more realistic model of the intellectual development process is a collection of
processes, often overlapping in time and thus largely happening concurrently.

---

[2]See [Ginsburg and Opper 1969]. Similar patterns occur in scientific research [Jeffreys
1957] [Kuhn 1963] and probably in animal learning as well.

Language acquisition is a domain in which the child can only use directed action in relatively limited ways. The repeated hearings of words in their varied but appropriate contexts must also be regarded as containing important ingredients of active participation (within the mind); the actions in the learner's repertoire may themselves be information-processing operations. The learning of the proper uses of any one word may happen over a period of several months, at the same time that many other words are gradually being learned.

In designing a computer program to carry out the steps of the circular reaction paradigm, one must be careful to not "get stuck in dead ends." Some kinds of explorations are bound not to find anything unusual and must eventually be abandoned if progress is to be made. Thus it must be easy to vary the mix of actions exercised from the repertoire and to focus attention on those most likely to lead to interesting or novel events.

8.3.2 Automatic Theory Formation

Douglas Lenat developed a program in 1975 called "AM" which demonstrated how the exploration of a space of concepts could be accomplished using a heuristic search procedure. His program began with a set of initial concepts of elementary set theory. The concepts were represented as frames. They were organized into an "ISA" hierarchy with more general concepts such as "object" or "conjecture" towards the top and more specific ones such as the concept of "ordered pair" near the bottom.

AM used a set of heuristic rules, organized into a production system, to expand its database of concepts. Typically it would perform such tasks as filling in properties and examples of existing concepts or creating a new concept using composition rules. It used a scheme for keeping track of which concepts and activities were most interesting. Associated with each object in AM was an "interestingness" value. Tasks were performed by AM in order of their interestingness, to attempt to find interesting new concepts. AM was able to discover the concept of prime numbers and to determine that it was an interesting concept. Eventually, after many hours of running time, AM became bogged down with uninteresting concepts, and nothing notable would happen. (Lenat attributed the stagnation to the fact that AM was not designed to invent new heuristics, and he later developed another system, "EURISKO," which could create heuristics.) However, the system was successful in demonstrating the methodology of automatic concept-space exploration in a mathematical area.

8.4   PYTHAGORUS: A LISP Program for Exploring Concepts in Geometry

8.4.1   General Remarks

This section presents a program which illustrates how heuristic search[3] may be used as the basis for exploring a space of concepts dealing with geometric figures. The features of this program are purposely limited, to keep it simple enough to be presented here in its entirety. The following aspects are included in the program: automatic concept formation using specialization; determination of examples of the concepts; evaluation of how interesting concepts are according to the relative numbers of examples that can be found for them; and overall direction of the exploration by "interest" estimates for the proposed tasks.

The particular space of concepts that PYTHAGORUS explores is a finite one. However, it would not be difficult to extend the program so that it could explore in an infinite space. As PYTHAGORUS tries to find examples of the concepts it has representations for, it performs "experiments" testing each member of the set of provided objects (the "toys") to determine whether it fits the definition of the concept. An alternative to providing a set of objects would be to give the program a procedure for generating new objects. It would be easy to write a function which returns a polygon with a random number of randomly selected vertices, each time it is called.

8.4.2   Task Creation

The initial agenda contains two tasks. One task requires that the system try to find examples for the general concept OBJECT. The other requires that the system try to create a more specialized concept from the general concept OBJECT.

If no new tasks were added to the agenda, the work of PYTHAGORUS would be over in a hurry. In order to keep the exploration going, additional tasks are created as new concepts are created and examples are sought for concepts. In the beginning, the system creates new tasks for itself faster than it can perform the tasks. Later, as more and more of the tasks performed fail to give rise to interesting concepts, fewer tasks are created, and the system finally stops.

After some examples of a concept have been found, two new tasks may be set up. First, a task to find more examples of the concept is set up if there are still objects which have not been tried as examples of the concept. Second, a task is set up to make a specialization of the concept, if no specialization already exists and if no such task is already on the agenda.

After making a specialization of a concept, a task is set up to make an alternative specialization, if possible. In addition, a task is set up to try to find

---

[3]The particular search method used in PYTHAGORUS is best-first search, which was described in Chapter 5.

examples of the new concept.

8.4.3 Implementation

PYTHAGORUS is a program that embodies some basic mechanisms for concept exploration. The structure of this program is as follows: There is an "agenda" (prioritized list of tasks) which is continually updated by the insertion of new tasks and the deletion of tasks that are completed. Each task is a specification for some activity. The function EXPLORE_CONCEPTS is a procedure which repeatedly takes the task of highest priority off the agenda and performs it with the help of other functions.

An item on the agenda has the form:

$$(\textit{interest-value }(\textit{task-specification}))$$

There are two kinds of tasks, and their specifications have the following forms:

- (MAKE_SPECIALIZATION concept-name)

- (FIND_EXAMPLES_OF concept-name)

The concepts under investigation are classes of geometric figures that can be derived from the most general class "OBJECT" using specialization through restrictive predicates. Since these predicates will be applied to actual geometric figures during the course of the program's exploration, we must define the representation scheme for the geometric figures. For this program, they are all polygons.

Let us now examine the details of the program.

```
; PYTHAGOR.LSP
; A program that explores a space of concepts
```

A polygon is represented as a list of points, and a point is a pair of coordinate values. The set of polygons used in the explorations is referred to as the "universe of objects" (these polygons are illustrated in figure 8.3) and it is defined as follows:

```
(SETQ BOX '((0 0) (0 5) (10 5) (10 0)) )
(SETQ SQUARE '((0 0) (0 10) (10 10) (10 0)) )
(SETQ ISOSCELES '((0 0) (5 5) (10 0)) )
(SETQ RIGHT_TRIANGLE '((0 0) (4 0) (4 3)) )
(SETQ TRAPEZOID '((0 0) (5 5) (20 5) (25 0)) )
(SETQ PARALLELOGRAM '((0 0) (5 5) (15 5) (10 0)) )
(SETQ RHOMBUS '((0 0) (4 3) (9 3) (5 0)) )
(SETQ MULTI '((0 0) (0 10) (4 15) (10 15) (15 10) (15 4) (10 0)) )
(SETQ LINE '((0 0) (10 0)) )
(SETQ DOT '((0 0)) )
```

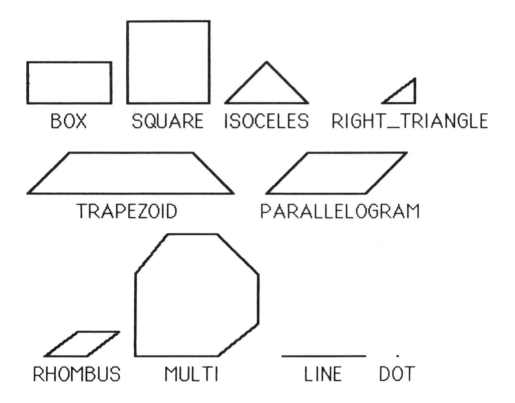

Figure 8.3: The universe of objects ("toys") manipulated by the PYTHAGORUS program.

```
(SETQ UNIVERSE '(BOX SQUARE ISOSCELES RIGHT_TRIANGLE TRAPEZOID
                PARALLELOGRAM RHOMBUS MULTI LINE DOT))
```

A collection of three predicates is provided for the purpose of forming specializations. The three predicates are (EQUALSIDES P), (NONZEROAREA P), and (MANYSIDES P). The argument P is a polygon.

```
(SETQ PREDICATES '(EQUALSIDES NONZEROAREA MANYSIDES))
```

The predicate EQUALSIDES uses four helping functions. The first of these is SIDE_LENGTH_SQ_LIST which makes a list of the squares of the lengths of the sides of the polygon. Second is SLSL, which does all the work for SIDE_LENGTH_SQ_LIST but refers to the value of local variable FIRST_PT which is established in SIDE_LENGTH_SQ_LIST. Third is SQ, which returns the value of its argument squared. The fourth helping function is ALLEQUAL, which returns T if all the elements in the list (which is its argument) are equal. The function SLSL also uses some coordinate-arithmetic functions, DX and DY which are defined later.

```
(DEFUN EQUALSIDES (P)    ; true if all sides have same length
   (ALLEQUAL (SIDE_LENGTH_SQ_LIST P)) )

(DEFUN SIDE_LENGTH_SQ_LIST (P) ; make list of lengths squared.
   (PROG (FIRST_PT)
         (SETQ FIRST_PT (CAR P))
         (RETURN (SLSL P))) )

(DEFUN SLSL (P)             ; helping function.
   (COND ((NULL (CDR P))   ; last side connects to 1st pt.
          (LIST (PLUS (SQ (DX FIRST_PT (CAR P)))
                      (SQ (DY FIRST_PT (CAR P))) ) ) )
         (T (CONS          ; other sides connect successive pts.
               (PLUS (SQ (DX (CADR P) (CAR P)))
                     (SQ (DY (CADR P) (CAR P))) )
               (SLSL (CDR P)) )) ) )

(DEFUN SQ (N) (TIMES N N)) ; return N squared.

(DEFUN ALLEQUAL (L)        ; true if all members of L are EQUAL.
   (APPLY 'AND
          (MAPCAR '(LAMBDA (XX) (EQUAL XX (CAR L)))
                  (CDR L) ) ) )
```

The predicate NONZEROAREA uses two helping functions, AREA and AREA1. Using AREA1 to do most of its work, AREA computes the area of the polygon by summing the areas (some positive and some negative) directly below each side; each of these areas is bounded by a quadrilateral consisting of the side of the polygon, a segment of the x axis and two vertical segments. Note that the function AREA assumes that the points of the polygon are listed in *clockwise* order, in order to have a non-negative result.

```
(DEFUN NONZEROAREA (P) (NULL (ZEROP (AREA P))))
; true if the area of P is not zero.
```

```
(DEFUN AREA (P)          ; compute the area enclosed by P
  (PROG (FIRST_PT)
        (SETQ FIRST_PT (CAR P))
        (RETURN (QUOTIENT (AREA1 P) 2))))
```

```
(DEFUN AREA1 (P)         ; helping function
  (COND ((NULL (CDR P))
         (TIMES (DX FIRST_PT (CAR P))
                (PY FIRST_PT (CAR P)) ) )
        (T (PLUS (AREA1 (CDR P))
                 (TIMES (DX (CADR P) (CAR P))
                        (PY (CADR P) (CAR P)) ) ) ) ) )
```

The third predicate in the collection, MANYSIDES, is true of a polygon if the polygon has more than six sides. It is defined very simply as follows:

```
(DEFUN MANYSIDES (P) (GREATERP (LENGTH P) 6))
```

Below are some helping functions for coordinate arithmetic. DX takes two points (which are coordinate pairs) and returns the difference $x_1 - x_2$. Similarly, DY returns $y_1 - y_2$. PY returns $y_1 + y_2$. XC and YC return the x and y coordinates, respectively, of a point, providing mneumonic representations for CAR and CADR.

```
(DEFUN DX (PT1 PT2) (DIFFERENCE (XC PT1) (XC PT2)))
```

```
(DEFUN DY (PT1 PT2) (DIFFERENCE (YC PT1) (YC PT2)))
```

```
(DEFUN PY (PT1 PT2) (PLUS (YC PT1) (YC PT2)))
```

```
(DEFUN XC (PT) (CAR PT)) ; get X coordinate of point.
```

```
(DEFUN YC (PT) (CADR PT)); get Y coordinate of point.
```

The procedure FIND_EXAMPLES_OF, in order to find examples of a particular concept, takes the list of objects not yet tried for the concept and tries three of them. (The number 3 was chosen to give a task granularity that permits the agenda mechanism to respond to subtle changes in INTEREST values of tasks, while still avoiding the heavy computational overhead that would be incurred if the number were 1.) FIND_EXAMPLES_OF puts any examples found onto the list of examples for the concept, and it updates the list of objects left to try. This function also updates the interest value for the concept in accordance with the results of the quest for examples.

FIND_EXAMPLES_OF and MAKE_SPECIALIZATION, its companion function, implement the key aspects of the program, and each of them has a long definition. FIND_EXAMPLES_OF takes a single argument, a concept (represented as a literal atom). The two PROG variables are used as follows: OBJECTS_LEFT represents the list of objects not yet tested as examples of the concept. X holds the object currently being tested.

```
(DEFUN FIND_EXAMPLES_OF (C)
  (PROG (OBJECTS_LEFT X)
        ; test 3 objects not yet tried as examples of C:
        (SETQ OBJECTS_LEFT (GET C 'OBJECTS_TO_TRY))
        (DO_N_TIMES 3       ; beginning of loop
          (COND ((NULL OBJECTS_LEFT)    ; if out of objects,
                 (PUTPROP C NIL 'OBJECTS_TO_TRY)  ; record it,
                 (GO NEXT)) )           ; and jump out of loop.
          (SETQ X (CAR OBJECTS_LEFT))   ; else, try next object:
          (SETQ OBJECTS_LEFT (CDR OBJECTS_LEFT))
          (PUTPROP C (ADD1 (GET C 'NUMBER_TRIED)) 'NUMBER_TRIED)
          ; Here's the test.  Apply the concept's defining pred.
          (COND ((APPLY (GET C 'PREDICATE) (LIST (EVAL X)))
                 ; an example has been found...
                 (PRINT
                   (APPEND (LIST X) '(IS AN EXAMPLE OF) (LIST C)))
                 (PUTPROP C
                          (ADDTOSET X (GET C 'EXAMPLES_FOUND))
                          'EXAMPLES_FOUND)
                 (PUTPROP C
                          (ADD1 (GET C 'NUMBER_FOUND))
                          'NUMBER_FOUND) )
                 ; but if the object is not an example...
                (T (PRINT (APPEND (LIST X)
                                  '(IS NOT AN EXAMPLE OF)
                                  (LIST C) ))) )
          )       ; end of loop.
        (PUTPROP C OBJECTS_LEFT 'OBJECTS_TO_TRY)

NEXT
        ; update the interest value for C:
```

```
(PUTPROP C (CONCEPT_INTEREST C) 'INTEREST)
; if there are still objects not yet tried,
;   enter a new task on the agenda to try 3 more objects:
(COND (OBJECTS_LEFT
          (PUT_ON_AGENDA
          (CONS ; compute interest val...
                  (EXAMPLES_TASK_INTEREST C)
                  (LIST (LIST 'FIND_EXAMPLES_OF
                               (LIST 'QUOTE C) )) ) ) )
        (T (COND (REPORTING
                  (PRINT '(OBJECTS EXHAUSTED)) )))) )
; if in the reporting mode, display the current agenda:
(COND (REPORTING (PRINT (APPEND '(AGENDA IS:) AGENDA))))
; if there is at least one example of the concept and no
; specializations for this concept have yet been created,
; and no tasks for such specialization are already on the
; agenda, create a new task to make a specialization of C:
(COND ((AND (GREATERP (GET C 'NUMBER_FOUND) 0)
              (NULL (GET C 'INCLUDES))
              (NO_SPEC_TASK C) )
          (PUT_ON_AGENDA
              (CONS   ; compute interest...
                  (SPEC_TASK_INTEREST C)
                  (LIST (LIST 'MAKE_SPECIALIZATION
                               (LIST 'QUOTE C) )) ) )
          ) )
; print out the current description of the concept:
(DISPLAY_CONCEPT C) ) )
```

The following function inserts an entry of the form (*interest-value* (*task-specification*)) onto the agenda, in its place, so that items are ordered, highest interest-value first.

```
(DEFUN PUT_ON_AGENDA (TASK)
  (SETQ AGENDA (PUT_ON_AGENDA1 TASK AGENDA)) )


; recursive slave to PUT_ON_AGENDA:
(DEFUN PUT_ON_AGENDA1 (TASK AGENDA)
  (COND ((NULL AGENDA) (LIST TASK))
        ((LESSP (CAR TASK) (CAAR AGENDA))
          (CONS (CAR AGENDA)
                (PUT_ON_AGENDA1 TASK (CDR AGENDA)) ) )
        (T (CONS TASK AGENDA)) ) )
```

The function NO_SPEC_TASK returns T if no MAKE_SPECIALIZATION task with concept *C* is on the agenda:

```
(DEFUN NO_SPEC_TASK (C)
  (NO_SPEC_TASK1 AGENDA) )

;recursive slave to NO_SPEC_TASK:
(DEFUN NO_SPEC_TASK1 (L)
  (COND ((NULL L) T)
        ((AND (SETQ TEMP (CADAR L))
              (EQ 'MAKE_SPECIALIZATION (CAR TEMP))
              (EQ C (CADR (CADR TEMP)))) )
         NIL)
        (T (NO_SPEC_TASK1 (CDR L))) ) )
```

Next is a function which computes the current interest value for concept using a formula that involves the "hit ratio" of number of examples found to number of objects tried. Letting r be this ratio, our formula is

$$\text{interest} = 400(r - r^2).$$

However, if no objects have yet been tried as examples for the concept, we define the current interest to be that "inherited" from the parent concept. In the body of CONCEPT_INTEREST, the first clause of the COND handles the case where none have been tried. The second clause computes the value according to a formula which is mathematically equivalent to that above, but works only with FIXNUM arithmetic, for efficiency.

```
(DEFUN CONCEPT_INTEREST (C)
  (COND ((ZEROP (GET C 'NUMBER_TRIED))
         (GET (PARENT C) 'INTEREST))
        (T (DIFFERENCE
             100
             (TIMES 4
                    (SQ (DIFFERENCE 5
                                    (QUOTIENT
                                     (TIMES 10 (GET C 'NUMBER_FOUND))
                                     (GET C 'NUMBER_TRIED) ) ) )) ) )) )
```

Another function for computing interest is the following one which computes the interest of a task to find examples of C. It is based on the formula

$$\text{examples\_task\_interest}(C) = 0.8\,\text{interest}(\text{parent}(C)) + 0.2\,\text{interest}(C).$$

This formula yields a value close to the interest of the parent of C, but adjusts this value slightly if there is experimental evidence so far that the interest of C is different from that of its parent.

```
(DEFUN EXAMPLES_TASK_INTEREST (C)
```

```
(QUOTIENT (PLUS (TIMES 8 (GET (PARENT C) 'INTEREST))
                (TIMES 2 (GET C 'INTEREST)) )
          10) )
```

The function PARENT, defined below, returns the parent concept of concept C. This function is used in the function EXAMPLES_TASK_INTEREST, above.

```
(DEFUN PARENT (C) (CAR (GET C 'ISA))) ; parent assumed unique
```

The interest value for a specialization task is computed by the next function as approximately ten times the parent concept's hit ratio:

$$\text{spec\_task\_interest}(C) = 10[N_{\text{found}}(\text{parent}(C))/N_{\text{tried}}(\text{parent}(C))].$$

```
(DEFUN SPEC_TASK_INTEREST (C)
  (QUOTIENT (TIMES 10 (GET C 'NUMBER_FOUND))
            (ADD1 (GET C 'NUMBER_TRIED)) ) ) ; avoids div. by 0.
```

A task of type MAKE_SPECIALIZATION requires that the system attempt to create a representation for a new concept by associating with a new atom the following:

1. a definition of the concept in terms of the parent concept, suitable for an explanatory printout,

2. a predicate that can be applied to any object to determine whether it is an example of this concept,

3. an interest value for the concept computed using a rule which takes into account the interest of the parent concept and the interest of the predicate used to form the restriction,

4. a list of objects that have not yet been tried as possible examples, initially the whole "UNIVERSE,"

5. a list of examples found (initially null),

6. a list of the predicates NOT used in the definition of this concept—this simplifies the procedure MAKE_SPECIALIZATION,

7. a list of the original (provided) predicates that have been used along the path from OBJECT to this concept (used in DISPLAY_CONCEPTS),

8. a list of the predicates that have been used to create specializations of this concept (initially null),

9. the number of examples found so far (initially 0), and

10. the number of objects tried so far (initially 0).

These items are put onto the property list of the atom under the following property types: DEFN, PREDICATE, INTEREST, OBJECTS_TO_TRY, EXAMPLES_FOUND, UNUSED_PREDICATES, PREDICATES_USED_IN_DESC, PREDICATES_USED_IN_SPEC, NUMBER_FOUND, NUMBER_TRIED.

   The function MAKE_SPECIALIZATION takes one argument, the atom for an existing concept. The two PROG variables, PRED and NEWC, are used to hold the predicate used to form a restriction of the current concept, and the literal atom that represents the new concept, respectively.

```
(DEFUN MAKE_SPECIALIZATION (C)
   (PROG (PRED NEWC)
        ; select a predicate not already involved in the parent
        ;  and not already used for a specialization of C.
        (SETQ PRED
              (SELECT_PRED (GET C 'UNUSED_PREDICATES)
                           (GET C 'PREDICATES_USED_IN_SPEC) ) )
        (COND ((NULL PRED)
               (COND (REPORTING
                      (PRINT
                        '(CANNOT FIND A WAY
                           TO SPECIALIZE FURTHER) ) ))
               (RETURN NIL) ) )
        ; indicate that the selected predicate is no longer
        ;  available for other specializations of C:
        (PUTPROP C
                 (CONS PRED (GET C 'PREDICATES_USED_IN_SPEC))
                 'PREDICATES_USED_IN_SPEC)

        ; allocate a new atom...
        (SETQ NEWC (NEW_ATOM))
        ; set up links in concept hierarchy...
        (MAKE_ISA NEWC C)
        ; register the list of unused predicates for
        ;  the new concept:
        (PUTPROP NEWC
                 (DELETE PRED (GET C 'UNUSED_PREDICATES))
                 'UNUSED_PREDICATES)
        ; possible examples might include all objects
        ;  in the universe:
        (PUTPROP NEWC UNIVERSE 'OBJECTS_TO_TRY)
        ; initialize the various counts for the concept:
        (PUTPROP NEWC 0 'NUMBER_FOUND)
        (PUTPROP NEWC 0 'NUMBER_TRIED)
```

```
; create the (possibly compound) PREDICATE which
;   tests an object to see if it is an example of
;   the new concept:
(PUTPROP NEWC
          (LIST 'LAMBDA '(OBJ)
                  (LIST 'AND
                          (CONS PRED '(OBJ))
                          (LIST 'APPLY
                                  (LIST 'QUOTE
                                          (GET C 'PREDICATE) )
                                  '(LIST OBJ) ) ) )
          'PREDICATE)
(COND (REPORTING ; if REPORTING enabled, show predicate:
   (PRINTM HERE IS THE NEW PREDICATE:)
   (PRINT (GET NEWC 'PREDICATE)) ))
; store the list of predicates that should be used
;   to describe this concept:
(PUTPROP NEWC
          (CONS PRED (GET C 'PREDICATES_USED_IN_DESC))
          'PREDICATES_USED_IN_DESC)

; put a task on the agenda to find examples of
;   the new concept:
(PUT_ON_AGENDA
    (LIST ; INTEREST = interest of parent concept.
        (GET C 'INTEREST)
        (LIST 'FIND_EXAMPLES_OF
        (CONS 'QUOTE (LIST NEWC)) ) ) )
; put a task on the agenda to make another
;   specialization of C
(PUT_ON_AGENDA
    (CONS (SPEC_TASK_INTEREST C)
            (LIST (LIST 'MAKE_SPECIALIZATION
                        (LIST 'QUOTE C) )) ) ) ) )
```

This function definition for MAKE_SPECIALIZATION would be even longer if it were not for the helping functions SELECT_PRED and NEW_ATOM. SELECT_PRED is used to select a predicate that is on the list of predicates available but not on the list of predicates already used along the current chain in the concept space.

```
(DEFUN SELECT_PRED (L1 L2)   ; return a member of L1 - L2
   (COND ((NULL L1) NIL)
          ((MEMBER (CAR L1) L2) (SELECT_PRED (CDR L1) L2))
          (T (CAR L1)) ) )
```

The function NEW_ATOM returns a new atom each time it is called[4]:

```lisp
(DEFUN NEW_ATOM ()
  (COND ((NULL ATOMS_AVAIL)
         (PRINT '(OUT OF ATOMS FOR REPRESENTING CONCEPTS)))
        (T (SETQ TEMP (CAR ATOMS_AVAIL))
           (SETQ ATOMS_AVAIL (CDR ATOMS_AVAIL))
           TEMP) ) )
(SETQ ATOMS_AVAIL '(C1 C2 C3 C4 C5 C6 C7 C8 C9 C10 C11
         C12 C13 C14 C15 C16 C17 C18 C19 C20 C21 C22
         C23 C24 C25 C26 C27 C28 C29 C30 C31 C32 C33
         C34 C35 C36 C37 C38 C39 C40))
```

The top-level control loop is implemented in the next function, EX-PLORE_CONCEPTS. This function executes tasks from the agenda until no tasks remain.

```lisp
(DEFUN EXPLORE_CONCEPTS ()
  (PROG (CURRENT_TASK)
  LOOP (COND ((NULL AGENDA)
              (RETURN '(MY INSPIRATION IS GONE))))
       ;select task at head of agenda:
       (SETQ CURRENT_TASK (CADR (CAR AGENDA)))
       (SETQ AGENDA (CDR AGENDA)) ; remove it from agenda
       (EVAL CURRENT_TASK)        ; perform current task
       (GO LOOP) ) )              ; repeat
```

Four functions that help construct the inclusion hierarchy for representing the concepts are listed below. They are similar to functions used in the LINNEUS program of Chapter 4.

```lisp
(DEFUN ADDTOSET (X SET)
  (COND ((MEMBER X SET) SET)
        (T (CONS X SET)) ) )

(DEFUN ADDSUBSET (X Y) ; form rep. that X is a subset of Y
  (PUTPROP Y (ADDTOSET X (GET Y 'INCLUDES)) 'INCLUDES) )

(DEFUN ADDSUPERSET (X Y); form rep. that X is a superset of Y
  (PUTPROP Y (ADDTOSET X (GET Y 'ISA)) 'ISA) )

(DEFUN MAKE_ISA (X Y) ; set up bi-direct. ISA link
  (AND (ADDSUPERSET Y X) (ADDSUBSET X Y)) )
```

---

[4]Some LISP systems provide a function GENSYM that actually generates new atoms, and it could be used here instead.

The initial state of PYTHAGORUS is established by the function INITIALIZE:

```
(DEFUN INITIALIZE ()
  (PROG ()
  ; Initialize the concept hierarchy to contain one concept,
  ;  OBJECT, from which specializations will be made.
  (PUTPROP 'OBJECT '(LAMBDA (X) T) 'PREDICATE)
  (PUTPROP 'OBJECT UNIVERSE 'OBJECTS_TO_TRY)
  (PUTPROP 'OBJECT PREDICATES 'UNUSED_PREDICATES)
  (PUTPROP 'OBJECT NIL 'PREDICATES_USED_IN_SPEC)
  (PUTPROP 'OBJECT 0 'NUMBER_TRIED)
  (PUTPROP 'OBJECT 0 'NUMBER_FOUND)
  (PUTPROP 'OBJECT 50 'INTEREST)
  ; One of the interest-computing functions requires that
  ;  OBJECT have a parent concept; therefore...
  (MAKE_ISA 'OBJECT 'DUMMY)
  (PUTPROP 'DUMMY 50 'INTEREST)
  ;
  ; Set up the initial agenda of tasks:
  (SETQ AGENDA '(
          (50 (FIND_EXAMPLES_OF 'OBJECT))
          (25 (MAKE_SPECIALIZATION 'OBJECT))
          )) ) )
```

For the purpose of monitoring the progress of the system, a function is provided which displays the important attributes of a concept:

```
(DEFUN DISPLAY_CONCEPT (C)
  (PROG ()
          (TERPRI) ; start a new line
          (PRINT1M CONCEPT:)(PRINT C)
          (PRINT1M OBJECTS WHICH HAVE:)
           (APPLY 'PRINTM (GET C 'PREDICATES_USED_IN_DESC))
          (PRINT1M SPECIALIZATION OF:)(PRINT (GET C 'ISA))
          (PRINT1M INTEREST:)(PRINT (GET C 'INTEREST))
          (PRINT1M EXAMPLES_FOUND:)
           (PRINT (GET C 'EXAMPLES_FOUND)) ) )
```

The utility function PRINT1M, used in DISPLAY_CONCEPT, prints a list (unevaluated) without parentheses and without a carriage return. PRINT1M is defined:

```
(DEFEXPR PRINT1M (L)
  (MAPCAR (FUNCTION (LAMBDA (S) (AND (PRIN1 S) (TYO 32))))
          L) )
```

In order to test the program, the following function is defined:

```
(DEFUN TEST ()
  (PROG ()
       (INITIALIZE)
       (EXPLORE_CONCEPTS) ) )
```

and then the function may be evaluated:

```
(TEST)
```

And for a more-detailed account of PYTHAGORUS's progress the following may be typed:

```
(SETQ REPORTING T)
(TRACE FIND_EXAMPLES_OF MAKE_SPECIALIZATION)
(TRACE PUT_ON_AGENDA)
(TEST)
```

8.4.4 Behavior and Limitations of PYTHAGORUS

PYTHAGORUS begins its exploration by generating examples of the initial concept "OBJECT" for which every polygon in the given universe turns out to be an example. The interest value for OBJECT is 0 because the criteria for a high interest value are that a concept have some examples, but not every element of the universe should be an example of the concept.

A full run of the program causes about five pages of output, without the REPORTING variable set to T. Two kinds of messages are displayed. One kind indicates the result of a test to see if a particular object is an example of a particular concept, e.g.,

```
(PARALLELOGRAM IS NOT AN EXAMPLE OF C3)
```

The other kind gives current information about a concept, e.g.,

```
CONCEPT: C11
OBJECTS WHICH HAVE: NONZEROAREA EQUALSIDES
INTEREST: 84
EXAMPLES_FOUND: (SQUARE)
```

Such a description is printed by the function DISPLAY_CONCEPT, which is called at the end of each examples-finding task. Displays like this for concept C11 occur four times. The last of them is as follows:

```
CONCEPT: C11
OBJECTS WHICH HAVE: NONZEROAREA EQUALSIDES
INTEREST: 64
EXAMPLES_FOUND: (RHOMBUS SQUARE)
```

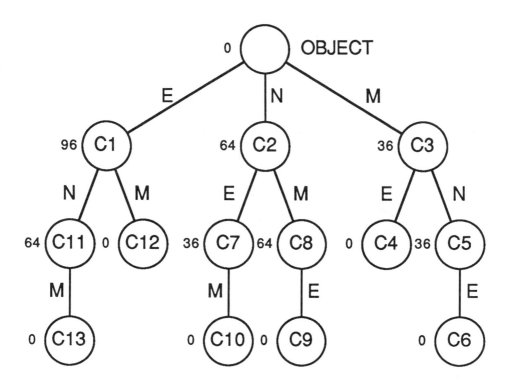

Figure 8.4: The space of concepts explored by the PYTHAGORUS program.

The interest value of 64 is lower here than in the first description, reflecting the change in the success rate in finding examples; SQUARE was found to be an example during the first group of three tests, but in all the remaining seven tests, only one more example, RHOMBUS, was found.

Many of the concepts that PYTHAGORUS generates are uninteresting because no examples exist. Most of these concepts we know to be mathematically equivalent, since they are essentially defined by conjunctions of the same predicates but in different orders. One of the exercises is concerned with the automatic recognition of equivalences of concepts.

The space of concepts in which PYTHAGORUS roams contains 16 elements (nodes). Only 14 of these are actually visited, because two of them are descendants of nodes with zero INTEREST. The search tree that is "traversed" by PYTHAGORUS is shown in Fig. 8.4 The order of creation of the nodes is not identical to the order of exploration of the nodes; each concept is created at most once, but it may be treated a number of times by tasks that try to find examples of it. The concepts are created in the order C1, C2, ... , C13. The order in which examples are first sought for each concept is: OBJECT, C3, C4, C5, C6, C2, C8, C9, C7, C10, C1, C11, C12, C13. This order is the result of the INTEREST values in combination with the tie-breaking behavior (which is to select the most-recently created task, rather than treat them in the order in which they were created).

One inefficiency of PYTHAGORUS is that it checks all objects when trying to find examples of a concept, even when that concept is very specialized (e.g., three levels down in the concept hierarchy). It does not take advantage of the fact that any object which is not an example of a concept C cannot be an example of any specialization of C. However, this inefficiency gives PYTHAGORUS the freedom to explore interesting specializations before their parent concepts are fully explored. The ability to explore a concept before its parent is fully explored would be especially important if the program used a polygon generator instead of a set of given polygons; otherwise, with an infinite number of possible examples to be tested, the program could never get past the first concept.

The heuristics used to compute interest values can be changed. For example, if one prefers that PYTHAGORUS explore the whole concept space before completing the example testing for general concepts, one can lower the interest value associated with tasks for finding examples.

8.4.5   Discussion

What are the possible benefits of developing concept-exploration systems? A program such as PYTHAGORUS does not possess sufficient expertise to be of use in practical problem-solving; e.g., in suggesting a new arrangement for the living-room furniture (which may be viewed as a problem of manipulating polygons). There are two standard answers to a question such as this, and there is another, better, answer to this particular question. The "standard" reasons for studying any kind of machine learning are (1) that through this research we hope to better understand human intellectual development, and (2) we seek to realize the potential for computer systems to build their own knowledge bases, so that experts and programmers do not have to spoon-feed them all that knowledge.

Concept-exploration techniques have a special significance. The whole approach itself seems to offer the beginnings of a methodology for formalizing conceptual knowledge. Mathematicians may be able, in the future, to rework fundamental subjects, such as abstract algebra and functional analysis, according to formal theory-formation guidelines, in such a way as to close gaps in current knowledge. The existence of such theoretical knowledge in a machine may allow the knowledge to be applied in new ways, because it may be organized in a scheme different from the traditional scheme.

What fields of study are amenable to automatic concept-exploration methods? In order to answer this, we recall the activities performed by PYTHAGORUS: creating concepts from existing concepts, and working with examples. The concept-formation activity may be seen as the theory-building part. The manipulation of examples is empirical, and the results of this activity guide the theory-building activity. Suppose we wanted a computer to build a theory about physics, say Newtonian mechanics. We would have to provide some initial concepts, perhaps concepts of space, time and matter. Operations would be needed that synthesize new concepts from existing ones. Perhaps more problematical is the provision of mechanisms to carry out physical experiments. The computer could control robot arms that would manipulate masses, strings, springs, etc., so that the computer could perform experiments much as one does in a college physics lab. Needless to say, empirically evaluating even simple physical concepts (the possibility of objects with negative mass, the existence of gravity, the law that "an object at rest tends to remain at rest") would require much more elaborate facilities than what is needed to find examples of the concept of a regular polygon.

Clearly, mathematics is an ideal realm for computer exploration, because experiments can be performed without robotics equipment, and in many cases, extremely rapidly. Also, by eliminating the need for physical experimentation, we largely avoid the problems of equipment breaking and interference from external factors.

However, concept-exploration methods are not limited to mathematics. There exist domains in which physical experiments can be done quickly and under computer control; these include electronics, electrochemistry, and perhaps molecular biology. Also, there are a number of subjects in which certain kinds of experiments may be performed completely in the computer, through simulation. Economics, evolutionary genetics, demographics, and molecular chemistry are such fields. If speed is not a concern, and the computer could place orders for experiments that would be performed by human scientists or technicians, then there seems to be no reason why the concept-exploration methodology could not be applied to any scientific domain.

Although the PYTHAGORUS program is not interactive, a concept-exploration program might be more useful if it could be interactively guided by a human. Besides directing the program's attention by occasionally overriding or adjusting the mechanisms that compute task and concept interest values, the human could provide terminology and descriptive comments for concepts, making it easier for humans to understand the computer's theory.

In order to make a program such as PYTHAGORUS interactive, one must provide for effective man-machine communication. The human user must be able to understand the program and give it commands or questions. Often, an interactive program is more understandable to a human user if it uses good graphics to display its current state or the data structures that the user is manipulating. For user input, a natural-language understanding capability is often desired (such techniques are described in the next chapter). A combination of graphical and textual communication may be best for such man-machine systems.

8.5 Concluding Remarks

In this chapter, we have examined two kinds of methods for learning about concepts. In the first group are techniques for finding a definition or classification rule from a set of examples and non-examples. This kind of learning may be termed "outside-in" because it begins with (part of) the extension of the concept and derives its intension (a logical predicate). On the other hand, the second group of methods computes the concept definitions analytically and mechanically without induction from examples. However, each of these concepts is explored by looking for examples of it, and the results of such exploration guide the development of additional concepts. This kind of learning may be called "inside-out" learning, because the system develops a concept's intension before exploring its extension. Learning from the outside in and from the inside out are complementary activities that might well be combined in future systems.

As the next section suggests, there is a large literature on machine learning. This chapter has presented only a few of the many ideas that have been developed. For every type of knowledge representation, there is a corresponding problem of devising a means to automatically create knowledge bases in it. For any form of mathematical model, there can be program designed to create such models. Machine learning has a long future.

8.6 Bibliographical Information

Early work on machine learning focussed on models for self-adapting pattern-recognition systems, including the "perceptron" [Rosenblatt 1962]. A good introduction to some of the numerical approaches to learning is found in [Nilsson 1965]. The application of a parametric learning method to an automatic game-playing system (for checkers) is described in [Samuel 1963]. The discovery of classification rules using combinatorial optimization and the "star" method is described in [Michalski 1980]. Some models of learning systems are described in [Buchanan et al 1977]. A cross-section of more recent work in machine learning is presented in [Michalski et al 1983] and [Michalski et al 1986].

Methods for interactive knowledge acquisition for expert systems are described in [Davis 1980], [Hayes-Roth et al 1981], and [Boose 1986].

A system for learning single concepts using induction is described in [Hunt et al 1966]. Methods for producing generalizations from sequences of structured objects are described in [Winston 1975], [Vere 1975], and [Hayes-Roth and McDermott 1977], and a survey of such systems is [Dietterich and Michalski 1981]. A systematic approach to learning concepts in which the possible final rules are grouped and represented by the bounds on their generality and specificity (the version-space method) was developed by Mitchell (see [Mitchell 1977]) and used in his "Lex" system; the Lex system learned heuristic rules applicable to solving integration problems in calculus [Mitchell et al 1981]. The computational complexity of inductive learning is discussed in [Valiant 1984] and [Valiant 1985].

Much of the motivation for designing systems that can theorize, creating concepts, making conjectures, and validating them empirically, stems from insights about the process of intellectual development, scientific inquiry and mathematical discovery that are elucidated in books like [Ginsburg and Opper 1969], [Jeffreys 1957] and [Polya 1954]. Polya's work provided direct support for the Ph.D. dissertation of Lenat, which is represented in slightly reduced form in [Lenat 1980]. One of the limitations of the AM program was that it could not modify its own heuristics. In an effort to provide a means for automatically improving heuristics, the EURISKO system was developed [Lenat 1983].

Another form of theorizing is the formulation of quantitative relationships in data. A description of one approach to the automatic discovery of scientific laws (using a program called "BACON") is in [Langley 1977].

An interesting collection of papers on machine learning is the compendium from a NATO Advanced Study Institute held in France [Simon 1976]; most of these papers are in English but some are in French. In addition to the papers, there are transcripts of discussions among the participants, which included several prominent researchers in machine learning.

References

1. Boose, J. H. 1986. ETS: A system for the transfer of human expertise. In Kowalik, J. S. (ed.), *Knowledge Based Problem Solving.* Englewood Cliffs, NJ: Prentice-Hall, pp68-111.

2. Buchanan, B. G., Mitchell, T. M., Smith, R. G., and Johnson, C. R., Jr. 1977. Models of learning systems. In Belzer, J., Holzman, A. G., and Kent, A. (eds.), *Encyclopedia of Computer Science and Technology*, Vol. 11. New York: Marcel Dekker, pp24-51.

3. Davis, R. 1980. Applications of meta level knowledge to the construction, maintenance, and use of large knowledge bases. In Davis, R. and Lenat, D. B. (eds.), *Knowledge-based Systems in Artificial Intelligence.* New York: McGraw-Hill.

4. Dietterich, T. G., and Michalski, R. S. 1981. Inductive learning of structural descriptions: Evaluation criteria and comparative review of selected methods. *Artificial Intelligence*, Vol. 16, pp257-294.

5. Ginsburg, H., and Opper, S. 1969. *Piaget's Theory of Intellectual Development.* Englewood Cliffs, NJ: Prentice-Hall.

6. Hayes-Roth, F., Klahr, P., and Mostow, D. 1981. Advice-taking and knowledge refinement: An iterative view of skill acquisition. In Ander-

son, J. R. (ed.), *Cognitive Skills and Their Acquisition.* Hillsdale, NJ: Lawrence Erlbaum, pp231-253.

7. Hayes-Roth, F., and McDermott, J. 1977. An interference matching technique for inducing abstractions. *Communications of the ACM,* Vol. 26, pp401-410.

8. Hunt, E. B., Marin, J., and Stone, P. J. 1966. Experiments in induction. New York: Academic Press.

9. Jeffreys, H. 1957. *Scientific Inference.* Cambridge University Press.

10. Kuhn, T. S. 1963. The structure of scientific revolutions. *International Encyclopedia of Unified Science,* Vols. I-II, The University of Chicago Press.

11. Langley, P. 1977. Rediscovering physics with BACON-3. *Proceedings of the Fifth International Joint Conference on Artificial Intelligence,* Cambridge, pp505-507.

12. Lenat, D. B. 1980. AM: An artificial intelligence approach to discovery in mathematics as heuristic search. In Davis, R. and Lenat, D. B. (eds.), *Knowledge-based Systems in Artificial Intelligence.* New York: McGraw-Hill.

13. Lenat, D. B. 1983. The nature of heuristics III. *Artificial Intelligence,* Vol. 19, pp189-249.

14. Michalski, R. S. 1980. Pattern recognition as rule-guided inductive inference. *IEEE Transactions on Pattern Analysis and Machine Intelligence,* Vol. PAMI-2, No. 4, pp349-361.

15. Michalski, R. S., Carbonell, J. G., and Mitchell, T. M. 1983. *Machine Learning: An Artificial Intelligence Approach.* Palo Alto, CA: Tioga Publishing, and Los Altos, CA: William Kaufmann, Inc.

16. Michalski, R. S., Carbonell, J. G., and Mitchell, T. M. 1986. *Machine Learning: An Artificial Intelligence Approach, Volume II.* Los Altos, CA: Morgan Kaufmann.

17. Mitchell, T. M. 1977. Version spaces: A candidate elimination approach to rule learning. *Proceedings of the Fifth International Joint Conference on Artificial Intelligence,* Cambridge, pp305-310.

18. Mitchell, T. M., Utgoff, P. E., Nudel, B., and Banerji, R. B. 1981. Learning problem-solving heuristics through practice. *Proceedings of the Seventh International Joint Conference on Artificial Intelligence,* Vancouver, pp127-134.

19. Nilsson, N. J. 1965. *Learning Machines: Foundations of Trainable Pattern-Classifying Systems.* New York: McGraw-Hill.

20. Polya, G. 1954. *Mathematics and Plausible Reasoning, Vol. I: Induction and Analogy in Mathematics, Vol. II: Patterns of Plausible Inference.* Princeton, NJ: Princeton University Press.

21. Rosenblatt, F. 1962. *Principles of Neurodynamics: Perceptrons and the Theory of Brain Mechanisms.* Washington D. C.: Spartan Books.

22. Samuel, A. L. 1963. Some studies in machine learning using the game of checkers. In Feigenbaum, E. A. and Feldman, J. (eds.), *Computers and Thought.* New York: McGraw-Hill, pp71-105.

23. Simon, J.-C. (ed.) 1976. *Computer Oriented Learning Processes.* Leyden, The Netherlands: Noordhoof International Publishing.

24. Valiant, L. G. 1984. A theory of the learnable. *Communications of the ACM*, Vol. 27, No. 11, pp1134-1142.

25. Valiant, L. G. 1985. Learning disjunctions of conjunctions. *Proceedings of the Ninth International Joint Conference on Artificial Intelligence*, Los Angeles, pp560-566.

26. Vere, S. A. 1975. Induction of concepts in the predicate calculus. *Proceedings of the Fourth International Joint Conference on Artificial Intelligence*, Tbilisi, USSR, pp281-287.

27. Winston, P. H. 1975. Learning structural descriptions from examples. In Winston, P. H. (ed.), *The Psychology of Computer Vision.* New York: McGraw-Hill, pp157-209.

Exercises

1. Which of the following situations is a case of learning? Explain why or why not in each case.

   (a) A weight lifter who was ill is now recovering. Each day, before practise, it is becoming easier to lift 300 lbs.

   (b) A pigeon walking on the ground spots a piece of bread. Knowing where the bread is, it picks it up in its beak and eats it.

   (c) A computer program, written in LISP, evaluates a function F on some arguments over and over again. The evaluation is initially slow because memory is almost full and the garbage collector runs frequently. Between some of these evaluations, the program frees a large area of memory, and then the successive evaluations of the function proceed more quickly.

(d) A program that solves problems is fed a lot of facts that have nothing to do with the problems it has to solve, and as a result, the time it takes to solve an average problem is lengthened.

2. Find another disjunctive-normal-form classification rule for the "warning" strings on page 288 that is reasonably short and does not use the proposition $M(x, 5, \mathrm{D})$.

3. Using the two sets of strings on page 288, determine classification rules with the following properties:

   (a) classifies the safe strings; and

   (b) classifies the safe strings and does not use negation in the left-hand side.

4. Develop a LISP program which can find classification rules for sets of strings such as those on page 288. Demonstrate its behavior, using the data in the text and a set of strings of your own.

5. Consider the sequence of arches and non-arches shown in Fig. 8.1 and described in the text. Suppose that a second arch, a_2, is presented to the learning system, thus extending the sequence, and that this arch (which still has two posts, but has a two-piece lintel) has the following logical description:

$$\mathrm{On}(b_2(a_2), b_1(a_1)) \wedge \mathrm{On}(b_3(a_2), b_4(a_2))$$
$$\wedge \mathrm{Adjacent}(b_2(a_2), b_3(a_2)) \wedge \neg \mathrm{Adjacent}(b_1(a_2), b_4(a_2)).$$

   (a) Draw a diagram illustrating a_2.

   (b) Determine the new classification rule that categorizes all five of the structures a_1, a_2, c_1, c_2, and c_3.

6. For the version-space example on page 294, $V(\emptyset, \emptyset)$ is given simply as "all rules in the rule language." Suppose we were to represent $V(\emptyset, \emptyset)$ as $\mathcal{V}(R_s, R_g)$; describe R_s and R_g. How many elements are in R_s, assuming that two rules are the same if they are conjunctions of the same set of literals?

7. On page 294 the version space $V(\{a, b\}, \{c, d\})$ is given. The learning process has apparently not been completed, since this version space still contains more than just a single rule.

   (a) Describe a fifth example (a third non-arch) that would cause the learning to converge on a single correct rule for the concept of *arch*.

(b) Show the version space that would result from putting your fifth example (from part a above) into Arch$^+$ instead of Arch$^-$. Does the learning process converge in this case?

8. The version-space approach to learning classification rules can be applied widely.

   (a) Make up a sequence of examples of poker hands that could be used to teach the concept of a "full house."

   (b) Provide a set of literals suitable for describing the hands (as conjunctive formulas).

   (c) Determine the sequence of version spaces that corresponds to your sequence of examples.

9. Develop a function "VS" in LISP which computes the version space for a set of training instances. The function should take as arguments a list of positive instances and a list of negative instances. Assume that each object is described by a conjunction of literals taken from a set of permissible literals bound to a global variable FEATURES. VS should return a pair of lists containing the most specific rules and the most general rules in the version space. Illustrate your program using the arches example in the text and/or using the poker-hands example from the preceding problem.

10. At the end of PYTHAGORUS's run,

    (a) which concept has the most examples?

    (b) which concept has the highest INTEREST value?

    (c) how many times have polygons been tested as examples of concepts?

11. In the PYTHAGORUS program essentially two activities are pursued: finding examples of concepts and the creation of new concepts. Clearly, a concept must be created before examples of it can be found. However, the relative rates of progress of these two activities can differ. The rates are affected by the interest values. Modify the functions which compute interest values so that PYTHAGORUS finds (a) as few examples as possible, and (b) as many examples as possible, before it creates its last concept.

12. Extend PYTHAGORUS, so that it performs a third kind of task: conjecturing about a concept. After a reasonable number of objects have been tried as examples of a concept C, a task should automatically be placed on the agenda that requires conjecturing about C. Consider two kinds of conjectures: 1. a conjecture that the concept C is empty, and 2. a conjecture that concept C is equivalent to another concept C'. Conjectures should be stored on the property lists of the concepts they involved. Once a conjecture has been made about a concept C, any further testing

of examples should be accompanied by further testing of the conjecture. If a conjecture then has to be retracted, the program should report the retraction.

13. Add the following features to PYTHAGORUS, making any modifications necessary to make the resulting system work smoothly:

   (a) an example generator that extends the universe of geometrical figures infinitely. The original universe should be included in the new one.

   (b) two new predicates that can be used to generate specializations.

   (c) a predicate generator that can generate predicates of the form (LAMBDA (P) (EQUAL (LENGTH P N))) where N is increased by 1 each time the generator is called. Note that this scheme allows generation of concepts such as triangle, quadrilateral, pentagon, hexagon, etc.

   (d) the ability to use the negation of a predicate as the basis of a restriction.

14. Incorporate into PYTHAGORUS a capability for using *functions* and objects to define new concepts. Then supply a set of functions that permits the program to generate a rich family of concepts. For example, the function HORIZONTAL_PROJECTION can be defined as taking a polygon as its argument and returning a pair (XMIN XMAX) indicating the horizontal extent of the polygon. With a particular polygon, say MULTI (as defined in the program), the function returns a particular value, in this case, (0 15). The combination of the function and the particular value may be used to create a predicate and, in turn, a restriction: "$P(x)$ is true if and only if the horizontal projection of x is (0 15)."

Chapter 9

Natural-Language Understanding

9.1 Introduction

9.1.1 Intelligence in Understanding Language

Natural languages such as spoken and written English, French, Chinese, etc., have evolved to allow human beings to communicate with one another. As we humans are lazy, we tend to try to minimize the effort needed to communicate (or put another way, we have learned over the generations to economize on words). We do this by giving just the right combination of facts and hints about something so that the listener or reader can infer the proper conclusion, or "get the right picture," etc. We usually avoid telling a listener something we think he/she already believes, except to establish a point of reference.

In order to achieve this economy, some problem-solving must take place at both ends of the communication channel. The speaker (sender) must determine what pieces of information must be presented explicitly to allow the listener to understand. The listener (receiver) must combine these bits of information with background knowledge and make the appropriate inferences. Finding an interpretation which is consistent with the speaker's sentences and the background knowledge may require a significant amount of problem-solving effort.

The study of natural-language understanding is therefore concerned with (a) the meanings typically conveyed through language and ways to represent those meanings, (b) the forms of phrases and sentences (syntax) and the ways that the constraints on form can be exploited to constrain possible meanings, and (c) the processes that can be used to derive interpretations of natural-language inputs by manipulating representations of the input and of the background knowledge. Clearly, the subject matter of Chapters 4 through 7 is all of potential use in understanding natural language, and that is a good reason for us to have left this subject until now.

9.1.2   Applications of Language Understanding

Perhaps the most obvious general application for the understanding of natural language by machines is to the man/machine interface; people should be able to speak to their computer, giving commands and asking questions, and the computer should perform the commands and answer the questions. Such a command might be, "Please recompute my taxes taking into consideration the charitable contribution of $100 to the Artificial Intelligence Society." Making oral commands in English promises to be more convenient for humans than typing commands. It would also be useful to allow typing to a computer in English. The time it takes for a human to learn to use a particular computer program could be reduced if the language of interaction could be English instead of obscure query languages, command languages, etc.

Apart from the convenience argument, there is a need for expert systems to obtain knowledge. Most of the accumulated knowledge of our modern civilization is written in books, in natural languages such as English. We have the technology to make machines read the physical characters printed on the pages of these books. We are gradually getting closer to having the technology that would permit computers to understand what they read. If computers could read and understand what they read, we would have a big lead on a solution to the knowledge acquisition problem.

9.1.3   Machine Translation

During the late 1950's a great hope developed that machines would be able to translate texts from one language into another. Projects were funded to develop systems that could translate Russian into English and vice versa. While these systems met with some success, researchers found it very difficult to get machines to do high-quality translation. The systems of the 1960's worked primarily by the use of dictionaries and syntactic mechanisms. They could not use semantic knowledge since little progress had been made towards effective representation of knowledge.

A well-known example that pointed out the limitations of automatic translation in the 1960's is the following: "The spirit is willing but the flesh is weak." This sentence, after being translated into Russian and back into English, became "The vodka is good but the meat is rotten."

The conclusion of the initial studies in machine translation was that purely syntactic methods can serve to produce rough translations; these translations can be helpful to scientists who want a general idea of what a paper written in a foreign language is about. But translations that are not knowledge-based are not of high enough quality or reliable enough to substitute for professional translations intended for careful reading or re-publication.

Some translators find that machine-produced drafts save some time in the process of producing polished translations. Others find that it is just as fast to perform the translation from the original foreign-language document as it is to polish a machine-produced draft. As the quality of machine translation improves, we may expect to see less expertise required of the human "translation polisher" to get a product of quality comparable to what now requires a full professional.

9.1.4 A Definition of Understanding

In order to describe or build systems that understand natural language, it is important to be clear about what we mean by "understand."

When a natural-language system serves as an interface to a computer system that takes commands and questions, it is easy to define what we mean by "understand:" a system *understands* when it takes the actions that the user intended. This definition is "operational." It is possible that a system could take the actions the user intends solely by accident; perhaps the user speaks or types incorrectly, but the computer system, because of a bug of its own, does what the user actually wanted. By our definition, the system would be understanding. We can strengthen the operational definition by insisting that the system can only be said to understand when the correct action is part of a general pattern of correct action in response to correct instructions from the user.

There are times, though, when this operational definition of "understanding" still does not seem adequate. Sometimes, systems do not respond after every user input. Even if they do, they may not respond in a manner that can really reflect whether or not they have understood. A system that accumulates knowledge without having a chance to apply it may or may not be understanding (in the general non-operational sense of the word). For such situations it can be useful to have a definition of understanding in terms of the *internal* behavior of the system, rather than the external behavior. A system *understands* some input when it creates an appropriate conceptual structure, makes appropriate changes to a conceptual structure, or makes an appropriate modification to its knowledge base. This definition is vague, because it leaves undefined the notions of "appropriate conceptual structure," and "appropriate changes" to conceptual structures or knowledge base. However, it gives an indication that understanding may involve the creation or modification of a representation within the system that is doing the understanding. According to Rich (1983), "To understand something is to transform it from one representation into another, where this second representation has been chosen to correspond to a set of available actions that could be performed and where the mapping has been designed so that for each event, an *appropriate* action will be performed." Rich combines the representation-changing aspect and the operational aspect in her definition of understanding.

"John gives Mary a bouquet of flowers."

Figure 9.1: Diagram for "John gives Mary a bouquet of flowers."

Note that understanding may also be viewed as temporary learning: an assimilation of the new input, and creation of a set of "bindings" of syntactic units with concepts (particular definitions of words) in the knowledge base (extended lexicon).

9.1.5   Representing Events with Case Frames

Let us now consider the way in which spoken or written language can represent such things as events and can describe situations.

In order to transmit information in communication, a message must *represent* the information. Language representations (spoken or written sentences) are sequences (e.g., either phonetic or lexical) and therefore linear or one-dimensional. On the other hand, many situations or experiences we might want to express are multi-faceted or multi-dimensional. (For example, an image of a landscape is two-dimensional.) This discrepancy in dimensionality means that some scheme is necessary to map experience or concepts into language. It also means that an inverse scheme is needed to map language representations back into representations that are closer to experience or thought forms. Let us look more closely at how such mappings might work.

A typical example of a situation that may be described by an English sentence is one in which there are two people (John and Mary), an inanimate object (a bouquet of flowers), and some action: "John gives Mary a bouquet of flowers." A diagram of the situation can help us get a perspective on this situation, and assign roles to each participant.

This sentence describes an event—an action, a process. This process is *giving*. The verb *to give*, of which "gives" is one form, specifies a particular kind of event, action, or process, in which the participants have particular roles: (1) there is a *giver*, someone or something which performs the giving, which is the agent of the activity; (2) there is a *given* (something which is given by the giver), in this case the bouquet; a more general role for it is the (direct) *object*; and (3) there is a *"givee"* whose role may be viewed more generally as that of *recipient* or even more generally as *indirect object*.

The process of understanding this sentence consists primarily of finding the kind of event being described, finding the participants in the event, determining the roles they play in the event, and appropriately affixing any additional information provided about the participants or the circumstances under which the event takes place. The most important clue in establishing the type of event is the verb. The verb not only sets up the possible roles that can be played in the event, but its position in the sentence helps to determine which roles are played by the participants. The main verb of a sentence may be regarded as a landmark. In this case it separates the agent (to the left of the verb) from the recipient and the direct object (both to the right of the verb).

The positions of the nouns around the verb are not, however, a completely reliable basis for assigning them their roles. The positions for each role may depend on the *voice* of the sentence. The sentence above is in the active voice. A passive-voice expression of the same situation is "A bouquet of flowers is given to Mary by John." Now the syntactic subject of the sentence is "a bouquet of flowers" even though "a bouquet of flowers" still plays the role of object in the event. The agent, John, is no longer the syntactic subject, but the object of the preposition "by." A computer program that is to construct the relational representation of the situation from an English sentence should construct the same situation for either of these two sentences. However, it could mark the relational representations differently to indicate the difference in "viewpoint" of the two sentences. The passive form, generally less common in usage, suggests that the listener or reader pay particular attention to the role of the object (in this case the bouquet) in the event, rather than to the role of the agent, the recipient or other participant.

The problem of constructing a semantic representation for a sentence is treated in more detail later in this chapter. Let us now consider all the levels of analysis that may be required in the process of understanding language.

9.1.6 Components of an Understanding System

The process of understanding natural language may be divided into a number of levels. These levels may not all be present in every system for understanding natural language, and it may not always be possible or appropriate to distinguish the levels. However, they are quite useful as a way of structuring the study of the subject. The levels are the following:

1. Signal (acoustical level). This is the form of input for speech understanding systems. A signficant amount of processing may be expended at this

level because of the volume of data involved, and the intensive nature of filtering operations. Analysis at this level generally includes the extraction of sound units called "phones."

2. Phonetic level. Raw phonemic information must be aggregated into phonological units or "phonemes." Phonemes can then be mapped into components of words (syllables).

3. Lexical (word) level. At this level, words and components of words are treated, including prefixes, suffixes, and other morphological forms and inflections.

4. Syntactic level. Words only form meaningful sentences if they are grouped according to grammatical rules. In order to prepare for interpretation of the sentence, the grammatical structure of the particular sentence must be determined by "parsing."

5. Semantic level. Assigning meaning to each word and phrase and to the entire sentence is usually the most difficult stage for designers of machines or programs that understand. Except for systems with fairly limited capabilities, a system must have and utilize a large body of knowledge about the subject ("domain") being discussed.

6. Pragmatic level. In addition to assigning meanings to words, phrases and sentences, there is sometimes a need for high-level control of a conversation; the system needs to determine whether or not the user understands something; it should monitor the interest or boredom of the user, and continually note the user's emotions. This level is concerned with overall planning and maintenance of the communications process.

In part because there are a large number of applications in which input is already in textual form, a treatment of speech processing (the acoustical and phonological levels) is not included in this text; however, several references on speech processing are mentioned at the end of the chapter. Neither is the lexical level, while quite interesting, discussed here. Therefore, we shall assume in the following two sections that sentences are input to a system as ASCII text, and that any words used are in a lexicon or word list accessible to the system.

9.2 Syntax

In order to interpret a sentence such as, "Show me the report on writing natural-language interfaces," it is necessary to determine the phrases that play certain standard roles in the sentence and to form an explicit representation of their structure. *Syntax* is the grammatical structure of sentences. Recovering the syntax of a sentence is called *parsing*.

9.2.1 Formal Languages

Formal languages are mathematical abstractions that may be used in modelling the syntax of natural languages. By making very precise definitions, it is possible to explore certain properties of languages (such as syntactic ambiguity) in a deep way. The study of formal languages has also permitted a systematic development of parsing techniques and an understanding of the computation time and space required for parsing.

A formal language is defined in terms of an "alphabet" and a "grammar" that determines the ways in which symbols of the alphabet may be combined into sentences. An *alphabet* is a finite set of symbols. For example, the set $\{0, 1\}$ is an alphabet. Another example is the set:

$$\{a, b, c, d, e, f, g, h, i, j, k, l, m, n, o, p, q, r, s, t, u, v, w, x, y, z\}$$

For a given alphabet Σ, a *string* over Σ is a sequence of zero or more symbols, each of which is a member of Σ. For example, the following are strings over $\{0, 1\}$:

```
101
000000000
1
0101
```

Note that the empty string (the sequence of length zero) is a string over this and any alphabet. In a formal language, a sentence is just some string of symbols that is well-formed according to the rules for the language.

A grammar is a scheme for generating sentences from elements of the alphabet, and a particular grammar is specified by describing the following four components:

1. an alphabet of symbols that may appear in sentences of the language (these are called the *terminal* symbols);

2. an alphabet of *nonterminal* symbols that may appear in partially-derived sentences but may not appear in actual sentences of the language;

3. a *start* symbol, a specified member of the nonterminal alphabet; and

4. a finite set of *productions*, each of which consists of a left-hand side string and a right-hand side string.

It is thus customary to describe a grammar with a 4-tuple.

An example of a grammar is the following (let us call it G_1):

$$G_1 = (\{a, b\}, \{S, A, B\}, S, P)$$

where P contains the productions:

$$S \to A$$
$$S \to B$$
$$A \to aa$$
$$A \to aSa$$
$$B \to b$$
$$B \to bBb$$

The productions operate on strings over a combined alphabet (which contains all the symbols of both alphabets for the grammar). The productions can be used to "re-write" a string by replacing an occurrence of the string on the left-hand side of the production by the corresponding right-hand side.

In order to determine whether a particular sentence such as "aabbbaa" can be generated by this grammar, we look for a way to start with the start symbol (in this case S), and keep applying productions to rewrite the current string so that we produce the desired string. Each string derived by applying a sequence of productions to the start symbol is called a *sentential form*. In this case, the following derivation can be found:

sentential form	how derived
S	(the start symbol)
A	(apply the production $S \to A$)
aSa	$A \to aSa$
aAa	$S \to A$
$aaSaa$	$A \to aSa$
$aaBaa$	$S \to B$
$aabBbaa$	$B \to bBb$
$aabbbaa$	$B \to b$

By placing some restrictions on the forms that productions may have, different classes of languages can be defined. Chomsky defined four important classes:

- Type-3 languages (also called "regular languages"). Each production has only a single nonterminal symbol on its left-hand side, and on its right-hand side has either a single terminal symbol or it has a terminal symbol followed by a nonterminal symbol.

- Type-2 languages (also called "context-free languages"). The left-hand side of each production must always consist of exactly one nonterminal symbol. (The example grammar above is context-free, and it generates a context-free language.)

- Type-1 languages (also called "context-sensitive languages"). The left-hand side of each production must not have a length greater than that of the right-hand side.

- Type-0 languages (also called "recursively enumerable languages"). Here there are no restrictions on the productions.

The most general of these four classes is the class of type-0 languages. Context-sensitive languages also form a very general class. However, because of the computational problems of dealing with these two general classes of languages, they have received relatively little study by computer scientists.

The most structured class is the type-3 or regular languages. For any regular language, it is possible to design a finite state machine that can sequentially process a string of symbols and determine whether it belongs to the language. However, regular languages are seldom adequate for modelling English. (They may be adequate for some simple natural-language front ends for things like operating system commands.)

The language class of choice for most serious implementations of natural-language understanding systems is the type-2 languages, or context free languages. Although these formal languages clearly have their limits, large subsets of English can be handled as context-free languages, and efficient parsing methods are known for them.

9.2.2   Context-Free Grammars and Languages

A major advantage of context-free languages over regular languages is that they can handle arbitrary levels of embedding, or, in other words, recursive structure. For example it is possible, in a context-free language, to define a prepositional phrase to be a preposition followed by a noun phrase, where the noun phrase may include a prepositional phrase itself.

Context-free languages are amenable to relatively efficient syntactic analysis (or "parsing") in comparison with general context-sensitive languages. The theory of parsing formal languages is well-developed, and many methods for the syntactic analysis of sentences in context-free languages have been studied.

These methods can generally be classified as either "top-down" or "bottom-up." A top-down parsing method starts with the start symbol of a given context-free grammar and successively applies productions, trying to derive the given input string. If a sequence of productions is found that transforms the start symbol into the target string, then that sequence, together with information telling where each production is applied in the sentential form, constitutes a *parse* of the sentence. A parse can be represented by a *parse tree*, which is a tree each of whose nodes corresponds to a sentential form, whose root corresponds to the start symbol, whose leaves all correspond to nonterminals, and such that N is a child of M if and only if the sentential form for M can be transformed into that for N by one application of a production. A bottom-up parsing method begins with the input string and attempts to derive the start symbol of the grammar by applying productions "backwards."

If a context-free grammar permits a sentence of its language to be derived in two or more distinct ways, the grammar is said to be *ambiguous*, and such a sentence is said to be ambiguous with respect to the grammar. Most grammars for English are ambiguous. For example, the grammar below (although very constrained) can generate the phrase, "the highest student's grade" by either of the derivations shown in Fig. 9.2.

$$S \rightarrow \text{the } A$$
$$A \rightarrow BA$$
$$A \rightarrow \text{grade}$$
$$B \rightarrow B \text{ student's}$$
$$B \rightarrow \text{highest}$$
$$B \rightarrow \text{student's}$$

The tree on the left associates the adjective "highest" with the noun "student" whereas the tree on the right associates it with "grade."

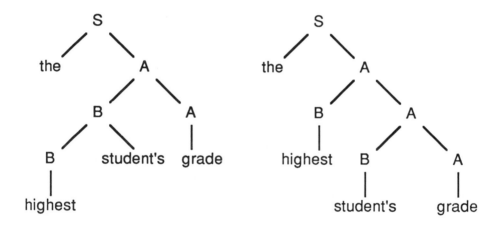

Figure 9.2: Two distinct parse trees for a phrase, showing grammatical ambiguity.

A grammatically ambiguous English sentence usually has only one (semantically) appropriate interpretation. However, because a parser is not usually concerned with meaning, it cannot choose the correct parse. Therefore, it is typically the parser's job to supply as many parses as may be necessary for a sentence to assure that a semantically appropriate one is found (if one exists). Since it is possible to construct highly ambiguous grammars (that produce sentences with many possible parses), a parser might stay fairly busy finding all possible parses for a sentence.

9.2.3 A Backtracking Parser in LISP

Some of the problems of parsing sentences of context-free languages can be easily seen if we consider an actual program for such parsing. The program described here uses depth-first search, implemented using a combination of looping and recursion. Each state of the implicit state space that is searched consists of a sentential form, a string of symbols derived from the start symbol of the grammar. The initial state is simply the start symbol. The goal state is the input sentence to be parsed.

Each production of the grammar may be regarded as an operator that, if applicable, may transform the current state into a new state. The program makes a few assumptions that ought to be mentioned. It assumes that there are no productions in the grammar that replace a nonterminal with the empty string. This ensures that the length of the sentential form grows monotonically with the number of productions applied. The program also assumes that a "leftmost" derivation is always acceptable as a result. A leftmost derivation is a sequence of applications of productions such that at each step, it is the leftmost nonterminal of the sentential form that is rewritten.

As presented, the program uses a grammar whose productions are as follows:

$$
\begin{array}{ll}
S \rightarrow NP\ VP & N \rightarrow \text{MAN} \\
NP \rightarrow NP\ PP & D \rightarrow \text{THE} \\
NP \rightarrow D\ N & V \rightarrow \text{RAN} \\
VP \rightarrow V\ AV & AV \rightarrow \text{FAST} \\
VP \rightarrow V & PP \rightarrow \text{OVER THERE}
\end{array}
$$

We begin the program by providing a representation for this grammar. Using the convention that S is always the start symbol of the grammar, and that any symbol mentioned in any production is part of the vocabulary of the language, it is only necessary to list the productions and to provide a way to distinguish the nonterminal symbols from the terminals. The grammar representation is shown below.

```
; PARSE.LSP - a top-down, backtracking parser
; for a context-free grammar

; Here is the grammar:
; The production rules for each nonterminal
;   are grouped together...
(PUTPROP 'S  '((NP VP))        'PRODUCTIONS)
(PUTPROP 'NP '((NP PP)(D N))   'PRODUCTIONS)
(PUTPROP 'VP '((V AV)(V))      'PRODUCTIONS)
(PUTPROP 'N  '((MAN))          'PRODUCTIONS)
(PUTPROP 'D  '((THE))          'PRODUCTIONS)
(PUTPROP 'V  '((RAN))          'PRODUCTIONS)
(PUTPROP 'AV '((FAST))         'PRODUCTIONS)
```

```
(PUTPROP 'PP '((OVER THERE)) 'PRODUCTIONS)

; This predicate distinguishes terminal symbols:
(DEFUN TERMINALP (W)
  (MEMBER W '(MAN THE THERE RAN FAST OVER)) )
```

Now the parsing functions can access the productions simply by using calls of the form (GET x 'PRODUCTIONS). First the top-level function, PARSE, is defined. It calls PARSE2 with parameters that correspond to the initial state.

```
; The top level parser function:
(DEFUN PARSE (INPUT)
  (PROG (CURRENT_PARSE MAXLEN)
        (PARSE2 'S NIL 1 INPUT (LENGTH INPUT)) ) )
```

The parameters of the call to PARSE2 indicate that the current leftmost nonterminal of the sentential form is S, that there is nothing to the right of this nonterminal, that the length of the unmatched portion of the sentential form is 1, that the entire input has yet to be matched against this sentential form, and that the length of the remaining input is the result of evaluating (LENGTH INPUT).

The function PARSE2 expands the leftmost nonterminal, trying all the productions for that nonterminal. In each case, it calls COMPARE to make sure that the terminal suffix of the new sentential form is consistent with the input. If it is, COMPARE makes a recursive call to PARSE2 to carry the derivation deeper. If the new sentential form cannot possibly lead to the goal (on the basis of length comparisons or terminal-symbol mismatches) COMPARE returns directly to PARSE2 without recursive calls. PARSE2 keeps track of the current parse, maintaining a stack of selected productions as the value of the atom CURRENT_PARSE.

```
; Function that actually applies productions
;   and does backtracking:
(DEFUN PARSE2 (X RIGHT S_LENGTH UNMATCHED U_LENGTH)
  ; X is leftmost nonterminal of current sentential form.
  ; RIGHT is the portion of the sentential form to the
  ;   right of X.
  ; S_LENGTH is the length of current form portion.
  ; UNMATCHED is the unmatched portion of the input.
  ; U_LENGTH is the length of UNMATCHED.
  (PROG (X_PRODUCTIONS P BETA TEMP)
        (SETQ X_PRODUCTIONS (GET X 'PRODUCTIONS))
  LOOP  (COND ((NULL X_PRODUCTIONS)(RETURN NIL)))
        (SETQ P (CAR X_PRODUCTIONS))
        (SETQ X_PRODUCTIONS (CDR X_PRODUCTIONS))
```

```
(SETQ CURRENT_PARSE
      (CONS (CONS X P) CURRENT_PARSE)) ; push onto stack

; apply selected production:
(SETQ BETA (APPEND P RIGHT))

; examine resulting sentential form:
(COMPARE BETA
         (SUB1 (PLUS S_LENGTH (LENGTH P)))
         UNMATCHED
         U_LENGTH)

; backtrack (pop):
(SETQ CURRENT_PARSE (CDR CURRENT_PARSE))
(GO LOOP)   ; go try next alternative
) )
```

The function COMPARE tries to match some terminal symbols of the current
sentential form with corresponding symbols in the input. BETA is usually not
an entire sentential form. All the terminal symbols to the left of BETA have
already been matched in outer contexts of the current recursive call, and so they
need not be matched against the input again.

```
; Function that matches terminal symbols in the sentential form
;   with the input and continues the parsing if on the right track.
(DEFUN COMPARE (BETA S_LENGTH UNMATCHED U_LENGTH)
  ; BETA is the relevant suffix of the current sentential form.
  ; UNMATCHED is the portion of the input remaining to be matched.
  (COND ((NULL BETA)                  ; nothing left of sent. form.
         (COND ((NULL UNMATCHED)   ; nothing unmatched: SUCCESS.
                (PRIN1 'PARSE:)    ; print ans. in reverse order.
                (PRINT CURRENT_PARSE) )
               (T NIL) ) )          ; something unmatched-no good.
        ((GREATERP S_LENGTH U_LENGTH) NIL) ; derivation too long
        ((TERMINALP (CAR BETA))      ; current symbol is a terminal
         (COND ((NULL UNMATCHED) NIL) ; if no input left, no good.
               ((EQ (CAR BETA)(CAR UNMATCHED)) ; symbols match--
                (COMPARE (CDR BETA)          ; try to match more.
                         (SUB1 S_LENGTH)
                         (CDR UNMATCHED)
                         (SUB1 U_LENGTH) ) )
               (T NIL)  ; case where terminal doesn't match.
               ) )
        (T ; we have reached a nonterminal in BETA;
           ; parse recursively:
```

```
(PARSE2 (CAR BETA)        ; new leftmost nonterminal,
        (CDR BETA)        ; new right portion,
        S_LENGTH
        UNMATCHED         ; remaining input.
        U_LENGTH) ) ) )
```

The following test function demonstrates the steps in parsing a simple sentence.

```
(DEFUN TEST ()
  (PROG ()
    (SETQ SENT '(THE MAN OVER THERE RAN FAST))
    (TRACE PARSE2)
    (PARSE SENT) ) )
```

One of the problems in top-down parsing is in letting the parser know when to stop a potentially-infinite sequence of expansions. The grammar provided for this example contains a *left-recursive* production, $NP \rightarrow NP\ PP$. After expanding NP, one gets $NP\ PP$, and after applying this again, one has $NP\ PP\ PP$. After k applications, one has the expression $NP\ PP\ \cdots\ PP$, where there are k copies of PP. Since this rule does not generate any terminal symbols, it does not immediately give rise to any mismatch, and so the process of expanding could go on for many cycles, without any mechanism to stop it. This program contains provisions to limit expansions using left-recursive productions. The means here is to keep an account of the current length of BETA and the unmatched portion of the input. If the length of BETA ever exceeds that of the remaining input, COMPARE fails, forcing backtracking.

Even so, left-recursive productions get expanded quite often, and they can lead to bad performance. Executing the TEST above causes 32 expansions of productions. If we use the slightly shorter sentence "THE MAN RAN FAST" then the number of expansions drops to 17. Interestingly enough, by simply eliminating the left-recursive production, this sentence causes only 9 production expansions.

9.2.4   Grammar for English

It has proved to be very difficult to write a grammar for the English language that encompasses most of the language that a literate adult can understand. Some general problems in constructing such a grammar are the following:

1. The variety of languages called English: Grammars for proper written (published, scholarly) English are naturally different from grammars of dialog. In order to understand a contemporary novel, it may be necessary to handle sentences such as, "The, uh, man ain't got no - uh, yuh-know, dough." In fact, there are clearly many personal versions of English, and it may be too much to expect one formal system to handle them all.

2. The evasiveness of words and phrases when it comes to classifying them into syntactic categories: A simple grammar will handle 90% of sentences in certain kinds of use but won't handle 100%, without admitting many kinds of ill-formed sequences of words. In English, phrases of one syntactic type can end up being used as another. For example, in "The fox jumped out from behind the rock," the phrase "behind the rock" is a prepositional phrase that functions as a noun representing a place. There are many adaptations of parts of speech: nouns serving as adjectives, nouns converted to verbs, etc., and these complicate the job of designing a good English grammar.

3. The size of the problem: Just the lexical part alone of English grammar is a large corpus of knowledge to represent. A significant part of a Webster's dictionary is taken up with spelling and part-of-speech information. In all likelihood, the parts of speech used in standard dictionaries are not accurate enough to permit good syntactic analysis, and a good English grammar would contain more kinds. Research projects have addressed the issue of providing a grammar for English, and several grammars have been proposed. These grammars typically require a large book to describe them.

As a result of these difficulties, designers of English-language interfaces to computer systems have often contented themselves with rather limited subsets of English. As we shall see, the problem of syntax is only a small part of the whole language-understanding problem. Semantics presents an even greater challenge.

9.3 Semantics and Representation

Before we discuss computational methods for understanding English sentences, it is worth elaborating on representations for meanings. Meanings can be expressed in terms of objects and relationships. By specifying the forms for the symbols which represent the objects and the relationships, we clarify semantic representation schemes.

Part of the problem in finding a good representation for sentence semantics is to determine the kinds of relationships that are to be communicated in a particular natural-language subset. Relationships involving quantity, time, space and beliefs, for example, warrant particular attention. Some of these relationships are explored in this section.

9.3.1 Lexicons

An English dictionary is a list of words with their meanings. It is a partial representation of the semantics of English. A difficulty in using standard dictionaries is that the definition for each word is described in words; it may be necessary to already understand the meanings of many words in order to understand the definition of a single new one. While lexicographers generally attempt to define words in terms of simpler or more familiar ones, sometimes the definition of a word may seem no clearer than the unfamiliar word itself. Nevertheless, many of the important syntactic and semantic aspects of words are given in a dictionary, and dictionaries often are effective in clarifying the meanings of words.

A *lexicon* is a knowledge base indexed for access by words (which are short character strings). It is usually assumed that the words represent concepts and that each entry in the lexicon gives a definition or description of a concept. In an AI system, a knowledge base could be implemented as a set of frames, with one frame per word, together with an index structure, possibly implemented as a B-tree, or more simply (but less efficiently) as a list of pairs of the form (*word pointer-to-frame*), where the list is ordered lexicographically.

While a lexicon represents knowledge about the words of a language and is therefore either a permanent or a slowly-changing structure, another structure or family of structures is needed to represent the semantics of the particular sentences that occur in dialog or reading. These structures are usually relations among semantic objects (e.g., word meanings).

9.3.2   Representing Events in Frames

In the introduction to this chapter, we discussed the notion of "case frames" that represent events in a scheme organized around a verb. Let us now elaborate upon this notion. It gives us a means to move above the lexical level, forming associations of word meanings—semantic structures which are essentially composites of meanings of individual words.

Let us consider a verb whose meaning is more subtle than the meaning of "give" (described earlier). Now we examine the verb "to buy." We may identify several roles that may be played by people or things in a buying event. These include the following:

1. buyer (the "agent" for the event);

2. seller (a sort of "co-agent");

3. merchandise (the direct object of the verb);

4. beneficiary (the indirect object); and

5. price (a role that is peculiar to buying and selling events).

Although we can refer to a buying event with the verb "buy," which is only three letters long, in actuality a buying event consists of a number of subevents, and the explicit representation of them requires a significantly more elaborate expression. We might describe this collection of subevents as follows:

- Buyer makes agreement with seller about ownership of merchandise and price.

- Ownership of merchandise is transferred from buyer to seller.

- Ownership of funds (in amount specified by the price) is transferred from buyer to seller. Alternatively, we can say that the seller's funds increase by the amount of the price, and the buyer's funds decrease in the amount of the price.

- Purchase is for benefit of beneficiary. The default implication is that the buyer gives the merchandise to the beneficiary soon after the purchase.

Let us now consider the example sentence: "Jill bought Mark a box of chocolates for $9.95 from the Dilettante for Valentine's Day." We can identify the type of event here as a buying event because "bought" is a form of the verb "buy." Then we may find which noun phrases play each of the roles in the event. On the basis of their sentence positions, the subject, indirect object and object can be labelled, and assigned to the roles "buyer," "beneficiary," and "merchandise." We depend on the fact that the sentence is in the active voice; in the passive voice, the grammatical subject might play the role of the beneficiary or the merchandise: "Mark was bought a box of chocolates by Jill for $9.95 from the Dilettante for Valentine's Day," or "The box of chocolates was bought by Jill for Mark for $9.95 from the Dilettante for Valentine's Day."

Let us now attempt to describe the semantics of "buy" through a more formal description of the subevents that take place in a buying event. Here is one quasi-logical description of these subevents (for the case without a beneficiary).

```
agree(buyer, seller, transaction)
is-part(transaction1, transaction)
is(transaction1,
    replace( owns(seller, merchandise),
             owns(buyer, merchandise) ) )
is-part(transaction2, transaction)
is(transaction2,
    both( increase-funds(seller, price),
          decrease-funds(buyer, price) ) )
```

Here we are saying that a buying event consists of an agreement of a buyer and a seller to a transaction; that there are two parts to the transaction (transaction1 and transaction2); that the first sub-transaction is a change of ownership of the merchandise from the seller to the buyer; and that the second sub-transaction is a transfer of funds as effected by increasing the seller's funds by the amount of the price, while decreasing the buyer's funds by the same amount. This description makes the assumption that money is manipulated by accounting (increasing and decreasing accounts) rather than being moved around or given and taken as if

Holding a Dinner Party	
roles, etc.	*fillers*
hosts:	Scott
guests:	Diane
invitees:	Diane, Erica
menu:	CAJUN2
event sequence:	invite guests—*invite(hosts, invitees)* plan menu—*plan(hosts, menu)* buy groceries—*buy(hosts, food)* cook—*cook(hosts, food)* entertain guests—*entertain(hosts, guests)* eat—*eat(guests, food), eat(hosts, food)* clean up—*wash(hosts, dishes)*

Figure 9.3: A script for holding a dinner party.

it were a physical object. Another way of describing the second sub-transaction would be as a change in ownership of an amount of money equal to the price.

In case there is a beneficiary, then the expression

`owns(buyer, merchandise)`

should be

`owns(beneficiary, merchandise).`

9.3.3   Scripts: Schemata for Chains of Events

While many verbs describe reasonably complex events, not all the events we may need to represent or describe have a verb that refers to them. Therefore, the case frame, while suitable for events organized around a single verb, needs to be extended to handle more complex kinds of events.

A natural way to allow more complex events to be handled by frames is to allow the main event to be represented as a list of subevents. The term "script" is sometimes used for such a frame. Scripts are used as schema for activity sequences that are usually considered as units. An example script for the activity sequence involved in holding a dinner party is shown in Fig. 9.3.

Each of the events in the script's sequence needs further elaboration. This could be done by linking each subevent slot to a case frame (or even another script) that describes that event in more detail, specifying the primary action, and the parties to that action, each in their appropriate roles. Another way to specify the events is to express them in a logical representation, or in some other formal language for describing events.

Let us now consider a story fragment and its relation to the script.

"Scott decided to have company for dinner. He invited Diane and Erica for Saturday night. Erica had a previous engagement, but Diane was free. After settling on a Cajun menu, he went to the market. Though out of shrimp, they had fresh catfish. When Diane arrived Saturday evening, Scott handed her a stiff Planter's Punch, and though she had never had blackened catfish before, she gave it a try and said she liked it. Scott offered her another punch."

Using a dinner-party script such as the one above, certain inferences about this particular story are facilitated. First, an understanding system would attempt to fill in as many of the slots in the script (or in schemata pointed to by the script) as possible, using the story. It would try to establish who or what fills each of the roles in the script. A correspondence between verbs in the story and actions in the script would be sought.

Here, after the dinner-party script has been selected as the most promising script for this story, the host is identified as Scott. Diane and Erica are readily determined to be invitees, and Diane is found to be a guest as well. Several of the events in the script correspond to verbs in the story. The story's verbs "invited," "settling," and "handed" can be seen to correspond to the script's verbs "invite," "plan," and "entertain," although handing is not entertaining in a strict sense (but handing a drink to someone can be considered as serving them a drink, and serving drinks may in turn be considered as entertaining). Information about some of the other events may be inferred from the story. For example, the phrase "he went to the market" implies that at least part of the buying event took place, since going to a market or store is normally a step in the process of buying groceries. Without any evidence to the contrary, it is appropriate to conclude that the buying event took place; thus the values in a script may generally considered to be defaults, true until shown otherwise. Although there is no mention of cooking in the story, from the script we may infer that cooking took place—that Scott did the cooking. With additional effort, we can conclude that the catfish was cooked.

The subevents in a script are normally considered as chronologically ordered. However, a more general kind of script may allow arbitrary ordering constraints on the subevents. A means for expressing such constraints is then needed. As an example, we might consider the first two events in the script for holding a dinner party, "invite guests" and "plan menu," as chronologically independent. This could be expressed by grouping them with special brackets, e.g., "[(invite guests) (plan menu)]."

There is a resemblance between scripts and plans. However, there is a fundamental difference between them. The existence of a plan implies that there is a goal which corresponds to it. On the other hand, scripts do not need goals. There may be a hierarchical structure within sequences of events in scripts, and this may be similar to hierarchical structure in plans. But again, the emphasis is different: scripts provide frameworks of understanding; plans provide the necessary steps toward a goal. In principle, one can develop plan-scripts that serve both functions.

To summarize, scripts are a variety of frame schemata that are well suited to representing sequences of events. They have most of the same advantages and disadvantages as a knowledge representation method that frames have: they do a good job of helping organize knowledge at the frame level; they don't help at the slot level; and they don't provide a means for organizing collections of frames.

Because frames and scripts do not provide support for slot-level semantics, a system based upon frames or scripts must utilize additional mechanisms for the detailed semantics. Thus we now consider some problems of representing semantics that frames don't help with.

9.3.4 Semantic Primitives

In order to avoid the problem of circularity that may occur in dictionary definitions, it has been proposed that a set of "semantic primitives" or atomic meanings be specified and used in combinations to represent more complex meanings. A particular meaning of any word then would either correspond to one of the given primitives or to a combination of them.

Two systems that have received considerable attention in the literature are one by Y. Wilks and one by R. Schank. The latter is now briefly described.

The "Conceptual Dependency" system consists of a number of primitive kinds of semantic objects and ways of combining them to produce arbitrarily complicated "conceptualizations." The semantics of "Pierre devoured the escargots" could be represented[1] as

(ACTOR (PIERRE) ACT (INGEST) OBJECT (ESCARGOTS)).

Actions, normally represented by verbs, are categorized into eleven types, five of which represent physical actions which people can perform: PROPEL, MOVE, INGEST, EXPEL and GRASP; two represent changes of spatial and other relationships of things to their environments: PTRANS (which indicates a change of location) and ATRANS (which indicates a change in an abstract relationship with an object); two refer to superficial aspects of communication: SPEAK (to utter a sound) and ATTEND (to direct one's perceptual attention); and two represent information-processing acts: MTRANS (transfer of information) and MBUILD (creation or modification of thoughts).

Most nouns can be classified into one of the following groups: those that represent physical objects, including animals and people, (these are given the name "Picture Producers"); locations, and times. Nouns that do not fall into any of these categories (e.g., earthquake, birthday party, happiness, question) may

---

[1]Notation adapted from [Riesbeck 1975].

represent events (and thus are expressible as conceptualizations) or states (and be represented with special primitives for handling states) or actions (and thus be handled with one of the eleven kinds of acts). This categorization of verbs and nouns helps lead to representations of the essential meanings of language expressions, and it facilitates the writing of programs that make inferences from the representations.

A conceptualization, like an English sentence, usually contains an agent (a picture producer) and an act (e.g., "Bill jumped."). However, a conceptualization might consist of a picture producer and an indication of its state or change of state (e.g., "Bill's face turned crimson."). One conceptualization may include another; in "Jill hurt Jack" there is a primary conceptualization that Jill did something, and a secondary conceptualization that the physical or emotional state of Jack changed for the worse; in addition, there is a causal relationship between the conceptualizations. The whole conceptualization comprises both of these and the causal link. As may be seen in the LISP-like example above, the Conceptual Dependency system incorporates notions of case (the roles played by nouns and subordinate clauses in relation to verbs).

It is beyond the scope of this chapter to describe all the details of the Conceptual Dependency system (this would require some fifty pages). The system provides primitives and combining rules suitable for representing the semantics of many everyday conversations and stories. It should be pointed out that the systems of both Schank and Wilks were designed pragmatically with the aim to support experimental systems for natural-language text comprehension. Semantic systems built upon logical foundations (such as that mentioned below) are an alternative approach.

9.3.5 Logical Forms

As we saw in Chapters 4 and 6, logic is attractive because of its simplicity in comparison to some other methods, and because of its ability to support deductive inference.

The limitations of logic (first-order predicate calculus) for sentence representation have largely to do with quantification; predicate logic gives only two choices: universal and existential, and the variables they may be applied to are restricted to represent elements of the domain, excluding functions and predicates. As mentioned in Chapter 7, the truth values provided by predicate logic, *true* and *false*, do not leave any leeway for uncertainty.

A number of variations on predicate logic have been proposed to better meet the needs for representing sentence semantics. One of these is Montague's "Proper Treatment of Quantification" (PTQ) and his semantic system based upon "Intentional Logic." Montague's system is logically well-founded and is rich enough to allow expression of very complex and subtle meanings. At present, it is difficult for the uninitiated to understand the Montague system because of its heavy dependence upon an elaborate logical framework.

9.3.6   The Semantics of Quantity

Because of their importance in AI systems, several specific issues in semantic representation are now discussed. The first of these is the notion of quantity.

In our everyday uses of English we employ quantitative notions of many sorts. We describe numbers of objects (e.g., "five apples") and quantity of substance (e.g., "lots of mayonnaise"). We refer to degrees of intensity (e.g., "she loved him very, very much"). We also may refer to objects or ideas, times, and places by number: e.g., "the second point you made," "on the fifth day," "north of the 45th parallel." Some essential quantitative notions that are needed for natural-language understanding systems are the following:

- numbers, such as counts of discrete objects.

- quantities: amounts of things. Amounts are values from a continuum of possible values. Amounts are linguistically related to collective nouns such as salt, water, and meat[2]. Many quantities are *measures*. A measure usually has at least two important aspects:

  - a physical substance, phenomenon or other notion which is measured, and

  - the units or scale on which an evaluation is given. (Note: we treat measurement of time and of space in separate subsections, because of their particular importance.)

  Relative quantities are often important in expressing meanings through natural language. Common notions of relative quantity are percentages, ratios, and proportions. Concepts of relative quantity are applicable both to discrete and continuous kinds of quantities.

- Relationships between quantities or numbers. Two classes of such relationships are these:

  - magnitude, e.g., greater, less than, equal, approximately equal; arithmetic relations, e.g., twice, thrice, half.

  - number-theoretic, e.g., rounder ($1.25 is rounder than $1.37), prime, relatively prime, etc.

Support for concepts of quantity such as these is an area that is not well provided for by pure first-order logic. However, it is possible to construct representations for these concepts in logical frameworks.

---

[2]It is sometimes difficult to distinguish a plural non-collective noun from a collective one. A somewhat ambiguous case is the sentence, "We saw a lot of deer cross the field." Here "deer" is plural and non-collective. On the other hand, "venison" is a collective noun; e.g., in the sentence, "We saw a lot of venison cross the butcher's counter."

9.3.7   The Semantics of Time

The designer of a natural-language understanding system should provide representations for the notions of time that are needed in the application area of concern. For example, in order to talk about children's stories, a set of concepts involving sequences of events, the past, days and other common units of time is appropriate. On the other hand, a conversation about a simulation of a VLSI circuit design may require concepts of gate delay, clock rise times, microseconds and nanoseconds, etc. Common concepts related to time typically fall into two categories: time objects, and temporal relationships.

Time objects include (a) points, (b) intervals, (c) repeated intervals (e.g., "On Tuesdays"), and (d) repeated points (e.g., "Every day at noon"). Such objects may be referred to in terms of events that are closely associated with them (e.g., "one gate delay" refers to an interval of time).

Some temporal relationships are the following:

- temporal precedence constraints. Special procedures may be needed that combine sets of constraints into new ones. Such procedures may sometimes be viewed as algorithms which compute intersections of sets of intervals and collections of intervals.

- relational binders of time:

    - "*When* John finished his program, he poured himself a drink."
    - "*After* John wrote his program, he poured himself a drink."
    - "*Before* John poured himself a drink, he wrote his program."

In addition to time objects and temporal relationships, there are certain temporal expressions which may denote a time object or temporal relationship indirectly. The terms *today, yesterday, tomorrow, now, next week,* etc. presumably are bound at the time of utterance.

There are usually three points of time that are related to a sentence. These are the time of utterance, the reference time, and the event time. Let us consider the sentence, "Just after I finished my assignment, the professor handed out the solution." The time of utterance is when the sentence was spoken or written by the speaker or writer. The reference time is the time when the speaker finished his/her assignment. The event time is the time when the professor handed out the solution.

It may often be necessary to understand quantification over time (or, as in this case, a type of event): "Whenever I finish an assignment, I go eat something." The meaning here is roughly equivalent to, "For all events involving my finishing an assignment, there is an event approximately coincident with it involving my going and eating something."

There are interesting problems for the designer of a natural-language understanding system related to keeping track of the temporal context. In a conversation there may be a number of time objects in the context:

A: "When I was on sabbatical, I lived in France for a while."
B: "Did you visit the French Alps?"
A: "Yes. I did some skiing there.
B: "What else did you do then?"

A more complicated example is this:

A: When I was a child, I did a lot of reading.
B: Did you read any of the "Hardy Boys" stories?
A: Yes, in my late childhood.
B: What else did you read then?
A: "The Little Engine that Could"

This sequence establishes two intervals of time, and proceeds to illustrate a possibly incorrect interpretation of a slightly ambiguous reference. The odd aspect of this conversation is that "then" in the 4th line seems to refer to the most recently referenced interval of time (the period of A's late childhood), but A's response in line 5 is the name of a story normally read in early childhood, and therefore this suggests that A interpreted "then" as referring to the first interval of time, A's childhood in its entirety.

If the conversation continued as follows, we see another interesting aspect of reference to time:

A: And what did *you* read then?
B: I wasn't yet born.

Presumably, by "then" A meant "during your childhood." However, B presumably took it to mean the absolute time interval during which A was a child, not B.

It should be clear that the proper resolution of "then" references requires reasoning about time and about the temporal aspects of the situation being discussed. The probable inconsistency of reading "The Little Engine that Could" in late childhood can only be detected with a knowledge of the reading level of this story and the reading expectations for children in late childhood.

In the second case, the ambiguity of "then" ought normally to be resolved in a way most likely to meet the expectation of the person asking the question. In this case, the answer "I wasn't yet born" seems not to be an answer that provides the kind of information that A was requesting. By reinterpreting "then" to be B's childhood, it becomes possible for B to provide the kind of information A is asking for.

9.3.8 The Semantics of Space

The designer of natural-language understanding system may need to provide representations for notions of space that are relevant to robot planning, human interactions with microworlds, and discussions about problems where space plays an important role (e.g., architect's advisor).

Words for spatial relations are a part of basic English (and any other natural language). "The phone is *to the left of* the computer." "The wine is *inside* the bottle." However, these relationships are often elusive when it comes time to decide what they mean in specific geometrical terms. (For example, if A is 1 unit to the left of B and one hundred units up from B, is A "to the left of" B?) Therefore, it is often helpful to be able to take advantage of constraints of the application in assigning meanings to these terms. (In the "Stone World" LISP example described later in this chapter, the cellular space used in the microworld suggests a specific semantics for several spatial terms.)

Analogous to the problem of resolving temporal references that use "then" is the problem of understanding the meaning of "there." If the spatial aspects of a discussion are important, it may be necessary to use a spatial-reasoning subsystem to properly interpret such references.

9.3.9 The Semantics of Knowing and Belief

One of the most challenging research areas in AI is the development of good systems for inferring people's beliefs from speech or text. Aside from the difficulty of extracting such information, achieving such inference implies that one has a good system for representing the beliefs. Such a system should support useful inferences about the other beliefs these people might hold and about the actions they might take as a result of their beliefs.

The natural-language part of the problem is difficult enough. The context of an utterance can play a very large role in the analysis. Satire and sarcasm, for example, are used to express beliefs indirectly. An unsophisticated computer system, when told, "Oh sure, pink elephants can fly," might accept this as a statement of literal fact. Another interpretation of it would be to assume that the speaker believes this to be fact, without assigning any degree of belief itself to the statement. A better interpretation is that the speaker wishes to cast doubt on (i.e., lower the degree of belief in) some other statement in the context.

Degrees of belief may be represented using such techniques as certainty values and distributions (such as those discussed in Chapter 7) and Dempster-Shafer theory. The semantics of certain qualified statements such as, "John believes it possible that the Loch Ness monster exists" can be represented using "modal logic." However, a discussion of such systems is beyond the scope of this text.

9.4   Computing Interpretations

In this section we consider two important methods that have been used to structure systems for automatic language understanding. One of these, the use of "semantic grammar," moves much of the work of extracting meaning from sentences onto the syntactic analyzer (the parser). The second scheme, the "augmented transition network," provides a framework in which semantic-analysis routines can be easily integrated with parsing. Later, we shall see how we can obtain the advantages of semantic grammars and augmented transition networks at the same time.

In a third subsection we consider some problems of *reference*: when does a noun phrase introduce a new object to the conversation, and when and how does a noun phrase refer to an object that is already subject to attention?

9.4.1   Semantic Grammars

Syntax was relatively well-understood by the late 1960's. By contrast, at that time, semantic analysis was viewed as a separate, mysterious process that would have to be studied in its own right. However, one practical method for building natural-language interfaces developed out of the opposite view: that since syntax is so well understood, we should modify the syntactic analysis of a sentence so that a maximum of the semantic analysis is performed at the same time. The technique called "semantic grammar" provides a way to do just that. While the method generally requires more elaborate grammars than normally used for syntactic analysis, the same parsing techniques can be used; context-free parsing is the only essential analysis technique needed. In this way it is possible for the semantic-grammar approach to exploit well-understood mechanisms.

Formally, there is no difference between a semantic grammar and a context-free grammar. However, in practice, a semantic grammar is a context-free grammar most of whose non-terminal symbols represent more specific categories of words than those of an ordinary context-free grammar for natural language do. For example, instead of having a general symbol ⟨noun⟩, a semantic grammar may have several more specific symbols: ⟨tool⟩, ⟨cut⟩, ⟨location⟩, ⟨work-piece⟩,

---

$S \to$ ⟨cut-verb⟩ a ⟨cut⟩⟨prep⟩ the ⟨work-piece-part⟩
                                with the ⟨tool⟩.
⟨cut-verb⟩ $\to$ bore | gouge | cut | drill | mill
⟨cut⟩ $\to$ hole | groove | rabbet | trough
⟨prep⟩ $\to$ in | along | into | through | across
⟨work-piece-part⟩ $\to$ ⟨component⟩ of the ⟨work-piece⟩
⟨component⟩ $\to$ flange | rim
⟨work-piece⟩ $\to$ baseplate | wheel assembly | assembly cover
⟨tool⟩ $\to$ minidrill | gantry drill |
                                dado cutter on the milling machine |
                                dado cutter on the portasaw

Figure 9.4: Semantic grammar for a (hypothetical) robotics application.

⟨component⟩ and ⟨work-piece-part⟩.

Let us consider an example of a semantic grammar that can be used to interpret commands in a subset of English for the purpose of instructing an industrial robot in the manufacture of some machine part. Here are some example sentences that this semantic grammar can handle:

"Bore a hole in the flange of the baseplate with the gantry drill."

"Gouge a groove along the rim of the assembly cover with the dado cutter on the milling machine."

The grammar is given in Fig. 9.4. The parse of a sentence with a semantic grammar contains the information necessary to build a semantic representation of the sentence; in fact, the parse itself may be considered a semantic representation. The overall action requested from a command such as one of the two above is specified by the verb of the sentence. The role that each noun plays in that action is apparent in the semantic-grammar parse.

On the other hand, there is a disadvantage in using the semantic grammar approach: except when describing very small languages, semantic grammars tend to have a great many productions, and so the parsing can be very time-consuming.

9.4.2 Augmented Transition Networks

Augmented transition networks (or "ATNs") were developed in an attempt to provide a practical framework for natural-language understanding.

In order to combine parsing with semantic analysis, it should be possible to attach semantic routines to specific parts of the parsing mechanism or grammar. An ATN can offer the following advantages: (1) The basic parsing scheme is easy to understand; the grammatical information is represented in a transition network, and consequently, an ATN is relatively easy to design. (2) Semantic analysis proceeds simultaneously with syntactic analysis, and semantics may easily be used to constrain parsing to resolve ambiguities.

The arcs of an ATN correspond to words and phrases. Each arc of an ATN is labelled with a specification of the condition under which the arc may be traversed. This is typically either a word, a phrase, a predicate to be satisfied by a prefix of the unscanned portion of the input sentence, or the name of another (or the same) ATN (in which case another ATN is called, possibly recursively). In addition to the condition on each arc, there is an action associated with each arc. The action may involve procedures that make partial interpretations, examine registers set by other actions, or perhaps do nothing at all. The ATN framework does not place any restrictions on the kinds of actions one can specify. Thus by deciding to use an ATN, one does not narrow the design alternatives for a system very much. However, the ATN approach seems to provide enough structure to a natural-language system to be helpful.

A sample transition network for parsing commands is illustrated later, and an implementation given.

9.4.3   Detecting and Resolving References

A system that constructs a semantic representation for a sentence builds a data structure (usually a graph) which is linked into a long-term memory or permanent knowledge base. Most meanings consist of interrelationships among objects. The objects may be classes of things (e.g., as in "Dogs are fun to have"), known individuals (e.g., "former president Carter"), unknown individuals (e.g., "a cat named Fuzzy"), or concepts (e.g., happiness). The objects may also be ones that have not been previously discussed but are in the immediate experience of the conversants: "You see that house? It needs a paint job."

When a system builds a representation, it is important that the correct objects be linked. A primary decision must be made about each noun phrase in the input sentences: Does it introduce a new object or does it refer to one that is already in the scope of the conversation? If it refers to a new object, then a representation of the object must be created. If the noun phrase refers to a pre-existing object, it is important not to create a second representation for it, because making inferences involving the object would become awkward or impossible.

In English, there are certain clues that help to reveal the newness or oldness of an object in a conversation. The pronouns *he, she, it, him, her, we*, and *they* usually refer to an old object—a person, group, or other object which already has been introduced into the conversation. The pronouns *I* and *you* refer to the transmitter and receiver of the message, respectively; these are old objects which do not need explicit introduction into the conversation. Occasionally, a pronoun such as *he* introduces a new object: "He who tells not the truth shall have a long nose." However, this form is relatively unusual and can often be detected by its use of a relative clause involving *who, which* or *that*.

Most noun phrases that do not consist of pronouns begin with a *determiner* such as *a, an* or *the* (these three words are commonly called "articles"). As was mentioned in Chapter 4, determiners such as *a, an* and *some* are said to be *indefinite*, and such a word often indicates that its noun phrase introduces a new object into the conversation. On the other hand, *the* is called *definite* and it usually signals that its noun phrase is not introducing a new object but refers to a concept that the speaker considers to be already in the experience of the listener. Unfortunately, English is sufficiently complicated that these rules are not adequate in some cases. The definite article can introduce a new object when the noun is followed by a relative clause: "The house which I just bought needs work." The listener may not be familiar with the speaker's new house; "the" indicates that the house is a particular one. Also, an indefinite article can refer to a concept well established in the listener's experience: "I always like a good wine." Here "a good wine" refers to the class of good wines (something well understood) and the indefinite article serves not to introduce something new but to generalize from "good wine" in the singular to the set of good wines. One way to handle new-or-old decisions is to assume that each noun phrase introduces a new object and then to merge objects when implications indicate that two objects should be regarded as the same.

The challenge of handling the new-or-old decision is probably not half as difficult as the problem of resolving references to old objects. The problem is most difficult with pronouns, because they are the least specific of the noun phrases and they offer ambiguity its greatest opportunities. The next sentence illustrates one instance of this problem.

> I'd never been tobogganing, but I took a train to Switzerland and gave it a try.

Two nouns in this sentence are placed so that *it* might well refer to them: *train* and *Switzerland*. The gerund *tobogganing* is used here both as an adverb modifying "had been" and as a noun, the antecedent of *it*. A system that didn't treat the gerund both ways could have trouble resolving the reference.

In some cases "it" is used to refer to an overall situation, event or experience, rather than some object that is explicitly mentioned: "She wined and dined me. It was great!" Here *it* refers to the speaker's particular experience of being wined and dined. Making this reference explicit requires the knowledge that wining and dining is an activity specifically oriented towards creating a pleasurable experience for the person who is the object of the action. Let us consider the similar-sounding example, "She took me to a performance of *Hamlet*. It was great!" The preferred antecedent of *it* in this case is *performance*. A performance is something for which it is usual to make an evaluation, and the explicit mention of *performance* together with the fact that it is a noun make it a stronger antecedent than the experience of being taken to the performance. However, if the speaker were to stress the word *took* heavily enough, the listener would then be inclined to accept the experience as the antecedent.

The general problem of resolving pronomial references may sometimes be solved using a constraint-oriented approach. First a set of candidate objects is identified; these objects are implicated either by their proximity in the text (or conversation) to the pronoun or by rules (e.g., rules that suggest events and experiences as possible antecedents). Then constraints and/or rules of preference are used to eliminate and/or order the alternatives. Some constraints may be simple (e.g., based on gender or number): "Jack and Jill went up the hill. She tumbled." The pronoun *she* cannot refer to Jack because they are incompatible in gender. In more subtle cases, we have a preference relationship that is only apparent after a fair bit of the meaning of the sentence has been extracted. For example, regarding the tobogganing example above, "giving something a try" is an effort often reserved for activities not yet experienced.

The above examples have illustrated some of the difficulties of determining references. These problems can be critical to the understanding of textual documents; inability to resolve a reference may lead to a complete failure to understand the text. Fortunately, however, there are modes of communication with natural language that are more robust. In a dialog, it is possible to ask a question about the referent of a word and then receive an answer. There need not be an impasse in the dialog due to failure to resolve a reference unless one party has no concept whatsoever of the thing being referred to by the other. Besides this "robustness" property, there are other interesting and useful aspects of dialog, and some of these are discussed in the next section.

9.5   Dialog Management

Unlike reading a text, participation in a dialog involves give-and-take, and each party to the dialog has some control over its course.

9.5.1   Modes of Conversation

There are different kinds of conversations that we might want a machine to participate in. The designer of a natural-language dialog system must take into account the kinds of conversations the system will handle. A system could be designed to handle one type of conversation only; another system might be able to shift modes and thereby exhibit greater sophistication. Here are some kinds of conversations:

1. Small talk. Much of human conversation may be considered small talk. The purpose of such conversation is generally to demonstrate goodwill and friendliness. It usually takes very little effort to understand small talk because most of it is predictable. For example:

   A. "Hi, John. How are things going today?"
   B. "Not too bad, Al. And you?"
   A. "Real good, ever since that downpour ended."

   Small talk typically tends to stick to subjects such as people's feelings, health, and the weather. Its expressions are often idiomatic or colloquial, and they may break the rules of "proper" English.

2. Question-and-answer (e.g., database querying). Some conversations are entirely focussed around the transfer of a single piece of information. One party to the dialog (the interrogator) wants to know a particular fact. The other party presumably has this information but needs to find out exactly what the interrogator wants to know. The dialog may proceed to narrow the range of subjects until the desired information is identified and can be transferred.

3. Database update or teaching. This mode is analogous to the previous one, except that the information will be transferred in the other direction.

4. Persuasion. One party is attempting to communicate a proposition and establish a high degree of belief in it by the other party.

5. Manipulation of emotions. While this mode is similar to persuasion in that it involves one party trying to bring about a change in the other, there are some particular strategies for emotional manipulation (e.g., flattery) that tend to be insufficient for persuasion.

This list is intended to be suggestive, and there are certainly other kinds of conversations.

In addition to kinds of communication, one can often differentiate *phases* of a conversation. Typical phases are the opening, body and close of a conversation.

9.5.2 The Phases of a Conversation

Before communication of key information is possible, certain aspects of the conversational context must be established. One of these is the identities of the parties to the conversation. These may be understood a priori, and not need explicit mention in the dialog, but without this information, the conversation will be limited. In the case of a human conversing with a computer, the computer may assume that it is always talking with "the user" and not need any particular identification from him/her. The human may not need to be told which program he/she is talking to, because he/she may have started up the program and obviously know which one it is. However, without being allowed to know the name of a user, it is likely that the computer is not able to build and maintain a model of the user's beliefs and preferences, and the conversation is likely to be a shallow one. The opening phase of a conversation may involve the following:

1. Greeting. This signals the commencement of the dialog, and it should wake up processes that seek to establish basic contextual information.

2. Establishing identities of parties to the conversation.

3. Loading the context. Any previously developed context for this communication partner should be retrieved and activated.

4. Determining the goals of the user. The purpose of the present conversation should be determined.

Much as "opening" and "endgame" refer to loosely defined phases in the playing of chess, the opening and close of a conversation do not have strictly defined boundaries. However, a conversation program can be designed to shift modes when certain developments have taken place in the dialog. For example, the opening could be considered complete when the identity of the user has been established. The beginning of the close of a conversation might be defined as the time when

1. the user types "goodbye," "see you later" or "gotta go," or

2. five minutes have elapsed without the user responding to a simple question.

During the close, the following may be involved:

1. a summary of conclusions reached during the body,

2. re-affirmation of the next meeting time,

3. courteous affirmation of the end of the conversation; e.g., "It was a pleasure to talk with you. Goodbye."

4. filing of conclusions reached for use on a future occasion,

5. clearing the current context in preparation for a fresh conversation with a potentially different user, or the same user on a different topic.

9.5.3   Monitoring Communication Effectiveness

The body of a conversation is generally where the purpose of the conversation is achieved. The degree to which the dialog needs to be controlled depends on what that purpose is. When the subject of communication is complicated or abstract, there is a greater chance for error (misunderstanding) than if the subject is simple and short. It is desirable to check for successful communication and take remedial action when problems are discovered. Demons (background processes) may monitor the following variables:

1. How well the user is understanding

2. The user's level of attention

3. The user's emotional disposition (happy, angry, etc).

If any of these variables is found to have a bad value, the course of the conversation should be adjusted before proceeding with the main flow. How such variables should be determined is a research question at present.

9.5.4   Schemata for Controlling Conversation

Somewhat beyond the state of the art is the design of a system that can converse flexibly in English with a user and persuade him or her to accept a political or religious argument. However, it is fun to imagine some of the mechanisms that could contribute to such a system.

Some conversations could be controlled with simple algorithmic strategies. A schema for persuasion is the following:

1. If the proposition is a simple fact, say so, and if possible, give its source (in this case the argument is complete); otherwise,

2. communicate the structure of the ensuing argument,

3. persuade the user of the premises,

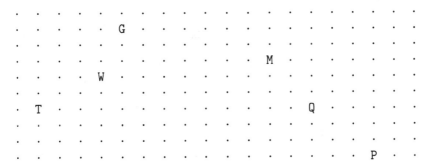

Figure 9.5: Map showing the initial state for Stone World.

4. persuade the user of the soundness of the rule of inference, and

5. demonstrate how the conclusion follows from the premises using the rule of inference.

This is just one schema for persuasion, and it uses a logical style. Another schema might involve identifying alternative beliefs and maligning their adherents.

9.6   An English Interface to a Microworld

9.6.1   System Description

In order to illustrate the interplay between a natural-language understanding system and the program it serves as a front end to, a miniature environment called "Stone World" is described. Stone World serves as a simulation environment in which actions can be taken. This world consists of a two-dimensional space (called "Stone Land"), a character called "Mace," and a set of objects some of which are movable and others of which are fixed. The 2-D space (Stone Land) is cellular, and any location in the space may be specified by a pair of integers giving the row and column for the cell.

The character Mace may be thought of as a man or as a robot who carries on some of the activities of a stonemason. Mace can move around in Stone Land according to commands given in natural language by the user. The objects in Stone World are the following: a tree, a pillar, a well, a quarry, a gem, and some stones. The gem and the stones are portable. Mace can be directed to pick them up and put them down. A map showing the initial state of Stone World is given in Fig. 9.5.

9.6.2   Network Description

The ATN used in the Stone World interface is shown in Fig. 9.6. The starting node for the main network is G1. The "accept" nodes are shown with double circles and are unlabelled. Arcs are labelled with either literal material or conditions. Conditions are shown in parentheses, while literal material is shown without parentheses. The symbol λ denotes the empty string. An arc involving λ is tried last, of all the alternatives from a node. Note that some conditions are predicates on the next word to be scanned. For example "(DIRECTION_ADVERB)" specifies that, in order to traverse the arc, a word of the direction-adverb type must be next. Other conditions are expressed as calls to subnetworks of the ATN. Thus "(NP1)" specifies that the subnetwork whose start node is NP1 is to be traversed, pushing the context within the main net. The phrase parsed by the subnetwork is considered scanned as the arc in the main net is traversed.

The network and parsing scheme are defined in such a way as to eliminate any possibility of backtracking. This results in some restriction of the language subset recognized by the system, but it greatly simplifies the parsing procedure and reduces the average time required to parse a sentence.

A typical command (sentence) that this ATN handles is:

PICK UP A STONE FROM THE QUARRY *

Note that "*" is used to terminate a sentence here, so that we can avoid the use of strings in LISP, and we implement more of the interface with standard functions. This command would be parsed by starting at G1 in the main net, and traversing a path as follows: The arc labeled "(TAKE_VERB) would be traversed since the predicate TAKE_VERB applied to PICK yields T; the arc labeled "UP" would be traversed. The arc labeled "(NP1)" would be traversed in accordance with the successful parsing of the subnet starting at NP1. The portion of the sentence scanned by the subnet would be "A STONE." Then the self-loop arc from and to node T4 would be taken, scanning "FROM THE QUARRY" since FROM satisfies DIR_PREP (that is, FROM is a directional preposition) and "THE QUARRY" would be successfully parsed by the subnet starting at DNP1 (which handles a directional noun phrase). Then the arc from T4 to LAST would be taken, scanning the * at the end of the sentence. Finally the λ arc would be traversed, taking the process to an accepting node.

9.6.3 Implementation

The program consists of two sets of functions and forms: those primarily used to implement the constraints of Stone World, and those primarily used in the natural-language interface.

We first describe how space and objects in Stone World are represented. Stone Land is represented as a 10 by 20 array (actually as a list of ten lists of 20 elements each). These elements are initially all set to "V" (for vacancy), and then objects are placed at particular locations with the help of the function SET_PLACE. The function SHOW, which displays Stone World, manipulates this representation directly. It uses helping functions SHOW_ROW and PRINT_PLACE.

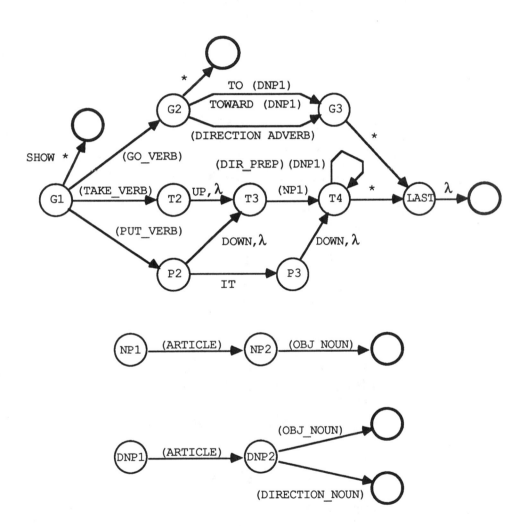

Figure 9.6: The Augmented Transition Network for the Stone World interface.

```
; STONEWLD.LSP

; A "Stone World" and a natural-language interface to it.
; This program demonstrates how a natural-language
; understanding program can be set up around a
; "micro-world".

(SETQ N_ROWS 10) ; dimensions of Stone World
(SETQ N_COLS 20)

; Let VR be a row of vacancies:
(SETQ VR '(V V V V V V V V V V V V V V V V V V V V))

; And here is the initially vacant array:
(SETQ STONELAND (LIST VR VR VR VR VR VR VR VR VR VR))

; This procedure puts an object at a place:
(DEFUN SET_PLACE (ROW COL OBJECT)
  (PROG ()
        ; replace atom at row=ROW, column=COL by OBJECT:
        (SETQ STONELAND
              (REPNTH ROW
                      (REPNTH COL
                              OBJECT
                              (GETNTH ROW STONELAND) )
                      STONELAND) )
        ; update the coordinates of the object:
        (PUTPROP OBJECT (LIST ROW COL) 'POSITION) ) )


; The following helping function replaces the Nth element
; of LST by ELT:
(DEFUN REPNTH (N ELT LST)
  (COND ((EQUAL N 1)(CONS ELT (CDR LST)))
        (T (CONS (CAR LST)
                 (REPNTH (SUB1 N) ELT (CDR LST)) )) ) )


; SHOW displays STONELAND on the screen.
; Note that (LOCATE I J) is a primitive function which puts
;   the cursor at row I, column J.
(DEFUN SHOW ()
  (PROG () (LOCATE 0 0)(CLS)(PRINTM STONE WORLD)
        (MAPCAR 'SHOW_ROW STONELAND) ; display each row.
        (LOCATE 18 0) ) ) ; move cursor to lower screen area.
```

```
(DEFUN SHOW_ROW (ROW)     ; display one row of STONELAND
  (PROG () (MAPCAR 'PRINT_PLACE ROW) (TERPRI)) )

; The next function prints one cell of Stone Land.
; There are 2 characters per cell, one of which is
; always blank (ASCII 32).
(DEFUN PRINT_PLACE (PLACE)    ;print PLACE (except V's as dots).
  (COND ((EQ PLACE 'V)(TYO 250)(TYO 32))
        (T (PRIN1 PLACE)(TYO 32)) ) )

; Place landmarks in STONELAND:
(SET_PLACE 5 5 'W)          ; well
(SET_PLACE 7 15 'Q)         ; quarry
(SET_PLACE 4 13 'M)         ; "Mace", the mason
(SET_PLACE 7 2 'T)          ; tree
(SET_PLACE 10 18 'P)        ; pillar
(SET_PLACE 2 6 'G)          ; gem
```

Now that the space and objects have been created, and the objects all have locations in the space, we need to specify more properties of the objects than just their locations. Some objects are portable and some are not. Also we initialize Mace as facing north and carrying nothing.

```
; stones and gems are portable; landmarks are not:
(MAPCAR '(LAMBDA (OBJ) (PUTPROP OBJ T 'PORTABLE)) '(S G))
(MAPCAR '(LAMBDA (OBJ) (PUTPROP OBJ NIL 'PORTABLE))
        '(Q W T P) )

(SETQ CARRYING NIL)            ; Mace starts out empty-handed
(SETQ LAST_DIRECTION 'NORTH) ; and facing north.
```

Next we define several functions which manipulate positions and directions. Before doing so, the four principal directions are declared:

```
(SETQ DIRECTIONS '(NORTH EAST SOUTH WEST))
```

The function CONTENTS provides a means to access values in the array STONELAND.

```
(DEFUN CONTENTS (I J)      ; returns contents of place I J.
  (GETNTH J (GETNTH I STONELAND)) )
```

The function NEIGHBOR_CONTENTS returns the contents of the particular cell neighboring Mace's current postion in the specified direction, or it returns the atom OFF_LIMITS if the neighbor would be outside STONELAND. The function NEIGHBOR_POS gets the coordinates of the neighbor. It uses the function VECTOR_ADD which returns the sum of two vectors.

```
(DEFUN NEIGHBOR_CONTENTS (DIR)
  (PROG (NEI_POS I J)
        (SETQ NEI_POS (NEIGHBOR_POS DIR))
        (SETQ I (CAR NEI_POS))
        (SETQ J (CADR NEI_POS))
        (COND ((OR (ZEROP I)
                   (ZEROP J)
                   (EQUAL I N_ROWS)
                   (EQUAL J N_COLS) )
               (RETURN 'OFF_LIMITS) )
              (T (RETURN (CONTENTS I J))) ) ) )


(DEFUN NEIGHBOR_POS (DIR)
  ; add the appropriate displacement vector to
  ; Mace's coordinate pair.
  (VECTOR_ADD (GET 'M 'POSITION)
              (COND ((EQ DIR 'NORTH) '(-1 0))
                    ((EQ DIR 'SOUTH) '(1 0))
                    ((EQ DIR 'WEST) '(0 -1))
                    ((EQ DIR 'EAST) '(0 1)) ) ) )

(DEFUN VECTOR_ADD (X Y)      ; return vector sum of X and Y
  (COND ((NULL X) NIL)
        (T (CONS (PLUS (CAR X)(CAR Y))
                 (VECTOR_ADD (CDR X)(CDR Y)) )) ) )
```

Several functions are now defined which carry out operations and/or perform tests for the legality of those operations. Some of these functions help Mace move, pick things up, or put them down. For example, the function MOVE is used to effect the change of Mace's position in the course of obeying a "GO" command. MOVE takes one argument, a direction such as NORTH. Then in the PROG body, it sets the value of POS to the pair of coordinates of the cell which is the neighbor of Mace's current position, in the given direction. Then, using a call to SET_PLACE, Mace's current cell is updated to be vacant, and this is shown on the screen by the call to PLOT. Then the atom M is written into Mace's new location and shown on the screen. The helping functions MACE_ROW and MACE_COL return the row number and column number, respectively, of Mace's current position.

```
(DEFUN MOVE (DIRECTION)      ; makes Mace move in direction
  (PROG (POS)
        (SETQ POS (NEIGHBOR_POS DIRECTION))
        (SET_PLACE (MACE_ROW) (MACE_COL) 'V)
        (PLOT 'V (GET 'M 'POSITION))
        (SET_PLACE (CAR POS)(CADR POS) 'M)
```

```
              (PLOT 'M POS) ) )

(DEFUN MACE_ROW () (CAR (GET 'M 'POSITION)))
(DEFUN MACE_COL () (CADR (GET 'M 'POSITION)))


; The next function returns T if OK to move
; in the specified DIRECTION:
(DEFUN MOVE_LEGAL (DIRECTION)
  (EQ (NEIGHBOR_CONTENTS DIRECTION) 'V) )

; Here is a function which makes Mace pick up the object
; that lies in the given DIRECTION:
(DEFUN TAKE (DIRECTION)
  (PROG (POS)
        (SETQ POS (NEIGHBOR_POS DIRECTION))
        (SETQ CARRYING
              (STONE_OR_GEM (CONTENTS (CAR POS)(CADR POS))) )
        (COND ((NULL (EQUAL POS (GET 'Q 'POSITION)))
               (SET_PLACE (CAR POS)(CADR POS) 'V)
               (PLOT 'V POS) ) ) ) )


(DEFUN STONE_OR_GEM (OBJ)    ; convert Q to S.
  (COND ((EQ OBJ 'Q) 'S) (T OBJ)) )

; The following function returns T if it is OK
; to take an object from the specified DIRECTION:
(DEFUN TAKE_LEGAL (DIRECTION)
  (AND (MEMBER DIRECTION DIRECTIONS)
       (MEMBER (NEIGHBOR_CONTENTS DIRECTION) '(Q S G))
       (NULL CARRYING) ) )


; In order to make Mace drop an object in a
; particular DIRECTION, the following definition
; is given:
(DEFUN PUT (DIRECTION)
  (PROG (POS)
        (SETQ POS (NEIGHBOR_POS DIRECTION))
        (COND ((NULL (EQUAL POS (GET 'Q 'POSITION)))
               (SET_PLACE (CAR POS)(CADR POS) CARRYING)
               (PLOT CARRYING POS) )) ; update screen
        (SETQ CARRYING NIL) ) )
```

```
; In order to make sure that it is OK to put an object
; down in a given DIRECTION, we define this function:
(DEFUN PUT_LEGAL (DIRECTION)
  (AND (MEMBER DIRECTION DIRECTIONS)
       (MEMBER (NEIGHBOR_CONTENTS DIRECTION) '(Q V))
       CARRYING) )
```

The following function is used to update the display of Stone World without redrawing it all.

```
(DEFUN PLOT (SYMBOL POS)     ; display SYMBOL at POS on CRT
  (PROG ()
        (LOCATE (CAR POS) (TIMES 2 (SUB1 (CADR POS))))
        (COND ((EQ SYMBOL 'V)(TYO 250))
              (T (PRIN1 SYMBOL)) )
        (LOCATE 22 0) ) )
```

Let us now describe the second half of the program, which implements the English-language interface to Stone World. Before we describe how the parsing procedure operates, we describe how the ATN is represented in LISP. Each node of the ATN is represented by an atom (e.g., G1). The arcs emanating from a node are represented by an expression which is stored on the property list of the atom. The expression is a list of the individual arc descriptions. Each arc is represented by a list whose first item is a pattern that must match the current portion of the input sentence if the arc is to be traversed. The rest of the list is a sequence of actions to be taken if the pattern matching is successful. If the arc leads to any node which is not a final node, then the last action for an arc has the form (NEXT N) where N is the name of the node to which the arc leads.

The function PARSE takes as its argument the current node in the ATN from which parsing is to proceed (or continue). It assumes that the global variable S contains, as its value, the remaining portion of the sentence being analyzed. PARSE has the job of attempting to traverse one of the arcs which leaves the current node by matching the value of S with the pattern for the arc. If the pattern matching is successful for an arc, then the corresponding actions are executed. Because of the way the arcs emanating from a node are represented, PARSE has only to take the list of arcs from the property list of the node, make some simple modifications to it and apply the COND function to it. The two modifications to the arclist are the following: (1) The pattern to be matched is embedded in a call to the MATCH function, and (2) a clause is appended to the list, corresponding to an "else" condition (to handle the situation when no arcs can be traversed from the current node, with the particular user input). The first modification is effected by the function ADDMATCH and the second is accomplished by the call to APPEND in the function PARSE itself.

The function NEXT, which is called as the last action in most of the arcs, functions mainly to call PARSE recursively to continue the analysis of the sentence after an arc has successfully been traversed.

```
;-------- Now for the Natural-Language Interface -----------

; The PARSE function starts the parse of the current
; string from NODE:
(DEFUN PARSE (NODE)
  (APPLY 'COND (APPEND (ADDMATCH (GET NODE 'ARCS))
                       '((T (PRINTM STUCK IN PARSE)
                            (SETQ INTERP '(NIL))
                            (SETQ SUCCESS NIL))) ) ) )

(DEFUN ADDMATCH (ARCLIST) ; make each compressed clause into a
  (MAPCAR '(LAMBDA (ARC)  ; legitimate COND clause.
                   (CONS (APPEND '(MATCH)
                                 (LIST (CONS 'QUOTE
                                             (LIST (CAR ARC)) ))
                                 '(S) )
                         (CDR ARC) ) )
          ARCLIST) )

(DEFUN NEXT (NODE)       ; displays progress and continues parse
  (PROG () (PRIN1 NODE)(TYO 32)(PARSE NODE)) )
```

Now the representation for our particular augmented transition network is presented. For each non-final node, we place a list of arcs on its property list.

```
; Here is the ATN for command analysis.
;   It is based on a semantic grammar:
(PUTPROP 'G1
  '(
    ((SHOW *)
     (SETQ S '(*))
     (SETQ INTERP '(SHOW_COMMAND)) )
    (((GO_VERB X)(* Y))
     (SETQ S Y)
     (SETQ DIRECTION_SLOT '(DIRECTION FORWARD)) ; default direc.
     (SETQ DISTANCE_SLOT '(STEPS 1))            ; default dist.
     (NEXT 'G2) )
    (((TAKE_VERB X)(* Y))
     (SETQ S Y)
     (SETQ COMMAND 'TAKE_COMMAND)
     (SETQ DIRECTION_SLOT '(DIRECTION UNSPEC)) ; default direc.
     (SETQ OBJ_SLOT 'STONE)                    ; default object
     (NEXT 'T2) )
    (((PUT_VERB X)(* Y))
     (SETQ S Y)
```

```
     (SETQ COMMAND 'PUT_COMMAND)
     (SETQ DIRECTION_SLOT '(DIRECTION FORWARD)) ; default direc.
     (SETQ OBJ_SLOT (LIST CARRYING))            ; default object
     (NEXT 'P2) ))
  'ARCS)

(PUTPROP 'G2
  '(
    ((*) (NEXT 'G3))            ; end of command
    ((TO (* X))                 ; "TO" arc
     (SETQ S X)
     (PARSE 'DNP1)              ; get destination info
     (NEXT 'G3) )
    ((TOWARD (* X))
     (SETQ S X)
     (PARSE 'DNP1)              ; get directional info
     (NEXT 'G3) )
    (((DIRECTION_ADVERB X)(* Y))
     (SETQ S Y)
     (SETQ DIRECTION_SLOT
           (LIST 'DIRECTION (NORMALIZE_DIRECTION X)) )
     (NEXT 'G3) ) )
  'ARCS)

(PUTPROP 'G3
  '(
    ((*)(SETQ INTERP (LIST 'GO_COMMAND
                            DIRECTION_SLOT
                            DISTANCE_SLOT))
     (NEXT 'LAST) ) )
  'ARCS)

(PUTPROP 'DNP1        ; sub-ATN for directional noun phrase
  '(
    ((*)(PRINTM THIS MUST BE A NAME)(NEXT 'DNP2))
    (((ARTICLE Z) (* Y))
     (SETQ S Y)
     (NEXT 'DNP2) ) )
  'ARCS)

(PUTPROP 'DNP2
  '(
    (((OBJ_NOUN W)(* Y))
     (SETQ S Y)
```

```
        (SETQ DIRECTION_SLOT (LIST 'TOWARD
                               (NORMALIZE_OBJECT W))) )
    (((DIRECTION_NOUN W) (* Y))
     (SETQ S Y)
     (SETQ DIRECTION_SLOT (LIST 'DIRECTION W))
              ) )
   'ARCS)

(PUTPROP 'T2
  '(
    ((UP (* X))       ; ignore particle "UP" if present here.
     (SETQ S X)
     (NEXT 'T3) )
    (((* X))
     (NEXT 'T3) ) )
   'ARCS)

(PUTPROP 'T3          ; get object (if any) of TAKE or PUT verb
  '(
    (((ARTICLE X)(* Y))
     (PARSE 'NP1)
     (SETQ OBJ_SLOT NP1)
     (NEXT 'T4) ) )
   'ARCS)

(PUTPROP 'T4
  '(
    ((*)
     (SETQ INTERP (LIST COMMAND OBJ_SLOT DIRECTION_SLOT))
     (NEXT 'LAST) )
    (((DIR_PREP X)(* Y))
     (SETQ S Y)
     (PARSE 'DNP1)
     (NEXT 'T4) ) )
   'ARCS)

; The next subnetwork parses a noun phrase and
; saves the result as NP1's value:
(PUTPROP 'NP1
  '(
    (((ARTICLE X)(* Y))
     (SETQ S Y)
     (COND ((EQ X 'THE)(SETQ DEFINITE T))
           (T (SETQ DEFINITE NIL)) )
```

```
      (NEXT 'NP2) ) )
   'ARCS)

(PUTPROP 'NP2
   '(
     (((OBJ_NOUN X)(* Y))
      (SETQ S Y)
      (SETQ NP1 (LIST (NORMALIZE_OBJECT X)
                      (CONS 'DEFINITE (LIST DEFINITE)) )) ) )
   'ARCS)

(PUTPROP 'P2
   '(
     ((DOWN (* X))    ; ignore particle "DOWN" if present here.
      (SETQ S X)
      (NEXT 'T3) )
     ((IT (* X))
      (SETQ S X)
      (NEXT 'P3) )
     (((* X))
      (NEXT 'T3) ) )
   'ARCS)

(PUTPROP 'P3          ; object seen already
   '(
     ((DOWN (* X))    ; ignore particle "DOWN" here, too.
      (SETQ S X)
      (NEXT 'T4) )
     (((* X))
      (NEXT 'T4) ) )
   'ARCS)

(PUTPROP 'LAST
   '(
     ((*)   (PRINTM I UNDERSTAND YOU)) )
   'ARCS)
```

The structure of the ATN has now been given. However, there remain particular tests and actions that occur in the arc descriptions which we haven't yet defined. Here we define them. Some of these functions such as GO_VERB are predicates that provide the interface with the ability to recognize common synonyms for the names of the actions, objects or directions that it understands.

```
; functions that support the pattern matching in the ATN:
```

```
(DEFUN GO_VERB (W) (MEMBER W '(GO MOVE HEAD WALK)))

(DEFUN TAKE_VERB (W) (MEMBER W '(TAKE PICK GRAB LIFT CARRY)))

(DEFUN PUT_VERB (W)
  (MEMBER W '(PUT DROP PLACE RELEASE POSITION LEAVE)) )

(DEFUN DIRECTION_ADVERB (W)
  (MEMBER W '(NORTH EAST SOUTH WEST NORTHWARD EASTWARD
              SOUTHWARD WESTWARD RIGHT LEFT UP DOWN
              STRAIGHT AHEAD)) )

(DEFUN DIRECTION_NOUN (W)
  (MEMBER W '(NORTH EAST SOUTH WEST)) )

(DEFUN DIR_PREP (W)
  (MEMBER W '(TO FROM TOWARD TOWARDS)) )

(DEFUN OBJ_NOUN (W)
  (MEMBER W
          '(QUARRY CORNER PLACE TREE WELL PILLAR STONE GEM) ) )

(DEFUN ARTICLE (W)
  (MEMBER W '(A AN THE)) )

; functions that support the actions on ATN arcs:
(DEFUN NORMALIZE_DIRECTION (W)
  (TRANSLATE W '((NORTHWARD . NORTH)(EASTWARD . EAST)
        (SOUTHWARD . SOUTH)(WESTWARD . WEST)(RIGHT . EAST)
        (LEFT . WEST)(UP . NORTH)(DOWN . SOUTH)
        (STRAIGHT . FORWARD)(AHEAD . FORWARD) )) )

; Here is a simple look-up function which
; looks word W up in DICT which must be a
; list of dotted pairs.  TRANSLATE returns
; the corresponding word or W if none.
(DEFUN TRANSLATE (W DICT)
 (COND ((NULL DICT) W)
       ((EQ W (CAAR DICT))(CDAR DICT))
       (T (TRANSLATE W (CDR DICT))) ) )

(DEFUN NORMALIZE_OBJECT (W)
  (TRANSLATE W '((QUARRY . Q)(TREE . T)(WELL . W)
              (PILLAR . P)(STONE . S)(GEM . G)
```

```
                (MACE . M)(YOU . M) )) )
```

The function ACT_UPON dispatches commands to the particular functions that can carry them out such as OBEY_GO, SHOW, etc.

```
(DEFUN ACT_UPON (L)      ; linguistic object
  (COND ((EQ (CAR L) 'GO_COMMAND)
           (SETQ SUCCESS T)        ;T until proven NIL
           (OBEY_GO) )
        ((EQ (CAR L) 'SHOW_COMMAND)
           (SHOW)
           (SETQ SUCCESS T) )
        ((EQ (CAR L) 'TAKE_COMMAND)
           (SETQ SUCCESS T)
           (OBEY_TAKE) )
        ((EQ (CAR L) 'PUT_COMMAND)
           (SETQ SUCCESS T)
           (OBEY_PUT) )
        (T (SETQ SUCCESS NIL)
           (PRINTM CANT SATISFY THAT KIND OF REQUEST) ) ) )
```

The function OBEY_GO begins by extracting the direction and number of steps parameters from the encoded command (which is the value of L, the argument passed to ACT_UPON). If the direction given is FORWARD then this is changed to the value of the global variable LAST_DIRECTION. Then a loop is begun which, in each iteration, attempts to move Mace one cell in the given direction.

```
(DEFUN OBEY_GO ()
  (COND ((AND (EQ (CAADR L) 'DIRECTION)
              (EQ (CAR (CADDR L)) 'STEPS) )
           (SETQ DIRECTION_SLOT (CADR L))
           (SETQ DISTANCE_SLOT (CADDR L))
           (SETQ DIRECTION (CADR DIRECTION_SLOT))
           (COND ((EQ DIRECTION 'FORWARD)
                    (SETQ DIRECTION LAST_DIRECTION) ))
           (SETQ NSTEPS (CADR DISTANCE_SLOT))
           (DO_N_TIMES NSTEPS
                  (COND ((MOVE_LEGAL DIRECTION)
                           (MOVE DIRECTION)
                           (SETQ LAST_DIRECTION DIRECTION))
                        (T (SETQ SUCCESS NIL)) ) ) )
        (T (SETQ SUCCESS NIL)
           (PRINTM CANT HANDLE COMPLEX DIRECTION OR DISTANCE) )
        ) )

(DEFUN CAADR (X) (CAR (CADR X))) ; a utility function
```

In order for Mace to pick up an object, the function OBEY_TAKE determines which object has been specified and which direction the object is to be taken from. Since the first element of L is the type of command (in this case TAKE_COMMAND), the parameters are in the remainder of L, and the form (SETQ PRMS (CDR L)) accesses them. If the user does not specify a direction, then the function FIND_DIR is called to determine which direction the object can be taken from. If the direction is specified as "THE QUARRY" then a special function FIND_DIR1 is called to determine the corresponding compass direction. Finally, if it is possible to carry out the resulting command, it is done. Otherwise the atom SUCCESS is given a value of NIL.

```
(DEFUN OBEY_TAKE ()
  (PROG (PRMS DIRECTION)
        (SETQ PRMS (CDR L))
        (SETQ OBJECT (CAAR PRMS))            ; thing to take
        (SETQ DIRECTION (CADAR (CDR PRMS)))
        (COND ((EQ DIRECTION 'FORWARD)
               (SETQ DIRECTION LAST_DIRECTION) )
              ((EQ DIRECTION 'UNSPEC)
               (SETQ DIRECTION (FIND_DIR OBJECT DIRECTIONS)) )
              ((EQ DIRECTION 'Q)
               ; handle Quarry direction as special:
               (SETQ DIRECTION (FIND_DIR1 'Q DIRECTIONS)) )
              )
        (COND ((TAKE_LEGAL DIRECTION)(TAKE DIRECTION))
              (T (PRINTM CANT TAKE THAT WAY)
                 (SETQ SUCCESS NIL) ) ) ) )


; The next function searches in the given
; DIRECTIONS to find the given OBJ:
(DEFUN FIND_DIR (OBJ DIRECTIONS)
  (COND ((NULL DIRECTIONS) NIL)
        ((EQ (STONE_OR_GEM            ; consider Q as S
              (APPLY 'CONTENTS (NEIGHBOR_POS (CAR DIRECTIONS))))
                 OBJ)
         (CAR DIRECTIONS))
        (T (FIND_DIR OBJ (CDR DIRECTIONS))) ) )


; The next function is like FIND_DIR, except
; that Q is not mapped to S.
(DEFUN FIND_DIR1 (OBJ DIRECTIONS)
  (COND ((NULL DIRECTIONS) NIL)
        ((EQ (APPLY 'CONTENTS
```

```
                    (NEIGHBOR_POS (CAR DIRECTIONS)) )
          OBJ)
       (CAR DIRECTIONS))
       (T (FIND_DIR1 OBJ (CDR DIRECTIONS))) ) )

(DEFUN OBEY_PUT ()
  (PROG (PRMS OBJECT DIRECTION OK)
        (SETQ PRMS (CDR L))
        (SETQ OBJECT (CAAR PRMS))        ; thing to put
        (SETQ DIRECTION (CADAR (CDR PRMS)))
        (COND ((EQ OBJECT CARRYING)(SETQ OK T))
              (T (SETQ OK NIL)) )
        (COND ((EQ DIRECTION 'FORWARD)
               (SETQ DIRECTION LAST_DIRECTION) ))
        (COND ((AND OK (PUT_LEGAL DIRECTION))
               (PUT DIRECTION) )
              (T (PRINTM CANT PUT THAT WAY)
                 (SETQ SUCCESS NIL) ) ) ) )

(DEFUN PRODUCE_REPLY ()
  (COND (SUCCESS (PRINTM OK, NEXT?))
        (T (PRINTM I CAN'T QUITE DO THAT ONE)) ) )
```

The function START is used to begin a session. It calls SHOW, which displays Stone World, and then the dialog with the user is begun. The function PARSE is called to begin the interpretation of each sentence of user input.

```
(DEFUN START ()         ; main program
  (PROG (INPUT DIRECTION_SLOT DESTINATION_SLOT OBJECT_SLOT)
        (SHOW)
        (PRINTM HEY YOU UP THERE! WHAT SHOULD I DO?)
        (PRINTM PLEASE END YOUR SENTENCES WITH * OR ?)
  LOOP  (SETQ INPUT (INPUT_SENTENCE))
        (SCROLL)
        (SETQ S INPUT)
        (PARSE 'G1)         ; analyze the English input in S.
        (ACT_UPON INTERP)   ; try to obey command or answer query.
        (SCROLL)
        (PRODUCE_REPLY)
        (SCROLL)
        (GO LOOP) ) )

(DEFUN INPUT_SENTENCE ()    ; get atoms until * or ?
  (PROG (TEMP)
    (RETURN
```

```
(COND ((TERMINATORP (SETQ TEMP (READ))) (LIST TEMP))
      (T (CONS TEMP (INPUT_SENTENCE))) ) ) ) )
```

```
(DEFUN TERMINATORP (ATM) (MEMBER ATM '(* ?)))
```

The following code is machine-dependent for the IBM PC; it is included here in keeping with the tenet that all programs presented in this text be complete and runnable without modification. It is a function to scroll a window that consists of the lower half of the screen.

```
(DEFUN SCROLL ()
  (PROG NIL
        (SET_REG 6 12)     ;CH = 12 = upper row
        (SET_REG 10 0)     ;CL = 0 = left col
        (SET_REG 7 24)     ;DH = 24 = lower row
        (SET_REG 11 79)    ;DL = 79 = right col
        (SET_REG 5 2)      ;BH = 2 = attribute for blank line
        (SET_REG 8 2)      ;AL = 2 = \#lines to blank
        (SET_REG 4 6)      ;AH = 6 means scroll active page up
        (BIOSCALL 10)
        (LOCATE 22 0) ) )
```

9.6.4 Sample Session

Once all of Stone World's definitions and other expressions have been loaded (and evaluated), a session is begun by typing:

```
(START)
```

This causes a map to be displayed (resembling Fig. 9.5) and the dialog is initiated. The lower portion of the screen serves as a dialog window, and in it soon appears the message:

```
HEY YOU UP THERE! WHAT SHOULD I DO?
PLEASE END YOUR SENTENCES WITH * OR ?
```

The user may then type a line such as the following, terminated with a carriage return:

```
WALK TO THE SOUTH *
```

The program then parses the command, displaying its progress by printing the labels of the nodes in the augmented transition network that it encounters:

```
G2 DNP2 G3 LAST_NODE
```

Soon, a positive acknowledgement appears:

I UNDERSTAND YOU

This is followed by an updating of the map to show the motion of the mason. The user might then type:

GO EAST *

The system will again parse and interpret the command and take the requested action. Using several such steps, the user can position Mace next to the quarry. Suppose that Mace is in the cell just north of it. The user may then type

PICK UP A STONE *

and this might be followed by the command

PUT DOWN THE STONE TO THE NORTH *

If the user then types

PICK UP A STONE FROM THE WEST *

the program responds (after giving the trace of its parsing) with the objection

CANT TAKE THAT WAY
I CAN'T QUITE DO THAT ONE

since there is no stone or quarry in the cell to the west of Mace.

     Since the quarry is an unlimited source of stones, it is possible for the user to make a complicated layout of stones, even though this would be somewhat painstaking. Several improvements to the program are suggested in the exercises. A session is terminated with control-C; creating a means of graceful exit is left as a trivial exercise.

9.7   Bibliographical Information

In order to solve the problems of natural-language understanding, knowledge of several kinds is needed. One must have linguistic knowledge: the morphology of words and syntax of sentences is one part; knowledge about the roles words can play and how these roles can be determined from the sentence is another. One must understand computer algorithms and data structures for constructing automatic language processing systems. One also must have knowledge about the domain of discourse, that can be represented in the understanding system and brought to bear on the interpretation process.

     Much of the linguistics background that is useful in building natural-language understanding systems is provided in the following books: [Fromkin and Rodman 1978] is a general and elementary book introducing linguistics. [Culicover 1982] provides thorough coverage of linguistic syntax. Semantics is the subject of

[Lyons 1977], and pragmatics is covered well from the linguistic point of view by [Gazdar 1979]. A good introduction to Montague semantics is [Dowty et al 1981]. A system for representing everyday situations, much of which is amenable to logical manipulation, has been proposed [Barwise and Perry 1983] and appears promising. A theory of language acquisition is presented in [Pinker 1984].

A compact survey of natural-language understanding systems is [Tennant 1981]. The role of syntax in language understanding by computers is treated in [Winograd 1983]. A mathematical introduction of formal languages is [Hopcroft and Ullman 1969]. An overview of AI with an emphasis on the representation of common-sense knowledge in "conceptual graphs" is [Sowa 1984]. A collection of articles was compiled by Minsky that cover relatively early efforts [Minsky 1968].

Computer systems that understand certain kinds of sentences in English are described in [Woods et al 1970], and [Wilks 1975]. The integration of a natural-language interface with a microworld was first successfully demonstrated by Winograd and is described in [Winograd 1972]. The details of several experimental programs for language understanding are described in [Schank and Riesbeck 1981]. A system of primitives for expressing meanings of words is described in [Schank 1972]. The use of noun cases in interpreting verb meanings is discussed in [Fillmore 1968] and [Bruce 1975]. The analysis of a speaker's purpose from the natural-language input is called "speech-act" analysis and is described in [Perrault and Allen 1980], [Searle 1969]. Semantic grammars were used extensively in the LADDER system [Hendrix et al 1978]. A syntactic formalism that facilitates semantics, known as "lexical functional grammars," is described in [Kaplan and Bresnan 1982]. A good discussion of practical issues in building natural-language interfaces is given in [Simmons 1986]. A text on data structures that covers methods (such as B-trees) suitable for implementing symbol tables and lexicons is [Standish 1980].

Computer systems for machine translation (e.g., from English to French) are now finding commercial use, although it is generally necessary for a human translator to post-edit the computer's output. The papers in an edited volume [Lawson 1982] describe not only current practice and systems under development, but also the colorful history of machine translation, a field which for many years was not considered respectable.

Computer understanding of human speech was the focus of an intensive research effort during the early 1970's under funding from the Defense Advanced Research Projects Agency. Two of the products of this effort are the HARPY system [Lowerre and Reddy 1980] and the HEARSAY-II system [Erman et al 1980]. A good introduction to speech understanding is [Newell 1975].

References

1. Barwise, J. and Perry, J. 1983. *Situations and Attitudes.* Cambridge, MA:

MIT Press.

2. Bobrow, D. and Collins, A. (eds.) 1975. *Representation and Understanding: Studies in Cognitive Science.* New York: Academic Press.

3. Bruce, B. C. 1975. Case systems for natural language, *Artificial Intelligence*, Vol. 6, pp327-360.

4. Culicover, P. W. 1982. *Syntax*, Second Edition. New York: Academic Press.

5. Dowty, D. R., Wall, R. E., and Peters, S. 1981. *Introduction to Montague Semantics.* Dordrecht, Holland; and Boston: D. Reidel Publishing Co.

6. Erman, L. D., Hayes-Roth, F., Lesser, V. R., and Reddy, D. R. 1980. The HEARSAY-II speech understanding system: Integrating knowledge to resolve uncertainty. *ACM Computing Surveys*, Vol. 12, No. 2, pp213-253.

7. Fillmore, C. J. 1968. The case for case. In Bach, E., and Harms, R. T. (eds.), *Universals in Linguistic Theory.* New York: Holt, Rinehart and Winston.

8. Fromkin, V. and Rodman, R. 1978. *An Introduction to Language*, Second Edition. New York: Holt, Rinehart and Winston.

9. Gazdar, G. 1979. *Pragmatics.* New York: Academic Press.

10. Hendrix, G. G., Sacerdoti, E. D., Sagalowicz, D., and Slocum, J. 1978. Developing a natural language interface to complex data. *ACM Transactions on Database Systems*, Vol. 3, pp105-147.

11. Hopcroft, J. E., and Ullman, J. D. 1969. *Formal Languages and Their Relation to Automata.* Reading, MA: Addison-Wesley.

12. Kaplan R. M. and Bresnan, J. 1982. Lexical-functional grammar: A formal system of grammatical representation. In Bresnan (ed.), *The Mental Representation of Grammatical Relations.* Cambridge, MA: MIT Press.

13. Lawson, V. (ed.) 1982. *Practical Experience of Machine Translation.* Amsterdam: North-Holland.

14. Lowerre, B., and Reddy, D. R. 1980. The HARPY speech understanding system. In Lea, W. (ed.) *Trends in Speech Recognition.* Englewood Cliffs, NJ: Prentice-Hall, pp340-360.

15. Minsky, M. (ed.) 1968. *Semantic Information Processing.* Cambridge, MA: MIT Press.

16. Lyons, J. 1977. *Semantics*, (2 volumes). New York: Cambridge University Press.

17. Newell, A. 1975. A tutorial on speech understanding systems. In Reddy, D. R. (ed.) *Speech Recognition: Invited Papers Presented at the 1974 IEEE Symposium.* New York: Academic Press, pp3-54.

18. Perrault, C. R., and Allen, J. F. 1980. A plan-based analysis of indirect speech acts. *American Journal of Computational Linguistics*, Vol. 6, pp167-182.

19. Pinker, S. 1984. *Language Learnability and Language Development.* Cambridge, MA: Harvard University Press.

20. Rich, E. 1983. *Artificial Intelligence.* New York: McGraw-Hill.

21. Riesbeck, C. K. 1975. Conceptual analysis. In Schank, R. C. (ed.), *Conceptual Information Processing.* New York: American Elsevier.

22. Schank, R. C. 1972. Conceptual dependency: A theory of natural language understanding. *Cognitive Psychology*, Vol. 3, pp82-123.

23. Schank, R. C., and Colby, K. M. (eds.), 1973. *Computer Models of Thought and Language.* San Francisco: Freeman.

24. Schank, R. C., and Riesbeck, C. K. (eds.), 1981. *Inside Computer Understanding: Five Programs Plus Miniatures.* Hillsdale, NJ: Lawrence Erlbaum Associates.

25. Searle, J. R. 1969. *Speech Acts.* Cambridge, England: Cambridge University Press.

26. Simmons, R. F. 1986. Man-machine interfaces: Can they guess what you want? *IEEE Expert*, Vol. 1, No. 1, pp86-94.

27. Sowa, J. F. 1984. *Conceptual Structures: Information Processing in Mind and Machine.* Reading, MA: Addison-Wesley.

28. Standish, T. 1980. *Data Structure Techniques.* Reading, MA: Addison-Wesley.

29. Tennant, H. 1981. *Natural Language Processing.* New York: Petrocelli Books.

30. Wilks, Y. 1975. An intelligent analyzer and understander of English. *Communications of the ACM*, Vol. 18, No. 5, pp264-274.

31. Winograd, T. 1972. *Understanding Natural Language.* New York: Academic Press.

32. Winograd, T. 1983. *Language as a Cognitive Process, Vol. 1: Syntax.* Reading, MA: Addison-Wesley.

33. Woods, W. A. 1970. Transition network grammars for natural language analysis, *Communications of the ACM*, Vol. 13, pp591-606.

34. Woods, W. A., Kaplan, R. M., and Nash-Webber, B. L. 1972. *The LUNAR Sciences Natural Language System*, Final Report, National Technical Information Service Report No. NTIS N72-28984.

Exercises

1. Describe as many of the interpretations for the following sentences as you can:

   (a) John, lying, told the truth.

   (b) Jennifer saw robots welding panels and grippers lifting subassemblies walking through the factory.

2. Determine the kind of event and determine the roles played by each participant (noun) in the following sentences:

   (a) Ivan programmed the computer to play chess in his spare time using LISP.

   (b) Last week, someone smashed the back window with a plank for a lousy old radio.

   (c) Ellen took the train from Montreal to Vancouver by way of Calgary.

3. Determine the number of times nonterminal symbols are expanded by PARSE2 in the job of parsing "THE MAN OVER THERE OVER THERE RAN FAST."

4. The discussion of left-recursive productions on p.336 gave some idea of how changing the grammar can affect the efficiency of parsing.

   • Write a small grammar G_1 for PARSE.LSP so that it can parse the sentence:

   $$S_1 = \text{``PARSERS DEAL WITH SYNTAX.''}$$

   • Now, by adding productions to G_1, obtain G_2 to parse

   $$S_2 = \text{``TRANSLATORS HANDLE SEMANTICS.''}$$

- Experimentally determine the number of expansions of nonterminals for each of the four combinations: S_1 with G_1, S_1 with G_2, S_2 with G_1, and S_2 with G_2. Of course, it should not be possible to parse S_2 with G_1. What does your experiment indicate about how the size of a grammar affects the efficiency of parsing with it?

5. In a grammar for a subset of English, is it necessary to provide a separate production rule for each (terminal) word? Suggest a way in which production rules for words could be represented efficiently.

6. Design and implement a bottom-up parser that uses depth-first search. How does its performance compare with that of PARSE.LSP?

7. Write a semantic grammar that can be used to parse the following sentences and ones similar to them: (1) "Compute the total of my itemized deductions for the month of November." (2) "Display a list of this month's messages from Jack." (3) "Erase that message." What are some of the other sentences that your grammar can parse? Now give an example of a sentence which seems related or similar to one of the three sentences above which your grammar does not handle.

8. In the following passage pronouns occur four times. What is referred to in each instance?

   " 'Twas a night fit neither for man nor beast. She was listing to starboard and we darn near called it quits."

9. For each of the following, judge whether the noun phrase in italics introduces a new object or refers to one already in the listener's experience. Explain your decision. Also, does the noun phrase refer to a class or an instance? Singular or plural?

   (a) *The man in the moon* smiled.
   (b) I saw *a nasty dog.* It barked.
   (c) *a certain U. S. president inaugurated in 1981*
   (d) *The best experience of my life* was being born.
   (e) *the best experience of your life*
   (f) *Skiing* is good at Sun Valley.
   (g) Jim bought *five apples.*
   (h) I love *your pecan pie.*
   (i) I love *your pecan pies.*

10. Modify the Stone World language interface to permit it to accept questions of the forms "Where are you ?" "What are you carrying?" and "Are you carrying a stone?"

11. Extend the Stone World program to understand distances in commands such as "MOVE WEST 5 STEPS *".

12. Add a feature to the Stone World program that enables it to be taught sequences of commands, so that the mason can be told to perform the entire sequence of operations with one new command.

13. Add one or more of the following features to the Stone World program:

    (a) an adversary: a new animate entity which moves on its own (perhaps using some pseudo-random scheme) and poses a threat to the mason.

    (b) the ability for the mason to "see" the objects that are more than one cell away, and to understand directions in terms of them. Then it could understand "Walk towards the tree." If done in conjunction with exercise 11, then the program should be able to handle commands such as "Head towards the tree for seven steps."

    (c) an ability for the mason to plan and solve problems, so that if the user enters a command such as "Place a stone next to the tree," and the mason is not carrying a stone, it will find a way to obtain one, then find a way to walk to the tree (possibly avoiding obstacles) and finally put the stone down.

    (d) new objects with interesting properties, including objects which may be visible to the mason from within a certain distance, and invisible to the user (not displayed).

14. Augment the program LINNEUS of Chapter 4 with a natural-language front end based upon an augmented transition network. The goal of this project should be to enlarge the number of sentence forms that can be handled by the program.

15. Add a natural-language front end to the probabilistic inference-net program of Chapter 7. The interface should allow the user to present input probabilities in sentences such as the following: "THE DECOR VALUE IS 0.88". The user should be able to ask questions about the structure of the network and the probability values in the network. Examples include these: "WHAT IS THE CURRENT PROBABILITY FOR POPU-LARITY", "WHAT NODES ARE IMMEDIATE PREDECESSORS OF OVERALL_FOOD_QUALITY", and even "WHY IS THE CURRENT PROBABILITY OF HYGIENE HIGH".

16. Add a user interface to the PYTHAGORUS program so that the user can do the following: (a) instruct PYTHAGORUS to proceed with concept exploration for a given number of steps (agenda tasks), (b) ask questions about the concepts that have been explored so far, (c) instruct the program to assign new names to existing concepts, and (d) instruct the program to alter the "interest" values for particular concepts.

Chapter 10

Vision

10.1 Introduction

10.1.1 The Richest Sense

Intelligent beings must obtain information from their environment. Perhaps the richest of the five sensing modalities of human beings is vision. Vision is essential to reading and to normal navigation through the world around us.

The large role for vision in human intelligence is suggested by the proportion of the brain that is dedicated to seeing. The occipital cortex, where visual signals are processed, together with portions of the cerebral cortex that appear to be dedicated to vision occupy approximately one fourth of the brain's volume.

A position can be taken that is even stronger. A number of writers have suggested that all thinking is visual in nature (e.g., [Arnheim 1969]). It is worth noting that there is experimental evidence supporting the view that consciousness is based upon the activation of visual representations of experience and plans (see [Kosslyn and Schwartz 1978]).

10.1.2 A Key Area of AI

Vision has been and continues to be a key area of artificial intelligence. The development of several general AI concepts is largely the work of researchers in computer vision. Early on, for example, neural network studies centered around the "perceptron" model, and several early studies of learning were tied to machine recognition of patterns. The notion of applying constraints to solve a problem was made explicit in early work on line-drawing analysis, and the relaxation paradigm for constraint satisfaction made its AI debut in vision. The "frame" approach to knowledge representation was in large part a suggestion for solving the problem of representing contextual information for machine vision.

The information-processing aspects of vision are particularly interesting because one is concerned simultaneously with spatial, geometrical relations, and symbolic, semantic structures. As is true for AI in general, some researchers in vision seek computational models that will improve our understanding of how humans do it, while others are primarily concerned with producing systems that are useful for applications in industry, medicine, commerce, etc. Vision by machine is sometimes called computer vision, pictorial pattern recognition, picture processing, automatic image analysis, scene analysis or image understanding.

10.1.3   The Challenge of Computer Vision

It has proven difficult to construct artificial vision systems that are capable of understanding indoor or outdoor scenes at a human level. A computer system has not yet been created that can look at an image and describe the scene depicted in words such as, "There is a tall oak tree to the left of a colonial-style house, and a blue Volvo is visible in the garage on the right side of the house."

There are several reasons why vision is such a challenging kind of artificial intelligence to achieve:

1. The world is three-dimensional, and the images from which a description must be formed are only two-dimensional projections.

2. Each pixel of an image represents the interaction of many processes, and it is difficult to separate these different influences. For example, a pixel's value may depend upon the illumination of the scene, the reflective properties of a surface in the scene (including color, texture, and specularity), fog or dust in the atmosphere, geometrical and chromatic distortions in the lens of a camera, characteristics of the imaging device, and the manner in which the image is digitized. Imaging devices such as vidicons introduce high-frequency noise into the image, and this is a common source of trouble for algorithms.

3. The volume of data in a good image is very large. In order to perform a simple operation such as filtering on a 512×512 image with 8 bits/pixel, several minutes of computer time may be needed. Certain edge operators may require hours on ordinary computers. Although parallel computers are being built for computer vision, they are not yet widely available.

4. In order to interpret an image intelligently, much knowledge is needed about the objects that may appear in the scene. The representation and use of this knowledge by algorithms must be coordinated.

10.1.4   Overview

This chapter discusses the most important issues in computer vision, and it presents an introductory sample of the many techniques which have been developed to address these issues. After a brief examination of human vision, we look at where images come from and how they are represented. Then we examine elementary manipulations such as filtering, and we proceed to the extraction of meaningful structures. The processes that contribute directly to vision are diagrammed below. Information flows primarily from bottom to top.

description
segmentation
preprocessing
sensing
image formation

After examining alternative methods of edge detection and segmentation into regions, and their supporting techniques, we consider the problems of analyzing shape. Representing and determining three-dimensional structure presents its own set of problems; we discuss these problems and a few of the methods that have been suggested to overcome them. Special heuristics for handling "blocks-world" scenes were important in the development of constraint techniques in AI, and so there is a brief discussion of vertex and segment labelling in line drawings.

10.1.5　The Physiology of Human Vision

A brief overview of the human visual system gives us a useful perspective from which to begin discussing the kinds of computing structures that can understand images as complex as natural scenes. Unlike most of the brain, the visual cortex has a regular structure that has been extensively studied, and an investigation of human vision seems to be more instructive for the design of machine vision systems than a general study of the brain is for designing most other kinds of AI systems.

The human eye receives information, encoded as structured light, from the environment. In most cases, the light is reflected by surfaces comprising a scene, and a two-dimensional projection of the scene is formed on the retina by the refractive components (cornea and lens) of the eye. The gross anatomy of the human eye is illustrated in Fig. 10.1a.

Intensities and/or colors of small spots of the image are sensed by rods and cones—specialized cells which produce electrical pulse trains in response to light. The rod or cone signals are gathered by long neurons called bipolar cells and transmitted to other neurons: amacrine cells and ganglion cells. The ganglion cells have axons which carry the visual signals out of the retina along the optic nerve. The electrical signals from the rods and cones are also transmitted to specialized neurons which may bias the sensitivity of adjacent rods or cones (this is probably the function of the horizontal cells). A schematic illustration of these retinal structures is given in Fig. 10.2a. An actual photograph of these retinal structures is shown in Fig. 10.2b.

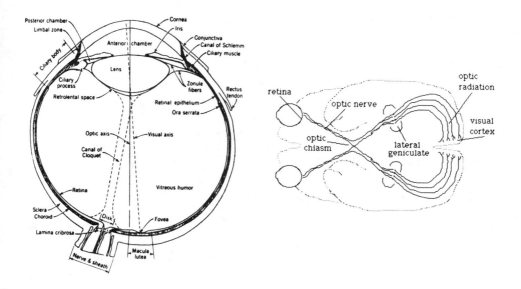

Figure 10.1: (a) The human eye (from [Polyak 1957], courtesy
of University of Chicago Press), and (b) the visual pathway.

The neurons are interconnected both in the retina and further back along the
"visual pathway" (see Fig. 10.1b) so as to detect a number of local phenomena
such as light-to-dark edges (in particular orientations), bars, spots, and changes
of intensity with time. After the optic nerves leave the eyes they cross at the
optic chiasm, where each splits and combines with the other. In this way, each
side of the brain gets signals from both eyes. The lateral geniculate body is
generally considered to be a relay station for visual signals, without significant
information-processing function.

The brain region called "area 17" is known to be responsible for a great deal
of the analysis of edges and contours required for perception. Experiments by
Hubel and Wiesel, in which electrodes were implanted into the visual cortex
of the cat, showed that there indeed exist neurons which fire only when very
specialized patterns (such as a dark vertical bar on a light background in a
certain position) are displayed in the cat's visual field. (These results helped
to encourage the development of computer image-processing operations such as
edge detectors.)

An interesting physical feature of the human retina is worth noting: the
retina is structured to have non-uniform resolution of detail; the region of highest
resolution is the *area centralis* or "fovea." Here the density of cone receptors is

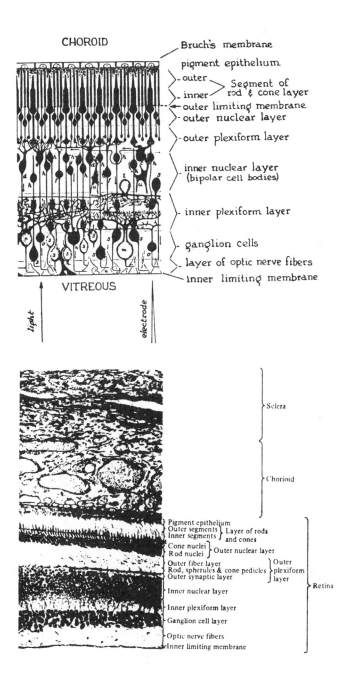

Figure 10.2: Cross section of neural material in the human retina: (a) schematic diagram, and (b) photograph (from [Polyak 1957], courtesy of University of Chicago Press).

roughly 150,000 per square millimeter. As the angle between the line of sight and the portion of the visual field of interest increases, the density of receptors drops significantly. This is illustrated in Fig. 10.3. This "multi-resolution" aspect of human vision finds a parallel in contemporary research in machine vision. The "pyramid" structures of section 10.2.11 is a manifestation of this.

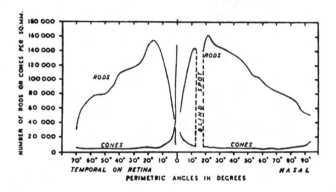

Figure 10.3: The density of rods and cones on the retina as a function of the angle from the visual axis (after [Pirenne 1967]).

10.1.6   Visual Illusions

In order to understand how a vision system works, it helps to be aware of its limitations. Visual illusions are important in the theory of human vision, because a theory is usually evaluated according to whether it is consistent or inconsistent with known facts and observations; visual illusions give us facts about errors that the human vision system makes.

Geometric illusions are a class of perceptions involving line drawings in which angles, lengths, colinearity and straightness do not appear as they really are. Some well-known examples are shown in Fig. 10.4a-d. These illusions suggest that spatial context and the organization of forms in a scene strongly influence human perception of these basic geometric characteristics.

Another class of illusions, the "subjective contour" illusions, illustrates how contextual forms can create the impression of edges or contours and foreground objects on a background. The "sun illusion," evoked by the drawing in Fig. 10.4e, is that there seems to be a disk in the center of the spokes that is brighter than the background. One has to work fairly hard not to see a contour surrounding this disk. This vivid illustration of the human propensity to perceive contours helps one understand why a large part of the research in machine vision has been directed to edge-finding algorithms. Closely related to the sun illusion is the perception of a triangle in Fig. 10.4f. The triangle is also perceived as being

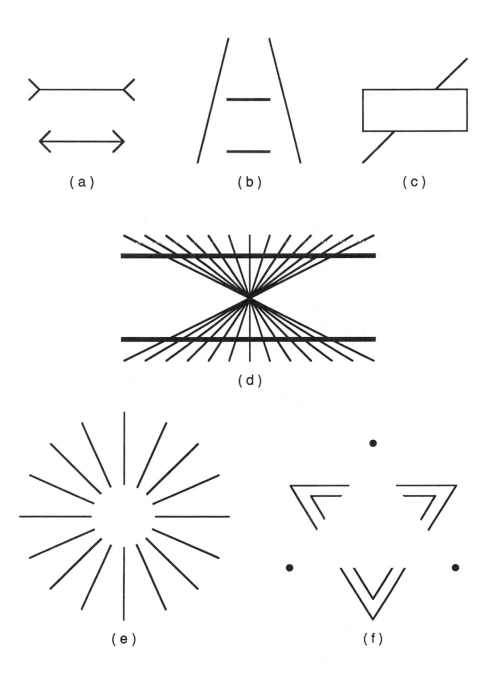

Figure 10.4: Visual illusions: (a) Mueller-Lyer, (b) Ponzo, (c) Poggendorff, (d) Zoellner, (e) "sun," and (f) triangular subjective contour.

brighter than its background.

A rather different sort of illusion is that elicited by Fig. 10.5. This is known as the Herman grid illusion. The spots that are perceived at the grid intersections can be partly explained by a theory of vision that employs a spatial-frequency model. Patterns that give rise to visual illusions in humans have been used as input to image-processing algorithms in attempts to test theories of vision, often with interesting results [Levine 1985].

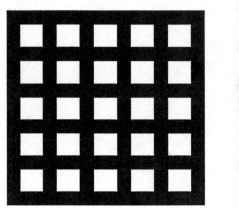 

Figure 10.5: The Herman grid illusion. Light spots are seen at the intersections of the dark lines, and dark spots are seen at the crossings of the white lines.

10.2   Image Formation and Acquisition

10.2.1   The Variety of Image Sources

Vision is a process of deriving an understanding of situations from their representations in images. In order to have a good understanding of vision, we first must understand what information is carried by an image and how the image has come to be a representation for a scene or situation. Images are formed through processes that are either physical, computational, or both.

Typically, images are the result of focussing light from a scene onto an image plane. Some images are produced by computer graphics systems. Some are produced by artists who employ both the information-processing capacities of their own brains and physical tools such as paintbrushes, pigments and canvasses. The kinds of image-formation processes that are most relevant to computer vision include not only optical focussing of light but also medical-imaging methods such as fluoroscopy, computerized axial tomography (CAT scanning), positron-emission tomography (PET scanning), ultrasound scanning, and magnetic-resonance imaging (MRI, sometimes called nuclear-magnetic resonance or NMR). Other imaging methods are also of importance in machine perception and vision. Pressure-sensitive "tactile arrays" allow a kind of spatial perception without light. Computer graphics and typesetting produce images that may contain arbitrary sorts of information, and specialized algorithms may be needed to analyze such images.

Remote-sensing processes such as LANDSAT satellite sensing record imagery that is formed optically. Images or ordinary indoor or outdoor scenes are formed by optical processes in our three-dimensional environment, and they are of particular importance for human and robot vision. Because of the large role played by this last kind of image-formation, we describe such processes in some detail below.

10.2.2 Scenes of Three-Dimensional Surfaces

Although images are formed by a wide variety of physical and computational processes, we can usefully describe image formation for a large class of scenes by one fairly simple model. (This model can be generalized to handle more physical factors.) The model we present involves the following entities situated in a three-dimensional space: a viewer, a surface (possibly curved), and a distant light source. These entities are diagrammed in Fig. 10.6.

The light source is assumed to be sufficiently far away from the surface and sufficiently small that the rays reaching the surface are practically parallel, and the intensity of light coming from the source is assumed to be uniform with respect to position. The surface is assumed to be "matte"—that is, to reflect incoming light so as to scatter it in all directions. Let us assume even more: that the surface is "Lambertian"—that the surface appears equally bright from any viewing angle on the same side of the surface as the light source.

The intensity of light that is reflected by the surface to the viewer in a small area dA depends upon several factors. The principal factors are these:

1. the intensity of the illumination, L, known as the *irradiance*,

2. the orientation θ_L of the surface at dA with respect to the direction of illumination. θ_L is the angle between the incoming rays of illumination and the surface normal at dA,

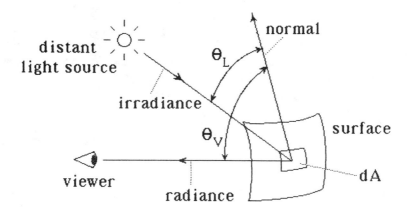

Figure 10.6: The light reflected from a small section of a surface.

3. the orientation θ_V of the surface at dA with respect to the viewer,

4. the solid angle σ (subtended by the viewer's optical system), whose vertex is a point in dA,

5. the reflectivity r of the surface, and

6. the size of the surface component, i.e., dA.

The solid angle σ is measured in *steradians*. One steradian is the amount of solid angle subtended at the center of a sphere of radius one unit by an area of one square unit on the surface of the sphere.

The amount of light that falls on the area dA is $L \cos \theta_L dA$. The amount of light reflected by the area dA in a particular direction does not depend on the directions, since the surface is assumed to be Lambertian. This amount of light, called the *radiance*, is usually measured in units of intensity of light per steradian, since the light may be considered to be radiating through a hemisphere from its center point in dA. The radiance R is given by

$$R = \frac{L \cos \theta_L dA r}{2\pi}$$

Thus the radiance is equal to the amount of light falling on the surface element (dA) times the reflectivity of the surface, divided by 2π, the number of steradians subtended by a hemisphere.

Finally, we can compute the amount of light reflected from dA to the viewer as

$$V = \sigma R = \frac{\sigma L \cos \theta_L dA r}{2\pi}$$

This model of the image formation process makes some strong assumptions, but it can provide a starting point for developing more sophisticated models.

With the use of more elaborate physics and mathematics, it can be extended to handle such attributes as

1. specular (i.e., non-Lambertian) surfaces,

2. wavelength-dependent illumination and reflectivity, and

3. diffuse light sources.

The image formation process is considerably more complicated if such phenomena as clouds, haze, translucent surfaces and secondary light sources (light reflected from surface serving to illuminate another) are taken into account.

10.2.3 Image Acquisition

Where humans and many of their animal relatives have retinal surfaces of minute light receptors to translate patterns of light into patterns of electricity, machines may also have surfaces covered with sensors. The solid-state CCD (charge-coupled device) cameras are examples of devices that have such sensitivity to light.

More economical sensors may be constructed by having not an array of sensors, but one sensor that is "multiplexed": scanned back and forth, up and down, through the visual field to cover all of the parts of the scene one may be interested in. In fact there exists an animal (a one-celled swimming creature, the female Copilia quadrata), that apparently has a scanning eye that moves rapidly across the visual field to obtain an impression of its surroundings (see [Gregory 1974]: Chapter 32: "The curious eye of Copilia," pp390-394).

An ordinary television camera is an example of a system that uses a scanning approach to image sensing. In this case, the optics are fixed and do not move with the scan, but an electron beam scans a stable image that is focussed onto a surface.

10.2.4 The Vidicon

The device most commonly used to transform optical images into electrical signals is the vidicon tube. Home video systems typically use the vidicon, and many computer vision systems work with it, as well. How a vidicon does its job is briefly described below.

An optical system is used to focus an image on the face of the vidicon which has a photoconductive surface. An electron gun in the tube is deflected either electrostatically or magnetically to scan the image. Since the resistance of the photoconductive surface is reduced wherever there is an increase of intensity in the image, the net current through the photoconductive surface varies according to the scanned image position. This continuously varying current is easily converted into a varying voltage, and the resulting signal is typically combined with scan-synchronization pulses and is output as a video signal.

An analog-to-digital converter (A/D converter) may then be used with sampling circuitry to convert the video signal into a series of integer values suitable for computer processing.

A typical commercial video digitizer allows a vidicon television camera to be plugged into its video input port, and it accepts commands from the computer in a form such as DIGITIZE X Y, where X and Y are to be in the range 0 to 511.

Digitizing systems that cost under US$2000 typically require 1/30 of a second to capture a 512 by 512 image from the video source.

The vidicon, while relatively inexpensive, has some disadvantages. The signal from a vidicon contains a large component of high-frequency noise; this noise can be partially filtered out, but often presents problems in image analysis. The vidicon is more vulnerable to geometric distortion of the image than some other devices such as the CCD array (described below); any abnormal fluctuation in the scanning circuitry usually causes a distortion in the scan pattern, and hence, in the image. Thirdly, a vidicon tube, like most vacuum tubes, is fragile and easily broken by vibration or shock.

10.2.5   Solid-State Image Devices

Most of the problems with vidicon tubes are overcome by using solid-state arrays of sensing elements. These arrays are highly durable, compact and not subject to geometrical distortions. Although the dynamic range (from dark to light) of solid-state devices has been relatively poor, the gray-scale capabilities of these devices has been improving. With rapid advances in integrated-circuit technology, solid-state imaging devices are also attaining higher resolution, and they are more likely to be manufactured in large batches at low per-unit costs.

The solid-state imaging device in widest use at present is the charge-coupled device array (CCD array). In a CCD system, a chip contains an array of zones each capable of storing a charge. After an initial charging, the charge begins to leak off at each zone roughly in proportion to the number of photons falling onto the zone. After a brief period of time, the charges remaining represent the image focussed on the array. Then, the charges are shifted out of the array through a coupling arrangement between zones, and the charge magnitudes are converted into a signal of varying voltages.

There are many variations of this solid-state imaging array. Some chips employ separate arrays for sensing and for buffering the image, so that the captured image is not degraded during the shifting time by the continued influence of photons. One can sometimes use a linear CCD array rather than a 2-D array to capture an image by scanning the array across the visual field, or by holding it fixed while the imaged object passes by on a conveyor belt. Today there is a trend toward integrating some processing logic with the sensing array all on the same chip; a possible use for such logic is to enhance the image through filtering or to compress it with a technique such as run-length coding.

It appears likely that solid-state imaging devices will eventually dominate the world of image acquisition just as the transistor has supplanted the triode vacuum tube for most uses.

10.2.6 Rangefinders

Particularly important in industrial robotics applications are devices which obtain a "depth map." Such devices are called rangefinders. In order to get a depth value for each pixel in an image, a device may use a number of possible methods. The "time-of-flight" method (with light or sound) involves measuring the time it takes for a pulse of light emitted by a laser or a front of sound waves to travel to and back from the object. Some popular instant cameras use an acoustical method of this sort to automatically focus the lens on whatever surface is in the center of the field of view. Sound waves are difficult to focus, and it is impractical to obtain good resolution with sonic echos; however, sonic-echo devices are useful in robotics for gauging proximity. Light, on the other hand, can be focussed well, but, because it travels so rapidly in relation to the circuitry used to measure its transit time, does not give good resolution in depth unless additional measures are taken. By modulating the laser light as it is transmitted and then measuring the phase of the arriving reflected light, resolution of better than 1 cm is possible. Using such laser rangefinders, good quality depth maps may be obtained, but it typically requires minutes or hours for a full image of 512 by 512 pixels.

Some rangefinders employ a "triangulation" method involving stereo imaging and/or structured-light techniques such as projecting a pattern of stripes onto the object being imaged. By illuminating only a single spot or line on the surface of an object at one time, a camera, viewing the object along a different axis from the illumination axis, records the spot or line either displaced or distorted, so that the depth of the surface at the spot or along the line can be readily calculated.

A third type of rangefinder uses the inverse-square law governing the fall-off of light intensity with distance from an object. In this method, the objects to be sensed are illuminated first by a lamp which is near the camera, and then by a camera farther away. By examining the degree to which the light intensity at a point changes, an estimate of the depth at that point can be computed. An inverse-square-law rangefinder is relatively inexpensive, but is not as accurate as a laser rangefinder, and it does not work well with specular surfaces or darkly-colored objects.

Rangefinders are generally "active sensing" systems because the operation of the device involves dynamically projecting light or sound on the objects to be sensed. It is not usually necessary to use an active sensor to obtain depth information; humans use passive means—binocular stereo, textural gradients, shading cues, etc. However, rangefinders can make the job of getting a depth map much easier than it would be using computational stereo, depth-from-texture, or other methods.

10.2.7   Sampling

If we try to express a scene as a two-dimensional matrix of numbers, we are faced
with the problem of deciding how big an array to use. For example, we might
try taking a sheet of graph paper having 100 rows and 80 columns, and place a
number in each box to represent a little square region of the scene. With each
number standing for a shade of gray, we could then reconstruct the picture by
coloring each square of the graph paper with the corresponding shade of gray.
If the resulting reconstruction looked like a good rendering of the original scene,
we would agree that the sampling rate was adequate. The term "sampling rate"
in computer imaging normally refers to the number of samples per unit area in
a picture. It is sometimes used to mean the number of samples per unit of angle
in the visual field, or just the total number of samples in a digital image. These
uses of the term are not the same but share an underlying common notion of
degree of detail.

A typical digital image for use in computer vision has 128 rows and 128
columns and allocates one byte of storage to each sample. Such an image therefore requires 16K bytes of memory or disk space. This size of image is popular
because it is often a practical compromise between the following considerations:

1. image fidelity: The higher the sampling rate (or spatial resolution), the
   more details can be represented in the image, the sharper the object edges
   can be, and the finer the textures that can be represented.

2. processing time: The lower the sampling rate, the fewer picture elements
   there are to process and the faster can a single image be processed.

3. memory requirements: The lower the sampling rate, the less memory is
   required to store the image. This can be particularly important when
   many versions of each image need to stored simultaneously.

4. cost of image acquisition equipment: The higher the sampling rate, the
   more expensive the cameras or digitizers usually are.

10.2.8   Aliasing

It is important to understand the relationship between the sampling rate and
the fidelity of the resulting representation. Although an image is a two-
dimensional signal, let us consider, for the sake of simplicity, the sampling of
a one-dimensional signal. If we have a slowly varying signal $y = f_1(x)$ as shown
in Fig. 10.7a, then the samples shown do a reasonably good job of representing
the signal. That is, it is quite apparent from the samples that the function
gradually rises and then falls. Now consider $f_2(x)$, shown in Fig. 10.7b. It os-
cillates at a higher frequency. The samples shown manage to capture one value
in each cycle of the oscillation. If we knew only about the samples, we might
conclude that the function being represented was constant. Even worse, the

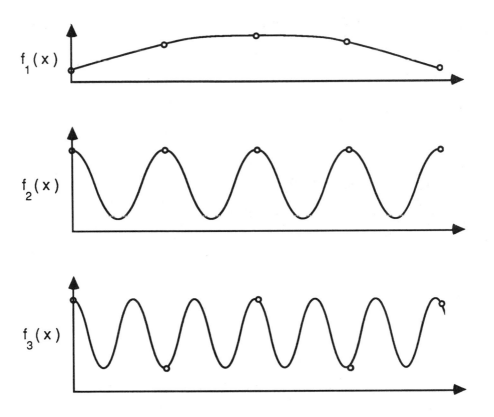

Figure 10.7: Sampling a function: (a) truthful sampling, and (b) aliasing with an apparent frequency of 0, and (c) aliasing with an apparent frequency of one-third of the original.

function $f_3(x)$ shown in Fig. 10.7c, which is oscillating 50% faster than f_2, gives a sampled signal that appears to oscillate at a frequency 50% slower than that of f_2 and only 1/3 that of f_3. This mapping of high frequencies into lower ones as a result of sampling is termed "aliasing."

It was proved by Shannon that in order to avoid aliasing of a particular frequency, it is necessary to sample the function with at least two samples per cycle. In other words, the sampling frequency must be at least twice the frequency of the highest-frequency component of the signal to be sampled.

Because aliasing is an undesirable effect that can lead to misinterpretation of images, it is important to assess the oscillations in an image to be sampled, and make sure either that the sampling rate is high enough to avoid aliasing or that the high-frequency components of the image are filtered out prior to sampling.

Each zone of the image that is represented by a single sample value is called a pixel. We also refer to the sample itself as a *pixel.*

10.2.9   Non-Rectangular Pixels

The numbers describing intensities or colors in an image need not be organized as a matrix of squares as on graph paper. The arrangement could be one of many little triangles. It could even be one of hexagons. In fact, it need not be a regular tessellation at all. For example, the printed guide sheets in a paint-by numbers set have regions of very irregular shapes and sizes. These arrangements, however, are not very general: a new one is needed for each picture, whereas the regular arrangements can suit a wide variety of pictures. It is easy to find examples of digital pictures in everyday life: cross-stitch samplers are digital pictures, and mosaic-tile murals are, also.

10.2.10   Quantization

"Quantization" describes the manner in which numbers are used to represent the intensities or colors at each sample point (or in each sample region). A very simple quantization scheme is to allow only two levels of intensity: black and white. This makes the representation very simple and compact: a single bit can represent each pixel. Such a method has the limitation that subtle differences among shades of grey in a scene are lost in the digital representation. A more general quantization scheme is to perform an analog-to-digital conversion for each pixel, to obtain a more accurate measure of its intensity. Typically, eight or sixteen bit values are used for this purpose.

The mapping of a continuous gray-scale into a finite number of values is usually done by the analog-to-digital converter hardware in a roughly linear fashion. Each continuous interval of input values which are mapped to a common output value is approximately equal in length to the other intervals.

10.2.11   Pyramids

When an image contains a variety of structures or objects in it, it may be useful to create several digitizations of it at different sampling rates. If the sampling rate (along a side) is doubled each time starting with the minimum resolution of 1 pixel for the whole image, the resulting collection of images is called a *pyramid.* A typical pyramid contains images of dimensions 1×1, 2×2, 4×4, 8×8, ..., 512×512.

A pyramid can just as easily be constructed from a digital image of dimensions, say, 512×512. First, the 256×256 level is constructed from the 512×512 original by taking 2×2 blocks of original pixels and creating a new pixel containing their average value. After continuing this process to the limit, a 1×1

image is constructed whose single pixel's value is the average value of the entire original picture.

Figure 10.8 illustrates a pyramidal representation for a picture of some human chromosomes taken with a microscope. Multi-resolution image-processing methods often operate on pyramid data structures.

10.3 Preprocessing

10.3.1 Low-Pass Filtering

Images can be economically digitized using a video camera together with an apparatus for sampling and holding the video output at a measured time point in the scan, and an analog-to-digital converter. However, as with most methods for image digitization, the results are "noisy." A noticeable amount of "snow" has been added into the image. This noise is a byproduct of the physical process of converting patterns of light energy into electrical patterns.

Noise wreaks havoc with many a computer algorithm for analyzing images. Therefore, an important step is eliminating or reducing the noise in an image prior to its analysis. When the scene to be analyzed is static, it may be possible to capture several similar images and average them together to form a single one in which the effects of noise are reduced. However, either because the objects in the scene are moving or for reason of time, or other constraint, it is often not possible to solve the problem of noise by averaging several images. Then, spatial filtering on the one image is appropriate.

10.3.2 The Two-Dimensional Discrete Fourier Transform

A form of the Fourier transform often is used as the basis for image filtering. The two-dimensional discrete Fourier transform (2DDFT) is an invertible mapping from an image to an equal-sized array of complex numbers that represent the amplitudes and phases of the spatial frequency components of the image. The 2DDFT, $F[u,v]$ of an N by N image $f(x,y)$ is defined by

$$F[u,v] = \frac{1}{N} \sum_{x=0}^{N-1} \sum_{y=0}^{N-1} f(x,y)e^{-2\pi i(ux+vy)/N}$$

where $i = \sqrt{-1}$. While u and v are typically taken in the range 0 to $N-1$ with the origin thus positioned at the lower left of the transform array, one may also set the range for u and v so as to position the origin in the center. The component $F[0,0]$ represents the zero frequency or constant component of the image, and it is sometimes called the "DC" (direct current) component. As the point (u,v) moves away from the origin, the spatial frequencies represented by $F[u,v]$ increase.

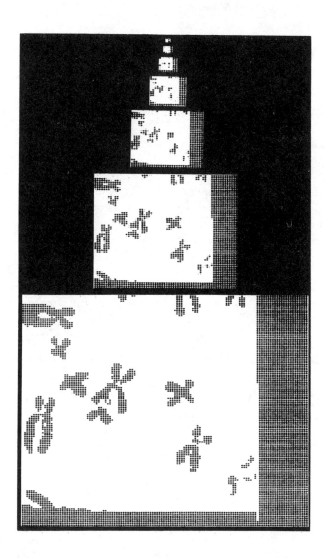

Figure 10.8: An image of human chromosomes represented as a pyramid.

Low-pass filtering of an image may be effected by setting the high-frequency components of the 2DDFT of the image to zero and then inverting the transformation by again applying the 2DDFT, but with a slight modification. The inverse 2DDFT is defined by

$$f(x,y) = \sum_{u=0}^{N-1} \sum_{v=0}^{N-1} F[u,v] e^{2\pi i (ux + vy)/N}$$

The 2DDFT (or the inverse 2DDFT) can be computed rapidly using the Fast Fourier Transform (FFT) algorithm. The FFT is applied to each of the rows of the image producing a partially transformed array $F[u,y]$, and then the FFT is applied to each of the columns of $F[u,y]$ to produce the 2DDFT $F[u,v]$.

10.3.3 Moving-Average and Median Filtering

The technique most often used for noise reduction is low-pass filtering. This is typically done by producing from the original $A[i,j]$ a new picture array $B[i,j]$ for which each element $b[i,j]$ is a weighted sum of values $a[i+p, j+q]$, $p = -2$ to 2, $q = -2$ to 2, where the weights are all positive and the highest weight is on the term where $p = q = 0$. In one dimension, this technique is called a moving average filter. In two dimensions, it is sometimes referred to as a neighborhood averaging filter.

An interesting filtering method which is based upon sorting rather than averaging defines $b[i,j]$ to be the median over the neighborhood of values around $a[i,j]$. Median filtering has the advantage that it tends to preserve the edges in a digital picture without smearing them. It always assigns to $b[i,j]$ one of the actual values from the original picture, rather than some fractional, in-between value that can occur with averaging.

10.3.4 Histograms and Thresholding

One way to judge the effectiveness of a picture digitization is to examine its histogram of pixel values. Like film exposure in photography, it is easy to under or over-expose digital pictures. It is easy to tell from a histogram whether there is a predominance of light pixels, or of black pixels, or whether the distribution is well balanced. The histogram may be described by

$$H[k] = \text{number of occurrences of value } k \text{ in } A[i,j].$$

A common technique in image analysis is to transform a gray-value picture (one representing each pixel value by several bits) to a binary (black/white) one by automatically choosing a threshold and then mapping all pixel values below the threshold to 0 and all others to 1. The selection of the threshold can often be done using the "valley" method, whereby the computer searches for two peaks in the histogram: one presumably corresponding to the pixels of the background and the other containing the pixel values from the object of interest. The valley is the minimum histogram value between the two peaks. Thresholding with the corresponding value of k often has the effect of segmenting the image into a single "object" region and a single "background" region. Image thresholding is an important operation in many machine-vision algorithms. It provides the simplest method for segmenting an image into groups of pixels according to their values.

10.4   Connectedness and Cellular Logic

10.4.1   Pixel Adjacency

The result of thresholding is a binary image—that is, an image whose pixels take on values of 0 or 1. It is usual to interpret pixels having value 1 as belonging to the objects of interest or the "figure" (sometimes called the foreground) and to interpret pixels having value 0 as belonging to the background ("ground").

Any pair of pixels that share an edge (i.e., side) is said to be *edge-adjacent* or "4-adjacent." (Note, however, that a pixel is not considered to be adjacent to itself.) A pixel in the interior of an image has four edge-adjacent neighbors. If a pair of pixels shares a vertex, they are said to be *vertex-adjacent* or "8-adjacent." The *4-neighborhood* of a pixel is the set of pixels that are 4-adjacent to it, plus the pixel itself. Thus there are generally five pixels in a 4-neighborhood. Only a pixel on the border of an image but not in a corner has a 4-neighborhood of four pixels; a pixel at the corner of an image has a 4-neighborhood of only three pixels. The *8-neighborhood* of a pixel consists of up to eight pixels which are vertex-adjacent to it, together with the pixel itself. The standard 4-neighborhood and 8-neighborhood are illustrated in Fig. 10.9.

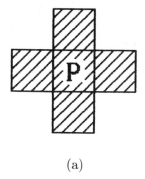

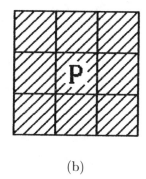

(a)   (b)

Figure 10.9: Edge-adjacent and vertex-adjacent pixels: (a) the 4-neighborhood of P, and (b) the 8-neighborhood of P.

10.4.2 Connected Sets of Pixels

A sequence of pixels $(P_1, P_2, \ldots, P_n)$ is a *4-connected sequence* if P_i is 4-adjacent to P_{i+1} for $i = 1, \ldots, n - 1$. The sequence is an *8-connected sequence* if P_i is 8-adjacent to P_{i+1}. Let S be a nonempty set of pixels (that is, a nonempty subset of the pixels of an image). S is *4-connected* iff either (1) for any two pixels A and B there exists a 4-connected sequence $(P_1, P_2, \ldots, P_n)$ of pixels in S such that $P_1 = A$ and $P_n = B$, or (2) S contains only one pixel. Similarly, S is said to be *8-connected* iff either any two pixels in S are the endpoints for some 8-connected sequence of pixels in S, or S is a singleton set.

We now define the concept of connected component. To be brief, we use the variable k in the definition so as not to have to give separate definitions for 4- and 8-connected components. A set S is a *k-connected component of the foreground* of a binary image I if the following conditions are all true:

1. S is a k-connected set of pixels;

2. the value assigned by I to each element of S is 1; and

3. there is no set S' satisfying both (1) and (2) that properly includes S.

The 4-connected components of the figure of an image are thus the maximal sets of ones that are each 4-connected. (Connected components can be defined for the background in a similar fashion.) Figure 10.10 shows a binary image that contains four 4-connected components of the foreground, two 8-connected components of the foreground and two 8-connected components of the background.

It is common for machine-vision software packages to contain a subroutine for determining the 8-connected components of the foreground of a binary image, and this is usually what is computed by a "connected-components routine."

It is interesting to note that an anomalous situation often arises when one examines the 8-connected components of both the foreground and the background. Intuitively, the diagonal set of ones in Fig. 10.11 divides the background into two halves. However, the background, as well as the set of ones, is considered to be a single component. In order to avoid this apparent contradiction, it is customary to compute 8-connected components only for the ones or foreground portion of the image, and if connected components of the background are needed, to compute 4-connected components of the ground. It is also interesting that no such anomalies arise when working with pixels based upon a hexagonal tessellation of the plane, and that the meanings of edge-adjacency and vertex-adjacency are equivalent in that context.

10.4.3 An Algorithm

A simple algorithm for finding the 8-connected components of the foreground of a binary image makes use of the depth-first search strategy introduced in Chapter

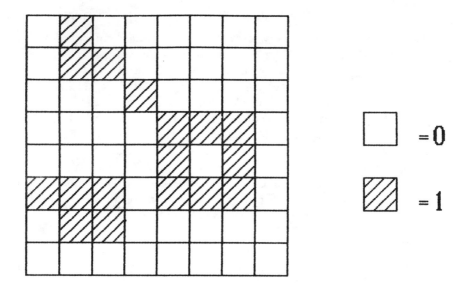

Figure 10.10: A binary image.

5. The algorithm begins by scanning the image left-to-right, top-to-bottom in search of a foreground pixel. As soon as one is found, it is used as the starting point for a depth-first search. The search identifies all the foreground pixels that can be reached from the starting pixel along 8-connected sequences of foreground pixels. Each of the pixels reached is marked as soon as it is first visited to prevent the search from getting stuck in a loop, and to allow the scanning procedure to skip over the pixels of components that have been found, when it is looking for a new starting pixel. The algorithm terminates when no new starting points can be found; that is, it stops when the scanning has passed the pixel in the lower-right corner of the image.

10.4.4   A Connected-Components Program in LISP

We now describe a LISP program that implements the algorithm just described. The input to this program is a binary image, represented as a list of lists. The output is a "components image" in which each foreground pixel has been replaced by the number of the connected component to which it belongs. The components are numbered starting from 1, in the order in which they are reached in the left-to-right, top-to-bottom scan.

The functions in this program are divided into three groups: those that manipulate the images directly (including simulating array accessing), those that define the search procedure, and functions to test the program and display the results. Let us begin by presenting the representation of the input image.

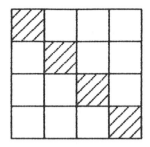

Figure 10.11: An anomaly: both the foreground and background are 8-connected.

```
; CONNECTD.LSP
; A program for connected-components labelling.

; Set up the input array:
(SETQ INPUT '(
   (0 1 0 0 0 0 0 0)
   (0 1 1 0 0 0 0 0)
   (0 0 0 1 0 0 0 0)
   (0 0 0 0 1 1 1 0)
   (0 0 0 0 1 0 1 0)
   (1 1 1 0 1 1 1 0)
   (0 1 1 0 0 0 0 0)
   (0 0 0 0 0 0 0 0) ))
```

The two functions GETVAL and STORE allow us to read and write a pixel's value in the simulated array IMAGE. (Some LISP implementations provide efficient array manipulations; GETVAL and STORE could be rewritten to take advantage of such features—or the array operations could be used in place of GETVAL and STORE.) The function GETVAL uses the function GETNTH (which was also used in the SHRINK program of Chapter 3). In order to keep our presentation of CONNECTD.LSP complete, the short definition is repeated here. Similarly, STORE calls the function REPLACENTH (also used in the STONEWLD program of Chapter 9).

```
; Array access routines:
(DEFUN GETVAL (I J) (GETNTH J (GETNTH I IMAGE)))

(DEFUN GETNTH (N LST)      ; return Nth element of LST
   (COND ((NULL LST) NIL)
```

```
          ((ZEROP N)(CAR LST)) ; (0 for first...)
          (T (GETNTH (SUB1 N) (CDR LST))) ) )

(DEFUN STORE (I J VAL)    ; store VAL at row I, column J in IMAGE.
   (SETQ IMAGE
         (REPLACENTH I
                      IMAGE
                      (REPLACENTH J (GETNTH I IMAGE) VAL) ) ) )

; Return a copy of LST where the Nth value
;    has been replaced by VAL:
(DEFUN REPLACENTH (N LST VAL)
   (COND ((NULL LST) NIL)
          ((ZEROP N)(CONS VAL (CDR LST)))
          (T (CONS (CAR LST)
                    (REPLACENTH (SUB1 N) (CDR LST) VAL) )) ) )
```

The function NEGATE, which negates all the numbers in a list structure, is used in this program to flag all the foreground (nonzero) pixels of the input image as "unvisited" before the connected-components search begins. NEGATE is defined below:

```
(DEFUN NEGATE (L)
   (COND ((NUMBERP L)(DIFFERENCE 0 L))
          ((ATOM L) L)
          (T (CONS (NEGATE (CAR L))
                    (NEGATE (CDR L)) )) ) )
```

A top-level function, CONNECTED_COMPONENTS, does nothing more than initialize the input image by "NEGATEing" it and then call SCAN to start the real work.

```
; Top-level function for finding connected components:
(DEFUN CONNECTED_COMPONENTS ()
   (PROG ()
         (SETQ IMAGE (NEGATE INPUT))
         (SCAN) ) )
```

The functions which define the search procedure are these: SCAN, DFS, and BRANCH. Their definitions are given below. The variable DIRECTIONS holds the adjacency definition desired for the formation of the connected components; each direction is represented as a displacement vector.

```
; Perform a raster-scan of the image looking for successive
;    connected components:
(DEFUN SCAN ()
```

```
(PROG (I J COUNT)
  (SETQ I 0)
  (SETQ COUNT 0)
  (DO_N_TIMES 8                      ; for each row...
    (SETQ J 0)
    (DO_N_TIMES 8                    ; for each column...
      (PRINT (LIST 'SCANNING I J))   ; show progress.
      (COND ((EQUAL (GETVAL I J)     ; is the pixel
                    -1)              ; unmarked, foreground?
             (SETQ COUNT             ; yes,
                   (ADD1 COUNT) )    ; up the count, and
             (DFS COUNT I J) ))      ; label the component.
      (SETQ J (ADD1 J)) )
    (SETQ I (ADD1 I)) ) ) )

; Depth-first search for more cells in the component:
(DEFUN DFS (COUNT I J)
  (COND ((EQUAL (GETVAL I J) -1)     ; be sure cell is foreg.
         (STORE I J COUNT)           ; label the cell, and
         (MAPCAR 'BRANCH DIRECTIONS) ); go in all DIRECTIONS.
        (T NIL) ) )                  ; don't search if cell is
                                     ; marked or background.

(SETQ DIRECTIONS                     ; 8-adjacency definition.
      '((-1 -1)(-1 0)(-1 1)(0 -1)(0 1)(1 -1)(1 0)(1 1)) )

; Attempt to continue search in direction DIR:
(DEFUN BRANCH (DIR)
  (PROG (II JJ)
        (SETQ II (PLUS I (CAR DIR))) ; determine row and col
        (SETQ JJ (PLUS J (CADR DIR))); of new cell.
        (AND (LESSP -1 II)           ; check array bounds...
             (LESSP -1 JJ)
             (LESSP II 8)
             (LESSP JJ 8)
             (DFS COUNT II JJ) ) ) ) ; OK, continue search.
```

The three search functions SCAN, DFS, and BRANCH work together. SCAN has the responsibility for finding new starting points for connected components. It marches across the image in raster-scan order. Whenever it finds a foreground pixel that has not yet been marked, it starts a new component by incrementing the count of components found and calling DFS to label the component. DFS has the job of marking the current pixel and causing the search to "fork" in all of the specified directions. It is the job of BRANCH to continue the search in each of these directions (each call to BRANCH continues the search in one of the directions). Note that DFS and BRANCH are co-recursive (each calls the other). These could have been combined into a single recursive function; however, by separating them, it is easy to use the "control fork" (MAPCAR 'BRANCH DIRECTIONS), which not only simplifies the code to effect the branching but makes it very easy to modify the set of directions in which the search is allowed to proceed.

The last two functions make it convenient to test the others. PRINT_IMAGE formats an array nicely. It assumes that each pixel only needs one character of output.

```
; Print an image array, nicely formatted:
(DEFUN PRINT_IMAGE (IMAGE)
   (COND ((NULL IMAGE) NIL)
         (T (PRINT_ROW (CAR IMAGE))
            (TERPRI)
            (PRINT_IMAGE (CDR IMAGE)) ) ) )


; Helping function for PRINT_IMAGE:
(DEFUN PRINT_ROW (ROW)
   (COND ((NULL ROW) NIL)
         (T (PRIN1 (CAR ROW))
            (TYO 32)
            (PRINT_ROW (CDR ROW)) ) ) )
```

The program is tested by the following pair of S-expressions.

```
(CONNECTED_COMPONENTS)   ; Test the program.
(PRINT_IMAGE IMAGE)      ; Display the results.
```

This program illustrates only one algorithm for labelling the connected components of a binary image. The problem is a very important one for machine vision, and apparently, a computationally challenging one even for very highly parallel computers. A class of theoretical devices for pattern recognition that were popular during the 1960's called "perceptrons" fell into disfavor when it was proved that they could not economically handle the connected-components problem [Minsky and Papert 1969]. Today, the development of algorithms and special hardware that can compute connected components efficiently on useful classes of images is an area of active research.

10.4.5 Cellular Logic and Parallel Operations

A digital image of size 512×512 has some quarter of a million pixels. Since analyzing the image at each pixel generally requires examining the neighborhood of a pixel (perhaps a 5×5 neighborhood), around 5 million value-examinations can be necessary for processing such a picture, let alone any of the arithmetic operations. These large volumes of data have prompted the design of parallel computers for machine-vision jobs.

Perhaps the most appropriate format for a parallel computer for vision is just the form of the image itself: a rectangular array of cells. For example the CLIP4[1] is a 96×96 array of simple processors, each interconnected with eight neighbors and to a central control unit. Each of these processors has its own local memory of 32 bits, each of which can be individually addressed. A program for the CLIP4 is stored only in the control unit, and there is just one program counter (in the control unit). Each instruction is read by the control unit and broadcast to all the cellular processors for simultaneous execution by each of them. Thus, for example, the controller might say, (in a manner of speaking) "clear your accumulator," and each cell would clear its accumulator. More interesting operations are those telling each cell to examine the values of its eight neighbors (edge-connected and corner-connected neighbors), and write a 1 to its own accumulator if it sees a particular pattern. Such machines also have the ability for each cellular processor to perform a one or two-input boolean function such as NOT, OR or AND on values stored in their local memories.

A one-step cellular logic operation may be specified by a boolean function of nine inputs:

$$x'_5 = F(x_1, x_2, x_3, x_4, x_5, x_6, x_7, x_8, x_9)$$

The nine inputs are the values of the 3 by 3 neighborhood centered around x_5:

$$
\begin{array}{ccc}
x_1 & x_2 & x_3 \\
x_4 & x_5 & x_6 \\
x_7 & x_8 & x_9
\end{array}
$$

For example, an operator to fill single-pixel holes is the following:

$$x'_5 = x_5 + (x_1 x_2 x_3 x_4 (-x_5) x_6 x_7 x_8 x_9)$$

Where "$x + y$" indicates boolean OR of x with y, and "$x\,y$" indicates boolean AND of x with y. This operation might be computed on a cellular array machine by reading x_1, then forming the product $x_1\ x_2$, etc. On a more powerful machine, the entire product might be computed in one step and the sum computed in a second and final step. Operations of this type can also be performed reasonably efficiently on special pipelined computers that map each neighborhood configuration into an output value using table-lookup means; such systems are commercially available from a variety of manufacturers.

By repeating one or more simple cellular-logic operations in a loop, more interesting operations may be performed. We will examine (in the section of this chapter on "shape") how various kinds of "thinning" operations may be repeated to shrink an object down to a single point or to produce a "skeleton" of the object.

---

[1]The CLIP4 (Cellular Logic Image Processor version 4) was developed at University College London during the 1970's [Duff 1978].

10.4.6   Erosion and Dilation

Two very important cellular-logic operations are "erosion" and "dilation." Actually, they may be defined for sets of points in the continuous plane as well as a cellular (discrete) space. The operations are based on the notions of intersections and unions of sets of points in the plane. Suppose A and B are sets of points in the plane. We assume $a = (x_a, y_a)$ is an arbitrary member of A and $b = (x_b, y_b)$ is an arbitrary member of B. The translation of a set C by $v = (dx, dy)$ we write $\tau_v(C)$. The erosion of A by B is the set:

$$\bigcap_{b \in B} \tau_b(A)$$

Thus, for each point of B, we make a translation of A. The intersection of all these translated versions is the erosion of A. If B consists of a single point, the result is just a translated (or perhaps untranslated, if that point is at the origin) version of A. If B contains two or more points, erosion produces a result smaller[2] than the original A. If we consider the sets of points now to be sets of pixels (i.e., those pixels in a binary image having values equal to 1), we have a notion of erosion that can be computed with cellular logic operations. Each translation can be done as a sequence of shifts in the array, and the intersections are easily computed with the AND operation on two values within each cell. Figure 10.12 illustrates the erosion of A by B where the origin is considered to be at the center of the 5 by 5 array, and elements translated from outside the array are taken as zeros.

0	0	1	0	1		0	0	0	0	0		0	0	0	0	0
1	0	0	1	0		0	0	0	0	0		0	0	0	0	0
1	0	1	1	1		0	1	1	0	0		0	0	0	1	0
1	0	1	1	1		0	0	1	0	0		0	0	1	1	0
0	0	1	1	0		0	0	0	0	0		0	0	1	0	0

Figure 10.12: Two binary images A and B, and a third: the erosion of A by B.

Dilation is the "dual" operation to erosion. The dilation of set A by set B is defined as the set:

$$\bigcup_{b \in B} \tau_b(A)$$

For example, if the set B consists of two horizontally adjacent pixels, the dilation of A by B is a set like A but one pixel wider everywhere. Any hole of width one or vertical channel of width one in A would also be filled.

---

[2]This assumes that A is a *bounded* set of points. This assumption is true for all practical examples.

```
0 0 0 0 0        0 0 0 0 0        0 0 0 0 0
1 1 0 1 0        0 0 0 0 0        1 1 1 1 0
1 0 1 0 0        0 1 1 0 0        1 1 1 1 0
1 0 1 1 0        0 0 1 0 0        1 1 1 1 0
0 0 0 0 0        0 0 0 0 0        1 0 1 1 0
```

Figure 10.13: Two binary images A and B, and a third: the dilation of A by B.

The two operations of erosion and dilation may be combined to produce other operations. Two such other operations are "closure" and "opening." The closure of A by B consists of the dilation of A by B, then eroded by $R(B)$, where $R(X)$ is X rotated by 180 degrees. If B consists of the "ell" image, closure of A by B has the effect of filling small holes and channels in A. However, at the edges of the array, there may be a loss of ones as a result of the convention that data outside the bounds of the array are taken as 0.

```
0 0 0 1 1        0 0 0 0 0        0 0 1 1 1
1 1 0 1 0        0 0 0 0 0        0 1 1 1 0
1 0 1 0 0        0 1 1 0 0        0 1 1 1 0
1 0 1 1 1        0 0 1 0 0        0 0 1 1 1
0 0 0 0 0        0 0 0 0 0        0 0 0 0 0
```

Figure 10.14: A, B, and the closure of A by B.

Similarly, the opening of A by B is defined to be A eroded by B, then dilated by $R(B)$. Opening has the effect of eliminating small, isolated fragments of A, or parts of A that are narrow or riddled with holes. Figure 10.15 shows an example.

```
0 0 1 0 1        0 0 0 0 0        0 0 0 0 0
1 0 0 1 0        0 0 0 0 0        0 0 0 1 0
1 0 1 1 1        0 1 1 0 0        0 0 1 1 1
1 0 1 1 1        0 0 1 0 0        0 0 1 1 1
0 0 1 1 0        0 0 0 0 0        0 0 1 1 0
```

Figure 10.15: The opening of A by B.

The analysis of shapes of two-dimensional objects using operations such as erosion, dilation, opening and closing is sometimes called *mathematical morphology*, and it has found numerous applications in industrial machine vision.

10.5   Edges and Lines

In order to compute the shape of an object in a picture, one must usually derive a representation of its boundary. The points in the image where the boundaries lie are generally places where the intensity changes abruptly. Various techniques have been developed to locate such places. These techniques usually involve the computation of a function of a neighborhood of values, such that the function yields a high value when there is a large change of intensity across the neighborhood (say, from left to right). Such methods are called "edge-detection" methods. Let us now examine several of them.

10.5.1   Local Differencing Methods

Let the original image be $A[i,j]$, and let the edge image (to be defined) be $E[i,j]$. Then Roberts' "cross operator" is:

$$E[i,j] = \sqrt{(A[i,j] - A[i+1,j+1])^2 + (A[i,j+1] - A[i+1,j])^2}$$

A more computationally-efficient edge operator is the "Absolute value of crossed differences" operator:

$$E[i,j] = |A[i,j] - A[i+1,j+1]| + |A[i,j+1] - A[i+1,j]|$$

Another variation is the following, which reorients the cross into a "plus:"

$$E[i,j] = |A[i,j-1] - A[i,j+1]| + |A[i-1,j] - A[i+1,j]|$$

Commonly used for edge detection is an approximate-gradient operator sometimes called the Sobel-edge operator:

$$E[x,y] = \sqrt{[(c + 2f + i) - (a + 2d + g)]^2 + [(g + 2h + i) - (a + 2b + c)]^2}$$

where a through i are the pixel values in a 3×3 neighborhood centered at (x,y) as follows:

a	b	c
d	e	f
g	h	i

Often, surprisingly good results may be obtained with a very simple edge detector for vertical (or similarly, horizontal) edges:

$$E[i,j] = A[i,j] - A[i,j+1].$$

Here, very negative results indicate a low-to-high-intensity edge and very positive results indicate a high-to-low-intensity edge. Thresholding the absolute value of this $E[i,j]$ gives a binary-image representation of the vertical-edge pixels in an image.

10.5.2   Compass Gradients

Operators based on 3×3 neighborhoods have been developed by Sobel (defined above), Kirsch, and Prewitt. One family of 3 by 3 edge operators is called "compass gradients." An operator in this family is computed by applying eight masks, one representing each of eight directions (North, Northeast, East, Southeast, South, Southwest, West, and Northwest). The mask returning the highest value indicates the direction of the edge, and this maximum value indicates the strength of the edge.

Two of the eight masks used for the Kirsch operator are shown below.

5	5	5
−3	0	−3
−3	−3	−3

5	5	−3
5	0	−3
−3	−3	−3

Two of the eight masks for one of several operators due to Prewitt are shown below.

1	1	1
1	−2	1
−1	−1	−1

1	1	1
1	−2	−1
1	−1	−1

10.5.3   A Vector-Space Approach

An interesting technique for edge detection is the Frei-Chen operator. In this method we consider each 3×3 neighborhood to be a vector in a 9-dimensional vector space. A linear transformation is applied to vectors in this space, to express them in terms of a special "feature basis." Each basis vector for the feature basis may also be expressed as a 3×3 array of values. The nine basis vectors may be arranged in three groups. The first group contains four vectors and defines the "edge subspace." The second group also contains four vectors and it defines the "line subspace." The third group consists of a single vector, and represents the "average subspace." The basis vectors are as shown in Fig. 10.16.

The intensity of an edge is computed as the square root of the sum of the squares of the projections of a neighborhood vector onto each of the four basis vectors of the edge subspace. Similarly, the line intensity is computed by projecting onto the line subspace and taking a root of sum of squares. This approach yields reasonably good results and has a formulation that is mathematically pleasing.

10.5.4   Heuristic Search for Object Boundaries

One way to avoid the problem of linking the disconnected edges usually obtained with edge-detection transformations is to trace edges directly in the image.

$$
\text{edge subspace} \left\{
\begin{array}{ccc}
1 & \sqrt{2} & 1 \\
0 & 0 & 0 \\
-1 & -\sqrt{2} & -1 \\[4pt]
0 & -1 & \sqrt{2} \\
1 & 0 & -1 \\
-\sqrt{2} & 1 & 0
\end{array}
\right.
\qquad
\begin{array}{ccc}
1 & 0 & -1 \\
\sqrt{2} & 0 & -\sqrt{2} \\
1 & 0 & -1 \\[4pt]
\sqrt{2} & -1 & 0 \\
-1 & 0 & 1 \\
0 & 1 & -\sqrt{2}
\end{array}
$$

$$
\text{line subspace} \left\{
\begin{array}{ccc}
0 & 1 & 0 \\
-1 & 0 & -1 \\
0 & 1 & 0 \\[4pt]
1 & -2 & 1 \\
-2 & 4 & -2 \\
1 & -2 & 1
\end{array}
\right.
\qquad
\begin{array}{ccc}
-1 & 0 & -1 \\
0 & 0 & 0 \\
-1 & 0 & -1 \\[4pt]
-2 & 1 & -2 \\
1 & 4 & 1 \\
-2 & 1 & -2
\end{array}
$$

$$
\text{average subspace} \left\{
\begin{array}{ccc}
1 & 1 & 1 \\
1 & 1 & 1 \\
1 & 1 & 1
\end{array}
\right.
$$

Figure 10.16: Frei and Chen basis for local neighborhood analysis.

An interesting method for contour tracing uses the heuristic-search approach of Chapter 5. A starting location in the image may be found by scanning the image with a simple edge detector such as a horizontal difference of two adjacent pixels, until a pair of pixels is found that is very likely to lie on an edge. The edge between these two pixels is vertically situated, and the initial direction for search may be chosen arbitrarily as upward (north). From that location on, the contour is extended by one edge element at a time by heuristically searching for the completion of the contour. With such a scheme, a good contour corresponds with an optimal or nearly optimal path through a state-space graph. The cost of a contour can be defined to ignore length, decrease as the average contrast across the contour increases, and decrease as the contour becomes relatively smooth. Figure 10.17 illustrates the choices for the second edge element in tracing a contour by such a means. The starting element is the segment between pixels P_4 and P_5, written (P_4, P_5). The contour may be extended taking either (P_4, P_1),

P_1	P_2	P_3
P_4	P_5	P_6
P_7	P_8	P_9

Figure 10.17: Contour tracing between pixels with heuristic search.

(P_1, P_2), or (P_2, P_5) as the next segment. One heuristic evaluation function which may be used is the following

$$C(\gamma) = \frac{w_1}{n} \sum_{i=1}^{n} \frac{1}{1 + |\alpha_i|} + \frac{w_2}{n - d + 1} \sum_{i=1}^{n-d+1} |\kappa_i|$$

where C gives the cost of path γ; n is the length of the path; w_1 and w_2 are weighting factors; the local contrast α_i is given by $V(P_{i_1}) - V(P_{i_2})$ where P_{i_1} and P_{i_2} are the pixels to the left and right, respectively, of the ith edge element in the path, and V gives the value of a pixel; and κ_i is the local curvature at the ith edge element.

The local curvature may be defined using a table-lookup scheme where a small number d of edge elements are examined, and the pattern of their relative directions determines what the local curvature value is. For $d = 3$ there are five possible relative configurations, after symmetry has been taken into account. These five patterns and their curvature values by one (albeit an arbitrary) assignment is shown in Fig. 10.18. Thus κ_i, the local curvature at the ith edge element, may be computed by examining the ith, $i + 1^{th}$, and $i + 2^{th}$ edge elements. The table of curvature values here takes only two angles into account at a time. If larger tables are used, considering three or more angles at a time, a greater degree of control can be attained.

The weighting factors w_1 and w_2 can be adjusted to regulate the relative influence of the contrast and the curvature. As with any edge-detection method, the success of this approach depends upon the quality of the edges present in the image. However, the method constructs contours that are connected, and it gets around the edge-linking necessary with other methods.

10.5.5 Gaussians, Laplacians and Zero Crossings

One approach to edge detection has gained influence among those who seek a computational model of human vision. This approach uses three steps, each of which has intuitive justification. First, the image is filtered with a two-dimensional "Gaussian filter" to reduce the effects of noise in the image. Next, a two-dimensional second derivative of the filtered image is computed. Thirdly,

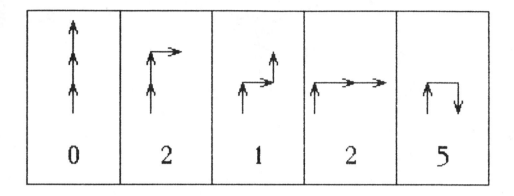

Figure 10.18: An assignment of curvature values to sequences of length 3.

the zero crossings of the second-derivative image are located and marked as edge elements. Let us discuss each of these steps in more detail.

The Gaussian function (sometimes called a "normal distribution") for a given pair of parameters μ and σ is defined as follows:

$$f_{\mu,\sigma} = e^{-(\mu-x)^2/\sigma^2}$$

The general shape of the Gaussian is that of a bell with sides asymptotically approaching zero as x goes toward plus and minus infinity. The parameter μ specifies the location of the center of the bell while σ controls how wide the bell appears. The Gaussian is desirable as a weighting curve in filtering because it clearly gives maximum weight to the signal point at $x = \mu$, and the weights for surrounding points taper off in either direction.

In two dimensions we can define a Gaussian *surface* analogous to $f_{\mu,\sigma}$ as

$$G_{\mu,\nu,\sigma}(x,y) = e^{-[(\mu-x)^2+(\nu-y)^2]\sigma^2}.$$

However, we usually have $\mu = \nu = 0$, and with the subscript σ understood, we use the simpler definition, $G(x,y) = e^{-(x^2+y^2)/\sigma^2}$.

In a discrete space, a Gaussian can be represented as an infinite array of samples. There is a computational disadvantage of the Gaussian in that it is an infinite curve and would overlap with an image so greatly as to require on the order of N^4 multiplications and additions to filter an N by N image. The fact that the Gaussian tapers off to the sides, however, allows one to approximate it well enough with only a finite number of samples. In practice, therefore, only a central portion of the Gaussian is used, the rest being treated as if it were zero.

A two-dimensional Gaussian function may thus be approximated by an array of values such as the following:

0.0	0.1	0.2	0.1	0.0
0.1	0.3	0.5	0.3	0.1
0.2	0.5	1.0	0.5	0.2
0.1	0.3	0.5	0.3	0.1
0.0	0.1	0.2	0.1	0.0

A seven-by-seven or even larger array could give a closer approximation to a true Gaussian, but would incur greater computational cost in filtering.

Once the image has been processed with a Gaussian filter, one may compute partial second derivatives $\partial^2/\partial x^2 G(x,y)$ and $\partial^2/\partial y^2 G(x,y)$ and combine them into the Laplacian:

$$\nabla^2 G(x,y) = \frac{\partial^2}{\partial x^2} G(x,y) + \frac{\partial^2}{\partial y^2} G(x,y).$$

This operator generally produces its strongest outputs where the gradient of the filtered image is changing most rapidly. The positions where the Laplacian passes through value 0 are the locations where the gradient (representing edge strength) goes through an extremum.

The zero crossings in the Laplacian can be obtained in the horizontal and vertical directions by scanning horizontally and vertically, detecting pairs of adjacent pixels where one has a positive value and the other has a negative value, or a triplet of pixels in which the outer two have opposite signs, and the middle one has value zero. If the edges in the original image are very gradual, or if the Laplacian is coarsely quantized, zero crossings of this form may not appear, even though the edges exist in the image. A wider latitude may be used for detecting zero crossings by allowing sequences of some number k of pixels, the $k-2$ middle of which are zero and the end pixels of which have opposite signs.

A computational shortcut can be taken to obtain the filtered and differentiated image from which zero crossings are extracted. It is possible to apply the differentiation operator directly to the Gaussian function once and for all, so that the image can be both filtered and differentiated with a single convolution operation. The resultant operator is called a $\nabla^2 G$ operator ("del-squared G"). In one dimension, a Gaussian and a $\nabla^2 G$ look as shown in Fig. 10.19a and b, respectively.

The two-dimensional versions of the functions in Fig. 10.19 are surfaces formed by rotating these functions around their central axes. Assuming this axis is at the origin, such a $\nabla^2 G$ operator may be described by the formula:

$$\nabla^2 G(x,y) = \frac{1}{\pi\sigma^4}(1 - \frac{x^2 + y^2}{2\sigma^2})e^{-(x^2+y^2)/2\sigma^2}$$

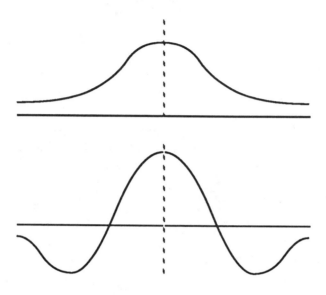

Figure 10.19: One-dimensional Gaussian (a) and $\bigtriangledown^2 G$ operator (b).

Because of its shape, this operator is commonly referred to as a "Mexican hat" or "sombrero" operator. There is evidence supporting the notion that the human visual system computes convolutions with $\bigtriangledown^2 G$ operators [Grimson 1980].

The results one gets by obtaining the zero crossing of the convolution of the image with a $\bigtriangledown^2 G$ operator are usually very sensitive to the value of σ used in the Gaussian. The use of a small value of σ typically leads to an intricate fabric of contours, while a large value of σ results in a few contours that are relatively smooth. By taking a whole set of contours using a range of values for σ one gets effectively a collection of edge images that represent edge effects in the image at different spatial frequencies. In many cases, the prominent edges in an image may be identified as those segments of zero-crossing contours that recur in several of the zero-crossing images. If this is true for a particular class of images, the class is said to satisfy the "spatial coincidence assumption." This assumption is conceptually equivalent to a statement that if an edge in an image is a prominent one, then the edge is visible in each of a series of representations at different resolutions.

Although the $\nabla^2 G$ approach to edge detection has not found much acceptance in practical applications of machine vision to date, it may find wider use as new computing systems reduce the computational penalty one currently incurs with the technique.

10.5.6 Edge Linking

Having found a set of pixels we believe to represent the contour of an object, we usually wish to extract from them a closed contour. Traditionally, the object is to obtain a "Freeman chain" (or "chain code") representation. The *chain code* for a boundary is a sequence of "elementary" vectors which, when linked end-to-end, follow the contour being represented. The elementary vectors are typically from a set of four, or of eight. Sets of four and eight elementary vectors are shown below:

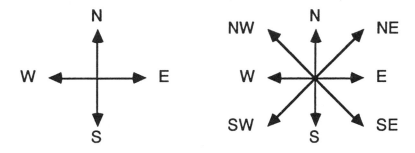

Figure 10.20: Elementary vectors for chain codes.

Note that each link in the chain can be indicated with two bits (if the four-directional code is used) or three bits (for the eight-directional code).

Extracting the closed contour is not always so easy. If there is noise in the original image, there may be gaps in the contour as found by the edge detector. There may also be spurious edge pixels which do not correspond to any actual edge in the original scene. These difficulties can sometimes be overcome through simple techniques. Incomplete contours, if the breaks are short, can be closed through a process of dilation.

If the edge information is represented in a binary image where pixels containing 1 are edge pixels, then simple gap closing may be effected by the following cellular logic operation: at each cell containing 0, set it to 1 if at least two non-adjacent neighbors (of its eight) are equal to 1. For example, the center pixel in the pattern below would be set to 1:

$$
\begin{array}{ccc}
0 & 1 & 1 \\
0 & 0 & 0 \\
1 & 0 & 0
\end{array}
$$

To close larger gaps, a more general method (which is essentially dilation) can be used: beginning with $E^0[i,j] = E[i,j]$ if $E^{(n-1)}[i,j]$ has a neighbor with value 1, then set $E^n[i,j]$ to 1. Gaps of length $2k$ pixels are closed in $E^k[i,j]$. This operation expands the set of edge pixels in all directions, not just along the gaps, and thus it is appropriate to follow k steps of gap filling by an equal number of steps of thinning.

Isolated edge fragments resulting from noise should be eliminated by related cellular-logic techniques. For example, any pixel without any neighbors having 1, is set to 0.

Another class of edge-linking techniques incorporates directional information into each edge primitive. Then gaps can be closed by extending edges in the directions they have at the gaps.

10.5.7   Relaxation Labelling

One method for cleaning up the results of edge detection involves the iterative adjustment of the edges to improve the extent to which the edge segments are locally consistent with one another. Let us describe a technique known as "probabilistic relaxation" for enhancing the results of local line detection in an image.

We assume that eight line detectors (each in a different orientation) have been applied to the image, and that from the results a set of nine probability values has been assigned to each pixel. Each probability value represents the strength with which a corresponding label is implied by the image at the pixel. Eight of the labels correspond to lines at the eight given orientations, and the ninth label is "no line." If none of the line detectors yields a high value, then "no line" is given a high value and the other labels are given low values. The nine values are constrained to sum to 1.0, and thus they are referred to as probabilities.

In each iteration of the algorithm, every pixel gets its probability values updated using a function of its current values and those of its neighbors. The updating strengthens the labels that are consistent with the current labelling information in the surrounding pixels, and it weakens labels that are inconsistent. The updating makes use of "compatibility functions" between labels of adjacent pixels. Let a_i and a_j be a pair of adjacent pixels, and let λ and λ' be labels. Then we say that r_{ij} is a *compatibility function* if $r_{ij}(\lambda, \lambda')$ gives a number between -1 and 1 indicating the degree to which λ and λ' are compatible. For example, let us assume that a_i is directly above (North of) a_j. If λ is a vertical-line label and λ' is a horizontal line label, then $r_{ij}(\lambda, \lambda') = -0.25$, and this indicates that they are somewhat incompatible; it is possible but unlikely that a contour in the image will make a 90° turn. On the other hand, if λ' is the same vertical-line label as λ, then the two labels are mutually supportive and $r_{ij}(\lambda, \lambda') = 1.0$ is an appropriate value.

Let $p_i(\lambda)$ and $p_j(\lambda')$ be the probability assigned to label λ in pixel a_i and the probability assigned to label λ' in pixel a_j, respectively. The updating should increase $p_i(\lambda)$ if $p_j(\lambda')$ is high and $r_{ij}(\lambda, \lambda')$ is close to 1. On the other hand, the updating should decrease $p_i(\lambda)$ if $p_j(\lambda')$ is high and $r_{ij}(\lambda, \lambda')$ is close to -1. If either $p_j(\lambda')$ is low or $r_{ij}(\lambda, \lambda')$ is close to 0, then the updating should not significantly alter $p_i(\lambda)$. An updating formula which possesses these properties is:

$$p_i^{k+1}(\lambda) = \frac{p_i^k(\lambda)[1 + q_i^k(\lambda)]}{\sum_\lambda p_i^k(\lambda)[1 + q_i^k(\lambda)]}$$

where

$$q_i^k(\lambda) = \sum_j c_{ij} \sum_{\lambda'} r_{ij}(\lambda, \lambda') p_j^k(\lambda').$$

Here the cij are weights that may depend upon the spatial relationship between pixels a_i and a_j. For example, if pixel a_i is at the center of the neighborhood below, then the values of c_{ij} for each neighboring pixel a_j could be as shown (the diagonal neighbors have weights roughly $1/\sqrt{2}$ of the others' and the weights sum to 1).

0.1	0.15	0.1
0.15		0.15
0.1	0.15	0.1

The formula says that in order to get the probability of label λ on pixel a_i for iteration $k + 1$, one computes the expression involving the iteration-k values of labels on a_i and its neighbors.

A relaxation-labelling operation of this sort can be useful in producing significantly cleaned-up line-element images, typically requiring on the order of ten iterations to clean up the image. Such a method cannot usually produce a globally consistent labelling, but it can reduce the number of local inconsistencies and ambiguities and is useful in simplifying the work of subsequent steps in the analysis of the image. This sort of improvement could be followed by a gap-filling operation (e.g., by dilation), or it could be used in conjunction with a method such as the heuristic-search boundary-finding method described earlier.

10.5.8   The Hough Transform

When analyzing scenes of the man-made world, straight lines are very important. Most buildings and many other artificial objects have straight lines as their edges. Being able to automatically find lines in an image is important. Although one can perform edge detection, attempt to link edges together, and then fit straight line segments to the edge sequences, this method runs into trouble when the noise in the image is very serious or if there are big gaps in the lines as a result of poor contrast or occluding debris or fog.

A straight line is a very highly constrained geometric object. Unlike an arbitrary edge sequence, it cannot continually change its direction as it extends in length; the direction cannot change at all. This means that even if we have only a few points of the image representing the line, we may still have more than enough information to determine the parameters of the line (actually two points is enough). We shall define the Hough transform to be an operation that maps an image $f(x, y)$ into another two-dimensional function $H(\rho, \theta)$, such that the value of $H(\rho, \theta)$ indicates the degree to which a line parameterized by ρ and θ is present in the image.

We now give a precise definition of the Hough transform and explain how it is computed. A common representation of a line in the plane is with an equation such as $y = mx + b$. This is sometimes called the "slope and intercept" representation since m represents the slope of the line (rise over run) and b gives the value of y at which the line crosses the y axis. The slope and intercept representation is not very appropriate for image analysis work because it breaks down for vertical lines (that is, $m = \infty$ for a vertical line), and vertical lines are very common in images (particularly in indoor scenes and outdoor scenes with buildings). A formulation that is more robust is the polar representation of a line:

$$\rho = x \cos \theta + y \sin \theta.$$

Each pair (ρ, θ) specifies a line.

If we assume that both the domain of the image $f(x, y)$ and the domain of the transform $H(\rho, \theta)$ is the whole continuous Euclidean plane, the *continuous Hough transform* (also known as the *Radon transform*) may be defined by:

$$H(\rho, \theta) = \int\limits_{-\infty}^{+\infty} \int\limits_{-\infty}^{+\infty} f(x, y) \delta(\rho, \theta, x, y) dx \, dy$$

where δ is an integrable delta function satisfying

$$\delta(\rho, \theta, x, y) = \begin{cases} \infty & \text{if } \rho = x \cos \theta + y \sin \theta; \\ 0 & \text{otherwise.} \end{cases}$$

The transform domain is called the *parameter space* or ρ–θ space. The transform is periodic, so that only values of θ in the range 0 to 2π need be considered. It is usual to consider the image as having value zero outside of a fixed square region, and one is usually interested only in values of ρ in some non-negative range $[0, \rho_{\max}]$. Note that each point of the image influences the values along a curve in the parameter space.

The usual means of computing Hough transforms for digital images is by partitioning the parameter space into cells and keeping a total of all of the contributions to each cell that have been accounted for so far. The whole transformation is effected by scanning the image array and for each pixel, determining the (ρ, θ) pairs that are affected, and adding the pixel's value (possibly scaled down by a constant) into the current total of each of the affected cells. The (ρ, θ) pairs are easily determined from the pixel coordinates (x, y) by computing $\rho_i = x \cos \theta_i + y \cos \theta_i$, for $\theta_i = 0, \ldots, 2\pi$, in suitable increments. The process of determining the (ρ, θ) pairs and accumulating the values is sometimes called "voting," since each image pixel "votes" for all the (ρ, θ) pairs that describe lines passing through the pixel.

In order to find the lines representing object boundaries in an image, using the Hough transform, the following sequence should be followed:

1. apply an edge-detection operator to the image obtaining a rough edge image;

2. compute the Hough transform of the rough edge image;

3. scan the transform to identify peaks and/or clusters of high values, and make a list of the (ρ, θ) pairs for these peaks; and

4. for each (ρ, θ) pair, examine the pixels along the specified line to determine the endpoints of the segment(s) along the line.

The Hough transform is thus only one step in the process of finding line segments in an image. Yet it is the crucial step which does the most to get around the problems of noise and gaps.

A disadvantage of the Hough transform is that it is computationally expensive to compute, requiring $O(N^2 M)$ "vote counting" steps for an N by N image, where M is the number of distinct values of θ used in the parameter space. The development of faster algorithms and special hardware for Hough or Hough-like transformations is a subject of current research.

With minor modifications, the Hough transform may be used to detect geometric objects other than lines. For example, to detect circles, the transform below may be used.

$$C(r, x_c, y_c) = \int\limits_{-\infty}^{+\infty} \int\limits_{-\infty}^{+\infty} f(x,y)\delta_c(r, x_c, y_c, x, y)dx\,dy$$

where δ_c is nonzero only if $(x - x_c)^2 + (y - y_c)^2 = r^2$. The parameter space for this transform is three-dimensional. The higher the dimensionality of the parameter space, the more costly the transform becomes to compute. Therefore, the useful variations of the Hough transform are generally of dimension not more than three or four.

10.6 Region Growing

In the previous section we have examined methods of edge detection, edge linking and line finding. There is an alternative approach to finding the boundaries of objects in an image. That is to first find the groups of pixels that belong to the same objects, and then to trace the boundaries of these groups. It is often the case that the pixels that belong to one object share some property; for example, their brightness values may all be within a small tolerance of each other.

The "region-growing" approach to image segmentation is primarily concerned
with the determination of these pixel groups or "regions." We begin our discussion of region-growing methods with a formal definition of "segmentation"which
includes a definition of "region."

A *segmentation* of an image can be formally defined as a set of regions
$\{R_1, R_2, \ldots, R_k\}$ that satisfies five conditions:

1. Each region is a 4-connected set of pixels of the image.

2. The regions are disjoint (and thus do not overlap).

3. The union of all the regions is the entire image.

4. Each region satisfies a "uniformity" predicate.

5. If R_i and R_j are adjacent regions, then the union of R_i with R_j does not
    satisfy the uniformity predicate.

For example, let us consider the digital image of Fig. 10.21a. Here we may
consider a region as "uniform" if all its pixels have the same value.

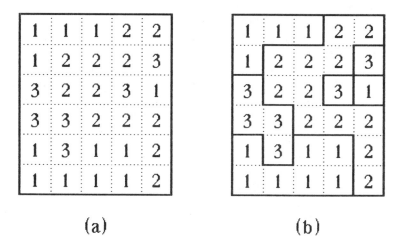

(a)   (b)

Figure 10.21: A digital picture (a), and its segmentation according to the criterion that a region is uniform if all its pixels have the same value (b).

This image contains only three different pixel values. However, a segmentation of it contains seven regions. Three regions have pixel value 1, one has value
2 and three have value 3. Notice that two of the regions with value 3 consist of
only a single pixel. These two regions cannot be merged because they are not
adjacent in the sense that they share one or more pixel edges.

In the previous example, there exists a unique segmentation for the image.
With a more liberal criterion for uniformity, there may or may not exist a unique

segmentation for an image. For example, we may declare that a region is uniform if its largest pixel value minus its smallest pixel value is less than or equal to 1. Several different segmentations with this criterion are consistent with Fig. 10.21a. Figure 10.22 shows three of them. Each of the first two has four regions. The first has one region containing both ones and twos (and three regions containing threes), while the second has three regions containing only ones and one region containing both twos and threes. The third segmentation shows how pixels with intermediate values may not always be grouped together.

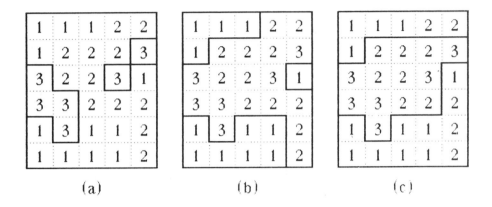

Figure 10.22: Three segmentations for the same image under the criterion that a region is uniform if its largest value minus its smallest value is less than or equal to 1.

10.6.1 Pixel-by-Pixel Region Growing

A segmentation using the criterion of Fig. 10.22 can be computed by starting from the upper left corner of the image, taking the first pixel to be part of the first region, and successively examining neighboring pixels (in some systematic fashion), adding them to the region so long as the criterion of uniformity remains satisfied. When no new neighboring pixels of any in the region can be added, one of those neighbors is taken as the starting pixel for a new region. And so this process continues until all the pixels are put into some region or other. Typically, a push-down stack is used to keep track of which pixels need to have neighbors examined (for example, a simple rule is: each time a new pixel is added to a region, place the four neighbors of that pixel on the stack). This algorithm is quite similar to methods used to fill regions on a graphics display screen with a particular color. It could be easily implemented in LISP by making some modifications to the program CONNECTD.LSP, presented on page 401.

10.6.2   Split-and-Merge Algorithm

One feature of the pixel-by-pixel approach to region growing is that it is computationally costly. The region uniformity predicate must be evaluated $O(N^2)$ times even if the final segmentation only has one region. An alternative approach evaluates that predicate less often, in the expected case, although perhaps over larger regions. In this approach, an initial partition of the image into square blocks is used as an approximation that is to be gradually transformed into the segmentation. The uniformity predicate is evaluated on each of these blocks. If it is true on a block, then that block can be a component of an even larger region. If it is not true on a block, the block is subdivided into four subblocks (of equal size) and the test is applied recursively to each one. When this splitting phase is complete, a set of square blocks, of various sizes, each satisfying the uniformity predicate, has been obtained. Next, a merging phase considers adjacent pairs of these blocks, merging such pairs into single regions whenever the predicate holds on their union. For most natural images, the computational effort in the split-and-merge algorithm is less than that required by the pixel-by-pixel method. Several phases of split-and-merge segmentation are illustrated in Fig. 10.23.

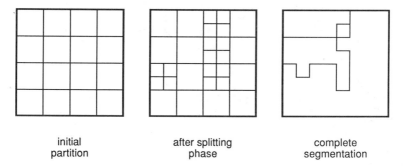

| initial partition | after splitting phase | complete segmentation |

Figure 10.23: Segmentation with the split-and-merge algorithm.

10.6.3   The Phagocyte Heuristic

One of the drawbacks of the straightforward approach to segmentation just mentioned is that results tend to be either messy, with many more regions than wanted, or overmerged, with things like sky and sea being combined into one large region. A simple means of taking shape information into account to offset some of the mischievous effects of pure pixel values is something called the "phagocyte" heuristic.

With this method, a pair R_1 and R_2 of adjacent regions is considered, having perimeters P_1 and P_2, respectively, and with a number W of elements (of the common boundary) that separate pixels whose intensity values differ by less than a constant c. The pair is merged if either W/P_1 or W/P_2 exceeds a threshold τ. Thus if, say, R_2 had a perimeter that is short in relation to W (the size of the weak part of the common boundary), then the ratio W/P_2 would be high, probably exceeding the threshold, and so R_1 would be merged with R_2. This is analogous to a phagocyte "swallowing up" another cell (as one may have come across in biology class). Figure 10.24 illustrates a typical merging situation for the phagocyte heuristic.

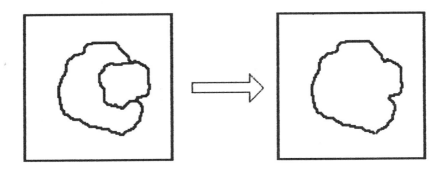

Figure 10.24: The phagocyte heuristic for region growing. The common boundary consists of W weak elements and S strong elements.

Another way to attack the problem of messy segmentations is "edit" the segmentations after they are computed with one of the above algorithms. They can be edited by examining each region, testing it for undesirable properties, and eliminating it if it has such properties. A region is eliminated by selecting a neighboring region and merging the two. A region may be deemed "undesirable" if it has the characteristics of regions arising from noise. Although slightly risky, a region consisting of a single pixel can usually be correctly eliminated, since imaging processes such as vidicons generate a considerable amount of "salt and pepper" (white) noise in the image that gives rise to spurious but small regions.

Another class of undesirable region is "transition" regions which result from the distortion of high-contrast contours by the digitization process. Where in the original scene there may have been a sharp boundary between the horizon and the sky, there may be a strip of pixels in the digitized image that are half land, half sky, and thus produce a region of intermediate brightness in the segmentation. Such transition regions may (usually) be identified using heuristics based on the numbers and kinds of neighbors they have, their widths, and the relationship between their pixels values and those of their neighbors. Once they have been identified, transition regions can be eliminated by forcing them to be merged with one of their non-transition neighbors.

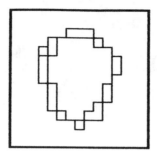

Figure 10.25: Transition regions.

10.6.4   Relational Descriptions

Once a segmentation has been computed, one is typically left with a two-dimensional array each of whose cells contains the identification number of the region to which it belongs. Often, however, a more symbolic representation is desired for the segmentation. In such cases, we can represent the relationships among regions using a labelled graph and eliminate much of the data. The nodes of such a graph correspond to the regions of the image, and the (directed) arcs indicate relationships such as "is to the left of," "surrounds," etc. Figure 10.26 illustrates a segmentation and a corresponding relational description.

The problem of analyzing a scene is then reduced to one of finding configurations in the relational description that match known patterns. It might not be a difficult job to test two relational descriptions for isomorphism: there are known algorithms for finding a one-to-one correspondence between the nodes of two labelled graphs that preserves arc connections. The problem is that the graph for an object usually changes as the illumination, orientation, and camera noise change. Thus we need ways to find best approximate matches between pairs of graphs. This is a very difficult computational problem, in general, and is the subject of ongoing research.

10.7   Shape Analysis

Intuitively, the shape of an object is the quality or form of an object which is invariant to translation, scaling, and rotation. Shape is dependent upon the arrangement of the object's component material in space; on the other hand, texture, color, and other reflective properties are not aspects of shape (although such surface properties can act as cues for inferring three-dimensional shape). The shape of a red square 3 cm on a side is *square*. In some sense, shape is everything that is left after one has determined the position, size, and orientation of an object, except for surface properties such as color. The shape of an object depends on the object's boundary, but not on its interior.

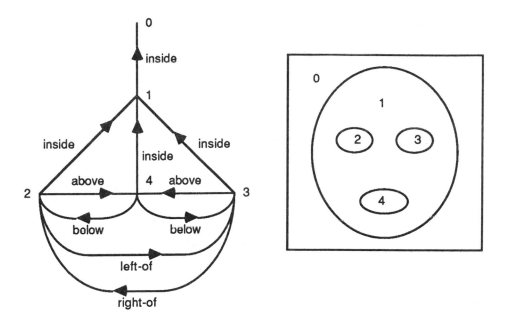

Figure 10.26: A picture segmentation (a), and its corresponding relational description (b).

Slightly more formally, we may define a *shape characteristic S* of a set of points in the plane or in 3-D space to be a function $S: \mathcal{P}(E^n) \to R$ which assigns a real number to each set of points in E^n (an n-dimensional Euclidean space). With $n = 2$, S is a 2-D shape characteristic, and with $n = 3$, it is a 3-D shape characteristic. This definition does not itself rule out parameters such as size, orientation and position; however, we can simply consider such parameters as poor characteristics of shape.

Shape is usually the most important visual aspect of an object for recognition, although color or texture can be very important in some situations. The fact that we recognize human figures and faces in cartoons drawn with only a few contour lines suggests how powerful shape is.

There are many shape characteristics which have been proposed or used for machine vision. In this section we describe a few of them. Our presentation will be in two dimensions. Most 2-D shape characteristics have analogous 3-D shape characteristics.

10.7.1   Circumscribing and Inscribing

Complex shapes are often described using their relationships to simpler ones. The most commonly used reference shapes are rectangles. The dimensions of a "bounding box" give an indication of the extent of an object along each of the coordinate axes. Sometimes called a "Ferret box," a bounding box is described by four parameters: the maximum and minimum x and y values occurring in the set of points. For a given set of points, the bounding box is unique provided that the set is bounded (i.e., the set does not extend infinitely far in any direction). However, translating or scaling the set must change the bounding box. Rotation usually changes the box as well. If we describe a bounding box only by its length and width, the result is a translation-invariant characteristic of the set of points.

A type of bounding box which is invariant to rotation as well as translation is the rectangle of smallest area, in any orientation, which completely encloses the object and which is described only by its length and width. Unlike the Ferret box, this bounding box may not always be unique for particular objects. For example, if the object itself is circular, then a bounding box may be rotated in any amount without changing the fact that it is a smallest rectangle enclosing the object. However, for most objects, this kind of bounding box is unique, and certain values, derived from the box, are useful shape characteristics.

The "aspect ratio" of the bounding box for an object sometimes is a good indication of how elongated the object is. For a Ferret box, the aspect ratio is:

$$\frac{y_2 - y_1}{x_2 - x_1}$$

and for a rotation-invariant bounding box, a ratio may be defined as length/width. In the latter case, the ratio is always greater than or equal to 1, because we define the length to be the longer of the two dimensions of the rectangle, unless they are equal. The aspect ratio is scale-invariant.

Just as one may use the characteristics of a box that *encloses* the object, one may also use features of the largest box that can be *inscribed* in the object. This is generally more difficult to compute, however, than a circumscribed box.

Another kind of circumscribing shape is the "convex hull" for an object. A set A of points is *convex* if for any two points $P \in A$ and $Q \subset A$, any point R situated on the line segment from P to Q is also in A. The *convex hull* $H(B)$ of a set B of points is the smallest convex set which contains B. The convex hull of an object is usually simpler in shape than the original. For example, a shape and its convex hull are shown in Fig. 10.27a and b. If one stretches a rubber band around a two-dimensional object the band takes on the form of the convex hull. There are numerous algorithms in the literature for computing the convex hull of a set of points.

In a cellular space the only truly convex sets are rectangular in shape, because any diagonal boundary line must be represented as a "staircase" of pixels, and such a staircase contains indentations (concavities). In general, the convex hull

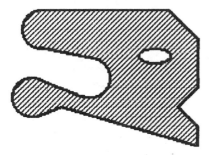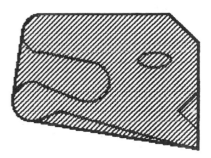

Figure 10.27: A shape (a) and its convex hull (b).

of the digital image of an object is different from the digital image of the convex hull of the object. It is interesting to note that the Ferret box (defined above) for an object is the smallest convex set including a set of pixels that may be accurately represented as a set of pixels itself. Thus the Ferret box may be considered as a form of cellular convex hull.

The Ferret box is usually so different from the true convex hull for a shape that it does not make sense to treat it as one. An enclosing form which is usually closer to the convex hull is one that permits staircases at 45° angles as well as horizontal and vertical boundaries. Such a hull has at most eight sides and is sometimes called the "octagonal closure" of the object. It can be efficiently computed by parallel computers that perform cellular-logic operations.

A useful shape characteristic based on the computation of the convex hull is the *convexity index* defined as the ratio of the area of the object to the area of its convex hull. The convexity index for a set of points may be as low as 0 for a very non-convex object, or as high as 1 for a truly convex one. The portion of the convex hull that is not in the object is called the *deficiency* and can be divided into two components: the "bays" which are indentations on the boundary of the object, and the "lakes" which are holes in the object. The ratio of bay area to object area gives another shape characteristic, as does the ratio of lake area to object area.

A largest convex set that can be inscribed in an object is sometimes called a *convex kernel*. Unlike the convex hull, convex kernels for an object can be non-unique. For example there are two convex kernels for the cross shown in Fig. 10.28. Computing convex kernels is more difficult than convex hulls.

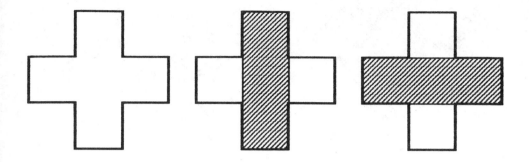

Figure 10.28: A shape having two convex kernels.

10.7.2   Integral Projections

A mapping from two-dimensional objects to real numbers effectively reduces the dimensionality of representation from 2 to 0. Some shape-analysis techniques work through the intermediate level of one-dimensional objects. An important class of such methods is known as "integral projections." An example of an integral projection is the following:

$$P(x) = \int\limits_{-\infty}^{+\infty} f(x,y)dy$$

If $f(x,y)$ represents a binary image, then $P(x)$ gives the number of pixels having value 1 in column x. Such projections are easily computed by scanning the columns of the image and totalling the pixel values in each one.

A useful pair of integral projections is a vertical one (as above) and a horizontal one (in which the integral is with respect to x instead of y). Then the problem of characterizing shape is reduced to describing one-dimensional functions. A binary image and its vertical and horizontal integral projections are illustrated in Fig. 10.29. Some characteristics of one-dimensional functions are: the number of peaks in the function, the number of non-zero intervals (connected components), and statistical moments.

10.7.3   Topology

Some characteristics of a set of points or pixels have more to do with how the pixels are connected than how their contours bend. The number of connected components in an image is one of these. Another is the "Euler number" which is defined as the number of 4-connected components minus the number of "holes," where a hole is an 8-connected group of background points or pixels that is

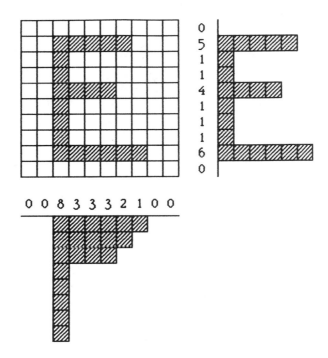

Figure 10.29: A shape and its horizontal and vertical integral projections.

entirely surrounded by object (foreground) pixels. A convenient shortcut exists for computing the Euler number of a binary image. If E is the Euler number, then

$$E = M - A + F$$

where M is the number of ones in the image, A is the number of edge-adjacencies of ones, and F is the number of occurrences of 2 by 2 blocks of ones in the image. Figure 10.30 shows three binary images and their Euler numbers.

10.7.4 The Medial-Axis Transform

In order to reduce 2-D shapes to simpler plane figures, one of a number of kinds of "skeletons" may be computed. The "medial axis transform" (MAT) can be defined for sets of points in the Euclidean plane in an elegant way. Let p_1 and p_2 be points in the plane. Then by $d(p_1, p_2)$ is denoted the Euclidean distance from p_1 to p_2. Let A be a set of points in the plane, and let p be a point (either in A or not in it). Then by $d(A, p)$ is denoted the shortest distance $d(q, p)$ for some point q in A.

We define $\mu(A, p)$ to be the set of points q in A where $d(q, p)$ is equal to $d(A, p)$. Thus $\mu(A, p)$ consists of the points of A which are closest to p. Clearly,

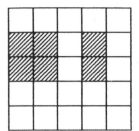 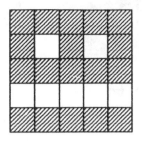 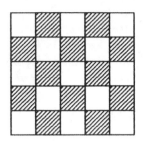

Figure 10.30: Three binary images and their Euler numbers: (a) 2, (b) 0, and (c) 12.

for any p in A, $\mu(A, p) = \{p\}$ and $d(A, p) = 0$.

The *medial axis transform* of A, denoted $\sigma(A)$ is defined to be:

$$\{p \text{ such that } |\mu(A, p)| \geq 2\}.$$

That is, the medial axis transform of A contains a point p if and only if p attains its distance to A at more than one point of A.

The medial axis transform of a rectangle consists of four diagonal line segments, open at one end, and meeting (if the rectangle is not square) on a fifth segment, also part of the medial axis transform. The segments are open at the corners of the rectangle, because each of the corners, being a member of the rectangular set of points, has only one member in its $\mu(A, p)$. The medial axis transform of a circle is its center. The medial axis transform of any convex set is empty.

For a filled-in shape, B, we may define the *boundary* $\delta(B)$ of B, as the set of all points q such that for any $\epsilon > 0$, there exists a point q' outside of B so that the distance between Q and q' is less than ϵ. That is,

$$\delta(B) = \{q \in B : \forall \epsilon > 0, \exists q' \notin B : d(q, q') < \epsilon\}.$$

The *endoskeleton* of a filled-in shape B is the intersection of $\sigma(\delta(B))$ with B itself. Similarly, the *exoskeleton* of B is that portion of $\sigma(\delta(B))$ that lies outside of B. Note that if B is convex, then its endoskeleton is non-empty but its exoskeleton is empty.

It is interesting to note that if A is a closed polygon, then $\sigma(A)$ consists of a union of portions of straight lines and arcs of parabolas.

The medial axis transform, exoskeleton, and endoskeleton have been applied to the problem of shape analysis of regions in computer vision. Although the Euclidean plane versions of these structures are quite sensitive to noise (minor variations of the shapes A or B), it is possible in practice to compensate for this to some extent.

It is interesting to note that the medial axis transform may be of use in path planning for robots. In a two-dimensional room with two-dimensional obstacles, a robot is to move from point A to point B. To minimize the chances of running into an obstacle, the robot may attempt to maximize its distance from the nearest wall or obstacle at all times. A natural way to achieve this is first to compute the medial axis transform (skeleton) of the room with the obstacles, then begin the journey by moving from point A to the closest branch of the skeleton, then follow the skeleton around the obstacles toward B, finally moving off the skeleton toward B (unless B is on the skeleton).

10.7.5   Digital Skeletons

Unless one is dealing with analytic representations of shape such as polygons, it can be very difficult to compute continuous skeletons for arbitrary sets of points in the plane. If one's shape is represented using a binary image, then digital approximations to the medial-axis transform can be employed.

One algorithm for obtaining a digital endoskeleton (internal skeleton) of a binary image is due to Stefanelli and Rosenfeld, and it is iterative in nature. It consists of the following:

At each step, each pixel is considered as a possible final point, and then for deletion and possibly deleted. There are two kinds of local conditions, the deletion conditions and the final point conditions. A point is deleted if it is a 1 and one or more of its four neighbors (to the north, east, south and west) is a zero. However, the four directions are tried one at a time, with deletion performed after each, thereby preventing a line of width two from being completely eliminated in one step.

A pixel is a final point if it has value 1 and, when scanning clockwise around the pixel, there are no cases in which a neighbor with value 1 is adjacent to another neighbor with value 1.

This algorithm produces a result which may be dependent upon the order in which the directions are tried. Directional preferences are generally inevitable in skeletonization schemes that yield skeletons of width 1.

10.7.6   Polygonal Approximation

In order to reduce the dimensionality of pictorial information, one may transform a two-dimensional-array representation of a shape to a (one-dimensional) string. The Freeman "chain code" provides a natural way to do this. For this method, the boundary of the shape is traversed, and the string is created by outputting a symbol at each step of the boundary, which indicates the direction of the boundary at that step. Codes based on 4 possible directions are often used, as are codes based on 8 possible directions. The strings which result are usually still more cumbersome than desired. Additional data reduction may be effected by approximating the chain-code representation by a polygon having a relatively small number of sides. Such an approximating polygon can be computed in many ways. A few of them are described here.

Since the chain-coded boundary may itself be regarded as a polygon, its vertices may be sampled to produce a new polygon with fewer vertices. For example the new polygon might contain every other vertex of the original polygon. This is "subsampling" the polygon. A disadvantage of this method of approximation is that there is no control of the error of approximation once the sampling interval has been fixed. Also, it may be that a good approximation would require different sampling intervals in different places in the boundary.

A second method, sometimes called "running approximation" takes a given error tolerance τ and tries to skip as many original vertices along the boundary as it can, but it must keep the distance from each original vertex in the interval to the vector of approximation less than or equal to τ. The problem with this method is that it tends to keep the error of approximation near τ even when a solution (using the same number of vertices) exists with zero error.

Both the subsampling method and the running-approximation method are "local" methods in the sense that the decision to keep a vertex for the approximation is made without considering all of the original vertices.

10.7.7   Ramer's Recursive Algorithm

A third method, known as Ramer's algorithm, uses a recursive approach. Like the method of running approximation, Ramer's method takes a given error tolerance and produces a solution in which the original vertices are within τ of a side of the new polygon. However, all of the original points are examined before Ramer's algorithm makes its first decision; it is not a local method. The polygon for Ramer's algorithm is not necessarily closed. Ramer's algorithm may be started by calling the recursive procedure with two arguments: the entire polygon (representing the portion to be approximated) and a pair of pointers to the first and last vertices (representing the current approximating segment for this portion). The procedure first checks to see if each vertex in the portion to be approximated is within a distance of τ of the approximating segment. If all vertices are, then the procedure returns the approximating segment. Otherwise, the vertex farthest from the approximating segment is identified, and used to create two new approximating segments (that improve the accuracy of the approximation). The portion to be approximated is also divided into two sub-portions by the chosen vertex. A pair of recursive calls to the procedure is made with the subportions and new segments. Ramer's algorithm tends to choose a good set of vertices for the approximating polygon more often than the running-approximation method does. The algorithm is reasonably efficient when the error tolerance is not too small.

10.7.8   Ramer's Algorithm in LISP

The ease with which polygons can be manipulated in LISP was apparent in
the PYTHAGORUS program in Chapter 8. Here, although the arithmetic we
perform on polygons is more substantial, the recursive structure of Ramer's
algorithm maps very neatly into LISP. We now describe a LISP program for
Ramer's algorithm.

The input to this program is a list of vertices, each of which is a pair with an
x-coordinate and a y-coordinate. This implementation assumes that the polygon
to be approximated is not closed; the first and last points must be distinct. It
is a simple matter to provide an additional function that will accept a closed
polygon as input and call the functions here to perform the real work, and this
is left as an exercise for the reader.

```
; RAMER.LSP
; A LISP implementation of Ramer's recursive algorithm
; for approximating a polygon with another polygon.

(SETQ TEST_POLY '((0.0 0.0)(0.0 4.0)(2.0 6.0)(4.0 6.0)
                  (6.0 4.0)(6.0 0.0)(4.0 -2.0)(2.0 -2.0) ))
```

The above-described polygon used as test data here is illustrated in Fig. 10.31.
(Additional examples are given in the exercises.)

Of the function definitions that make up the program, the first three,
RAMER, RAMER1 and SPLIT, embody the algorithm itself. Most of the remaining functions support the computation of distance information.

The function RAMER is the top-level function. However, it does nothing
more than call RAMER1 to do the real work and then affix the last vertex of
the polygon to complete the solution. RAMER1 calls the arithmetic function
ERRORS to determine the relative distances of each vertex from the segment
that connects the first and last vertices. It checks the maximum of these errors
against the value of TOLERANCE, and if the error is within the tolerance,
RAMER1 returns the first vertex of the polygon as the approximation (the last
vertex is omitted to simplify the APPENDing of partial solutions). If the error
exceeds the tolerance, then the polygon is split at the vertex of maximum error
(the function SPLIT does this), and RAMER1 returns the result of appending
the approximations of the two subpolygons (which are computed with recursive
calls to RAMER1).

```
(DEFUN RAMER (POLY)
  (APPEND (RAMER1 POLY)(LIST (LAST POLY))) )


; return polygonal approx. of POLY, without last point:
(DEFUN RAMER1 (POLY)
  (PROG (ERROR_LIST LASTPOINT POLY1)
```

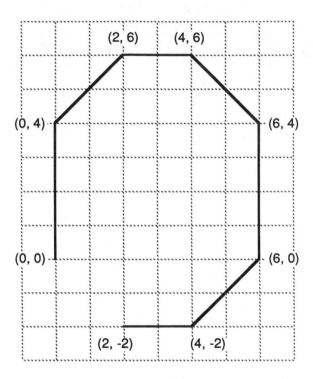

Figure 10.31: The test polygon used as sample data in RAMER.LSP.

```
(SETQ LASTPOINT (LAST POLY))
(SETQ ERROR_LIST (ERRORS POLY))
(SETQ EMAX (APPLY 'MAX ERROR_LIST))
(COND ((GREATERP TOLERANCE EMAX)      ; if approx. OK,
        (RETURN (LIST (CAR POLY))) ) ; return 1st point.
      (T (SETQ POLY1 (SPLIT POLY ERROR_LIST EMAX))
        (RETURN (APPEND (RAMER1 (CAR POLY1))
                        (RAMER1 (CADR POLY1)) )) ) ) ) )
```

The function SPLIT takes three arguments: POLY: a polygon to be split, ERROR_LIST: a list of the vertex error values as computed for making the decision of whether or not to split, and EMAX: the value of the maximum in this list. It returns two lists, each representing a subpolygon of POLY, breaking POLY at the position in ERROR_LIST where value EMAX is found.

```
(DEFUN SPLIT (POLY ERROR_LIST EMAX)
  (COND ((EQUAL (CAR ERROR_LIST) EMAX)     ; at pt. of max error?
```

```
                (LIST (LIST (CAR POLY)) POLY) )  ; yes, return 1st vertex
                                                 ; and POLY itself.
        (T (SETQ TEMP                            ; no,
                    (SPLIT (CDR POLY)            ; SPLIT the CDR of POLY
                           (CDR ERROR_LIST)
                           EMAX) )
            (CONS (CONS (CAR POLY)(CAR TEMP))    ; put CARs back on.
                  (CDR TEMP) ) ) ) )


; Return list of approximation errors for internal points of POLY
(DEFUN ERRORS (POLY)
  (PROG (X1 Y1 X2 Y2)
        (SETQ X1 (CAAR POLY))
        (SETQ Y1 (CADAR POLY))
        (SETQ X2 (CAR LASTPOINT))
        (SETQ Y2 (CADR LASTPOINT))
        (RETURN
          (CONS 0.0 ; Error for first point is clearly 0.
                (MAPCAR '(LAMBDA (P)
                           (DIST3 (CAR P)(CADR P) X1 Y1 X2 Y2) )
                        (CDR POLY) ) ) ) ) )
```

The function DIST3 takes as arguments the coordinates of three points, which we may call P_0, P_1, and P_2. It calculates the square of the distance from P_0 to the line *segment* whose endpoints are P_1 and P_2.

```
(DEFUN DIST3 (X0 Y0 X1 Y1 X2 Y2)
  (PROG (S01 S02 S12)
        (SETQ S01 (DISTSQ X0 Y0 X1 Y1))
        (SETQ S02 (DISTSQ X0 Y0 X2 Y2))
        (SETQ S12 (DISTSQ X1 Y1 X2 Y2))
        (COND ((LESSP S01 S02)
                  (COND ((LESSP (PLUS S01 S12) S02)
                            (RETURN S01) )
                        (T (RETURN
                              (PDIST X0 Y0 X1 Y1 X2 Y2) )) ) )
              (T (COND ((GREATERP S01 (PLUS S02 S12))
                            (RETURN S02) )
                        (T (RETURN
                              (PDIST X0 Y0 X1 Y1 X2 Y2) )) )) ) ) )
```

In case the minimum distance between the point and the line segment is not achieved at one of the endpoints but in the interval between them, it is necessary to compute the distance (squared) between the point P_0 and the *line* passing through P_1 and P_2. Thus PDIST computes the square of the perpendicular distance from the point (X0 Y0) to the line that passes through points (X1 Y1) and (X2 Y2). It first computes $a = x_1 - x_2$, $b = y_1 - y_2$, $c = x_0 - x_1$, and $d = y_0 - y_1$. Then it uses the formula:

$$\left[D(P_0, line_{P_1, P_2}) \right]^2 = \frac{(ad - bc)^2}{(a^2 + b^2)}$$

By comparing the square of the distance with the tolerance directly, the costly square-root operation (required to obtain the actual Euclidean distance) is made unnecessary.

```
(DEFUN PDIST (XO YO X1 Y1 X2 Y2)
   (PROG (A B C D TEMP)
          (SETQ A (DIFFERENCE X1 X2))
          (SETQ B (DIFFERENCE Y1 Y2))
          (SETQ C (DIFFERENCE XO X1))
          (SETQ D (DIFFERENCE YO Y1))
          (SETQ TEMP
                (DIFFERENCE (TIMES A D)(TIMES B C)) )
          (RETURN (QUOTIENT (TIMES TEMP TEMP)
                             (PLUS (TIMES A A)(TIMES B B)) )) ) )
```

The square of the distance between P_1 and P_2 is $(x_1 - x_2)^2 + (y_1 - y_2)^2$ and is computed by DISTSQ.

```
(DEFUN DISTSQ (X1 Y1 X2 Y2)
   (PROG (A B)
          (SETQ A (DIFFERENCE X1 X2))
          (SETQ B (DIFFERENCE Y1 Y2))
          (RETURN (PLUS (TIMES A A)(TIMES B B))) ) )
```

The function LAST, used to identify the last vertex in the input polygon, has the straightforward definition below.

```
(DEFUN LAST (L)
   (COND ((NULL (CDR L))(CAR L))
         (T (LAST (CDR L))) ) )
```

In order to test the program, the following code enables tracing and initiates processing the test polygon.

```
(TRACE RAMER PDIST SPLIT)

(DEFUN TEST ()
   (PROG ()
      (SETQ TOLERANCE 5.0)
      (PRINT (APPEND '(APPROX_OF_TEST_POLYGON)
```

```
                    (RAMER TEST_POLY) ))
    ) )

(TEST)
```

This test results in a three-segment approximation to the seven-segment int-put polygon. This is displayed (overlaid on the original) in Fig. 10.32.

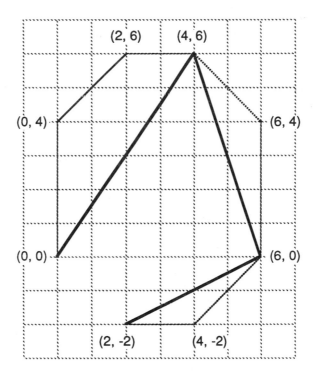

Figure 10.32: The result of Ramer's algorithm on the test polygon, with TOLERANCE = 5.

10.8 Three Dimensions and Motion

Although there is a wide variety of applications for two-dimensional machine-vision methods, thorough analysis of indoor or outdoor scenes requires that three-dimensional descriptions be produced. Robots that work or navigate in a three-dimensional environment are likely to need 3-D vision techniques. In this section, representations and vision algorithms for 3-D structures are discussed.

10.8.1   Representations for 3-D Objects

Whereas two-dimensional objects are represented by such data structures as two-dimensional images and lists of line segments, 3-D objects can be represented by 3-D images, by collections of surfaces, space curves, and combinations of 3-D primitives. The number of mathematical and computer representations that have been developed for 3-D structures is very large. Let us consider a few of them.

Some 3-D structures are just collections of points in 3-D space. When finite, such a collection can be represented as a list of ordered triples. Other structures such as polyhedra can be described as relations on finite sets of points, and so they can be represented as a list of triples together with a representation of the relations. 3-D surfaces described as surface patches also can be represented in terms of points in space called "control points."

10.8.2   3-D Arrays

A series of sectional images of a human brain, created with a CAT scanner, effectively represents a 3-D density function $f(x, y, z)$. A natural representation for this is as a 3-D array of numbers. Alternatively, the domain of this function can be segmented into volumes divided by surfaces; these surfaces can be represented together with indications of the density within each volume.

Three-dimensional solids may also be represented by 3-D arrays. Just as a binary image represents the shape of a 2-D object, a 3-D binary array can handle a 3-D shape. Because the number of cells (called *voxels*) is equal to N^3 where N is the number of cells in one row of the array, the memory requirement for the array is large if N is anything but small. In order to represent a 3-D binary array more efficiently, an "octree" can be used.

10.8.3   Octrees

An *octree* is a tree structure each of whose nodes corresponds with a cube-shaped volume of the 3-D array; the root of the tree corresponds to the whole array. Each non-leaf node in an octree has eight immediate descendant nodes. Any node except the root corresponds to one of the eight octants of the cubical volume that its parent node correponds to, where the octants are the spaces formed by bisecting the cube three times using mutually-orthogonal planes parallel to the cube's faces. Each node of an octree is marked as "full," "empty," or "mixed." A full node correponds to a volume that is completely contained in the object being represented. An empty node's volume is totally disjoint from the object's. The volume for a mixed node contains some object and some empty space. Memory is saved by only allowing mixed nodes to have children. An octree can be computed from a 3-D binary array by building a complete tree up to the root, determining the labels for each node, and then pruning off all the descendants of nodes that are full or empty.

Both 3-D binary arrays and octrees belong to a class of representations called "spatial-occupancy" methods. Spatial-occupancy methods can handle complexity of shape very well, provided that high spatial resolution is not needed. For high spatial resolution, methods that use explicit representations of coordinates are generally preferable.

10.8.4 Generalized Cylinders

A method of 3-D shape description which has proved versatile and efficient for many applications is called "generalized cylinders." An ordinary cylinder is a geometric object that can be described in terms of its axis (a line segment) and its cross section (a circle). A *generalized cylinder* is a structure having an axis which is an arbitrary space curve, and whose cross section may vary along the curve and is not restricted to be circular; each of a generalized cylinder's cross sections may be a different planar, simple closed curve. The cross sections are assumed to form a continuous surface. A representation for a generalized cylinder can consist of a list of cross-section curves (represented with some 2-D method) together with a space-curve representation (e.g., with a 3-D chain encoding, a 3-D polyline by a list of vertices in 3-space, or a 3-D spline curve) of the axis, and with a list of the points along the axis to which the specified cross sections correspond.

10.8.5 3-D Structure from 2-D Images

The fact that we humans are skilled at determining three-dimensional relationships in a scene given only a (flat) photograph is a good reminder that it is possible to deduce much 3-D structure from a 2-D projection. To be sure, the projection process "throws away" information in the scene, and without any knowledge about what the world is like, it would not be possible to correctly reconstruct the 3-D structure. Without world knowledge, the interpretation of the image is *underconstrained.*

However, the world operates only in certain ways; for example, an opaque object in front of another one hides it or hides part of it. Trees, houses, people, roads and cars have certain ways of appearing, and when we see a tree standing in front of a car, we perceive the car as one complete object, even though its image is divided by that of the tree. The fact that the tree's region divides the car's region is a depth cue telling us that the tree is in front of the car. Our knowledge of the world provides enough constraining information so that a reasonable interpretation can usually be made. Even with much world knowledge, the 3-D structure is usually still underconstrained; there may always be some details of the situation being examined which can not be determined. Answering the question "was there a rabbit behind the house?" is beyond the ability of a vision system if neither the image nor the system's world knowledge can provide evidence one way or the other. We must be happy if a vision system helps us answer a reasonable set of questions (but not all questions involving 3-D scene structure) about the observed situation.

Two of the methods for determining depth-related information in a scene, from a single image, are called "shape from shading" and "shape from texture."

10.8.6   Shape from Shading

As graphic artists are well aware, a surface such as that of a sphere can be given a three-dimensional appearance by shading it. In the other direction, it is possible to compute the 3-D shape of a surface from the shading information in an image. To explain how this is done, we first introduce the "gradient space."

Suppose that the surface is represented by $z = f(x, y)$, and that z is the depth of the surface from the viewer at image position (x, y). For a small change in x or in y there is a corresponding change of z. These changes are given by $p = \partial z / \partial x$ and $q = \partial z / \partial y$. The pair (p, q) denotes the *gradient*. The space of possible values of (p, q) is called *gradient space*. Since the gradient of a plane in space is constant, a plane or section of a plane is represented in gradient space as a point.

Let us assume that the surface in the scene is Lambertian (i.e., matte), so that it reflects light uniformly in all directions. The intensity of the reflected light depends only upon the angle of incidence θ_i and not on the angle of reflection. The intensity of reflected light is given by $R = r \cos \theta_i$. Thus, given the magnitude and direction of the incident light, the orientation of the surface, and the reflectance of the surface, the radiance, which corresponds to the image intensity, can be found. Fixing the light-source intensity and direction, and fixing the reflectance, the intensity of the reflected light is a function of orientation: $R = G(p, q)$. The function G is called a *reflectance map*.

Given a value of R, the amount of light reflected, the set of possible pairs (p, q) such that $R = G(p, q)$ forms a curve in gradient space called an *iso-intensity* curve. The value of R therefore does not uniquely determine the surface orientation (p, q) but constrains it. With the help of additional constraints, it is possible to recover the surface orientation. Additional constraints can be obtained from vertices in the edge image of the scene (if the surface is polyhedral), or from continuity of the gradient across the surface (if the surface is smoothly curved).

Information about the orientation of a surface can also be obtained using cues other than intensity in the image. Some other kinds of cues are: the coarseness and directionality of textures on the surface, the relative motion of parts of the surface (requiring a sequence of images to analyze), and the 2-D shape of the projected boundaries of a surface.

10.8.7   Stereo

Several forms of stereo imaging can be used to obtain depth information in an image. The best-known method is binocular stereo. Humans use this method in normal 3-D vision, and can also use it with stereograms to obtain the sensation of 3-D perception. For example, the random-dot stereogram of Fig. 10.8.7, when viewed such that the images seen by each eye are aligned, evokes the perception of a square protrusion from the otherwise flat surface. This stereogram was gen-

Figure 10.33: A random-dot stereogram.

erated by making two copies of a random binary image and displacing the black dots within a square region in the right-hand copy horizontally by a distance of two pixels. The two-pixel-wide column uncovered by the square is randomly re-filled. The fact that humans can perceive depth from random-dot stereograms is evidence that our visual system does not require meaningful features in order to perceive depth, and so the perception of depth seems to be a lower-level process than the recognition of features or objects.

Algorithms have successfully been devised for computing depth information from a stereo pair of images. The general structure of the different stereo algorithms is similar. It consists in obtaining separate images of a scene from two distinct viewpoints, with a known relative orientation. The two images are put into correspondence by locating and matching various features, and then depth information is computed from the relative disparities of the features in the two images. The most difficult part of this process is usually obtaining the correct correspondence between the features of the two images. If the two viewpoints are separated by much of a distance, the two views of the same scene can be dramatically different so that a feature in one image may not have any counterpart in the other. If the viewpoints are very close together, the correspondence aspect is easier, but there will not be enough disparity between the images to get accurate depth information.

Other methods of stereo imaging are motion parallax and photometric stereo.

In motion parallax, one camera takes a sequence of images of the scene from different viewpoints. Although it is easier to get images with great disparity this way, the positions of the viewpoints may not be known with as much accuracy as with binocular stereo. With photometric stereo, a scene is imaged from a single viewpoint two or more times, with the position of the light source different each time. Using the shape-from-shading method, enough constraints can be built up to obtain local surface orientation. References for more details on stereo techniques are given at the end of the chapter.

10.8.8   Motion

The visual perception of motion is important in robotics and numerous other application domains. The simplest dynamic image-analysis task is "change detection." Change detection has practical applications in the security industry; a single night watchman can monitor a large building with the help of video cameras and change-detection equipment. Industrial robots can handle a wider variety of jobs or perform manufacturing functions more quickly if they can visually follow moving objects and pick them up, weld, paint or inspect them in motion. Visual navigation systems, such as an automatic driver for a car, need the ability to determine motion parameters of objects so as to avoid collisions.

Although the goal of motion analysis is usually to extract the parameters of motion in order to predict the future positions of objects moving in the scene, motion analysis has other uses. Sequence of images can help solve the noise problem that plagues the analysis of static images. For example, it is easier to see the moving heart in some ultrasound pictures than to find the heart in a single (static) picture from the same sequence. The redundancy of information in a sequence of images allows the effects of noise to be overcome; however, a system must either determine the motion parameters in the sequence or put the key features of the moving object in each frame into correspondence in order to take advantage of the redundancy. Another use of motion is to gain additional constraints for determining 3-D structure. For example, an image of a uniformly-illuminated white cylinder with an irregular sprinkling of small black dots is difficult to interpret as a cylinder, if viewed perpendicular to its axis; there are no shading cues and the texture is not regular enough to help. However, if the cylinder is rotating around its axis, it shape is obvious. The motions of the dots give the shape away.

Computational methods for analyzing motion from images fall into several categories. "Correspondence" or feature-matching techniques try to put the prominent features of a pair of images (representing the scene at different times) into correspondence. Once such a correspondence has been found that is self-consistent, the spatial disparities of the features may be used to estimate the velocity of scene objects relative to the camera.

Another class of methods is useful in estimating the velocity of the observing system through its environment: optical-flow determination. If the observer is moving forward, the static objects in the environment seem to stream by. The optical-flow field is represented by a 2-D array in which each cell holds a 2-D velocity vector. Each vector $V(x, y)$ represents the rate at which the surface element represented at point (x, y) in the image seems to be moving. The surface element is the one closest to the observer along the ray from the viewpoint which passes through the image plane at (x, y). If the observer's visual axis is along the direction of motion, the velocity field will have a *focus of expansion* at its center. Around a focus of expansion, the velocity vectors point away, and the magnitudes of the vectors are small near the focus, gradually increasing as the radius from the focus increases. Algorithms for finding the focus of expansion usually have, as their main problem, determination of the optical flow field. If there is not enough visual contrast in the environment, it may only be possible to compute reliable velocity vectors for a few locations in the array. Interpolation may sometimes be used to fill in flow information; or the focus of expansion may sometimes be derived directly from a sparse set of velocity vectors.

Another method for analyzing motion in image sequences assumes that most of the scene is static, and that the moving objects are large in relation to the frame-to-frame movement. By subtracting the previous frame from the current one, the regions where changes have occurred can be readily identified. Furthermore the regions can be labelled as "accretion" or "depletion" regions according to whether they have positive or negative pixel values in the difference image. A moving object which is brighter than its background gives rise to an accretion region at the end of the object in the direction of motion. It is trailed by a depletion region, where the object has just been but no longer is. A line drawn through the centroids of a pair of accretion regions (or depletion regions) arising from the same object gives the direction of motion for the object. By treating the history of a pixel's values in the image sequence as a single vector value for the pixel, segmentation of the image into regions can be performed using uniformity predicates which are sensitive to such properties as the rate of change of the brightness; the result of such a segmentation is a motion map.

10.9 Blocks-World Heuristics

A collection of vision techniques have been developed for analyzing line drawings of toy blocks. These techniques, while not very useful in practice, have been influential in the development of general methodology not only for vision but for other kinds AI problems. For example, the general idea of labelling graphs according to constraints is a product of this work. For this reason, it is appropriate to examine these methods.

Let us suppose that we have available a clean line drawing of a scene of some blocks on a table. On the basis of the shapes and connections of the lines in this drawing, it is possible to determine the correspondence between regions in the drawing and the blocks in the scene. Two noteworthy studies of this problem are by Guzman and by Waltz. They are briefly described below.

10.9.1   Guzman Labelling for Line Drawings

The objective is to find objects such as rectangular prisms and pyramid-shaped blocks through an analysis of the junctions of lines in the drawing. A typical line-drawing for Guzman's method is shown in Fig. 10.34.   Each vertex (junction)

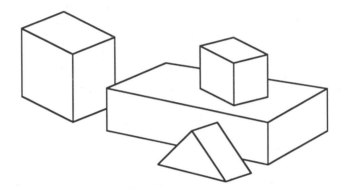

Figure 10.34: A line drawing for analysis by Guzman's method.

is classified according to the number of lines meeting there and the angles they form. The basic kinds of vertices are: *fork, arrow, ell, tee, kay, ex, peak,* and *multi.* These are shown in Fig. 10.35.

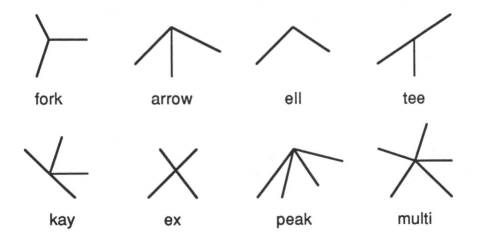

Figure 10.35: The eight types of junctions for Guzman's method.

After each junction in the line drawing has been classified, the regions defined by the lines are "linked" on the basis of the junctions. A link between two regions means that they may belong to the same object. When a pair of regions is doubly linked, the pair is interpreted as belonging to the same object. The rules for linking are as follows:

1. fork: three links are created, one across each of the three arms of the fork.

2. arrow: one link is put across the shank of the arrow.

3. ell: no linking done.

4. tee: if two tees can be found with colinear stems, tops toward one another, the pair is said to match. In this case the two regions to one side of the stem line are linked, as are the two on the other side of the stem line; however, this linking is not performed if it would link a background region to a non-background region.

5. ex: the lines forming the 180-degree angle get links across them.

6. peak: like the arrow, links are put across all lines except those making the obtuse angle.

Guzman developed additional rules to handle more complex cases. Others later greatly elaborated the junction-based approach. However, the first steps by Guzman were significant in showing how junction information could be used to get an interpretation for the scene.

10.9.2   Huffman-Clowes Labelling

Huffman, and independently, Clowes developed a more rigorous technique for labelling line drawings of blocks. They considered not only the junctions where line segments meet, but also the types of lines themselves. They identified four line types: convex edges, concave edges, occluding edges with object on the right, and occluding edges with object on the left. These are illustrated in Fig. 10.36.

Taking some of the angular junction configurations used by Guzman (only those where two or three lines meet), they worked out the possible ways that the lines at these junctions could be labelled. For example, the number of ways a fork, arrow, or tee junction can be labelled is $4 \times 4 \times 4$, and the number of ways an ell can be labelled is 4×4. With ells, forks, arrows, and tees, we have some 212 different junction possibilities. The interesting fact, however, is that not all of these combinations correspond to possible situations in scenes. To find out which actually occur, we can enumerate the possible ways a scene vertex can be produced. Let us imagine a point in space where three perpendicular planes intersect. These planes divide space into eight octants. Depending on how many of these octants are full of matter or empty, we may have a corner at the point or not. In general, if the number of full octants is odd, we have a

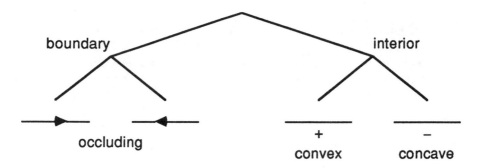

Figure 10.36: Four types of lines for Huffman-Clowes labelling.

corner. (However, if only two diagonally-related octants are full, or are empty, we also have a corner, but we assume that in our line drawing, no more than three lines come to a junction.) For these cases where corners exist in this three-dimensional situation, consider the possible views of the corners. Assuming we only view each corner from empty octants, the actual number of different labelled junction configurations is only 16, but one of these can occur in three different orientations, so that we have a total of 18, as shown in Fig. 10.37.

Starting with a line drawing of the same type as for Guzman's method, we can usually find a labelling using Huffman-Clowes labels using a straightforward technique known as "Waltz filtering" or "discrete relaxation." We begin by associating with each junction in the drawing a list of all the possible labels that could go there (e.g., a list of six for an arrow junction). We then make note of the fact that a line segment must have matching line types at each end. This allows us to eliminate from the sets at the endpoints of each line, junction labels that have no consistent counterparts at the other endpoint. For most legal line drawings, this process terminates with unique labels at each junction, and the convergence is rapid.

10.10   Bibliographical Information

A general reference on biological vision systems is [Gregory 1974] and a very readable introduction to human vision is [Gregory 1972]. References on the physiology and neurophysiology of the visual system include [Polyak 1957], [Hubel and Wiesel 1962] and [Kuffler and Nicholls 1976]. Visual illusions have been of interest for many years. Sources of illusions are [Coren and Girgus 1978] and [Gregory 1968]. Stereo human vision using random-dot stereograms was introduced by [Julesz 1975]. One of the motivations for studying machine vision is the hope of obtaining good models for human vision. [Crettez and Simon 1982] is an example of such a model. A book that presents human vision and machine vision in juxtaposition is [Levine 1985]; this book includes hundreds of references, as well. A theory that takes psychological as well as computational evidence

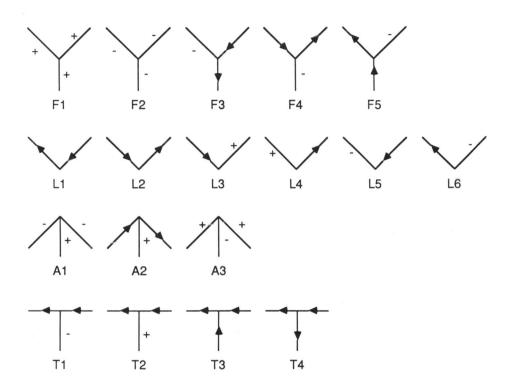

Figure 10.37: The eighteen junction configurations of Huffman and Clowes.

into consideration is outlined in some detail in [Marr 1982], where particular emphasis is given to binocular stereo vision.

Pattern recognition in digital images began to be investigated in the early days of artificial intelligence [Uhr and Vossler 1963]. For a time great interest was focussed on "perceptrons," neural-network-like models which seemed potentially very powerful; that interest largely subsided when some limitations of perceptrons were discovered [Minsky and Papert 1969].

The study of picture processing, concerned largely with thresholding and non-linear approaches to edge detection, took place largely during the late 1960's and early 1970's. Good introductions to that are [Rosenfeld and Kak 1976] and

[Pavlidis 1977]. A number of good algorithms, as well as the relationship of image processing to graphics, are described in [Pavlidis 1982].

Vision research at the surface, line-drawing, and object levels was funded largely by the U.S. Dept. of Defense Advanced Projects Agency, starting with Roberts' well-known study [Roberts 1963], and followed by other studies primarily at M.I.T. [Winston 1975]. More recently the boundaries between pattern recognition, picture processing, and ARPA-style computer vision have begun to fade, and there has been a realization that low-level and high-level processes must usually be integrated to obtain useful vision systems. A good survey of research literature relevant to machine vision is [Ballard and Brown 1982]. A somewhat less imposing introduction is [Nevatia 1982].

The physics of image formation has been extensively studied [Horn 1977], and models of the process have been used to design algorithms that determine surface shape and reflectance properties [Horn 1986].

Low-level vision may be treated as a two-dimensional signal processing problem. A thorough reference with this perspective is [Pratt 1978]. The use of Gaussian filters and Laplacians in computational models of human vision was argued by Marr, Hildreth, Grimson, and Poggio [Marr and Hildreth 1980], [Grimson 1980], [Marr, Hildreth and Poggio 1979]. The spatial coincidence assumption which justifies the use of zero crossings of the Laplacian as edges if they occur at several resolution levels is also the implicit justification for an edge-detection method that uses pyramids [Tanimoto and Pavlidis 1975]. Another way to obtain the effect of a $\nabla^2 G$ operator uses a difference of Gaussians [Burt 1981] and seems to have some computational advantages over the Laplacian. A relatively concise introduction to image transforms such as the Fourier transform is [Andrews 1970]. A computationally efficient method for the 2-dimensional discrete Fourier transform computes the 2DDFT directly in a recursive manner [Naccarato and Chien 1979].

Edge detection, treated in most of the image-processing texts, goes back at least to [Roberts 1963]. A vector-space approach to edge detection is given in [Frei and Chen 1977]. The extraction of linear features is described in [Nevatia and Babu 1981]. Line and curve enhancement using "relaxation" is described in [Zucker et al 1977]; the relaxation approach was subsequently adopted in numerous other vision experiments. The Hough transformation described here is an adaptation of the "point-to-curve transformation" of [Duda and Hart 1973]. A number of more recent studies of Hough transforms and a generalized version are mentioned in [Ballard and Brown 1982]. Hough's patent for a pattern-recognition device used the slope-and-intercept representation of a line as the basis for the parameter space [Hough 1962]. The continuous Hough transform is a special case of the Radon transform [Deans 1981]. The use of heuristic search for boundary finding was developed in [Martelli 1976].

Recent work on low-level vision has focussed on the issue of computational speed. The algorithms based on cellular logic are attractive because they can be executed by very parallel processors [Preston et al 1979], [Duff 1978, 1980],

[Rosenfeld 1981], [Tanimoto 1983], [Uhr 1984]. Hierarchical data structures and their impact on low-level vision are assessed in [Tanimoto and Klinger 1980]. A variety of multi-resolution image-analysis methods are described in [Rosenfeld 1984]. The digital skeleton algorithm described in this chapter is from [Stefanelli and Rosenfeld 1971].

Segmentation has received much attention in the literature. The thresholding approach was successfully developed by [Ohlander et al 1978]. Early work on the region-growing approach, and the introduction of the phagocyte heuristic is described in [Brice and Fennema 1970]. One survey of region-growing methods is [Zucker 1976]. Another treatment of the problem is [Riseman and Arbib 1977]. The split-and-merge method is described in [Pavlidis 1977]. Color information enlarges the possibilities for segmentation methods [Ohta et al 1980].

Shape-from-shading methods were developed by Horn and further extended by Woodham [Horn 1975], [Woodham 1978]. A general scheme for separating the different factors in the scene-formation process, called "intrinsic images" is presented in [Barrow and Tenenbaum 1978]. The analysis of image sequences and motion analysis are essentially the same subject, and they are treated in [Huang 1981]. A method for computing 3-D shape from texture information is in [Kender 1979]. Another method for determining 3-D structure from an image is in [Kanade 1981]. Representations for 3-D structure are surveyed in [Faugeras 1983], and the octree method, introduced in [Jackins and Tanimoto 1980], is related to the "quadtrees" used for two-dimensional map data [Samet 1984].

The labelling of line drawings received much attention during the early 1970's. Building on [Guzman 1968], important studies were made by [Clowes 1971], [Huffman 1971], [Mackworth 1973] and [Waltz 1975].

A number of complete systems for computer vision are described in [Hanson and Riseman 1978], and the techniques in the ACRONYM system in particular are described in [Brooks 1981].

References

1. Andrews, H. C. 1970. *Computer Techniques in Image Processing.* New York: Academic Press.

2. Ballard, D. H. and Brown, C. 1982. *Computer Vision.* Englewood Cliffs, NJ: Prentice-Hall.

3. Barrow, H. G., and Tenenbaum, J. M. 1978. Recovering intrinsic scene characteristics from images. In Hanson, A. R. and Riseman, E. M. (eds.), *Computer Vision Systems.* New York: Academic Press, pp3-26.

4. Brice, C. R., and Fennema, C. L. 1970. Scene analysis using regions. *Artificial Intelligence*, Vol. 1, pp205-226.

5. Brooks, R. A. 1981. Model-based three dimensional interpretations of two dimensional images. *Proceedings of the Seventh International Joint Conference on Artificial Intelligence*, Vancouver, pp619-624.

6. Burt, P. J. 1981. Fast filter transforms for image processing. *Computer Graphics and Image Processing*, Vol. 16, No. 1, May, pp20-51.

7. Clowes, M. B. 1971. On seeing things. *Artificial Intelligence*, Vol. 2, pp79-116.

8. Coren, S. and Girgus, J. S. 1978. *Seeing is Deceiving: The Psychology of Visual Illusions*. Hillsdale, NJ: Lawrence Erlbaum Associates.

9. Crettez, J.-P. and Simon, J.-C. 1982. A model for cell receptive fields in the visual striate cortex. *Computer Graphics and Image Processing*.

10. Deans, S. R. 1981. Hough transform from the Radon transform. *IEEE Transactions on Pattern Analysis and Machine Intelligence*, Vol. PAMI-3, No. 2, pp185-188.

11. Duda, R. O. and Hart, P. E. 1973. *Pattern Classification and Scene Analysis*. New York: Wiley.

12. Duff, M. J. B. 1978. A Review of the CLIP Image Processing System. *Proceedings of the National Computer Conference*, pp1055-1060.

13. Duff, M. J. B. 1980. Propagation in cellular logic arrays. *Proceedings of the Workshop on Picture Data Description and Management*, Asilomar Conference Grounds, Pacific Grove, CA, IEEE Computer Society, August, pp259-262.

14. Faugeras, O. D. 1983. 3-D shape representation. In Faugeras, O. D. (ed.), *Fundamentals in Computer Vision: An Advanced Course*. Cambridge, England: Cambridge University Press, pp293-303.

15. Frei, W. and Chen, C. C. 1977. Fast boundary detection: a generalization and a new algorithm. *IEEE Transactions on Computers*, Vol. C-26, No. 2, October, pp988-998.

16. Gregory, R. L. 1968. Visual illusions, *Scientific American*, Vol. 219, No. 5, 1968, pp66-76.

17. Gregory, R. L. 1972. *Eye and Brain: The Psychology of Seeing*, Second Edition. New York: McGraw-Hill.

18. Gregory, R. L. 1974. *Concepts and Mechanisms of Perception*. New York: Scribner's.

19. Grimson, W. E. L. 1980. A computer implementation of a theory of human stereo vision. AI Memo 565, Artificial Intelligence Laboratory, Massachusetts Institute of Technology, Cambridge, MA.

20. Guzman, A. 1968. Computer recognition of three-dimensional objects in a visual scene. Technical Report MAC-TR-59, Artificial Intelligence Laboratory, Massachusetts Institute of Technology, Cambridge, MA.

21. Horn, B. K. P. 1975. Obtaining shape from shading information. In Winston, P. H. (ed.), *The Psychology of Computer Vision*, New York: McGraw-Hill, pp115-155.

22. Horn, B. K. P. 1977. Understanding image intensities. *Artificial Intelligence*, Vol. 8, No. 2, pp201-231.

23. Horn, B. K. P. 1986. *Robot Vision*. New York: McGraw-Hill and Cambridge, MA: MIT Press.

24. Hough, P. V. C. 1962. Method and means for recognizing complex patterns. U. S. Patent 3069654 (December 18, 1962).

25. Huang, T. S. (ed.) 1981. *Image Sequence Analysis*. New York: Springer-Verlag.

26. Hubel, D. H., and Wiesel, T. N. 1962. Receptive fields, binocular interaction and functional architecture in the cat's visual cortex. *J. Physiology*, Vol. 160, pp106-154.

27. Huffman, D. A. 1971. Impossible objects as nonsense sentences. In *Machine Intelligence 6*. Edinburgh: Edinburgh University Press.

28. Jackins, C. L., and Tanimoto, S. L. 1980. Oct-trees and their use in representing three-dimensional objects. *Computer Graphics and Image Processing*, Vol. 14, pp249-270.

29. Julesz, B. 1975. Experiments in the visual perception of texture. *Scientific American*, Vol. 232, pp24-43.

30. Kanade, T. 1981. Recovery of the three-dimensional shape of an object from a single view. *Artificial Intelligence*, Vol. 17, pp409-460.

31. Kender, J. R. 1979. Shape from texture: an aggregation transform that maps a class of textures into surface orientation. *Proceedings of the Sixth International Joint Conference on Artificial Intelligence*, Tokyo, pp475-480.

32. Kosslyn, S. M. and Schwartz, S. P. 1978. Visual images as spatial representations in active memory. In Hanson, A. R., and Riseman, E. M (eds.), *Computer Vision Systems*. New York: Academic Press.

33. Kuffler, S. W. and Nicholls, J. G. 1976. *From Neuron to Brain.* Sunderland, MA: Sinauer.

34. Levine, M. D. 1985. *Vision in Man and Machine.* New York: McGraw-Hill.

35. Mackworth, A. K. 1973. Interpreting pictures of polyhedral scenes. *Artificial Intelligence*, Vol. 8, pp99-118.

36. Marr, D. 1982. *Vision.* San Francisco: W. H. Freeman.

37. Marr, D. and Hildreth, E. 1980. Theory of edge detection. *Proceedings of the Royal Society, Ser. B*, Vol. 207, London, pp187-217.

38. Marr, D., Hildreth, E., and Poggio, T. 1979. Evidence for a fifth, smaller channel in early human vision. AI Memo 541, Artificial Intelligence Laboratory, Massachusetts Institute of Technology, Cambridge, MA.

39. Martelli, A. 1976. An application of heuristic search methods to edge and contour detection. *Communications of the ACM*, Vol. 19, No. 2, pp73-83.

40. Minsky, M. and Papert, S. 1969. *Perceptrons: An Introduction to Computational Geometry.* Cambridge, MA: MIT Press.

41. Naccarato, D. F., and Chien, Y. T. 1979. A direct two-dimensional FFT with applications in image processing. *Proceedings of the IEEE Computer Society Conference on Pattern Recognition and Image Processing*, Chicago, IL, Aug. 6-8, pp233-238.

42. Nevatia, R. 1982. *Machine Perception.* Englewood Cliffs, NJ: Prentice-Hall.

43. Nevatia, R. and Babu, K. R. 1981. Linear feature extraction and description. *Proceedings of the Seventh International Joint Conference on Artificial Intelligence*, Vancouver, pp639-641.

44. Ohlander, R. B., Price, K., and Reddy, D. R. 1978. Picture segmentation using a recursive region splitting method. *Computer Graphics and Image Processing*, Vol. 8, pp313-333.

45. Ohta, Y., Kanade, T., and Sakai, T. 1980. Color information for region segmentation. *Computer Graphics and Image Processing*, Vol. 13, pp222-241.

46. Pavlidis, T. 1977. *Structural Pattern Recognition.* New York: Springer-Verlag.

47. Pavlidis, T. 1982. *Algorithms for Graphics and Image Processing.* Rockville, MD: Computer Science Press.

48. Pirenne, M. H. 1967. *Vision and the Eye*, Second Edition. London: Chapman and Hall.

49. Polyak, S. L. 1957. *The Vertebrate Visual System*. Chicago, IL: University of Chicago Press.

50. Pratt, W. K. 1978. *Digital Image Processing*. New York: Wiley.

51. Preston, K., Jr., Duff, M. J. B., Levialdi, S., Norgren, P. E., and Toriwaki, J.-I. 1979. Basics of cellular logic with some applications in medical image processing. *Proceedings of the IEEE*, Vol. 67, No. 5, pp826-855.

52. Riseman, E. M., and Arbib, M. A. 1977. Segmentation of static scenes. *Computer Graphics and Image Processing*, Vol. 6, pp221-276.

53. Roberts, L. G. 1963. Machine perception of three-dimensional solids. Technical Report 315, Lincoln Laboratory, Massachusetts Institute of Technology, May. Also in Tippett, J. T. (ed.) 1965. *Optical and Electro-Optical Information Processing*. Cambridge, MA: MIT Press, pp159-197.

54. Rosenfeld, A. and Kak, A. C. 1976. *Digital Picture Processing*. New York: Academic Press.

55. Rosenfeld, A. 1981. *Picture Languages*. New York: Academic Press.

56. Rosenfeld, A. (ed.) 1984. *Multiresolution Image Processing and Analysis*. New York: Springer-Verlag.

57. Samet, H. 1984. The quadtree and related hierarchical data structures. *ACM Computing Surveys*, Vol. 16, No. 2, pp187-260.

58. Stefanelli, R., and Rosenfeld, A. 1971. Some parallel thinning algorithms for digital pictures. *Journal of the ACM*, Vol. 18, No. 2, pp255-264.

59. Tanimoto, S. L. 1983. A pyramidal approach to parallel processing. *Proceedings of the Tenth Annual International Symposium on Computer Architecture*, Stockholm, Sweden, June 14-17, pp372-378.

60. Tanimoto, S. L. and Klinger, A. (eds.) 1980. *Structured Computer Vision: Machine Perception Through Hierarchical Computation Structures*. New York: Academic Press.

61. Tanimoto, S. L. and Pavlidis, T. 1975. A hierarchical data structure for picture processing. *Computer Graphics and Image Processing*, Vol. 4, pp104-119.

62. Uhr, L. 1984. *Algorithm-Structured Computer Systems and Networks*. Orlando, FL: Academic Press.

63. Uhr, L. and Vossler, C. 1963. A pattern recognition program that generates, evaluates, and adjusts its own operators. In Feigenbaum, E. and Feldman, J. (eds.), *Computers and Thought*. New York: McGraw-Hill.

64. Waltz, D. I. 1975. Understanding line drawings of scenes with shadows. In Winston, P. H. (ed.), *The Psychology of Computer Vision*. New York: McGraw-Hill, pp19-91.

65. Winston, P. H. (ed.) 1975. *The Psychology of Computer Vision*. New York: McGraw-Hill.

66. Woodham, R. J. 1978. Reflectance map technique for analyzing surface defects in metal castings. AI Memo 457, Artificial Intelligence Laboratory, and Ph.D. Dissertation, Massachusetts Institute of Technology, Cambridge, MA.

67. Zucker, S. W. 1976. Region growing: Childhood and adolescence. *Computer Graphics and Image Processing*, Vol. 5, pp382-399.

68. Zucker, S. W., Hummel, R., and Rosenfeld, A. 1977. An application of relaxation labelling to line and curve enhancement. *IEEE Transactions on Computers*, Vol. C-26, No. 4, pp394-403.

Exercises

1. How many bytes of storage are required for an image of size 512 by 512 with 2 bits per pixel?

2. What is the difference between the radiance and the irradiance? Describe a situation in which some light plays both roles at the same time.

3. Why is radiance measured in terms of light energy per steradian?

4. Suppose that a 128 by 128 digital image is used to represent a scene of a dark house behind a white picket fence. What is the maximum number of pickets that would be distinguishable in the image?

5. Make a collection of visual illusions. Devise a series of image-processing operations for each illusion to help explain why the illusion is perceived. Some of the operations you may want to use are: low-pass filtering, edge detection, endpoint detection, and Hough transformation.

6. Plot a histogram for the 8 by 8 image shown below. Choose a threshold using the "valley" method. Show the results of thresholding with this value and also with the values T=.5 and T=5.5.

```
6 2 5 0 0 5 2 6
2 6 0 4 4 0 6 2
5 0 6 1 1 6 0 5
0 4 1 6 6 1 4 0
0 4 1 6 6 1 4 0
5 0 6 1 1 6 0 5
2 6 0 4 4 0 6 2
6 2 5 0 0 5 2 6
```

7. Use canned software or write your own program to experiment with some elementary image processing techniques. Print out, describe or demonstrate the effects of applying each technique to a digital image of your own choosing.

   (a) median filtering with a 3 by 3 neighborhood;

   (b) gray-value histogram;

   (c) thresholding using the mean value in the image;

   (d) edge detection with the Roberts cross operator;

   (e) filtering with a Gaussian kernel over a 5 by 5 neighborhood;

   (f) computing a Laplacian or $\nabla^2 G$ over a 5 by 5 neighborhood;

   (g) detecting zero crossings in the Laplacian or $\nabla^2 G$ image; and

   (h) two-dimensional discrete Fourier transform.

8. Describe the following three methods for breaking a picture up into parts for analysis:

   (a) thresholding

   (b) edge detection

   (c) region growing

   What are some advantages and disadvantages of each method?

9. Write a program that inputs (1) an image and (2) a desired number of regions and tries to find a threshold (using binary search) that produces a number of connected regions as close to the desired number as possible.

10. For the binary images A and B shown below, apply dilation (by B) to A three times followed by erosion three times. The desired image is given by $(((((A \oplus B) \oplus B) \oplus B) \ominus B) \ominus B) \ominus B)$. What is the result?

```
0 0 0 0 0 0 0 0
0 0 0 0 0 0 0 0
0 0 0 1 0 1 0 0              1 1 1
0 0 1 1 0 0 1 0              1 1 1
0 0 0 1 0 0 1 0              1 1 1
0 0 0 0 1 0 0 0
0 0 0 0 0 0 0 0
0 0 0 0 0 0 0 0
```

              A   B

11. In an N by N binary image, what is the maximum number of connected components possible for the foreground and for the background if

   (a) 4-connected components are counted for each of the foreground and background?

   (b) 8-connected components are counted for each of the foreground and background?

   (c) 8-connected components are counted for the foreground and 4-connected components are counted for the background?

12. (a) Modify the LISP program for connected components so that it labels 4-connected components.

   (b) Produce a variant of the program, which labels the background 8-connected components as well as the foreground connected components.

   (c) Produce a variant of the program which uniquely labels each 8-connected component of the foreground and each 4-connected component of the background.

   In each case, test your program on the binary image of Fig. 10.10.

13. The number of connected components in an image is sometimes used as a feature of the image. Discuss the variance or invariance of this feature under the following kinds of transformations. Can any of these operations increase the number of components?

              (a)   rotations   (d)   dilation
              (b)   translations   (e)   erosion
              (c)   scale changes

14. Several steps are necessary to develop a program for tracing contours in an image using heuristic search.

    (a) Write a function which computes the local curvature κ_i using the table-lookup method.

    (b) Write a function that computes the cost of a contour.

    (c) Write a function which scans an image with a simple edge detector and chooses a starting location for tracing a contour.

    (d) Using your functions for parts (a), (b) and (c), develop a program that employs best-first search to construct a contour in an image. Demonstrate your program using image data (either synthetic or from a scanner or digitizer).

    (e) Modify your evaluation function so that a path is penalized if it wanders back on itself at any point other than the starting point.

    (f) Change the relative influence of contrast and curvature in the evaluation function and describe the resulting changes in the contours computed by your program.

15. Describe an evaluation function (for the tracing of contours using heuristic search) that would bias the program to trace circular contours of a fixed radius.

16. (a) Write a program that computes a segmentation of an image. The uniformity predicate for a region is satisfied if the maximum value in the region, minus the minimum value, is less than or equal to epsilon. You may choose to do this by making modifications to CONNECTD.LSP as suggested on page 421.

    (b) Take an image and segment it with the program of part a. Now rotate the image 180 degrees by reversing the order of the bytes in its file. Segment the rotated image using the same value of epsilon. How do the results compare (besides being rotated)?

17. Consider the point data shown in Fig. 10.38.

    (a) Describe (in words) the result of applying a least-squares line fit to this data.

    (b) Describe the Hough transform of the data and how this transform should be interpreted.

18. Find the maximum value of TOLERANCE that causes the RAMER program to produce a four-segment approximation of the test polygon in the text.

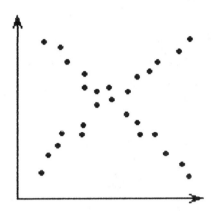

Figure 10.38: Noisy point data.

19. Compare the results of approximating the two open polygons of Fig. 10.39 using the RAMER program with a TOLERANCE of 5.0. The LISP representations for the polygons are:

```
(SETQ SINE '((0.0 0.0)(1.0 2.0)(3.0 -2.0)(5.0 2.0)
             (7.0 -2.0)(9.0 2.0)(10.0 0.0) ))
(SETQ COSINE '((0.0 2.0)(2.0 -2.0)(4.0 2.0)
               (6.0 -2.0)(8.0 2.0)(10.0 -2.0) ))
```

Which result is preferable and why? Describe how Ramer's algorithm could be extended to produce approximations that meet the same tolerance requirement but require fewer segments to do approximations when it is possible to get by with fewer.

20. Modify RAMER.LSP to handle polygons that are *closed* rather than unclosed. Make up two or three test polygons and use them to demonstrate that your program works correctly.

21. Use or write a program that computes the horizontal and vertical integral projections of a 32 by 32 binary image and detects and counts the peaks in these projections.

   (a) Study and describe the resulting features for images of the capital letters A, E, I, O, and U.

   (b) Study and describe the features for all the capital letters.

   (c) Write a program that attempts to recognize the capital letters by using these features.

   (d) Improve the performance of your recognizer by adding additional features to it, of your own design.

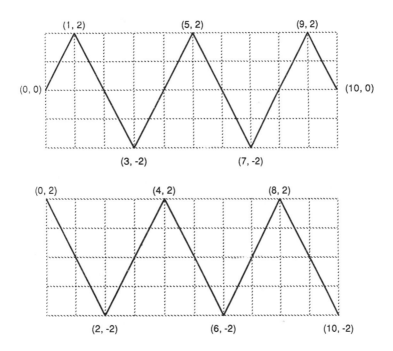

Figure 10.39: Polygons "SINE" (a) and "COSINE" (b) for use with the RAMER program.

22. One of the difficulties of vision is that a three-dimensional scene, when digitized as an image, is represented in a two-dimensional array. What are some ways in which the depth information in the scene can be inferred?

23. Let us suppose that all thinking is visual in nature.

    (a) Suggest some of the operations that a computer designed to "think with images" might perform.

    (b) How could the memory of such a system be organized?

    (c) How could such a system possibly solve problems?

    (d) What are some of the mechanisms that would be required to support such visual thinking?

24. (Term project) Develop a program that is capable of analyzing pictures of cups and saucers on a table top and which reports on its analysis. The program should successfully recognize: a cup in isolation in different orientations, a saucer in isolation in different orientations, and a cup-and-saucer combination. What does your program report when it looks at a stack of two cups? An overlapping pair of saucers?

Chapter 11

Expert Systems

11.1 Introduction

The previous chapters of this book have focussed on particular techniques of artificial intelligence. These ideas and methods may be likened to the chemical elements; they are the basic building blocks of larger, more complicated entities. We now wish to examine some of the possibilities for compounds, alloys and other mixtures, which can be formed to meet particular, practical needs.

In this chapter we use the term *expert system* to refer to a computer system or program which incorporates one or more techniques of artificial intelligence to perform a family of activities that traditionally would have to be performed by a skilled or knowledgeable human. (However, an expert system need not replace a human expert; it may play the role of a colleague or an assistant to the human.) Expert systems may be thought of as the delivery vehicles for AI techniques. Artificial intelligence is *applied* to a real-world problem by incorporating it into a piece of software or a hardware/software combination, and the resulting system is what we call an expert system.

This chapter addresses several issues related to the application of artificial intelligence in systems that automate or support problem-solving, diagnosis, advising, decision-making and control. The process of developing an expert system shares much with software engineering in general, and yet it requires additional considerations regarding the construction and appropriate use of knowledge bases. Expert systems are often very complex, and they may require the successful integration of several diverse components. The interfaces among these components must be carefully specified, because the information that must pass across them often consists of semantic representations, and their meanings must not be accidentally distorted as they move from one part of the system to another. Special software tools are needed in the design, debugging and maintenance of expert systems. Expert systems may place heavy demands on computer hardware, and special parallel architectures can help to meet such needs.

461

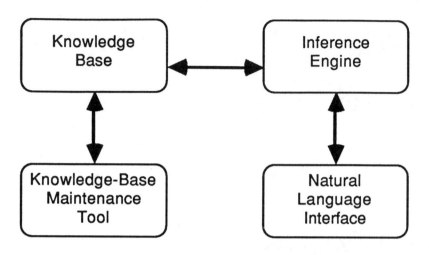

Figure 11.1: The typical structure of an expert system.

11.2   Integration of AI Techniques

11.2.1   Design Methodology

In Chapter 3 the typical structure of a production system was illustrated (see
Fig. 3.1). There, a base of production rules was coupled to a database of state
information and a control scheme or interpreter. We may generalize such a
structure, obtaining that shown in Fig. 11.1. The knowledge base may consist
of production rules, but may also take other forms: semantic networks, frames,
relational database plus inference rules, etc.

The inference engine is the procedure which generates the consequences, conclusions or decisions from the existing knowledge. It may be a rule interpreter or
it may be the routine which updates certainty values in a probabilistic inference
network.

Relatively simple expert systems can often be constructed effectively, making
use of the production-rule format of Chapter 3. The development of such a
system can be easier than that for systems requiring multiple AI techniques.
Here is an overall design cycle for relatively simple rule-based systems:

1. Define the problem and determine whether it is an appropriate one for
   which to build a rule-based expert system.

2. Construct the rule base. This may involve a knowledge engineer working
   together with an expert.

3. Debug and refine the rules.

In order to cover a broader class of applications, a somewhat more lengthy design process is needed. The steps of this process are as follows:

1. Define the nature of the tasks to be accomplished by the system.

2. Define the nature of the knowledge available. (Are there facts known with certainty together with inference rules, is the knowledge probabilistic, does the knowledge consists of mathematical models, or is it a semantic system of some sort?)

3. Choose appropriate mechanisms for representation and inference.

4. Define the interfaces required to integrate the components.

5. Tailor the components if necessary.

6. Construct the knowledge base.

7. Debug and refine the knowledge, and any other system components, as necessary.

For some of these steps, computer-based tools are available (and some kinds of tools are discussed below).

The power of this second approach is that a wider variety of AI techniques may be incorporated in the expert system, as needed. The greater challenge arises from the diversity of possible ways the techniques may be combined and from the increased complexities of some of these combinations.

11.2.2 Ways to Combine AI Techniques

Here are some of the ways in which the elementary AI techniques can be combined to produce more complex components to meet particular needs:

- Combine two knowledge-representation methods, such as semantic networks and frames. Each node of the semantic network is associated with one frame.

- Combine a knowledge representation method with an inference method (this may require some knowledge-representation conversion when the knowledge is accessed). For example, we could use a resolution theorem prover with a semantic network; a link in the net could easily be converted into a unit clause whose predicate symbol corresponds to the arc label and whose two arguments correspond to the labels on the nodes that are connected by the link. With the semantic net containing only facts (i.e., the equivalents of atomic formulas), the network must be augmented with a set of additional formulas which includes rules to allow useful deductions to be made.

- Combine a machine-learning method with a visual feature-extraction procedure. For example, the learning algorithm for single concepts could be
  applied to sets of images using characteristics of the images such as the
  numbers of connected components of area greater than 50 pixels when
  each image is thresholded with the "valley" method. The result would be
  a method for learning about classes of images in terms of the numbers of
  regions (of this particular type) that they contain.

These combinations certainly do not exhaust the possibilities, but they are
meant to suggest the sorts of combinations a designer can create.

11.2.3   Incorporating Numerical Models

The capabilities of expert systems would be greatly restricted if they were limited to knowledge bases consisting of rules, frames, semantic networks, and facts
represented in the predicate calculus. Many natural (e.g., the weather) and
man-made systems (e.g., a nuclear power plant) can be modelled with sets of
differential equations. A good mathematical model should be regarded as an
important piece of knowledge about such a system. An expert system for evaluating the safety of nuclear reactors might include, as one of its components, a
runnable mathematical model of a typical reactor; the advice it would give to
its users would be based in part upon the outcomes of simulations that it would
perform.

The development of mathematical models for nuclear reactors and other such
systems is not generally considered to be within the domain of artificial intelligence. However, such model-building might be considered to be AI if it were
done automatically by a learning or model-building program. Also, it may be
necessary to modify a model to make it compatible with the rest of an expert
system, and this may require that an expert and a knowledge engineer work
together. For example, if the reactor expert system needs margins of error in
order to make safety recommendations, then the model might need to be modified to maintain intervals or probability density distributions instead of scalar
parameter values.

In order to integrate a numerical model into an expert system, it may be necessary to program the model in LISP, or to make it efficiently callable from LISP
even though it is written in, say, Fortran. Incorporating a mathematical model
in an interactive software system may lead to long response times and frustrated
users. It may well be worth incorporating rapid approximation techniques that
allow useful feedback to the user or to the executive portion of the expert system,
so that detailed calculations are only performed when such accuracy is actually
needed.

11.3 Tools

Tools are very important in developing expert systems. An expert system usually contains a complicated body of knowledge that may give rise to complex behavior. During development, a set of rules may be inconsistent and/or incomplete. (Indeed, there may still be inconsistencies and omissions even after delivery.) Tools that assist in the organizing and editing of sets of rules can help the designer to understand his rule base and detect problems. The behavior of an expert system may be difficult to trace, and tools for tracing can help the designer to find all of the state changes that are of interest during a chain of inferences.

The designer should be able to use the computer to the fullest in the complex information-engineering task of constructing an expert system. Most expert-system construction tools fall into the following categories: "shells," expertise transfer systems and knowledge-base editors, and graphical-display tools. Bases of commonly-needed knowledge can be useful building blocks, and they may be packaged with various browsers, editors, and/or interfacing or conversion routines.

11.3.1 Shells for Rule-Based Systems

The term "shell," for an expert system, usually refers to all of the system's software except the application-specific knowledge. The shell includes the access procedures for the knowledge base, the inference procedure, and various additional modules.

A shell may support only one or several knowledge-representation schemes. It might provide only logical inference capability or it may provide others: probabilistic, inductive, etc.

One of the first shells to be constructed and put to use was EMYCIN ("Empty MYCIN," derived from the MYCIN medical expert system by removing the application-specific knowledge). A few of the many commercially available shells include ART ("Automated Reasoning Tool"), OPS5, OPS83, M.1, S.1, KEE ("Knowledge Engineering Environment") and Knowledge Craft. A much more detailed list is given in [Waterman 1986].

Such systems can be very useful for rapid prototyping of expert systems. These shells can facilitate knowledge-base construction by providing good knowledge-representation facilities. However, the work of actually formulating the knowledge is not the job of a shell; this generally requires interactive dialogs between a knowledge-base building tool and one or more humans.

11.3.2 Knowledge-Base Construction

Two sorts of aids may be found for building knowledge bases. One sort conducts an "interview" with an expert, asking the expert repeatedly for information. It builds up a relational structure from the expert's responses. These tools are called *expertise-transfer* systems.

The other sort of aid is a structured editor that allows a trained knowledge engineer to easily add information to the knowledge base (or delete or modify the information). For example, such a system may allow the user to view a list of production rules, add and remove them, with the system checking the rules' syntax. Many of the commercial shells include such editing capabilities (e.g., KEE).

An advantage of direct interviews between an expert and the system is that the middleman (knowledge engineer) is eliminated with possible economic saving. Also, if the knowledge engineer is only marginally competent, the quality of the resulting knowledge base may be higher.

On the other hand, a good knowledge engineer will understand the difficulties of the knowledge-transfer process, and bring a familiarity with knowledge-representation schemes and their limitations to the task. He/she may also be able to provide the sort of flexibility and assistance to the expert that no existing automatic-interviewing system can.

11.3.3 Graphical Representations

Another class of tool is concerned with the display of knowledge and inference processes, so that the designer can understand them. Certain schemes for knowledge representation suggest graphical-display procedures. For example, a frame may be displayed as a rectangular box whose contents are the slot-filler pairs, each displayed in a separate horizontal "slot" inside the box. A semantic network may be displayed as a graph, embedded in the plane, or even as a three-dimensional network to be moved through, with the assistance coordinate-transformation software and/or hardware.

It is the desire to maximize the understandability of the representation that suggests that innovative graphical-display techniques be used in the presentation of various types of knowledge. Most geographic information should obviously be displayed with appropriate maps, for example.

Different designers may prefer different representations for the same kinds of knowledge. Some designers have a general preference for visual presentation over the textual, and they claim to think visually; for such designers, graphical presentations are desirable. Others may prefer the textual or symbolic representations for most information.

11.4 Hardware

The performance of expert systems depends not only on the software but on the hardware as well. General-purpose computers may be appropriate for many AI applications. However, there are various ways in which computer hardware may be tailored to AI's special needs. One approach is to design the processor to efficiently execute programs written in a particular language, such as LISP. Another approach is to provide several or many processors that can run concurrently in a cooperative fashion, speeding up inference and problem-solving process through parallel processing.

The added speed afforded by appropriate hardware can reduce the user's waiting time during an interactive session, or it can allow a larger space of states to be searched in problem-solving, possibly improving the quality of the solutions that are found.

11.4.1   LISP Machines

A LISP machine is a computer specially designed to execute LISP programs efficiently. Most existing LISP machines are single-user workstations with bit-mapped graphic display and mouse input. Examples include the Symbolics 3600 series systems, the Xerox 1100 series (running Interlisp-D), and the Texas Instruments "Explorer."

The Symbolics system achieves efficiency by using microcoded functions for operations such as CAR and CDR. Space is saved using "CDR coding" of linear lists; the links in a linked list are removed whenever it can conveniently be done, reducing both memory requirements and the likelihood of page faults in the virtual memory system. Garbage collection is performed incrementally to give the user the appearance of uninterrupted processing during interactive sessions.

11.4.2   PROLOG Machines

A PROLOG machine is tailored to the efficient execution of Horn-clause logic programs. Unification must be very fast, since it is performed very often. Pattern matching must also be efficient.

Some PROLOG programs can take advantage of parallel processing, when it is available. Two kinds of parallelism are common for PROLOG: "AND parallelism" and "OR parallelism." It is common for a rule in PROLOG to have several subgoals (literals on the right-hand side of the rule). For example the rule

```
Head(x) :- Subgoal1(x,y1), Subgoal2(x,y2), Subgoal3(x,y3).
```

has three subgoals. If the variables y1, y2 and y3 are distinct, then the subgoals can be processed in parallel, saving time. This concurrency is known as AND parallelism since each concurrent subgoal is a conjunct of the rule. If one subgoal instantiates a variable that is an argument to a subsequent subgoal, then the latter cannot be processed until the former has been satisfied, preventing the use of AND parallelism on the particular pair of subgoals. This is often the case, and consequently AND parallelism cannot be expected to yield large savings.

On the other hand, OR parallelism can be quite helpful. When a particular goal is to be satisfied, there may be several rules whose heads match the goal. With OR parallelism, each of these rules may be processed simultaneously. There are no ordering constraints among them.

It is common to measure the speed of a PROLOG machine in LIPS (logical inferences per second).

For such purposes, "logical inference" may not necessarily refer to the complete application of a rule; it may simply refer to the partial unification of two atomic formulas: the detection and processing of a single disagreement where one term is a variable.

While computer architectures have been proposed to exploit AND and OR parallelism in PROLOG programs, other efforts have been directed at more general purpose parallel-processing systems. Some of these are described in the following subsection.

11.4.3   Parallel Architectures

In order to provide the computational power needed by AI applications, two broad families of parallel architectures have been explored. A parallel computer in the first family consists of a multiplicity of processing elements that perform operations in lockstep, perfectly synchronized like soldiers marching to a drum. Although at any one time they all perform the same operation, the data being manipulated are generally different. This sort of system is termed "SIMD" (Single Instruction stream/Multiple Data stream).

The other family is referred to as "MIMD" (Multiple Instruction stream/Multiple Data stream) architectures. A member of this family consists of a collection of processors, each with its own program counter and instruction-interpretation unit. Such a system may employ its processors in multiple executions of a single program, or the processors may each run a different program. If they execute the same program, then at any particular time they need not all perform the same step of the program as would be the case with an SIMD system.

A common form for an SIMD computer is a two-dimensional array of processing elements, each interconnected to its four or eight near neighbors. Such systems are very appropriate for low-level vision, where each processing element can handle the computations for a single pixel or small region of an image.

Another way to use an SIMD system is to apply it to a combinatorial optimization problem such as the "travelling salesman" problem or the painted squares problem (see Chapter 5); we can assign one processing element to each of the candidate solutions and let each processing element work through the computation that determines whether the candidate satisfies all the criteria for being a solution. In the case of the travelling salesman problem, the job of each processing element might be to compute the cost of one particular tour and test this cost against a given threshold.

An MIMD system can be used in a myriad of ways. One interesting approach is to decompose a state-space search problem so that each processor is responsible for searching a portion of the space. This can be effected by parallelizing the search of the successors of a node whenever there are enough processors available to do so. Such a scheme requires a means for allocating processors to tasks dynamically.

It is also possible to parallelize a rule-based system: each processor is given one or more rules that it is responsible for. With condition-testing performed in parallel, the time to find rules that can fire is greatly reduced. If the action portion of a rule consists of several sub-actions, it may be possible to parallelize their execution, as well.

The technical problems of dynamically assigning processor to tasks— computing rule subconditions and sub-actions, searching subsets of trees—are only of few of the many challenging problems currently under investigation that deal with parallel computing in AI.

11.5 Examples of Expert Systems

Since expert systems have been expensive to develop, most existing ones have addressed problems in fields where there is a high potential economic payoff. Manufacturing, medicine, and financial management are three such areas. Let us briefly examine three existing systems.

11.5.1 XCON: A Configurer for VAX Computers

Among the rule-based expert systems that have proved successful outside of the research laboratory, perhaps none is better known than XCON. Originally named R1, XCON was developed jointly by Carnegie-Mellon University and Digital Equipment Corporation. XCON inputs customer orders for VAX-series computers and decides how to configure the orders, providing detailed descriptions of spatial layouts of components, assignments of various circuit boards to their slots, and choosing the lengths of cables, etc. XCON performs a job in seconds that previously required skilled technicians approximately 20 minutes to complete, even with the use of an editing program on a computer.

XCON was begun using OPS4, and soon after was using OPS5. A sample rule from XCON's rule base is the following one for placing power supplies into VAX 11/780 systems:

```
IF:   The most current active context is assigning a power supply
      and an SBI module of any type has been put in a cabinet
      and the position it occupies in the cabinet (its nexus)
          is known
      and there is space available in the cabinet for a power
          supply for that nexus
```

```
        and there is an available power supply
THEN: put the power supply in the cabinet in the available space.
```

The development of XCON suggests that expert systems can be useful at an early age and gradually be improved and extended over time. With approximately 800 rules, XCON was successfully configuring VAX 11/780 systems in 1979. In 1981 it used about 1500 rules and could configure VAX 11/750 systems as well. Rules were gradually added to handle PDP-11's, MICROVAX's and the 11/725 and 11/785 systems, so that by 1983 XCON contained some 3000 rules. According to its developers, the level of effort put into the project was nearly constant (four full-time people over about five years); this suggests that the primary work in producing such a system is in designing the rules, since the rule base grew at a roughly constant rate over the project period.

11.5.2   CADUCEOUS: An Internal-Medicine Consultant

Perhaps the largest medical expert system developed to date, CADUCEOUS helps a physician to diagnose diseases of the internal organs from information about a patient's symptoms, medical history and laboratory tests. The knowledge of CADUCEOUS consists primarily of the descriptions of some 500 diseases in terms of over 3500 conditions. A strength of this system is its ability to correctly diagnose patients who have several diseases simultaneously. Originally having the name INTERNIST-I, the system was developed at the University of Pittsburgh, and it has been used on an experimental basis.

11.5.3   TAXMAN: A Corporate Tax Law Advisor

Developed at Rutgers University, TAXMAN is an expert system that helps the user to understand legal concepts related to taxation in a corporate environment. TAXMAN employs frames to represent tax law, corporate tax cases, and correspondences among cases (which assist in understanding the cases). By creating and using correspondences between a hypothetical or current situation and previous cases, TAXMAN could assist with planning of legal argumentation, which in turn could support litigation, out-of-court negotiation, or business decision-making. The development of TAXMAN has helped to open the domain of legal reasoning as a field for expert-systems research.

11.6   Limits of Expert Systems

To put expert systems in perspective, we need to understand their limitations and the potential pitfalls in using them. We consider limitations not only of present day systems but future systems as well.

11.6.1 Quality of Knowledge

An expert system is limited by the quality of the knowledge that it contains. Even when a system's knowledge is very good in a particular area, it may be poor or nonexistent outside of the narrow area. If the performance of the system drops suddenly as it gets slightly outside its area of strength, it is said to have a "knowledge cliff." A knowledge cliff can be both bad and good. It is usually bad to get poor performance from any system, especially when it is only "slightly" outside its domain of expertise. On the other hand, a system with a knowledge cliff can more easily be identified as outside its domain of expertise (because its recommendations and observations may be obviously bad), and this may help prevent its use for such cases.

11.6.2 Speed of Inference

Speed of inference is most critical in competitive situations and situations where optimal or nearly-optimal solutions are needed in a fixed amount of time. Game (e.g., chess) playing, and military decision and control environments are particularly sensitive to the speed of the information processing in expert systems. The most time-consuming applications of AI tend to be those whose problems are formulated as combinatorial search problems or as rule-application where the lengths of inference chains can grow beyond, say 10.

Machine learning may be the mode of artificial-intelligence activity with the greatest potential to soak up computer cycles. Many learning problems are expressed as combinatorial optimizations such that the better the solution to the optimization problem, the better the system learns what it is supposed to.

Expert systems that solve narrowly-focussed sorts of problems can generally operate efficiently. However, as the context in which the system can operate grows, the time it takes to solve a particular problem generally grows as well. Thus there is a tradeoff between speed and generality in expert systems.

Similarly, in domains such as language understanding and vision, as more ambiguity is tolerated, the interpretation speed is reduced.

11.6.3 Proper and Improper Use

Misuse of expert systems falls into two categories: accidental and malicious. While various precautions can be taken to reduce the likelihood of misuse, it is a limitation of expert systems that this possibility cannot be entirely eliminated.

Accidental misuse may become more and more likely with an expert system that allows a human to become alienated from a position of informed responsibility. The human-machine team for problem-solving has thus far generally been human-directed. The user typically directs the system to perform database searches, particular numerical computations, etc., and then thinks about the results and continues the process. Expert systems can tip the balance: the human might no longer be the "wiser" member of the team and might no longer *feel* accountable for the team's recommendations; the human may be tempted to give up his/her last vestige of critical thinking. (Additional discussion of the limitations of artificial intelligence may be found in Chapter 12.)

11.7   Bibliographical Information

Some good general references on expert systems are [Hayes-Roth et al 1983] and [Waterman 1986]. A collection of papers that introduces AI and then discusses its applications is [Andriole 1985]. The commercial potential for expert systems is described in [Winston and Prendergast 1984]; this record of a workshop involving both technical and business leaders includes transcripts of the discussions.

The issue of integrating numerical techniques with AI techniques is addressed by several papers collected in [Kowalik 1986]. The issue of organizing knowledge for expert systems according to the type of problem-solving it is for is treated by [Chandrasekaran 1983]. Parallel architecture is treated in [Hwang and Briggs 1984]. The massively parallel "Connection Machine" designed for AI problems is described in [Hillis 1985].

A system for expertise transfer through computer/expert interactions is described in [Boose 1986].

Summary descriptions of nearly two hundred expert systems are given in [Waterman 1986]. The XCON system (also known as R1) is described in [McDermott 1982]. The CADUCEOUS expert system (originally named INTERNIST-I) is described in [Miller et al 1982]. The TAXMAN system is described in [McCarty and Sridharan 1980, 1981].

References

1. Andriole, S. J. (ed.) 1985. *Applications in Artificial Intelligence.* New York: Petrocelli Books.

2. Boose, J. H. 1986, ETS: A system for the transfer of human expertise. In Kowalik, J. S. (ed.), *Knowledge Based Problem Solving*, Englewood Cliffs, NJ: Prentice-Hall, pp68-111.

3. Chandrasekaran, B. 1983. Towards a taxonomy of problem solving types. *The AI Magazine*, Winter/Spring, pp9-17.

4. Hayes-Roth, F., Waterman, D. A., and Lenat, D. B. (eds.) 1983. *Building Expert Systems.* Reading, MA: Addison-Wesley.

5. Hillis, W. D. 1985. *The Connection Machine.* Cambridge, MA: MIT Press.

6. Hwang, K. and Briggs, F. A. 1984. *Computer Architecture and Parallel Processing.* New York: McGraw-Hill.

7. Kowalik, J. S. (ed.) 1986. *Coupling Symbolic and Numerical Computing in Expert Systems*. New York: North-Holland.

8. McCarty, L. T. and Sridharan, N. S. 1980. The representation of evolving system of legal concepts: I. Logical templates. *Proceedings of the 3rd CSCSI/SCEIO Conference*, Victoria, British Columbia. pp304-311.

9. McCarty, L. T. and Sridharan, N. S. 1981. The representation of evolving system of legal concepts: II. Prototypes and Deformations. *Proceedings of the Seventh International Joint Conference on Artificial Intelligence*, Vancouver. pp246-253.

10. McDermott, J. 1982. R1: A rule-based configurer of computer systems. *Artificial Intelligence*, Vol. 19, No. 1, pp39-88.

11. Miller, R. A., Pople, H. E., Jr., and Myers, J. D. 1982. INTERNIST-I: An experimental computer-based diagnostic consultant for general internal medicine. *New England Journal of Medicine*, Vol. 307, No. 8, pp468-476.

12. Waterman, D. A. 1986. *A Guide to Expert Systems*. Reading, MA: Addison-Wesley.

13. Winston, P. H. and Prendergast, K. A. (eds.), 1984. *The AI Business: Commercial Uses of Artificial Intelligence*. Cambridge, MA: MIT Press.

Exercises

1. Describe how a rule base might be integrated with a numerical model of meteorological activity to automatically make weather predictions of the sort given in newpapers or on television.

2. Make up a set of three to ten rules for choosing the best computer-programming language for a software development task. Incorporate such factors as the development time available, importance that the software be free of bugs, the expected number of times the software will have to be modified to meet future needs, and programmer familiarity with the language. Describe what an expert system should be able to do that uses these and additional rules.

3. Develop a graphical tool that can display portions of inclusion hierarchies such as those created by the LINNEUS program of Chapter 4.

4. Develop a graphical tool for manipulating a probabilistic inference network. The tool is to consist of two parts:

    (a) a graphical editor for probabilistic inference networks, and

(b) an updating display routine that shows the updating of the current probabilities of nodes.

The tool should be integrated with a set of functions for performing the computations, such as those used in the INFNET.LSP program in Chapter 7.

5. Develop a graphical tool to support the design of augmented transition networks such as that used in the STONEWLD program of Chapter 9. The tool should be able to display an ATN as a graph, and to permit editing the ATN interactively.

6. Develop an appropriate natural-language interface and couple it to a rule-based "wine advisor" that uses rules such as those mentioned in Chapter 6, Section 6.7.

7. Describe a means that could help prevent the inadvertent use of an expert system for problems outside its domain of expertise.

Chapter 12

The Future

12.1 Where is AI Going?

In this chapter we discuss the future of artificial intelligence and the relationship between AI and human culture. There is good reason to attempt to predict what the future holds in store for us. Man is a planning animal. It is in our nature to attempt to control our destiny: to have food on the table tomorrow, to be prepared for any dangers, to continue the existence of our species.

However, there is an inherent difficulty that any prognosticator has: there is a thin line between appearing provocative and appearing foolish. In order to be provocative, it is generally necessary to predict something new and unexpected. At the same time, anyone who readily accepts the prediction and does not find it "foolish" finds it to be consistent with his/her own current beliefs, and it is thus to some extent already "expected" and not very provocative. Someone who finds the prediction so unexpected as to be inconsistent with his/her beliefs is apt to judge it foolish. Nonetheless, it seems worthwhile to give consideration to even the far-flung possible eventualities, because these may be the ones which change us the most.

We begin our discussion with some trends in the technology. Then we examine a few of the possible benefits and detrimental effects that AI may have on our economy, society and culture.

12.1.1 Better Integration

In Chapter 11 we identified the key to applying AI as the integration of AI techniques with other information-processing technology. Achieving such integration presents many challenges. Some of these are involved with creating standard forms for knowledge representation and transmittal and getting these standards accepted. Others are to understand the useful interactions among the various kinds of subsystems.

Much work needs to be done to develop methods to couple numerical models with non-numerical knowledge representations. Such couplings may require systems of decision and quantization. Furthermore, qualitative models may be needed to augment the quantitative ones, in order to support qualitative reasoning at acceptable speeds.

The information technologies that need to be integrated are diverse. Besides the above-mentioned numerical models, such technologies include computer networks and telecommunications, databases, computer graphics, speech and other acoustical techniques, robotics, process-control, parallel electronic computing, optical computing, and possibly biochemical information-processing technology.

12.1.2 More Mature Application Methodologies

The discipline of software engineering arose in response to the need to develop complex software systems for many applications. Design disciplines such as software engineering provide standard procedures for producing solutions to certain classes of problems. Because of the complexity and often open-ended scope of AI applications, traditional software design methods are not adequate. One problem is that the specifications of what function the AI software is to perform are much more likely to change as the system is developed than would be the case with, say, a payroll-computation program. The methodology for AI must support the experimental aspect of AI development and allow the system to grow organically from a small kernel prototype to the complete applications system.

We can expect that there will be very general and useful AI development methodologies available in the future. In applying artificial intelligence, new ways are being discovered to classify and solve problems. By developing new tools and step-by-step procedures for the design of expert systems, methodologies are evolving that eventually will allow the successful application of AI to many more fields than have been tackled so far.

12.2 Economic Benefits

In the past, in order to develop an expert system for a class of problems, it was necessary that there be a high potential for economic benefit; this was needed to justify the great expense of developing the system. This criterion will continue to guide most serious applications of artificial intelligence techniques for some time. However, as the costs of computing systems continues to fall, and AI technology becomes more widespread, we can expect to see many expert systems developed for reasons such as their intrinsic interest.

It is obvious that successful expert systems can bring economic rewards to their creators, owners and users. By cheaply performing a task that otherwise requires an experienced professional, labor costs may be greatly reduced. However, it is worth mentioning that expert systems have some potential advantages over human experts.

12.2.1 Advantages of Expert Systems

The fact that software can be easily copied means that expert systems can permit a wider distribution of operational expertise than would be possible when only a limited number of human professionals have such expertise.

Software, when protected from damage, can remain intact for arbitrarily long periods of time. Thus one can gain a permanence of expertise relative to the temporary life cycle of the human professional. A company with valuable expertise may be able to help assure its longevity by embodying it in software.

Whereas human professionals in fields such as medicine have great difficulty keeping abreast of the latest practical recommendations, expert systems can be rapidly updated and distributed electronically, allowing the end user or patient to benefit from new advances.

The commitment of knowledge to a knowledge base can make it more convenient to validate and/or ratify than it would be if the knowledge were never recorded in the formalism.

12.2.2 AI Pushing Computer Technology

Research in AI has had a positive influence on other aspects of computer technology. For example, the development of the LISP language in the late 1950's helped spread knowledge of symbolic-programming constructs into the mainstream of programming-language design. Some of the most advanced programming environments have been developed in response to the needs of AI researchers. The heavy computational requirements of AI applications has stimulated the development of parallel processing and special-purpose integrated-circuit chips. Automatic programming technology is beginning to have a positive impact on software development as algorithm generators and smart data structures come into use.

12.3 Social Growing Pains

While AI promises economic benefits to its creators, vendors and many of its users, like any new technology its development is likely to cause some problems and a certain amount of chagrin for some people. By taking over various mental activities from people, there will be some who lose their jobs; others will lose their sense of involvement in the information-processing activities—planning, diagnosing, understanding— that go on in the world.

12.3.1   Labor

As the automobile replaced the horse-drawn carriage, stable attendants and carriage drivers were replaced by auto mechanics and motorcar chauffeurs. Robots are replacing some assembly-line laborers in factories.

AI will probably lead to the replacement of various professionals by computers and by teams of researchers and knowledge engineers that supply and maintain expert systems. In the future, a good medical clinician will rely on a great deal of computer-delivered expertise. The top medical people will probably all be researchers involved in improving the knowledge bases that the clinicians are using. These medical people will use AI in their work; their experiments will be designed in interactive dialogs, as will the results.

Some clinicians are bound to resent the lowering in status their profession may undergo, while most will probably welcome the improved quality of service they can deliver with the new technology.

Unlike previous technological changes, however, the "AI revolution" may lead to fundamental changes in the way people regard their own brains and belief systems.

12.3.2   The Possibility of Greater Confusion

Book knowledge is being transformed into interactive-system knowledge. While this has the benefits of making the knowledge operational, providing automatic access to the relevant facts and rules, and providing the computational power to bring simulation models to life, there is also a greater potential for confusion with expert systems than with books. Particular knowledge bases, unlike books, are readily modified. Thus, they may grow, whereas a single book is a static repository of knowledge. A professional who "goes by the book" is one who uses a fixed, documented procedure for his or her actions. To say that one "goes by the expert system" may not imply the same degree of stability and conservatism, particularly if the knowledge base of the expert system can evolve in an uncoordinated way.

12.3.3   User Responsibility and Alienation

Once the user of an expert system begins to trust its judgment, he/she may be tempted to avoid the intellectual effort required to check the machine's arguments or even to feel "in touch" with the reasoning processes. Without intellectual responsibility, the user will grow lazy and will lose his/her sensitivity to many subtleties of the planning, diagnosis, or other problem-solving task. Once the user's awareness is reduced, the likelihood of misunderstanding increases; the user is apt to take the computer's advice out of context or to slip up in more direct ways. For example, a medical clinician who routinely prescribes medication for various illnesses with the assistance of an expert system could cause a patient subtantial harm with a careless misinterpretation of the system's advice. The kind of "de-personalization" that often occurs in bureaucracies could manifest itself in worse ways if the bureaucrats are even further removed from the concerns of the people they "serve" than they already are.

To prevent apathy among those involved in the distribution and use of AI will be a challenge. Part of the solution may be to place liability on all of the parties involved, rather than only the client, only the designer, or only the vendor. The parties are the following: the designers of the expert system, including any separate parties who build the knowledge base, inference engine or other utilities; the vendor, who sells the product and claims it useful for the purchaser's business; the user, who operates the program, feeding it inputs and interpreting its outputs; the client, who provides details of his problem and is partially responsible for implementing the solution. On the other hand, justice would seldom be served if all the parties are routinely help liable for the negligence of only one of them.

Research is needed in the design of systems that encourage the users to take a responsible, intellectually active role in problem solving wherever there are substantial penalties for misinterpretation.

12.3.4   A Human Identity Crisis

Artificial intelligence poses a kind of psychological threat to people whose sense of identity is based on their (possibly misguided) perception of the difference between a mind and a machine. "I think, therefore I am" was Rene Descartes' way of proving his existence to himself. To many people, a more apt belief is "I think, therefore I am not a mere machine." If these people come to believe that machines can think, and they believe that machines are inferior entities, then they will probably feel disheartened and possibly threatened. Indeed, there is a controversy among philosophers, theologians, and others about the relationship between the concept of person (or, more specifically, *mind*) and the concept of machine (or, more specifically, artificial intelligence).

One can imagine that AI techniques might provide a new means with which to evaluate systems of beliefs, including religious beliefs. Dimensions of such evaluations might include logical and qualitative consistency, the relationship between evidence and generalizations, and the "utility" of dogma and other teachings in helping to satisfy human needs. In fact, it is possible to think of the problem of planning man's future as a kind of state-space search. While some people may welcome the new ways of thinking about human activity on earth, others may find the new ideas disturbing, particularly if they find the ideas both compelling and in conflict with cherished beliefs.

12.3.5   The Sorcerer's Apprentice

Perhaps the greatest danger of any new technology is that we may lose control
of it, or that its power may fall into the hands of those who use it against human
interests. One unfortunate but possible role for AI is that of the magic in *The
Sorcerer's Apprentice*. Researchers may learn just enough about AI technology
to put it into motion, initially for the good of man; but it may turn out that
they are unable to stop it from becoming a menace. A similar story is that of the
Frankenstein monster, created with good intentions but successful only enough
to be able to terrorize mankind.

Recognizing this problem, Isaac Asimov laid down his "Three Laws of
Robotics" which are as follows:

1. A robot may not injure a human being, or, through inaction, allow a
   human being to come to harm.

2. A robot must obey the orders given to it by human beings except where
   such orders would conflict with the First Law.

3. A robot must protect its own existence as long as such protection does
   not conflict with the First or Second Law.

Unfortunately, it would appear to be very difficult to create a piece of AI software that is capable of making the discriminations that would allow it to actually
follow the three laws. Acting as an advisor to a human, a program would probably not be able to tell whether the advice was going to be used for injuring
human beings. Thus the problem is this: an AI system could probably be put
together with some mechanism that attempts to obey the laws, but it would not
be intelligent enough to ensure that the laws are really obeyed in the long run
and in the general sense of the word *injure*.

Artificial intelligence technology is information technology, and it is capable of
being transmitted relatively rapidly. There is thus a somewhat greater potential
for it to move into irresponsible hands than, say, explosives technology. This
puts an extra measure of responsibility for the proper use of AI on its developers
and vendors.

12.4   Cultural Benefits

12.4.1   Refinement of Human Knowledge

In the course of reformulating our knowledge of history, philosophy and nature
(to mention just a few areas), academicians and knowledge engineers have an
opportunity to attempt to resolve ambiguities and eliminate inconsistencies in
the knowledge. Such attempts might lead to such improvements in the knowledge
that interesting new truths can easily be inferred.

Machine learning research is introducing new methods of formalizing and validating knowledge, including not only techniques of inductive inference, rule formulation and clustering, but also "ratification," and methods for the justification and explanation of knowledge.

It is conceivable that "knowledge refineries" could be set up to facilitate the production of high-quality knowledge bases. These institutions could function commercially and/or as parts of educational or government research establishments. If the management of knowledge can be entirely automated, one can imagine electronic networks in which autonomous agents produce, refine, buy, sell and otherwise exchange knowledge like commodities options or like electrical power.

12.4.2 Improvements to Human Language

The reformulation of human knowledge is a process that brings to attention the strengths and weaknesses of the languages that the knowledge has been recorded with. With our present-day knowledge of syntax, semantics and formal knowledge-representation methods, we can improve the natural-language representation of the knowledge for human readers at the same time that we put it into AI-usable form.

As the elements of artificial intelligence become more widely known, people will use these concepts in the course of describing everyday situations and solving various problems in their lives. For example, someone might describe his own reasoning in the terms of production systems: "My *Don't eat smelly fish* rule fired and I threw the ripe package in the garbage."

Analogies to AI concepts are bound to be used inappropriately on occasion, and yet they offer many new expressive opportunities. While the development of mathematical logic undoubtedly led to more rigor in the works of many writers, AI enlarges the set of concepts we can bring to bear in relating our knowledge to other people. It gives us alternative names for the certainties of statements, ways to describe what we see and hear, and new ways in which to describe our beliefs.

12.4.3 New Ways of Seeing

Vision technology can provide "ways of seeing." In the future, it will be possible to generate specific image transformations which correspond with forms of artistic interpretation.

The imposition of familiar structure on random data is the activity of a psychoanalysis patient interpreting a Rorschach-test ink-blot diagram; computer-vision systems can be made to hallucinate in similar situations and to display surrealistic or schematic representations of the perceived results. Systems may also be made to reconstruct scenes in particular styles, in caricature, or adhering to particular resource constraints such as amounts of various colors, shapes of component forms, number of pixels, etc. Such capability could have a profound effect on the graphic arts, advertising, and educational sectors of society.

12.4.4 Revitalization of Intellectual Pursuits

The excitement in artificial intelligence is giving a new vigor to intellectual activities in general. The questions AI asks of each field are essential ones:

- "What are the goals of the field?"

- "What is the nature of the knowledge in this field?"

- "How is this knowledge changing?"

- "How is new knowledge acquired?"

- "How is the knowledge to be used or appreciated?"

- "How does the knowledge in this field relate to that in other fields?"

By helping to focus attention on inconsistencies, AI is encouraging rethinking of old issues. Its techniques are offering new ways of solving old problems, and new questions are becoming apparent.

12.5   Bibliographical Information

Discussions of the economic promise of expert systems may be found in the references for Chapter 11. The social and economic impact of AI is discussed in [Feigenbaum and McCorduck 1983]. Excellent chapters on the psychological, philosophical and social impact of AI may be found in [Boden 1977]. The impact of AI upon religious thought is discussed in [Wiener 1964] and [LaChat 1986]. Isaac Asimov's famous "Three Laws of Robotics" may be found in [Asimov 1950].

The prospect of AI as a new medium for knowledge is discussed in [Stefik 1986], and the notion of "knowledge refineries" is introduced in [Michie 1975].

References

1. Asimov, I. 1950. *I Robot.* New York: Gnome Press.

2. Boden, M. *Artificial Intelligence and Natural Man.* New York: Basic Books.

3. Feigenbaum, E. A., and McCorduck, P. 1983. *The Fifth Generation: Artificial Intelligence and Japan's Computer Challenge to the World.* Reading, MA: Addison-Wesley.

4. LaChat, M. R. 1986. Artificial intelligence and ethics: An exercise in the moral imagination. *AI Magazine*, Vol. 7, No. 2 (Summer), pp70-79.

5. Michie, D. 1983. A prototype knowledge refinery. In Hayes, J. E., and Michie, D. (eds.), *Intelligent Systems: The Unprecedented Opportunity.* Chichester: Ellis Horwood, pp57-69.

6. Stefik, M. 1986. The next knowledge medium. *AI Magazine*, Vol. 7, No. 1 (Spring), pp34-46.

7. Wiener, N. 1964. *God and Golem, Inc.* Cambridge, MA: MIT Press.

Appendix A

Summary of LISP Functions

Listed here are the built-in LISP functions that are assumed to be available for the programs in the text. They are listed alphabetically. Functions marked with a dagger ($\dagger$) either are peculiar to the dialect of LISP used here, or have some notable system-dependent properties.

(ADD1 N): Returns 1 plus the value of N. Reports an error if overflow occurs in the addition. If N is represented as a FIXNUM, then the arithmetic is performed on 16-bit integers represented in 2's complement form. If N is represented as a FLONUM, then the arithmetic is performed on IEEE Floating Point Standard 64-bit numbers.

(AND X1 X2 $\cdots$ Xn): Successively evaluates the Xi until one is found with value NIL (in which case AND immediately returns NIL), or they are all found to be non-null, in which case AND returns T.

(APPEND L1 L2 $\cdots$ Ln): Returns the result of concatenating the lists L1, L2, etc. The arguments are not altered as they are with NCONC.

(APPLY FUNC ARGLIST): The function is applied to the arguments which are given in the list which is the value of ARGLIST. The value of FUNC may be either an atom which is the name of a function, or it may be a LAMBDA expression defining a local function.

(ATOM X): Returns T if the value of X is an atom, and it returns NIL otherwise.

(BIOSCALL N)$\dagger$: Calls a ROM-resident BIOS function. Arguments for the BIOS function are set up using SET_REG. N specifies a software interrupt number.

(BOUNDP X): Returns T if the value of X is bound.

(BREAK X)[†]: As soon as this function is evaluated, the interpreter stops further evaluation and prints "BREAK:" followed by the result of evaluating X. It then enters a "READ-EVAL-PRINT" loop similar to that at the top level. Local variable values can be examined or changed, and functions can be executed as if at top-level. To continue the evaluation of an expression after a BREAK, type the atom RESUME. BREAK always returns NIL. (An escape to the top level can be obtained by typing control-Break.)

(CAAR X): This is equivalent to (CAR (CAR X)).

(CADAR X): Equivalent to (CAR (CDR (CAR X))).

(CADDR X): Equivalent to (CAR (CDR (CDR X))).

(CADR X): Equivalent to (CAR (CDR X)).

(CAR L): Returns the first element of a list or dotted pair.

(CDAR X): Equivalent to (CDR (CAR X)).

(CDDR X): Equivalent to (CDR (CDR X)).

(CDR L): Returns all but the first element of a list, or returns the right-hand side of a dotted pair.

(CLS)[†]: Clears the screen.

(COND (C1 E1) (C2 E2) $\cdots$ (Cn En)): Successively evaluates the Ci until one is found that is not NIL. Then the corresponding Ei is evaluated and returned as the value of the COND. It is permissible to follow each Ci with more than one Ei. In this case, if Ci is the first non-null condition, the E's immediately following it are successively evaluated and the value of the last one in the group is returned as the value of the COND expression. This feature is called an "implicit PROG."

(CONS A B): Constructs a new dotted pair whose left half is the value of A and whose right half is the value of B. If the value of B is a list, then (CONS A B) has the effect of creating a new list like B, but containing the value of A as an additional element at the front.

(DEFEXPR FNAME (L) FN_BODY): Defines a "FEXPR" or user-defined special form. When the FEXPR is called, there may be any number of arguments to it; they are all passed to the FEXPR unevaluated in a list, bound to L.

(DEFPROP A V P): Associates value V with property P on the property list for atom A. DEFPROP is similar to PUTPROP, except that A, V and P are not evaluated and generally do not need to be quoted.

(DEFUN FNAME (ARG1 ARG2 $\cdots$ ARGn) FN_BODY): Defines a normal, user-defined function. This function will take a fixed number of arguments, when called, which are always evaluated before being bound to the formal arguments of the function definition. Such a function is known as an "EXPR."

(DEF_SEG N)[†]: Defines a segment for the PEEK and POKE functions.

(DIFFERENCE N1 N2): Returns the result of subtracting the value of N2 from the value of N1, or it reports overflow or underflow.

(DOSCALL)[†]: Calls a DOS function using the assembly language instruction INT 21H, as described in the DOS manual. Arguments are passed using SET_REG and GET_REG. It is useful for setting the time and date, and for miscellaneous I/O functions.

(DSKREAD 'D:FILENAME.EXT)[†]: Searches disk D for a file named FILE-NAME having extension EXT, and if found, reads the text in that file as LISP input. Note that the disk drive designation is optional, as is the extension of the filename.

(EQ A1 A2): Returns T if A1 and A2 have values stored in the same memory location. It is a valid and efficient way to test two literal atoms for identity. However, it is not valid as a test for the equality of composite S-expressions or numbers.

(EQUAL X1 X2): Used to test two arbitrary S-expressions for equality.

(EVAL X): Applies the evaluator to the value of X.

(FUNCTION FN)[†]: Is defined here to have the same effect as QUOTE. Some LISP compilers require that function atoms be quoted using FUNCTION.

(GET A P): Searches the property list for the atom which is the value of A for an entry of the form (value(P) . X) for some S-expression X and if found, returns whatever X is. Otherwise, it returns NIL.

(GET_REG N)[†]: Returns the contents of an 8088/8086/80286 accumulator register following a call to BIOSCALL. The number N specifies which register: 0 = AX; 1 = BX; 2 = CX; 3 = DX; 4 = AH; 5 = BH; 6 = CH; 7 = DH; 8 = AL; 9 = BL; 10 = CL; 11 = DL.

(GO A): See PROG.

(GREATERP N1 N2): Returns T if the value of N1 is numerically strictly greater than the value of N2.

(LESSP N1 N2): Returns T if the value of N1 is numerically strictly less than the value of N2.

(LIST X1 X2 $\cdots$ Xn): Returns a list of the values of the arguments.

(LOCATE I J)†: Positions the cursor on the screen at row I, column J. The upper-left position of the screen is at I=0, J=0.

(MAPCAR FN ARGLIST): Applies the function given by the value of FN to each element of ARGLIST and returns a list of the results.

(MAX N1 N2 $\cdots$ Nk): Returns the maximum of its arguments.

(MEMBER ELT L): Returns NIL if ELT is not a (top-level) member of the list L; otherwise, it returns T.

(MIN N1 N2 $\cdots$ Nk): Returns the minimum of its arguments.

(NCONC X Y): Attaches Y to the end of list X by a non-copying concatenation; NCONC resembles APPEND with two arguments except that X is modified rather than copied. Circular lists can be created using (NCONC X X), where X was any normal list.

(NULL X): Returns T if the value of X is NIL.

(NUM_EQ N1 N2)†: Returns T if the numeric values of N1 and N2 are equal. It is not defined if either N1 or N2 is non-numeric.

(NUMBERP X): Returns T if the value of X is a number; otherwise, it returns NIL.

(OR X1 X2 $\cdots$ Xn): Evaluates the Xi until one is found which is not NIL (whence OR immediately returns that value) or until they are all found to be NIL (whence OR returns NIL).

(PEEK N)†: Returns the value (0 to 255) of the byte stored at offset N of the segment last declared with a call to DEF_SEG.

(PLIST A): Returns the property list of the atom which is the value of A.

(PLUS N1 N2 $\cdots$ Nk): Returns the sum of the arguments, or reports overflow.

(POKE N B)†: Stores B (which should be in the range 0 to 255) at offset N of the segment last declared with DEF_SEG.

(PP X)†: Pretty-prints the value of X. This is a good way to display function definitions within LISP.

(PRIN1 S): Prints the S-expression and leaves the cursor at the position just after the last character printed.

(PRINT S): Prints an S-expression and a carriage return and line feed after it.

(PRINT_DATE)[†]: Prints the current date, as maintained by DOS.

(PRINTM E1 E2 ⋯ En)[†]: Prints the unevaluated arguments separated by spaces, followed by carriage return and line feed.

(PRINT_TIME)[†]: Prints the time of day according to the computer's time-of-day clock.

(PROG (X1 X2 ⋯ Xn) Y1 Y2 ⋯ Ym): The Xi are taken to be local variables (current bindings of them are saved at entry to the PROG and restored at exit). The forms Y1, Y2, etc. are considered in order. If form Yi is atomic, it is skipped. Otherwise it is evaluated. If a form such as (GO Yk) is encountered, the LISP interpreter immediately begins searching the sequence of Y1, Y2, etc. to find one which is EQ to Yk. If one is found, control transfers to the Yj immediately following Yk. Thus, a "GOTO" is executed. If a form such as (RETURN Z) is evaluated, the PROG immediately is exited with the value of Z as its value. If the last Ym is evaluated and is not (nor does it contain) a GO or RETURN form, the PROG is exited with the value NIL.

(PUTPROP A V P): Places value V on the property list for atom A, associated with the property P.

(QUOTE X): Returns its argument unevaluated. One may also use the single-quote character to indicate a quoted S-expression. For example, '(A B C) = (QUOTE (A B C)).

(QUOTIENT N1 N2): Returns the integer-division quotient of N1 divided by N2. Reports an error if the value of N2 is 0.

(READ): Returns an S-expression that is typed at the keyboard by the user.

(REMAINDER N1 N2): Returns N1 mod N2. Reports an error if the value of N2 is 0.

(RETURN X): See PROG.

(RPLACA X Y): Replaces the CAR of X by Y; X is "permanently" modified.

(RPLACD X Y): Replaces the CDR of X by Y; X is "permanently" modified.

(SET A X): The value of X is assigned to the atom which is the value of A. If the value of A is not a literal atom, an error is reported.

(SET_PLIST A L)[†]: Makes the value of L become the new property list for the atom which is the value of A.

(SET_REG N1 N2)[†]: Sets an 8088/8086/80286 accumulator register prior to a call to BIOSCALL. N1 indicates which register (as explained for GET_REG) and N2 is the integer value to be placed in the register.

(SETQ A X): The value of X becomes that of A. Argument A is not evaluated.

(SUB1 N): Returns the value of N minus 1. Reports an error if underflow occurs in subtraction.

(SYS_BREAK)[†]: Terminates evaluation and prompts the user for either escape to top level or for access to the local binding environment. This function has the same effect as the user's typing control-Break.

(SYS_PRM N)[†]: Returns the LISP system parameter designated by N. If N=1 then the maximum number of LISP cells allowed in the system is returned. N=3: the total number of bytes allocated for strings (names of atoms) is returned; N=4: the number of bytes used so far for strings is returned; N=5: the number of times the garbage collector has been invoked in the current session; N=6: the current value of the pointer for the stack of protected temporary results (this stack has 512 bytes allocated).

(TERPRI): Prints a carriage-return and line-feed.

(TIMES N1 N2 $\cdots$ Nk): Returns the product of the arguments, or reports overflow.

(TRACE F1 F2 $\cdots$ Fn): Makes each function Fi a traced function. Note that the Fi are unevaluated and should not be quoted. Any function can be traced, be it a system function, library function, or user function. If any Fi is not a literal atom, the function aborts to the BREAK error handler.

(TYI)[†]: Waits for a key to be typed on the keyboard and returns an integer ASCII code value for it. If the key typed was an extended scan key (such as the *Ins* key or one of the cursor-arrow keys), the value returned is $256 + x$, where x is the second scan code value. For example, if the cursor-up arrow key is typed, TYI returns 328.

(TYO N)[†]: Prints the character whose ASCII code is given by the decimal integer N. Note that if N=7 then this causes a beep to sound. Graphics can be created by printing special characters of the IBM PC's extended character set.

(UNBIND X): Unbinds the atom which is the value of X. That is, if X has a binding in the current environment, it is removed.

(UNTRACE F1 F2 $\cdots$ Fn): Turns off trace mode for each Fi. If no arguments are given, all traced functions are made untraced. If any Fi is not a literal atom, UNTRACE aborts to BREAK.

(WRITECHAR CHAR ATTRIBUTE COUNT)[†]: Displays the character whose ASCII value is CHAR on the screen with given ATTRIBUTE, according to the IBM PC Technical Reference Manual, allowing color, blinking, underlining, etc. Display is at the current cursor position, with COUNT copies of the character.

(ZEROP N): Returns T if the value of N is zero; otherwise, it returns NIL.

Author Index

Subject Index

THE ELEMENTS

of

Artificial Intelligence

A									E
atom									Expertise
Sx S-expression	**R** Production rule	**I** ISA hierarchy	**K** State space	**Pc** Predicate calculus	**Pr** Probability	**C** Concept formation	**L** Lexicon	**Ir** Image representation	**Sh** Shell
Cs CONS	**Dn** Discrimination network	**F** Frame	**D** Depth-first search	**Rn** Resolution	**B** Bayes' rule	**V** Version space	**Sy** Syntax	**Sg** Segmentation	**Ie** Inference engine
Cd COND	**Pa** Pattern matching	**Sn** Semantic net	**As** A* algorithm	**U** Unification	**Fz** Fuzzy logic	**H** Heuristic	**S** Semantics	**Q** Relaxation	**N** Numerical model
Df DEFUN	**X** Formula manipulation	**Cn** Constraint	**Pl** Planning	**Ht** Herbrand's theorem	**Sf** Sufficiency factor	**Cr** Circular reaction paradigm	**Pg** Pragmatics	**M** Morphology	**In** Integration
Mp MAPCAR	**Fc** Forward chaining	**Rd** Relational database	**Ab** Alpha-beta search	**P** Prolog	**Ds** Dempster-Shafer calculus	**Di** Discovery	**At** Augmented transition net	**Z** Depth	**Pp** Parallel processing

529

AI Software Offer

A LISP interpreter for the IBM-PC, XT, AT, and compatibles is available from SoftWave. This interpreter runs all the LISP programs and supports the programming exercises in *The Elements of Artificial Intelligence.*

The SoftWave LISP package includes the following:
- All LISP programs from the text, on diskette.
- The SoftWave LISP interpreter.
- User manual.

To order, send name and address with check or money order in the amount of US$38 or as shown below, or VISA/MasterCard number to:

SoftWave
P. O. Box 31607
Seattle, WA 98103

- -

Check one:
- [ ] Single-computer license: $38.
- [ ] Industrial site license: $190.
- [ ] Educational site license: $95.

VISA/Mastercard # _____

Name: _____

Street: _____

City: _____ State: _____ Zip: _____

Please allow up to 4 weeks for delivery.